News Clippings From Price, Castlegate, Helper, Cleveland, Scofield, Utah 1882 - 1899

Including: Wellington, Spring Glen, Green River, Winter Quarters, Molen, Emery

Some of the names include: Alger, Allanti, Allred, Anderson, Angle, Arrowsmith, Assadoorian, Atkison, Autio, Avery, Babcock, Ballard, Ballentyne, Ballinger, Beal, Beardsley, Bearnson, Beatle, Beddoes, Bergen, Beveridge, Birch, Bishop, Blake, Bodie, Bodle, Borr, Bowngren, Branch, Branco, Brinker, Brinkerhoff, Brock, Broderick, Brothers, Brown, Bryner, Buffmire, Bryson, Bunce, Bunderson, Burch, Burnfield, Burns, Burr, Burrows, Butts, Caffey, Callaway, Cameron, Capo, Carava, Carr, Carter, Castle, Cavigilo, Checketts, Christensen, Citerio, Cole, Conner, Cook, Coombs, Cowley, Cox, Cunningham, Daniel, Davies, Davis, Dickinson, Dimick, Donaldson, Dorius, Downard, Draper, Dumayne, Dunlerson, Durant, Eddy, Edwards, Eldredge, Emerson, Empey, Erickson, Evans, Ewell, Farrer, Farrish, Fawcett, Fetherstone, Fisk, Fitch, Fitzgerald, Floyd, Foote, Forrester, Frandger, Frandson, Fransden, Frantzen, Frekleson, Frost, Fuller, Fulmer, Garboda, Garden, Garling, Geiger, Gentry, Gibson, Glazer, Gould, Grames, Grimes, Griffin, Grundvig, Hall, Hallred, Halverson, Hammell, Hammond, Hansen, Harkness, Harrison, Hawkins, Hawks, Hill, Hoffman, Holdaway, Holley, Holliday, Hood, Horn, Horsley, Howard, Hutchinson, Ingles, "Jane-Red-Jacket" Jeffs, Jensen, Johnson, Jones, Keepers, Kenner, Killpack, Koekt, Kofford, Kuriz, Lamph, Larson, Lay, Lee, Leigh, Leonard, Lewis, Liddell, Link, Llewellyn, Long, Lord, Lowenstein, Lister, Lundal, Maceabee, Mangum, Marlotti, Marsh, Marsing, Martin, Mathis, Marzznia, McCune, Mead, Metcalf, McFarlane, McIntire, McKendrick, McMullin, Millburn, Miller, Montague, Moore, Muhlestein, Mulholland, Murcardeni, Myers, Nelson, Nickerson, Nielson, Nixon, Moyes, Oliphant, Olsen, Overson, Oveson, Oviatt, Pace, Padfield, Palmer, Palva, Parmley, Parmerly, Parrott, Passetio, Pattenson, Pearson, Perkins, Petersen, Peterson, Petty, Pittman, Poltiens, Potter, Powell, Pratt, Price, Pugh, Pulsipher, Rasmussen, Raums, Rees, Reese, Reeves, Reid, Rhoades, Richards, Ricks, Roberts, Roper, Ross, Rosser, Rougeri, Rowe, Ruggeri, Santachi, Saraceno, Savage Scalzo, Scofield, Seaboldt, Seeley, Sharp, Shaw, Shipp, Shultz, Simmons, Singleton, Smith, Snow, Snyder, Soderburg, Somers, Sorensen, Southworth, Spafford, Stagg, Staker, Stearns, Steen, Stevens, Stokes, Stone, Stowell, Street, String, taylor, Tell, Tergerson, Terry, Thayn, Thayne, Thomas, Thompson, Thordarson, Tidwel, Tilley, Touner, Travis, Tuttle, Vacher, Vale, Valentine, VanBuren, Vance, Vanlenyee, VanNatta, VanNotta, VanWagner, Wade, Wakefield, Walinia, Walker, Wallaco, Ward, Warf, Warren, Wartnia, Webb, Westover, White, Whitmore, Whitney, Wilcox, Williams, Wilson, Wiseman, Wisberg, Woodward, Woolley, Wright, Young, Zabriskie, Zaccrea, Zerbe, Zwellen, and many, many more.

Some of the articles are easier to read than others, please consider that they are 100 years or more old.

Compiled from the Deseret News (Utah), Deseret Evening News (Utah), Deseret Weekly (Utah), Eastern Utah Advocate (Utah), Eastern Utah Telegraph (Utah), Iron County Record (Utah), Logan Journal (Utah), Ogden Daily Enquirer (Utah), Ogden Daily Standard (Utah), Provo Daily Enquirer (Utah), Salt Lake Herald (Utah), Salt Lake Telegram (Utah), Salt Lake Times (Utah), Salt Lake Tribune (Utah), Vernal Express (Utah), Washington County News (Utah),& contributions from other regional papers.

Often while working on family history (genealogy) I wonder about more than is listed on the pedigree sheets and am so grateful for their sacrifices and love for the generations to follow

JUDGES OF ELECTION.

THE APPOINTMENTS MADE BY THE COMMISSION YESTERDAY TO ACT IN NOVEMBER.

EMERY COUNTY.

Castle Dale Precinct—Orange Seely, John K. Reid, James H. Wilcox.

Ferron Precinct—John E. King, Hiram S. Stephens, Warren S. Peacock.

Huntington Precinct—Ira B. Whitney, M. E. Johnson, C. W. Caldwell.

Moab Precinct—William H. Allred, L. B. Bartlett, Thos. M. Pritchett.

Price Precinct—Fred E. Grames, Levi Simmons, Mat Simmons.

The judges for Schofield not yet appointed.

DIED.

Price—At Pleasant Valley, Emery Co., December 7th, in the 61st year of her age, Mary Price, wife of John Price. Deceased was a native of Pendarron, Glamorganshire, Wales, and had been a faithful member of the Church for 35 years. She died in the faith.

CASTLE VALLEY.

PARTICULARS OF A TRIP AND VISIT TO CASTLE VALLEY.

For the following we are indebted to J. F. W.:

"The journey to Castle Valley, a hitherto remote, desolate region beyond the line of frequent travel, is now made with comparative ease in one day from Salt Lake City. Taking the D. & R. G. train at 7.40 a.m., by courtesy of the General Agent, Mr. Lamborn, we skirted up the valley of the Jordan, often on the river's bank, through the narrows and around the northern shore of Utah Lake to Provo, where lunch is taken, and the little train pursues its way past Springville and over a wide expanse of bench land, lying below the mountains. The Spanish Fork Canyon is entered and the road becomes quite picturesque as it passes by the rugged gorges, opening on either side. In many respects, particularly in the chimney rocks, the mountain scenery resembles that of Echo Canyon about the 'Witch's Rocks' and in the vicinity of the town of Echo.

At Clear Creek station the ascent commences to be quite difficult and continues so to the summit; from the latter point, however, the train glides over the smooth steel rails very rapidly to Pleasant Valley Junction, where we arrived at five p. m., and were hospitably entertained by Mrs. Southworth, former landlady of the Lake Point Hotel. At this station, the last opened for regular travel, we boarded a lumber car on the "construction train" and sped round the point of the mountain where Fish Creek and White River join to form Price River. Along the sinuous banks of the latter, the long train of cars, having loaded with ties, dashed by the tie companys and saw mills in the canyon at fearful speed. The road is so crooked that horseshoe curves are frequent and we found it quite interesting to keep track of the North Star, appearing first on one side of the car and then the other with such rapidity as to be bewildering to the star-gazer. The scenery in Price River Canyon is very beautiful, reaching its highest attraction at Castle Gate. The latter is the opening made by the stream through a wall of rugged rock rising on one side like a slender promontory reaching into the sky. This promontory, extends from the mountain down to the roadside where it is cleanly cut from base to summit, 500 feet above, appearing like a thin slab of red sandstone set on edge.

At Price, to be called hereafter Castle Valley Station, where we arrived at 9 o'clock p.m., we were welcomed by Bishop Frandson and Counselor E. W. McIntyre. A ward has been organized here with about 35 families, scattered along the river for several miles. They, however, have located a townsite and are now engaged taking the water out to cover it. The prospects are that quite an important town will spring up at this point, as the railway company will erect a round house and perhaps some shops; it will be the market and shipping town for Castle Valley and the broad extent of land capable of cultivation when the water is brought on to it will alone surround the town with the elements of prosperity and wealth.

In the morning we left Price for Huntington, distant twenty-seven miles. The beautiful weather, balmy, warm and spring-like made the journey very pleasant, while the wonderful, ever changing scenery was a source of constant delight. The following description of this road was written by Brother Johnson, a member of the Young Men's Association at Huntington:

'The road between Huntington and Price River, Emery County, Utah, is over rolling hills und hollows, and interspersed with deep gorges and washes that have been caused by the action of the turbulent waters that had gathered from the adjacent hillsides during thunder-showers, and rushed frantically along in their wild career to the Gulf of California, far away in the Sunny South.

On either side of the road at intervals can be seen table lands or mesas, which are composed principally of slate rock covered slightly with a light blue clay. And the scene might become monotonous but for the splendid range that stretches as far as the eye can reach in every direction, dotted here and there with herds of stock ranging from one bunch of sand or Gramma grass to another, a distance of many miles.

There is also another feature of this road worthy of note, and that is, the tendency it has to create a hope within the weary traveler as he wends his way over sand-ridge and desert plain. He can always see a gentle rise of ground just ahead, and he hopes he can obtain a good view when he gains the top, and so he can (of another hill). But when he does get sight of the river he has gained the top of just a baker's dozen of these hills and crossed as many valleys or flats, and 20 miles north and 10 east. The Twin Peaks are about half way between the two traveled streams Huntington and Price.'

At Huntington conference was held. The meetings were numerously attended by Saints from all of the settlements in Emery Stake except Moab, on Green River, 150 miles away. The new log meeting house, the best of the kind we have seen in the Territory, accommodated the people comfortably. The instructions given were eminently practical, Apostle F. M. Lyman engaging with his customary interest in the spirit and business of the conference. A High Council was chosen, many ordinances attended to and the Stake and Ward organiza-

tions so far perfected as the circumstances of the people at present require Saturday evening a conference of Y. M. M. I. A. was held.

On Sunday evening we drove to Castledale, ten miles, and held meeting, and were hospitably entertained by President C. G. Larson and family. On Monday we continued our southern journey to Ferron, distant fifteen miles, where we met with the Saints and spent a very enjoyable day at the comfortable home of brother M. W. Molen. The next day we drove early to Orangeville, ten miles on our return and held meeting in the new school house, which was packed to its utmost capacity. After dining with Bishop Robertson we drove on with Judge Elias Cox to Huntington, where we attended the regular meeting of the Young men's Association and listened to the interesting exercises.

By our return to Price we had seen enough of the Castle Valley country to convince us of its future outcome. There is land and water enough to supply a large population, the productiveness of the soil has been tested, and was found last year to be very profitable, as high as forty bushels of wheat to the acre being raised. The towns already platted and those contemplated, start with fair prospects, and through the blessing and favor of Providence the Saints of Emery Stake, who now number nearly 1,400, have every reason to expect large additions to their numbers, and that the barren wastes of Castle Valley, which they have secured, will yet bloom and 'blossom as the rose.'"

EMERY STAKE CONFEREN[CE]

The Quarterly Conference of E[m]ery Stake was held at Hunting[ton] meeting house March 3, 1883.

There were present on the sta[nd] Apostle F. M. Lyman, Juni[us] Wells, Assistant Sup't Y. M. M. A.; President C. G. Larson a[nd] Counselors, Bishops, President[s] Quorums, etc.

After opening exercises Preside[nt] Larson congratulated the people [of] Huntington on having such a co[m]modious house to hold conference [in.] Spoke at some length on the bles[s]ings of God to us in this fronti[er] Stake; also gave a report of h[is] travels to Moab, Grand Va[lley; said] he believed the people in the diffe[r]ent wards were united both tem[porally] and spiritually in the buil[d]ing up of Zion.

Bishop Elias Cox, of Hunting[ton] Ward, Bishop Frederick Olsen, [of] Ferron Ward, Bishop Jasper Rob[ert]son, of the Orangeville Ward, a[nd] Bishop Olsen, of Castle Dale Wa[rd] gave reports of their respect[ive] wards.

Apostle F. M. Lyman spoke [en]couragingly to the people in reg[ard] to building up new settlements. [All] his instructions were listened [to] with marked attention by [the] Saints. He announced the foll[ow]ing programme of meetings in [the] different settlements:

Castle Dale at 7 o'clock Sun[day] evening, Ferron Ward Monday 2 o'clock, Orangeville Tuesday [2] o'clock, Price Ward Wednesd[ay] 2 o'clock.

Singing and benediction.

After singing and prayer El[der] Jos. W. Moore spoke a few word[s on] the blessings of God to our peo[ple] and gave a favorable report of [the] High Priests Quorum.

Elder N. T. Guyman gave a g[ood] report of the Seventies of Em[ery] Stake.

Elder Junius F. Wells was su[r]prised to see so many together [on] the first day of conference; spok[e at] some length to the young, show[ed] the blessings in store for the fai[thful.]

His remarks were listened to [with] rapt attention.

[A]postle F. M. Lyman spoke at [som]e length in regard to the organ[izati]on of a High Council for Emery [Sta]ke, showed what kind of men [ar]e necessary to be chosen as [Hig]h Councilors. Made a few re[mar]ks on the celestial law of God [and] also on the Word of Wisdom; [sho]wed the blessings that would ac[cru]e from living up to these laws. [Si]nging and benediction.

Sunday, 10 a.m.

[T]he house was crowded to over[flo]wing.

[A]fter opening services the statis[tica]l report was read by J. R. Reid, [Sta]ke Clerk, also the report of the [Sun]day schools of Emery Stake.

[A]postle F. M. Lyman presented [the] general authorities of the [Ch]urch and Stake, who were unani[mo]usly sustained.

Prest. Larsen said there was one ... ... that was not reported this ...ference, on what is known as ...ddy Creek, it should have been ...orted in the Ferron Ward.

Elder Junius F. Wells spoke in ...ard to the Saints instructing ...ir children in the doctrines of our ...y religion when they are young. ...postle F. M. Lyman spoke a few ...rds on punctuality.

...inging and prayer.

...During the recess between fore-...on and afternoon meeting, a ...esthood meeting was held, at ...ich time the following brethren ...re ordained and set apart to fill ... positions named: As members ... the High Council of Emery ...ake, Charles Pulsipher, Anthon ...llsen, Peter Johnson, A. J. Jew...., John Donaldson, Sylvester H. ...x, Jos. W. Moore, Andrew C. ...nsen, Jasper Petersen, Geo. Fran... was ordained and set apart as ...shop of Price Ward, with E. W. ...cIntire and Caleb B. Rhoades as ... Counselors. John F. Wakefield ...s set apart as First Counselor to ...esident Jos. W. Moore, High ...iest's Quorums of the Emery Stake ... Zion. The following brethren ...re called as members of the High ...ounsel: J. H. Taylor, of Orange-...le; Mads Larsen and E. Homer, ... Ferron.

2 p. m.

...After singing and prayer the Sac-...ment was passed. President O. ...ely and President Rasmus Jus-...nsen each said a few words of en-...ouragement to the Saints. Prest. ...arsen hoped we had learned some-...ing by coming to Conference, that ...e would take with us to our homes ...d put in practice.

Apostle F. M. Lyman spoke with ...ergy on the following subjects: ...e sacrament, repentance, word of ...isdom and tithing. He asked for ...e blessing of God to be on this ...nd and on everything pertaining ...ereto, that the Saints might be ...essed in all things.

President Larsen said this Con-...rence would now be adjourned un-...l the first Saturday and Sunday in ...ne, to meet at Orangeville.

Apostle Lyman thanked the peo-...e for coming together, also the ...oir and the band for making mu-...c for us. The Huntington and ...rangeville choir combined, sang: ...his is my Commandment."

Benediction by Elder Junius F. ...ells.

J. K. REID,
Clerk of Emery Stake.

Salt Lake Herald
June 3, 1883

DEPUTY REGISTRARS.

EMERY COUNTY.

S. J. Harkness, Scofield precinct.
Job. H. Whitney, Castle Dale, pre-
    cinct.
John D. Kilpack, Ferron precinct.
John F. Wakefield, Huntington
    precinct.
O. H. Warner, Moab precinct.
Caleb B. Rhoads, Price precinct.

Correspondence.

MARSHALL PASS,
State of Colorado,
June 6th, 1883.

For Deseret News:

[A]t an elevation of 10,857 feet, [whe]re snow is to be found many [hun]dred feet below us, I remember [...] For the last two hours we [hav]e been circling around the tops [of] these beautiful, verdant and [heav]ily timbered mountains. From [whe]re I now sit I see a tank that [has] been in view from the moving [trai]n that has appeared to circle [aroun]d it, at different angles for the [last] 70 minutes. Passengers com[ing] it is with difficulty they [brea]the.

[W]e have now left the waters that [flow] into the Pacific—through the [Gun]nison, Grand and Colorado riv[ers] and have commenced our de[scen]t leaving the head waters of the [Ar]kansas river as they speed on [thei]r way to the Atlantic, through [the] great Mississippi.

[T]he engineering skill—displayed [in l]aying out this road and in the construction of these massive Locomotives, with eight driving wheels, drawing immense trains of loaded cars around curves at angles so very acute, (as to cause an engineer, it is said to whistle "down breaks" on one occasion, when he became a little confused, thinking he was about to collide with another train—when, lo! he had mistaken the rear end of his own train for that of another,) over a grade of 270 feet to the mile, is something very remarkable, to say the least, while the thrilling sensation experienced by the traveler as he passes through the "Castle Gate," whose massive pillars tower 400 feet above the Pass, the Castle Valley and "Black Canyon," present most romantic views, with rocky heights reaching 2,600 feet above the rapidly flowing Gunnison.

President Woodruff is now seated near me and excitedly exclaims, "If I could spare time to follow that stream for ten miles, I could supply my family with trout for a year." It appears that he got on the train at Price, Emery County, and reports to have traveled 80 miles by wagon in the last four days over Castle Valley, mostly of clay formation, very barren, as it seldom snows in winter, and rains in summer are not to be relied upon. Five meetings were held at Orangeville, where the people of the Stake assembled in Conference, under the presidency of C. G. Larsen, also one at Castledale and one at Huntington, where a good spirit prevailed amongst the Saints, and much good instruction was imparted.

In the latter place Bishop Elias Cox resigned, and Chas. Pulsipher was ordained Bishop in his stead, and two Counselors, and two High Counselors were selected and set apart to fill vacancies. The people are busy putting in crops, making ditches, etc. The five streams on the west side of the valley are quite high, the smallest of which contains as much water as Little Cottonwood, and the largest as much as the Jordan. They are known as Price, Huntington, Cottonwood, Farren and Muddy.

The Stake is prosperous and numbers over 1,600—over one-third of whom are under eight years of age.

While much of the scenery on this route is magnificent, we have seen no game, with the exception of a prairie dog or two to-day.

I am just reminded by a person sitting near me that there is other game in the country as he has heard of panthers being in the mountains, and he himself and two other persons were traveling from Heber City, Wasatch Co., through the country extending south a distance of 200 miles, where their provisions gave out, and they were without food for two or three days, but they luckily found a huge porcupine, so large and fat he says it took all three of them to get it upon their pack animal. (I presume they were not as strong as the porcupine, inasmuch as they were all grown men, and they could eat little else than the soup). Upon this they subsisted two days until they reached a settlement. He, however, says game is much more plentiful in these parts than it was then, inasmuch as the Indians do not hunt it as much and it is eight years since he passed through such a strait.

I have just met our townsman John W. Snell, who reports that he has marketed in colorado and vicinity over 1,800 bushels of Utah potatoes, in the last 30 days.

NONNAC.

Deseret News
February 6, 1884

Pleasant Valley Mines.—Superintendent Wm. G. Sharp returned a few days ago from Scofield, Pleasant Valley. The Utah Central mine is still burning, but not so extensively as hitherto. Another attempt was made last week to put out the fire and recover the bodies of the McLeans, but it only resulted in taking out some of the burning material. Another effort will be made shortly. Mrs. McLean, widow of one of the dead miners, is feeling better and has moved down to Provo.

The Pugsley mine, about half a mile from the other claim, is now being worked, and coal shipping is going on at the rate of 100 tons per day. This mine was purchased by the Utah Central Company of Phillip Pugsley, hence its name. It had not been worked to any extent prior to the burning of the other mine, which has rendered its development necessary.

Salt Lake Tribune
August 1, 1884

P. V. JUNCTION AND SCOFIELD NOTES.

Dr. Grass, M. D, is located at P. V. Junction.

Soldier Summit has an immense double snow shed

A new Mormon meeting house is to be log erected at Wales.

"Bob" Beatty is clerking in Mr. Williams store, Wales

There are are four saw mills and plenty of timber near P. V. Junction.

The Indians near P. V. have some fine horses and are fond of horse-racing.

Some forty cars of coal go down to Salt Lake and Provo from Scofield every day.

Pleasant Valley Junction is 93 miles from Salt Lake City, and Scofield, 113 miles.

Earl & Thomas have a general merchandise store at Scofield, and are doing a good business.

A new depot, similar to the one at Provo, and machine shops will soon be built at P. V. Junction.

Water froze in buckets at the station at Scofield the night of July 15th Winter clothing and underwear is a luxury.

Numerous fishing parties are camped along Fish and Mud Creeks, and are catching large numbers of the finny tribe.

The weather at P. V. Junction and Scofield is very cool and pleasant, two pairs of heavy blankets being used at night to keep comfortable.

Several bears, a panther and lots of deer have been seen around Wales, and as soon as the game law is up, sportsmen will have a "picnic."

Southworth Co. are agents for The Tribune at this point, and also have a general merchandise store, two lodging houses, and the St. James Hotel.

Mr. Scott Elliott has a herd of 10,000 sheep grazing on ground near Soldier Summit. These sheep yield over 6,000 pounds of wool annually

The Utah Central Coal mines at Scofield is still on fire despite all efforts to smother the fire. A new tunnel has been started about two hundred feet above the old one.

Soldier's Summit is over 4,000 feet above Salt Lake City, and about 8,000 above the sea. Much fine scenery can be observed from the cars on the way up and down Spanish Fork Canyon.

Since the D. & R. G railroad started up, the towns along the road have livened up considerably, having been very dull while the washout and legal troubles compelled the stoppage of the trains.

Walter Southworth, the genial proprietor of the St James Hotel, will be missed from P. V. for a short time, as he visits Ogden, Salt Lake and Provo, on business connected with the forthcoming excursion.

Numerous Indians, of the Ute tribe are camped within six and seven miles of P. V, and frequently bring large quantities of deer, bear, and wild cat skins in, to trade for supplies They report swollen streams of water during the last two months.

Rev. Erastus Smith, of Provo, delivered an interesting lecture upon "Temperance" last Saturday evening, in the dining room of the Rio Grande Hotel, and on Sunday night preached a sermon—having a large attendance both nights.

Two sons of the Indian who died from drinking too much liquor near P. V. Junction, have a herd of cattle and horses numbering 900 head, and evidently don't know what to do with them—neither wishing to sell nor to keep and feed them.

Two paraffine, or wax mines, have been worked near here, one being owned by a German Co in Kyune Canyon, and the other by Mr E. Covington, near Soldier Summit. This wax is worth from 15 to 17½ cents per pound, and is shipped to Chicago, New York, St. Louis and San Francisco, where it is used in coating varnish, making candles, wax dolls, etc.

The fishing and hunting in Pleasant Valley is of the finest kind, and many yarns are told in regard to it. One that was told to me yesterday was to the effect that a Salt Lake man came out here last week, caught such a quantity of fish that he died of physical exhaustion before he could drag the trout down the canyon to catch a freight train. This may be a strong story, but there are certainly numerous streams to fish in, besides excellent grouse, rabbit and sage hen hunting.

I took a run up to Scofield and the D & R G coal mines the other night with Conductor Abbott. Mr. Abbott very courteously pointed out the numerous places of interest in Pleasant Valley as we climbed up the canyon, and also showed me through the coal mines. This was a treat, as coal in all sorts of shapes, sizes and quantities could be seen, little mules chewed their hay and wagged their tails in their stables 500 feet under the ground, the air passages for fresh air, and in fact a hundred interesting things I saw, made the visit a pleasant one.

Scofield is certainly a coal mining camp, as well as Wales, both towns being inhabited by coal-miners and their families. Conductor Abbot, the gentlemanly conductor of the Pleasant Valley branch of the D & R G, showed me through the coal mines of the D. & R. G. at Wales, and it certainly was a treat. There is enough coal in these mines to supply Utah for the next hundred years, and it is of the best quality. There is at present but very little work being done at the mines, not over 50 men being at work.

Pleasant Valley Junction is a railroad town of about four hundred population, and is the terminus of the first freight division out of Salt Lake. A round house, of eleven stalls is here, built at a cost of $30,000, besides three general merchandise stores, four hotels and restaurants, two barber shops, five saloons, a bath house, and several lodging houses. The location of the town is to be changed from its present location, as the railroad company wish to build new switches on the land. The houses and building will be torn down and rebuilt some 40 or 50 feet to the east of their present location.

Scofield is 4,600 feet above Salt Lake City, and 8,000 above the sea, and yet fine lettuce, radishes and other garden vegetables are raised.

BILLY MORTON.

Deseret News
August 6, 1884

Accidentally Drowned.—About 7 o'clock in the evening of July 26 a little child twenty-two months old, son of Mr. John D. Lewellyn, of Scofield, Utah, was missed from home and could not be found. The people turned out enmasse and searched up and down the creek, among the hills and in every nook and corner where it was thought possible the child might be found. Search was kept up until morning, but owing to the darkness it was not successful until after daylight, when the body of the child was found in the creek. He had been found twice attempting to cross the creek on the railroad bridge, and it is supposed that in making the attempt the third time, unobserved, he had fallen in. His head and face were badly bruised and discolored by the fall. This is the eighth child out of a family of nine that has been taken away from this earth to a better home. The parents have the sympathy of the entire community in their sad bereavement.

PLEASANT VALLEY.

"THE GAZETTEER" fiend is around in this section.

SMALL GAME is reported as being plenty and close at hand. We'll see.

COAL SHIPMENTS from this locality are not so brisk as in former years; yet a good business is being done.

WILL AND Joe Sharp are among the many Salt Lakers one meets at Schofield and other parts along the line.

SCOTT ELLIOT, the "sheep king," was among the passengers on to-day's train. He has a large bunch of "mutton" over in Castle Valley.

A SWITCH has lately been put in at the Utah Central coal mine, under the supervision of Will Sharp. It is of great convenience, and will save its cost in three months.

AN EXTENSION is being made to the snow sheds at Soldiers' Summit, which will be of great advantage during the winter, avoiding, to a much greater extent, the danger of the cut being filled by drifts.

THE SCENERY along the railroad between Salt Lake and the coal mines, especially in Spanish Fork canyon, is greatly enhanced in attractiveness by the vari-colored autumn leaves that cover the hillsides.

THE "PLEASANT VALLEY Pullman" is what the denizens call the "caboose" that serves as passenger, mail, freight and express car between Pleasant Valley Junction and the Winter Quarters coal mines. It should be replaced with a new and better one.

WEDNESDAY'S EAST-BOUND train ran into a horse between Mill Fork and Clear Creek stations; but fortunately with no damage to the coaches or passengers. When the train left it was not known whether the animal was dead or not. The affair caused no excitement, and was noticed but by few of the passengers.

JOHN READING, Salt Lake's florist, is here, and ships a car-load of evergreens on Thursday. This is the second carload this season. Some of the present lot will be used in Liberty Park, and will add much to the attractions of that locality. This is a new industry, and one that promises to be a successful one. It has been proven that at least 75 per cent. will grow. It is intimated that a great many lawns will be graced with these beautiful trees ere long.

ARGEETEE.

P. V. COAL MINES, Oct. 15, 1884.

P. V. PARAGRAPHS.

In and About the Southern Coal Fields.

No snow here yet. The weather is as pleasant as in Salt Lake.

Bub Beatie and B. H. Young, Jr., are among the social lights in Winter Quarters precinct.

Fish Creek abounds in trout. The finny beauties can frequently be seen as they jump to the surface.

Mrs. B. F. Cummings, of Logan, who has been on a visit to her relatives, leaves here to-morrow for home.

Winter Quarters has one saloon, and the bar-keeper puts in his spare time—he has plenty—in mending shoes.

It is estimated that, with judicious management, and one or two red-hot stump speeches, Capt. Smith, the Liberal candidate, will receive at least three votes from this precinct alone.

A joint meeting of the residents of Winter Quarters and Schofield precincts was held at the new schoolhouse last evening to consider the feasibility of using the house in common for a school this winter. It was decided so to do, and the advantages of the joint school will be apparent to all.

The Herald reaches us at about 7 p. m. each day. The mail facilities, however, are not as good as could be wished for. I do not know where the fault lies. Some are inclined to say it is at P. V.

Junction, but letters from Salt Lake are sometimes several days on the road, whereas, if posted in time, they should reach here within 10 hours of leaving your city. The express business is not so well managed as it might be either. A package was received here recently that had been only six days on the road—a distance of 18 miles.

Game in "the valley" is very scarce; a party has just returned, and report they found no shooting of any consequence between this place and Hale's Siding in Fish Creek Canyon. In the mountains near the latter place, however, and indeed in almost any part of Fish Creek Canyon, grouse are plentiful in the foot hills. One party returned this evening with twelve grouse, after spending an hour in the vicinity of Hales'. Four bears were exhibited here a day or two ago, having been killed a couple of miles above the P. V. mines. Dead deer are brought into town nearly every day, but they are very scarce in comparison with a couple of years ago. One who hunts deer now is a hunter in a double sense.

The P. V. coal mines are running about eighty men, the U. C. forty, and the Mud Creek about thirty, thus giving employment to 150 miners, and furnishing sustenance to 1,000 persons within a radius of three miles. About 400 tons of coal are shipped daily from the three places. This, however, does not represent the capacity of the mines by any means. It is claimed that if cars could be obtained 1,000 tons could be shipped daily from the P. V. mines—three in number—alone, with no prospect of exhaustion within a generation. There is enough coal in this place alone to supply Salt Lake with fuel until a Liberal Delegate is elected to Congress.

ARGEETEE.

P. V. Coal Mines, Oct. 17, 1884.

DEATHS.

BABCOCK—At Price, Emery County, Daisy Augusta, infant daughter of John and May Augusta Henchett Babcock.

ACCIDENTAL KILLING.

Particulars of the Death of Anthony Kelly.

COAL MINE, SCOFIELD, Utah,
December 20, 1884.

To the Editor of THE HERALD:

On the 17th inst., Anthony Kelly, a miner, was killed in No. 2 tunnel, in the Pleasant Valley coal mines, by the falling of the top of the room. After he was buried in the debris he spoke two or three times, and the men worked diligently to get him out, but he only lived a few minutes. The next day his brother took his body to Salt Lake City for burial. He was aged 36, unmarried and formerly of Pennsylvania, where his parents are now living.

The place where Mr. Kelly was killed is not where he was working, or the place of his work, but quite a distance therefrom. His brother testified that he was going out to inform the driver of a "fall" when a second "fall" came upon him. But some are of the opinion that he was pulling down the top coal and pulled it upon himself. There is some circumstantial evidence in favor of this, and the clearing away of the debris will settle this question, for if he was working there his tools will be found. However, the matter was purely accidental. The accompanying is the inquest.   PHONSO.

CORONER'S JURY VERDICT.

TERRITORY OF UTAH,
WINTER QUARTERS PRECINCT,
SANPETE COUNTY.

An inquisition holden at Coal Mine Station, in Winter Quarters Precinct, Sanpete County, on the Seventeenth day of December, A. D., 1884, before David J. Williams, Justice of the Peace in Winter Quarters Precinct, in said County, upon the body of Anthony Kelly, there lying dead, by the jurors upon their oaths do say, that the said Anthony Kelly came to his death by the accidental falling of a clod from the roof of room in the Pleasant Valley Coal Mines, Wednesday, December 17th, between the hours of 10 and 11 o'clock a. m.

In testimony whereof, the said jurors have hereunto set their hands the day and year aforesaid.

B. H. YOUNG, JR.,
J. M. BEATIE,
THOMAS PORTER,

Attest my hand, this seventeenth day of December, A. D., 1884,

DAVID J. WILLIAMS,
Justice of the Peace.

Bound Over. — "J. B.," writing from Price, Emery County, on the 13th inst., sends us an account of the trial of Captain Hawley. D. & R. G. Special Agent, on the evening of the 12th, before E. W. McIntyre, Justice of the Peace at that place. The charge, which was preferred by Mr. Marsh, the man whom Hawley ejected from his office, was for assault and robbery. The robbery part of the charge was not sustained, it appearing from the evidence that though Captain Hawley forcibly seized possession of the office which Mr. Marsh had occupied, containing private as well as company property, and without showing any authority for such action, there was no intention on the part of the captain to steal anything, but simply to examine the papers, after which they were left in charge of a clerk. The charge of assault, however, was proven and Captain Hawley was bound over in the sum of $500 to await the action of the Grand Jury of the First District Court. Our correspondent states that considerable interest is felt at Price over the probable action of the Grand Jury, as, if the case be brought into court, it will likely be shown to what extent a special agent of the railway can go without showing papers for his authority when asked to do so.

Deseret News
January 28, 1885

CANAL MAKING IN EMERY COUNTY.

PRICE, Emery Co., Utah,
Jan. 19, 1885.

Editor Deseret News:

The thermometer has ranged near zero here for the last three weeks, with snow ten inches deep. Yet we have a good turn out of men and teams at work on our city canal ditch. We have some heavy cuts and fills to make which the frost does not materially interfere with. We have four miles of ditch to make to get the water to our townsite, which we expect to complete in time to plant gardens, trees, etc.

The health of the people on this river is good; no sickness of any kind.

Yours respectfully,　　　H. W.

Salt Lake Herald
March 15, 1885

APPOINTMENTS as notaries public were issued yesterday by Secretary Thomas, to Thomas C. Bailey and C. E. Pomeroy of this city, Parlin Macfarlane, of Ephraim, Sanpete County, and Fred. E. Grames, of Price, Emery County.

Salt Lake Herald
March 29, 1885

Judges for Weber and Emery Counties.

EMERY COUNTY.

Scofield—Robert McKekney, D. M. Holdway, John Eden.

Hungtington—Philander Birch, H. S. Loveless, G. W. Johnson.

Castle Dale—James Jeffs, Orange Seeley, Joseph Dennison.

Molen—H. S. Peacock, Hans C. Hansen, Seth Wherehand.

Ferron—William Taylor, Jr., M. H. Fugat, John J. Loveless.

Muddy — Samuel Miller, Aloz. C. Lozenbee, Miles Miller.

Moab—L. B. Bartlett, John Schaffer, Thomas Pritchett.

A BREEZE FROM PRICE.

A Reminder to the Provo Grand Jury.

THE D. & R. G. PRICE AGENCY.

Clarence Marsh Explains His Position, and Wants to Know Where His Case Has Gone.

PRICE, UTAH, April 18th, 1885.

To the Editor of THE HERALD.

When convenient, and if consistent, will you kindly allow me space in your valuable paper for publication of this statement, as also the two enclosed letters. In your issue of January 17th last, an article appeared headed, "The Special Agent," which article set forth the duties of a special agent, and the authority vested in that character by the D. & R. G. W. Ry. The article, after strongly eulogizing the great ability, the fine stature and the invaluable aid this self-styled Captain Hawley was to the receiver, also set forth charges against my character, and endeavored to brand me a thief and liar, and one unworthy of trust. A summary of the article also appeared in the San Francisco Chronicle. On January 24th following, I made a reply to the same, and also promised the public that the whole case should come before the Grand Jury at Provo, for investigation.

The case duly came up before the Grand Jury in Provo, at its last sitting, but up to this time the case has not been heard. Hawley claims the case was thrown out of court. Hawley's bondsmen are released. Hawley has not been arraigned. Briefly stating the evidence given there: One reliable man testified that Hawley told Bancroft, the receiver, when starting from Salt Lake with his complaint made and signed by one saloonkeeper, one man who acts as an agent for the company who bitterly hates Mormonism, but who has a wife in the east from whom he is not been divorced and who is now living in this country with another woman to whom he is not married and raising a family by, also signed by a drunken employee; that he did not think the complaint amounted to anything; that he expected trouble if he entered Marsh's office without authority. Bancroft answered by saying throw him out, we will stay by you. The balance of evidence given proved that Hawley refused to show authority three times; that he assaulted me; broke open cash drawer of two separate companies; gave away some of my personal effects, assaulted me and robbed my office of all my personal letters and myself afterwards compelled to pay over $179 collected by three unauthorized agents; also that the Express company said Hawley was not in their employ and I should have resisted his entrance; also that no notice of Hawley's appointment to any position in the service was ever made by Bancroft or any other officer. I also wish to state that the letter of resignation mentioned in Mr. Bancroft's letter is a stolen document and not official, as same was never mailed, but taken from my office by Hawley and acted on to avoid a civil case.

I also wish to state that the cause for Mr. Bancroft's actions cannot at present be made public by me but will without doubt in time when I shall be able to set forth my charges before those who are Mr. Bancroft's employers as well as mine.

I have been out of employment, with a family to support, since January last. I have spent considerable of my savings and have tried every endeavor to have my case come before the court for investigation, where a poor man should be able to have his grievances heard as well as the unreliable representative of a corporation. After receiving so many inquiries from my many friends and former employers, some of whom are readers of your paper, asking what had become of the case of Hawley, and begging I had not allowed it to go unnoticed, I kindly ask the publication of the above for their information, and by it I think they will see the abuse I have been subjected to, and the treatment received for respecting the sovereignty of the law, as also the precedent established by the law in Utah in favor of a blackmailing, self-styled detective. Yours truly,

CLARENCE MARSH.

W. H. BANCROFT, RECEIVER, DENVER & RIO GRANDE WESTERN RAILWAY,
OFFICE OF SUPERINTENDENT.

SALT LAKE CITY, Utah,
March 15, 1885.

Clarence Marsh, *Esq., Price, Utah:*

Dear Sir:—For your information and in answer to yours of the 15th inst., I will enclose a copy of a letter written to Mr. Maddison. It fully explains itself. You resigned your position with the Company. I have never made any charges against your character, therefore, there is nothing to retract. If other people have made charges, you must look to them to answer them.
Yours truly,
W. H. BANCROFT,
Receiver.

THE GUARANTEE CO. OF NORTH AMERICA,
HEAD OFFICE, 260 James St.,
MONTREAL, March 31, 1885.

INSPECTION DEPARTMENT.

Mr. C. *Marsh,*
Price, Emery Co., Utah:

Dear Sir: Replying to your letter dated 15th, I have pleasure in stating that we have nothing against you, and any application you may make shall have our best consideration.
Yours truly,
E. RAWLINGS,
Managing Director.

THREATENED LYNCHING AT PRICE.

A LECHEROUS SCOUNDREL ALMOST SWUNG INTO ETERNITY SEVERAL TIMES AT THE END OF A ROPE.

PRICE, Emery County, Utah,
July 2, 1885.

Editor Deseret News:

A few days ago we had the arrival of a new section boss, James Bergen by name, sent here to take charge of a crew of Chinamen on the D. & R. G. Railway. Shortly after his entrance into the town he made himself very conspicuous by telling people around the railway station of his

INTENDED FUN

with "Mormon" women, etc. Some of our boys thought he would bear a little watching, and accordingly paid a little attention to his movements in the evenings, not for a moment expecting that the brute would use open daylight for his hellish purpose.

Yesterday afternoon, July 1st, Sister Nelson, who lives on a farm about two miles down the river, came to town to do some trading at a store, and on her return, in the middle of the afternoon, she was followed up by this devil in human form—James Bergen—who, by fast walking, soon caught up with her, and, about three-quarters of a mile from the nearest house, made

INDECENT PROPOSALS

to her, and offering her money. The poor woman, though very nervous and frightened, attempted to shame him by talking to him, but this only made the fellow worse, and he not only indulged in the most vulgar language but also proceeded to expose his person; whereupon Mrs. Nelson fled homeward, screaming for help, and escaped her follower.

The news flew like an electric flash from one end of town to the other, and aroused general indignation. Some of the boys concluded to ride him on a rail, and were just proceeding to do so, when about a dozen masked men arrived on the spot, took the scamp in charge, and led him quietly to a telegraph pole. The bystanders could come to no other conclusion for a moment than that some

LYNCHING

was near at hand, especially when a short, heavy-set man was noticed in the rear, with a long rope. The masked men moved about as if they had been drilled for the purpose. The strictest order prevailed, and very few words were spoken, but amid the silence the rope was fastened around the prisoner's neck, who, imagining by this time that perhaps the next minute would find him in eternity, broke out in a torrent of supplications for mercy, telling the would-be lynchers of his good standing in Christian religious society, as also his respectable family relations.

A young man climbed the telegraph pole, with the loose end of the rope, which was done in less time than it takes to tell it, and the brute was then asked if he had anything to say before swinging. The doomed section boss stuttered some few sentences and then offered up

HIS PRAYER

to the Holy Mary and others, the prayer indicating that he was either a Methodist or a Catholic.

After his prayer was finished the crowd swung him up a foot or two from the ground, and, letting him down, told him to pray again. After the second prayer they again

SWUNG THEIR MAN

a little way up, and again let him drop. This was repeated three or four times, and at last when the lynchers thought it was all he could stand he was asked if he would leave immediately if they would spare his life. This offer was accepted with thanks and gratitude, and a few moments after a fellow was seen marching on the railway track towards the east, with a speed which would do credit to a good young horse, occasionally looking back, as if apprehending danger from the citizens of Price, and we hope by this time that Mr. James Bergen is safe among his Christian friends in Colorado, and taken care of by them, where he can sit down quietly and relate the incidents of his four days' visit to Utah and his experience among the "Mormons."   C. H.

Salt Lake Democrat
September 17, 1885

Bishop David Williams, of Pleasant Valley, is in the city, and says that the colony at Price, Utah, is getting houses, irrigating ditches and all conveniences ready as fast as possible for a prosperous season next summer. A Colorado market for produce is being opened up, and a road has been made from the Indian agency to their settlement.

Salt Lake Herald
October 7, 1885

From the Coal Mines.

Mr. David Williams, of the Pleasant Valley Coal Mines, in Winter Quarters Canyon, is in the city. His contract with the owners of the property expired on the first of the present month. During the years that the mines have been under his charge, Mr. Williams has been untiring in his endeavors to promote the comfort and prosperity of the miners in his employ, and his many acts of kindness will be missed by the miners in the valley.

Mr. Williams is not yet decided as to what business he will go into, but in whatever he may take hold of, all who know him will wish the best of success.

His son, David J., is established at Price, on the D. & R. G., and it is quite probable that a colony will soon take up quarters there.

It is understood that Will Williams will remain in the employ of the coal company at Winter Quarters, and if so, the company will have made a wise selection.

CAPTURE OF A HORSE THIEF.

PRICE, Emery Co., Utah,
Sept. 29th, 1885.

Editor Deseret News·

Our quiet little burg was last Thursday aroused from its usual peaceable situation, by a party who were traveling through the country on their way to Oregon, who came to town and reported that a horse had been stolen the day previous from their camp about thirty-five miles east from here. The owner of the horse was anxious to get his animal back, and while speaking to a crowd of people present, he offered the liberal reward of $150 for the capture of the thief and the return of the horse.

Our respected townsman and farmer, Charles Johnson, who is of a very quiet disposition, and never says a great deal, after a moment's consideration remarked, "I guess I will take your $150." He was soon authorized as "deputy constable by the proper authority," and shortly after his gigantic form was seen on a horse, slowly making his way out of town in a southerly direction, as though he was taking a ride for the benefit of his health.

It is a general custom among such officers of the law, when going after a desperado, to arm themselves to the teeth, but it was different with friend Johnson; he went on his way without any weapons of any kind, relying upon his physical strength, of which a wise providence has meted out to him an abundance. He traveled through Huntington, Castle Dale and Ferron Creek, and by inquiring found that his man was only a short distance ahead of him. He traveled along and arrived at a place called Muddy, 70 miles from here about two o'clock at night, where he happened to see by moonlight the horse in question, tied to a corral fence. Our deputy concluded to camp by the same corral, so he took the saddle off his horse and sitting coolly down called in his wandering thoughts, and reflected on past, present and future. A moment after he noticed some bedding close to the house, and supposing somebody slept there he paid some little attention to the moving of the quilts

About daybreak on Friday morning the man in the bedding had perhaps had sleep enough, and commenced moving about in the quilts uncovering his face, to see if the sky was free from clouds, but suddenly a voice from our unarmed deputy came like a rushing of many waters. Arms up, young man! And although the thief had a heavy six-shooter at his side, the command given by Mr. Johnson was promptly obeyed.

The man in authority told his prisoner that he guessed they would both return to Price, as he thought they had a little urgent business to attend to in Squire McIntire's office, to which the prisoner consented, and on their return they started: but, lo and behold! on the road, between Muddy and Ferron creek, the prisoner snatched from Johnson the six-shooter, which the deputy had taken from him and was carrying himself, and attempted to escape. But the officer grappled with him, got hold of the weapon and after it had been once discharged without doing harm to either of them, and after a fall to the ground the prisoner again mounted. Very little was said, but Johnson told him kindly, if he made another attempt like that, he would get hurt. Nothing happened to mar their peace during the balance of the journey, and they arrived safe at Price yesterday (Sunday) afternoon.

This morning at nine o'clock the prisoner whose name is George Wright, was brought into the justices court, where he plead guilty to the two charges preferred against him—grand larceny, and attempt to disarm an officer and judge E. W. McIntire bound him over in the sum of $1,000 to appear before the grand jury in the First Judicial District at Provo. The bond not being furnished the deputy will tomorrow take his man to Provo.

The following commissions were issued on Wednesday:

Elias H. Cox, superintendent of district schools, Emery County.

William H. Branch, selectman, Emery County.

H. P. Rasmussen, justice of the peace, Molen Precinct, Emery County.

J. T. Farrer, justice of the peace, Thomas Farrer, constable, Blake Precinct, Emery County.

David Miller, justice of the peace, Muddy Precinct, Emery County.

S. J. Harkness, justice of the peace, Joseph M. Fairbanks, constable, Scofield precinct, Emery County.

Chinese Depredators. — Our correspondent "C. H.," writing from Price, Emery Co., gives us an account of the recent arrest and trial before a justice's court at that place of a couple of Chinamen who had been caught stealing vegetables from a garden. It seems the Celestials in question took advantage of the absence of most of the residents from their homes while attending the Sabbath meeting to sneak into the garden of a citizen by the name of Marsh and go to digging up and appropriating turnips and other vegetables. Mrs. Marsh arrived upon the scene in time to catch the depredators at their work and on ordering them out of the garden was threatened with violence and probably only saved by the timely interference of two young men.

On being brought into court the culprits plead guilty, and for some reason known only to the justice, that functionary let them off with the ridiculously low fine of $2.50 each.

Cases of theft from the Chinese railroad employes are becoming so common that nothing that can be stolen by them is now considered at all safe without it is secured by locks or bars. Not only are such tools as people usually leave outdoors about their premises carried off by the pilfering rascals, but pigs and chicken also.

Our correspondent relates that during the silent hours of the night recently he was awakened from his slumber by his pig squealing, and without stopping to dress himself he hastened out to his pig pen. Just as he arrived there two Chinamen who were in the act of trying to secure the porker sprang from the pig pen over the fence and made off across the prairie. Bent on capturing the marauders, he gave chase, but had not gone far when he stepped in a bed of prickly pears, and was glad to get back to the house and remove the thorns from his feet.

The people of Price, as may naturally be expected, feel indignant over the action of the D. & R. G. Railway in forcing the presence of the thieving Mongolians upon them, and our correspondent says if the company is really too poor to employ white men to replace them on the section they would prefer to donate the difference in the rates of wages to having their present infliction.

Deseret News
October 21, 1885

Pleasant Valley Notes. — On last Friday afternoon the D. & R. G. round house at Scofield was destroyed by fire, being completely consumed. Close to it was the lumber yard of David Eccles, and for a time there was imminent danger that the lumber would take fire also. Had it done so a vast conflagration would have been the result, as immense quantities of lumber are lying in the yard. The round house was located about one and three-quarter miles from the Winter Quarters (D. & R. G.) coal mines. A caboose was quickly run up to the mines and returned loaded with miners who came to aid in putting out the fire. A startling rumor was started about the time the flames began to subside. It was to the effect that the nightwatchman, who usually slept in the round house during the day, had been consumed in the burned buildings. It was afterwards settled, however, that such a calamity had not happened.

For several years past Bishop David Williams, of the Pleasant Valley ward, has had the management of the D. & R. G. coal mines, but with the month of September his contract expired, and the management of the mines was assumed, on October 1st, by the Pleasant Valley Coal Company, whose officers will in future conduct the business of mining the coal. Bishop Williams had at the mines a store and stock of general merchandise which he sold out to the P. V. Coal Co., when the change took place. The Bishop has removed his family from the mines to the town of Scofield, about two miles distant, where he talks of engaging in mercantile business, stock raising, etc.

The output of coal from the D. & R. G. mines during the last few days has exceeded 500 tons per day. The force of miners is being rapidly increased, every train to Pleasant Valley having on board black diamond diggers, many of whom take their families with them. At the Utah Central mines there is also quite a rush.

The population of Pleasant Valley probably numbers at the present time 1,000 souls, which number is being rapidly augmented. Starting at Pleasant Valley Junction, on the main line of the D. & R. G., is a branch road about 17 miles long, reaching to the coal mines in Pleasant Valley, and forming the only avenue of communication between the valley and the outside world. A great deal of fault is being found with the management of this branch line, and the accommodations afforded passengers going over it are certainly anything but pleasant and comfortable. Travelers are compelled to ride in a caboose attached to a coal train, which seems not to be governed in its arrivals or departures by any time card. It is set down in the time table as leaving P. V. Junction at 4:10 p.m., but frequently it does not depart until late at night. During the present influx of miners and their families into Pleasant Valley, it often happens that women and children are detained in this caboose hours and hours after the time at which they should have reached their destination, and in consequence they suffer great inconvenience and anxiety, and find themselves landed in a strange place late in the night.

ORGANIZATIONS EFFECTED AT PRICE.

PRICE, Emery County, Utah,
November 4th, 1885.

Editor Deseret News:

Blessed are their feet who bring glad tidings and make the hearts of the people rejoice.

This can truly be said by the people of Price Ward, for the blessed visits from our brethren and sisters from your city, who lately have been here, and displayed wisdom, which only a higher power than man can inspire. As Daniel said, "There is a God in heaven who revealeth secrets." So we can testify that no other power than that of the Almighty could have brought to pass what has been wrought out for this Ward in the last few days.

On the 27th of last month we were apprised of the arrival of Apostles Young, Lyman, and Grant, who, on the following day at well-attended meetings, reorganized the Price Ward.

Bishop Frantzen, who had arrived a few days previous from a long absence to the west, was allowed as Counselors, John Pace and John Mathis, who both had the endorsement from the whole community and were unanimously sustained by all the Saints.

Besides organizing the ward, the Apostles spoke to the assembled Saints with a power which no man can speak with unless the treasures of heaven are revealed to him. After being fed with the word of eternal life in the discourses delivered by those inspired of the Most High, we bid them a hearty farewell and God speed, and the people here went to their usual occupations with new vigor and energy. None conceived the idea that another similar feast was awaiting us, until last evening when, like electric flashes the news spread up and down the river among the Saints that our worthy sister Eliza R. Snow Smith and sister Elizabeth Howard, from Salt Lake City, and sister Larson and her counselor for the Relief Society of Emery Stake, had arrived and that the Saints were summoned to meet at ten o'clock this morning.

Representatives from all the districts in the ward made their appearance in our large, commodious meeting house, where our sisters organized the Primary Association with Sister Eldredge as president, whose nomination received a hearty response from the Saints.

The good presiding sister gave some very valuable instruction for our young folks, which were wise and timely.

Again before two o'clock in the afternoon, people from all quarters commenced gathering about the meeting house. This meeting was for the purpose of arranging a Relief Society, which object was accomplished, with our worthy and esteemed Sister, Sara Cox, as president, and Sister Pace and Sister Empey as her counselors. These ladies who have been chosen and set apart for the offices mentioned have already proven themselves worthy of the confidence which the Saints have placed in them, and after meeting this afternoon, when congratulations followed, the words, "God bless you, sister," were heard from all directions.

So we feel to thank and bless our visiting bretheren and sisters, and to say, Call again soon.   C. H.

CORRESPONDENCE.

YOUNG MEN ORGANIZED IN PRICE.

PRICE, Emery County,
Utah, Nov. 14th, 1885.

Editor Deseret News:

The organization of the Young Men's Mutual Improvement Association for Price Ward took place on Sunday evening, the 8th inst., with the following officers: Ernest Horsley, president; Albert Bryner and Arthur W. Horsley, counselors; Eugene E. Branch, secretary; Erastus Olsen, asssistant secretary; Brigham McIntire, treasurer; Charles Webb, librarian.

Those young men, all born in the covenant, spoke with a power and determination in favor of the cause of God which almost made the old folks present feel that they had better take a back seat, and let the heroes occupy the pulpit henceforth, as their sermons almost made the mountains echo with joy.

May heaven strengthen them in their responsibility through all future events, is the desire of   C. H.

Salt Lake Herald
December 30, 1885

PLEASANT VALLEY ITEMS.

Dull Trade---Christmas---Railroad Matters.

This has been the mildest winter experienced in this valley since its settlement. Snow is only a few inches deep as yet.

December has been a very slack month for the coal trade, the mines not more than making expenses. In consequence of dull times, about 200 men have gone to seek employment in other mines. It is believed that the force in Winter Quarter's mines will be reduced to 100 men.

On Christmas Eve there was a raffle at Scofield for a silver cornet, valued at $75. C. H. Bliss was the lucky person, but claiming that music was left out of his composition, and that would never be able to perform on even a corn stalk violin, he immediately proceeded to turn the instrument over to his wife, who is spending the holidays in Salt Lake.

The Pleasant Valley Assembly Hall was decorated on Christmas with two large, well filled Christmas trees, and the din of a multitude of happy children was heard for three prolonged hours.

Messrs. Sharp, Carpenter, Young, Beatie, Nelson, Abbott, McKeckney, Angus, Ferguson, and others with friends from below, are making the best of the season and enjoying themselves hugely.

There have been some complaints about the U. S. mail lately. It is brought to the station between 10.30 and 12 p. m. and kept there till 10 a. m. next day before taking to the office. It has even been kept there till 3 p. m. next day. I think the cause of this is the railroad company keep their men on duty sixteen to twenty hours for work that can be performed in five or six. The men were heard to say they only got fourteen hours' sleep, last week. They make two trips per day to P. V. Junction and this is about four hours' work, and the switching that is to be done here is but little at present. A passenger coming to this place, arrives at P. V. Junction at 3.30 p. m., and has to wait till about 10 p. m. and often later, before he can start for Scofield. If there was any necessity for such proceedings it would be excusable, but as it is, it is hoped the company will make the desired change.

On Christmas Eve, the Springville Dramatic troupe descended on us unawares and announced they would play the Two Orphans and Nature and Philosophy on the evenings of the 25th and 26th. Notwithstanding the dull times and the severe criticisms of the Provo *Enquirer*, the theatre was crowded at both performances. The acting exceeded the expectations of everybody, and it is decidedly better than any traveling troupe that has ever visited us. We have critics here who have seen the play produced in prominent theatres, one of whom says he has seen it performed by seven different troupes from New York to San Francisco and all say this home company played it well. At any rate they will be welcome if they visit us again.

P. V.

PLEASANT VALLEY, Dec. 26, 1885.

Deseret News
March 24, 1886

DEATHS.

BRYNER.—At Price, Emery Co., Utah., Maggie Marie, daughter of Albert and Marie Bryner; born September 3, 1885; died March, 8, 1886.

Deseret News
May 5, 1886

DEATHS

PERKINS—At Price, Emery County, Utah, Emily Alice, daughter of Nephi and Emily Jane Perkins; born January 8, 1883, died April 24, 1886.

EMERY COUNTY ITEMS.

PRICE, Emery County, Utah,
April 29th, 1886.

Editor Deseret News:

Our little burg, Price, filled with its industrious and enterprising inhabitants, is prospering under the blessings of a wise Providence, who has promised he will help those who will help themselves in all things.

The peace, prosperity and happiness which reign among the Latter-day Saints in this Stake of Zion would almost indicate that the millenium, or the peace reign, which the divine writings tell about, had commenced. But by reading the newspapers, which relate the savage measures adopted by our Christian (?) friends, and the hostility to our progress, manifested by our kind (?) U. S. Officials and their gang of intruders, we come to the conclusion that we are living on the eve of the reign of Babylon, and we feel that the morning will soon dawn upon us, when the King of kings, and Lord of lords will take his reign upon this planet.

We have no time here at Price, to spend in courts, or before prying prosecutors; we all here despise their actions. Their zeal, is worthy of a better cause. We are very busy in our different occupations endeavoring by our labor to provide for those who depend upon us for their support; and above all things we are very careful to keep all the laws of God, and not break any constitutional law of the land. We feel sorry, for those who are persecuted for their religion, and our prayers ascend daily that the Lord God will hasten the time when His will may be done on earth as it is done in the heavens.

The Saints here in this Stake have been working energetically this spring in purchasing and planting fruit trees.

Last fall our school trustees were successful in securing the services of Prof. I. W. Nixon, of St. George, to teach our day school, which he has done for two terms, to the great satisfaction of all concerned. He has had an average of 50 scholars, some of whom have received education in the more advanced branches.

The making of the new road from here to the Uintah Reservation is now under the superintendency of Mr. G. Goss, and in a few weeks the transportation between those two places will be in order, to the great convenience and benefit of all concerned.

Our fellow-townsman Brother Nephi Perkins, lost by the hand of death, a few days ago, his bright little girl, Emily Alice, three years old. The necessary preparations for her burial were attended to in due time, and the funeral service appointed, at which time the little corpse appeared as if in a sound sleep, and some of the visitors had the idea that the child was not dead. The heartbroken mother was persuaded, by close observation, that there was still hope for her darling's recovery. So, the funeral was wisely postponed till next morning. Neighbors and friends again gathered, and service was held under the presidency of Bishop Frantzen. The weeping mother and the visitors appeared by the coffin to take their last look on the beloved child, when suddenly one of the visitors exclaimed that the child was not dead, which, after due consideration, caused another postponement till the following day, when at last it was considered safe to bury the child, as mortification had set in to a very great extent.

The first of May will be celebrated in grand style at Price.   C. H.

DEATHS.

SIMMONS.—At Price, Emery County, Utah, May 5th, 1886, Jonathan Simmons, born in Nauvoo, Hancock County, Ill., Feb. 22nd, 1843.

Gone to the Bad.—During the greater part of the time for nearly a year past, the firm of D. J. Williams & Co., of Price, Emery County, have had in their employment a man named C. Halvorsen, a native of Denmark, who, however has lived in different places in this Territory for many years. He was a man of more than average intelligence, and was quite prominent and very generally respected in the community in which he resided. Since he removed to Price he has been in straightened, almost destitute circumstances, and Williams & Company have given him employment, more out of sympathy and respect than because he was really a valuable hand.

Recently the firm reluctantly began to suspect him of stealing goods and money from the store, and yesterday had a search warrant issued, resulting, as we learn by private advices, in the recovery of several hundred dollars worth of goods which he had stolen. He was held in $2,000 bonds to await the action of the grand jury on a charge of grand larceny.

The fall of Halvorsen from the standing of an honest man, respected by his neighbors and fellow citizens, to the low level of a thief and robber of his friends and benefactors, has produced a profound sensation throughout Emery County.

Election Judges.—The Utah Commission has appointed the following-named judges of election for Emery County:

Moab precinct—S. B. Bartlett, Walter More, Thos. Pritchette.

Blake precinct—Josephus Gammage, Robt. Hatrick, Nephi Purke.

Price precinct—Fred Grames, Wm. F. Williams, Wm. Noyes.

Huntington precinct—G. W. Johnson, Thomas Wakefield, H. S. Loveless.

Lawrence precinct—Henry Roper, Philander Birch, Robt. Hill.

Orangeville precinct—Frank Carroll, Hyrum Huntington, E. M. Cox.

Muddy precinct—Miller Miller, Jacob Marchy, Geo. Merrick.

Wellington precinct—John Hallred, J. D. Wright, Hyrum String.

Scofield precinct—D. W. Holdaway, John Eden, A. H. Earll.

DEATHS.

ROPER—At Huntington, Emery County, Utah, on June 26th, 1-86, after two days' illness, Charlotte Elizabeth Mellor, wife of Henry Roper.

Deceased was born January 16, 1842, at Leicester, England, was baptized in 1852 and emigrated with her parents in 1856, helped pull a handcart across the Plains in Captain Martin's company. She was an affectionate wife, a loving mother of 13 children, 12 of whom survive her, and who, with her husband and numerous relatives and friends are left to mourn her departure.—COM.

Took His Own Life.—Our readers will remember references made in these columns to the conduct of one C. Halvorsen, an employe in the store of D. J. Williams & Co., at Price, Emery County, who had been detected in stealing considerable quantities of goods from his employers. About two weeks ago he was committed to await the action of the grand jury, and was sent to the county seat, Castle Dale. The jail there, is unsuitable for confining prisoners, and Halvorsen was permitted to stay at the house of Orange Seeley, Esq., where he was subjected to a strict surveillance.

Information reached Price a few days ago that Halvorsen was having every opportunity to escape from custody should he so desire, and that there existed in Castle Dale a strong belief that he was innocent of criminal conduct. This information led the firm of D. J. Williams & Co., and also the Justice who committed Halvorsen, to address letters to some of the county officers assuring them that prisoner's guilt was flagrant and unquestionable, and urging that, in the interest of justice, he should be confined until until bailed out, suggesting that he be removed to Provo for safe keeping.

The purport of these letters was communicated to Halvorsen, who began to manifest the greatest anxiety lest he should be sent to Provo. On Friday last Mr. T. E. Grames, of Price, accompanied by two of his neighbors as witnesses, went to Castle Dale to prove up on some land. Halvorsen, learning of their arrival and acting upon the supposition that they had come to take him to Provo, took a knife and, retiring to the shelter of some willows on the bank of a ditch not far from Mr. Seeley's house, cut his throat in a horrible manner. He gashed the fore part of his neck in a shocking way before finally severing the cord of life. He was absent from the premises of Mr. Seeley about half an hour before being missed, when a gentleman present suggested to Halvorsen's son, who was also present, that he go and look for his father. He started out and in a few moments discovered his father's lifeless body in the willows, the throat mangled as above described.

Halvorsen had evidently formed the determination to take his own life before he would go to Provo; and it seems evident that he had decided to commit suicide anyhow. He left some letters, in which he confesses his guilt, and intimates a purpose to destroy his own life. In one letter he declares his wife, who is highly esteemed by all who know her, to be entirely innocent of any connection with his crimes.

A gentleman intimately acquainted with Halvorsen, expresses the opinion that his mind was, to some extent at least, unsound, as several years ago he had his skull fractured, and has at times acted strangely. This is probably a just conclusion. His funeral was held at Price on Sunday last, and was the termination of quite a sensational chapter of the history of Castle Dale. The deceased leaves several small children.

Off For Price.

Two companies of soldiers, accoutred as if for hard work, with pick and shovel, marched down to the D. & R. G. depot yesterday, and were taken aboard a special bound for Price, Emery County. They will camp twelve miles north of Price, and will work on the road opened by Geo. Goss to the new Fort Duchesne with a view to making it practicable for the transportation of military supplies, the Price route being much shorter than the other way by the U. P. Major Bush, Captain Baker and Lieutenant Byrne were in command of the detachment.

Deseret News
October 6, 1886

DEATHS.

REESE.—At Scofield, Emery County, from the result of an accident William, son of Levi P. and Ann Reese, aged 7 years and 10 months. He died on Sept. 20th and was interred on the 22nd. Great sympathy was shown to the parents in their sad bereavement.

Ogden Herald
November 26, 1886

Price.

From a letter received by a gentleman in this city, we learn that Price, Emery County, is becoming quite a busy town. The freighting of government supplies to Fort Duchesne and the Indian reservation furnishes employment to a great number of men. During this winter there are some seven or eight hundred thousand pounds of freight to be hauled. The distance is about ninety-five miles, and the pay is one cent per pound. It is said this does not always pay expenses, still, the applications for freight to haul are numerous.

Oats at Price are $1.50 per hundred, potatoes are 60 cents, butter 25 cents, and eggs are 20 cents per dozen. Other supplies cost in about the same ratio.

Salt Lake Herald
December 3, 1886

Price Mercantile Company.

The Price Mercantile Company have filed a copy of their articles of incorporation with the Secretary of the Territory. The object and pursuit of the incorporators is to carry on a general merchandise business at Price, Emery County, Utah. The capital stock is placed at $40,000, and this is divided into 4,000 shares of $10 each. The following are the stockholders and the amount held by each:

D. J. Williams.	1,000
Emm. W. Cummings, Salt Lake	100
W. F. Williams, Price	1
B. F. Cummings, Jr.	1
Martha Williams, Price	1

The officers of the new company are: President, David J. Williams; Vice-President, W. F. Williams; B. F. Cummings, Jr., Secretary and Treasurer. The duration of the incorporation is placed at twenty-five years.

Deseret News
December 29, 1886

DEATHS.

LLEWELLYN.—At Scofield, Emery Co., Utah, Susannah, beloved wife of David Llewellyn, of palpitation of the heart. Deceased was born August 2, 1819, at Dursley, Gloucester, England; baptized into the Church of Jesus Christ of Latter-day Saints, March 19, 1880. Sister Llewellen always bore a faithful testimony of the Gospel, and has laid her body down, with the hope of a glorious awakening on the morning of the first resurrection.

THE STONE MURDER !

Louis Steen, the Slayer, Implicates Three Others.

THE COLD-BLOODED KILLING !

The History of the Murderer, Who Proves to be a Youth About 19 Years of Age.

PRICE, UTAH, January 22.
To the Editor of THE HERALD.

I telegraphed you last evening in reference to the killing of Homer J. Stone. The particulars are as follows: Stone was keeping a restaurant here. A young man about 20 years of age, named Louis Steen, had an order on Stone for $2.50. Stone refused payment, when the fellow began pulling off his coat, and said that unless payment was made, he would take it out of his hide.

STONE THEN PULLED A PISTOL,

and told him not to come that game. This happened at about 5 p.m., and the parties soon separated, and the matter dropped, or at least Stone supposed that it had. In the evening, Stone went up town, and learned that the fellow had been endeavoring to borrow a pistol, and had made threats that he would kill him. Stone made the remark to some of the boys who were with him that he thought he had better have him arrested, but the boys ridiculed the idea, and said the fellow did not have sand enough to shoot a cotton-tail, and so they let it go at that. Stone then went into the lower part of town, to visit a tent where a lot of teamsters were stopping, and as he was returning, about 8.20 p.m., he had arrived nearly opposite Brig. Young's place of business, at which point he turned to go home. One of his companions invited Stone to go in and take a drink, but refused, and when pressed said he would go in and take a cigar, and as he did so a man jumped in front of them. Stone was heard to exclaim: "Here, now, don't you come that!" At this

THE FELLOW FIRED AND STONE FELL

forward on his face. The murderer ran away and disappeared in the dense darkness. Some of the boys ran to Stone, picked him up, and asked him if he was hurt. No response was made, and the poor boy gave one groan and died. It is earnestly hoped and believed that the man who did the shooting will be found, although he has not been apprehended up to the present writing. Stone's brother and other relatives were telegraphed the sad news. Stone had many friends in this place, and was a jolly good fellow. Peace be with him evermore.

THE MURDERER CAPTURED.

PRICE, UTAH, January 23, 1.53 a.m.
Special to THE HERALD.

The last thirty-six hours have been the wildest ever seen in this section of the country since the advent of the Little Giant. Owing to the circumstances surrounding the affair, there was no doubt in the minds of anyone but that Steen was the murderer of Homer J. Stone, and he has been persistently sought for. Louis Steen was arrested here to-night. He is 19 years of age. Sheriff Turner came down and worked up the case.

The murderer's confession implicates three others, who will be arrested at once. Steen is a son of Theodore Steen, postal clerk on the Union Pacific ten years ago, and a nephew of Otto and John Steen, of Wahoo, Nebraska.

All efforts to get any later news than that given above, failed, although the telegraph office was kept open until 3 o'clock.

THE MURDER CASE.

The Killing of Homer J. Stone Under Investigation.

A CLEAR CASE AGAINST STEEN. — THE CASE AGAINST THE OTHERS NOT YET DEVELOPED.

At a few minutes before 11 o'clock this morning Louis Steen, Samuel B. Woolley, William B. McCloskey and James Haley, who were under arrest on the charge of murder, were brought in from the penitentiary. They were securely handcuffed, but the irons were removed in the Marshal's office, and the defendants issued into the clerk's room, where the preliminary examination was to be held.

A large number of witnesses and spectators were present, Sheriff Turner, of Utah County, who made the arrests, being among the number. District Attorney Dickson conducted the prosecution, and Judge P. H. Emerson appeared for defendants Woolley, McCloskey and Haley.

The defendants were then arraigned before Commissioner McKay, and listened to the reading of the complaint charging them with the crime of murder, in having engaged in the unlawful killing of Homer J. Stone, at Price, Emery County, Utah, on Friday, January 21, 1887. A plea of not guilty was made for each, Steen speaking scarcely above a whisper, while his associates gave their reply in positive language.

The Commissioner asked Steen: Have you any counsel?

Steen (in a whisper)—No, sir.

Commissioner—Do you desire any?

Steen—Yes, sir.

Commissioner—How old are you?

Steen—Eighteen years.

Commissioner—Have you any money to pay an attorney?

Steen—No, sir.

Mr. Dickson suggested that Judge Emerson and Mr. Evans, who appeared for the other defendants, also take care of Steen's interests, but they declined.

Judge E. D. Hoge was then requested to act, but said he had done so much of that class of business that he did not relish it. He would not positively refuse, but would prefer if an attorney from the judicial district where the crime was committed would take the case.

A. G. Sutherland, Sen., of Provo, finally consented to act as counsel for Steen.

Dr. Hall, of this city, was the first witness, and testified to having examined the body of Homer J. Stone, on Jan. 25. He described the course of the bullet, which had entered at the back, just below the right shoulder blade, had passed through both lungs, severed the principal blood vessel leading from the heart, and came out at the left breast. The ball had ranged upward, and the wound inflicted was necessarily fatal.

William Henry Reeves was the next witness. He testified that he was from Cleveland, O.; on the night of the shooting he was with Stone at the saloon where Steen asked him to settle a bill of $10, and had afterward stayed with him until the shooting, at which time he was 10 or 15 feet in advance. He turned and saw a person whom he believed to be Steen run away from the scene. His version of the affair does not differ materially from the account already published. The order on Stone, which the defendant was trying to collect, was in favor of Paul Meyers, for $10, and Meyers had offered Steen one half if he could get Stone to pay it.

Wm. F. Williams also testified. He was shown a pistol and identified it as the weapon that Steen confessed having used in the commission of the crime. He had listened to the defendant's confession, in which he stated, in addition to the account already given, that he borrowed the pistol from S. B. Woolley, telling the latter that he had had a row with Stone, and wanted to defend himself. Woolley had remarked that he also had a grudge against the deceased. Another of the defendants, Wm. McCloskey, had told him that if Stone had treated him as he had Steen, he would call him out and brain him. Steen had then gone in search of Stone, and when he met him made a second demand for payment of the bill. This was again refused, and the defendant drew his pistol from his belt. Stone placed his hand on his pistol and called "None of that;" he then turned and tried to get away, when Steen fired. The two were then about ten feet apart. The murderer stopped a moment, then ran off. He crossed the river to the deserted village of Cleveland, but after wandering around until the next night, came and gave himself up. He said, in the presence of quite a number of witnesses, "I may as well tell it all first as last. I am the man who killed Stone." He further claimed that he had been encouraged to the deed by other parties.

At the conclusion of Mr. Williams' testimony, the Court took a recess. The case was to be proceeded with at a later hour this afternoon.

DEATHS.

BROWN—At Scofield, Emery County, Utah on January 23d, 1887, of pleuro-pneumonia, Elizabeth, daughter of Thomas and Elizabeth Brown; deceased was born on the 8th of November, 1861, in Ayrshire, Scotland, consequently was in her 25th year. *Mill. Star* please copy.

Deseret News
February 16, 1887

CORRESPONDENCE.

HUNTINGTON, Emery-County,
January 26, 1886.

Editor Deseret News:

The appearance of this county is anything but inviting, as it has a sterile, forbidding appearance; in fact, it looks as though when the floods descended that this part of the country was where they struck the earth and washed it into deep washes, leaving flat-topped hills quite picturesque in appearance, some at a distance appearing feudal castles of antiquity; much so that you expect to see the sentry pass along the battlement from tower to tower or to see coming toward you a train of armored knights with all the accoutrements of feudal warfare. One might, indeed, easily look upon one of the old castellated rocks and closing the eyes dream over and of those romances that we have read in youth and imagine that one of those scenes of fiction was before him, but awakening he finds himself in Castle Valley, Emery County, Utah, and sees around him the barren, dreary look that the country at nearer view presents. And we venture to say that no people but the "Mormons" would have thought of redeeming it and causing it to yield to the husbandman, for it was naturally so forbidding and the labor to get the water out was so great that any people less united in their efforts could never have accomplished so great a task, at so great a risk, for the land before the water is applied looks as though nothing would grow. Yet by the use of fertilizers and the irrigation of it at

proper times it can be redeemed and made to produce fine crops. The corn crop is exceptionally good. Vegetables of all kinds prosper and yield in abundance in answer to proper care. Price is the first town reached in this county and has sprung into some importance since so much freight has been shipped from that point, but our agricultural district is not yet fully developed. The ditch is lagging, but it is expected to be completed in the spring.

From Price

THE ROAD TO HUNTINGTON

runs south over a broken country. The town of Huntington lies on the south side of the creek, on a gradual sloping place inclining to the east, and is platted in squares, the roads running north and south, and east and west. The town is one mile square and is building up quite rapidly. Water has been taken out at great expense, and they are enlarging the canals now made, and another large ditch is being taken out on the north side of the creek, that will, when completed, cover about seven thousand acres of land in the district called Cleveland, which lies about three miles northeast from Huntington.

A coal vein has been developed by D. C. Robbins about eight miles from Huntington, which yields a most excellent article of coal. The vein is about eight feet thick and has a solid rock ceiling and floor.

Two marriages took place in Huntington on Monday, the 24th. Miss Emma Jane Loveless, daughter of Sheriff Loveless, to Mr. A. D. Dennie. A feast and dance followed the ceremony, in which was manifest a great amount of enjoyment. Peace prevails; all seem to be prospering and none are in want of the necessaries of life.

L.

Deseret News
February 23, 1887

Daily Mail Wanted.—Complaints come from Price, Emery County, that people in that region who get their mail distributed there — especially residents of Huntington, Castledale, Orangeville and Ferron—do not receive it till four or five days old from here. The mail that leaves here on Friday gets to Price the same evening and remains till the following Tuesday, and so on; and the only way this state of things can be cured is by a daily mail. We understand the people there are getting up a petition to Postmaster General Vilas, and this is the proper thing to do.

Salt Lake Herald
February 25, 1887

In November last, C. C. Anderson, of Price, Utah, was badly injured by the explosion of giant powder, which had been cached in the ground where he was digging. He was brought to this city for treatment, and is now able to be around. He is totally blind, however, one eye being blown out of the socket and the other so badly injured as to deprive him of sight. Anderson has a poor old mother who is dependent upon him for support, and the case would certainly seem to be one worthy of the most charitable consideration of citizens.

Deseret Evening News
March 2, 1887

DEATHS.

LARSEN.—At Molen, Emery County, Utah, February 9th, 1887, of diphtheria, Oluf Larsen. Born January 2, 1866, at Wenaysel, Denmark. He leaves a wife and one child. He emigrated to Utah with his parents, Savend and Johanne Bretta Larsen, in 1873, lived in Ephraim, Sanpete County, for... years; went with his parents to Castle Valley in 1877; was a bright and promising young man, second counselor to the Bishop, also first counselor to the Y. M. M. I. A. and assistant secretary to the Sunday school. [COM.

SUNDAY SCHOOLS IN YOUNG SETTLEMENTS.

PLEASANT VALLEY WARD,
March 1, 1887.

Editor Deseret News:

Sunday, the 27th of February, was a day memorable in the history of this ward. Our Sunday School held its quarterly review, and a splendid time was enjoyed. Great credit is due to those who took an active part in training the young people, the rendering of the exercises being a complete success. Although we have had many reviews, not one could be compared to that which was conducted on Sunday. It shows that a lively interest is being taken in the instruction of the young, in instilling into their minds the principles of truth and a desire to cultivate the love of music, solos, choruses, part singing, duetts, recitations, dialogues and speeches were the order of the exercises, and to give preference to any, would be an act of injustice, for all did well. Much credit is due to Assistant Superintendent Eden for the arduous task he has performed in getting classes of small children and teaching them to sing. No one, until lately, would undertake to do this. Brother Eden anticipates leaving here and settling in Castle Valley. When he does so, our Sunday School will sustain a loss. In connection with other duties, he is leader of the Sunday School musical department and is organist. The Sunday Schools in this part of the Territory are in a flourishing condition.

The roll will, I believe, total somewhere about 230, with an average attendance of 175. This is good considering that our ward is out small in numbers and that we occupy an isolated position in the "Tops of the Mountains." Our superintendents, Brothers Richards, Parmley, Eden and Page—there being a branch at Scofield over which Assist. Supt. T. P. Page has control—are men of energy and full of zeal in so noble a cause. On Sunday our large meeting house was crowded at both sessions (afternoon and night), all available space being occupied, and considering there were so many mothers present with babes in their arms, and the crowded state of the house, remarkable quietness prevailed.

W. LAMPH, Ward Clerk.

Fatal Accident.

Deseret News.

At Scofield, on the 28th, at noon, William Murray, a section hand, was thrown off a hand car, by a dog knocking against his feet, the hand car going down grade at a fair rate of speed, and fracturing his skull. He died instantly. An inquest was held and a verdict rendered in accordance with the above. Murray was a quiet, unobtrusive man, a widower about forty years of age. His only known relative is a sister, a Mrs. Mason, living near Solomon City, Kansas.

SHOOTING AFFRAY AT SCOFIELD.

A Couple of Enraged Ruffians Undertake to do Up a School-master and get Badly Worsted.

A shooting affray took place at Scofield on Tuesday evening which though not attended with fatal results will probably land one scamp and perhaps two, in the penitentiary. Mr. C. H. Bliss a young School teacher in Scofield, was the person assaulted, and he came in last evening and gave us the following particulars:

At the coroner's inquest held over the body of W. B. Murray, the section hand killed on Monday, Mr. Bliss was called to testify. It appears that previous witnesses in the case, intimidated by the bluster of the fellow White, who had charge of the car from which Murray fell, in their testimony had estimated the speed of the car, at the moment Murray was killed, at much less than it really was. When Mr. Bliss took the stand, however, he gave the speed at 20 miles per hour. This put the section boss pugilist into an almighty bad temper, and he was very soon on the trail of the impertinent witness that refused to take alarm and accommodate his testimony to the threats of what he looked upon as a braggart and a ruffian. Accordingly on Tuesday evening while Mr. Bliss was at the depot attending to some express business, he suddenly found himself confronted by the belligerent railman who had equipped himself with a friend and a pistol for the express purpose of doing up the young pedagogue with neatness and dispatch.

Sticking his nose very close into Bliss' face he opened the interview by assuring Bliss in "his own peculiar way" that he was not entirely a truthful person and that his mother was a canine of the commoner sort, etc. Bliss thought it none of his concern if she was, whereupon White became sore displeased and struck Bliss in the face. The latter at this backed up a few steps, and observing White and his partner Thomas Loyed still following him up and continuing their threats, he drew a knife from his pocket and ordered them to stand back. White then took out his pistol, saying that he would make him use his knife since he had been to the pains of exhibiting it. Here a struggle ensued which for a moment seemed to mean certain death of one, if not both of the persons engaged. After two shots had been fired, one of them passing through Bliss' right side and the other grazing his wrist, and several sever stabs had been inflicted upon White, the struggle came to a sudden ending through Bliss fortunately and dextrously wrenching the pistol from his opponent.

White and his companion are at this writing under arrest awaiting an examination before Commissioner Hill.

The Verdict.—Yesterday the jury in the case of the People vs. Lewis Steen, who killed Homer J. Stone on the 21st of January last, at Price, Emery County, returned a verdict of guilty of murder in the second degree, with a recommendation to the mercy of the court. The youth of the defendant doubtless cut an important figure in the case. Sentence will be passed on Monday.

EMERY COUNTY ITEMS.

A Budget of News from a Lively and Growing Section.

PRICE, Emery County, Utah,
March 31st, 1887.

Editor Deseret News:

Rapidity and solidity characterize the growth of the settlements and business enterprises of Castle Valley which embraces the bulk of the population of Emery County. Especially is this true of the town of Price, which has certainly been a lively place for some months past.

Ever since the murder of Stone in January last, the citizens of this place have been bringing a pressure to bear upon the county authorities, with a view to having them provide better means for maintaining the law than have heretofore existed here. As a result bids have been called for on the construction of

A JAIL AT PRICE,

which will soon be in process of erection. In addition to a jail the town will also need a patrolling officer, until the disorderly element that so abounds here shall be taught that the place is governed in a civilized manner.

Frequently of late ominous reports of threatened Indian troubles at one or both of the Indian agencies in Wasatch County, have reached here. It is said that the Indians threaten to begin hostilities as soon as "the grass is a finger length high." But your correspondent is satisfied, from conversing with individuals well acquainted with the temper of the Indians, that the war spirit is confined to a few evil disposed uncompahgres at the Ouray agency, and is not felt at all at the Uintah agency.

The most important business event of recent occurrence in this country was the opening here to-day of the new store of the Emery County Mercantile Company, and it is not too much to predict that the occurrence will

MARK AN EPOCH

in the commercial history of this section. In personnel, experience and facilities for buying low this company is a strong one, and a unique and highly advantageous feature of it is that it embraces representatives of eastern jobbing houses dealing respectively in dry goods, groceries, etc. In one sense, therefore, this company may be said to buy its goods from its own members.

The new store is certainly worthy of a brief description. The outer walls and roof are of iron, which, being nicely painted, looks first rate, and, being fire-proof, greatly reduces the cost of of insurance. The interior of the building is admirably and handsomely fitted up with counters, shelving, etc., and is as convenient and fine looking a retail salesroom as one need wish to see. The size of the building is 25x50 feet. A brick-paved cellar, the full size of the building, is chock full of goods.

THE MANAGER

of the new store is L. M. Olsen, Esq., late superintendent of the Ephraim Co-op., whose success in that position was remarkable. The manner in which he has arranged his new domain proves him a thorough merchant. The intention is to do a jobbing trade as well as a retail business, and the company opens with a stock of merchandise both large enough and varied enough to meet all probable demands. In every line of general merchandise their store embraces a department, the stock of which is remarkably complete. The new store is in fact an emporium from whence our entire county may be supplied, hence the importance to this region of this enterprise.

Two or three months ago, at Green river station, east of here, there was a

GREAT EXCITEMENT

over the discovery of some petroleum springs. Several gentlemen prominently connected with the D. & R. G. became members of a company whose object was to develop the discovery. But we hear no more of the enterprise. There have been rumors of mineral discoveries between here and Fort DuChesne, but no important locations have been made. Farming and stock raising, the latter especially, will continue to be the leading industries of this region.

A SMALL BAND OF GYPSIES

reached our town on the 28th inst., and during the afternoon a row occurred between some of them and a number of freighters. The trouble seems to have been occasioned by the re-

fusal of one of the freighters to pay one of the Gypsy women two dollars for telling his fortune. A good deal of liquor had been drunk that day by the freighters concerned, and for a time there was danger of a general move among them to drive the dusky itinerants out of town. The trouble did not go that far, however.

Incredible as it may seem, the Gypsy woman received many a dollar fee from persons here, for telling the latters' fortunes. If the fool-killer and an undertaker would follow a band of Gypsies, both would find business lively. Respectfully.

CASTLE VALLEY.

Emery County Notes.—Mr. Wm. Howard, of Huntington, Emery County, sends the following, under date of April 4th:

We have had a very dry, warm winter, which has enabled us to get our canals and ditches in running order a month earlier than usual.

The farmers have been putting in crops for the last six weeks, and if we do not have a storm soon, the grain will have to be watered up.

A year ago, Huntington spent about $1,200 in fruit trees, mostly from the Geneva Nurseries, which as a general thing, have done well. Although their trees are small, yet they have splendid roots, with plenty of small fibres, which cause the tree to grow very rapidly when set out. Some that I bought from this firm last year sent forth new limbs over three feet long last season. Mr. Geo. Ipsom of this place also bought in a large lot of fruit trees

from the Woodbury nurseries, but the great trouble with them was they did not have root. As a consequence, a great many of them died. Most of us feel well to think we have got splendid orchards started.

The people of Cleveland (which is destined to be a large settlement), about six miles northeast of Huntington, are now very busy on their canal. They expect to get water out soon enough this spring to raise crops this coming summer. A great many of the share holders of the canal are Pleasant Valley coal miners, who have taken up land and made some improvements on it, in most cases enough to fill the law, but who have to go back to the mines to earn means to support themselves and families. On account of no water being within six or seven miles of their land, they can as yet do no farming.

The health of the people generally is good.

Deseret News
May 4, 1887

A Child Scalded.

Scofield, Emery County,
April 26, 1887.

Editor Deseret News:

On the 25th inst. a child belonging to John G. Timothy, of this place, was severely scalded, through the overturning of a teapot; the teapot was resting on the stove. The mother had the child in her arms and upon her going to do something put the child down close to the stove. The child reached out its hand, caught hold of the teapot and upset

the scalding contents over its head, face and right side. The clothes, when taken off brought the skin away with them. The sufferings of the child were fearful. Everything that human skill and experience could do, was done to alleviate the pain of the little one, and at the time of writing the child is doing as well as can be expected.

The weather here has been very changeable of late, and as a consequence there are a few suffering from severe colds. Work is very slack at present. Yours respectfully,
W. L.

HORSE THIEVES CAPTURED

THREE DESPERADOES NOW IN JAIL IN PROVO.

On Tuesday night, the 17th inst., there were stolen from parties in the vicinity of P. V. Junction, Utah County, three horses, three saddles, three guns, two or three pistols and a fine field glass. The next night Constable Frank Hoover, of P.V., telegraphed the fact to Sheriff Turner, at Provo, and on Thursday the Sheriff, after sending the news to officers in various directions that they might be on the lookout, started out after the thieves. At P. V. Junction warrants were obtained for Ben. Marsh, a one-armed man whose home is in Salt Lake City, Frank Ellis, or McDonald, and a third person whose name was unknown, these being the suspected parties.

Sheriff Turner and Constable Hoover started on Thursday evening for Fort DuChesne, but after going sixty miles they learned that they were on the wrong scent, and retraced their steps to P. V., reaching there Sunday morning. In the meantime word had been received that another gun had been stolen from Charles H. Taylor's, at Price, Emery County, and that the house of Mr. Avery, at Farnham, had been broken into. This indicated that the thieves were working south, and the sheriff and constable took the next train for the Lower Price crossing.

Prior to this, however, Constables Fred. Grames and H. Bryner, in company with Jackson Cole, of George C. Whitmore's ranch, and some others, had started on the same trail. This posse came up with the fugitives at the Lower Price crossing, and steps were taken to capture them. It was known that they were well armed and desperate, and that two of them had taken refuge in the brush across the river.

Notwithstanding the great danger to which he exposed himself, Jackson Cole urged his horse into the stream, forded it, and before the thieves were aware of it, had got within shooting range and covered them with his rifle. They did not for a moment suppose that a single man would perform such a daring feat, and believing they were surrounded and taken at a disadvantage surrendered, and in a short time after were placed in irons by the officers. The third person of the trio was then discovered to be Joseph Mulligan, as he gave his name, a late arrival from Colorado.

An examination of the prisoner's effects showed that, had they had an opportunity to fight, it would have fared badly with the other party. They had all the weapons that had been stolen, and were provided with a plentiful supply of explosive cartridges. All of the plunder except the field glass was recovered, and on the arrival of the train, a few minutes after the capture, the three prisoners were given into Sheriff Turner's custody.

The whole party then returned, and an examination was held before Justice Smith, at P.V., on Monday, and the defendants held to await the grand jury's action. McDonald's bail was fixed at $2,000, and that of Marsh and Mulligan at $1,000 each. In default of sureties the trio are now languishing in jail at Provo.

McDonald was but recently liberated from the Penitentiary, where he had served a term for grand larceny. Marsh is the person who was indicted with another man for robbery committed near the Opera House in this city. His companion was convicted and punished, but the indictment against him was dismissed a few months ago. Of Mulligan's antecedents nothing is known.

The capture was an arduous task and was well done. The ranchmen and others in the vicinity gave the officers every assistance in their power, and made the arrest of the gang practicable.

DEATHS.

LAY.—At Price, Emery County, May 27th, 1887, of measles, Samuel Orson Lay, son of Robert and Emily Lay. Born May 29th 1886.

Pleasant Valley.

A correspondent, "J. K. P.," writing from Scofield, Pleasant Valley, on the 30th ult. says that work in the coal mines has been slack for some time past and there don't seem to be much chance for times to liven up very soon. The miners barely make a living; some with large families experience hard times in making ends meet. It is anticipated that the saw mills will soon start up again, which will have a tendency to make times better.

The meeting house (at what is commonly called the "Y") is nearly completed. The cost will not exceed $1,000. The Saints in this part of the vineyard have been very much in need of a comfortable place to meet in, having to travel about two miles to the Pleasant Valley Ward meeting-house.

The next move ought to be to get an organ for the new building.

Professor Thos. Hardee has organized a singing class and is teaching vocal music. He is a very efficient and successful music teacher.

An enjoyable party was given last Friday evening in the new Assembly Hall which was kept up till 12 o'clock and all that were present expressed themselves on leaving that they never enjoyed themselves better. James Gatherum and John E. Ingles deserve a word of credit for their judicious management of the affair.

Two schools are running in full blast, disseminating the well attended.

Salt Lake Herald
June 26, 1887

THE SCOFIELD MINES.

The Course of a Great Coal Vein.

BLACK DIAMOND TREASURES.

Salt Lakers Engaged in the Hunt for Wealth—Superintendent W. G. Sharp's Theory.

To the Editor of THE HERALD.

I have neglected to say "dear," because you know how dear editors are, and, therefore, this diplomatic word is always understood. I can't get your paper, I have not got a Bible (left it at home by mistake), I have found a nice edition of Chambers' Encoclopedia, have a nice hotel and plenty of paper and ink, the spell comes on me to write something; while I recall the editor's prayer, write on one side, as the Virginian did when he spit tobacco juice on the outside of Charles Dickens' clothes while on a Pennsylvania canal-boat. That is the Virginian spit; Dickens swore, and the boat went on, so with me, only one side is to be daubed and I go on.

I think Scofield did a better thing for the world when he built the Pleasant Valley Railroad up to these coal mines, than old Hannibal did when he fought his army up to and upon the Appian way, or Napoleon when he made the sullen Cossack heat his tea kettle over the raging flames of the Kremlin; because in the discovery and opening up of these coal mines we and ours are enabled to keep our feet warm in winter, and others by means whereof can make steam for all utilitarian uses. Scofield did not make a success of either his coal mines or his railroad, but he led the way, like Columbus, barring the latter's chains and most cruel death. He led the way, but the enterprising Coloradoans won the stakes, not a tithe of which is taken down yet.

IT IS SUMMER SEASON

now, and not very many miners are employed. Winter it seems is the harvest moon; still even now a good train of coal is run out every day to be taken on thence by the D. & R. G. Western, for immediate consumption. Here we found a couple of Superintendent John Sharp's sons; one engaged in superintending the work in the coal mines and the other an extensive railroad contractor; and James X. Ferguson, merchandise; A. H. Earll, merchandise and Oliver Kimball, the champion merchant of Alta in former days. All of these gentlemen appear to be enjoying themselves. Scofield is a small place, consisting of 600 or 800 inhabitants, mostly engaged in coal mining. The town contains three or four stores and the usual number of saloons, billiard tables, etc., found in mining towns. There are two extensive coal mines at this place, the first known as the Utah Central Railway Coal Mine, which is probably one of the most famous coal mines of the world, both for quality and quantity. The second is the Pleasant Valley Coal Company's mine, which furnishes quite as famous coal for the market.

The former is on the left hand side of town, and the latter on the right; both within a radius of one and a half miles from the centre of the town.

MY CHIEF GEOLOGICAL ADVISER

was Mr. William G. Sharp, superintendent of both of these mines, who is a young man scarcely 30 years of age—a real Agassiz in his way. He is fond of fishing and hunting and can digress on geology and mines without limit. For a young man he has had an extensive experience, having been connected with the statisticians bureau of the United States service for quite a long period. He showed me the inside workings of the former mine in detail; it consists of an enormous vein of 28 to 30 feet in thickness, whose walls are true and it extends into the mountain on a raise of scarcely one foot in 100 in length.

The main tunnel into the mine is something over 1,000 feet in depth; there are divers lateral tunnels, drifts and chambers leading into this main tunnel from either side, all of which are in this vein of coal.

The coal itself is conveyed to the mouth of the tunnel (whence it is dumped in railroad cars) on a train which is on the decline of about one foot to to the 100 in length. The empty cars are drawn back to the head of the tunnel and drifts by mules, hence it will be seen that in the incline of the vein towards the mouth of the tunnel, as before mentioned, the force of gravity has furnished the chief operative power for working this mine.

In the southeasterly lobe of

THE UTAH CENTRAL MINE

a large fault occurs, some 50 feet in width. The vein is found on the southeasterly side of this fault, the upper strata of which is some few hundred feet below the line of the hanging wall on the northwesterly side, but explorations on the former side show that the hanging wall in and about it is on the raise, and hence it is expected that within a few hundred feet the vein will attain its position as shown on the northwesterly side. Indeed, it must be so, or else the vein (which in its entirety has been formed by one cause, originating in one geological period) would not crop out in Castle Valley, in the same formation—sandstone—and at about the same elevation above sea level. The lateral action causing the upheaval of the low range of mountains hereabout, has nothing to do with the original deposits made on a level whence the coal is formed. The disturbances occurred after the deposit was made. Some years ago, it will be remembered, a fire occurred in the northwesterly lobe of this mine, in what is known as the Pugsley tunnel; two men lost their lives through it. This working was sealed up and has not since been opened. At the extreme northwesterly end of the workings of the Pugsley tunnel another fault occurs in this vein, directly under a lateral ravine or gulch.

Mr. Sharp made a very interesting statement to me in regard to faults generally in veins, whether of coal or silver, and his experience has led him into both classes. His remark was this: He had noticed that faults occurred at the lowest angle of depression, between adjoining hills, or mountains; why in the .... of .... it should be thus he

fact existed. There is a large hill in which this vein is situated, in either extremity of which are

TWO LATERAL RAVINES

leading off at right angles from the main gulch or canyon below. Beneath these ravines these faults occur. Most of us who are accustomed to mining, admit the main point as stated by Mr. Sharp. The fault between the Alice and Magna Charter, in the "Fraction," so-called, at Walkerville, Montana, is a familiar instance. This occurs in the depression, (beneath the surface, of course), between two hills; another instance is found in the Queen of the Hills mine in Dry Canyon, Utah. In it is the largest and probably the hardest spot to find the vein, on the opposite side of the fault, extant, and yet these lateral ravines occur. In the latter, as all will readily understand, other influences bear on the fault question; the fault occurs directly under the general cone of the mountain, the decline of which on the Soldier Canyon (opposite) side is much steeper than on the Dry Canyon lobe; here then two influences operated instead of one. It may be averred that the idea is mere theory; but after all, who so able to tell a reasonable story as he who has to give an account of every nickel he expends, give a good reason for his experiments on and about the foibles of nature, and who, in the end, in order to be accredited a successful mining superintendent, must in some way or other be able to prove to stockholders, who usually want that the credit side of his cash account shows a balance in favor of his mine; if in running tunnels, drifts, etc., at a cost of $10 to $20 per foot, his cash account gets the swamp it makes no difference; profits or consumption are his only alternatives, headaches and faults do not count.

Hence it was that in one hour's time Mr. Sharp turned over to me a few leaves in the book of nature, pointing out in a brief, but very clear way, the evidences which she presents to a practical and observing eye. I shall, in justice to myself, here add, that I never spent an hour in my whole life in a more agreeable way than with this very accomplished and genial young scientist, if I may be permitted to use the expression. Those who look into and upon the labyrinth of nature with a clear, cool eye and draw from such inspection well wrought conclusions, based on practical experience, may not shine for the present in the pages of history, but how about the future, when an impartial record is made up and the balance sheet shows that the author has contributed one grand idea to the tomes of that which the poverty of the English language feebly denominated "science."

And finally, let me add, that from my experience I had much rather be a lawyer than a mining superintendent, for, among others, the following reasons: The lawyer can, with some show, tell his client that the jury were ignorant, biased or bribed, the court mistook the law, or did not know it, and finally that the law itself is wrong. Such is, among

A MULTITUDE OF OTHER THINGS,

the opportunity to shift, after the genious of Sunderland, the responsibility; not so with the mining superintendent, he must meet Cæsar face to face, whose decrees are incorrigible and inflexible; science tallies not except at the end of pointed arrow, circumscribed only by tinted hues of the rainbow, where are found the ducats, labelled not "in God we trust," but "success." We are told even now that God is love, and that He

is just, a lawyer does not, of certainty, need either of these ingredients mixed or mingled with his constitution or character, because if it were said he loves God as well as his fellow men (and their fees) the cruel world would give him no credit for it—he covenanted to do all this when he became a lawyer; on the other hand, if the command, "be just" be hurled at him he can answer with an emphasis equal to that of Paul at the time of his wonderful conversion, "here am I," and patting his breast, answer, "this is Old Justice itself. I have *no sins*; the love (for fees) and justice which this noble breast carries is as boundless as the universe and as potent and fathomless as the tides and depths of the mighty ocean; errors, if any, were not of my hand or heart, things were wrong in the court, the jury box, and last, but not least, with the law itself," but not so with the mining superintendent; nature is his god, and the laws of this deity have no apostles to expound them, no vicegerent to bestow absolution or sprinkle incense and holy water on the tomb or grave of his errors and mistakes. He must travel back into the geological history of the world for millions of years and then take out his note book and write, and then draw his conclusions from the evidences which she has been laying by for him; if he makes a mistake no excuse suffices, the world call him an ass; if he makes a hit then the stockholders quaintly asks, "where are your dividends promised last month?"

Mr. Sharp

DOES HIS OWN ENGINEERING

and planning; thus he combines in himself the sciences of a geologist, mining engineer and mining superintendent. He claims for the coal of the Utah Central mine that, by actual experiment, it will make more steam when used for motive power than any other coal to his knowledge in the Rocky Mountain region. If so, this subject is worthy of the most serious consideration by consumers of coal for heating and steam generating purposes.

In referring to this opinion of Mr. Sharp's, I do not do so from the fact

that some persons might consider him a mere theorist, but I consider his opinion worthy of consideration, based upon critical and extended experience.

THESE TWO COMPANIES

possess more than three square miles of coal lands, the title to all of which has been obtained from the government of the United States; but this is not all, as extensive as the possessions of these two companies are, the limit of these coalfields is of a very much wider range.

In conversation with Mr. Sharp while at Scofield, and with Mr. George Goss, (who is connected with the P. & R. G. Western Railway Company,) they both agree that the coal-fields at and near Scofield extend over into Castle Valley, which lies nearly parallel with Pleasant Valley for its length, (about 20 miles,) and then swings around toward the west, and eventually ending at or near Salina in Sevier County. The Pleasant Valley coal-fields are separated from those in Castle Valley by a low range of mountains extending nearly northeast

80 miles; but the coal croppings are very much more extensive

IN CASTLE VALLEY

than in Pleasant Valley. The Castle Valley coal-fields can be reached by a railroad running out from Price Station on the D. & R. G. Western, extending southwesterly up and along this valley. When we come to consider the fuel question for the Rocky Mountain region, and the number of fire sides and persons that must be kept warm, then we can estimate the incalculable value of these coal-fields to the general public. Practically these fields yet remain unpurchased from the government; they are yet open to the hand of industry and the purse of enterprise.

This idea is advanced by those who know. Let the Legislature of Utah adopt, and the Territorial authorities enforce a local traffic law, whereby the product of these coal fields can be landed in the Salt Lake basin, on the same terms per ton per mile as freight is landed from Chicago or New York, and then we can have coal, and good, too, as cheap as $3 or $4 per ton, instead of $6 or $7. Here is a point for a chamber of commerce or a board of trade, much more beautiful to the public than wine suppers or beef *a la mode*.

It is not probable from present indications that the Pleasant Valley coal-fields extend into the San Pete Valley which lies some 20 or 25 miles on the southwest and nearly parallel to Pleasant Valley. X X X.

PLEASANT VALLEY, Scofield, Utah.

Deseret News
July 20, 1887

DEATHS.

McINTYRE.—At Price, Emery County Utah, July 7th, 1887, Ella, youngest daughter of John and Alice McIntyre, aged 2 years and 3 months.

Deseret News
August 24, 1887

An Infant Drowned.

"W. L.," writing from Scofield, August 18th, gives the following account of a sad casualty that occurred in Winter Quarter's Cañon, near the D. & R. G. coal mines:

"A sad fatality occurred here about 9 o'clock this morning, whereby the infant son of Mr. Samuel Coombs lost his life.

It appears that the child, who was about 14 months old, was just beginning to walk. Being left alone for a few minutes, by some means it got outside of the house to a wash tub, which contained but a little water left over from washing the day before. Standing by the tub the child lost its balance and fell face downward into it. The absence of the child caused the mother to inquire for it. One of the older children went outside to look for him, and ran in and told the mother that the child was in the tub. It was instantly taken out and every means were used to restore it to consciousness, but in vain; it was suffocated. Great sympathy is shown for the bereaved parents, as this is their second child lost by drowning. The body will be taken to Spanish Fork for interment.

Deseret News
October 5, 1887

Commissioned.

The following commissions were issued by Governor West yesterday:

A. E. Keeler, justice of the peace, Park City, Summit County.

John Brunton, justice of the peace, Bingham, Salt Lake County.

John C. Duncan, justice of the peace, Ferron, Emery County.

E. W. McIntire, justice of the peace, Price, Emery County.

J. A. Farrar, justice of the peace, Blake, Emery County.

Wm. Wood, Sr., Justice of the peace, Minersville, Beaver County.

Swen Nielsen, Justice of the peace, Fairview, Sanpete County.

JONES.—At Scofield, Emery County, Utah, about 10 o'clock on Saturday night the 17th inst., after an illness of nine weeks, Margret, wife of Thomas D. Jones, aged 61 years.

Deceased was born in Merthyr Tydvil South Wales and was baptized in that branch and in the year 1842 and labored with others in distributing tracts and church works among her friends and has always been steadfast in her belief of all the principles of the Gospel and bore a strong testimony to its truth. Deceased emigrated from Tteorky to Utah on the 23d of Oct. 18-1, arriving at Provo Nov. 11th of the same year; removed to Pleasant Valley Ward. She leaves a husband, a daughter and 6 grand children, with a large circle of friends to mourn her loss.

Mill. Star, please copy.

Deseret News
October 26, 1887

LAMPH.— At Scofield, on October 10, 18-7, of abscess of the liver, Daniel Lamph, late of Spennymoor, Durham, England, aged 35 years and 4 months.

Deceased was born on the 10th of June, 1832; baptized on the 10th of October, 1881; emigrated to Utah on the 13th of the same month, and died on the above date at the residence of his son William, after a very short illness.—COM.

Millennial Star, please copy.

Salt Lake Herald
November 17, 1887

Sad accident.

To the Editor of THE HERALD.

A sad accident occurred here on Tuesday, November 8th, in the drowning of two small children, one a little girl 5 years old, Anna Eliza McKendrick, daughter of Charles H. and Mary E. McKendrick; the other, a small boy 4 years old, Joseph Benton Powell, son of John A. and Sarah J. Powell. On November 3d, these children went with their mothers down to the river, to witness the baptizing of their cousin, Robert Powell, and other children. On the 8th, they, along with Willie Powell, went to the river to play at baptizing. Josie and Eliza took hold of hands and waded out in the stream up to their waists, when they ducked under. Willie, the child who remained outside, waited for them to come up again. The girl came to the surface once and then disappeared, when terror-stricken Willie ran to the house and told his mother that Josie and Eliza had gone way down in a deep hole. The mothers of the two unfortunate children rushed frantically to the river's brink, only to find their beloved little ones cold and stiff in the arms of the grim monster, Death. The boy had been washed up on the beach about thirty yards below. The girl went with the stream about fifty yards, when the braids of her hair caught on a snag and held her floating in the water.

The obsequies were held on Friday, the 11th, when the little darlings were interred side by side. Yours truly,

C. H. VALENTINE,

PRICE, EMERY Co., Nov. 13, '87.

A VEIN OF ANTHRACITE.

A Valuable Discovery Reported near Price, Utah

Mr. B. H. Young, of Price, is in the city, and bids fair to become a bloated bondholder ere long if his expectations, which are based upon substantial reasons, are fulfilled. For several years past, Mr. Young has made his home in the south—at the Pleasant Valley coal mines, and other places, and during this time has gained a thorough knowledge of the country surrounding those places. About a month ago, while out in the mountains near Price and about fourteen miles from the railway, he discovered a vein of coal, samples of which have been brought to this city, and competent experts have pronounced it to be anthracite of the very best quality. If this be true, and there seems to be no reason to doubt it, the find will prove to be an exceedingly valuable one, and one that will have a big influence upon the coal trade in this section. Although plentifully supplied with the bituminous article, which exists within the borders of Utah in sufficient quantities to supply half the world, anthracite has never before been discovered, and all that is used in this Territory is brought from Colorado. Several prominent gentlemen are endeavoring to get an interest in the matter, and further developments will be watched for eagerly. Anthracite is an article we have scarcely looked for, and its discovery goes to prove what has so often been stated—that our resources, numerous as they are, have not all been discovered.

DEATHS.

CHRISTIANSEN.—At Muddy, Emery County, Utah Territory, Nov. 3d, 1887, Mary, wife of Bishop Caspar Christiansen, of lung fever.

Deceased was born August 1st, 1842, in Denmark; was baptized in October, 1864, and came to the United States in 1869. She lived in Minnesota six years, and in 1875 came to Utah, settling in Spring City. In 1881 she removed to Muddy, where she resided until her death. She leaves a husband and eight children, and was an industrious wife and loving parent.—COM.

Millennial Star, please copy.

DEATHS.

HARRIS.—At Winter Quarters, Sanpete Co., Dec. 29th, 1887, of convulsion of the brain, Catherine Harris, daughter of Thomas Phelps and Catherine Harris, aged 12 years.

PITTMAN.—At Winter Quarters, Sanpete Co., January 3rd, 1888, of brain fever, Amy, beloved wife of John Pittman, aged 28 years. Deceased was married quite young and bore to her husband 9 children, 6 of whom are now left to mourn her loss. The bereaved family have the sympathy of the entire community.—COM.

THOMAS.—At Scofield, Emery Co., Jan., 1888, of stomach disease, Isaiah D., son of Evan S. and Margaret Thomas, aged 3 years. —*Millennial Star* and Welsh papers please copy.

Deseret News
January 25, 1888

Cold.

A correspondent writing from Scofield, Emery County, gives an account of the cold weather in that section. He says that on Saturday night coal oil froze in the lamps, and at 6:30 p.m. on that day the thermometer indicated 50 degrees below zero at the mouths of Mud Creek and Winter Quarters Cañon.

Deseret News
March 7, 1888

Deputy Registrars.

The Utah Commission yesterday made the following appointments:

Sanpete County—Fayette, Wm. M. Scott; Gunnison, James M. Robbins; Maxfield, Peter A. Mortensen; Petty, John Patten; Manti, E. W. Fox; Ephraim, Peter Schwalbe; Spring City, Jacob Johnson; Chester, E. J. Conrad; Wales, H. C. Lamb; Fort Green, Geo. Wilson; Moroni, N. L. Eliason; Mt. Pleasant, J. D. Page; Fairview, H. C. Brunson; Milburn, S. E. Jensen; Thistle, Wm. N. Tidwell, Jr.; Winter Quarters, E. L. Carpenter.

Emery County—Castle Dale, Carl Wilberg; Blake, J. P. Farrar; Ferron, J. W. Williams; Huntington, J. F. Wakefield; Muddy, J. T. Lewis; Molen, J. D. Kilpack; Moab, C. J. Boreen; Orangeville, J. K. Reid; Price, A. Ballanger; Schofield, S. J. Harkness; Wellington, R. B. Thompson.

Utah Enquirer
March 13, 1888

DIED.

Leigh.—At Price, Emery County, March 2, 1888, of lung fever, Epaphro C., son of Sarah Chailln and John D. Leigh; born July 2, 1887.

Davies—At Scofield, Emery County, on the 25th of February, of whooping cough, Ann B., infant daughter of John F. and Mary B. Davies, aged 8 months. *Millennial Star* please copy.

Deseret News
March 14, 1888

OBITUARY.

WOODWARD.—James Woodward, son of James and Laura Woodward, was born in Kingston, Upper Canada, July 22nd, 1817; his father, James Woodward, came over from England to America shortly after the war of 1812, and died while Brother Woodward was quite young; the latter lived (most of the time) among strangers, until April, 1842, when he left New York State and went to live with an uncle by the name of Asa Read, who lived in Portage County, Ohio, where he joined the Church, being baptized on the 23d of July, 1842, by Samuel Phelps. He was re-baptized in Kirtland April 6th, 1843, and ordained an Elder by Lester Brooks and John Young. In the spring of 1844 he was ordained a Seventy and set apart in the 29th Quorum; in the same winter he joined the Nauvoo Legion and was elected a corporal. From the time Brother Woodward joined the Church until the time of his death he was a faithful member and always bore a strong testimony to the truth of the Gospel.

He passed through a great many of the trials and persecutions with the Saints, and of late years took an active part in the Sunday schools, and otherwise taught the young the duties they owe to the Lord. He also held several political offices and was a selectman of Emery County when he died, on the 6th day of October, 1887, from dropsy and heart disease. He left a large lot of relatives and friends to mourn his loss.—[COM.

Salt Lake Herald
March 16, 1888

Accidentally Killed.

SCOFIELD, Utah, March 15, 1888.—[Special to THE HERALD].—William Johnstone was killed here this morning, by being run over by an engine on the railroad track. Very little information can be obtained in regard to him. Age, about 51; he had a father in England a brother in Australia and two children, whereabouts unknown; has lived a number of years in Utah, principally around Ogden, being employed as engineer and sawyer. William Johnstone is thought by some to be an alias, and that his right name is William Morrison. Possibly this may be the means of making this known to some of his relatives.

Deseret News
April 11, 1888

DEATHS.

LEWIS.—At Schofield. Emery Co., March 27th, 1888, of measles, Emma Jane, daughter of Daniel and Letitia Lewis, aged 3 years and eight months.
Millennial Star and Welsh papers please copy.

LAY.—At Price, Emery County, March 21, 1888, of whooping cough, Silas Emanuel, son of William R. and Emily Konner Lay; aged 5 months and 25 days.

BRYNER.—At Price, Emery County, March 30, 1888, of pneumonia, Casper Harmon, son of Harmon C. and Edith Miles Bryner; aged 5 months.

WARREN.—At Price, Emery County, March 31, 1888, of quick consumption, Hattie May, daughter of William Z. and Mariah Powell Warren; born March 14, 1887.

Utah Enquirer
June 1, 1888

P. V. COAL MINES.

The Extensive Mining Being Done In The District.

A correspondent writing to the *Tribune* from Schofield, under date of May 24th, says:

The first four months of this year were the most active in coal operations the Pleasant Valley mines ever had. From January 1st to April 30th. inclusive, the shipments were:

Pleasant Valley mine	60,207 tons
Utah Central mines	20,000 "
Total	80,207 tons

The Pleasant Valley Company sent out eighty thousand tons in 1887, while this year their output was three-fourths that amount in one-third of a year. While the local demand for coal was much larger this than last year, the Southern Pacific Company was a purchaser to the extent of sixty thousand tons. Between January 30th and April 28th coal was shipped from here to the extent of 4716 cars, making very lively times for the railway boys. At present 175 men are employed at the Winter Quarters mine operated by the Pleasant Valley Company, and 55 by the Utah Central mine, making a total of 230 men in all. Miners are paid eighteen cents per ton after screening over half in screens. The average slack in the coal mined is about twenty per cent of the total. The Winter Quarters mine is ten feet thick, is worked by a main tunnel run on a level, from which drifts have been run upwards in places of a fourth of a mile from which rooms are run 21 feet wide, with pillars between 27 feet wide. These rooms are worked from two drifts, 400 feet apart, and after meeting in the middle, all the pillars are drawn out except next to the drifts, which are left for the purpose of keeping the opening good. In time these remaining pillars are taking out thus getting the entire coal seam, permitting the ground to come down from above. The Utah Central mine has a vein 28 feet thick, which is all taken out except four feet at the top that is left to keep the mine in proper shape while working. Both mines are well managed by W. S. Sharp, who for the past two years has had their superintendence. Scofield Station keeps the agent, Mr. Shermer, and an assistant pretty busy in handling their shipments. To-day they filled out way bill numbered 7170, indicating how many they had made since January 1st. As each way bill represents a car, the number tells how many cars of coal have gone out, except that there were a few, a very few, cars of merchandise. With the increasing demand for fuel, this fine coal mining district promises to become a much greater producer. The amount and quality of coal here, and the fine facilities for mining and shipping, warrant the prediction, that the coal business here is only in its infancy.

SCOFIELD, Utah, May 24.

Two Wards.

By letter from Brother Evan S. Thomas, we learn that, on the 17th, the ward heretofore known as Pleasant Valley Ward, was divided into two. The upper portion of the ward, located in Winter Quarters Cañon, retains the old name. Thomas J. Parmley was made Bishop, and Hyrum Richards and Isaac Whimpey were made his Counselors.

That portion of the ward embraced in the town of Scofield, takes that name. John T. Balantyne was ordained Bishop, and Thomas P. Page and John R. Davis were chosen as his Counselors. These changes were made by Apostle H. J. Grant and Presidents A. O. Smoot and David John of Utah Stake.

CASTLE VALLEY.

The Home of the Prairie Dog—Immense Deposits of Coal — Improvements in a Naturally Forbidding Region — Phenomenal Increase of Bees.

HUNTINGTON, Emery County.
July 2, 1888.

Editor Deseret News:

The first account the writer ever remembers concerning Castle Valley was given by some of his comrades in an Indian expedition in 1866, who had followed a party of marauding Red Men into this region, in the hope of recovering from them some of the cattle they had stolen from Sanpete settlements, and they, like the majority of the ancient Israelites sent to spy out the promised land, did not view it with the eye of faith. They gave it a very hard character. They found it so dry and parched that scarcely any vegetation except prickly pears were to be seen, and probably not one of the whole command imagined the valley would ever be inhabited by white men. The country generally has

A MOST FORBIDDING APPEARANCE;

consisting of uneven plains, broken occasionally by deep gullies or washes furrowed out by the streams which course down from the mountains on the west or by cloud-bursts or freshets to which the region has doubtless been subjected for ages. The name of Castle Valley has been derived from the peculiar mountains which surround it, or rather hem it in on the west, and which have a castellated appearance, with their mesa tops and many colored, bare and precipitous sides as they tower up for hundreds of feet, showing the effects of the erosion which as reduced them from what they doubtless once were—an elevated level plain—to what they are today.

THE SOIL

in the valley is light colored and more or less impregnated with mineral, and the early settlers must certainly have had a good deal of faith to ever attempt to raise a crop on it. But it is a great deal better than it looks. The mineral though similar in appearance must be unlike in nature to that with which the soil in the lower portions of many other valleys throughout the Territory abounds. It does not interfere materially with the growth of crops, which when plentifully supplied with water, an element with which, fortunately, the country is bountifully provided, grow rapidly and luxuriantly though the surface of the soil may be almost white with the salts with which it is everywhere more or less impregnated. Lucern yields three good crops during the season and many other crops do as well here as in the lower valleys generally, while trees and vines grow unusually rank. The country is not, however, so well adapted for the raising of small grain as many other valleys are, although much of it is grown here.

Brother Orange Seeley, who is now one of the counselors to President C. G. Larsen of this the Emery Stake, but who was then a resident of Mount Pleasant, Sanpete, was the first to attempt a settlement of this region. He ventured into the south end of the valley with a herd of cattle in 1875 and continued to occupy it as a herd ground and experimented a little at raising a crop until 1878, when a number of others from Sanpete were called to join him in establishing settlements in the valley and contending with the numerous

PRAIRIE DOGS

inhabiting it for a subsistence. It is pretty safe to say that no people but Latter-day Saints would have been likely to succeed in the undertaking, but they have persevered in the midst of all manner of discouragements and will doubtless continue to do so until Castle Valley becomes a fruitful region and a desirable place for a home.

The first village arrived at on entering the valley by train, and the only one located on the line of railway is

PRICE.

The townsite contains, in addition to the railway station and a couple of well-patronized and thriving stores, perhaps not more than twenty-five dwellings and a saloon or two, the invariable adjunct to a railroad town, but the ward includes a great many persons living on ranches up and down Price River and about twenty families who are establishing a settlement seven miles distant, to the south-east, called Wellington. The last mentioned is likely soon to become a ward of itself and an extensive one too, as it has ample room on the broad and comparatively level plain which it occupies to spread out and plenty of water to irrigate with. Price, proper, is likely to develop hereafter faster than it has d ne, as after a long and laborious struggle the residents have at last succeeded in completing their canal and bringing water to their gardens.

Twenty-three miles south of Price, after traversing a rolling prairie which contains scarcely a green thing to break the monotony of its sterility,

HUNTINGTON,

the largest settlement of the county, is reached. The town contains perhaps 150 families, but the ward includes about fifty more, located farther down the stream eastward in what are known as the

LAWRENCE AND CLEVELAND

branches. The latter is destined to become one of the largest wards of the Stake. It is about seven miles distant from Huntington and much of the soil it includes is as good as can be found in the valley. It has a canal fifteen miles long, just completed this year at a cost of 30,000 which is expected to irrigate 10,000 acres, but should the water prove sufficient, which is very doubtful as the whole of the stream is already utilized, at least 15,000 acres more could be cultivated and irrigated by it. Many of those who have located farms in Cleveland and helped to construct the canal are miners who are employed during a large portion of the year at Schofield. The canal at Huntington does not exceed three miles in length, and yet it cost $20,000. It passes through a tunnel 300 feet long and was was quite difficult to construct in other places owing to the unevenness of the ground.

CASTLE DALE,

the county seat, located ten miles south of Huntington, is a pleasantly situated village containing a grist mill and planing mill and some very well built residences. This settlement is well supplied with water as is also

ORANGEVILLE,

situated on the same stream, about three miles westward. The latter place is well supplied with shade trees, chiefly the native round leafed cottonwood, very similar in appearance to the Canadian poplar, and a very thrifty variety of box elder, which has a fresh looking, green bark and a differently shaped leaf to the box elder trees found in other portions of the Territory. Fruit trees and vines also appear to do well here, as indeed they do in nearly all the settlements of the valley. The writer had the pleasure of attending a Stake conference of the Y. M. M. I. A. in Orangeville and also meetings held under the auspices of the Young Men's Associations in Castle Dale and Huntington. For lack of time he was unable to visit the villages of Ferron, fifteen miles south of Castle Dale, Molen, three miles east and Muddy, fifteen miles south of Ferron, but learned that those settlements were in a prosperous condition, the last mentioned being especially noted for the energy and perseverance of its inhabitants in the matter of canal making. The feats they have accomplished in that line are, simply marvelous.

No country in the world is better supplied with

COAL MINES

than is Castle Valley, which, however, are as yet undeveloped. Immense veins crop out in numerous places around the mountain sides and in some instances can be traced for miles in the valley. Many veins have been consumed by fire and at least one is said to be still burning, as tradition says it has been for the last thirty years. The attention of eastern capitalists has already been attracted to the coal deposits of this region, which experts declare to be the most extensive they have ever seen, and it is not at all unlikely that the next decade will witness the construction of branch lines of railway into this valley for the development of the mines and a great influx of popula-

tion. In the meantime the present inhabitants are laying the foundation for permanent prosperity by the development of the agricultural resources of the country and rendering all the more easy to extract the mineral wealth with which it abounds when the time comes to do so.

The climate of Castle Valley which is extremely dry, seems especially adopted for

THE CULTIVATION OF BEES

which seem to do better here than any other part of the Territory. Indeed, it is doubtful if any place in the world excels it in this line. Numerous cases are cited of swarms increasing three or four fold already during the present season with a prospect of their still continuing to multiply and yield honey for some months before the season is over. Thus has this region, originally so uninviting in appearance, its compensating advantages and, through the industry of its inhabitants and under the blessing of the Almighty, is it being made a pleasant abode.   G. C. L.

Salt Lake Herald
August 28, 1888

IMMIGRANTS COMING.

Names of the Company Now En Route to Utah.

Following is a full list of the company of Saints which left Liverpool on the 11th instant, on the steamship *Wisconsin*:

For Pleasant Valley - Isaac, Catherine, Henry, John, Taileson and Hector Evans; Christina. Mary, Alelander and Richard Stuart.

For Morgan—Minnie and Louise Heywood; John and Ann Hardman.
For Scofield—John Hunter.
For Echo—George Beveley.

Salt Lake Herald
September 4, 1888

Notes From Pleasant Valley

THERE are five stores, all doing an average trade; also a saloon which, in its line, is not dead.

THE last, but not least, is the coal industry, which employs many men continually getting out the darky metal. Owing to the slackness of trade, miners can only get about one-half time; but time will commence to liven up next month and the workmen will then feel jubilant and jolly, as they have plenty to do and their purses are full. They can then dress well, eat plenty and have the best in the market.   A RAMBLER.

MOST of the men are busy mining coal, hauling lumber and in various other occupations in which the people are engaged. In the mountains southwest of the valley, there are five steam saw mills, which, on an average, cut from 10,000 to 12,000 feet of lumber per day. To keep these mills running, they keep many hands constantly employed getting out timber, making roads, hauling lumber, etc. This lumber is mostly shipped to Provo and Salt Lake City, and is hauled into the valley at from 40,000 to 50,000 feet per day.

PLEASANT VALLEY is about seven miles long by one to two wide. It is shut in on either side by low hills and mountains, upon which countless herds of sheep, cattle and horses roam. The valley is taken up and made into fine pastures and meadow lands. Your correspondent could not but note the difference from what it was before the iron horse was heard in these parts; then some few stockmen made this their summer home and came here to pasture their stock and to make butter, cheese, etc. Now you find two very thriving villages, Scofield and Winter Quarters. The former contains 125 families and the ward is presided over by Bishop Ballentyne; the latter contains 115 families and is presided over by Bishop Parmerly. There are two day schools in session, with an enrollment of seventy pupils.

SCOFIELD, August 31st, 1888.

Deseret News
September 19, 1888

DEATHS.

BOTT.—At Price, Emery County, Utah, Karl Bott; born June 11, 1850, at Wurttemburg; died September 8, 1888. He leaves a wife and four small children.

Salt Lake Herald
October 12, 1888

THOMAS HOWELLS, employed at No. 3 mine at Winter Quarters, near Scofield, met his death a couple of days ago through a heavy mass of coal falling upon him. The mines which had been closed down for a couple of days in order that his comrades might attend his funeral services, were opened again yesterday morning. The deceased was about 26 years of age and unmarried.

VISIT TO EMERY STAKE.

Brothers Goddard and Willes Rapidly Recovering.

HUNTINGTON, Emery Co.,
Nov. 17, 1888.

Editor Deseret News:

Since the communication of your correspondent, which left here on the 14th, relative to our sad misfortune, we deem it not only a duty we owe to our many friends, but a pleasure to record the wonderful power of God, our Heavenly Father, in so rapidly restoring the shattered tabernacles of two of His fragile servants. Through the anointing of oil and the prayer of faith, we have been the recipients of God's blessings in a marvelous degree, that not only makes our own hearts rejoice, but fills our many ministering friends with astonishment and gratitude. The minor bruises and scratches have nearly all disappeared, and the more serious injuries, which caused us the most acute pain and helplessness are rapidly giving way.

One week ago this morning we left our homes and the "city we love so well," on an official visit to this Stake of Zion. We traveled on the Utah Central as far as Springville, and after partaking of the hospitality of Bishop Packard and family, were detained four hours on account of an accident on the D. & R. G. This delay made it about 10 o'clock p.m. when we arrived at Price, Emery County. We then wended our way to Elder Lars M. Olsen's house. He having gone to conference to be held at Ferron, 50 miles distant, his house was left in charge of a housekeeper, who had retired to rest.

We were soon ensconced in a warm room, and also refreshed in our inner man. After a good night's rest, and an early breakfast we looked around for a conveyance to take us to Huntington, and thence to Ferron, where the quarterly conference was held. We found two teams about to start, one owned by Brother Howard, son of William Howard of Salt Lake City, and the other by Brother McNiven. Either of them offered to take us, but one of Brother Howard's horses being sick, it was deemed wisdom to accept the kind offer of the latter, and after carefully wrapping us up in blankets and quilts, to keep us warm, we started on our journey of twenty-three miles. We shall never forget the careful and unselfish treatment we received at his hands. On reaching the verge of that steep and ever to be remembered descent, he got out of the wagon and cautiously examined the same before starting down, little dreaming what an experience awaited him that had never transpired with him before, for we had no sooner passed the brow of the hill, his horses being held with a tight grip, than one of the bits broke in the mouth of one of the horses, and the ring also on the other bit, thus loosening their head gear, and away they went, turning over the wagon and all its contents.

The result of that fearful occurrence having been stated in a previous communication, we will simply say that we feel ourselves so much improved that we anticipate with the help of the Lord a glorious time tomorrow (Sunday) in meeting with the children in their Sunday school, and also with the Saints of Huntington in their general assemblies. It is difficult for us to imagine any circumstance to arise that could draw deeper on the sympathy and the most unremitting attention and generosity of the Saints of Huntington. Long will be cherished in our memories their love and tender regard towards us.

On Thursday night our room was literally besieged with about 20 of the sweet singers of Israel, making over 30 occupants for over two hours. After their beautiful serenade, some remarks were called for, and made by one whose name is attached to this letter. It was a soul stirring time, and we are here in the midst of our friends, resting and taking care of ourselves. We are glad and thankful to the Lord that we came to Emery County, and though it is our first, we sincerely hope and believe it will not be our last visit.

We labor in the interest of the Sunday Schools of Zion; it is our meat and our drink and has been for many years, and going around from school to school, to offer a few words of encouragement to both children and teachers, and to give timely suggestions to Stake and local superintendents, and sometimes an occasional song, all backed up by the blessing of the Lord, fills our cup of rejoicing.

Should no unforeseen circumstance arise, we may possibly leave here on Monday, travel as far as Price, and on Tuesday afternoon start for home per the D. & R. G. as far as Springville, then per the Utah Central to Salt Lake City, on Wednesday.

GEORGE GODDARD,
WM. WILLES.

Deseret News
December 5, 1888

DEATHS.

HARDY.—In Scofield, Emery County, Nov. 00, 1888, of a complication of disorders, Mary Jones, wife of Thomas L. Hardy.

She was born July 28, 1818, at Tondu, near Bridge End, Glamorganshire, South Wales; came to Utah in 1883, and soon afterwards was baptized. She was the mother of eleven children, seven of whom are living, who, with her husband, are left to mourn her loss. She died a faithful Latter-day Saint.—[COM.

Salt Lake Herald
January 10, 1889

THOMAS BROWN, a coal miner, engaged in mine No. 3, Winter Quarters, was killed on Tuesday, by the coal caving in upon him. His funeral services occurred yesterday. He leaves a wife and family.

Utah Enquirer
January 11, 1889

SCOFIELD BURGLARY.

Fowler and Turner Do Some Neat Work.

THEY SECURE THE TWO GUILTY PARTIES

And Effect the Recovery of the Stolen Goods.

On the day after New Year's Sheriff Thomas Fowler received a dispatch from Scofield, Emery County, requesting him to go there on the next D. & R. G. train, as three stores there had been robbed. The Sheriff realized there might be considerable work to be done, so he invited his old companion, ex-Sheriff J. W. Turner, to accompany him. The officers arrived at Scofield at 6 o'clock that same night, going direct to the U. C. Railway Co. office. There they learned that Earl's store, in which the Postoffice is situated, had been robbed of a quantity of men's underwear, some gloves, and money from the drawer, as well as some registered letters containing over $80.00 in currency, and about $20.00 in stamps taken from the Postoffice department. The store of David Eckles had also been broken into, and a quantity of gold-plated and silver watches, watch charms, finger rings, etc., stolen therefrom. The Utah Central Railway Company store had been served the same way and four overcoats, gloves, shirts, and some money that had been left in the drawer taken from it. The whole amount from the different stores reached nearly $400. In each case the thieves had broken the fastenings of the doors to effect an entrance.

It was some time after the officers arrived at Scofield before they could get a starting point. The store of Mr. Earl had been burglarized on New Year's Eve, and the other two on New Year's night. Thread after thread of information caught onto by the officers was followed up, search warrants were sworn out and several houses searched. Finally two warrants of arrest was placed in Sheriff Fowler's hands, and he corraled two men, on whom suspicion rested. The only clue with the first man arrested was that on New Year's night he had started home to his boarding-place, reaching there about 3 o'clock on the morning of January 2d. In returning to his room mate a watch that he had borrowed to wear while he went to a party, there was a new gold-filled chain attached to it. The next day he asked his partner for it, saying it was a gift from his uncle, and that he did not care to have it worn for common use.

After keeping these two suspicious parties, that had been arrested, from talking together for two nights, and following up every thread that the officers caught on to from the good people there, who rendered the officials every assistance possible, the goods were all found buried in the mines. The watches and chains had been placed in tin cans, and the clothing in sacks, all the articles then being buried in the coal dust at the mine.

The County Attorney of Emery county was sent for, and at the examination one of the arrested men revealed how the whole thing had been done. From the man's tale it appears that they had buried the money under the ties of the tramway in the mines.

The officers are jubilant over their success, and for the assistance the good people of Scofield rendered them. The names of the two men arrested are Thomas Murchie and William Craig. Both are transient miners, and had been working in the coal mine at Scofield. They were bound over in the sum of $2,500 bonds to await the action of the next grand jury at Provo, in default of which Sheriff Fowler brought them to Provo, and they languish in jail.

The two officers seriously think somewhat of locating near the mine. They say a mine that they can dig silver, gold, greenbacks, and clothing from is better than any Sheriff's office in the Territory.

Utah Enquirer
January 25, 1889

A short time ago Samuel Roberts, Jr., had his toes crushed in an accident at Price, Emery County. It was found necessary to amputate the big toe to-day.

Utah Enquirer
February 22, 1889

Scofield.

An entertainment was given under the auspices of the Y. M. & Y. L. M. I. A. and the Scofield Ward Sunday school on the night of Feb. 16, 1889, consisting of songs, duetts, solos, dialogues, etc. Our choir leader, Thos. L. Hardy, and party, rendered two pieces with credit and applause, especially in "The Sailor's Chorus." All that took part did well, and the piece was greatly appreciated by all in the room. T. C. Reese and and party, from Winter Quarters Coal Mine, rendered a few pieces in a creditable manner. Mr. Reese is a splendid comic singer. Mr. J. E. Ingles, our Irish comedian, came out in full colors and done his part up in good shape. The farce, entitled, "Dutch Justice," was quite laughable. It was remarked by some that in the way this piece was rendered that it would be hard to beat it. Our little meeting-house was crowded to overflowing. It was announced that the programme would be repeated in three weeks, with a slight change, and it is to be hoped the public will turn out in the future, and be as liberal as in the past, in helping to support and sustain two of the most useful institutions for the advancement of the youth.

The Young People's Association was organized February 10, 1887, and has flourished ever since. We have a good library, and it is the calculation to enlarge it as soon as possible.

The Sunday school is in a flourishing condition, and all that are officiating in that great cause deserve praise for the zeal and energy in which they are conducting the same.

ONE OF THE BOYS.

SCOFIELD, February 11, 1889.

Utah Enquirer
April 23, 1889

DEPUTY REGISTRARS.

Another Batch Appointed by the Utah Commission.

EMERY COUNTY.

Precinct.	Name.
Castle Dale	Carl Wilberg
Blake	J. F. Farrer
Malen	J. S. Killpach
Ferron	J. W. Williams
Muddy	John T. Lewis
Orangeville	J. K. Reed
Price	A. Ballinger
Wellington	R. B. Thompson
Huntington	J. T. Wakefield
Larence	Elias Thomas
Scofield	S. J. Harkness

Utah Enquirer
May 31, 1889

DIED.

EDWARDS.—In Pleasant Valley, Utah, May 21, 1889, Margaret Edwards, wife of Ed. Edwards formerly of Pen-heol-gerrig, Merthyr-Tydfil, Wales. Sister Edwards was born in South Wales in 1821, was baptized into the Church of Jesus Christ of Latter-day Saints in 1849, by Elder Wm. Richards, since which time she has proven faithful to the principles of truth and salvation. Sister Edwards has been a resident of Spanish Fork since her arrival in Utah; but for some two or three years her health has been failing. Hoping to restore her health she went on a visit to her son William and family at Scofield, Pleasant Valley, when she died on the 21st of May, 1889. With national fidelity the Welsh of that place made an appropriate demonstration of respect towards the deceased and her relatives. The remains were conveyed to Spanish Fork, where suitable services were held; Elders John Moore and T. C. Martill delivering the funeral sermons and Elder Wm. Creer offering the prayer.—*Millennial Star* please copy.

NOT DEAD.

Elder Snow Arrives From the Southern States.

The Manti *Sentinel* announced on Friday the death of Elder John Snow, now on a mission to the States, giving his residence as Manti. No particulars were given. The only missionary in the States whose name was similar to the above was Elder John O. Snow, of Orangeville, Emery county, who has been quite ill for some time past. Monday morning the following special telegram was received:

PRICE, Utah, September 2, 1889.—Elder John O. Snow has arrived home safe. He is improving in health.　　　D. O. ROBBINS.

Elder Snow is the son of Warren S. and Maria B. Snow, and was born in Provo, October 16, 1859.

L. S. Pond returned to his camp on the D. &. R. G. at Price, Utah, to-day. He was accompanied by Miss Clara Whittle and Mrs. Jos. Hendricks, who expect to be gone about two months.

Scofield.

An entertainment was given under the auspices of the Y. M. & Y. L. M. I. A. and the Scofield Ward Sunday school on the night of Feb. 16, 1889, consisting of songs, duetts, solos, dialogues, etc. Our choir leader, Thos. L. Hardy, and party, rendered two pieces with credit and applause, especially in "The Sailor's Chorus." All that took part did well, and the piece was greatly appreciated by all in the room. T. C. Reese and and party, from Winter Quarters Coal Mine, rendered a few pieces in a creditable manner. Mr. Reese is a splendid comic singer. Mr. J. E. Ingles, our Irish comedian, came out in full colors and done his part up in good shape. The farce, entitled, "Dutch Justice," was quite laughable. It was remarked by some that in the way this piece was rendered that it would be hard to beat it. Our little meeting-house was crowded to overflowing. It was announced that the programme would be repeated in three weeks, with a slight change, and it is to be hoped the public will turn out in the future, and be as liberal as in the past, in helping to support and sustain two of the most useful institutions for the advancement of the youth.

THE Young People's Association was organized February 10, 1887, and has flourished ever since. We have a good library, and it is the calculation to enlarge it as soon as possible.

THE Sunday school is in a flourishing condition, and all that are officiating in that great cause deserve praise for the zeal and energy in which they are conducting the same.

　　　　　　ONE OF THE BOYS.
SCOFIELD, February 11, 1889.

Deseret Weekly
September 28, 1889

AT PLEASANT VALLEY.

A creditable entertainment was given in Pleasant Valley Ward meeting house a short time ago, the programme for the evening consisting of choice selections of music by the leading talent of the Ward, in glees, solos, duets, trios, sentimental and comic songs, recitations and negro melodies. The proceeds of the entertainment will go to aid in immigrating the family of Brother Thomas Griffiths of this Ward.

Another entertainment was given at the Theatre Hall, Scofield, Sept. 14, 1889, with but little change in the programme. This was to help to defray the expense of making an addition to the Pleasant Valley Ward meeting house, and was not as successful as was expected, for the reason that there was not a stove in the house and it was a cold night.

A glee club will be organized in this ward tomorrow evening, the 16th inst. We have the talent here for a good club.

EVAN S. THOMAS.

SCOFIELD, Utah, Sept. 16, 1889.

Salt Lake Herald
December 7, 1889

David Williams Dead.

Yesterday morning a dispatch received by A. L. Williams, Esq., announced the death of his father, David Williams, at Price, Emery county, where he had been engaged in a general mercantile business for some months. Something over a year since, deceased returned from a prolonged stay in Wales, his native country, and soon after became a severe sufferer from asthma, which was the cause of death. For several months the disease grew steadily worse, and at times caused terrible distress.

In or about the year 1878 deceased became manager of the D. & R. G. Pleasant Valley coal mines, and had charge of them until near the close of 1885. He was a capable business man, an excellent geologist, and was widely known and much respected in business circles, and by hundreds of his countrymen in Utah and Idaho.

The funeral services will be held in the Fifteenth ward meeting house at 11 a. m. to-morrow (Sunday) for which reason the Sabbath school will adjourn one hour earlier than usual.

Friends and acquaintances of the deceased are invited to be present.

Death of a Good Man.

David Williams whose death occurred on the morning of Dec. 6th, 1889, at Price, Emery County, was the son of David and Sarah Williams, and was born in Blaenavon, Monmouthshire, Wales, Dec. 16, 1827, and hence was aged nearly 62 years. He embraced the Gospel in its fulness in the year 1847, and was soon after ordained a Teacher, and then a Priest. In 1849 he was ordained an Elder and called to the ministry. He traveled as a missionary four years, principally in North Wales, and labored with marked zeal and success. He married Miss Sarah Williams on May 29, 1847; migrated to St. Louis in January, 1855, and was president of the Welsh Saints who formed a considerable part o the large company on the ship. He remained in St. Louis about one year, when he went to Kingston, Ill. He remained there but a short time when he removed to Canton, Ill., where he located in the fall of 1856.

He was at this time in very poor circumstances financially, but he set to work with a will and soon improved his pecuniary condition. He was a coal miner, at which calling he worked. After a time he purchased a tract of coal land in the town of Canton, which subsequently became valuable property. He also acquired two other tracts of coal land near Canton. In December 1875, Elder B. F. Cummings, Jr., who was traveling in Illinois as a missionary, met him. He had long been separated from intimate association with the Saints, but his faith in the Gospel as taught by the Prophet Joseph Smith was firm and bright, and at his request he was rebaptized by Elder Cummings, January 8th, 1876.

He immediately took an active part in extending the work of the Gospel in Canton and vicinity, which had now commenced to open up in a very gratifying manner. Owing to the facilities Brother Williams had for furnishing employment, scattered Saints found, and converts made by the Elders in that region were invited by him to come to Canton, and in a few months a branch of about fifty members existed there, of which he was president.

At the opening of the year 1876, he was a wealthy man, and was using his means generously to forward the work of the Gospel. But business reverses overtook him in rapid succession, and before the middle of 1877 he was compelled to make a settlement with his creditors which left him in poverty. The settlement made, he had but a few hundred dollars left. He now made preparations to gather to Zion, and out of his scanty funds he generously assisted a score or more members of the Canton branch to pay their fares to Utah. He arrived in Ogden August 9, 1877, and a few days later came to this city, almost without a dollar. But he and his family were happy and cheerful. He began the business of a retail coal dealer in a small way, in which he continued for some months when, early in the year 1878, he was called on a mission to the Southern States. He responded and labored in that field eleven months when he was honorably released.

He was an excellent geologist and an experienced coal mine manager, and soon after his return from his mission he became manager of the D. & R. G. coal mines, at Pleasant Valley, in October, 1880.

The mines were rapidly developed under his control and soon quite a community of miners and their families were gathered there. Many of these being Latter-day Saints, a branch of the Church was organized of which he was made president. In 1883 Pleasant Valley Ward was organized and he was ordained [a Bishop and set apart to preside over it.

He continued in this position till December, 1885, when he went on a mission to Wales. For a time he labored as a traveling Elder, but later became president of the Welsh mission, with a numerous and energetic corps of missionaries under him. During his administration that mission assumed an activity it had not known for many years. He spent his own money freely to foreward it, and labored with great zeal and energy. It was while he was president of the Welsh mission that Jarman created great excitement in that country. Repeatedly Brother Williams was surrounded by howling mobs, who thirsted for his blood; but physical fear was an emotion unknown to him, and he never shrank from either danger or duty.

He returned to Utah in November, 1888. During the three years of his mission, asthma, a disease from which he had long suffered more or less, became deep seated, and he never obtained relief from it. Notwithstanding his broken health, he could not brook inactivity, and in May of this year he opened a general mercantile business at Price, Emery County. From that time until his death he suffered terribly at frequent intervals. He passed away like a child falling to sleep.

Brother Williams was a good and a remarkable man. He was a natural leader, and gifted with rare abilities in some directions. To look into his clear, blue, earnest eyes and doubt his honesty, was impossible. He decided the most important matters instantly, and was generally guided by a correct intuition. In his business plans and enterprises it was nearly always a leading object to provide employment or aid for others, and he has planned for and helped to feed thousands. Ingratitude which is so often the reward of the philanthropic worker, never swerved him from his purpose to labor for the welfare of others. He was a father to his employes.

As a parent he was solicitous for and devotedly attached to his children; as a husband he was tender and affectionate; as a business man he was intelligent and thoroughly reliable; and as a Latter-day Saint he lived and died faithful to the obligations of the Gospel, having a firm assurance of his election to a glorious resurrection.

He leaves two wives and was the father of fourteen children, seven of whom survive him. He also had a large number of grandchildren. These, with hundreds of his countrymen living in this region, and a host of other friends and acquaintances, will cherish his memory as that of a man worthy of their esteem and affection. Peaceful be his rest.

Mill. Star, please copy.

Utah Enquirer
December 24, 1889

W. W. ROBERTS, a coal miner, at Winter Quarters, was killed a day or two ago by a premature blast.

Deseret Evening News
December 27, 1889

Encouraging Signs.

SPRING GLEN, Emery County, December 24th, 1889.—[Correspondence of the DESERET NEWS].—At the present time we feel doubly blessed here in the progress which has been made.

Our canal company was incorporated three years ago. We have a 300 foot tunnel on our ditch; our main efforts have been centered upon it, and it is nearing completion. A meeting house has been dedicated, and we are now building rapidly upon our town lots.

Spring Glen has a very cleanly location, all the recent storms having failed to render its sandy streets muddy and disagreeable. We are six miles below the celebrated Castle Gate coke works, on Price river.

At the Stake Conference on November 11th and 12th, Apostle F. M. Lyman set apart Brother Heber J. Stowell (formerly of Ogden) as our bishop. Shortly afterwards the stake presidency visited us, holding two meetings and setting apart Brother Edward Fulmer as first, and Brother A. J. Simmons as second counsellors.

The people are trying with much zeal to improve their condition, and have always been quite united in public affairs.

We are large landholders and have generally evinced a willingness to divide our holdings with our friends when they come and want to settle near us. This part of the valley possesses more than ordinary facilities in range, timber, water and water power, market for produce, and labor for the unemployed.

T. PRATT, Ward Clerk.

Utah Enquirer
December 31, 1889

Marriage Licenses.

Marriage licenses have been issued to John Wilson and Mary Maud King, of Payson; to Gabriel Ocklander and Cary Johnson, the former of Scipio, Millard county, and the latter of Santaquin, Utah county; to Thomas Dryburgh and Maggie Meldrum, of Provo; to Erastus Olsen, of Price, Emery county and Sarah M. Cox, of Spanish Fork, Utah county.

Y. M. M. I. A. Conference at Scofield.

Quite a good time was had at the Y. M. M. I. A. conference held at Scofield, December 29th. Elders G. H. Brimhall and N. L. Nelson and Sister Zina D. Lyons were present from Provo. After the usual opening excerises President J. K. Purcell gave a brief sketch of the workings and advancement of the association during the past year.

Sister Zina D. Lyons gave the young people some very good advice, and proceeded to organize a Young Ladies Association.

The ladies chose Matilda Wilcox as their President and Kate Russell and Jennet Adamson as her counselors. They were unanimously sustained.

After the choir sang, President G. H. Brimhall arose and gave some instructions regarding the order and power of the Priesthood. He branched off somewhat on mutual improvement, his remarks being interesting and instructive. He then presented the following names to be sustained as officers of the Y. M. M. I. A.: J. K. Purcell president and J.E. Ingles and Thos. Bute, counselors.

The evening session of the Y. M. M. I. A. was held, at which Professor John Nelson lectured on the principles of "Eternal Progress," which was instructive and interesting, being quite a treat for the young and the old.

Deputy Registrars.

Appointments made by the Utah Commission:

EMERY COUNTY.

Blake—J. J. Ferron.
Wellington—R. B. Thompson.
Price—A. Ballinger.
Huntington—J. F. Wakefield.
Lawrence—Elias Thomas.
Castle Dale—Carl Welberg.
Orangeville—J. H. Reid.
Molen—J. D. Kilpack.
Muddy—J. J. Lewis.
Scofield—S. J. Harkness.
Moab—Henry Crouse.
Ferrin—J. W. Williams.

DIED.

SHARP.—At Scofield, Emery county, Utah, March 3, 1890, Josephine, daughter of Joseph R. and Maude E. Sharp. Born March 1, 1890.

SCOFIELD NOTES.

An Unpleasant Day with a Pleasant Termination.

The last season has been a bad one for this town. Work has been slack in the mines, and as a consequence money is scarce. A great many persons have moved away. Up at Winter Quarters there are quite a number of houses empty. The staff of men at the R. G. mine has been reduced, and those who are left make better wages. The trouble during the last winter was on account of there being too few cars. The railroad guage had been changed to the broad, and a sufficient number of broad guage cars could not be secured.

The streams here are very high and there is still a quantity of snow higher up in the mountains, so that it is expected there will still be higher water. This great mass of snow and the backward season have interfered with the lumber business, and none of the saw mills have yet begun the season's work.

This district has been interested in the land contest excitement, which is not settled yet, and there have been some jumping of claims. How it is all going to end it is hard to tell. There is much talk and some threats of lawsuits and land office contests, which will tend to cause bad feeling and difficulty.

The season has been backward, and the weather is still cold, but the stretches of meadow across the Pleasant Valley are very pretty. Flocks of sheep are now being pastured on the grass-covered mountains in this region.

I crossed the mountains from Thistle to this place over a very rough road, fording the swollen streams, which at times were quite dangerous. I intended to pass over the mountain and down Huntington Creek to the town of Huntington, but the deep snow in the head of the canyon forced a change of plans, so I intend to cross over the mountain and down Gordon Creek to Price.

A SUBSEQUENT LETTER.

While at Scofield, Emery County, on the evening of May 21st we intimated our intention of crossing the mountain into Castle Valley.

We were, however, advised to beware of the streams and not venture to ford in swollen places. Eventually we decided upon taking a road which crosses a steep mountain at the head of Gordon Creek Canyon.

At 8 o'clock next morning we were fairly on our journey, the mountain road being so steep that the horse had some difficulty in getting along. By slow stages we continued to ascend until, looking backward, the cragged range of the Wasatch bordering the lower valleys seemed down below us. All the gorges were filled with snow, forming a bright and interesting picture, while all around us were massive snow banks.

Into one of these we suddenly plunged, and horse and buggy sank. For a time it appeared as though further progress was impossible, but undaunted, we went to work and presently lifted the vehicle to the crest of the snow, and soon horse and buggy were moving again. But when the descent of the road began we found ourselves in a greater difficulty than before. Large banks of snow met us on the steep down grade, and at times the horse plunged and the conveyance crowded until our seats were anything but safe. On we plunged—now in a snowdrift, now in mud, until the creek-bed was reached. The canyon being so narrow, the road had been made down the channel of the creek, and the rapidly melting snow had gorged the latter, cutting out the road, so that at times the horse stumbled into great holes and the buggy seemed at times to stand on end. For long distances we traveled on the crest of the snow and the creek roared under us, while to the left of the mountain sides bloomed wild flowers.

Hope presently grew stronger within us; but, soon afterwards, to our dismay, we were confronted by fallen trees which apparently blocked our way. Searching around we found a stick which answered as a handspike and with this the lighter trunks were turned so that we could pass.

We journeyed on till noon had passed, when we reached an old mill site; but there was no mill.

After further struggles we found a neat ranch, where the kind people provided us with refreshment and we felt that our day of trial and adventure was nearly ended.

TRAVELER.

Deseret Evening News
June 12, 1890

EMERY STAKE.

PRESIDENT—C. G. Larsen, Castle Dale.

COUNSELORS.—Orange Seeley, Castle
Dale; Wm. Howard, Huntington.

Emery County, Utah.

WARDS.	BISHOPS.
Castle Dale	Henning Olsen
Ferron	F. Olsen
Huntington	C. Pulsipher
Molen	L. S. Beach
Emery	C. Christensen
Orangeville	Jasper Robertson
Price	Geo. Frandsen
Cleveland	Samuel N. Alger, P. E.
Lawrence	Calvin W. Moore
Spring Glen	Heber J. Stowell
Castle Gate	William Lamph, P. E.
Upper Price	F. Ewell, P. E.
Wellington	Jefferson Tidwell, P. E.
Wilsonville	Sylvester Wilson, P. E.

Ogden Daily Standard
June 25, 1890

DIED.

BALLINGER—In this City, at the residence
of J. M. Atkinson, June 23d, of meningitis.
Grace, daughter of Alpha and Ella Ballinger, of Price, Emery county, Utah, aged 18
months and two days.

Deseret Evening News
August 19, 1890

Spring Glen.

From Brother J. H. Van Natta o
this place we learn that the
settlers have almost completed
the construction of a tunnel, 355
feet long, through solid rock, for a
canal. The latter will be eight
miles long, will head in Price
river, and will cover a large amount
of excellent land.

Spring Glen is situated between
Price and Castle Gate, and the
people have petitioned the county
court of Emery County to establish
a precinct there. The petition has
been referred back to have the people of Price and Spring Glen to agree
upon the dividing line of their
precincts. The new one will probably be established in September.

ELEVEN car loads of cattle passed
through Grand Junction Saturday
morning from Price, Utah, con-
signed to a firm in Omaha.

Ogden Daily Standard
August 26, 1890

Teancum Pratt, of Spring Glen, Emery county, was released from the penitentiary yesterday, having served a six months' term for unlawful cohabitation, and 30 days for the fine imposed. When Mr Pratt appeared for sentence at Provo, he was quite ill, his leg having been broken in an accident. He came into court on crutches, and up to the present he is unable to dispense with them. His health has been seriously affected by incarceration in the situation in which he has been placed.

Salt Lake Times
September 13, 1890

A Child's Sad Death.
Manti Sentinel.

At Molen, Emery county, Owen Anderson, a child about twenty months old, was drowned by falling into a hole containing about a foot of water, Sunday, Aug. 24.

Deseret Evening News
September 29, 1890

NAMES
OF
PRESIDENCY AND BISHOPS
OF THE
Organized Stakes of Zion.

P. E. means Presiding Elder.

Where a Ward has no post office of its own the nearest post office to it, and the one at which the residents obtain their mail, is given in parenthesis.

EMERY STAKE.

PRESIDENT.—C. G. Larsen, Castle Dale.

COUNSELORS.—Orange Seeley, Castle Dale; Wm. Howard, Huntington.

Emery County, Utah.

WARDS.	BISHOPS.
Castle Dale	Henning Olsen
Ferron	F. Olsen
Huntington	C. Pulsipher
Molen	L. S. Beach
Emery	C. Christensen
Orangeville	Jasper Robertson
Price	Geo. Frandsen
Cleveland	Samuel N. Alger, P. E.
Lawrence	Calvin W. Moore
Spring Glen	Heber J. Stowell
Castle Gate	William Lamph, P. E.
Upper Price	F. Ewell, P. E.
Wellington	Jefferson Tidwell, P. E.
Wilsonville	Sylvester Wilson, P. E.

County Register
October 16, 1890

NOTICE FOR PUBLICATION.

No. 627.

Land Office at Salt Lake City, Utah, Oct. 1st, 1890.

Notice is hereby given that the following-named settler has filed notice of his intention to make final proof in support of his claim, and that said proof will be made before the County Clerk of Emery Co., Utah, at Castle Dale, Utah, on Nov. 29th, 1890, viz:

Hiram A. Southworth, D S No 10876 for the N ½ N E ¼ Sec 7 Tp 14 S R 10 E.

He names the following witnesses to prove his continuous residence upon, and cultivation of, said land, viz:

Heber J. Stowell, Frank M. Ewell, Harry Thompson, Walter Grimes, all of Spring Glen, Emery Co., Utah.

FRANK D. HOBBS, Register.

BOOTH, WILSON & WILSON, Att'y's.

IN CASTLE VALLEY.

Description of the Various Wards of the Emery Stake of Zion.

[Correspondence of the DESERET NEWS.]

For the purpose of making a tour through the Emery Stake of Zion in the interest of Church history, I left Salt Lake City on the 5th inst. and arrived at Price station (125 miles from the city) in the evening. Next morning in company with Prest. Geo. Q. Cannon and Elder John Morgan, who had arrived during the night, I continued the journey by team (Bishop Geo. Frandsen, of Price taking us in his carriage) to Orangeville, a distance of 32 miles, where we attended the Stake quarterly conference on that and the following day. After the conference Prest. Cannon and Elder Morgan returned home and I proceeded to gather historical information concerning the Emery Stake of Zion. In visiting the various wards and settlements for that purpose I have held meetings with the Saints in nearly every place and have had a good time generally. Last Sunday evening I also spoke to a respectable congregation of Saints and strangers in Castle Gate, a mining town in Price Canyon, and yesterday attended a ward conference at Spring Glen, where the Stake Presidency was in attendance, and today, in connection with that Presidency and Bishops Geo. Frandsen of Price, and H. J. Stowell of Spring Glen, I attended the ward conference at Wellington on which occasion the Bishopric of that new ward was made complete by the setting apart of Geo. W. Eldredge to act as first and Robert

A. Snyder as second counselor to Bishop A. C. McMullen. In these ward conferences much good and practical instruction was given suitable for the circumstances surrounding the Saints in this new country, and the Spirit of God was poured out in a great measure upon all present causing the hearts of the Saints to rejoice exceedingly. After the afternoon meeting today Prest. C. G. Larsen and his counselors (Orange Seely and William Howard) returned to their homes in Castle Dale and Huntington, and I returned to Price, where, in the hospitable home of Bishop Geo. Fraubsen, I am finishing my historical gleanings as regards the Emery Stake, preparatory to leaving for other parts of the country.

The Emery Stake of Zion embraces nearly all of Emery County, Utah, and consists of eleven organized wards, which, named in geographical order, commencing from the north, range as follows: Spring Glen, Price, Wellington, Cleveland, Huntington, Lawrence, Castle Dale, Orangeville, Ferron, Molen and Mudday. Three of these settlements are situated on Price River, three on or near Huntington Creek, two on Cottonwood Creek, two on Ferron Creek and one on Muddy Creek, all in what is generally known as Castle Valley. This valley has well defined boundaries on the west and north where lofty mountains separate it from other valleys and tracts of country, but on the east and south it extends into an almost unexplored region so far that even the earliest settlers here are unable to define its boundaries. It is, in fact, an open country, traversed by low mountain ranges, barren hills, deep gulches and washes, etc., and in many places it is absolutely impassable for teams. Even men on horseback often encounter great difficulties in getting through, and in some instances are compelled to travel a distance of twenty-five miles or more in order to advance five miles in a straight line. But in the western part of the

valley, near the eastern base of the Wasatch mountains, where all the settlements are located, there are comparatively fine tracts of country, which after being brought under cultivation, can most properly be termed an oasis in the desert. Generally speaking, Castle Valley is more suited for pastural than agricultural pursuits. Still the people have made, and are now making, farming a decided success, as in many instances the amount of grain raised per acre compares very favorably with that produced in the most fertile parts of our Territory. The culture of bees has, of late years, been proven to be a very successful industry and it is now generally acknowledged that Castle Valley produces the best honey in Utah, and perhaps the best in the United States. As an example of what can be done as regards quantity I may state that during the past summer Brother Caleb B. Rhoades of Price, produced 5,500 pounds of honey from 22 stands of bees. Noah T. Guyman of Orangeville, and John Zwahlen of Ferron, have been nearly equally successful in their bee culture the present season. The great natural wealth of Castle Valley, however, seems to be its immense coal fields. The coal is found in inexhaustable quantities in the several canyons in the mountains west. The veins, so far discovered, ranges from six to eleven feet in thickness and the coal is of the most excellent quality. But until railways shall have been built to the different places where these immense coal deposits have been discovered they are of course comparatively valueless, except for local consumption.

The Saints in Castle Valley have made great progress during the last few years, and their towns and villages begin to assume the appearance of comfort and prosperity. More settlers, however, are needed and anyone in need of a home who is not afraid to face the hardships and dangers of a new country, will be made heartily welcome by the

people of this valley.

Castle Dale, pleasantly situated on the north bank of the Cottonwood Creek, 32 miles southwest of Price, the nearest railway station, is the headquarters of the Emery Stake and the county seat of Emery County. It contains the best flouring mill in the county, and the only one, except the little Pioneer mill at Orangeville on the same creek (Cottonwood). Castle Dale has 58 families belonging to the Church and a few non-members. Henning Olsen is Bishop. A new meeting house, which, when completed, will be the most commodious public building in the county, is in course of erection, and will probably be completed next spring. Two of the Stake Presidency (President C. G. Larsen and his first counselor, Orange Seeley) reside in this place.

Orangeville is the other town on Cottonwood Creek. It is situated about three miles west of Castle Dale, not far from the mouth of Cottonwood Canyon, in which very extensive coal-fields have been discovered. There is considerable talk just now about constructing a railway from a point on Price River to these mines. Orangeville can boast of having produced more fruit, so far, than any other settlement in Emery County, and is also surrounded by some choice farming lands. This town has 60 families belonging to the Church, over whom Jasper Robertson presides as Bishop. He is also probate judge of the county.

Ferron, a fine little town on Ferron Creek, is reached by traveling 11½ miles in a southwesterly direction from Castle Dale. The town is situated on the north bank of the creek on a hill side sloping gently to the south. Across the creek, south of the townsite, is a compact body of good farming land. Ferron has the finest and most commodious meeting-house (known as the Social Hall) in the Emery Stake, and a number of comfortable private residences. The strength of the Saints here is 63 families, and Frederick Olsen, a man of sterling qualities, is the Bishop.

Three miles east of Ferron is Molen, an outgrowth of Ferron. It is a pleasant little neighborhood, and the townsite is situated on the north side of Ferron Creek, near where the old Gunnison trail crosses that stream. There is some of the best farming land in the county, but as the quantity is very limited as also water wherewith to irrigate it, Molen will perhaps never become a very large place. Lyman S. Beach, with H. P. Rasmussen and Hans C. Hansen, presides as Bishop over the 23 families of Saints who reside here.

After traveling 16 miles through a genuine desert country—broken and desolate—in a southwesterly direction, the townsite of Emery (formerly called Muddy) is reached. It is situated in the north end of a large valley extending toward the Fish Lake Mountains on the south. From here the lofty peaks of the Henry Mountains are also seen toward the southeast. To convey the water of Muddy Creek onto the lands where Emery is situated a long and expensive canal had to be constructed, which for a distance of 1230 feet is tunnelled through a mountain-ridge. This was done at an expense of nearly $50,000. And as the community which had to do this immense labor was poor, it has indeed been a heavy task. But it has been accomplished, and the prospects before the enterprising people of Emery are now very bright compared to what they were a few years ago. The Emery Ward numbers 46 families of Saints, and Wm. G. Petty, one of the founders of Pettyville, Sanpete County, presides here as Bishop.

Lawrence, named in honor of C. G. Larsen, President of the Emery Stake, is a village and farming district situated on Huntington Creek, eight and one-half miles northeast of Castle Dale. To it has the reputation of being the best grain producing district in the county. In 1888 13,000 bushels of small grain was raised in this little settlement, which numbers only twenty-four families. No other settlement in the Stake, even those much larger, produced an amount equal to that. Calvin W. Moore, formerly a member of the "Mormon" Battalion, is the Bishop of Lawrence Ward.

Huntington, the metropolis of Emery County, is pleasantly situated on the north bank of Huntington Creek, nine and one half miles northeast of Castle Dale, surrounded by good farming land. This growing town is the home of 153 families of Latter-day Saints, presided over by Bishop Charles Pulsipher, a son of the late President Zelah Pulsipher. Here also reside Henry Harriman, one of the first seven Presidents of the Seventies, now over eighty-six years of age, Geo. W. Johnson, another Church veteran, Wm. Howard, second Counselor in the Stake Presidency, and others of prominence and note. A fine meeting house is here also in course of erection, and the town is fast assuming the appearance of comfort and wealth.

Northeast of Huntington is a fine open tract of country, said to be the finest in the county, in the midst of which the settlement known as Cleveland is pleasantly situated. The recently surveyed townsite on which the people are now preparing to build, is seven miles northeast of Huntington, but as yet the settlers live in a very scattered condition on their respective quarter sections. They number thirty families of Saints and have recently been organized into a ward, with Lars P. Oveson, a man of enterprise and ability, as Bishop. To convey the water of Huntington Creek onto the farming lands of Cleveland, a canal, fifteen miles long, had to be constructed, at a cost of $35,000.

Price, on the Rio Grande Western Railway, is favorably situated on the north bank of Price River, 125 miles from Salt Lake City and twenty-two miles northeast of Huntington. The "Mormon" population of Price Ward, consisting of forty-five families, reside mostly on the townsite near the railway station, and are commencing to feel more comfortable and satisfied than formerly. It has required considerable hardship and energy to redeem this part of the county from its desert sterility, but through perseverance and patience the object has been accomplished, and Price now has the appearance of comfort and enterprise. This is the shipping point for the whole country lying southward, and also to the government post situated ninety miles to the northeast. George Frandsen, late of Mount Pleasant, Sanpete County, presides as Bishop over the Price Ward.

Wellington, named for Justus Wellington Seeley, Jr., one of the early settlers and leading men of Emery County, is a scattered settlement lying on both sides of Price River below Price Station. The townsite, which was partly surveyed yesterday, is on the north side of the river, about six miles southeast of Price. The people intend to build on it at once, and move together as fast as possible. Jefferson Tidwell is the pioneer settler of this part of the country, which now has thirty-three families of Saints, presided over by Bishop Albert E. McMullin. This ward is an outgrowth of the Price Ward.

Spring Glen is another outgrowth of the Price Ward. It contains all the Saints (23 families) residing in and below Price Canyon. The recently surveyed townsite is situated in a fine cove on the east side of the river, six miles northwest of Price Station, and a number of the settlers have already built on it, although the canal which is to convey the water of Price River on to the site and surrounding farming lands, is not yet completed. The cost of constructing said canal will perhaps amount to $15,000 or more, as it must be tunneled part of the way through a rocky ridge. But as this tunnel which is 340 feet long, is nearly completed, the water will perhaps be brought on to the lands for which it is intended next spring. About six miles above Spring Glen townsite is the mining town of Castle Gate, which has sprung into existence during the last two years. Here coal mining and coke burning is carried on already on a large scale, and about five hundred men are employed. The rocks and mines belong to the Pleasant Valley Mining Company and is superintended by Mr. Sharp, son of Bishop John Sharp, of Salt Lake City. Among the men employed by the company are quite a number of brethren who have recently been organized into a branch of the Church under the Presidency of Wm. T. Lamph, as a part of the Spring Glen Ward. Regular meetings and Sunday schools, which are often visited by strangers employed at the mines, are held every Sabbath, and everything points in the direction of a Ward being organized here in the near future.

ANDREW JENSON.
PRICE, Emery County, N. S.,
    November 25, 1890.

IN GRASS VALLEY.

For the purpose of making a tour through the Emery Stake of Zion in the interest of Church history, I left Salt Lake City on the 8th inst. and arrived at Price station (125 miles from the city) in the evening. Next morning in company with Prest. Geo. Q. Cannon and Elder John Morgan, who had arrived during the night, I continued the journey by team (Bishop Geo. Frandsen, of Price taking us in his carriage) to Orangeville, a distance of 32 miles, where we attended the Stake quarterly conference on that and the following day. After the conference Prest. Cannon and Elder Morgan returned home and I proceeded to gather historical information concerning the Emery Stake of Zion. In visiting the various wards and settlements for that purpose I have held meetings with the Saints in nearly every place and have had a good time generally. Last Sunday evening I also spoke to a respectable congregation of Saints and strangers in Castle Gate, a mining town in Price Canyon, and yesterday attended a ward conference at Spring Glen, where the Stake Presidency was in attendance, and today, in connection with that Presidency and Bishops Geo. Frandsen of Price, and H. J. Stowell of Spring Glen, I attended the ward conference at Wellington, on which occasion the Bishopric of that new ward was made complete by the setting apart of Geo. W. Eldredge to act as first and Robert A. Snyder as second counselor to Bishop A. E. McMullen. In these ward conferences much good and practical instruction was given suitable for the circumstances surrounding the Saints in this new country, and the Spirit of God was poured out in a great measure upon all present causing the hearts of the Saints to rejoice exceedingly. After the afternoon meeting today Prest. C. G. Larsen and his counselors (Orange Seely and William Howard) returned to their homes in Castle Dale and Huntington, and I returned to Price, where, in the hospitable home of Bishop Geo. Frandsen, I am finishing my historical gleanings as regards the Emery Stake, preparatory to leaving for other parts of the country.

The Emery Stake of Zion embraces nearly all of Emery County, Utah, and consists of eleven organized wards, which, named in geographical order, commencing from the north, range as follows: Spring Glen, Price, Wellington, Cleveland, Huntington, Lawrence, Castle Dale, Orangeville, Ferron, Molen and Muddy. Three of these settlements are situated on Price River, three on or near Huntington Creek, two on Cottonwood Creek, two on Ferron Creek and one on Muddy Creek, all in what is generally known as Castle Valley. This valley has well defined boundaries on the west and north where lofty mountains separate it from other valleys and tracts of country, but on the east and south it extends into an almost unexplored region so far that even the earliest settlers here are unable to define its boundaries. It is, in fact, an open country, traversed by low mountain ranges, barren hills, deep gulches and washes, etc., and in many places it is absolutely impassable for teams. Even men on horseback often encounter great difficulties in getting through, and in some instances are compelled to travel a distance of twenty-five miles or more in order to advance five miles in a straight line. But in the western part of the valley, near the eastern base of the Wasatch mountains, where all the settlements are located, there are comparatively fine tracts of country, which after being brought under cultivation, can most properly be termed an oasis in the desert. Generally speaking, Castle Valley is more suited for pastural than agricultural pursuits. Still the people have made, and are now making, farming a decided success, as in many instances the amount of grain raised per acre compares very favorably with that produced in the most fertile parts of our Territory. The culture of bees has, of late years, been proven to be a very successful industry and it is now generally acknowledged that Castle Valley produces the best honey in Utah, and perhaps the best in the United States. As an example of what can be done as regards quantity I may state that during the past summer Brother Caleb B. Rhoades of Price, produced 5,300 pounds of honey from 22 stands of bees. Noah T. Guyman of Orangeville, and John Zwahlen of Ferron, have been nearly equally successful in their bee culture the present season. The great natural wealth of Castle Valley, however, seems to be its immense coal fields. The coal is found in inexhaustable quantities in the several canyons in the mountains west. The veins, so far discovered, ranges from six to eleven feet in thickness and the coal is of the most excellent quality. But until railways shall have been built to the different places where these immense coal deposits have been discovered they are of course comparatively valueless, except for local consumption.

The Saints in Castle Valley have made great progress during the last few years, and their towns and villages begin to assume the appearance of comfort and prosperity. More settlers, however, are needed and anyone in need of a home who is not afraid to face the hardships and dangers of a new country, will be made heartily welcome by the people of this valley.

Castle Dale, pleasantly situated on the north bank of the Cottonwood Creek, 32 miles southwest of Price, the nearest railway station, is the headquarters of the Emery Stake and the county seat of Emery County. It contains the best flouring mill in the county, and the only one, except the little Pioneer mill at Orangeville on the same creek (Cottonwood). Castle Dale has 58 families belonging to the Church and a few non-members. Henning Olsen is Bishop. A new meeting house, which, when completed, will be the most commodious public building in the county, is in course of erection, and will probably be completed next spring. Two of the Stake Presidency (President C. G. Larsen and his first counselor, Orange Seeley) reside in this place.

Orangeville is the other town on Cottonwood Creek. It is situated about three miles west of Castle Dale, not far from the mouth of Cottonwood Canyon, in which very extensive coal-fields have been discovered. There is considerable talk just now about constructing a railway from a point on Price River to these mines. Orangeville can boast of having produced more fruit, so far, than any other settlement in Emery County, and is also surrounded by some choice farming lands. This town has 66 families belonging to the Church, over whom Jasper Robertson presides as Bishop. He is also probate judge of the county.

Ferron, a fine little town on Ferron Creek, is reached by traveling 11½ miles in a southwesterly direction from Castle Dale. The town is situated on the north bank of the creek on a hill side sloping gently to the south. Across the creek, south of the townsite, is a compact body of good farming land. Ferron has the finest and most commodious meeting-house (known as the Social Hall) in the Emery Stake, and a number of comfortable private residences. The strength of the Saints here is 63 families, and Frederick Olsen, a man of sterling qualities, is the Bishop.

Three miles east of Ferron is Molen, an outgrowth of Ferron. It is a pleasant little neighborhood, and the townsite is situated on the north side of Ferron Creek, near where the old Gunnison trail crosses that stream. There is some of the best farming land in the county, but as the quantity is very limited as also water wherewith to irrigate it, Molen will perhaps never become a very large place. Lyman S. Beach, with H. P. Rasmussen and Hans C. Hansen as Counselors, presides as Bishop over the 26 families of Saints who reside here.

After traveling 18 miles through a genuine desert country—broken and desolate—in a southwesterly direction, the townsite of Emery (formerly called Muddy) is reached. It is situated in the north end of a large valley extending toward the Fish Lake Mountains on the south. From here the lofty peaks of the Henry Mountains are also seen toward the southeast. To convey the water of Muddy Creek onto the lands where Emery is situated a long and expensive canal had to be constructed, which for a distance of 1240 feet is tunnelled through a mountain-ridge. This was done at an expence of nearly $50,000. And as the community which had to do this immense labor was poor, it has indeed been a heavy task. But it has been accomplished, and the prospects before the enterprising people of Emery are now very bright compared to what they were a few years ago. The Emery Ward numbers 46 families of Saints, and Wm. G. Petty, one of the founders of Pettyville, Sanpete County, presides here as Bishop.

Lawrence, named in honor of C. G. Larsen, President of the Emery Stake, is a village and farming district situated on Huntington Creek, eight and one-half miles northeast of Castle Dale. It has the reputation of being the best grain producing district in the county. In 1888 13,000 bushels of small grain was raised in this little settlement, which numbers only twenty-four families. No other settlement in the Stake, even those much larger, produced an amount equal to that. Calvin W. Moore, formerly a member of the "Mormon" Battalion, is the Bishop of Lawrence Ward.

Huntington, the metropolis of Emery County, is pleasantly situated on the north bank of Huntington Creek, nine and one-half miles northeast of Castle Dale, surrounded by good farming land. This growing town is the home of 133 families of Latter-day Saints, presided over by Bishop Charles Pulsipher, a son of the late President Zerah Pulsipher. Here also reside Henry Harriman, one of the first seven Presidents of the Seventies, now over eighty-six years of age, Geo. W. Johnson, another Church veteran, Wm. Howard, second Counselor in the Stake Presidency, and others of prominence and note. A fine meeting house is here also in course of erection, and the town is fast assuming the appearance of comfort and wealth.

Northeast of Huntington is a fine open tract of country, said to be the finest in the county, in the midst of which the settlement known as Cleveland is pleasantly situated. The recently surveyed townsite on which the people are now preparing to build, is seven miles northeast of Huntington, but as yet the settlers live in a very scattered condition on their respective quarter sections. They number thirty families of Saints and have recently been organized into a ward, with Lars P. Oveson, a man of enterprise and ability, as Bishop. To convey the water of Huntington Creek onto the farming lands of Cleveland, a canal, fifteen miles long, had to be constructed, at a cost of $35,000.

Price, on the Rio Grande Western Railway, is favorably situated on the north bank of Price River, 125 miles from Salt Lake City and twenty-two miles northeast of Huntington. The "Mormon" population of Price Ward, consisting of forty-five families, reside mostly on the townsite near the railway station, and are commencing to feel more comfortable and satisfied than formerly. It has required considerable hardship and energy to redeem this part of the county from its desert sterility, but through perseverance and patience the object has been accomplished, and Price now has the appearance of comfort and enterprise. This is the shipping point for the whole country lying southward, and also to the government post situated ninety miles to the northeast. George Frandzen, late of Mount Pleasant, Sanpete County, presides as Bishop over the Price Ward.

Wellington, named for Justus Wellington Seeley, Jr., one of the early settlers and leading men of Emery County, is a scattered settlement lying on both sides of Price River below Price Station. The townsite, which was partly surveyed yesterday, is on the north side of the river, about six miles southeast of Price. The people intend to build on it at once, and move together as fast as possible. Jefferson Tidwell is the pioneer settler of this part of the country, which now has thirty-three families of Saints, presided over by Bishop Albert E. Mc-Mullin. This ward is an outgrowth of the Price Ward.

Spring Glen is another outgrowth of the Price Ward. It contains all the Saints (23 families) residing in and below Price Canyon. The recently surveyed townsite is situated in a fine cove on the east side of the river, six miles northwest of Price Station, and a number of the settlers have already built on it, although the canal which is to convey the water of Price River on to the site and surrounding farming lands, is not yet completed. The cost of constructing said canal will perhaps amount to $15,000 or more, as it must be tunneled part of the way through a rocky ridge. But as this tunnel which is 840 feet long, is nearly completed, the water will perhaps be brought on to the lands for which it is intended next spring. About six miles above Spring Glen townsite is the mining town of Castle Gate, which has sprung into existence during the last two years. Here coal mining and coke burning is carried on already on a large scale, and about five hundred men are employed. The rocks and mines belong to the Pleasant Valley Mining Company and is superintended by Mr. Sharp, son of Bishop John Sharp, of Salt Lake City. Among the men employed by the company are quite a number of brethren who have recently been organized into a branch of the Church under the Presidency of Wm. T. Lamph, as a part of the Spring Glen Ward. Regular meetings and Sunday schools, which are often visited by strangers employed at the mines, are held every Sabbath, and everything points in the direction of a Ward being organized here in the near future.

ANDREW JENSON.
PRICE, Emery County, U. T.,
November 25, 1890.

THE JURY LIST.

68	H. N Fugate	Ferron	Emery
69	A Peterson	Richfield	Sevier
70	Frank Carro'l	Orangeville	Emery
71	Joseph J Jensen	Richfield	Sevier
72	Samuel P Snow	Orangeville	Emery
73	B Middlemass	Richfield	Sevier
74	John H Scott	Huntington	Emery
75	Peter Erickson	Richfield	Sevier
76	Frank P Long	Price	Emery

Eastern Utah Telegraph
January 16, 1891

—Our estimable hostess, Mrs. E. Mathis, of the Mathis House, has just returned from Salt Lake, with a fine assortment of carpets, curtains and fixtures for the new hotel.

—The town of Castle Gate, but little more than a year old, is a veritable little city with it's electric lights, coke ovens, and the extensive coal works of the P. V. Coal Co.

—Mrs. Curly, wife of H. H. Curly, born at Vineyard Haven, Mass. died at Ft. Du Chesne Jan. 6th 1891. Deceased was 29 years old highly accomplished and beloved by all who were favored with her aquaintance. Mr. Curley Passed through Price yesterday on his way to Vineyard Haven with the remains where they will be interred.

Valentine–Petersen.

On Sunday evening, Jan. 11th, 1891, at the residence of C. H. Valentine, in Price, Utah, Mr. C. C. Valentine and Miss Lovina Petersen were united in the holy bonds of matrimony, Esq. Valentine, officiating.

Mr. Valentine is one of the live young business men of Price, possessing the confidence of the people of Emery county where he is well acquainted, and is at present in the employ of the Gilson Asphaltum Co's. store in Price. The bride for sometime has been a resident of Brigham City, Utah, is an accomplished lady, and will be a valuable acquisition to the society of Price. The TELEGRAPH congratulates.

Salt Lake Herald
January 20, 1891

THE INITIAL number of the *Eastern Utah Telegraph*, published at Price, Emery county, Utah, has made its appearance. It is a six column eight-page paper, and gives evidence of becoming a credit to the town in which it is published.

—Hiram Thayne, son of Esq. J J. Thayne, of Wellington, died yesterday.

—W. I. Williams, operator at Helper, made us a call yesterday and subscribed for the TELEGRAPH.

—Mr. David Williams' children have been quite sick for the last week, but are improving now.

—The County Superintendent of this county has made the following disposition of federal school funds in this county:

Wellington	$305 67
Price	722 09
Scofield	930 3o
Huntington	1355 58
Cleveland	3o5 67
Lawrence	323 o9
Castle Dale	877.79
Orangeville	7o8 8o
Ferron	478 11
Molen	221.50
Emery	385.41
Green River	
Castle Gate	429.71
Total	$6844 35

—County Court met on the 15th inst. and adjourned the 17th to meet again March 2nd. A large amount of County business was transacted. The old jail, with lot, at Price, was ordered sold and notice issued that sale would take place at March term of court, an excellent move on the part of the court as this property is of no value to the county and is valuable to Price as it gives more attainable business property and thereby assists in the growth of our city. A jail has no business in the center of the city, as our Provo neighbor can testify.

C. H. Cook was appointed Justice of the Peace of the new precinct of Spring Glen. G. N. Perkins was appointed constable.

On Monday evening, Jan 26th a social was given at the residence of John D Llewellyn Esq, in Castle Gate in honor of the birth day of Capt. John L. Smith About 9 o'clock P. M , a great many guests assembled and dancing was engaged in until a late hour, a most enjoyable time being had All the available room was occupied and hardly another person could have gained admittance so great a number of the citizens having to express their friendship for Captain Smith. During the evening the dancing was interspersed with toasts and the singing of solos which were very appropriate and interesting and which assisted in making the evening pass away very pleasantly.

Capt. Smith has many friends because of his kind and gentlemanly demeanor, all of whom united in wishing him prosperity and happiness and many returns of his "thirty eighth birthday".

The stockholders of the Spring Glen Canal Co having completed the tunnel in their ditch of 368 feet wish to celebrate the event Friday afternoon and night, Jan 30th, at Spring Glen, and cordially invite all of their friends to be present. The Programe is as follows:

During the afternoon the school children and all others desiring, will visit the tunnel.

The gathering for a Picni: Supper at 6 o'clock and supper at 7. During which time, instrumental music and other amusements will be furnished. After which will be a short literary pro:; : : as follows.

First, Music.

Second, Speech by Orator of the day.

Third, Vocal Music.

Fourth, Speech.

Fifth, Music—Instrumental.

Sixth, Stump Speech

Seventh, Music—Song by Miss Laura Thompson,

Eighth, Speech.

Ninth, Music—by the Band,

Other exercises may be given if time will permit.

After literary exercises a social dance will be given—dancing until 12 o'clock, free to all.

By Order of Board of Directors

H J STOWELL, Pres
J. H VANNATTA, V. P.
H. A. SOUTHWORTH, Sec'y.
T. H JONES, Treas.
F. M. EWELL Director.

Eastern Utah Telegraph
February 5, 1891

NOTICE.

Notice is hereby given that there will be a meeting of the shareholders in Price Water Company at the School House in Price, Emery County Utah, on the 14th day of Feb. 1891 at 7.30 o'clock p. m. for the purpose of electing officers for the ensuing year and for the transaction of such other business as may properly come before the meeting.

Dated Price Emery county Utah, Feb. 2nd 1891.

C. H. VALENTINE,
Sec'y.

MARSING—We regret to chronicle the sad occurrence of the deaths of Chester A. Marsing, born June, 2nd, 1890, who died January 30th 1891, of Scarlatina, and John Henry Marsing, born May 21th 1880, who died February 2nd, 1891, of diphtheria, both the sons of N. L. Marsing, of Price. The bereaved family have the sympathy of the entire community in their affliction

—On account of too much work we were delayed one day in going to press and if our readers will pardon us this time we will try and do better.

Castle Gate School Report.

We have 65 mames on roll with a daily average attenlance of 14.

For the week ending Feb. 13 Miss. Mary Coombs and Jennie Touner are are reported for good deportment.

Lilla Sanchit, Jean Sanchit, Joe Coclit, Sam Coombs and Lewls Coombs were neither absent nor tardy.

IDA H. BALDWIN, Teacher.

—W. E Cowley, of Cleveland, was visiting his daughter, Mis Arthur Gibson, last week and called at our office He is as well posted on Utah's early history as any one we have yet run across and is impressed with the belief that both gold and silver ore abound in paying quantities in the San Rafael range in Emery county He will read the TELEGRAPH in the future

—The dam for the new reservoir will be 350 feet long, 80 feet wide at the bottom and 15 feet wide at the top, the reservoir costing between $1,500 and $2,000. On the upper side there will be two layers of stone to strengthen the dam and prevent washing Several men and teams are at work and will soon have the reservoir completed H. E. Atkeson is superintending the construction of the reservoir and will push it to completion as rapidly as possible.

—Polly P. Warren shot and killed a mountain lion on Meadow Creek yesterday morning. Mr. Warren had wounded the lion and it was making for him when he shot it the second time and killed it. It measured eight feet

—The annual meeting of the Price Water Co was held at the school house Saturday, 14th, inst. The yearly report showed a very satisfactory state of affairs The following officers were elected for the ensuing year Pres, L M. Olson; Vice Pres, C. H. Taylor, Treasurer, C. H. Valentine, Directors, A. Ballinger, Henry Mathis, A. A. Mulholland and C. H. Empey.

—The telegraph line to Ft. Du Chesne has been repaired and is again in working order. The trouble was caused by one of the wires becoming loose and being pressed against the pole at times by the wind prevented the current from passing Messrs Kelliher and Gibson deserve credit for their promptness in hunting up th difficulty.

County Register
February 21, 1891

A Manti Correspondant under date of 13, writes: The following weddings took place this week: David Zabriskie, of Price, Emery Co., and Mary Ellen Sorenson, of Spring City.

Eastern Utah Telegraph
March 5, 1891

Wellington Notes.

Yesterday was the last day of our District School It was spent in recitations, Songs and Dialogues by the pupils until 12 o'clock when there was a recess of one hour, after which the children assembled at the new meeting house and enjoyed themselves in a dance. There was a dance in the evening for the adults All passed off quietly and all seemed to enjoy themselves.

Our new meeting house is now ready for meetings and amusements

The health of the people here is good with the exception of some bad colds, owing to the sudden changes of the weather.

B E. E.

—We Are informed that Frank Nickerson's family have the diphtheria.

—Mr. Barlow's little boy has been quite sick for the past week, but is now improving.

—Frank Hallem has been very sick with pneumonia, both lungs, but is convalescent now

—We are under many obligations to Dr. Hoyt for assistance rendered during the past two weeks.

—Mr. and Mrs. Robt. Fuller, of Green River, came up on No. 3 last evening and will spend a few days in Price They are stopping at the Mathis House.

PRICE.

SOMETHING ABOUT THE TOWN OF PRICE AND ITS PROSPECTS WITH MORE NEXT WEEK.

The town of Price is situated about midway between Ogden, Utah, and Grand Junction, Colo, at an elevation of about 4000 feet above sea level. The location is upon a beautiful plateau sloping very gently to the south until it reaches the Price river, a stream of clear water supplied with gushing, sparkling fluid from mountain springs in the Wasatch Range. The river furnishes an abundance of water to irrigate a large extent of country now laying vacant within a few miles of town.

In making the above statement regarding the amount of water flowing in Price river it is to be understood that the water will have to be stored up in reservoirs and saved during the season when not wanted for watering crops. At this time, for instance, there has been no land watered from ditches since last August and during the time from August until this writing there has been water enough wasted if it had been stored up for future use, allowing for the amount that would have evaporated, to watered at least five times as much land as is now under cultivation, and this amount of good government land lying within a short distance from this place holding out an inviting hand to the home seeker

By reason of the sheltering of the Wasatch, Book and Cedar mountains the climate is mild and beautiful, the summers are warm but the evenings are always cool, spring and fall genial and kindly, and the winters are so open that horses, cattle and sheep thrive with out shelter on the hills and valleys in every direction from town.

Price is the largest shipping and receiving point between Ogden and Grand Junction with but two exceptions Salt Lake and Provo During the month of December of last year there was recieved at this point 1,618,-197 pounds of freight, and there was forwarded from here, during the month, 673,585 pounds In Emery county and tributary to Price there are already over 65,000 acres of land now cultivated in hay, grain and fruits Besides the products of the soil, there are large numbers of cattle, horses and sheep. which add no small amount to the wealth and prosperity of this community. To the West, North and South there are millions of tons of coaking coal, while to the East, North east and South east there is an inexhaustible amount of Parafine and Asphaltum. In the valleys and among the mountains near by are unmistakable signs of good gold, copper and silver mines, many of which we believe will be developed to a paying basis during the present year.

The supply of water for the people of this, our little city, will be from a beautiful reservoir, now under construction, and located about a quarter of a mile north of the business part of town, fully sixty feet above the foundation of the buildings now completed

The reservoir will be supplied from Price Water Company's canal which will afford an abundance of water power for a good Grist Mill, Electric Light plant and other small machinery. It is admitted by every thinking intelligent man that there will be between Grand Junction and Provo a city of no small magnitude and we believe that Price will be that point. We are willing to admit, however, that in the near future Cisco, Thompson Springs, Green River and Castle Gate have the natural advantages to make good and lively points

DAVID WILLIAMS

David Williams, Sr.—This is the next oldest house in our place, now under the management of David Williams Jr. This old firm occupy a large two story building with a basement under the entire house. While Mr Williams does a strictly ready pay business, his pleasant deportment has won for him many friends throughout this country. He carries a general supply of every thing wanted by farmers, mechanics or stockmen, and always sells at bottom prices, and his business is such that it would be called large in other towns

EMERY COUNTY MERCANTILE CO.

Of the business firms of our city we will mention, First—the Emery County Mercantile Co. of which L. M. Olson is manager, which commenced business March 30th 1887, with a small capital and uncomfortable building, they have grown and prospered until they now occupy trading rooms 46x50 feet, which are always filled to their utmost capacity with dry goods, groceries, clothing, boot, shoes, hardware, and furniture. Under these rooms there is a very large cellar used as a store away for unbroken packages. Besides this the company have a large ware house where one can always see tons of flour, feed, grain & etc., to this is added a large inclosure containing at least 15,000 square feet which is well filled with iron, wagons, lumber and agriculturial implements. This company by their fair and honorable business way have built up a trade that amounts to very nearly $100 000 annually.

GILSON ASPHALTUM COMPANY.

Next in order is the Gilson Asphaltum Co This company is the Successor of S S. Jones, now of Provo, having bought out Mr Jones July 5th, last year, and they are the owners of the only developed Gilsonite Mines in the world. They have the government contract for freight to DuChesne, loading here with supplies for the Fort and Agency their teams return loaded with Asphaltum which is loaded on the cars here and shipped east by almost every regular freight train that passes the Station. Some days several cars go at a time. It is needless to say that this company is doing a very extensive business and it is whispered that their business will be more than doubled before mid summer. They carry every thing wanted by the people, from a needle to a wagon.

PRICE TRADING COMPANY.

This company have just fairly opened up in business with a fine new large store building, good ware house and a large cellar all of which are filled with bright, clean, new goods. The company is composed of four of our best leading citizens. They cannot help doing what is already apparent, namely a first-class business. They also carry every article wanted by a western family.

THE OASIS SALOON.

Is kept by J. B. Milburn. Mr Milburn has been in business as long as any man in our town, and the "Oasis" has always been conducted in a careful manner. Outside of his business Mr. M. is always ready to lend a helping hand to every enterprise, either in the town or the country.

THE MAGNET

Is kept by F. B. Lang. As with the "Oasis," so with the "Magnet," but few men have made more friends than F. B. Lang. We know that many people are prejudiced against the liquor trade but we doubt if any town in Utah can furnish better and more popular men than the proprietors of the "Oasis" and "Magnet."

MATHIS HOUSE.

This new and well furnished house is kept by Mrs. Emma Mathis, who is experienced in the hotel business

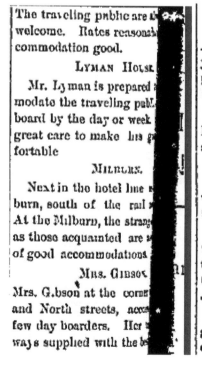

The traveling public are [...] welcome. Rates reasonab[...] commodation good.

LYMAN HOUSE.

Mr. Lyman is prepared [...] modate the traveling pub[...] board by the day or week [...] great care to make his g[...] fortable

MILBURN.

Next in the hotel line [...] burn, south of the rail [...] At the Milburn, the strang[...] as those acquainted are [...] of good accommodations [...]

MRS. GIBSON

Mrs. Gibson at the corne[...] and North streets, acco[...] few day boarders. Her [...] ways supplied with the be[...]

ATTORNEYS

A. Ballinger, County [...] Attorney, for Emery cou[...] yer of good merit and [...] promptly to any busines[...] his care.

S. K. King, Atty, [...] Burlington, Colo, where [...] a very large practice is h[...]

KING & HO[...]

Real Estate and [...] will sell Farms, Town L[...] Claims, & etc.

We have given above [...] tial list of the business [...] town. We have beside[...] Carpenters, Blacksmith[...] & etc.

What we want next [...] gon maker. A Tin[...] do well.

But, above all of … more and better scho… no better place in the … first-class College or … Price, as this is the pri… point for a territory … miles in width by one … fifty in length, much … susceptible to settlem… vation.

To The Scholars.

It is hoped the much dreaded "yellow flag" that has been floating so much in our community for the last six weeks, has disappeared for good. Although the scare is still present, I think one week longer will give that ample time to disappear.

If all is well next Monday, we will open school at the school house.

There will be only one school, all grades being included in it. We do not desire to rush the children into school if there is any possible danger of exposing them to disease. There is no doubt but that the danger will be over by next Monday, and the children should not be deprived of their schooling any longer. The trustees will be pleased to receive suggestion on the subject.

H. G. MATHIS,
Trustee

Eastern Utah Telegraph
April 2, 1891

—W. J. Powell, of Salt Lake, was in town last week. Mr. Powell is an old settler of Castle Valley and says he has full faith in the rapid growth of this country.

—A shooting affray occurred at Scofield last Sunday. Two parties who were in a quarrel got into a scramble for the possesion of a pistol which was discharged inflicting a painful but not dangerous wound upon Albert Green.

—E. T. Wilson and J. J. Thayne were among the Wellington people who were trading in Price this week.

—J. Whitmore of Wellington, cousin of J. M Whitmore, was in town Sunday.

—The remains of Mrs. Charles Marsh were removed from near Mr. Marsh's house to the summit of the hill in the north part of Mr. Marsh's land. He and his son, Clarence, intend getting water on the hill and by planting trees around the grave beautify the spot. No better location could have been selected.

—The following Emery County people were in Salt Lake last week A. J. Jeffs, Ben Jeffs, Mrs. O. J. Anderson, John Peterson and wife and Wellington Seeley, of Castle Dale, and Jos Johnson, E Cox and J L Brasher and daughter, of Huntington, and Bishop Franclsen and daughter J. B. Milburn and wife, Seren Olson and wife and Drs Hoyt and Harvey, of Price

A Sad Accident.

On last Saturday the thirteen year old son of Charles Johnson, who lives three quarters of a mile southeast of town, was going to water his horse when Mr. Johnson was startled by the cry of his little daughter of "Oh! my brother." Jumping from the house Mr. Johnson was compelled to witness the horse running at full speed dragging the boy after him, with the halter fastened to the boys wrist. The horse ran around the corral jumping across an old potato pit then into the lane and on toward town. The horse being young and active his speed only seemed to increase until lost to view in the direction of town. When he reached town he stopped with other horses near Mr. Horsley's corral. William Peterson saw the horse running and made haste after him but only to find the boys lifeless body fastened to the rope. On examination it was found that the childs neck was broke, skull fractured and very much bruised up otherwise. Mr. and Mrs Johnson have the heart felt sympathy of the entire community

Deseret Weekly
April 18, 1891

THAT, TERRIBLE TALE ABOUT THE THOMAS FAMILY.

WE HAVE already noticed the story which has gone the rounds of the press concerning the alleged suicide of one Thomas Thomas who, with his family, had "escaped" from Utah and were on their to Wales. It was stated that "he resided at Scofield near Salt Lake City, and because he refused to join the 'Mormon' Church life was made unbearable to him and the alternative was offered to him to join the Church or be killed." He managed to escape with his family, and on his way east, imagining that the "Mormons" were pursuing him, he jumped from the train into a river and was drowned.

The widow with her children excited the deepest sympathy, and a subscription was taken up for them so that they were able to pursue their journey and sailed from New York for Wales.

We denounced the story as false on its face and expressed the hope that some of the people of Scofield, which is about a hundred miles from this city, would send us the facts in the case. We are in receipt of the following letters and signatures which we think are sufficient to stamp the story as a complete falsehood, made up in the first place, no doubt, as a newspaper sensation. The first of these letters is from a "Mormon" source:

SCOFIELD, April 3rd, 1891.

To the Editor of the Deseret News:

Your issue of March 31st contains an editorial article, "A Terrible Tale of Woe," which refers to statements circulated by eastern newspapers respecting Thomas Thomas and family, emigrants from Scofield to Wales. It is claimed the said Thomas Thomas committed suicide by jumping into the Detroit River to escape his pursuer who he said was a "Mormon." It is also stated that the "Mormons" of Scofield demanded he and family should join their Church, and on their refusing to do so, threatened to kill them and made life unbearable to them.

Now we, the undersigned "Mormon" residents of Scofield, wish to make it known to all the world, if possible, that while Thomas Thomas and family resided among us, which they did for about five years, they were never urged to join the Church, much less threatened with death should they refuse to do so.

Nothing could be farther from the truth than the statement that they were interfered with, and they were well respected by all who knew them.

(Signed) *Mormons*—John F. Andersen, Frances Nelson, John L. Nelson, John O. Nelson, Mary B. Davis, John F. Davis, Mary Lewis, Samuel Davis, Emma Boweter, Jr., Tha. Davis, Emma Boweter, Sr., David W. Lewis, Sarah Jane Reese, William E. Lewis, Alice C. Whimpy, William B. Boweter, Jr. Mary E. Whimpy, William Boweter, Sr. Martha A. Whimpy, Isaac Whimpy, Emily J. Whimpy, J. K. Parcell, Rachel Davis, Andrew Pugmire, Sarah Donaldson, Vernilo Avery, Mary Pugmire, Charles T. Greenland, Sarah R. Avery, Herbert Savage, Rachel Greenland, John Street, R. J. Savage, Edwin Street, M. A. Hartshorn, John F. Davis, S. A. Bennett, Rachel Evans, Rachel E. Evans, Rachel Evans, Glatice Davis, Mary Ann Davis, Mary Jane Davis, Evan S. Thomas, Margaret Thomas, Thos. T. Parmley, Margaret A. Thomas, David J. Thomas, Brigham M. V. Goold, Catherine Goold, Henry E. Greenland, Mary Ann Parmley, Richard T. Evans, Esther Ann Greenland, William Leyshon, Martha Evans, George W. Reese, Emmaly Leyshon, Evan Evans, Jane Reese, Joseph S. Thomas, Rachel Evans, Frederick Thomas Edwards, Ann Thomas, Sarah, Bedows, William Powell, Hannah Watson, John Potter, Mary Evans, J. L. Boulden, M. O. Boulden. William T. Evans, Mary Jones, John A. Jones, Sen.,

Sarah Jones, John A. Jones, Jun., Elizabeth Richards, David Jones, Mary Ann Evans, Thomas M. Richards, Sebelia Evans, David T. Evans, E. A. Bird, William Evans, Sarah Ann Williams, Joseph Richards, Mary Richards, Hyrum Richards, Mary C. Richards, Thomas Cox, Sen., Hannah Richards, George Cox, Jane Cox, Thomas Cox, Jun., Mary Pitman, William Cox, Mrs. A. Wallace, Andrew Wallace, Margaret H. Williams, Mrs. Gwen Street.

The accompanying letter and list are from non "Mormons" in Scofield:

SCOFIELD, Emery Co., Utah,
April 4th, 1891.

Editor Deseret News:

We the undersigned, non-Mormon residents of Scofield, Emery County, Utah, protest against statements published by Eastern and some Western papers, that Thomas Thomas and family had to flee from here or join the Mormon Church to save their lives.

Our experience with the Mormon people of Scofield is that any person can live peaceably among them and that all persons have their own free will and choice as to whether or not that they join the Mormon Church, and it is our firm belief that the said Thomas Thomas had no cause whatever to leave Scofield on any Mormon pretence, as he was well respected by all who knew him

(Signed) *Non-Mormons*—Thos. W. Snowden, Jas. Wimber, T. H. Thomas, W. H. Myers, B. B. McDonald, James Wallace, Jr., J. M. Beatie, J. W. Kissoll, Fannie Mearweather, Arena Wimber, Sarah Rosser, Della Hughes, Martha Young, Mary Ann Evans, Mary L. Jones, Mary A. Pitman, Wm. Moore, S. J. Harkness, Mattie Harkness, Wm. Edwards, A. H. Earll, A. Forrester, A. Mearweather, Henry J. Hughes, Wm. Bird, Jos. Williams, Daniel Pitman, Mesbach Pitman, William Street, John T. Williams, Wm. H. Williams, Edward Thomas, Wm. Thomas, Robert Davis, George Watson, Mary Watson, Christiana Padfield, Mrs. J. M. Beatie, Jos. Nealon, Edward Jones, James Wallace, Sen.; Jas. McNabb, David Evans, Mathias Patinson, John Haddon, David Haddon, John Pitman, Walter Donalson, Samuel Radfield, Jun.; Thomas E. Edwards, Wm Rosser, Julius Bearnson, John A. Christean, Samuel Padfield, Sen.

If the foregoing is not sufficient evidence of the untruth of the story which has been so extensively copied as proof of the intolerance of the "Mormons," we think the following will satisfy the most incredulous:

SCOFIELD, Emery Co., Utah,
April 3, 1871.

Editor Deseret News:

Dear Sir:—I wish to correct the statement published in the eastern papers of the troubles of a family by the name of Thomas, said to be from Salt Lake City. The above family lived at Winter Quarters coal mine, Scofield, Emery County, Utah, about four years and a half, where the man Thomas Thomas and his son worked in the mines, and in the early part of February he decided to return to Wales with his family. Mr. Thomas expressed himself in that way ever since the last advance in the wages of miners made in South Wales, and on the night before he left camp a Mormon gave him a present of nine shillings of the English money, for which the Mormon had no use in this country.

Mr. Thomas and family started for Wales the last Wednesday in February. The occasion was one that showed respect to the family, who shook hands with all their surrounding friends both Mormons and non-Mormons. The story that the Mormons demanded that they should join the Church, and on their refusal to do so the Mormons threatened to kill them and made life unbearable to them, is false and without foundation, and a lie. The following postal card was received last night, addressed to William E. Edwards, Scofield, Emery Co., Utah, dated March 28, 1891:

398 WEST STREET, New York.

Yours to hand this day. Thomas Thomas and wife, and four children left and gone to Wales. They sailed two weeks ago.

ENOCH EVANS.

Yours truly,   EVAN S. THOMAS.

Thus, it turns out that not only is the story about the persecution of this family untrue, but that the man did not commit suicide as related, as he with his family sailed from New York for his old home in Wales about three weeks ago.

Will some of the papers that published the falsehoods, now kindly find space for the truth? We doubt it. The practice is to publish any absurdity that reflects unfavorably on the "Mormons," and suppress any refutation of the falsehood no matter how positive and reasonable and well substantiated it may be. Most of the anti-"Mormon" tales that are told by the newspapers with such gusto, and by some sectarian preachers with so much affected honor and shocked piety, have as little foundation in fact as the terrible tale of woe made up by reporters about the Thomas family.

Eastern Utah Telegraph
April 23, 1891

—County Collector Killpack was in town this morning.

—Postmaster Ovitt, of Cleveland, was in town Tuesday.

—T. Pratt, Esq, of Holper, was on our streets Saturday.

—Sheriff Loveless is busy distributing fruit trees over the county. We are glad to see so many trees being planted and predict bountiful returns to those putting out orchards.

—Bishop McMullen, of Wellington, called last Saturday and paid us one years subscription. If the people of Emery county could only realize what a pull it is and has been for us to run a paper here they would run tio around and pay their subscriptions. It is a small—very small—matter to you but a very important one to us. In every community one or more persons should take hold and get subscribers for the TELEGRAPH. Individuals residing in a community can do a great deal to help the paper along and not miss the time, and their assistance would be greatly appreciated.

Eastern Utah Telegraph
April 30, 1891

Wellington Notes.

There will be a grand ball in the Wellington meeting house on the evening of May 1, 1891. All are invited.

Bishop McMullen's teams started for the Post with freight last Tuesday.

The prospect for getting the water on our townsite this summer is quite good.

The ball here last Monday night was a grand success

B. E.

EMERY ITEMS.

A few days since a cellar occupied as a dwelling by a family here was burned up. The lady had gone a short distance to the creek for water and when she returned had barely time to drag her two small children from the cellar in time to save them. All of their household effects and clothing were burned. The people at once furnished the destitute family assistance which was at the time greatly needed. One of the children set fire to the paper on the wall of the cellar which caused the trouble.

The farmers are busy putting in their grain and if all is well a bountiful crop may be expected as a large acreage will be put in.

Some talk has been made of a large saw mill being erected here but as yet nothing definite has been learned.

Two children have died from La Gripp this spring.

Supt. Olson, made our school a visit a few days since and in the evening delivered to our citizens a fine lecture on education and the school laws of the Territory.

Our fond hopes are that a railroad will soon be built through Emery so that we can have communication with the outside world.

Our people have fully liquidated the debt against the public organ which is now used in our church and Sunday school.

ETTA WILLIAMS.

Local News Price

BORN—To Mr. and Mrs. Robert Fuller, on Saturday, April 25th, a girl. Dr. Hoyt reports the mother and child doing well.

—Mrs Hall, and daughter, went to Castle Gate last Monday, where they have employment in the new hotel.

—Ephraim Dimick, was up from Wellington Tuesday. He says the crops are looking well in that section of the county He will read the TELEGRAPH.

—Last Tuesday, Mrs. Markey, landlady at the section house, dislocated the shoulder of her little son by lifting him too suddenly by the hand Dr Hoyt reduced it and the little one is improving very rapidly.

—Born on May 2 to Mr. and Mrs. Henry Empey, a girl, mother and child doing well Dr. Hoyt says that Utah is sure to be populated for most all of the babies are girls.

—While in Castle Gate a few days since a TELEGRAPH representative called on Manager Caffey at Magnolia Hall who spared no pains to make the time pass pleasantly. The Hall is the best conducted saloon in this country and is run about right.

—William J. Powel & Co,. are building a reservoir about four miles below Cleveland the dam of which is 550 feet long and twenty five feet high The dam will be 100 feet wide at the base and twelve feet at the top, and will make a body of water a mile long by a half a mile wide with an average depth of fifteen feet. Around the lake they intend to plant a great number of shade trees of all varieties and in a few years the people of Cleveland will have a fine summer resort while the lake will afford good skating in the winter. The company are arranging to put fish into the lake and supply it with boats by means of which pleasure parties can sail on its placid waters. About $4,000 has been expended already on the dam which will soon be pushed to completion Why are there not more of these artificial lakes made in Emery county? Along the numerous streams in the mountains and in every settlement in Castle Valley artificial lakes can be constructed and upon their banks groves of trees planted and thousands of dollars thereby added to the wealth of the county, besides making Castle Valley a pleasant place to live

—Just as we go to press we are informed that the infant son of Erastus Anderson died yesterday and was burried to-day. The parents have the heartfelt sympathy in their bereavement.

—DIED —On Sunday morning the infant daughter of Mr and Mrs A. E Gibson. The sympathy of the community is extended to the afflicted parents in their great loss.

NOTICE.

I hereby give notice that on
and after June first the "Magnet" saloon will be turned over
by me to Messrs. HUTCHINSON
& FULLER, and all parties indebted to me are hereby requested to call prior to that
time and settle.

F. B. LANG.

Eastern Utah Telegraph

Price

May 22, 1891

—J. Wilson, of Wellington called
at this office Monday and reports the
crops looking well down the river.

—Mr. and Mrs J C. Vance, of
Wellington were among the visitors
to this office this week. They will
read the TELETRAPH in the future.

Deseret Weekly

June 20, 1891

DEATHS.

WILLIAMS.—At Castle Gate, Emery county,
Utah, May 19th, 1891, Blanche Walters, the beloved wife of Watkin Williams; aged 33 years.
Deceased was born July 20, 1858, at Pengarud-
du, Glanmorganshire, Wales. She was the
mother of seven children, five of whom are
left to mourn her loss. She was a loving wife,
a kind and affectionate mother, and an estimable friend.

Millennial Star and Welsh papers, please
copy.

LORD.—May 20th, 1891, at Castle Gate, Emery
county, Utah, of convulsions, Ida May, infant
daughter of William Thomas and Charlotte J.
Lord; aged five weeks.

Eastern Utah Telegraph

July 10, 1891

Died.

Mr. Neilson, father of Joseph and
Nells Neilson, of Cleveland, died on
Monday, the funeral occurring Wednesday. Father Neilson was one of
our most respected citizens, past
eighty years of age and was respected
by all who knew him

—Esquire J. C. Vance, of Wellington, was in town Thursday and as
usual called at the TELEGRAPH sanc-
tum to discuss politics.

—Fred. Grames came in from his ranch in Nine Mile Canyon this week and will remain in Price for sometime cutting hay for R. A. Powell.

— —W. K. Crowley was up from Cleveland Wednesday. He reports fine prospects for crops and the heaviest Lucern that has been seen in years.

PRICE RIVER.

A Letter From One of the First Men of the Town.

SALT LAKE CITY, Utah, }
July 1, 1891 }

Editor Price Telegraph:

DEAR SIR—I am one of the oldest residents of Price. I located the eighty acres upon which stands the town. My home property is in the Price precinct and I therefore should be interested in the welfare of the place. It is too well understood to need comment, that the necessity of good water to make a home desirable makes it of the greatest importance to furnish healthy water if possible without regard to cost; and many towns have to convey it from twenty to thirty miles, in order to preserve the health of the people. It was well demonstrated that the plague of London was owing to lack of drainage and the "fouling" of the water. It may not be thought that most of the water we drink passes off through the pores of the skin and the unhealthy portion is left to be worked off by the kidneys and the blood, thus preparing the body to

matters any contagious disease that may be floating in the air—such as diptheria, typhoid fever and all other such diseases, and, when the water we drink is unhealthy, they often become malignant and defy the judgment of the best of doctors. Without delineating any further, let us look at the water of Price River. It being taken out above Helper

The Spring Glen people who use the ditch to be used for farm and city purposes and all the waste water, after passing over their farms, city lots and manured land, will go into the river, to be taken out again at Powell's ditch and the Price City ditch, and after being used over their lands, brought through corrals, pig pens and chicken coops, will go into the river, to be used and taken out again into the Grames ditch and used upon farms as before, the waste water going into the river to again be ... ditch and ... used by the ... farm and

...frequently been so low that parties below the Town ditch could not get water to drink only from pools in the bed of the river, that horses and cattle would pass through and refuse to drink. Then, there is no wonder at diptheria becoming so malignant as to make almost every case fatal. Now, there is no need of such a state of affairs. The water being taken out above Helper will be conveyed in a ditch near to the head of the Price town ditch and can be put into it and carried through the Price ditch, which can be extended on towards Wellington and the people of Wellington can connect their ditch with the Price ditch, thus having a drinking stream above all irrigation running for sixteen miles, which having passed in the open air and sunlight, will be much more healthy and better than when it first left the river. Each settlement can add...

...original water right sufficient for domestic use and when water can be had let all lands below the ditch, which is not covered by ditches already out, be irrigated from the main ditch, but under all circumstances retain enough for domestic purposes, and, by so doing, we will advance the value of our homes 500 per cent, and retain the health of our families. That, if there is not something done to keep pure the water we have to use for culinary purposes Price Precinct will soon become a slaughter yard for ourselves and children.

Dr. Pike, and all other doctors, who have seen the mode of the waters of Price River, make the same statement. Yours truly,

J. C. Busch.

Salt Lake Times
August 5, 1891

MURDER NEAR PRICE.

An Aged Man Killed and Buried in a Shallow Grave Near His Home.

PRICE, Utah, Aug. 5.—A murder committed five miles from this place, about two weeks ago, has just come to light. Ben Buchanan, an aged recluse, was missed from his ranch about the 17th of July, but as his team, harness and wagon were also missing, no importance was attached to the circumstance until about the 25th of July, when a search party was organized. A rancher living at Farnham came to town and reported that on the 17th two men passed his house driving Buchanan's team. The search party immediately went to Buchanan's ranch, and found a shallow grave in a dry wash. Buchanan's body, with his two dead dogs, was found, rolled up in blankets and covered with about six inches of earth. He had been shot through the head.

To Whom it May Concern.

I have this day sold to Albert Bryner, of Price, Emery County, Utah, about fifty head of cattle, ranging in age from one to six years and all branded [brand] four E combined, on right ribs, and [brand] marked with a crop off of left ear and under bit in the right ear.

R M WATSON.

No. 1094

Land Office at Salt Lake City, U. T., Aug 22, 1891.

Notice is hereby given that the following named settler has filed notice of his intention to make final proof in support of his claim, and that said proof will be made before the Clerk of the County Court of Emery County, U. T., at Castle Dale, U. T., on Saturday, October 10, 1891, viz: Thomas Gale, H E., No. 8406, for the N W.¼ of N E ¼ and E.½ N W.¼ Sec. 7 and S. E. ¼ of S W ¼, Sec. 6, Twp. 13 S., R 11 E.

He names the following witnesses to prove his continuous residence upon and cultivation of said land, viz:

Thomas Lundal, Robert A. Snyder, Edgar Thayn, William J. Tidwell, all of Wellington, Emery County, U T.

FRANK D HOBBS,

133-oa3t. Register.

—Joseph Burch came down from Salt Lake Sunday and on Monday went up to Helper to commence platting the new townsite

Floods at Price.

From Bishop Frandsen of Price, Emery county, who is in this city, we learn that quite a freshet from a cloud burst occurred about five miles above Price on Thursday last, resulting in the washing away of the banks of the canal by which the canal was supplied with water, for a considerable distance, and more or less damage to the stacks, crops in the field and the dwellings of several residents of that vicinity. The storm did not extend to Price, although the sound of it was plainly heard there. The crops generally throughout Emery county are fully up to the average. Lucern is better than usual.

A family by the name of Garling living in an isolated condition midway between Price and Spring Glen are having a serious time with the diphtheria, one child having died and three others being badly affected with the malady, though improving.

DEATHS.

RICHARDS.—At Scofield, Emery county, August 18th, 1891, Mary Richards, widow of Thos. Richards, aged 74 years. She was born in Llanelly, Carmarthenshire, South Wales. She joined the Church in the fall of 1847. She was very kind to the Elders in feeding them and giving them a place to rest. She died as she had lived, a faithful Latter-day Saint, with a hope of a glorious resurrection.

WILLIAMS.—At Castle Gate, Emery County, May 19, 1891, Blanche Williams, wife of Watkin Williams. She had given birth to a boy and a girl on the previous day.

September 13th, Watkin Williams, Jr., and on the 16th of September, Blanche Williams, son and daughter of Blanche and Watkin Williams, both born May 18th, 1891. They were affectionately cared for till their decease by Mr. and Mrs. Rees A. Lewis.

LLEWLYN.—At Castle Gate, September 16, 1891, of cholera morbus, Margaret, daughter of Job Llewlyn; born January 17, 1889.

Eastern Utah Telegraph
October 16, 1891

Salt Lake Herald
November 24, 1891

CRUSHED TO DEATH

An Estimable Young Man at Castle Gate the Melancholy Victim.

Late information from Castle Gate confirms the rumor concerning the death of James Forrester, which was announced in THE SUNDAY HERALD's special telegrams.

It appears he went into the slack bin of the coal crusher on his own account, and while there the coke hopper was put under to load. This caused the slack to give way in the center, drawing the young man into it in such a manner that he could not extricate himself, and he was completely suffocated.

James Forrester had been a cripple for some time and was the more unable to assist himself by reason of that misfortune. He was an exemplary young man, not yet 27, and was held in high regard by the entire community. The mines were closed in respect to his memory and his funeral was largely attended.

Logan Journal
November 25, 1891

Marriage Licences.

Jacob Carrick, of Scofield, Emery Co., Utah, to Sarah Williams of Salt Lake City, Utah.

Delinquent Tax list of Emery County, Utah

EMERY PRECINCT

Names	County Territorial and School tax	Special. School tax
Allred, Isaac	$2.50	$0.87
Albertson, Rasmus	4 10	.77
Bradrick C. H	.2 25.	81
Green, Brothers	28 37	6.2.
Jones, T J	2.18	28
Lone Tree Stock Company	7 17	1.34
Miller, Samuel	2 41	31
Miller, Miles	1 90	22
Miller D P	.2 00	22
Miller, John E.	. 1.50	12
Olson, O T	7 15	1 68
Olson, Lewis	2.23	31
Pratt, Davice	8 75	1 92
Smith, Alfred	3 62	06
Woodberry, W J	3 23	50

FERRON PRECINCT

Names	County Territorial and School tax	Special. School tax
Behnnin H S	3 15	
Behnnin, E. C.	2.12	
Burdich, M S	2 83	
Burrison, Peter	3 35	
Conover, A G	11.25	
Fredrickson Rasmus	5 60	
Huntsman, Edward	5.90	...
Halverson, Lewis	2.00	
Hitchcock, Frank	3 83	
Hitchcock, John	5.13	
Jensen, C K	4 05	
Jensen, Albert	8 38	
Jensen Christian	2.15	
King John E	15 75	
Klug Robert F	5 23	
Lorendhal S M	7.00	
Mills, H G	5.55	
Nelson, Christian	4 80	
Nelson Hyrum	9 02	
Olsen, Fredr'ck jr	8.27	
Olson Ole	42.00	
Olsen, Levy	7.23	
Pettey, H A	3 00	
Pettey, George A	9 00	
Ralph, John	10.50	
Stevens, A H	5 53	
Stevens, William	1.23	

MOLEN PRECINCT

Names	County Territorial and School tax	Special. School tax
Alder, Niels	2 15	
Cook J H	9 87	
Kofford, George & Co	3 25	
Peterson Peter F	4 00	
Swasy, Joseph	8.90	...

ORANGEVILLE PRECINCT.

Names	County Territorial and School tax	Special. School tax
Anderson, Andrew	17 25	
Curtis, William H	3 25	
Curtis, John S	6.35	
Curtis V E	5 57	
Crawford, G	5.00	
Childs P A	5.12	
Fox, George	3.55	
Fullmer James	1.27	
Hudson Thomas	17 65	2.51
Houskeeper, T F	5.70	
Jenks, Ben	5.47	...
Miles & Swasy	7.25	
Moffitt, C. A	8.10	
Parry, John L	3.30	
Stillson, G. A	2 57	
Swasy, Siddny	13 05	
VanBuren, A C	7.25	

CASTLE DALE PRECINCT

Names	County Territorial and School tax	Special. School tax
Christensen Andrew	2 25	31
Dounleen, Joseph	9 75	2.18
Hadley, John	3 00	50
Jeffs, James	13 05	3 19
Johnsen Peter	3 00	50
Kofford William	3 00	50
Lake, Robert	2.75	43
Olsen Henning jr	2 25	31
Olsen, Andrew N	8 50.	1 87
Olsen, Jorgenia Mrs	4 50	-
Olsen Nad	13 75.	3 05
Olsen, John	2.25	31
Swasy Charley	67 40	16.10
Seely, J L	4 95	98
Sowell James N	2.10	27
Turner, William	3.85	71

LAWRANCE PRECINCT

Birch, P C		13.83
Burgess, H L		4.10
Day, A. N		9.85
Day, Ira A		6.45
Hill, Robert W		9.45
Miller Christian		6.5
McArthur S C		2.37
Moore, Lewis A		1.53
Roper, Henry		4.50
Reynolds, R B		8.45
Tanner B A		4.50
Tanner, A M		3.00

HUNTINGTON PRECINCT

Allen, Shalon		2.02
Black, Isaac		2.25
Burgess Hyram		3.15
Cram, L D		4.80
Chase Samuel		2.75
Cox Allen		4.00
Cordingly Bros		10.10
Gardner A C		4.55
Green W J		5.00
Robbins & Harmon		8.50
Herriman, Henry H		8.75
Herriman, H S		2.00
Inge, J A		2.25
Jorgensen, N C		3.60
Jones, John		2.80
Jones, Hyrum		10.50
Lott, J W		2.50
Mangum, E F		3.15
Ottostrum, Hyrum		4.70
Onard, J W		3.75
Smith, O A		8.70
Tylor, D M		8.85
Wakefield, Thomas		10.35
West, John A		7.00
Washburn D A		8.73
Wa..., L S		5.95

Youn... CLEVELAND PRECINCT

CLEVELAND PRECINCT

John P	3.70	2.70
Johnson,	3.87	2.37
Johnson, M. ...rgret Mrs	9.15	8.75
Jensen, Ole C	1.80	8..
Williams, John	1.85	85
Wells, Thomas		

PRICE PRECINCT

	4.73	1.8
Anderson Joseph	13.05	6.12
Birch, Joseph	11.45	5.21
Bryner, Henry	2.65	8.
Mongul, M S	6.05	2.12
McIntire E W		1.2
McKindrick, C H		1.8.
McIntire, J H	4.15	1.60
Mann, Samuel	4.00	1.12
Grames, Albert	3.25	
Grames, Charles	3.53	
Grames, Charles	3.25	1.18
Hatch, Abraham	2.50	75
Jensen, C F		17.22
Powell, John A	53.63	
Powell, Robert A	24.40	11.70
Smith C M	1.05	.21
Thompson, R B	8.00	2.50
Warren Frank	2.75	1.37

Spring Glen Precinct

Babcock W. H.	10.15	1.87
Ewell F M	10.05	4.52
Ewell, F M Jr	10.05	4.02
Stowell, H J	4.95	1.8
Vannitta J H	14.20	6.80

CASTLE GATE PRECINCT

Hewelyn, Jobe	1.45	
Hewelyn John	2.01	
Wade, Henry	16.85	

SCOFIELD PRECINCT

Andersen John F	2.25	62
Adamson Hyrum	2.10	50
Burrows, David	8.00	2.5.
Burrows, W L	8.25	4.12
Burrows W. O	13.00	6.00
Birch, John	1.73	87
Cattle, William C	2.18	51

Cramer Antone	3 00	1 u
Curtis, Perry	1 75	87
Davis Rodrich	3.25	1 12
Fife, William	1 90	45
Granger L	.35 85	12 31
Green, D. D	2 30	45
Hing, Sam	4.50	1 75
Hentrichson B A	16.75	8 87
Hunter, Andrew	2 90	5u
Hunter, Adam	2.00	50
Jensen, O. J	1 90	45
Jensen, Christian	1 70	85
Kimball, O G	16.15	8.57
Lloyd, W W	1 75	87
Leysben, William	1 75	87
Masters, William	4 00	1 50
McLeac, Neph L	2.40	70
Mayweather, Frank	3 00	50
Metcalf, J W	2.25	63
Morris, Edward	1 75	87
Price, John L	2 50	75
Pattersen, Thomas	3.15	87
Parce L, J. K	5.87	2 43
Robbins, Charley	2 0J	50
Sharp, J K	15 00	7 00
Trivler, J. R	4 00	1.50
Thomas T H	3 90	1 45
Stewart, Andrew	2 00	50
Hunter, & Comp	11 00	5 00
Llewelyn, Isiah	2 25	62

WESTERN QUARTERS PRECINCT

Bennett, Benjamin	1 25	87
Evans, William	1 75	87
Gardner, Ira	7 00	3 00
McLean, Angus	2 00	50

WELLINGTON PRECINCT

Critterdon Hyrum	4.50	2 50
Avery, R W	11 45	4.36
Hill, Henry	2 12	89
Hill, George	5 40	3 36
Milburn George B	4.35	2 68
Roberts, B M	11 13	5 00
Watson R N	3.60	2 08
Ionog, George H	6 70	4.56
Yeager, George	2 20	90

WOODSIDE PRECINCT

Curtis, Joseph	2.52
Hutchison, Mrs	2 50
Hutchison, J H	2.37
Prssett, L R	2.42

BLAKE PRECINCT

Gammage, Josephine	11 95
Harris, N U	1 10
Fuller, R. L.	2 40

NINE MILE PRECINCT

Kimball, Isaac	2 50
Russell, John	3.35
Shaw, Fred	4.30

TRANSITORY.

Dean, James	20 1o	9 55
Downs, John	8 90	
Davidson, Bros	3 50	
Eldridge & Argyle	78.50	
Hallevan Michal	49 40	12 1o
Kempton H B	11 05	5 05
Lunt & Mynder,	9 75	
Lunt, Shed	21 00	
Moroni Coop Herd,	121 75	
Miller P M	4 90	
Okey Charley	8 25	
Sidwell John	8 90	
Thomos, Frank	28 75	
Thomas Mat	42 00	
Withmore George C.	160 00	17 20

J D KILLPACK, Assessor and Collector
Emery County, Utah

Eastern Utah Telegraph
December 18, 1891

—Miss Della Nixon left Wednesday for her home at St. George. Miss Nixon has made Price her home for a long time, and her presence will be missed by a large circle of friends.

—Prof. Monroe will open a night school, at Price, after Holidays. Instructions will be given in Penmanship, Book Keeping and practical Mathematics

Eastern Utah Telegraph
December 25, 1891

H. A. Atkison has been appointed Deputy Sheriff at Price, and has filed his bonds

—The dance Friday night at the Williams Hall was a success in every particular. About 40 couple were present.

Deseret Evening News
December 29, 1891

At Price, Utah, on Monday afternoon J. J. Kinsman was instantly killed by accident. Kinsman was a brakeman on Conductor Stewart's freight train, and was in the act of making a coupling when his foot caught in a frog, pinning him fast, while the parts of the train were approaching to be coupled. He made every effort to extricate his foot, but without avail. He was instantly killed.

His body was horribly crushed and mangled. The deceased was a resident of Grand Junction, Colo., to which the body was conveyed last night on the east bound passenger No. 2. He leaves a wife and one child. The news, when broken to Mrs. Kinsman, prostrated her entirely. They have been married a little over a year.

Eastern Utah Telegraph
January 1, 1892
Price

—John T. Owenes, the armless man who plyes the violin and banjo with his feet, was in town the first of the week. Mr. Owens furnished the music for the dance at the William's Hall Monday night. We pronounce him a first-class performer.

—A Mr. Pratt from Salt Lake was in town several days this week preparing to prospect in Whitmore canyon.

—Price is badly in need of better water facilities A six inch hole in the ground with a windlass over it would be an improvement.

—A Happy New Year

—About 10 inches of snow fell Tuesday and Tuesday night.

—Ira Lyman had the misfortune to cut his thumb

Lawrence Locals.

Snow.

Holidays.

Good Health prevails.

The Dance Christmas night was well attended. Good Music and a good time in general, and a good supper, we would judge. as it took most of them one hour and fifteen minutes to dispose of it

Amos M Tanner and Elizebeth Slaw, both of Lawrence, were united in the holy bonds of matrimony on the 23rd of Dec. A free dance at night was a feature of the occasion that will long be remembered by those in attendance.

HON. L. M OLSON,

of Price, Emery county, Fourteenth representative district, who enjoyed the distinction of coming out victor in the famous campaign against Hon. Abe Hatch, is the youngest of nine children. He was born May 17, 1851, in Vermland, Sweden. Both parents died before he was six years old. From 1860 to 1868, he lived in Christiania, the capital of Norway, from which place he emigrated to Salt Lake city in 1868, walking almost every step of the way from Laramie, Wyoming. He attended the University of Deseret during 1875, and that period embraces all his school days. He afterward taught school at Ephraim, which he made his home, and in 1878 he spent three years in a visit to his native home. On his return in 1881, he resumed his former vocation of school teaching. In 1882 he was elected a city councilor; in 1883 was appointed superintendent of Ephraim Co-op. and also filled the vacancy in the office of city treasurer. In 1887 he moved to Price, Emery county,

to take charge of the Emery County Mercantile company. In 1889 he was elected county superintendent of district schools against his Liberal opo\nent, Mr. Milles. He was renominated in 1891 by acclamation and re-elected against his Republican opponent.

The vote on the final count stood: Olsen (Democrat), 532; Hatch (Republican), 404; Kimball (Liberal), 42.

THE JURY LIST

W L Burrows, Schofield, Emery county.

Newburn Butts, Castle Gate, Emery county.

Henry Wade, Castle Gate, Emery county.

John D Llewellyn, Castle Gate, Emery county.

Michael Conner, Price, Emery county.

John E Reid, Orangeville, Emery county.

T J Farrer, Green River, Emery county.

Oliver Harmon, Huntington, Emery county.

DEATHS.

BRYNER.—January 23rd, 1892, at Price, of la grippe, Mary Evaline, daughter of Albert and Moriah Bryner, aged 16 months and 2 days.

Salt Lake Tribune
February 25, 1892

SOCIABILITY AT SCOFIELD.

There was a leap-year ball held at the meeting-house Thursday evening, January 21st, which all pronounce as having been the best, most enjoyed, and most successful hop ever had in Scofield. The committee, the Misses Katie Russell, Maggie Strang and May Strang, deserve great credit for their efforts, which resulted so successfully.

For some time past William Potter, ex-saloonkeeper, has been missing cigars and cigarettes from his stock, which he stored away after closing out his saloon. Some young men of the town were observed smoking quite often since the thefts began who previously had seldom partaken of the luxury of a cigar. Their favorite brands were also observed to be identical with those Mr. Potter had lost. Suspicion naturally pointed toward them being the guilty parties. Sunday last Mr. Potter took out a search-warrant, and accompanied by Officer Lloyd, found about 200 cigars and a large quantity of cigarettes (about one-third of amount stolen) hidden in a hay stack on the premises where the persons suspected reside. The two boys, whose ages are 10 and 12 years respectively, acknowledged their guilt when accused, and were arrested. At the hearing given by Justice Harkness Wednesday night, it transpired that the boys were acting as a sort of agent for older persons, who consumed the stolen goods. Their paternal, when approached with the search warrant, unloaded several boxes of cigarettes, which he said he supposed were stolen by some one else's boys and hidden in his stack. A young man who is supposed to be sweet on a sister of the two young miscreants is the particular person referred to as the consumer of the "Havanas." He makes no denial of having known the goods to have been stolen, and went to the stack whenever he craved for a smoke. He is also to explain his position before the grand jury with the two boys. All are now under bonds, and will likely decide from personal experience that "Honesty is always the best policy."

BIRD'S EYE VIEWER.

Deseret Weekly
March 19, 1892

DEATHS.

THOMAS—At Scofield, Emery County, Utah, March 7, 1892, of dropsy. Frederick Thomas, aged 65 years, 5 months and 10 days.

Deceased was born September 26, 1826, in Pont-y-Gwaith, Merthyr, Glamorganshire, South Wales, and was baptized into the Church of Jesus Christ of Latter-day Saints May 4th, 1848, by Elder William Morgan. He was ordained a Teacher two months later, and to the office of a Priest during the same year, being set apart to preside in the latter quorum. He was ordained an Elder in the fall of 1849, and was set apart as clerk. He continued to act for fifteen years in that branch of the Church. On April 22nd, 1867, he buried his wife Susan, and in 1868 married again. On October 11th, 1874, he and his family journeyed with other Saints to Utah, staying at Ogden six years, and then moved to Logan, where he remained nine years, and then moved to Pleasant Valley ward. He has always been steadfast in his belief in all the principles of the Gospel and bore a strong testimony of its truth. He leaves five sons, three daughters and twenty-eight grandchildren, also a large circle of friends, to mourn his loss.—[COM.

Millennial Star, please copy.

The Pleasant Valley mines are located at Scofield; they are connected with the Rio Grande Western by a branch fifteen miles long and are 112 miles from Salt Lake City by rail. There are two veins worked here, one thirteen and one twenty-eight feet in thickness. The output is used by the Union Pacific and Rio Grande Western for engine fuel and for commercial purposes, being sold in all towns from Colorado to Idaho. The Union Pacific own mines at Scofield, from which they mined in 1890 200,000 tons of coal.

The Castle Gate mines are at the station of that name on the main line of the Rio Grande Western. They are 111 miles from Salt Lake by rail. There are several veins worked here, the largest being fourteen feet thick. This is the only coal so far found in Utah that will coke. A set of eighty coke ovens is now in operation there. In 1890 there were 7778 tons of coke made there, which was sold to the Salt Lake smelters at $18.50 per ton. The Pleasant Valley company mined in

1890 at Scofield and Castle Gate 234,487 tons of coal. The Castle Gate coal is used all over Utah and is shipped as far west as San Francisco.

The Castle Valley mines are situated southwest of Castle Gate, and are not worked at present, as they have no rail communication. The U. P. in 1890 located a line to them from Juab, and purchased most of the right of way with the intention of taking the coal southwestward on the line they were building toward Pioche and Los Angeles. All work was suspended on these lines in October, 1890. The distance by rail from Salt Lake would be 130 miles.

The Cedar City and Kanarra mines are at the southwestern extremity of the coal belt. They have no rail communication, and are mined only for domestic use in the adjacent towns. The veins are from four to twelve feet in thickness.

At Winter Quarters.

The residents of Winter Quarters celebrated Pioneer Day on Monday last in good style. The forenoon programme of exercises embraced prayer, vocal and instrumental music (the Winter Quarters brass band having been present), and addresses. Nuts and oranges were distributed among the juveniles. There were sports for the youngsters in the afternoon and an excellent time was had all round.

Work in the coal mines has started up. Men are coming into camp daily. The Y. M. and Y. L. M. I. A. held a conjoint meeting last Sunday evening before a large audience. All are pleased with the new manual.

The health of the people is good.

EVAN S. THOMAS.

Scofield, Emery county, Utah, July 26th, 1892.

GOSSIP FROM CASTLE GATE.

EDITOR TRIBUNE:—Last Saturday was pay day for the coal miners.

Superintendent W. G. Sharp of the Pleasant Valley Coal Company spent the first of the week at Scofield and Winter Quarters.

Captain J. L. Smith, who has been very sick for the past two weeks, is able to be around again.

The Mormons have finished their new meeting house and hold services each Sunday, with a good attendance. The hops that are given in the church each week afford a larger attendance and are greatly enjoyed by the old folks as well as the young.

Mrs. M. J. Keenan has gone to Cedar Rapids, Neb., for a short visit with relatives and friends.

School opened last week, with Miss Hazle McCormick as teacher. The average attendance is about seventy-five. Miss Hazle is well liked by the scholars, and every one wishes her success as a teacher.

Mr. and Mrs. H. A. Nelson returned from Springville Tuesday, where they had been making a short visit with Mrs. Nelson's father and mother.

Mr. and Mrs. Ferg Ferguson returned the first of the week from Salt Lake, after a two weeks' visit. Ferg bet on Corbett and is happy.

Mr. E. L. Carpenter was up from Zion last Saturday, paying off the miners and other employees of the coal company.

Scott M. Miller has gone to Provo for a few days.

Dr. H. B. Asadoorian was called to Pleasant Valley Junction Monday to see an injured Rio Grande Western Railway section man.

Mr. and Mrs. Graver Lewis are celebrating the arrival of a five-pound boy at their home. Mr. and Mrs. Wade of the Wade Hotel also had free beer on tap last week. It is a boy also.

Mr. and Mrs. Joe Patterson of Winter Quarters mine, who were recently married, gave a party Tuesday night. Those attending from here were: Mr. and Mrs. H. A. Nelson, Mr. Robert Forrester, wife and Mrs. Forrester's sister, who have just arrived from Scotland; Mr. Sandy McLean and Miss Reece. All report having a good time.

John W. Ray, agent Rio Grande Western Railway at this place, has been very sick since his return from Salt Lake last week.

The coal mine is running as usual, the output of coal being from twenty to twenty-five cars per day.

Mr. J. X. Ferguson, who has been in charge of the Wasatch Store Company here for several days, has resigned his position, and has been in Salt Lake several days, making arrangements to start a big store of his own at Helper. May he meet with success is the wish of all.

Messrs. William Parmley and Samuel Rowley were elected delegates to the county convention to represent the "Republicans" of Castle Gate. Judging from the amount of political wire pulling that is being done here, the office of Justice of the Peace must be very remunerative to hold. The leading candidates in the field are Harry J. World and Henry J. Schultz.   S.

CASTLE GATE, Sept. 24, 1892.

ELECTION JUDGES.

More of Them Appointed by the Utah Commission Today.

The Utah commission appointed the following judges of election this morning:

Salt Lake Herald
October 29, 1892

EMERY COUNTY.

Spring Glen Precinct—John Y. Biglow, R.; J. T. Fitch, R.; George V. Perkins, D.

Castle Dale—Carl Milberry, D.; William Laber, R.; Richard Miller, R.

Orangeville—E. M. Moore, D.; F. W. Fail, R.; H. M. Reid, R.

Ferron—H. W. Curtis, R.; F. A. Killpark, R.; Andrew Nelson, D.

Morlan—David Killpark, D.; Seth Wareham, R.; Charles Wayman, R.

Cleveland—Samuel Wells, R.; John Eden, R.; F. J. Marsing, D.

Lawrence—Llewellyn Lewis, D.; Ira A. Day, R.; P. C. Birch, R.

Muddy—J. T. Lewis, R.; John Edmondson, R.; Jens P. Olsen, D.

Scofield—A. H. Earle, R.; F. J. Lewis, R.; J. R. Parcell, D.

Winter Quarters—Samuel Padfield, R.; John Patten, R.; Thomas S. Parmley, D.

Castle Gate—R. D. Wilstead, R.; John Bermidge, D.; Scott M. Miller, R.

Price—E. Lynch, R.; J. B. Milborn, R.; J. M. Whitmore, D.

Wellington—S. H. Grundvig, R.; William Tidwell, R.; R. H. Snyder, D.

Minnie Maud—E. C. Lee, R.; J. H. Kimball, R.; A. J. Russell, D.

Huntington—William H. Burgess, D.; John H. Colt, R.; Curtis W. Caldwell, R.

Woodside—S. H. Pressett, R.; Felix Pressett, R.; C. H. Hutchinson, D.

Blake—R. P. Johnson, D.; Thomas Farrer, R.; William Shafer, R.

THE HERMIT'S DEATH.

August Nelson Charged with the Murder.

The Old Man was Found Buried With Two of His Dogs Near Price, Utah.

The Buchanan murder case is now on trial at Provo, a jury having been secured when court adjourned last evening.

James Buchanan was an old man of eccentric habits who lived the life of a hermit, near Price, U. T., on the Rio Grande Western road. He rarely ever sought human companionship, his favorite company being a couple of well-bred dogs. There was a very general belief among those who knew Buchanan that he had

A CONSIDERABLE SUM OF MONEY

stowed away, as he usually got good prices for anything that he marketed, and rarely spent a cent more than was absolutely necessary for his existence.

One day his absence from home was talked of by his neighbors. But little notice was taken of this, as it was a custom of his to hitch up his team, drive off, without saying a word to anyone of his destination and be absent several days. A visit to the hut in which Buchanan passed his nights revealed nothing of a suspicious nature, and when it was found that his team was not in its usual place, they concluded that Buchanan had taken another of his mysterious journeys and would return in a short time.

Several days passed by, however, and the old man did not return, and one afternoon a neighbor, in crossing the Buchanan property, was attracted to a spot from which came a foul stench. An investigation proved that Buchanan, in company with his two dogs, had

BEEN KILLED AND BURIED

there. The body was exhumed and decently reinterred.

Suspicion attached to a couple of men named August Nelson and N. Larsen, semi-tramps, who had been seen on and around Buchanan's ranche.

Sheriff Fowler started on their trail, and some months afterwards, Nelson was arrested; an indictment was promptly found by the grand jury, and Nelson is now facing the consequences of the awful deed.

The prosecution claims to have evidence that will surely convict Nelson, but the officers have been unable to locate Larsen.

The taking of testimony will begin this morning.

Salt Lake Herald
November 4, 1892

FROM EMERY COUNTY.

Hon. A. D. Gash Carries Away an Audience and 36 Democratic Recruits Obtained.

Correspondence of THE HERALD.]

SCOFIELD, Oct. 31, 1892.—A Democratic meeting was held at Winter Quarters to hear the principles of Democracy expounded by the Hon. A. D. Gash of Provo city. He commenced by speaking of the tyranny exercised by kingly power by taxing the people without giving them representation. He also paid a glorious tribute to the memory of Thomas Jefferson, the great founder of Democracy. He then went on amidst thunderous applause to show how the Republican party was taxing the poor people for the special benefit of the rich, showing that the protective tariff is only an oppression of the working men, and proving conclusively that the Democratic party was and is the upholder of human liberty. After speaking for two hours and ten minutes he closed the greatest speech that was ever made in Winter Quarters amidst tremendous cheering.

Thirty-six came forward and signed the Democratic roll, among them being some who had been looked upon as doubtful. We then had music by the band, after which several songs. The meeting gave three cheers for Grover Cleveland, Adlai Stevenson and Joseph L. Rawlins and the straight Democratic party, and the meeting closed with a vote of thanks to the speaker.

We safely say that Winter Quarters will be heard from on the 8th of November and help to swell the majority for Joseph L. Rawlins and Democracy.

ROBERT HOWARD, Secretary.

Salt Lake Herald
November 9, 1892

ACCIDENTAL DEATH.

H. J. Hammell Crushed to Death at Scofield.

SCOFIELD, U. T., Nov. 8.—[Special telegram to THE HERALD.]—An accident occurred today at the Pleasant Valley Coal company's Winter Quarters mine by which H. J. Hammell came to his death. The deceased was working on a coal pillar and had to use a ladder to light a shot. In carrying his ladder to a place of safety the blast caught him and buried him underneath the coal. He was badly crushed and died in a few hours. Deceased was a native of Belguim and only came to this country about one month ago. He leaves a wife and four children.

Salt Lake Herald
November 19, 1892

EMERY COUNTY.

Precinct.	Rawlins.	Caruon.	Allen.
Blake	5	11	16
Castle Dell	46	32	1
Cleveland	1	49	31
Ferron	30	12	
Huntington		40	3
Lawrence	9	42	
Muddy	25	6	
Nolen	3	30	
Orangeville	18	4	
Price	52	59	
Scofield	30	65	1
Spring Glen	30	8	41
Wellington	19	12	3
Winter Quarters	21	22	
Woodside	24		20
Minnie Moore	8	1	2
Castle Gate	6	10	
Total	461	365	118

Rawlins' plurality, 96.

County Officers—Clerk, Carl Wilberg; recorder, Carl Wilberg; assessor, Henry Wilson; collector, Wyatt Bryan; attorney, Chris Johnson; sheriff, H. G. Mathias; treasurer, H. C. Miller; surveyor, W. H. Tredwell; coroner, William Taylor; selectmen, H. M. Furgate, E. H. Cox, J. L. Boulder.

On the question of the removal of the county seat to Price, the vote stood: Yes, 819; noes, 332.

An error in THE HERALD yesterday made Dr. Wilcox coroner of Davis county, when it should have read John Wayman. The selectmen are W. M. Needer, D. C. Lee and David Cook.

Vernal Express
February 16, 1893

KILLED ON THE RIO GRANDE.

William A. Reese Cut to Pieces Near Castle Gate.

CASTLE GATE, Utah, Feb. 6.—[Special to the Salt Lake Herald.]—A man by the name of William A. Reese met his death to-day on the track two miles below this town in a horrible manner by being literally cut to pieces by a freight-train.

It appears that he lately came here from Winters Quarters, where his home and family are, presumably to seek work. He has been drinking heavily of late and was last seen at Helper. It is evident from the place that he was found that he was on his way back to Castle Gate, taking the railroad track as the best road to get there.

Within two miles of the mines he must have got sleepy and sat down or was drunk and fell down across the track, but how long he remained in that position nobody can say. The grade is a little steep just there, and when the freight came rushing along when in sight of the man lying across the track, the engineer could not bring the train to a standstill untill Reese was dragged 800 feet from where the engine struck him being scattered on the frozen snow and ice on the river. What could be found was gathered up and brought to Castle Gate, and an inquest will be held tomorrow before H. J. Shultz, justice and acting corner of this place.

Salt Lake Herald
March 22, 1893

ACCIDENTS IN THE MINES.

Two Men Killed and Nine Injured During the Year.

On September 7, 1892, Richard Hunter, a miner in the Union Pacific No. 1 Pleasant Valley mine, was injured by a falling rock from the roofing, while at work in the mine. He was not at first considered fatally injured, but succumbed and died from his hurts on September 11, 1892.

Henry Hamel, a miner in the Pleasant Valley Coal company's Winter Quarters No. 2 mine, was killed by a premature blast on November 8, 1892, about three tons of coal falling upon him.

NON-FATAL ACCIDENTS.

The number of non-fatal accidents was nine, the list including a boy, seven miners and a locomotive engineer.

Salt Lake Herald
July 14, 1893

MORE DEPUTY REGISTRARS.

EMERY COUNTY.

Muddy—S. M. Williams.
Ferron—(To be filled by the resident county registrar).
Molen—J. H. Cook.
Orangeville—Frank Carroll (Independent).
Huntington—V. D. Crain.
Cleveland—L. P. Overson.
Castle Dale—R. C. Miller.
Lawrence—Philander Burch.
Price—Soren Olson.
Wellington—H. F. Hanson (Republican).
Woodside—C. O. Moore (Republican).
Blake—J. T. Farrer (Republican).
Minnie Maud—F. E. Grames (Republican).
Spring Glen—C. H. Cook.
Castle Gate—H. J. Schultz (Republican).
Scofield—S. J. Harkness (Republican).
Winter Quarters—J. M. Beatie.

A New Hand Loom.

Mr. James Peterson of Price, Emery county, Utah, has just invented a patent hand loom for the purpose of weaving woolen cloth. It is stated that this hand loom will weave from 75 to 100 yards per day. If is a fact it is one of the greatest inventions of the day. This would indeed be a Godsend to our poor people during these hard times. This loom is made entirely out of wood. Mr. Peterson wishes some person to assist him to get a patent on the invention He feels quite confident that he has an invention that will sell readily and make the owners rich. Further information can be had by addressing James Peterson, Price, Utah.

Last Sunday evening, says the eastern Utah *Telegraph*, published at Price, Emery county, the 12-year-old son of Robert Powell met with a very severe accident which may prove fatal. The boy was riding a colt which he thought was perfectly gentle. He was riding along slowly and sitting on sideways; but getting tired of his position thought he would get on straddle. Just as he went to raise his leg the horse became frightened, throwing the boy off and kicking him. The back portion of the skull was crushed.

PLEASANT VALLEY HISTORY.

WINTER QUARTERS, Pleasant Valley, Utah Co., Utah, Nov. 6, 1893.— This place has nothing at all in common with old Winter Quarters, founded by the Saints on the Missouri river in 1846; it is even asserted by the old settlers here that the Winter Quarters in Nebraska were not thought of by those who named this Winter Quarters in Utah. This more modern town or mining camp perhaps derives its name from the fact that winter with its almost perpetual snows and frosts bids defiance to any other atmospheric condition for about nine months out of every twelve. The altitude at the mouth of the mines is nearly 8100 feet above the level of the sea, while Scofield, two miles distant, is 7832 feet above sea level. Winter Quarters is situated in a narrow canyon which extends westward from the extreme south end of Pleasant Valley. The log houses and cabins which shelter the miners' families are mostly situated on the more sunny side of the canyon on the mountain slope. They are strung along for a distance of over one mile, part of them above and part of them below the mouths of the three principal mines.

The Latter-day Saints meeting house is perched on the hillside about half a mile below the mines. It is a log building in T shape, each of its two parts measuring 20x40 feet. Of the 429 souls, or seventy families, of which the Pleasant Valley ward is composed, the larger half reside at Winter Quarters and the other part in and below Scofield.

A great proportion of the Saints at Winter Quarters are Welsh, while quite a number of those at Scofield are of Scotch extraction. Meetings and Sunday schools are held separately in both places every Sabbath, generally well attended, except when the weather is so severe that out-door exercise is out of the question, which happens quite frequently in the dead of winter. There are also separate Relief Societies, Primary Associations and Y. M. and Y. L. M. I. Associations, in all of which much good is being accomplished and the members generally take a lively interest in the exercises.

Scofield is an incorporated town (not city) situated in the extreme south end of Pleasant Valley on a nice level flat, opening out into the valley northward, with a canyon extending southward, and another one (Winter Quarters canyon) westward, while the mountains form the natural townsite boundaries on the east and west.

The Union Pacific coal mines are situated east of Scofield, a short distance up the mountain slope; but they are not being worked at present, nor have they been for several months past. In consequence of this quiet a number of men are out of employ-

ment, while others have found work at the Winter Quarters mines above. The distance from Scofield to Pleasant Valley junction, on the Rio Grande Western railway is sixteen miles by rail; to Fairview, Sanpete county, it is about twenty-four miles by nearest wagon road, and in order to reach Huntington, Emery county, by mountain road, the traveler must go nearly forty-five miles.

Pleasant Valley proper is about four miles long from north to south, and its average width is a little over a mile; its surface consists mostly of meadow land, and there are about a dozen summer ranches located at different points in the valley. Mud creek, on which Scofield is situated, enters the valley from the south, while Fish creek, the larger stream of the two, comes in from the west. The junction of the two streams is in the lower or north end of the valley where Fish creek enters a canyon eleven miles long, through which the railroad also passes. Near the mouth of this canyon, where Fish creek and White river come together and form Price river is situated the railway station known as Pleasant Valley Junction. When the railroad company had their roundhouse and

machine shops here a few years ago this was quite a lively town, and its questionable population helped very materially four years ago to steal Salt Lake City, but now it is a poor shadow of its former self. As a conclusive proof of this I may say that the last saloon there had to close down a few weeks ago for lack of patronage.

Besides the Mormon population in Pleasant Valley there are quite a number of Gentiles, but so far as I can understand a friendly feeling exists between the two factions, and the election tomorrow will be carried on strictly on national party lines.

Active work in the Pleasant Valley coal mines was carried on as early as 1875, but as the coal had to be hauled out by teams the business was unprofitable until 1879, when the Pleasant Valley railroad was first built up to the mines. Then followed several years of prosperity, the output from the mines sometimes amounting to 900 tons a day from the Winter Quarters mines alone. At present there are about three hundred men employed at the mines, and the daily shipments amount to about 500 tons.

The first ecclesiastical organization in Pleasant Valley dates back to Dec. 22, 1881, when a branch of the Church of Jesus Christ of Latter-day Saints was organized here with David Williams as President. In 1883 the branch

was organized into a regular Bishop's ward; and from 1888 to 1890 there were two wards in the valley, one at Winter Quarters, called the Pleasant Valley ward, and the other at Scofield. Owing to the removal of one of the Bishops in 1890, the two wards were amalgamated into one, and the present Bishop is Thomas B. Parmley who acts with Hyrum Edwards and John E. Ingles as counselors.

I may add that there is a respectable Latter-day Saint meeting house at Scofield, a lumber building 22 x 40 feet, nicely situated in the center of a block which is enclosed with a lumber fence. The buildings of the town consist of small lumber structures, and they are all in plain view, as there are no trees or shrubbery of any kind to hide them from the gaze of the visitor. Until the Lord shall be pleased to temper the elements to a considerable extent Scofield will never rank as a fruit growing or grain growing neighborhood. Nothing in this line except a little rye has ever matured in the valley.

Last night I addressed an appreciative congregation of Saints and strangers at Scofield and today I am historically engaged. The San Juan and San Luis Stakes are next on the program.

ANDREW JENSON.

Deseret Weekly
December 16, 1893

THE EUROPEAN MISSION.

[*Millennial Star, Nov. 27.*]

ARRIVALS—The following missionaries arrived Sunday morning, November 19, per Cunard Steamer Lucania, all for the British mission: J. B. Patterson, of St. Johns, Arizona; Francis Clarke, of Eden, Utah; E. S. Horsley, of Price, Utah; H. J. Mulliner of Kanarra, Utah; Wm. Blain, of Spring City, Utah; Francis Cundill, of West Jordan, Utah. They were accompanied by Mrs. H. L. James, of Salt Lake City, who is on a visit to relatives.

Ogden Daily Standard
December 17, 1893

Death of Mrs. Powell.

Died at the home of her son, Robert A. Powell, near Price, Emery county, Utah, on Wednesday morning, December 13, 1893, at 10 a. m., Mrs. Gemima Powell, in the 80th year of her age.

Mrs. Powell was born near the city of Cincinnati, Ohio, where spent a portion of her early life. Leaving the scenes of her birth place she went with her parents to Nauvoo, where some years later she was married. A few years after her marriage and during the persecutions of the Latter-day Saints in her community, her husband was wounded, having his skull broken by a mob for refusing to assist in the persecutions of the Latter-day Saints. Neither she nor her husband had at this time joined the Saints.

After her husband had recovered they started for Salt Lake city, where both husband and wife joined the Church of Jesus Christ of Latter-day Saints. They made them a home where the city of Ogden now stands. The land where the depot stands was once owned by them. Some time after settling here the husband was drowned in attempting to cross the river. The widow remained at the old home for some time, after which she removed to Salt Lake city. Leaving Salt Lake she went to Pondtown, near Tintic, where she lived for several years. For the last five or six years she has made her home with her son, Robert A. Powell, near Price, spending a portion of her time with her daughter, Malinda Garnmage, at Green River, Utah.

Mrs. Powell has always lived a consistent member of the Church of Latter-day Saints ever since she connected herself with that people. She has "fought a good fight;" she has "kept the faith" and has gone to her reward. Peace to her soul.

Mrs. Powell leaves three sons, two daughters and a host of friends to mourn her loss. In the midst of life we are in death.

W. B. D.

Ogden Daily Standard
January 18, 1894

Neighborhood News.

Helper, Utah, Jan. 15.—In spite of frost and snow the people of Helper are enjoying the best of health. The farmer smiles to see the snow come down, as it promises him an abundant supply of water, while the cattleman rides by with downcast eye, and as he thinks of the many cattle that will ere long mingle their bones with the dust, or rather the snow, murmurs in a subdued voice, "When the Spring Time Comes, Gentle Annie."

* At the present there are two petitions in circulation for the purpose of dividing Emery county. One petition asks for the county seat to be at Price, and the other for Helper. We hope to win, and win we must.

Spring Glen district has lately been divided and one part will hereafter be known as Helper district.

Deputy Sheriff John Bryner met with a mishap at a dance the other night through a little misunderstanding with a party from Castle Gate. The result is that Sheriff Jack is peeking out from under a handkerchief with one eye.

Salt Lake Herald
February 26, 1894

Killed by a Coal Car.

The Eastern Utah Telegraph gives the following account of a fatal accident at Castle Gate:

Joe Hancock, a young man employed in the coal mines at Castle Gate, as car driver, had the life crushed out of him instantly last Saturday, by a car passing over his body. He was standing on the front part of the car driving his mule as usual, when he became overbalanced, falling in front of the car, which was heavy loaded with coal. It crushed his body almost to a jelly. He was about 21 years old and his parents reside at Spring Glen. He having worked in this neighborhood considerable, he was pretty well known in these parts, and his many friends will be sorry to learn of his sad death.

Salt Lake Herald
March 14, 1894

Land Office Filings.

Ferra L. Young, of Huntington, Emery county, yesterday filed in the land office homestead entry 10874, for 160 acres in section 2, township 15 south, range 8 east.

Joseph H. Proctor, of Mt. Pleasant, Sanpete county, made final proof on his desert entry 3236 for 160 acres in section 12, township 15 south, range 4 east.

Lars H. Olson, of Price, Emery county, filed a contest against the timber cutting entry made by John A. Johnson on May 22, 1884, for 160 acres in section 11, township 15 south, range 10 east. He alleges that Johnson has failed to either cultivate the tract or plant it to trees.

Salt Lake Herald
April 20, 1894

DIED.

OLSON—At Price, Emery county, April 18, 1894, of croup, Laurientius Magnus Olson, son of L. M. and Birdie Olson; born at Salt Lake city, February 26, 1892.

Funeral today, April 20, from No. 44 East North Temple street, Salt Lake city.

Friends of the family respectfully invited to attend.

Provo Daily Enquirer
April 18, 1894

CARBON COUNTY.

The Fight for the County Seat.

CITIZENS' CONVENTION.

A Rousing Meeting Held At Helper—Candidates Nominated.

The Carbon County Citizens' convention assembled at Helper on Friday, April 13, 1894, as per call by committee of citizens.

The hall was profusely decorated with bunting and banners, and everybody seemed inclined to make the first county convention of the new county one to be long remembered by its participants·

Wellington's delegation arrived early in the day and were at work instanter for the interests of their section.

Not until the arrival of the train from the west, at 12:30 p. m., did the town begin to take on convention airs, as it brought down the Scofield, Winter Quarters and Castle Gate delegations, accompanied by the Castle Gate Brass band, which played many fine selections, while everyone had a word of praise as to its merits.

Promptly at 3 p. m., Mr. J. Tom Fitch called the convention to order, stating the object of the convention was to put in the field for election on May 1st, a full county ticket.

Mr. J. X. Ferguson of Helper, was elected temporary chairman, and B. F. Caffey secretary.

Chairman appointed the following named as a committee on credentials: J. B. Roberts of Wellington; H. J. Stowell of Spring Glen; Thos. Durkin of Helper.

A recess of 15 minutes was taken for committee to prepare report.

The committee duly reported as follows (the report being adopted;)

The following named delegates are entitled to seats in this convention:

Castle Gate—B. F. Caffry, Andrew Young Sr., Wm. Chappell, Grover Lewis, Thos. Cox Sr.

Spring Glen—Jas. Rooney, Jas. X. Ferguson, T. H. Jones, H. J. Stowell, Thos. Durkin.

Wellington—John L Wilson, W. N. Bliss, J. B. Roberts.

Scofield—Jos. R. Sharp, F. P. Gridley, Henry Wilson, J. F. Valentine.

Winter Quarters—Robt. McKechney, Wm. Powell (proxy,) T. T. Reese (proxy) Geo. Martin (proxy).

Minnie Maud and Price precincts not having any delegation.

The chair appointed committees as follows.

On Permanent Organization.—F. P. Gridley, Scofield; T. F. Durkin, Helper, Grover Lewis, Castle Gate.

On Resolutions—J. R. Sharp, Scofield; B. F. Caffey. Castle Gate; H. J. Stowell, Spring Glen; J. L. Willson, Wellington; T. F. Durkin, Helper.

Convention took a recess for one hour, at the end of which the chairman called the convention to order.

The committee on permanent organization reported, recommending that the temporary organization be made permanent. The report was adopted.

The committee on resolutions submitted the following:

Resolved, That we, the delegates of this convention, place in nomination a full county ticket for Carbon county.

Resolved, That the said officers be so distributed to the several precincts of Carbon county as shall be most equitable and just to the respective voters, here represented, of said Carbon county.

Resolved, That all nominations be voted on by ballot.

Resolved, That we, the delegates, uphold and sustain the nominations of the Citizen's Independent convention; and that we will support the ticket placed in nomination for Carbon county by this convention.

The report of the committee was unanimously adopted.

Nominations of officers being in order, the chair appointed the following as tellers to count the ballots of the convention: Messrs. Valentine, Lewis and Durkin.

SELECTMEN.

Mr. J. L. Willson nominated Peter Liddel of Wellington af selectmen.

Mr. Cox, Sr., nominated Andrew Young of Castle Gate for selectmen.

Mr. J. R. Sharp put in nomination F. P. Gridle of Scofield.

Mr. Jas. Rooney nominated J. L. Boulden of Winter Quarters.

Mr. Liddell, Mr. Young and Mr. Boulden having received majorities of the ballots, they were declared the unanimous choice of the convention.

SHERIFF.

Mr. Jas Rooney placed the name of Thos. Lloyd of Scofield before the convention, and he was declared the choice of the convention by acclamation and on suspension of the rules.

B. F. Caffey nominated Dr. H B. Assadorian of Castle Gate for county coroner.

J. B. Roberts nominated A. Ballinger of Price.

Dr. Assadorian secured the nomination.

J. L. Willson nominated Mr. W. A. Thayn of Wellington for county surveyor. Mr. Thayn received the nomination.

Thos. Cox, Sr., presented the name of Jos. R. Sharp for clerk and recorder. Mr. Sharp received the nomination, every vote being cast for him.

COUNTY SUPT. OF SCHOOLS.

W. N. Bliss presented the name of H. A. Southworth of Price No other names being presented, Mr. Southworth was declared the unanimous choice of the convention.

TREASURER.

Thos. Cox, Sr., nominated John Forester of Castle Gate for treasurer.

J. L. Willson nominated J. Tom Fitch.

On ballotting, Mr. Fitch received the majority of the votes; and his nomination was made unanimous.

ASSESSOR AND COLLECTOR.

Jas. Rooney placed the name of S. J. Harkness before the convention for assessor and collector. Robt. McKeeny of Winter Quarter presented the name of Henry Wilson of Scofield. Harkness received a majority of the votes and was declared nominated.

COUNTY ATTORNEY.

J. B. Roberts nominated J. X Ferguson for county attorney, who was the unanimous choice of the convention.

After a recess of fifteen minutes the chair called the convention to order, and the minutes were read and approved, after which a vote of thanks was tendered Mr. Jas. Rooney for the use of the hail; also to the chairman and secretary for their services.

The following named gentlemen were chosen as the campaign committee, to conduct the election to a successful issue:

J. Tom Fitch of Helper, chairman; B. F. Caffey, Castle Gate; J. L. Willson, Wellington; Henry Wilson, Scofield; Robt. McKeeney, Winter Quarters.

After giving three rousing cheers for the ticket that had been nominated, the convention adjourned.

Every one was loud in praise of the amity and good cheer that governed the progress of the convention, all parties being entirely satisfied with the work and choice of the first convention of Carbon county.

J. X. Ferguson,   B. F. Caffey,
      Chairman,   Secretary.

Ogden Daily Standard
April 27, 1894

Carbon County Candidates.

Carbon county Republicans have nominated the following list of candidates for office, to be voted for at the special election to be held on the 1st of May:

For Clerk and Recorder—H. A. Nelson, of Castle Gate.

For Assessor and Collector—David Holdaway, of Price.

For Treasurer—Robert Forrester, of Castle Gate.

For Prosecuting Attorney—J. Schness, of Winter Quarters.

For Sheriff—C. H. Cook, of Spring Glen.

For Surveyor—W. J. Tidwell, of Wellington.

For Superintendent of Public Schools —Joseph W. Davis, of Price.

For Selectman—Eugene Santechi, of Castle Gate; F. P. Gridley, of Schofield; E. O. Lee, of Minnie Maude.

Salt Lake Herald
May 4, 1894

Licenses to wed were issued yesterday to Frederick Dungerd, aged 55, and Hannah C. Dale, aged 41, both of this city, and to Elliott Miller, aged 25, of Spring Glen, and Sarepta Vickers, aged 25, of Nephi.

THE CARBON COUNTY RETURNS.

Official Canvass of the Votes Cast at the Election the First of May.

Messrs. J. M. Cohen, John T. Lynch and Alfales Young, who were appointed a board to canvass the votes polled in the Carbon county election, met yesterday afternoon, and the returns being all to hand, completed the canvass.

Of the thirteen county officers voted for, the Republicans elected ten, the Democrats two and the Citizens one.

The two candidates, Thayn for Surveyor and Davis for Superintendent of Schools, returned as Democrats, were on both tickets.

The Utah Commission will meet to-morrow to ratify the canvass and issue the certificates of election. The returns by precincts were as follows:

FOR COUNTY SEAT.

	Price.	Scofield.	Wellington, Helper per ton.	
Castle Gate	37	..	30	1
Helper	1	..	29	..
Minnie Maude	18	..	..	..
Price	91	..	3	..
Scofield	9	62	2	..
Spring Glen	9	..	8	..
Wellington	22	..	24	..
Winter Quarters	31	17	2	..
Total	218	62	98	1

Price declared duly chosen.

COUNTY OFFICERS.

Clerk of the County Court—

	J. E. Ingles, Dem.	H. A. Nelson, Rep.	Jos. R. Sharp, Cit'n.
Precincts.			
Castle Gate	7	37	22
Helper	..	1	29
Minnie Maude	9	9	23
Price	17	72	4
Scofield	11	11	20
Spring Glen	8	3	7
Wellington	4	13	30
Winter Quarters	21	17	12
Total	77	163	143

Nelson, Republican, elected.

County Recorder—

	J. E. Ingles, Dem.	H. A. Nelson, Rep.	Jos. R. Sharp, Cit'n.
Castle Gate	7	38	23
Helper	..	1	29
Minnie Maude	5	9	..
Price	17	72	4
Scofield	11	19	41
Spring Glen	8	3	7
Wellington	3	13	31
Winter Quarters	19	18	13
Total	76	164	147

Nelson, Republican, elected.

County Assessor—

	Wm. Miller, Dem.	D. Holdaway, Rep.	S. J. Harkness, Cit'n.
Castle Gate	12	22	24
Helper	..	1	29
Minnie Maude	9	9	..
Price	12	78	4
Scofield	8	22	22
Spring Glen	15	2	1
Wellington	4	17	26
Winter Quarters	19	18	13
Total	79	190	119

Holdaway, Republican, elected.

County Collector—

	Wm. Miller, Dem.	D. Holdaway, Rep.	S. J. Harkness, Cit'n.
Castle Gate	12	32	24
Helper	..	1	29
Minnie Maude	9	9	..
Price	12	78	4
Scofield	8	32	22
Spring Glen	15	2	1
Wellington	4	17	26
Winter Quarters	19	18	13
Total	79	189	113

Holdaway, Republican, elected.

Prosecuting Attorney—

	J. B. Schiness, Rep.	Jas X. Ferguson, Cit'n.
Castle Gate	30	23
Helper	1	29
Minnie Maude	18	..
Price	85	8
Scofield	15	40
Spring Glen	3	11
Wellington	14	31
Winter Quarters	41	8
Total	207	160

Schiness, Republican, elected.

Sheriff—

	R Farrish, Dem.	C. H. Cook, Rep.	Thos. Lloyd, Cit'n.
Castle Gate	20	21	17
Helper	..	1	29
Minnie Maude	9	9	..
Price	19	69	6
Scofield	7	3	51
Spring Glen	7	4	7
Wellington	3	11	52
Winter Quarters	25	5	17
Total	102	123	161

Lloyd, Citizen, elected.

Treasurer—

	A. H. Ehril. Dem.	J. J. Fitch. Clt'n.	J. Forrester. Rep.
Castle Gate	8	19	6
Helper		28	4
Minnie Maude	5		9
Price	13	3	12
Scofield	14	28	19
Spring Glen	8	5	4
Wellington	5	23	13
Winter Quarters	23	7	50
Total	84	119	175

Forrester, Republican, elected.

Surveyor—

	W. A. Thayn. Dem.	W. J. Tidwell. Rep.
Castle Gate	36	32
Helper	29	1
Minnie Maude	9	9
Price	22	70
Scofield	46	16
Spring Glen	12	6
Wellington	35	12
Winter Quarters	30	29
Total	219	169

Thayn, Democrat, elected.

Coroner—

	H. B. Asadorian. Rep.	J. H. Eccles.	I. Llewellyn.
Castle Gate	61		
Helper	30		
Minnie Maude	15		
Price	78		
Scofield	48	1	1
Spring Glen	13		
Wellington	45		
Winter Quarters	29		
Total	321	1	1

Asadoorian, Republican, elected.

Selectmen.

	J. B. Beattie, Dem.	G. C. Johnson, Dem.	Thomas Cox, Sr., Dem.	E. Santschi, Rep.	F. P. Gridley, Rep.	E. C. Lee, Rep.	Thos. L. Boulhan, Citizen.	Peter Liddell, Citizen.	Andrew Young, Citizen.	C. H. Sturges
Castle Gate	16	5	29	40	28	27	7	15	39	
Helper	20		1	1	1	7	7	23	2	
Minnie Maude	5	7	5	8	5	11				
Price	22	13	19	68	71	74	1	5	4	
Scofield	21	11	16	12	24	17	6	20	23	31
Spring Glen	8	3	4	8	8	7	7	7	7	
Wellington	6			10	13	14	26	35	34	
Winter Quart's	32	21	23	17	14	12	3	8	5	4
Totals	135	53	33	163	159	157	133	142	29	

The three Republicans, Gridley, Santschi and Lee, head the list.

Superintendent of District Schools—

	J. W. Davis. Dem.	H. A. Southworth. Citizen.
Castle Gate	52	14
Helper	1	20
Minnie Maude	18	
Price	89	5
Scofield	34	28
Spring Glen	11	5
Wellington	16	31
Winter Quarters	41	8
Totals	262	122

Davis, Democrat, elected.

PRECINCT OFFICERS.

CASTLE GATE

Justice of the Peace—
Robert Williams 79
H. J. World 47
Thomas Cox, Sr., Dem.

World, Republican, elected.
Constable—
Grover Lewis 47
Ed Edwards 15

HELPER

Justice of the Peace—
Peter A. Smith 25
Constable—
J. H. Brady 25

MINNIE MAUDE.

Justice of the Peace—
A. J. Russell 15
E. C. Lee 3
Constable—
Frank Smith 17

PRICE

Justice of the Peace—
C. W. Allred 7
E. W. McIntire 74
Constable—
Jake Kofford 13
E. Anderson 70

SCOFIELD.

Justice of the Peace—
Henry Wilson 51
S. J. Harkness 2
Constable—
Thomas Lloyd 2
C. J. Jensen 47
John S. Price 3

SPRING GLEN.

Justice of the Peace—
J. M. Miller 9
John T. Rowley 2
C. H. Cook 9
Constable—
A. J. Simmons 11
J. H. Ewell 1
J. N. Perkins 1

WELLINGTON.

Justice of the Peace—
L. Jensen 32
E. Thayn 10
Constable—
S. H. Grundrig 34
J. B. Roberts 7

WINTER QUARTERS.

Justice of the Peace—
S. A. Harrison 22
S. D. Reese 16
Constable—
Joseph Loveridge 27
Joseph Richards 22

Salt Lake Herald
July 29, 1894

THE UTAH COMMISSION.

MORE DEPUTY ELECTION REGISTRARS APPOINTED YESTERDAY.

CARBON COUNTY.

Castle Gate—Harry World.
Spring Glen—Elliott Miller.
Helper—James X. Ferguson.
Wellington—John Maxmullen.
Winter Quarters—J. M. Beatie.
Scofield—Charles A. Robinson.
Minnie Maud—Fred Grames.
Price—J. H. Sarvis.

EMERY COUNTY.

Castle Dale—R. C. Miller.
Cleveland—H. H. Oviatt, sr.
Ferron—T. O. Borreson.
Huntington—C. D. Cram.
Lawrence—P. C. Bearch.
Muddy—S. M. Williams.
Molen—N. C. Larsen.
Orangeville—George Fox.

Deseret Weekly
August 18, 1894

The quarterly conference of the Emery Stake of Zion convened at Price, August 5th and 6th, 1894. Elders John H. Smith and Heber J. Grant, of the Council of the Apostles, the Stake presidency, and many of the leading members of the Priesthood from the various wards were present. The brethren of Price had prepared a comfortable bowery, and President Larsen called for the attention of the audience at 10 a. m. After singing and prayer, the condition of the Stake was reported by President Larsen. He said the health of the people was good. Peace generally prevails. The Stake and ward organizations are complete with few exceptions. Meetings are well attended, yet there are a few very careless members among us who need laboring with. Money is scarce, but we have prospects of a most bountiful harvest.

Bishops Fransden of Price, McMullin of Wellington, and Fulmer of Spring Glen then reported their wards, corroborating in almost every particular the president's statements.

Elder John Henry Smith followed. He was pleased to meet with the Saints of Emery Stake under such favorable circumstances, and felt thankful to hear such good reports from the Stake and wards. He said the Gospel embraces all truth and will exalt all who observe its laws. He encouraged all to beautify their homes and make a grove for public gatherings in every ward. He thought the aged in our midst were not treated with that respect and veneration that they deserved; this is displeasing before the Lord; we show our love of God by aiding His children.

At 2 p.m. the sacrament was administered by the Priesthood of Price, after which Elder O. Seeley spoke briefly. Bishops Lamph, of Castle Gate, and Ovesen, of Cleveland, reported their wards.

Elder Heber J. Grant occupied the remaining time on the subjects of improvement, faith, home industry and the Word of Wisdom. He said that if for no other reason the Saints should observe the Word of Wisdom from a financial standpoint, as one million dollars is sent out of Utah every year for tea, coffee and tobacco. The speaker made much merriment by asserting that the hearts of the Latter-day Saints were all right but their heads or (judgment) needed fixing.

At the second day's services, Elder William Howard made opening remarks, commenting on the good instructions of the previous meetings and explaining some of the differences between Latter-day Saints and other religions of the world. He urged parents to set worthy examples.

Bishops Moore, of Lawrence, Johnson, of Huntington, Olson, of Castle Dale, and Robertson, of Orangeville, thought their wards about the same as others reported.

Elder Smith next spoke on the evils of cigarette smoking, especially among the boys; said leading officers in the Priesthood by all means should keep the Word of Wisdom. Church government and prayer were each beautifully explained by the speaker. Mothers were asked in the most earnest manner, to teach their little ones to lisp the name of their Creator in prayer.

At 2 p.m. Bishop Olsen, of Ferron, and Counselor Williams, of Emery, reported their respective wards as in good condition. Elder Uriah Curtis, superintendent of the Sunday schools of Emery Stake, spoke of the good work being done in the schools since adopting the new system.

The totals of the Stake statistical report were then read.

Elder Grant explained that only those teachings that we put in practice did us any good; economy should be practiced in all our expenditures; idleness should be discouraged among this people. Round dancing and getting into debt were both spoken against. "Do not get what you cannot pay for at once."

The General and Stake authorities were sustained.

A Priesthood meeting was held Sunday evening and almost the entire time taken upin urging the brethren to keep the Word of Wisdom.

The meetings were all well attended and an excellent spirit prevailed. Singing was beautifully rendered by the choir of Price, Wellington and Spring Glen, under the direction of Brother Cox, of Price.

A. E. WALL, Stake Clerk.

CARBON COUNTY DEMOCRATS.

County of Black Diamonds in Line For Success.

Price, Utah, Sept. 12.—[Special to The Herald.]—The Democracy of Carbon county met at Price on Tuesday and selected a new county committee, named delegates to the territorial Democratic convention, arranged for a joint meeting of Emery and Carbon to select three candidates for the constitutional convention, and set on foot plans for a vigorous local and district campaign.

At 2 p. m. the Price cornet band summoned the unterrified to the place of meeting and a temporary organization was soon effected, with Hon. L. M. Olson, as chairman, and Emmett Lynch as secretary.

Committees on Credentials—J. P. Hite, H. Fiak, J. L. Wilson, T. Rhodes, Thomas Faris; and on organization and order of business, composed of H. J. World, Joseph Jones, and E. Miller, were named, and submitted unanimous reports, making the preliminary organization permanent with all but one precinct represented.

D. O. RIDOUT, JR., TALKS.

During the absence of the committees the convention was briefly addressed by Hon. D. O. Rideout, jr., of Salt Lake county. For half an hour he presented the cause of Democracy in able and eloquent terms, and in a manner to both charm and entertain. He was greeted with loud and repeated applause.

TO CONFER WITH EMERY.

The chair announced that a delegation of five from Emery county were present and desired to confer with a like number from Carbon for the purpose of arranging a joint convention for the two counties. On motion B. F. Caffey, J. H. Van Natta, G. C. Johnson, H. Miller and John Haweny were appointed.

J. H. Sarvis, B. F. Caffey, Thomas E. Davis, J. H. Van Natta and Emmett Lynch were then named as delegates to the Territorial Democratic convention, after which a new county central committee was chosen, consisting of E. L. Harman, Minnie Maud, J. S. Thomas, Winter, Quarters; J. M. Fossett, Wellington; J. H. Sarvis, Price; H. J. World, Castle Gate; L. M. Olson, Price, and Nathan Miller, Spring Glen.

Hon. L. M. Olson was made chairman and J. H. Sarrris secretary of the new committee.

ALL FOR RAWLINS.

Emmett Lynch presented a resolution endorsing the territorial and national platforms of 1892 as well as the doctrines laid down in the address issued by the Democracy at the convention of June 16, 1894, and concluding with a hearty endorsement of the official acts of Delegate Rawlins in the last Congress and requesting the delegates to Salt Lake to work for his renomination.

This brought forth the most enthusiastic cheers, as did every reference to the distinguished young Democrat made during the day, and was unanimously adopted.

REGISTRATION MATTERS.

Several of the registrars for Carbon county met Hon. J. R. Letcher, chairman of the Utah commission, here and had a talk over matters pertaining to their work. At the close of the convention the people assembled in the Bowery and listened to a talk from Mr. Letcher on questions affecting the double election machinery and the importance of selecting good men to the constitutional convention.

Ogden Daily Standard
October 17, 1894

JUDGES OF ELECTION.

Utah Commission Makes the Following Appointments.

EMERY.

Blake, A D Thompson, D, R P Johnson, D; G A Stanton, R.

Castle Dale, C E Larsen, D; John W Lake, D; G H Branor, R.

Cleveland, Lewis Larson, D; George T Oviatt, D; Adolph Axelson, R.

Ferron, Robert E King, D; R W Curtis, D; James Henry, R.

Huntington, J F Wakefield, Sr, D; D M Tyler, D; J E Johnson, R.

Lawrence, Ole N Tuft, D; Henry Roper, D; L Lewis, R.

Molen, James H Cooke, D; Edward Larson, D; H O Hanson, R.

Muddy (Emery), Nephi Williams, D; H C. Larson, D; P V Banderson, R.

Orangeville, A O Van Buren, D; Charles H Oliphant, D; H W Reid, R.

Woodside, J E Randall, D; Jacob Coleman, D; Eli Randell, R.

CARBON.

Castle Gate, B F Caffey, D; William Ingall, D; Robert Williams, R.

H[....], J H Van Natta, Thomas Rhodes, D; John A Bigelow, R.

Minnie Maud, E L Harmon, D; G C Johnson, D; J A Lee, R.

Price, J P Hurt, D; C H Empey, D; J B Millburn, R.

Spring Glen, William Miller, D; John T Rowley, D; C H Cooke, R.

Scofield, W C Burrows, D; N L McLean, D; O G Kimball, R.

Winter Quarters, T J Palmer, D; Thomas Farrish, D; J B Schiness, R.

Wellington, George A Wilson, D; E E Branch, D; H F Hansen, R.

Deseret Evening News
December 31, 1894

IN THE COAL REGION.

"Traveler's" Notes in Carbon County and the Near Vicinity.

Work in the coal mines in Pleasant Valley is slack; for the last month the men have not put in over half time. The mines are in excellent condition to turn out a large amount of coal if worked up to full capacity. The Pleasant Valley company's mine at Winter Quarters could put out twelve hundred ton a day if crowded. This is a well managed and admirably arranged mine, turning out an excellent quality of coal. F. J. Parmley is in charge. The coal is hauled out by an electric motor and they have a real underground railway on which one may ride for over a mile into the tunnel at the rate of fifteen miles an hour. Your representative took this ride, seated on some grain sacks in a coal car. The sensation was peculiar as we dashed along trying to keep our nerves steady and hold onto the miner's lamp that had been given us. The sudden turns, the gloom of darkness only lit up by the glare of the electric light on the motor and the feeble light of a miner's lamp made it quite a sensational ride. We must have walked at least eight miles visiting the different workings. There are at present about 250 men employed in and around this mine. The company has just erected an addition to their barn, 30x40 feet, to accommodate their animals, of which they have quite a number.

The Wasatch Store Co. run a store in connection with the mine and the day before Christmas distributed 125 turkeys to their patrons as a Christmas present.

The Latter-day Saints have a comfortable meeting house and a live ward organization, and hold meetings at Winter Quarters and at Scofield, which are well attended.

The U. P. mine at Scofield has now about one hundred employes and there is a store in connection with this mine. Ingles & Ballantyne also do quite a business. The postoffice is kept by Mr. Earl, about half-way between the two mining camps, and is out of the way for each. There should be a change and a postoffice established at Scofield, centrally located, and one at Winter Quarters, to accommodate the people, as the present arrangement is very unhandy and expensive.

The Pleasant Valley Mining Co. is now opening another excellent mine opposite the present workings that when properly developed will give them unexcelled facilities to produce coal in large quantities and will establish this as a permanent coal mining center. There is considerable snow on the ground here and prospects of more, while the air at this altitude is quite cold, as we are about 7,832 feet above the sea level, and can feel the difference in the air between here and Salt Lake valley.

Wm. Howell is now acting as agent for the DESERET NEWS in this locality and has quite a nice circulation.

NOTES AT CASTLE GATE.

The scene at Castle Gate looking down the canyon from above the town is quite brilliant at night, as the coke ovens send up a red glare that is relieved by the brighter light of the big electric lamps. There are now about fifty coke ovens in active operation here; the mine is kept running quite regularly and all the slack it produces is made into coke. The vein of coal in this mine is not very thick, being only between four and five feet, yet it is very hard and makes fair coke. It lies on the top of a big ledge of sandstone, while there is another ledge above it. The mine is partially lit up by electricity and the coal drawn out by the electric cable, and all the shots in blasting the coal are fired by electricity in the evening after the men are out of the mine. The dust in this mine is apt to explode, hence the precaution to fire the shots while the men are out. The mine is also regularly watered to keep the dust damp to prevent accidents.

This mine is located in Price canyon about twelve miles from that town, and there are now about 250 men employed in and around it, while there are about 50 men employed at the coke ovens. This place is on the main line of the R. G. W. near the famous Castle Gate and about six miles from Helper, the end of division, and where the railway company have a round house and shops.

The Latter-day Saints have a ward organization here and a respectable meeting house. Wm. T. Lamph is the Bishop. The people here are not without amusements. A local company is now rehearsing to give a theatrical performance on New Year's eve. The camp boasts a very good brass band that would do credit to a more pretentious place.

Snow has been falling here for the last two days, and the weather has been cold. Trains are passing on time. The officers elected in this county went to Price to qualify yesterday. Yet the question who the selectmen were to qualify before has not been settled. The law says they are to go before the probate judge, but there has been no probate judge appointed for this county, so they have none to approve their bonds. Some of the people feel to criticise Uncle Grover for not gratifying somebody's ambition to become probate judge.

David L. Evans will look after the interests of the DESERET NEWS at Castle Gate from now on and the subscribers will get good service.

TRAVELER.

CASTLE GATE, Carbon Co., Dec. 29, 1894.

Deseret Evening News
January 10, 1895

Scofield and Winter Quarters.

A sad accident happened at the U. P. mine at Scofield on Wednesday, January 2nd, to D. D. Green, a miner.

He was working at a piece of coal, standing on a ladder, when the coal broke away, knocking him down and fatally injuring him. He died on Monday at 11 o'clock. He was about 45 years of age and leaves several children, some of which are quite small, with no mother, she having died some time ago.

Three men by the name of Lloyd and one by the name of Smith killed a beef at Scofield belonging to a Mr. Whitmore, of Price, for which they were bound over to await the action of the grand jury in bonds of $300 each.

We are having winter in earnest now, both snow and frost.

The flanger runs between Scofield and Winter Quarters pretty often to clear the track.

The Latter-day Saints in this part hold their fast meetings on the first Sunday in each month. Last Sunday being the first in the new year, many new resolutions were made. We had a very interesting meeting at Winter Quarters, several young men and young women bearing faithful testimonies. A MORMON BOY.

Deseret Evening News
January 30, 1895

Scofield and Winter Quarters.

SCOFIELD, Jan. 28, 1895.—We are having very cold weather up here. This morning at 5 o'clock it was thirty-two below zero.

Things are pretty quiet at present. The Winter Quarters mine has not worked for several days, for want of cars, the railroad blockades out west being the cause. The Scofield mine has worked fourteen days this month, which is much better than usual.

Robbie Burns was not forgotten at Scofield this year, a grand ball being held in commemoration of the 136th anniversary of his birthday.

Charles Greenland lost a little girl, three years old, last Saturday, croup being the cause.

Mr. J. B. Shiness left for the capital this morning.   A MORMON BOY.

Provo Dispatch
February 11, 1895

NEWS FROM SCOFIELD.

Plenty of Snow The Carbon County Teachers Meet—Shipping Coal to California—Other Matters.

SCOFIELD, Feb. 10.—[Correspondence DISPATCH.]—After a week of fine weather a foot of snow was added to the already deep coat that Scofield has had all winter. If abundance of snow in the mountains means good harvests, then the farmers will be blessed this year. The snow is nearly fence high up here.

The Carbon County Teachers association met here on Friday last. They discussed educational questions during the afternoon session, and in the evening the following program was rendered: Trio, "Old Kentucky Home;" soprano solo, "The Lover and the Bird," Mrs. R. Hood; comic song. "There Are Moments When One Wants to be Alone," J. H. Davis; recitation, "The Black Horse and His Rider," Mrs. Conyingham; duett, "The Lost Ship," Jno. H. Davis and Jno. Hood; address on county school teaching by Superintendent J. Davis; instrumental duett, "Hear Me, Norma," Jno. Hood and Miss M. Strang; comic song. "Sneezing," Mr. Webb; recitation, Mr. Rose of Wellington; address. "Experience in School Teaching," Mr. Webb of Winter Quarters; recitation, Mrs. Conyingham.

A crowded house greeted the performers and the numbers were well rendered. Credit is due Mrs Conyingham of the Scofield school for the manner in which the affair was conducted. Superintendent Davis was well pleased with the condition of the school here.

The U. P. mine has only worked one day this month owing to lack of orders. The Winter Quarters mine is working every day, they having received a heavy order from California.

The work on the old Rio Grande mines, Nos. 1 and 3 is being pushed as rapidly as possible. The rock in which the tunnel is being driven is very hard, and the progress is slow. Superintendent Sharp came up from Castle Gate the other day and examined the tunnel. He has called for bids on the rockwork as the quickest way to get through it. A great many bids are in, as the lucky bidders are sure of a year's employment. The bids will be opened on Tuesday next.

The sickness which attacked so many children here in the beginning of the year has disappeared.

The Y. L. M. I. A. have issued invitations to a ball on Valentine's evening. It promises to be a success.

        J. H.

Deseret Evening News
March 4, 1895

Scofield and Winter Quarters.

SCOFIELD, Feb. 28, 1895.—The coal trade has fallen off and the general cry here is dull times. The P. V. Coal company has given notice to their employes at Winter Quarters that there will be very little work for some time, and advises those who were going to leave in the spring to do so now.

There are several cases of scarlet fever at this place. Mr. Lee Gordon lost a son last Monday from it, aged 2 years and three months.

Superintendent Grilley, of the U. P. mine, has tendered his resignation.

Superintendent H. A. Nelson, of the Wasatch Store company, came up from Castle Gate today.

The vote for constable for Winter Quarters resulted in a tie at the last election. There has been no action taken in the case since. Will the News please inform us what should be done and who should do it.

A MORMON BOY.

Provo Dispatch
March 9, 1895

NEW SUIT FILED.

L. M. Olson of Price, Emery county, is suing the Price Water company for $170 00 and for $415.00, and costs. He alleges that the officers of the company fraudulently and without the knowledge of himself transferred to A. M. Horsley and C. H. Taylor 170 shares of his stock in the company; also that they did fraudulently transfer to A. Ballinger and C. H. Taylor, 415 shares of the stock of M. Conner whose claim against the defendants, Mr. Olson has purchased. Horsley, Ballinger and Taylor are alleged to be officers and directors in the defendant corporation.

Provo Dispatch
March 14, 1895

SCOFIELD NEWS.

Henry Freckleton's Arm Ground to Pieces.

RARE PRESENCE OF MIND.

Expense of Forming the New County of Carbon—A Musical Contest Coming—Miss Arrowsmith's Light Sentence Complained of—Other Matters.

SCOFIELD, March 12,—[Correspondence of THE DISPATCH.]—This place is enjoying a season of very expensive quietness. The mines here and at Winter Quarters are almost at a stand still. The U. P. mine has only worked three days this month, and only four days in February. Winter Quarters mine has only worked two days this month. At the last named mine a notice is up asking men who intend leaving for their farms to do so at once as the company does not wish to discharge men.

The latest event on the tapis is the arranging for an "eisteddfod" or musical contest to be held here in June next. A committee of thirteen has the affair in hand and they are pushing matters with energy. Three hundred dollars will be given prizes to be divided among the choirs and soloists who may compete. A prize of $100 will be given for the best rendition of "The Last Rose" by a choir of from thirty to sixty voices, and a prize of $60 for the best rendition of "The Summer," by a choir. Fifty dollars is offered for the brass band which renders "The Witch Dance" best. There will be a male chorus prize; one for a female chorus; a cornet solo; piccolo solo; solos for bass, baritone, tenor, contralto, and soprano, duetts and quartetts. Altogether the affair promises to be a grand one, and if proper encouragement is given it will be a success.

A very serious accident occurred yesterday at Castle Gate, whereby a man by the name of Harry Freckleton lost his arm. He was employed running an electric hoisting engine, and while moving around he slipped and fell forward. His arm was caught in the cogwheels and ground to pieces in an instant. He had presence of mind enough to pull away from the engine or he would likely have lost his life, he reached with his other hand and secured a hatchet and cut his sleeve loose in order to free himself from his perilous position. He was entirely alone and had to walk some distance in the mine before finding help. He was taken to the hospital in Salt Lake this morning.

Selectman Ballantyne has just returned from Price where he has been attending the county court. The court is now thoroughly organized with Judge Olsen at the head, and they ran through a large amount of business last week. They audited all the accounts of the last court and attended to all matters pertaining to county business. The expenses attached to creating the new county of Carbon amounted to $1689.47, and the other expenses for running the county without salaries was $2,404.47 from the creation of the new county until the close of 1894. The amount for salaries was $2,099.98.

A great deal of indignation was expressed when the news of Miss Arrowsmith's light sentence reached here. A great many people think that there is a premium set upon crime now-a-days, and that when a crime is committed, to avert punishment, all that is needed is a cleverly worded petition. The great question in the minds of the people here is whether the mail service is safe now when male handlers get off so easy after stealing money and valuables from the mail intrusted to Uncle Sam. The amounts said to have been taken by this girl Arrowsmith would pay quite a number of $25 00 fines.

Talk about spring! There is about two feet of the beautiful in this neck o' the woods, and the prospect is that it will stay several weeks yet.

The news of President Smoot's death was received here with many expressions of sorrow. The venerable president held a very warm corner in the hearts of the people here. Bishop Parmley attended the funeral services.

J. H.

Salt Lake Herald
March 17, 1895

DIED.

FREKLESON—At St. Mary's hospital, this city, Saturday, March 16th, at 3 a. m., Henry Frekleson; born July 16, 1863, at Slamannan, Scotland.

Funeral will be held at Castle Gate, to which place the body will be shipped.

Deseret Weekly
April 13, 1895

SCOFIELD AND WINTER QUARTERS.

SCOFIELD, April 8, 1895.—The U. P. mine is working from four to six days a month which makes things very quiet. The Winter Quarters mine is working nearly full time since the No 5 mine at Almy stopped.

Mr. J. M. Loveridge has been appointed constable for Winter Quarters precinct by the county court to succeed himself. Joe makes a very good officer and keeps the boys pretty straight.

Thos. Farish had quite an experience the other day in trying to cross the mountains from Castle valley to Pleasant valley on horseback. After wallowing through the snow till nearly dark he encountered a drift so deep and soft that he was compelled to turn back, and had it not been for Miller Bros.' ranch, where he found food and shelter for the night, he might have perished. The next day he got back home and concluded to leave his horse and take the stage to Price, thence to Scofield by rail.

We are pleased to state that Brother Richard T. Evans is recovering from the severe attack of brain fever from which he has been suffering. His parents are up from Castle Dale and are assisting his wife to nurse him back to health.

Dr. Smith has been appointed quarantine physician for this district.

A MORMON BOY.

Deseret Weekly
April 27, 1895

SCOFIELD, April 16th, 1895.—Levi Reese Jr., was killed at Castle Gate, Sunday evening last, by jumping on the westbound passenger train, just for fun. He missed his hold and fell between the cars as the train was moving at a good speed. Death was instantaneous. He was 22 years of age, unmarried. The funeral took place at Scofield today. Quit a number of people came up from the Gate.

Alex Wilson got his foot crushed in the Winter Quarter's mine and has gone to the hospital at Salt Lake for treatment.

SCOFIELD, May 6, 1895.—We have had considerable snow the last week and part of the time it was quite cold. Things are very quiet in these parts, not much building or improving, but Mr. Frank Merewether is preparing to build an addition to his residence.

England and Iceland joined hands in wedlock the other day in the persons of John Carrick, of Winterquarters, 25, and Eva Goodmanson, 20, of Spanish Fork.

Prof. John Hood has been teaching the school children of Schofield music for about two months and last Friday evening they gave a concert which reflected great credit upon both instructor and performers.

SCOFIELD, May 8th, 1895.—Mr. John P. Johnson, of Winter Quarters, had a baby boy die yesterday of pneumonia. He was 18 months old. He will be buried at Scofield tomorrow.

The Eisteddfod that is to take place here in June promises to be a grand success. The committee has made arrangements with the railroads for a rate of one-half fare from all points in Utah. They have already received letters from several places asking about places to stay at.

A MORMON BOY.

SCHOFIELD, May 21, 1895.—The U. P. Coal company is paying their employes today for the month of April.

The district school house is being repaired by Contractor John Eccles. Among other improvements a bell is to be placed in a neat tower on the west end of the building.

Wednesday evening, May 22nd, a concert and ball will be given by the Schofield contest choir.

Supt. W. G. Sharp visited the Winter Quarters mine today.

Supt. J. P. Gridley made a flying visit to Schofield yesterday. Mr. Gridley spends most of his time of late at the Ham's Fork mines in Wyoming.

MORMON BOY.

Scofield and Winter Quarters.

SCOFIELD, June 10th, 1895.—We have had considerable snow here lately and it is rather chilly yet.

The Winter Quarters mine is working half time, while the Scofield mine is working about one third time.

Some of the boys up at Winter Quarters have been in the habit of making a disturbance around the meeting house during choir practice, etc., until it became unbearable, so the other day the constable rounded up seven of them and took them before the justice. They were fined $5.90 each, including costs.

There has been considerable sickness among the children hereabouts, caused, it is claimed, by the inclemency of the weather.

Everybody and their cousins at Winter Quarters are cleaning up their yards, which is giving the camp quite a respectable appearance.

The county court of Carbon county has adopted a code of quarantine regulations affecting all parts of the county not included in the limits of incorporated towns, which if adhered to strictly, should materially aid in preventing the spread of contagious disease.

Sheriff T. Lloyd has returned from Price, where he has been attending the county court.

Mrs. T. J. Parmeley is visiting friends at Coalville.

Mr. and Mrs. J. R. Davis, of Spanish Fork, are spending a few days with their sons. MORMON BOY.

SCOFIELD, June 10th, 1895.—We have had considerable snow here lately and it is rather chilly yet.

The Winter Quarters mine is working half time, while the Scofield mine is working about one third time.

Some of the boys up at Winter Quarters have been in the habit of making a disturbance around the meeting house during choir practice, etc., until it became unbearable, so the other day the constable rounded up seven of them and took them before the justice. They were fined $5.90 each, including costs.

There has been considerable sickness among the children hereabouts, caused, it is claimed, by the inclemency of the weather.

Everybody and their cousins at Winter Quarters are cleaning up their yards, which is giving the camp quite a respectable appearance.

The county court of Carbon county has adopted a code of quarantine regulations affecting all parts of the county not included in the limits of incorporated towns, which if adhered to strictly, should materially aid in preventing the spread of contagious diseases.

Sheriff T. Lloyd has returned from Price, where he has been attending the county court.

Mrs. T. J. Parmeley is visiting friends at Coalville.

Mr. and Mrs. J. R. Davis, of Spanish Fork, are spending a few days with their sons.   MORMON BOY.

Scofield Eistedfodd.

There are about 2500 at Scofield celebrating the eistedfodd. Prominent Welshmen are present from all parts of Utah. Arthur L. Thomas was given an ovation and delivered an address. Following Governor Thomas's remarks came the day's contests. The prize for the tenor was awarded to R. J. Thomas of Salt Lake; for tenor and bass duet to William T. and Richard T. Evans of Winter Quarters. The prize for the best recitation was divided between Mrs. H. Anderson and Hector Evans of Scofield. Evan Stephens's chorus, "Mother's Lullaby," was won by the Scofield Ladies' Club, led by John Hood. Best comic song, Peter Elliott, Salt Lake; soprano solo, Miss Davies, Lehi, contralto, Mrs. John Hood, Scofield.

CAUGHT IN A CAVE-IN.

A Finlander named Koski, was ——ed by a cave-in at a coal mine in a ——named Winter Quarters and brought to Salt Lake last night. —— operation will be performed by physicians today and until this is —— the extent of his injuries will n—— known.

SCOFIELD'S BIG EVENT.

IT WAS A SUCCESS FROM START TO FINISH.

Prizes Were Scattered to All Parts of the Territory, and the Efforts Made By All Were Praiseworthy in the Extreme.

Scofield, June 27.—(Correspondence of The Herald.)—Our great musical contest, the eisteddfod, is over and the people have departed for their homes. The affair was a splendid success from every point. The committee having the affair in charge worked assiduously and the result is that Scofield will more than likely hold an annual eisteddfod for the encouragement of the divine art. The adjudicators were authorized in our circulars to divide prizes, and they exercised this authority with a vengeance, as the report will show. As a consequence, the people from the different places, friends of the contestants, all think they are the favored ones, which is a happy state of affairs and an extraordinary one for the adjudicators to produce. They seemed to strive to please everybody, so that the committee might be induced to continue eisteddfod work in future years.

The officers selected by the committee all arrived on Tuesday and at 3 o'clock ex-Governor Thomas, J. J. Davis (Fenan Ddu), Prof. E. Beesley, Prof. L. D. Edwards, Prof. H. E. Giles, together with members of the committee, mounted the stand and the eisteddfod was declared open. A. L. Thomas, as president of the day, was introduced, and he made a speech extolling the Welsh people to a great extent and ended by wishing success to the eisteddfod.

At the conclusion of this address J. J. Davis addressed the Welsh people in their native tongue.

Mr. J. R. Sharp, of Scofield, then called the contestants for the tenor solo forward, and the following gentlemen responded: W. T. Evans, Winterquarters; Thomas Snowden, Scofield; Thomas Farrish, Castle Valley; R. J. Thomas, Salt Lake. The solo was "Anchored," and Mr. Thomas was declared the winner.

The tenor and bass duett, "The Two Sailors," was the next number, but there was only one entry, W. T. and R. T. Evans, of Winterquarters. They were highly complimented for their rendition and were awarded the prize.

The recitation for adults, "The Polish Boy," called forth two contestants, Mr. Hector Evans and Mrs. Hannah Anderson, and the prize was equally divided.

The next number was the ladies' chorus, "Mother's Lullaby." Only one chorus entered, the Scofield ladies' chorus led by Mr. John Hood. The adjudicators declared their rendition to be very fine and extended compliments to them.

Second Session.

The second session opened with Mr. J. R. Sharp as president, A. L. Thomas having been urgently called to Salt Lake.

The first on the programme was the comic song contest. There were five entries, and the prize was awarded to Peter Elliot, of Salt Lake. The songs caused a great deal of enthusiasm.

The contralto solo, "He Shall Feed His Flock," from the Messiah, was the next contest. Mrs. Mary Hood was the only contestee, but she gave an excellent rendition of it, and was highly complimented by Prof. Edwards.

The choir contest on the Welsh Glee, "The Summer," was the next numbrr. The entries were Scofield, John Hood, leader; Winter Quarters, T. C. Reese, leader; Castle Valley, Thomas Hardee, leader. The prize of $50 was divided between Scofield and Castle Valley. The former had six points against them and the latter had four points. The decision was very unsatisfactory and not in accordance with the marks placed on the copies of the adjudicators. The copies show that Scofield was entitled to the prize by heavy odds, but they took their medicine as it was administered.

Third Session.

This session opened on Tuesday morning at 2 o'clock with J. R. Sharp in the chair. The first on the programme was the adjudication of Welsh and English poetical composition. J. J. Davis, the adjudicator, gave the decision on the Welsh poetry in Welsh. The subject was, "The Freedom of Our Country," but only one composition was received. However, the adjudicator gave the composer a good adjudication, pointing out the errors and praising the good points in such a style as to show the poet how to improve.

There were two compositions on the English poetry, subject, "Freedom of Our Country." The prize was awarded to James Dunn, of Tooele, who tendered a fine composition on the subject. The adjudication on this was also delivered in an excellent manner.

The next contest was the bass solo, "The Wolf." John Hood was the only entry, but he won an excellent report from the adjudicators, who said the rendition was such as might have been expected from a professional.

The recitation for children was won by Annie Snowden, of Scofield.

The male voice catch was the next number. The Huntington (Castle Valley) Glee club was the only entry. They sang "Call John," and were awarded the prize.

The impromptu lecture called forth eight contestants. The speakers were confined to five minutes, but some only occupied half a minute. The adjudicators declared for D. C. Woodward, of Castle Valley; John James, Salt Lake, second; and R. W. Gibbs, Scofield, third.

This number caused much laughter and applause.

Only one brass band entered the contest—the Castle Gate band—but they rendered the contest piece, "The Witch Dance," in excellent style.

Prof. Edwards paid them a glowing tribute for their rendition. The $45 and metranome were awarded to them.

Fourth Session.

The interest of the whole contest centered in this session. The building was crowded to suffocation and many could not obtain admission. After an opening selection by the Castle Gate brass band, the male chorus contest was announced.

There were two entries, Scofield and Winterquarters; the former led by John Hood and the latter by T. C. Reese. Both choruses were horribly rendered, but the former was by far the best rendition. The points were 14 against Scofield and 25 against Winterquarters; but the adjudicators, in a vain effort to please all, divided the prize giving $15 to Scofield and $10 to Winterquarters. This caused a great deal of indignation.

The baritone solo was next announced. Four contestants appeared: W. T. Evans, R. T. Evans, Andrew Hood and John James. The adjudicators were not satisfied as to John James and R. T. Evans, and they were requested to sing again. The prize was awarded to Mr. Evans, but here again the adjudicators were censured. Mr. James is a cultured baritone and gave an excellent rendition, but the prize was awarded to Mr. Evans, although there is no doubt in the minds of any listener as to Mr. James' superiority.

The excitement at this point was intense, but suppressed. The choir contest on the chief piece was the cause of the excitement. The same choir which sang in "The Summer," entered for this contest. They sang in the following order: Scofield, Winterquarters, Castle Valley. The adjudication was: Scofield four points against; Winterquarters six points against; Castle Valley six points against. The prize of $100 was then divided as follows: Scofield, 30; Winterquarters, $30; Castle Valley, $40. Anyone can see that there is something wrong here. The choir with the least points against got the least money, while the choir with six against received the most. The Scofield choir sang the piece "The Last Rose," according to the metranome time marked on the copies. The first movement is 88; the second movement 96 and the third movement 88. Castle Valley sang it: First movement 48; second movement 108; third movement 48 or 50. This was not taken into consideration at all by the adjudicators. The copies used by Mr. Edwards in adjudicating show only four points against Scofield, while they show seven points against Castle Valley. Winterquarters rendered the piece in a horrible style and consequently should not have been considered at all, but they were awarded the same amount as Scofield. Aside from this Prof. Edwards said to Mr. Hood, the leader of the Scofield choir, before leaving Scofield, that he did not want any feelings to exist, and that Scofield would expect to have another eisteddfod and he did not want to hurt it. He added: "It is enough for you to know that you are the best man, and the prize will make little difference to you. You are a young man with a bright future before you." When this is taken into consideration there is little doubt as to the fairness of the adjudication. The people here and at Winterquarters are indignat over this work.

The concert in the evening, in which the successful contestants took part, was also crowded and the songs were all excellent. If it were not for crowding your columns an extended report would prove interesting.

Prof. H. E. Giles proved an efficient accompanist and deserved the excellent opinion in which the people of this place hold him. By the way, Provo does not appreciate the excellence of Prof. Giles as it should do. He is a gem of a musician, an accompanist of extraordinary ability and withal modest in his accomplishments, which adds greater charm to him as a man. He has earned laurels here and a warm corner in the hearts of the people.

The railroad company generously tendered the committee the use of the roundhouse and the committee converted it into a bower of beauty by decorations of evergreens and bunting. It has a seating capacity of 1,290, and each session was well crowded.

Salt Lake Herald
July 5, 1895

REGISTRARS NAMED.

UTAH COMMISSION HAS BEGUN ITS ANTE-ELECTION LABORS.

Carbon County.

Castle Gate, W. T. Lamph; Helper, Thomas Rhodes; Minnie Maud, E. L. Harmon; Price, P. I. Olsen; Scofield, J. E. Ingle; Spring Glen, Thomas Rowley; Wellington, E. E. Branch; Winter Quarters, J. M. Beatle; Garfield county.

Carbon Condensations.

[ENQUIRER Correspondence.]

The Republican party organization of Carbon county is being admirably managed. Recently the committee met and elected the following as the officers: A. Ballenger, chairman; James Rooney, vice-chairman; C. B. Snyder, secretary. The committee, including the foregoing, consists of J. K. Ferguson, of Helper; J. A. Harrison, of Castle Gate; S. A. Harrison, of Winter Quarters; W. H. Donaldson, of Scofield; F. M. Ewell, Spring Glen; Geo. A. Wilson, Sen., of Wellington, and E. C. Lee, of Lee's.

W. L. Pickard, Salt Lake's well known wool man, stopped off here on the 24th on his return from Uintah, where he had been making some wool negotiations.

Dr. Hathenbruck was in Price on Wednesday.

Elder R.J. Dugdale, of Provo, preached in the Latter-day Saints meeting house on Sunday.

The Price Trading store has all week been the usual center of business activity. Scarcely a day has passed for a month or more that has not found from 25 to 50 teams surrounding this hive of trade.

D. W. Holdaway is a popular assessor and collector. The Republicans made an excellent choice when they elected him to that office.

Rio Grande Western trains, both "going and coming," are every day crowded with passengers.

Price has a brass band that any Utah town may be proud of.

Mrs. C. B. Snyder is a genial hostess. Under her discipline the Price hotel is a model home for the wayfaring drummer.

The office of the Castle Valley News is situate next door to the Price post office. Patrons and friends are invited to give the News a call.

Hon. A. Ballenger makes a most efficient county chairman for the Republicans, and C. B. Snyder, the secretary, is no slouch.

Ladies' Republican clubs are being organized in Carbon county. The ladies of Emery county should commence, without further delay, to organize. The ladies in both counties will be a tower of strength for the party that secured for them the franchise.

County Clerk Braffett is an accommodating gentleman.

Mr. Charles Taylor, manager of the Price Trading Company, took a business trip to Salt Lake Thursday, to be gone three or four days.

Work on the town hall is to be pushed ahead vigorously. The building which is to have a fine rock foundation, with ample basement, and brick walls, will be 50x70. The town board, realizing its inability by reason of limited funds in the town treasury, together with several other public spirited citizens, are drawing upon their personal resources to pay the cost of this structure. It is needless to say that the town board is Republican.

It is amusing to notice the silly assertions made by the local Democratic sheet to the effect that the Republicans object to the women voting. The writer of such stuff should be better posted on past and present history. The Republicans first declared in favor of woman suffrage and a Republican Constitutional convention then went to work and actually gave women the right to vote. We suggest to the writer aforesaid that he familiarize himself with the constitution; he will find just such a provision there, and put there —too, by a body of Republicans.

Carbon county's population is making steady growth. The following figures, from a recent official enumeration, bear out this fact: Price 604, Castle Gate 843, Minnie Maud 142, Scofield 593, Spring Glen 215, Winter Quarters 612, Wellington 429, Helper 258, grand total 3696. In the county the totals as to sex are: Males 2316, females 1350.

A foot ball game between the citizens club vs. The Wanderers club, at Castle Gate on Wednesday was won by the former. The score stood 1 to 0. A one mile foot race between Wm. Bell and Alma Jones for a purse of $10 was won by the latter.

Selectman Ballentyne was in from Scofield on Tuesday.

Mr. Sam. M. Whitemore was in Price this week on business.

A new Salt Lake asphaltum company has been organized and representatives of the company are here in Price. It is whispered around that the new company has made some very fine locations but just where, nobody seems to know.

Price in a short time will have completed a stock yard, second to none in this Western country. This yard will be 210 feet square, with three shoots, a lane 200 feet long running through the whole. There will be five partitions 38x74, and at the rear of the main yard there will be a smaller yard 160 feet square. The whole will contain 26 gates, which are of a new patent, and claimed to be of the very best. Each post is put in the ground 42 inches. The Rio Grand Western is putting in the yards. Nine men are employed under the foremanship of Mr. Geo. Restine.

PRICE, July 26, 1895.

SHOOTING AT SCHOFIELD.

Thomas Llewlyn Badly Wounded By W. C. Burrows—A Quarrel Over Hay Land—Other Newsy Items.

SCOFIELD, July 25.—The haying season has begun here and, as usual, quarrels are also beginning. The first row of the season occurred shortly after 6 o'clock this evening, and as a result, Thomas Llewelyn is lying at his ranch with a bullet hole through his leg, the work of W. C. Burrows, one of the oldest settlers in this valley. Llewelyn has settled on a school section and he has made improvements and cuts the hay each year. Part of this section is cut off by Mud creek and this part, which contains about three acres, joins the lower end of Burrows' ranch. This afternoon about 2:30 Burrows and a hired man named Sturgess, proceeded to cut the hay on the detached portion of the school section. Shortly after 6 o'clock Llewelyn rode up on horseback and stopped his horse in front of Burrows' team and ordered the man Sturgess to quit cutting the hay or he would blow their brains out. Sturgess replied that he would cut it as he was hired to do. Mr. Burrows took a hand in the parley, and using a wooden-toothed rake, tried to make Llewelyn's horse move. Llewelyn struck Burrows over the head with a black-snake whip. He also cut a gash on Burrows' hand. After some more scuffling Llewlyn jumped from his horse and advanced toward Burrows with the butt end of the whip raised. When about four yards apart, Burrows drew his pistol and shot Llewelyn. This is the story as told by Burrows to your correspondent this evening.

After the shooting Llewelyn's boy rode into Scofield for Dr. Smith, who attended, and made the wounded man as comfortable as possible. The wound is not a very dangerous one.

W. C. Burrows immediately after the affair also rode to Scofield and gave himself into the hands of Sheriff Lloyd. He was taken before Judge John Webber and made a deposition to the above effect, and was placed under $500 bonds. The affair has caused a profound sensation in this locality as both men are well known. Your correspondent was unable to see Mr. Llewelyn in order to get his version of the shooting.

Another accident occurred this evening. Miss Ellerbeck, of Salt Lake, is here visiting with Mr. and Mrs. Art. Campbell, and a riding party was formed this evening. While passing along the street a little boy jumped in front of Miss Ellerbeck's horse, and she was unseated. She was thrown quite heavily to the ground, but was able to take her seat in the saddle again and ride home.

Pioneer day was observed here in a suitable manner. The citizens gathered in the bowery in the morning where a programme of speeches, songs, etc., was rendered. Andrew Hood was orator of the day, and in an able manner he traced the history of the pioneers. In the afternoon racing and other sports was indulged in. In the evening the cantata "Strange Visitors" or "A meeting of the Nations" was presented at the school house to an immense crowd by the school children under the direction of Mr. John Hood. The singing and patriotic drill were highly appreciated by the audience. The children were in the costumes of the various countries and carried the flag of the country they represented. The day was magnificently spent.

Jessie, the 17 year old daughter of John Cunningham, is very ill with blood poisoning. Dr. Smith is attending the case.

The mines are almost at a standstill. The Winter Quarters mine is expected to run better next month.

Mr. F. P. Gridley, the genial superintendent of the Union Pacific mine at this place has resigned, and Mr. J. R. Sharp has been appointed to succeed him for the present. The appointment is a very satisfactory one to the employees as Mr. Sharp is a man of marked ability and will look after the interests of both employer and employee.   J. H.

BRIEF LOCAL PARAGRAPHS.

SCOFIELD, July 25, 1895.—The citizens of Scofield and Winter Quarters joined together in a grand celebration of Pioneer Day, which was held in the meeting house lot of the former named place. Everything went off nicely and without a hitch.

In the evening the children of Scofield, under the leadership of Mr. John Hood, rendered a cantata entitled, "Strange Visitors, or a Meeting of the Nations." The entertainment was well attended and was spoken of very highly.

This has been the poorest month for work at the mines for many years. We are only getting one day a week. People are compelled to run behind in order to get enough to live on. They live in hopes, however, of times getting better soon.   MORMON BOY.

Provo Daily Enquirer
August 28, 1895

CARBON COUNTY.

Its Legislative Ticket Chosen— County Convention.

Representative to Legislature:—James X. Ferguson;

County Supt. of Schools:—I. B. Roberts.

The above ticket was nominated at the Carbon County Republican convention held at Helper, Saturday, Aug. 24th.

County Chairman Ballinger called the meeting to order.

Mr. D. W. Holdaway was made temporary chairman, with I. B. Roberts secretary.

The secretary read the call as published in the News. Roll was called of the different delegations, showing a full delegation from every precinct but Minnie Maud, which was not represented.

The different committees were elected as follows, with a member from each precinct:

Committee on credentials:—Wm. Thompson, J. Harrison, T. H. Jones, I. B. Roberts, Thomas Lloyd, J. Y. Biglow, A. W. Horsley.

Committee of resolution:—Wm. Thompson, Dougal Wright, T. H. Jones, G. A. Willson, J. W. Smith, L. A. Doles, Mrs. D. W. Holdaway.

Committee on permanent organization and order of business:—W. Thompson, Benj. Cartar, Mrs. Jane Babcock, Brig Jones, John Strang, Mrs. E. W. Eldredge and P. A. Smith.

After the appointment of the committees, a thirty minutes recess was taken, so that the committees could prepare their reports. After the recess the chairman called the convention to order. The committee on credentials reported through James Harrison, of Castle Gate, showing a full delegation from every precinct except Minnie Maude. The report was adopted.

The committee on resolutions made their report in which they welcomed the women and declared in favor of silver at 16 to 1, which was received with much applause.

The committee on permanent organization and order of business reported. D. W. Holdaway was made permanent chairman, with I. B. Roberts secretary.

The first business was the election of seven delegates to the State convention at Salt Lake Aug. 28. The following were elected: H. A. Nelson, Castle Gate; Thomas Loyd, Scofield; Wm. Thompson, Winter Quarters; A. Ballinger, Price; J. X. Ferguson, Helper; D. W. Holdaway, Spring Glen; I. B. Roberts, Wellington, and R. G. Miller delegate at large.

The next business before the convention, was the nomination of a Representive to the Legislature. A member of the Scofield delegation placed in nomination James X. Ferguson, and H. A. Nelson, of Castle Gate, nominated R. G. Miller. After three tie ballots, there was a motion for a 10 minutes recess, in which to discuss the two candidates. Some talk followed in favor of the two candidates, several of the delegates stating that they would not change their vote if they stayed there a week and showed it on the 4th ballot, which resulted 18 to 18. After this they took another recess. After the meeting was again called to order, and the convention about to ballot again, Mr. Miller arose and in a neat speech withdrew his name, and asked the entire delegation to support Mr. Ferguson. Mr. Miller was loudly applauded. A unanimous vote was then taken for Mr. Ferguson.

The superintendent of public schools next came up. Mr. Smith of Scofield, believing in the Republican principle of woman's suffrage, placed in nomination, Miss Sadie Kimball of Scofield. G. A. Willson of Wellington, placed in nomination Mr. I. B. Roberts. The vote resulted as follows.

Miss Kimball 20, Mr. Roberts 16. Mr. Ballinger questioned the legality of a woman, acting as school superintendent, as it was a Territorial office and women did not have the franchise in Territorial matters. A motion was made to leave it to the central committee, to appoint another candidate if they found that Miss Kimball could not act. The motion was lost. The secretary read a section from the Territorial Statutes which settled the question. Dr. Smith made a motion that the convention reconsider the vote and withdrew Miss Kimball's name. Mr. Roberts was then elected by acclamation.

Mr. James Harrison of Castle Gate, was elected a member from Carbon Co. on the Territorial central committee.

The county central committee of Carbon county was elected as follows: Chairman, A. Ballinger, Price; Vice-president. Geo. A. Willson, Wellington; J. W. Smith, Scofield; Dougal Wright, Castle Gate; 8, A. Harrison, Winter Quarters; J. X. Ferguson, Helper; F. M. Ewell, Spring Glen; W. J. Tidwell, Wellington; D. W. Holdaway, Price; F. C. Lee, Minnie Maud.

The following delegates were elected to attend the Judicial convention at Mt. Pleasant Sept. 10th: W. J. Tidwell, J. W. Smith, H. A. Nelson, Geo. Frandsen, T. C. Reese, F. M. Ewell, James Rooney.

Sensational convention at Price, Sept. 21st: Thomas Lloyd, 8, A. Harrison, E. W. McIntyre, T. H. Jones, L. A. Dole, Dugal Wright, Geo. A. Wilson.

The convention then adjourned.

Deseret Weekly
August 31, 1895

EMERY STAKE CONFERENCE.

The quarterly Conference of the Emery Stake of Zion was held in the Ferron meeting house Sunday and Monday, Aug. 11th and 12th, 1895. Elder John H. Smith, of the Apostles, the Stake presidency, and most of the Bishops and leading officers of the Stake were present on the stand.

Sunday morning at 10 o'clock, Elder Larsen president of the Stake, reported the Stake as in a very satisfactory condition. He felt proud of the Saints over whom he presided. Said the health of the people was generally good. Spiritually they are improving, and the Lord is blessing the elements for their sakes, so that an abundant harvest is at hand. The presidency had visited eight of the wards in the last quarter. The Stake and ward officers seemed to be working in perfect harmony. Advised all to "seek first the kingdom of God," etc.

Bishops Hyrum Nelson, Henning Olsen, and L. P. Ovesen corroborated the president's report.

Elder J. H. Smith then spoke at length on the subject of fast offerings; said each family should at least donate the worth of their usual breakfast once each month to the poor. If funds should accumulate they will be a safeguard against a time of great need. Those who give to the poor lend to the Lord, and a blessing will surely follow. The owner of a small farm and a house with one room should never feel poor.

2 o'clock p.m.—The sacrament was administered by the Priesthood of Ferron Ward.

Elder O. Seeley, of the Stake Presidency, said it was seventeen years since he led a company of Saints into this valley to make homes. The people moved from place to place in the then desolate land trying to find the most suitable place to settle. Now hundreds of farms are being cultivated, and through the blessing of God producing heavy crops.

Bishops Counselor A. J. Allen and Bishops C. W. Moore, Jasper Robertson and George Frandsen reported their wards as in a fairly prosperous condition.

Elder John Henry Smith occupied the remainder of the time encouraging the people to assist in the erection of the Pioneer monument. He explained how nearly all nations show their respect for the achievements of their illustrious countrymen, by building some kind of a structure to their honor, and pointed out many instances of the same. The memory of Brigham Young will ever be cherished in the hearts of this people, but it is justly due to that noble man, and his associates, that we erect this structure as a matter of history, if for no other reason.

A Priesthood meeting was held directly after the afternoon service, in which much valuable instruction was given.

Monday, Aug. 12th, at 10 a. m., Counselor Wm. Howard reminded the Saints of their many duties in the Gospel. We should utilize every blessing within our reach, for the Lord is very kind to us.

Elder F. M. Ewell reported the Spring Glen ward, and Bishops H. P. Rasmussen and W. G. Petley spoke in glowing terms of the good people in their respective wards.

Elder J. H. Smith then gave a powerful discourse on the first principles of the Gospel, tracing the hand dealings of Providence with His people from Father Adam down to the dispensation of the fullness of times.

At 2 p. m. the general and local authorities were unanimously sustained.

High Counsellor J. H. Taylor and Patriarch Alex Jameson each made a few timely remarks, after which Brother Smith made his closing speech, urging in forcible language the necessity of keeping all the commandments of God. Said he was a strong believer in the doctrine that no son or daughter reared in the house of prayer would be lost.

Elder Larsen exhorted all to follow the excellent teachings given so freely during this most enjoyable conference.

Meetings were all well attended notwithstanding the busy time, harvesting, etc. The teachings of Brother Smith were greatly appreciated; also the sweet singing of the Ferron choir under the direction of Prof. L. P. Thomas.   A. E. WALL, Clerk.

Salt Lake Tribune
September 5, 1895

ACCIDENTAL DEATH.

Inquest Upon the Body of George S. Edwards at Castle Gate.

[TRIBUNE SPECIAL]

Castle Gate, Utah, Sept. 4.—In the inquisition before Coroner H. B. Asadorian upon the body of George S. Edwards, who was killed as reported by your correspondent yesterday, Jurors William T. Lamph, M. Beveridge and Andrew Lester returned a verdict of accidental death.

George S. Edwards was a native of Pennsylvania, but has been the last ten years in the coal mines of this section, where he is well known. He was past representative of the Knights of Pythias lodge at Northfield, British Columbia, and was today buried under the auspices of the Knights of Pythias lodge No. 13. About sixty of the members turning out, and to the sad, sweet strains of the Dead March in Saul, played by the Castle Gate brass band, the funeral procession wended its way to the graveyard, where Grand Representative Baker of Rocky Mountain lodge, Salt Lake City, officiated as prelate, and with the beautiful Pythian burial rites performed, all that was mortal of George S. Edwards were laid to rest.

Deseret Evening News
September 11, 1895

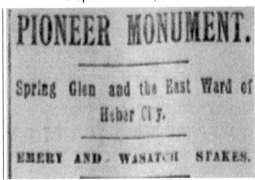

PIONEER MONUMENT.

Spring Glen and the East Ward of Heber City.

EMERY AND WASATCH STAKES.

The Fund Has Nearly Reached Nine Thousand Dollars Total.

CARD FROM THE FIRST PRESIDENCY

Salt Lake City, August 20, 1895.

Contributions in aid of the monument to be erected in Salt Lake City in memory of Brigham Young and the pioneers, should be sent by those charged with the duty of collection as frequently as possible to Heber M. Wells, Salt Lake City, who will see that same are properly acknowledged.

We earnestly hope that all the people will respond generously and promptly to this call, to the end that the monument may be completed at the earliest possible date.

WILFORD WOODRUFF,
GEORGE Q. CANNON,
JOSEPH F. SMITH,

First Presidency of the Church of Jesus Christ of Latter-day Saints.

ACKNOWLEDGMENTS.

The Brigham Young Memorial association acknowledges receipt of the following contributions to assist in the building of the Pioneer monument:

From Spring Glen ward, Emery Stake:

T Pratt	$ 1 00
Anna E Pratt	50
Sarah E Pratt	50
Thomas Rhodes	20
Martha Rhodes	20
Thomas W Rhodes	15
Joseph E Rhodes	15
Martha M Rhodes	15
Karl A Rhodes	15
J R Ingles	75
Lizzie Ingles	15
J R Ingles Jr	25
Wm Miller	25
Margaret Miller	25
Maggie Miller	25
George Miller	25
Nathan Miller	50
Lillian Miller	50
Everett Miller	50
F M Ewell	50
Fannie Ewell	25
Periot Ewell	25
Wm Ewell	50
Lillian Ewell	50
Thos Haycock	5
Alma Haycock	5
Jessie Haycock	5
Mary A Haycock	50
Joshua Wiseman	25
Harriet Wiseman	10
Jacob Wiseman	10
Frank Wiseman	10
Sarah Wiseman	10
Florence Wiseman	10
Lydia Wiseman	10
T H Jones	25
Minnie S Jones	10
Christine S Jones	10
Dora M Jones	10
Margaret Hansen	45
J T Bigelow	1 00
Mary E Bigelow	1 00
Irvin Bigelow	50
Jane Babcock	50
Lyda Babcock	10
Vardus Babcock	10
Total	$13 10

Subscribed by members of the East ward, Heber City, Wasatch Stake,

Per Bishop R S Duke............. 49.30

Previously acknowledged:

From Bannock Stake............. 104.50
" Bear Lake Stake............. 129.61
" Beaver Stake............. 15.35
" Box Elder Stake............. 61.45
" Cassia Stake............. 71.10
" Cache Stake............. 253.94
" Davis Stake............. 329.50
" Emery Stake............. 97.51
" Juab Stake............. 253.35
" Kanab Stake............. 25.00
" Malad Stake............. 151.25
" Maricopa Stake............. 107.95
" Millard Stake............. 163.90
" Morgan Stake............. 29.55
" Oneida Stake............. 209.00
" Panguitch Stake............. 92.00
" Parowan Stake............. 76.20
" Salt Lake Stake............. 2700.05
" San Juan Stake............. 59.45
" Sanpete Stake............. 335.85

" San Luis Stake............. 49.40
" Sevier Stake............. 72.21
" Snowflake Stake............. 80.90
" Star Valley Stake............. 25.75
" St. Joseph Stake............. 125.60
" St. Johns Stake............. 42.90
" Summit Stake............. 151.75
" St. George Stake............. 347.08
" Tooele Stake............. 201.15
" Utah Stake............. 724.80
" Uintah Stake............. 6.20
" Wayne Stake............. 80.85
" Wasatch Stake............. 150.90
" Weber Stake............. 160.65
" Eastern States............. 53.10
" North Western States..... 58.00

Total.........................$8980.45

Today's acknowledgment:

From Spring Glen.................. 13.50
" Heber East Ward............ 49.30

Grand Total.................. $8952.55

Deseret Weekly
September 14, 1895

Deputy Registrar Rowley, of Spring Glen reports a most uncalled for condition of affairs on Gordon creek, Carbon county, says the Price Advocate. He found there several families of children between the ages of six and fourteen years who had never seen the inside of a school house. In one family alone are five children who are totally and densely ignorant. The parents live about ten miles from Spring Glen and all very poor. It would appear that something should be done at once in order that these children no longer be deprived of their right to something in the way of an education.

At Castle Gate, while excavating for the new bicycle track, George S. Edwards was, without warning, crushed to death by the sudden fall of a mass of dirt and rocks, says the Price, Carbon county, Advocate. He had no chance for his life as the mangled and bruised body showed when recovered. Pat Walsh, who was working with him, was thrown down but not seriously injured. A coroner's jury rendered a verdict of accidental death. George Edwards was a prominent Knight of Pythias and took great interest in the founding of the order here. He came originally from Pennsylvania, but has been working in this vicinity for a number of years. He had a host of friends many of whom followed his remains to the grave on Wednesday, Sept. 4.

Spanish Fork Herald
September 20, 1895

old, survive her. The funeral was held in this city on Thursday of last week.

Mrs. Buffmire was well known here and was a very popular young woman, her sterling traits of character winning friends and making her a general favorite with people among whom her lot was cast. It is sad that one so gentle and earnest should be called to the Great Beyond almost at the beginning of an active and useful life among the people of the earth, but the all-wise Father in Heaven doth all things for the best, and the bereaved husband and little one will find comfort in the conscionesness that she is with the chosen ones of God.

Mrs. Buffmire's maiden name was Mary Jane Rowe, and she was born in Wales 23 years ago. She had been in America eleven years, and was married to Mr. Buffmire about seven years since.

A younger sister who was absent in Colorado was unable to reach here in time for the funeral. This was the first time she had been separated from her sister during a life time of 21 years.

Obituary.

At Helper on the morning of Tuesday, Sept. 10, 1895, Mrs. G—. Buffmire, a daughter of Mr. Lewis Rowe, of Schofield, and a niece of Mr. Owen Rowe of this city, departed this life after a brief illness. A husband and three children, the youngest of whom was but nine days

Deseret Weekly
September 28, 1895

SCOFIELD, Utah, Sept. 18, 1895.

We are unusually quiet here for this time of year. Last year at this time we were sending away one thousand tons of coal per day, and working six days per week, while now we are working half a day now and then, making from one to two days a week. A number of people have left here in search of a place where they can make a livelihood.

Mr. and Mrs. Frank Meriwether buried one of their twin boys last week at three weeks old. Mrs. G. Buffmyre, who was a resident of Scofield for many years died at Helper last week, and was buried at Spanish Fork. She leaves a husband and three children, the youngest but a few days old.

We are having beautiful weather, the nights being more mild than is usual in this altitude at this season of the year.

The mammoth edition of the EVENING NEWS is grand. It is interesting to us who have grown up with the country, who are eye witnesses to what is related in those pages, as also to strangers.

Some of our boys have been out hunting bear of late. They have been successful in killing four.

A Finland lady gave birth to twins on Friday last.

The health of the people at Scofield and Winter quarters is pretty good at this writing, there being but one case of disease, and that of typhoid fever, the patient is a little girl of Chris. Jensen's our Scofield tailor, formerly of Springville.   MORMON BOY.

Deseret Evening News
October 9, 1895

ELECTION JUDGES.

EMERY COUNTY.

Blake. Ira R. Browning D., A. D. Thompson D., Thomas Forrer R.

Castle Dale. C. E. Larsen D., A. G. Livingston D., Orange Seeley R.

Cleveland. L. P. Overson D., G. B. Oviatt D., W. E. Cowley R.

Ferron. Frederick Olsen D., George W. Perry D., Fred Kilpack R.

Huntington. William Huster D., John T. Wakefield Jr. D., Alonzo Brinkerhoff R.

Laurence. Henry Roper D., Ole N. Tuft D., C. W. Moore Sr. R.

Molen. H. C. Hansen D., E. H. Barton D., L. S. Beach R.

Muddy (Emery). John Lewis Jr. D., Heber C. Petty D., John Williams R.

Orangeville. A. C. Van Buren D., Andrew Anderson D., F. W. Fall R.

Woodside. Eli Randall D., F. H. Worley D., William Turner R.

CARBON COUNTY.

Castle Gate. Alfred J. Reese D., Robert Howard D., H. A. Nelson R.

Helper. H. A. Miller D., J. H. Van Natta D., James Rooney R.

Minnie Maud. G. C. Johnson D., David Smith .. Isaac Kimball R.

Price. Seren Olsen D., Joseph Jones D., C. B. Snyder R.

Scofield. Thomas H. Thomas D., Charles A. Robinson D., O. G. Kimball R.

Spring Glen. A. J. Simmons D., William Miller D., T. H. Jones R.

Wellington. Peter Liddell D., L. H. Jackson D., Newton Hill R.

Winter Quarters. T. J. Parmley D., Thomas Farrish D., J. B. Schivess R.

Provo Daily Enquirer
October 11, 1895

Scofield's Big Rally.

[Correspondence.]

At Scofield, Hon. F. J. Cannon, spoke Wednesday evening to the largest gatheering ever seen here. Fully 150 people were turned away unable to get within hearing distance. From Winter Quarters, a mile distant, everybody came to hear the "Little Giant." A torch light procession was formed at Winter Quarters which marched to Scofield, where they joined in with those of Scofield. A shot gun club was in line and made the air fairly ring with volleys. Red fire was burned in abundance, and every thing was ablaze with enthusiasm.

The meeting was held in the school house. Jos. Sharp was chairman, and made a beautiful speech in presenting Mr. Cannon, introducing him as the first Senator from the State of Utah.

Mr. Cannon was given a perfect ovation and talked to the people for two hours on the issues of the day,

Col. A. D. Gash of Provo was billed to speak to the people of Winter Quarters at the same time, but alas! for poor Abe, he was not in it.

Abe had just five persons in the house, including himself, when the people en mass formed in their procession and started for Scofield, a mile distant. Poor Abe looked like he was lost in the wilderness.

SOAPEL.

SCOFIELD, Utah, Oct. 20, 1895.—
Mrs. M. Williams, aged 82 years, died
at Winter Quarters on Friday, of old
age. She was the oldest person in the
place; was a native of Wales. She
died in full faith of the Gospel. The
funeral services were held in the
Winter Quarters meeting house. The
remains were being interred at Scofield.

The mines here are working pretty
well now, but are not running things
as is usual at this season of the year.

The germs of scarlet fever still lurk
around this place and occasionally new
cases break out. John Cunningham
lost a child last week and has two more
down with the dread disease. Robert
Bishop, who has a ranch between here
and Price, has six children sick with
the fever.

Quite a number of the Utah county
farmers come up here for their winter's
coal. They bring vegetables with
them to pay for the fuel.

The P. V. Coal company had a car
load of machinery come the other day
for No. 1 mine. Mr. N. Smith, their
mason, is here from Castle Gate building an addition to the power house at
Winter Quarters.

MORMON BOY.

SCOFIELD, Oct. 31, 1895.
There is considerable sickness again
in Scofield and Winter Quarters,
especially among the children. Several families are quarantined for scarlet fever. Mr. and Mrs. S. A. Harrison's infant boy died this morning.

The P. V. Coal Co. is having considerable trouble with the No. 1 mine at
Winter Quarters, mining through 400
feet of rock and 750 feet of coal to encounter more rock. It is hoped, however, the second fault or jump will not
be as serious as the first.

The Kimball mine is kept quite
busy furnishing coal to the teams that
come from Utah Valley.

Brother Andrew Hood and the Sunday school children of Winter Quarters have started to practice for a concert, the proceeds to go to the Sunday
school.

MORMON BOY.

EMERY STAKE SUNDAY SCHOOL CONFERENCE.

The annual Sunday School Conference of Emery Stake convened at Castle Dale, Nov. 2nd and 3rd, 1895. Present on the stand, Elders K. G. Maeser and Thomas C. Griggs, of the Sunday school union board, Stake superintendent N. E. Curtis, first assistant Alexander Jameson, Bishop Olsen, of Castle Dale, and two ward superintendents.

The Price Sunday school was reported by Assistant Superintendent Jos. Jones and Brother James Peterson gave the report of Castle Dale Sunday school. Elder Thomas C. Griggs, of the Union board, occupied a short time, giving instructions on how to govern local schools and a brief account of Sunday schools in general. Brother K. G. Maeser outlined the exercises that should be carried out in the Sunday schools and made especial remarks on concert recitations.

In the afternoon the report of the Ferron school was presented by J. E. King. The second intermediate department of the Castle Dale school rendered an exercise which was worthy of praise. Brother F. M. Ewell, of Spring Glen, reported the Sunday school over which he was presiding. The necessity of encouraging each other in Sunday school duties; the mode of governing ourselves in regard to the Sacrament and other topics were ably treated by Elder Griggs. Elder Maeser illustrated the way in which to teach by precept and example; the way to sustain and be sustained; the necessity of officers and teachers handing in excuses for absenting themselves from school—the consecutiveness of excuses from an individual not to exceed three without a forfeit of position, which position should be filled by someone else.

Sunday, Nov. 3rd, 10 a. m. The Huntington Sunday school was reported as being in a good condition by Supt. O. J. Harmon; Supt. Ole M. Tuft reported the Sunday school of Laurence as being poorly supported. A review on the life of the Savior was given as an exercise by the primary department of the Castle Vale school, followed by an exercise on the crucifiction and resurrection of the Savior. Supt. J. C. Snow reported the Orangeville school as being in a condition favorable to success. Brother Thomas C. Griggs addressed the congregation on the topics of ideals, cheerfulness, order, punctuality of officers, teachers, choristers and pupils; duties of Elders, secretaries, and the ways of dismissing schools.

The following questions were anawered by Brother Maeser: Shall a teacher continue to teach who uses tobacco? No; no teacher should teach by precept who cannot teach by example. Who should be set apart in Sunday schools? School officers only should be set apart. A congratulation was extended by Brother Maeser to the pupils who had taken part in class exercises, for their complete answers.

A Teacher's meeting was held at 12 o'clock, at which Bro. Maeser explained the object of having teachers' meeting, by comparing them to an engine room where all the forces were to be originated and be prepared for activity. The following topics were spoken upon very comprehensively: plans, methods of teaching, order, including place, cleanliness, quietness, class exercises, how to teach, disorderly pupils, Sacrament, nickel day, and the caution never to teach by compulsion but always by love. In reference to the above Bro. Griggs was very instructive.

Conference reconvened at 2 p.m., and the Sacrament was administered by Elders Bold Peterson, and Peter Franson, of Castle Dale. The general and local officers were presented by State Secretary J. B. Jewkes and sustained by the people. Bro. J. N. Killpack, of Molen, reported the Sunday school of which he was superintendent as following the plans adopted by the Union board, or nearly so. The 1st intermediate department of Castle Dale school gave an exercise on Lehi and his family, conducted by Miss Peterson and Sister Anderson.

Stake Superintendent U. E. Curtis gave the report of the Stake announcing that it is more progressive this year than it has ever been before. He explained the courses of study that had been pursued by the union of Castle Dale and Orangeville during the past winter in relation to carrying out the instructions given at Provo. He further announced that he had instructed the various wards to do likewise. He concluded by presenting the methods used in Orangeville Sunday school.

Brother Maeser by way of endorsement to the remarks of Brother Curtis, added further instructions on the duties of Sunday school teachers and of obligating teachers which should not be done contrary to the teacher's free agency.

Elder C. G. Larson expressed himself as being pleased with the rapid improvement that had been made during the past year. He extended his thanks and gratitude to all who had taken part and especially to Brother Maeser and Griggs, who had come so far to see us. Asst. Stake Supt. Alex Jameson added his mite to what had been said, and gave very appropriate instructions. Elder Griggs congratulated Brother Larson on his vast number of Sunday school children, and commended Brother N. E. Curtis on his labor. The conditions that would have favored his absence from conference were related, but he added that his duty stood foremost of all things. His appreciation of the choir, janitor and all who had taken active parts were extended; and he concluded by giving good advice and well wishes to all.

Brother U. E. Curtis made appropriate closing remarks.

J. D. JEWKES, Stake Secretary.

Deseret Evening News
December 24, 1895

Fire at Winter Quarters—Notes.

SCOFIELD, Dec. 21, 1895.—A fire broke out at the residence of Archibald Anderson at Winter Quarters on Thursday evening, Dec. 19th at 8:30 o'clock. The house (a frame) and all its contents were consumed in less than an hour.

The family barely escaped with their lives. Mrs. Anderson, who was sick in bed at the time, and a baby four days old, were somewhat scorched while getting out of the house.

Pay day came to both of the mines here this week to gladden the hearts of the people for Christmas, that is, those who were fortunate enough to get a good pay.

The coal trade is beginning to slacken off, and the mines are not working so steady.

Seven inches of snow fell here last night.

MORMON BOY.

Salt Lake Herald
December 27, 1895

Wedding Bells.

CASTLEGATE, Dec. 25.—During the week the people of Castlegate have been marrying and giving in marriage. Peace has now been declared between the north and the south for Castlegate appropriated one and Spring Glen contributed one. The last couple who helped to continue the matrimonial excitement were Alma Jones, of Spring Glen, and Miss Elizabeth Williams, of Castlegate. Their reception was a huge affair and everything was in harmony.

The masquerade ball at the K. of P. hall on Xmas eve, was the greatest social event that has occurred here for many years. The right kind of ladies and gentlemen had the affair in hand to make it a success. The committee rewarded a neat sum to the best dancers. Bob Wilson and Margaret Ann Thomas, of Castlegate, were the lucky ones and another lady whose name was not given received a turkey for the best costume.

Christmas day was observed in the usual quiet and delightful way by the people of Castlegate. An interesting programme was rendered before a large crowd of people in the K. of P. hall at 10 o'clock a. m.; a dance for the children was indulged in; candy, nuts, etc., were distributed among "Utah's best crop."

Logan Journal
January 2, 1896

T. H. Jones, the well known Spring Glen ranchman proprietor of the Price meat market, met with a very painful accident a few days ago which may result in crippling his strong right arm. Mr. Jones was making one of his regular trips to Castle Gate last Thursday and at a bad place in that very bad road turned out to let a team pass. In starting again one of the wheels struck a big rock and Mr. Jones was thrown out. In trying to save himself he fell on his right wrist badly fracturing it. Fortunately Mr. Jones was not alone. J. W. Foote was in the rig with him and surgical aid was at once secured. The injured arm is doing quite nicely but a man with Mr. Jones' active disposition feels ill at ease when bandaged up.—Price advocate.

State Game Warden Heath wired to Price for the arrest of all parties in possession, or concerned in the handling of the big consignment of venison which was spirited out of town a few days ago. The Advocate don't believe the local authorities have backbone enough to make a single arrest for the offense known to have been committed. For several days that the 500 carcasses were stacked up here nothing was done looking toward the enforcement of the law. Local parties having a pull were probably too heavily interested in the shipment to be interfered with. Good thing.—Price Advocate.

Deseret Weekly
January 18, 1896

SCOFIELD, Jan. 10, 1896.

Thomas C. Rouse, a resident of Winter Quarters, died at the Holy Cross hospital, Salt Lake City, January 5, 1896, of asthma. He was born December 5, 1830, at Tredegar, Monmouthshire, South Wales; July 14 1854, he married Miss Ann Davis. He was noted as a choir leader both in Tredegar and in Merthyr Tydvil, in the years 1859 and '60. He was very faithful in the Church at that time and was thought a great deal of by the Saints and traveling Elders. He came to America in 1866, lived in Pennsylvania eleven years, moved to Iowa in 1877, and came to Utah in 1889. He has lived at Winter Quarters the last four years. He was president of the board of district school trustees; also president of the Carbon County Cambrian association, and a member of the executive committee of the Cambrian Association of Utah.

He leaves a wife, seven children and thirteen grandchildren to mourn his loss. The funeral services were held in the Winter Quarters meeting house, Jan. 9th. A large concourse of relatives and friends followed the remains to their last resting place in the Scofield cemetery.

Several other children are sick in the camp. We have had frequent extreme changes in the weather recently which seems to have caused a great deal of sickness. MORMON BOY.

Manti Messenger
February 7, 1896

Green River Ritings.

Miss Pearl Getty of Willow Bend, is one of the most plucky young ladies in the Green River Valley. On Jan. 29th, while her father and brother were absent from the ranch, her mother, while walking in the yard, noticed a moving object on the very edge of one of the high cliffs that surround the Bend, and called her daughter to look at what she supposed was an antelope. Pearl, on seeing the animal, ran for her Winchester rifle and succeeded in getting to the foot of the cliff unobserved, whereupon she drew the rifle and taking steady aim fired; the animal leaped into the air and came tumbling down the cliff within twenty yards of his slayer's feet. It proved to be a fine large mountain sheep, one which an old hunter would have been exceedingly proud of

Much interest was taken in the miner's meeting Feb 1st, at Gammage's hall. It was largely attended by the miners and citizens. A committee was appointed to draft by-laws and constitution of the proposed Green River mining district

Geo A. Stanton had a severe attack of rheumatism last week and was laid up for several days.

Will Valentine and Joe Ross have finished their work building a wagon road around the side of the mountain. This will shorten their distance to town about two miles.

BRONCHO.

Salt Lake Herald
February 20, 1896

CASTLEGATE, Feb. 18.—Judge Johnson held court at Price Thursday, Friday and Saturday. Several cases were disposed of. In the case of Brownlee et al., for libel, the defendant was sentenced to six months; appealed.

There is great joy in camp today on account of the news that the Badly mine in Marysvale district has been sold. All the stockholders are residents of this country, some being very poor men who have had a hard struggle to pay their assessments. Now that the prospect of being tolerably rich is in view they have got an extra swagger on their gait.

Two deaths have occurred here, one being an Italian by the name of Baptiste Melano. The poor fellow had laid on a bed of sickness for quite a long time suffering from chronic Bright's disease. The other was an Icelander by the name of J. H. Johnson. His death was caused by pneumonia superinduced by typhoid fever. He leaves a wife and family. He was formerly a resident of Spanish Fork.

Mr. Alfred Haycock, of Nephi, is with us on a visit to his brothers, whom he has not seen since his coming to this country some eight or nine years ago. After taking in the sights, he says that Nephi is good enough for him. He will return Thursday. A grand leap year ball was held at Price on Valentine's day, quite a number of the elite of Castlegate went down; a special coach being chartered for that purpose. The English speaking miners are pulling out of the mines. They have strong reasons for doing so, some going to the silver and gold mines and others going to plant corn. Mercur's boom is setting them crazy. Sunday being a beautiful day, the whole army of bicyclists were out in sweaters and bloomers taking their exercises.

Deseret Weekly
March 7, 1896

SCOFIELD, March 1, 1896.—George R----, aged 73, an old resident of Winter Quarters, died yesterday from natural causes. He is a brother to Thos. C. Reese, who died about two weeks ago as mentioned in the NEWS.

Times are very dull here and everything is very quiet.

March is coming in like a lion; it has been snowing and blowing all day.

Mr. Edward Reese, of Salt Lake, was here last week and organized clubs of the Populist party, both at Scofield and Winter Quarters.

J. J. Davie, of Provo, made a business trip to Scofield last week.

MORMON BOY.

Deseret Weekly
March 28, 1896

ITEMS FROM SCOFIELD.

SCOFIELD, March 15, 1896.—Mr and Mrs. N. L. McLean buried a baby yesterday. It was born Thursday evening and died on Friday. The mother is getting along as well as can be expected.

A Finlander had his leg broken a few days ago at Winter Quarters mine. Dr. Smith set the limb and the patient is getting along nicely.

The mines worked half time last week.

The machinery and other preparations at the No. 1 mine at Winter Quarters are now complete, and will commence operations tomorrow. The engine is placed in the tunnel about 1,800 feet from the outside. The grade is just sufficient for the loaded cars of coal to draw the rope to the outside from where the empties are attached to be drawn in. This mine is now quite extensively developed, and is a very fine property. The P. V. company could now produce at Winter Quarters from 1,600 to 2,000 tons of coal per day.

The health of the people in this section is pretty good; there has been very little sickness for the last few months.

John Wilber, justice of the peace of Scofield, has resigned and the county court has appointed John Strang to fill the vacancy.

Wm. Rosser and his mother have moved from Winter Quarters to Salt Lake City, where they intend to make their home in the future. Mr. Rosser is interested in the Haruscrabble mines and expects to work there when they get the mill started.

A subscriber to the NEWS has failed to receive his paper of late and has lost several papers. Can you not find out if anybody is making himself too familiar with other people's mail?

Bro. J. A. Newren, second counselor to our Bishop has gone to Sanpete for the summer. MORMON BOY!

PLEASANT VALLEY NOTES.

SCOFIELD, March 29, 1896.—The miners in these parts will get about ten days in, this month.

The P. V. Coal Co. are making some changes. Hereafter they will have the coal at Winter Quarters loaded with shovels instead of with forks as heretofore. They are working mines No. 1 and 2 alternately.

The coal orders are pretty slow and the prospects for the summer are not very encouraging. Quite a number of people are leaving; many of them have farms.

A good many families who used to depend on the mines here for a living have taken up homesteads in Castle Valley. They work on their farms in the summer and come back to the mines for the winter. Most of them have been struggling hard to make themselves homes, and will soon be independent of the mines.

Brother and Sister John G. Goold, old residents of Winter Quarters, are moving to Salt Lake where they will make their future home. They are getting up in years and they find this high altitude and long winters very severe on them.

Mrs. E. Keenan will hereafter keep a stock of millinery in connection with her dressmaking establishment at Scofield.

A marriage license has been taken out by Andrew Autio, 26, and Aliina Raumia, 20, both of Winter Quarters (Finlanders.)   MORMON BOY.

SCOFIELD, April 6th, 1896.—Brother James W. Gatherum was very seriously hurt in the U. P. mine at Scofield on Thursday last by falling from a ladder about twenty feet. He was picking some coal, when it gave way suddenly, knocking him off the ladder. He fell with the back of his head on some large pieces of coal, cutting a large gash, in which Doctor Smith found it necessary to put several stitches. Brother Gatherum is recovering, but is quite badly bruised up.

The Castle Gate Dramatic company came to Scofield last Friday and presented to the satisfaction of all present Damon and Pythias. The house was well filled and the company returned on Saturday rejoicing.

John P. Meakin, G. C., visited the local Knights of Pythias here on Friday. He went to Price on Saturday.

The scarlet fever has made its appearance in Winter Quarters again, in the family of John Christian.

Willie, the 11-year-old son of Wm. Powell, while out playing the other day, fell and broke his arm. This is the third time the boy has had the same misfortune.   MORMON BOY.

Court at Price.

Judge Johnson is holding a term of court at Price. The following jurors were empaneled: W. H. Sturges, Scofield; M. H. Beardsley, Helper, Samuel Harrison. Winter Quarters, E. D. Fullmer, Spring Glen; E. C. Lee, Minnie Maud; Levi Simmons, Price; George Drury, Spring Glen; Eugene Miller, Castle Gate; Fred Grames, Minnie Maud; C W. Allred, Price; S. J. Padfield, Jr., Winter Quarters; J. J. Bearnson, Winter Quarters; John Holley, Castle Gate, Henry Fiack, Price The vanire was ordered,

A number of naturalizations were effected, most of the applicants being residents of the coal-mining camp of Castle Dale as follows: Henry Wade and Richard White, natives of England, Christmas Davis, Thomas W. Lewis and James Evans of Wales, and Louis Allanti, Christopher Sainaghi, Peter Gerz, Calso Daniel, Carlo Ruggeri and J. Palva of Italy

The motion to re-tax costs and set aside verdict in the case of Wilson vs. Milner was set for 10 a. m. May 12th.

The second libel case against editor S. H Brownlee was called up for trial, but owing to the uncertainty of the whereabouts of the defendant, who a short time since made his exit through a 6x11 inch hole in the county jail, the hearing was postponed indefinitely.

WILLSON IS ACQUITTED.

Jury Out Ten Minutes — Jurors Drawn and Cases Set.

Price, Utah, May 13.—The noted case against Taylor Willson, charged with assault with intent to commit rape, has come to an end in a verdict of "not guilty." Clara Jones Tidwell, the wife of James Tidwell, charged that Willson came to her house on the night of July 9, 1895, and entering her bedroom, committed the offense charged. Defendant denied that he entered the house at all, or saw the woman that night; he went to get help for a sick nephew, and failing, went back and stayed up all night with the sick boy. The jury, M. H. Beardsley, Samuel Harrison, E. C. Lee, Levi Simmonds, George Denny, S. J. Padfield, Jr., J. J. Beardson and John Holley, were out but ten minutes, finding a verdict of "not guilty."

JURORS DRAWN.

By order of Judge Johnson, twenty-five jurors were drawn to serve during the July term of court. The selection was as follows: Henry Wilson, Scofield; B. F. Caffey, Castle Gate; John T. Reid, Helper; J. S. Patterson, Scofield; H. D. Allred, Wellington; Edward Morgan, Scofield; S. J. Harkness, Scofield; Thomas Brown, Winter Quarters; J. M. Loveridge, Winter Quarters; J. M. Beatie, Winter Quarters; Thomas Gale, Wellington; C. H. Empey, Castle Gate; William Miller, Spring Glen; Angus M. Lean, Castle Gate; Thomas Rhodes, Helper; H. J. Stowell, Spring Glen; O. G. Kimball, Scofield; Joseph Burch, Wellington; J. H. Thomas, Scofield; William Fitzsimmons, Helper; John L. Nelson, Castle Gate; P. A. Smith, Helper; I. D. Lyman, Price; W. L. Burrows, Scofield; Nephi L. McLean, Scofield.

The venire was issued returnable the first Monday in August at 2 p. m.

The following cases were set for trial:

August 5th—George C. Whitmore vs. D. & R. G. W. railway; W. C. Burrows vs. O. G. Kimball

August 6th—I. M. Olsen vs. Price Water company; Harriet Walton vs. Walton.

The motion made by Attorney James A. Williams to set aside verdict and judgment in the case of Bruce Wilson vs. George B. Milner was denied, and leave was granted to amend cost bill.

Judge Johnson ordered the following entry:

"In consideration of the disqualification of the Judge of this court to act in certain cases now pending, he having acted as counsel for the parties of record, the Hon. William M. McCarty, Judge of the Sixth Judicial District court of the State of Utah, is hereby invited and requested to attend at the July term of this court, in and for Carbon county, to transact such business as may properly come before the court."

An adjournment was then taken, subject to the call of the Judge.

Deseret Weekly
May 30, 1896

SCOFIELD, Utah, May 19, 1896.—The coal trade is very quiet and it is feared we will not get in ten days' work this month.

Work on the elevator at Winter Quarters has progressed very slowly on account of the inclemency of the weather. The new boiler is being put in place today.

Mr. S. J. Harkness, a respected and old time citizen of Scofield, has sent his family to Massachusetts, where they will make their home. Mr. Harkness intended joining them in the fall but his wife met with an accident in Chicago, having her foot run over by a street car, so Mr. Harkness, fearing it might be worse than they cared to tell him, started after them last Thursday.

The bicycle fever is beginning to take effect at Pleasant Valley. Quite a number of new wheels have arrived recently. With a little work on the road a very nice run could be had of about seven miles around the valley which is nearly egg shaped with the town at the smaller end.

Mr. Frank Sturges, who is boiler inspector for the Hartford Insurance company, spent Sunday at Winter Quarters. He is moving his family to Salt Lake City, where he will have his headquarters hereafter instead of at Denver.

Quite a number of people were out yesterday prospecting for diamonds, one of our store-keepers having lost one out of his ring.

Miss Maggie Strong left yesterday to spend a few days at Provo.

MORMON BOY,

Salt Lake Herald
May 30, 1896

Scofield Siftings.

Coal trade is light and the boys are not getting in much time.

The elevator at Winter Quarters is fast nearing completion and will soon be in active operation.

Mrs. S. J. Harkness, with her children, recently departed for Massachusetts. In Chicago Mrs. Harkness met with a very painful accident having her foot run over by a street car. On learning of the accident S. J. Harkness departed immediately for Chicago, to accompany Mrs. Harkness to her destination.

The bicycle fever has struck the valley, a number of machines have recently been purchased.

Frank Sturgess, boiler inspector for the Hartford Insurance company, Sundayed in Winter Quarters.—Advocate.

Deseret Weekly
June 6, 1896

SCOFIELD, May 26, 1896.

There is not much going on here except at the elevator that is being built at Winter Quarters.

The men working at the U. P. mine here anticipate better times if the proposed new management of the Oregon Short Line and Utah Northern takes hold of this mine.

Summer weather has suddenly dawned upon us up here and the streams have greatly swollen the last few days.

Superintendent W. G. Sharp and Surveyor General Snow have been at Winter Quarters for several days looking over the coal fields.

J. V. Long of the new management of the Castle Valley News was in Scofield yesterday in the interests of that paper. He and W. W. Hack have leased the plant and are going to try their luck in the newspaper business.

J. E. Ingles is building a new dwelling house near his old one.

Andrew Hood, superintendent of the Sunday school at Winter Quarters, is getting up a cantata with the children, to be given Friday evening, May 29th.

MORMON BOY.

Deseret Weekly
June 20, 1896

Castle Valley News: Mr. Jukes of Grangeville died last week of old age. ......Bishop Lamph's house in Cleveland was burned this week......John Huntington of Orangeville died of pneumonia a few days ago.....John Downard had a narrow escape from a vicious cow which he was driving through Soldiers' canyon Wednesday. The horse he was riding was gored to death but he was not hurt.

SCOFIELD, June 13.—Scofield and Winter Quarters are very quiet these days, as the coal business has gone down and the ice business is on top. But we look for our little burgh to be enlivened soon, as the time is drawing nearer for the great event of the year in this part, the Eisteddfod. It is expected that fully a thousand people will visit Scofield at that time. There will be good fishing and it will be a nice opportunity for the city folks to take a trip to the mountains.

The eight hours pay does not agree with the day men and drivers here very well, but the eight hours work is all right, and is quite acceptable, even if the days' wages are cut in some instances. The working people look upon it as a great benefit for the future, and that there will be a much smaller per centage of illiteracy among miners and others.

Winter Quarters is badly in need of a postoffice. If a person writes a letter in the evening, he cannot get it any further than the Scofield office for about thirty-six hours, and it will not reach Salt Lake until the third day.

MORMON BOY.

Deseret Evening News
July 21, 1896

Winter Quarters Notes.

SCOFIELD, July 20, 1896.—The work at Winter Quarters is better this month than it was last. There is still not enough for the number of men here.

The Scofield mine is working about half time.

Mrs. John Hood is still quite ill.

Ed. Morgan and Hugh Hunter will start for England in a few days on a pleasure trip.

There has been considerable sickness among children lately and Dr. Smith has been kept quite busy.

W. H. Donaldson, has been appointed justice of the peace of Scofield in the place of John Strang who has removed from the precinct.

MORMON BOY.

SCOFIELD EISTEDDFOD.

A grand Eisteddfod was held at Scofield, Carbon county, July 28th and 29th, 1896, under the auspices of the Carbon County Musical association. There was a fair attendance of well dressed and respectable people, and the proceedings gave general satisfaction.

The Eisteddfod was opened by singing the chorus Star Spangled Banner, by the audience, led by Prof. H. E. Giles.

Address by Governor Heber M. Wells, who spoke in favor of the Eisteddfod, and said he considered it an honor to be called to preside over its meetings. His patriotic speech was well received by the audience.

Tenor solo, Ye Breezes that Blow, sung by W. T. Evans, to whom was awarded the $5.

Mr. Ferguson of Provo was called for a comic song and responded to the satisfaction of the audience.

The prize of $5 was awarded to Hugh Hunter, Scofield, for playing "Pibroch of Donald Dhu," on the Highland military bagpipes.

Contest recitation for adults, "Asleep at the Switch," three contestants; the prize of $3 was awarded to Libby Walton, Scofield.

Soprano and alto duett, "Love was playing hide and seek" (Gwent), was rendered by the Swinger Brothers; no contest. The boys have done well under the circumstances. They are the favorites of the whole camp.

Organ and solo selection by Prof. Giles.

There was no contest on the ladies' chorus, "Spring Morning;" the prize of $15 was awarded to the Scofield Chorus Club, which sang very well.

The afternoon session was closed by singing "The Land of my Fathers," by Wm. T. Evans, the audience joining in the chorus.

The Tuesday night session was opened by singing "America" by the audience, led by Prof. Giles.

Address by Hon. J. R. Sharp, who took the chair, as Governor Wells had to go home. He paid a tribute to the Welsh and the Scotch for their patriotism and love of music and literature. His address was a master-piece, and ought to be printed.

There were two contestants for the bass solo, The Mighty Deep; the prize of $5, was awarded to John Wood, Scofield.

Mr. Hunter played Mrs. McClow Highland Fling on the bag pipes, Mr. Ferguson dancing in the Highland costume.

Prof. John P. Meakin of Salt Lake city, another Celt, recited The Drummer. It was very comical, and was encored.

The Winter Quarters, male voice club, sang Invocation to Harmony (Stephens;) the baton was awarded to William T. Evans, the conductor, but the prize of $50.00 was withheld until the next Eisteddfod.

Singing the comical song, The Man that broke the bank of Monte Carlo, by Peter Elliott, Salt Lake city.

Singing, Clamoring Over the Hillside, by Swinger brothers; very good and was encored.

Singing, the Pilgrim's Chorus, by the Scofield choir, under the leadership of John Hood; no contest.

Adjudication by John J. Davies of the eighty lines of English poetry, subject, Utah; prize, $3; of the compositions that of James Dunn of Tooele, the best; the poem was read by Prof. Meakin, who recommended it to be printed, for the use of literary meetings, concerts, etc.

Adjudication by John J. Davies of the eighty lines of Welsh poetry; subject, Music; prize, $3, which was awarded to Isaac Evans, Castle Dale.

Contest selection, Best song of singer's choice; four competing; Peter Elliott and Richard T. Evans equally worthy.

Contest recitation for children, Little Jo; three competing; the prize awarded Annette Ferguson, Castle Gate.

Contest selection, Welsh song, two competing, Wm. T. Evans took the prize.

Thomas Giles of Provo took the prize of $3 for playing the organ solo, Washington Post March.

The last session was opened by singing in Welsh, The Lamb of My Fathers, by Wm. T. Evans, the audience joining in the chorus.

Contest in singing the soprano solo My Western Home (Stephens), Jennie Morgan, Winter Quarters, and Alice Browning, Salt Lake, competing; both sang well, the prize awarded to Miss Browning.

Tenor and bass duet, Flow Gentle Deva; prize $5, awarded to Evans Brothers.

Baritone solo contest, Noble Boy of Truth, four contestants; the $5 prize awarded to John B. Evans, Castle Dale.

Comic recitations by Professors Meakin and Giles—encored.

Contest selection of comic song—two competing; the prize of $2 awarded to Prof. Meakin.

Singing the second piece in the grand choral contest, "Daybreak," (Brooms.) by the Scofield choir; the second prize of $50 was awarded the choir, and the gold medal to the conductor John Hood.

A vote of thanks was given to Gov. Wells and Hon. J. R. Sharp for their good services as president and conductor, and also to the adjudicators Smythe and Davies for their just adjudications during the Eisteddfod.

Mr. John Hood, chairman of the committee, and Levi Jones, secretary, worked like beavers; Ed. Morgan, Hugh Hunter, Thomas Brown, John W. Lloyd, Hector Evans, John L. Price, Wm. Edwards, Frank Mereweather, H. H. Earl and others have done commendable work, and labored under unfavorable circumstances to make the musical festival a success. The committee will make their financial sheet balance even.

They intend to hold it annually and set the one for next year earlier in the season.

The Rio Grande Western round house was well seated and decorated for the occasion. The weather turned out to be very favorable and the people enjoyed one of the most interesting and enjoyable Eisteddfods ever held in Utah. BRUTUS.

Salt Lake Herald
August 20, 1896

Scofield Siftings.

SCOFIELD, Aug. 19.—Scofield has just lost two very pleasant visitors, Miss Alice Bowring of Salt Lake and Miss Arlie Orchard of Ogden. The two young ladies have been the guests of Mr. and Mrs. Campbell.

Professor Makin's class in elocution is getting along very nicely. Claude Rinke, one of the professor's pupils, shows signs of some day becoming a great orator. The Makin family will give an entertainment here before long.

The choir of the late Eisteddfod held in this city not long ago, gave a very delightful dance last Wednesday evening. Refreshments were served.

Scores of parties going fishing and hunting can be seen daily in this little valley. The fish are very plentiful.

The mines at Winter Quarters are working constantly, while the U. P. mine works but six or seven days out of the month.

Miss Beatie is visiting here for a week or two.

Next Friday night at the Union Pacific hotel there will be given a party in the honor of Miss Wamoi Brunker, who is visiting with Mr. and Mrs. Makin.

Salt Lake Herald
August 30, 1896

Coal fight over. C. S. Martin sells Rock Springs, Castle Gate and Diamond lump, $4.75; P. V. and Winter Quarters lump, $4.50; all kinds nut, $4.25.

CARBON COUNTY NOMINEES.

Republicans and Democrats Put Up County Tickets.

[TRIBUNE SPECIAL.]

Price, Utah, Sept. 16.—The Republican convention of Carbon county was held at Castle Gate Monday the 14th. Permanent organization was formed as follows: Samuel Harrison, chairman; Louis Wright, secretary.

Sixteen delegates were present and resolutions adopted as follows:

Resolved, That is be the sense of the convention that we decline sending any delegates to the Mt. Pleasant convention to nominate McKinley electors.

Resolved, That this convention elect seven delegates to attend the silver convention to be held at Salt Lake September 24th.

Resolved, That we are in favor of perpetuating the principles of silver at the ratio of 16 to 1 and the protection of American industries as enacted in the platforms of the Republican party of Utah in the past.

Resolved, That we elect a full Republican county ticket.

Resolved, That this convention elect seven delegates to attend the convention at Ogden to nominate a member to Congress, said delegates to work for a silver nominee.

The following county ticket was chosen by acclamation:

Representative in the State Legislature—Oliver G. Kimball, Scofield.

Clerk and Recorder—W. H. Donaldson, Winterquarters.

County Attorney—J. W. Warf, Wellington.

Collector and Treasurer—Lars Frandsen, Price.

Sheriff—Gus Donaut, Castle Gate.

Surveyor—Robert Forrester, Castle Gate.

County Commissioners—A. Liddle, Wellington; Mike Beveridge, Castle Gate; Lewis Jones, Winterquarters.

Delegates chosen to attend the conventions at Salt Lake and Ogden—H. Finck, I. B. Roberts, J. B. Schinness, Joseph R. Sharp, F. M. Ewall, H. Wade and Lydia Liddle.

Delegates to attend the Twelfth district Senatorial convention to be held at Price—H. Finck, J. C. Moser, Wm. Boyter, F. M. Ewall, Abe Liddle, J. E. Patterson and Lars Frandsen.

THE DEMOCRATIC TICKET.

The Democratic county convention for Carbon was held at Price on Tuesday afternoon. The committee on resolutions roasted the Citizens' party movement as being against the taxpayers' interests.

Delegates chosen to attend the State convention—Wm. T. Lamph, John Nicholson, J. Engles, Don Johnston.

Delegates to the Senatorial convention—G. A. Wilson, Jr., Wm. Miller, J. I. Wilson, J. H. Vannatta.

The following county ticket was nominated:

Representative—Wm. F. Lamph.

County Commissioners — Edgar Thalne, Wm. Miller, Andrew Hood.

Treasurer—A. Briner.

Assessor—G. A. Wilson, Jr.

Sheriff—Hermann Briner.

Surveyor—R. Forrester.

Prosecuting Attorney—J. W. Warf.

There was considerable dickering on the Prosecuting Attorney's nomination. L. O. Hoffman, present incumbent, was nominated, but Warf, also the Republican nominee, was unanimously chosen.

Four of the nominees were not present, and little enthusiasm was shown, each treating his nomination as a matter of course.

Both Democratic and Republican tickets are considered weak for this county, and will have a hard time to win.

John L. Wilson was chosen chairman of the county committee and J. Dexter Smith secretary.

HEAVY PRICE RIVER FLOOD.

IT CAUSED A LANDSLIDE ABOVE HELPER.

The Big Bridge at Price Washed Out and the Bridge at Wellington Reported Gone—Great Damage Done.

Correspondence Tribune.]

Price, Sept. 21.—A flood came down Price river Saturday night which was greater than any yet known here by the oldest resident. The streets of Price were good-sized rivers, and canals and town ditches were ruined. It will cost the county many hundreds of dollars to repair the roads and bridges. The big bridge over the river at Price was washed out, and it is reported that the bridge at Wellington also went out. There were numerous washouts along the Rio Grande Western track between here and Castle Gate and between Price and Lower Crossing. The trains were delayed several hours.

A landslide occurred above Helper, where rocks weighing many tons were washed onto the track. Thousands of dollars' damage has been done to ranches on the river bottoms, and much grain in the shock was carried away.

Fences and ditch flumes were taken out like straw, and hundreds of ties and poles came down in the flood. The citizens of Price, Spring Glen and Wellington lose nearly all their grain crops, and several houses were partially inundated. J. M. Whitmore and three others who were across the river attending to the constructing of the telephone line to Huntington, Emery county, had a very narrow escape. They had just started to come back over the river bridge, and when on the Price side the flood came in such torrents that the wagon had to be abandoned, and two of the party waded back over the bridge, while the other two unhitched the horses and rode back, but by this time the bridge was swaying, and the water reached over a hundred yards on either side of the banks. The men were covered with mud and soaked from head to foot, but finally got out, and waited on the other side of the river until Sunday morning at 10 o'clock, but their wagon was washed down-stream. Anxiety is felt for people residing at Wellington and Farnham, as much water emptied into the river between here and those places, and there is a number of houses close to the river.

Great damage was also done in Box canyon, where ranches and stock were carried away before the flood. Hundreds of acres of farming land is covered with debris and from three to six feet of quicksand. The sight of ruined farms is pitiful, indeed, and numerous citizens are contemplating borrowing their winter's flour, instead of sending to Green River to gather their grain and have it threshed.

WHAT CAUSED THE DAMAGE.

The Going Out of the Desert Lake Dam Washed R. G. W. Track.

Correspondence Tribune.]

Price, Sept. 22.—Early this evening it started to rain, and has continued steadily for several hours. The streets are again streams of muddy water, and another severe flood is imminent if the storm continues all night.

Already there are several trains tied up on account of washouts, and two miles below Price the water is running in torrents over the track so that westbound trains are held on the other side. Other washouts are reported along the line, and traffic will be almost entirely suspended for several hours.

DAM GOES OUT.

A report was brought in today that the reservoir dam at Desert lake, some twenty-five miles south of here, had been washed out, doing great damage. The heavy rains of the past few days have also caused floods in the Huntington and Cottonwood rivers in Emery county and the farms located along these streams have suffered severely.

WASH AND LANDSLIDE.

Sept. 23.—Later.—The flood last night has caused the Rio Grande Western "a peck of trouble." There are numerous washouts, the worst of which are between Green River and Sunnyside; Price and Spring Glen. The construction crews and section men are repairing as rapidly as possible.

The flood took out a strip of track about three miles west of here, and there is reported a big wash and landslide between Castle Gate and Pleasant Valley Junction. Temporary repairs will allow the local passenger trains to resume their runs by evening.

SCOFIELD, Sept. 15.—B. F. Lewis of Winter Quarters had the misfortune to bury his baby boy, three months old, on Saturday.

John Kissell departed this life Sept. 13, 1896, at Winter Quarters, Carbon county, Utah. He was born Nov. 28, 1827, at St. Austle, Cornwall, England; joined the Church in the year 1886; came to Utah in 1887, and settled at Richfield; moved from there to Winter Quarters January, 1895. The funeral services were held in the meeting house on Tuesday afternoon. The remains were interred in the Scofield cemetery by the side of his wife who died last November.

MORMON BOY.

OBITUARY NOTES.

RASMUS MADS ENGELSTAD.

EMERY, Emery County, August 25, 1896.—Rasmus Mads Englestad departed this life the 22nd day of August, 1896, at Emery, Emery county, Utah. He was born September 19, 1812, at Lyrigdahl, Listjerke ludicial district, Christiansands, Stift, Norway, consequently he was 84 years, 11 months and 3 days old when he passed peaceably away. In 1850 he took passage on the steamer North America, for San Francisco, Cal., where he remained and occupied his time in digging gold, farming. He went from San Francisco to Sacramento in the latter part of December, 1856, where he heard the Gospel preached by Elder George Q. Cannon for the first time. On the 9th day of February, 1857, he was baptized by Elder George Q. Cannon; in April of the same year he went to Carson valley, Nevada, and remained there till the first companies of Saints started to Salt Lake City, where he arrived August 17, 1857. He commenced to work on the Salt Lake Temple on the day of his arrival; was ordained an Elder by Doctor Samuel Sprague on the 18th of September; was ordained a Seventy in the Fourteenth quorum by President Millen Atwood on the 28th day of December, 1857; married Annie Margrette Olsen Hanson (a widow) on the 25th of March, 1858; was in the move from Salt Lake City to Santaquin; in 1860 moved to Fairview, Sanpete county; stayed there four years; in 1864 moved to the Muddy, St. Joseph; moved to Mt. Carmel, Long Valley, Kane county, in 1871. At the aforesaid place he had a nice home and a good farm and orchard, but in later years the floods came and took his fruit and shade trees and all his improvements and two-thirds of his city lot. He has been a subscriber to the DESERET NEWS for thirty-six years. He took the weekly paper when he had to pay six dollars a year. He was branch clerk for a number of years; was counselor to Bishop Bryant Jolly for about eighteen years. His wife preceded him about seven months ago. He came to this place to spend his last days with his daughter Anna Engelstad Keel. He had been here about a month. He died as he had lived a faithful Latter-day Saint. He leaves a daughter and a number of grandchildren to mourn his loss.

ALFRED SMITH.

ELIZABETH R. BROWN.

Elizabeth Robb Brown departed this life at Winter Quarters, Utah, September 6th, 1896. The funeral services were held in the Winter Quarters mee ing house, on Tuesday the 8th. Consoling remarks were made by Elders Andrew Gilbert, Thomas E. Davies, Wm. Coulthard and Bishop T. J. Parmley. Deceased was born December 28th, 1843, at Dreghorn, Ayrshire, England, and was the daughter of David Robb and Elizabeth Todd. She was married to Thomas Brown, December 31st, 1860. They had five sons and two daughters, of whom two sons and one daughter are living. Brother Brown came to Utah in July, 1883 Sister Brown, with the youngest child, following in 1884, and the rest in 1886. They settled at Scofield. The husband and father was killed in the Winter Quarters coal mine on the 7th of January, 1889.

The funeral of Sister Brown was very largely attended. She was buried in the Scofield cemetery.   W. H.

Millennial Star, please copy.

COAL OFFERS.

There were in all seven bids for the coal contract, as follows:

Haim Bamberger Coal company—Diamond, Rock Springs, Black Butte and Castle Gate, car load lots, joint building and police station, $4.50; Emigration canyon, $5.50; Parley's and City Creek, $5.75; crematory, $4.75; same, less than car lots, joint building and police station, $4.75; Emigration canyon, $5.75; Parley's and City Creek, $6; crematory, $5. Winter Quarters and P. V., car lots, joint building and police station, $4.50; Emigration canyon, $6.25; Parley's and City Creek, $6.50; crematory, $5.50; same, less than car lots, joint building and police station, $4.50; Emigration canyon, $5.50; Parley's and City Creek, $5.75; crematory, $4.75. Slack—Diamond, Rock Springs, Castle Gate and Winter Quarters, joint building and police station, $3; Emigration canyon, $4; Parley's and City Creek, $4.25; crematory, $3.25.

D. J. Sharp—Anthracite, sizes 1, 2, 3 and 5, car lots, $9.75; Castle Gate lump, car lots, $4.50; nut, $4; slack, $3; ton lots, $4.75, $4.25 and $3. Rock Springs, car lots, lump, $4.50; nut, $4; slack, $3; ton lots, $4.75, $4.25 and $3. Rock Springs (Peacock), car lots, lump, $4.50; nut, $4; slack, $3; ton lots, $4.75, $4.25 and $3. Diamond, car lots, lump, $4.50; nut, $4; slack, $3; ton lots, $4.75, $4.25 and $3. Winter Quarters, car lots, lump, $4.25; nut, $4; slack, $3; ton lots, $4.50, $4.25 and $3. Winter Quarters, car lots, lump, $4.25; nut, $4; slack, $3; ton lots, $4.25. Pleasant Valley, car lots, lump, $4.25; nut, $4; slack, $3; ton lots, $4.50, $4.25 and $3.

Utah Coal company—Rock Springs, Castle Gate, Diamond and Black Butte, retail, delivered, $4.75 per ton; car load, mine weights, delivered, $4.50. Pleasant Valley, Winter Quarters, Grass Creek and Weber, retail, $4.50; car load, $4.25. All kinds of nut coal, retail, $4.25; car load, $4; slack, delivered, $3.

Weber Coal company—Weber coal, lump, $3.85; pea, $1.85; free on board cars at Salt Lake.

C. S. Martin—Rock Springs, Sweetwater, Castle Gate and Diamond lump, $4.25; Winter Quarters and Pleasant Valley lump, $4; Weber and Almy lump, $3.75; Rock Springs, Sweetwater, Castle Gate and Winter Quarters nut, $3.75; Weber and Almy nut, $3.25; Rock Springs, Sweetwater, Castle Gate, Winter Quarters and Pleasant Valley slack, $2.75; Almy and Weber pea coal, $2 (cash prices). Car load lots, free on board cars in Salt Lake.

Miller & Miller—Diamond, Rock Springs, Castle Gate and Black Butte, car load lots, in yards, $4.25; delivered, $4.50; Pleasant Valley, Winter Quarters and Weber, $4 and $4.25; nut, $3.75 and $4; slack, $3.

W. J. Wolstenhome—Rock Springs, Castle Gate, Winter Quarters and Diamond mine slack, $3, delivered; Rock Springs, Castle Gate and Diamond nut, car load lots, $4.50; Winter Quarters, Pleasant Valley and Weber, lump, $4.25; anthracite, $9.75; nut coal, $4. Extra prices for delivery: Crematory, 25 cents per ton; high pipe line, 50 cents; Emigration water works, $1; Parley's canyon, $1.

The bids were referred to the chairmen of the following committees: Sanitary, waterworks, fire and police and control of joint building.

CARBON COUNTY.

Heavy for Bryan but Mixed on County Officers.

Correspondence Tribune.]

Price, Utah, Nov. 4.—Election day has at last come and gone, and the people of Carbon county at least have evidenced by their ballots that they were far from being unanimous, or even a little bit harmonious, in selecting the county's officers. In the selection of State candidates it will be seen by the table giving the vote by precincts that they were a little more united, and the vote polled gives but a small majority for the Republican, Independent Republican ticket. This, in the case of R. S. Collett and M. E. Johnson for Senator from the Twelfth district will hardly avail Mr. Collett anything, as Uintah county has given Johnson a majority of 284, and Emery county (his home) is almost certain to poll him a large majority, which San Juan and Grand counties cannot overcome.

Mr. Collett is by far the most popular man, and the result of the election is almost without explanation, but the Democrats claim that the Populists of Uintah county voted to a man for their candidate.

During the campaign a thorough canvass was made of the counties of eastern Utah by both Republicans and Democrats and numerous meetings held, but the people were somewhat disappointed at not having an opportunity to hear such orators as Senator Cannon, Hon. W. H. King and others who were billed to visit us. Some of them now ask if the Republican central committee really thought that this remote portion of the State was strong enough, powerful enough and intelligent enough to need no assistance, no building up, and could be taught no more?

There were more votes cast for McKinley electors than was expected, and though defeated, the people are heart and soul with Bryan.

The Carbon county ticket as elected shows a mixed-up state of affairs. One Citizens' party, one Republican and one Democratic Commissioner, a Republican Clerk and Recorder, a Democratic Treasurer and a Republican Assessor. The Surveyor and Attorney were on both the Democratic and Republican ticket, and the Sheriff elected was nominated by the Republicans and indorsed by both the Independent Republican and Citizens' party. If any county in the State can show such an impartial selection, Carbon will give in.

No trouble was experienced at any of the polls, and very few tickets had to be thrown out. An amusing thing at Castle Gate came under my observation. A gentleman there actually crossed all three emblems, and then went on down the ticket and voted for the men of his choice. He didn't want much, and lost it all.

The County Commissioners will meet Monday, the 9th instant, and officially canvass the returns, which we believe will show but little variation either way.

PRECINCT OFFICERS.

First Precinct, Winter Quarters—Joseph S. Thomas (Dem.), Justice of the Peace. Mathias Pattinson, Jr., (Dem.), Constable.

Sixth Precinct, Price—William Burr (Dem.), Justice of the Peace. Louis Smith (Dem.), Constable.

Eighth Precinct, Wellington—J. C. Vance (Dem.), Justice of the Peace. J. S. Birch (Rep.), Constable.

Fifth Precinct, Spring Glen—A. J. Simmons (Dem.), Justice of the Peace. H. J. Stowell (Dem.), Constable.

Fourth Precinct, Helper—J. H. Van Natta (Dem.), Justice of the Peace. Harrison Miller (Dem.), Constable.

Third Precinct, Castle Gate—Andrew Young, Sr., (Dem.), Justice of the Peace. Thomas E. Edwards (Rep.), Constable.

Deseret Weekly
November 7, 1896

SCOFIELD, Oct. 28, 1896.—On Monday we were suddenly changed from fine autumn to bleak winter, and it has been snowing and blowing ever since.

Last Sunday the Pleasant Valley ward conference was held. Elder Reid Smoot of the Stake presidency was up from Provo. The afternoon meeting was held in the upper part of the ward (at Winter Quarters) and the evening meeting in the lower part (at Scofield). The Saints enjoyed themselves very much. The different organizations of the ward are in a flourishing condition.

Both Schofield and Winter Quarters have excellent day schools, with two teachers each. There are prospects also for having night schools, and we are in a fair way for intellectual advancement during the winter.

The P. V. Coal company's mines are working pretty steadily now, and the old hands who work on their farms in the summer are about all back to their "Winter Quarters."

James H. Hood of Salina is spending a few days at Scofield among his relatives. MORMON BOY.

Deseret Evening News
November 27, 1896

Scofield Notes.

SCOFIELD, November 25th, 1896.—Robert Pedon while riding on the train to Winter Quarters to work at the mines got his foot caught between two flat cars and bruised it quite badly, though no bones were broken. He will be laid up for some time.

The work at Winter Quarters has dropped off to about half time. This company's mine at Castle Gate is working steady, the orders having gone from here to the Gate on account of the superiority of that coal over this.

The Union Pacific mine here is working better than for a long time past.

Mrs. T. H. Thomas is now running the Union Pacific hotel.

Hugh Hunter, who went to Scotland last August, returned to Scofield last week. He reports having a very nice visit and a pleasant voyage.

James Russell, foreman of the U. P. mine, and wife are visiting friends at Rock Springs, Wyoming.

MORMON BOY.

Deseret Evening News
December 11, 1896

NAMES
OF
PRESIDENCY AND BISHOPS

Emery Stake.

President: C G Larsen, CastleDale, Counselors: Orange Seeley, Castle Dale; Wm Howard, Huntington.

Emery County, Utah.

WARDS.	BISHOPS.
Castle Dale	Henning Olsen
Cleveland	L P Ovesen
Emery	Alonzo Brinkerhoff
Ferron	Hyrum A Nelson
Huntington	Peter Johnson
Lawrence	Calvin W Moore
Molen	Hans P Rasmussen
Orangeville	Jasper Robertson

Carbon County, Utah.

Castle Gate	William T Lamph
Price	Earnest S Horsley
Spring Glen	Edwin Fullmer
Wellington	A E McMullin

Salt Lake Herald
December 16, 1896

Infanticide at Scofield.

Cache Valley News: A lively sensation, involving an estimable young lady and a polished young male resident of Winter Quarters, is being hushed by the parties interested, but as it is understood that the officers are posted there may yet be some unpleasant diclosures. Your correspondent is not able at present to fully verify the rumors afloat wh'ch attach responsibility for infanticide upon the persons alluded to. Suffice to say that a dead infant was found in Mud creek one day last week which gave evidence of having had a natural birth and a cruel and unnatural death. Evidence points strongly toward a certain couple, and the near future may be expected to bring out the facts, unless the efforts of the guilty parents succeed in suppressing the investigation.

Deseret Weekly
December 19, 1896

ECHOFIED, Dec. 11th, 1896.—Wm. C. Reese shot his brother Evan on Wednesday evening the 9th inst. The ball from a 32-caliber pistol entered the front and left side of the head, striking the skull bone and coming out on the same side about four inches from the place of entrance. Dr. J. W. Smith was called and dressed the wound. It appears to be not so very serious as at first thought. He bled very freely, but was able to appear in court next day. He refused to prosecute the brother who did the shooting, after the arrest was made. William has a family and Evan boards with him. He and the lady of the house were the only witnesses. They say they were having a friendly scuffle for the gun when it was accidentally discharged, but the neighbors say whisky and a family row did it.

The mines have been working good for a couple of weeks, and the railroad boys are worked nearly to death.

Wm. Palmer, the oldest band on the road, is laid up with a lame back, but hopes to be able to get out again in a few days.

Coal Mine Inspector T. Lloyd is visiting the mines here this week.

Frank F. Strang, 21, and Mrinthrie Palmer, 18, both of Scofield, have taken out a marriage license.

Two deaths have occurred at Winter Quarters since our last writing, one a four-months-old baby of Mr. and Mrs. J. J. Bearnson, and the other an infant baby of Mr. and Mrs. Joseph Richards.

Mr. James P. Johnson, who was injured by the train while working on the yard at the Winter Quarters mine about six weeks ago is still unable to work, and having a wife and six small children it comes pretty hard on him. Mr. Johnson's back was injured and he thinks it will be a long time yet before he can work.

MORMON BOY.

Deseret Evening News
December 22, 1896

Scofield Notes.

SCOFIELD, Dec. 21, 1896.—A sensational article appeared in the Castle Valley News of Dec. 11, purporting to be a correspondence from Scofield, telling about an infanticide. It was an incorrect statement, however, the officers having thoroughly investigated the case, and having concluded that the writer, whoever he may be, sought to injure the people of Scofield and Winter Quarters. The citizens are greatly worked up over it. The article was signed "Mormon Boy," and many blamed the correspondent of the DESERET NEWS, but investigation has proved that he was not the writer, who is unknown.

Two deaths occurred here on Saturday. Both were children about one year old. The cause of death was pneumonia. One was the child of Mr. and Mrs. Charles Robinson, the other of Mr. and Mrs. A. Arnason.

Scofield school district has levied a special tax of one-half of one per cent, and Winter Quarters one of one and one-half of one per cent; the latter district is to build a school house, which it very much needs.

Frank F. Strang and Miss Marinthria L. Palmer were married on Saturday evening at the residence of the bride's parents at Scofield. The ceremony was performed by the justice of the peace at Winter Quarters.

The Winter Quarters choir is getting up a concert to be rendered on Wednesday evening, the 23rd; the proceeds to go toward getting a new organ for the ward.

Brothers Hinckley and Wilson of the Utah Stake presidency Y. M. M. I. A. were with us on Saturday and Sunday, and gave the Saints some valuable instructions on mutual improvement work. WM. HOWELLS.

Deseret Evening News
December 29, 1896

Scofield and Winter Quarters.

SCOFIELD, Dec. 28, 1896.—Brother and Sister John E. Ingles lost their infant child by death on Tuesday last. It was buried at Ogden.

Mr. and Mrs. Joseph M. Loveridge's baby girl three months old died on Sunday morning.

Mother Reese, widow of the late George Reese, is quite ill.

Our merchants did a very good business for the holidays and everybody seemed to have a merry Christmas.

The people of Winter Quarters expect to have a postoffice soon. They need it very much, as the present service is a great inconvenience to them. The petition for the office has been sent to Senator Cannon, who will present it to the postmaster general.

The Carbon county court will meet on the 31st to wind up the business of the term and to transmit the office to the commissioners elect. WM. HOWELLS.

Scofield and Winter Quarters.

SCOFIELD, Jan. 6, 1897.—The two weeks old infant of Mr. and Mrs. John Cunningham died on Tuesday, the 5th inst.

Coal mining has slackened off at Scofield, and the people are anxiously awaiting the settlement of the U. P. and Short Line matter, hoping for the entire separation of the two, as that would no doubt give the Scofield miners steady work to supply the latter road with coal.

The New Year came in very quiet, the boys having had a merry time and spent their money on Christmas.

The people of Winter Quarters had a New Year's greeting that not many towns in the West could get. As the New Year was coming in a serenading party came around, and we were gradually awakened by beautiful strains of an old Scotch air which was played by the Scotch laddie, Mr. Hugh Hunter, and as the echoes from the bagpipes were dying among the evergreen pines on the side of the canyon, a Welsh air, by Mr. Wm. L. Jones on his harp and Mr. Richard D. Reese with his piccolo, was struck up. The sweet music upon the crisp night air was most beautiful.

Mr. Andrew Hood, county commissioner-elect, has qualified, but commissions for our precinct officers have not arrived yet.

Mr. W. H. Donaldson has gone to Price to do the clerical work for Carbon county for the next two years.

There is so little snow in the mountains here that some people begin to entertain fears for the coming season 's crops. WM. HOWELLS.

COAL MINER KILLED.

GEORGE MARTIN CRUSHED IN WINTER QUARTERS MINE.

When Taken Out He Sought to Write a Letter to His Wife, but Fainted Away—Body Brought to this City.

Last Thursday an accident occurred in the Winter Quarters coal mine at Scofield which resulted in the death of George Martin, a miner and a former resident of this city. Martin, in company with Gus Buffmire, had been working in one of the drifts, where a large amount of coal had been taken out. Some one called Buffmire and he turned to leave the drift. At that moment the whole wall bulged out and toppled over, completely burying Martin, who was working close to its base. Buffmire's movement saved him, for the mass of coal only struck him on the shoulder and hurled him to one side, so that he escaped without injury, save a few bruises.

He summoned assistance and work was quickly begun on the rescue of the unfortunate Martin, who lay buried under a foot or more of rocks and coal. Only a few moments of vigorous work on the part of his friends was necessary to enable the rescuers to reach the body of the man. He was unconscious, but was still breathing, and on being taken into the air recovered sufficiently to be able to speak. His first words were of his wife, and he requested writing materials, that he might inform her of the accident. They were quickly procured, but though he tried to rise he was unable to hold the pen, and in an instant he fainted away from the pain of his injuries. His body was frightfully mangled, one side being crushed almost to a jelly, while the bones of his legs and arms were fractured in many places.

The officials of the Pleasant Valley Coal company, which owns the mine where Martin was injured, immediately chartered a special train to bring the unfortunate man to this city for treatment, but before they had proceeded more than a dozen miles he began to grow weaker from pain and loss of blood, and a few moments later he died.

The remains of the dead miner were brought to this city Saturday by his widow, and yesterday the funeral occurred from Joseph E. Taylor's undertaking rooms on First South street.

Martin's aged mother lives at 529 South Second East street, and his widow and infant child are at present staying with her. They are in very poor circumstances, and the loss of the bread-winner of the family will be most keenly felt. A brother of the deceased lives on Elm avenue and a sister lives in West Jordan.

Deseret Weekly
January 23, 1897

SCOFIELD, Jan. 14, 1897.—George
Martin, a miner working at No. 7
mine at Winter Quarters, was completely buried by falling coal at about
4:30 this afternoon. Dr. Smith starte
to take him to the hospital at Salt
Lake by special train but only got as
far as Scofield, two miles, when the
injured man died. This was about two
hours and a quarter from the time of
the accident. Martin is about 35, and
leaves a wife and two children.

The two weeks old baby of Mr. and
Mrs. John Jones died on the 13th inst.

The wife of Richard D. Reese gave
birth to twins on Tuesday night, the
12th, one of which died next day.

WM. HOWELLS.

Deseret Evening News
February 11, 1897

Scofield Notes.

SCOFIELD, Utah, Feb. 9, 1897.

To the Editor:

There is considerable sickness at
Scofield and Winter Quarters and
several deaths have occurred at the
latter.

Lewis Jones buried a baby today
seven months old. Hector Evans lost
one a year old, and Wm. L. Jones
parted with a girl four years old.

John H. Davis of Spanish Fork took
his son Roderick home yesterday from
Winter Quarters quite ill.

No. 2 mine at Winter Quarters has
been closed and the company is taking
out the machinery. The miners have
been put into No. 1 mine, which
crowds the mine very much, there being six men in an entry and three in
each room.

The coal trade is very dull at present. In the U. P. mine a number of
the single men have been drawn out.

There is just enough snow in Pleasant Valley to make good sleighing.

Wm. Edwards has moved into the
boarding house at W. Q.   H.

CLEVELAND.

Miss Agnes Oviatt our post mistress, has been very sick for a week past

The little girl of Mr. and Mrs Ovirwn is quite sick. Perhaps this accounts for the pre-ence of Hon L. P Or rsen Sunday night and Monday.

David H. Tilley, a little boy of Mr. and Mrs. J. R Tilley has been suffering considerable the last ten days from a stomach complaint, but is now some better.

The infant of Mr. an l Mrs George Oviatt is very sick. Otherwise our little town is doing fairly well.

The music and elocution club is preparing a grand entertainment to come off in the near future

Last Sunday our town was a little more dismal than h nsual, but perhaps Price can account for this? The semi-annual stake conference

A double wedding in Cl veland next Wednesday night. Paired this way Henry Rasmussen to El z beth Ann R chards, Steppe Johnson to Emma Ward.

The Y. L. M. I. A. will celebrate their anniversary February 18, and wind up with a dance in the opera house.

He arrived In the home of fellow-citizens Mr. and Mrs. Sam l N. Alg r, all well, especially the father.

I just now learned of the death of David H. Tilley. It is a very sad ending. The parents have hoped on to the last. He was a young lad in apparent good health. The immediate cause I have not learned, only that his stomach was in a very serious condition.

We also record the death of the infant of Mrs and Mr Geo. Oviatt

CASTLEGATE.

On Monday morning the dead body of a man was found in one of the empty coke ovens. It appears that one of the coke loaders was looking for some part of his screening apparatus and on looking around for it discovered it in the oven and a man apparently asleep upon it. Finding that the man would not awaken by shouting, he got into the oven and and found the man dead. On searching the body, papers were found, which showed that the person, was by name, J J. Brazier, and that he had lately come from Butte, Montana. Other articles were found among which was a bottle of laudanum wh ch suggested suicide. As he was seen alive and apparently well on Saturday. An inquest was held before Justice of the Peace Harry Duerden, who empaneled Henry Wade, Andrew Young sr. and W. T. Lamph as jurors. Several witnesses was

sworn, two said that they had only seen the man when he was found, one had seen him on Saturday washing himself at the water pipe of the oven in which he was found and had seen him on Sunday laying down, but thought him asleep, as many travellers called there to pass the night, it being a warm spot. Dr. Asadoorian made a post mortem examination to see if it was really a case of self dis truction He came to the conclusion that the man died from heart failure, superinduced by hunger and a dose of narcotic, not sufficient of the poison being taken to kill him A verdict to that eff ct was accordingly brought in. He was a man about 35 years ol l, medium size, was respectably dressed, was a member of K. of L of Butte City, was in good standing and was a cook by profession These facts were supposed by articles found on him and by persons to whom he applied for work Messages were sent to Butte for information regarding his indentification and disposition of the body. If none is forth coming the body will be buried here

Another shooting scraps occurred Saturday night between two Italians. As luck would have it no one was hurt. The parties interested are under arrest and will have trial before Judge Durden. We hope that a lesson will be taught these fellows. No use giving names, as I might as well write hieroglyphics.

Angus McL an won the case between him and Milburn of Price, which was appealed.

A number of Castlegate residents went down to the district court and took out their citizen papers.

Quite a few of old timers have paid us a visit this week among whom we saw Messrs W. Parmley, W. S Carr, John Beveridge, Robert Howard and others.

County Commissioners Thorn and Hool were inspecting the place for bridging the river and we hope that the bridge will soon span the stream as it is just now a bad crossing.

The Italians gave a dance in the K. of P. hall Saturday evening.

The Price meat peddlers had a bad runaway on Saturday afternoon about a mile below town, damaging their wagon considraly. The horses ran to Helper before they could be stopped. We are informed that the owner got bruised up some.   W. Tell.

SCOFIELD.

A glee club has been organized at Winter Quarters with Owen Rowe as conductor. The club, with the talent already enlisted, hopes to be able to give the public a rare musical treat on St. David's day, March 1. It is intended to give the entertainment at Scofield.

During the past week the flanger has been busy as has the section men in removing the snow from between the rails, on account of the heavy snow that fell last week.

John Beddoes, of Winter Quarters, met with a very painful accident on last Wednesday, receiving a very bad cut over his eye. Dr. Smith took four stitches in the wound. Mr. Beddoes will be laid up for some time.

The little four year-old daughter of Mr. and Mrs. W L. Jones died on Wednesday and was buried on Friday. The bereaved parents have the sympathy of the entire community.

The little eight months-old child of Mr. and Mrs. Lewis Jones died on Saturday.

If a girl is dancing with a gentleman at a party and the couple stop a while is it proper for the girl to propose going on again or that she should wait for her partner to propose?

[The above, we take it, was for the editor to answer and the following reply comes from the society editor. "we will say that it is proper for the girl to 'propose', especially when the gentleman is inclined to be bashful Should there be more "proposing" on the part of the ladies there would be fewer old bachelors Yes, by all means let the ladies propose".—Ed]

Remember the grand masquerade ball at Price town hall next Monday evening everybody will be there. Good music furnished by Evans Brothers of Castlegate Come and enjoy yourself. Washington's birthday only comes once a year

The sheet and pillow case masquerade ball to be given at Helper, Monday night, February 22, is for the benefit of the widows and orphans of Helper and should be well patronized.

E. E. Branch of Wellington, was in Price the first of the week

Assessor W. J. Tidwell was seen at the capital of Carbon, Monday.

Mrs. Fred Grames and children of Nine Mile are visiting in Price for a few days.

Miss Helge Ericason of Cleveland, is visiting her sister Mrs. H. C. Smith, this week.

WELLINGTON

A party of Price young men who visited our place to participate in the dance on Friday night defined to the satisfaction of all, the difference between gentlemen and hoodlums. After leaving the hall they began yelling, firing pistols and cutting and slashing with their whips, a few innocent bystanders receiving the force of the lash Boys, a plenty of anything is enough. We have had enough of this kind of thing and would prefer hoodlums to give this place a wide berth.

A number of the boys are down from the tie camps getting supplies They report work progressing nicely.

Will Liddell spent Sunday at home and returned to the sheep camp on Monday.

The health of our community is good.

Under the management of the new choir leaders, Jones and Liddell, we are pleased to note a very decided improvement in that part of the Sabbath exercises.

Died —Agnes E. Oviatt, daughter of Henry H. and Sally R. Oviatt, born May 7, 1866 in Circle valley, Piute county, Utah, died February 10, 1897, at Cleveland, Emery county. Utah of inflamation of the bowels. Sister Agnes Oviatt was one of the few young ladies that was loved and respected by all who knew her, being always on hand to give assistance to those that were in need. At the time of her death she held the position of president of Y. L. M I A. which she had filled for five years to the entire satisfaction of all concerned. She was also secratary and treasurer of the Sunday school from the time it was first organized in Cleveland up to the time of her death. She also held the position of treasurer of the relief society of the Cleveland ward for several years, and in all her labors was always punctural and energetic. She was a faithfull Latterday Saint and died as she had lived, in full hope of a glorious resurrection.

LAWRENCE.

The ground is still covered with a good coat of snow and sleighing continues to be one of the enjoyments of the season, though the weather has moderated considerable and the spring winds are making their appearance.

Tuesday evening a meeting was held for the purpose of reorganizing the Y. M. M. I association. Jos. Johnson and D C. Woodward were present. The latter attended to the business part of the meeting after which each of the new officers expressed their willingness to work in their respective positions. The new president, O. M. Miller with his assisting officers will no doubt carry the work on successfully. After the business was transacted Johnson spoke of the M I work and the benfits therefrom

CLEVELAND

It has been very cold here the last week and the sleighing remains good. Cleveland is the possessor of many and varied patterns of sleighs. The make covers styles from the landing of the pilgrims up to the very latest, barring the "Trilby."

A young lady of this place received the mitten from Price the other day.

During the winter the general health of the people has been good. Of late a numbe have been confined with bad colds, mostly among the children, but nothing serious is known.

A number of wagons are being loaded, filled for Moab

Arrangements are being made by the school for the celebration of Washington's birthday. "Come to the crowd" and have a good time

For some time many of the people have been busy storing up ice, preparing for warmer weather.

Alma Soderburg was a Castledale visitor Saturday and Sunday.

Wednesday and Saturday are mail days It would be a fine thing to have a daily mail

The wedding ceremonies of Henry Rasmussen and Miss Richards was postponed for one week on account of the death of Miss Agnes Oviatt.

Good drinking water is a scarce article with us. Our leading men must have, ere this, realized the necessity of action looking to remedying this great health distroyer, filthy water. No one can doubt that with pure water the health of the people would immediately improve It is the imperative duty of our citizens to earnestly endeavor to remedy this evil

SCOFIELD

Our people who own Castle valley ranches are very much elated over the 6 inch fall of the beautiful On the faces of our young people we notice a perceptible grin the cause of which is also apparent Many are taking advantage of the good sleighing and the laughter of the merry makers is in harmony with the jingle of the sleigh bells

The year '97 has brought us a five foot ten inch constable, and a four and a half foot justice of the peace Both gentlemen are to our liking—democrats They have their sleeves rolled up, ready for business.

The assembly hall at Scofield was closed on Sunday on account of the building undergoing needed repairs All the people went to Winter Quarters

Since No. 2 mine at Winter Quarters was closed down No. 1 mine has been, to some extent, crowded The main entries are running three shifts in order to open up the mines and to make more room for miners.

What is rapidly becoming the favorite dance, was given last Monday night by the boarding boys at Winter Quarters Another will be given on next Saturday night. Will, take a tumble; Jack J. is after you. No scrapping allowed here.

Eastern Utah Advocate
February 25, 1897

MOLEN.

Our school has been closed the last week on account of the illness of the teacher, G. A. Weggeland. Mr. Weggeland is rapidly recovering and it is hoped school will resume early this week.

The entire sporting fraternity and otherwise of eastern Utah are cordially invited to attend the horse races here on March 4, 1897. It will be a kind of an annex to the show at Washington, We have the best track in the entire valley. Many speedy animals will enter.

The plague, la grippe, has just about spent itself here. None were exempted, all suffered alike. There was no serious cases.

The rancher is a happy man these days The long, cold winter accompanied by continued snowfall will put the ground in excellant shape for early farming and an abundant yield is confidently expected.

CASTLEGATE.

Being like a good many here, under weather, we were unable to send our weekly budget for the last week's issue. We were confined to our bed by an attack of la grippe and the grippe having such a grip we were unable to wield the faber. However, the grippe having lost its grip we are to the front once more. There are a number qu te ill from bad co'ds, a few of which being unable to work. Among this numb r is W. C. Cameron and W. H. Lawley.

Mrs Hy Wilcox had a severe attack of neuralgia of the heart which came near taking the good la ly from this mundane sphere, but close attention on the part of Dr Asadoorian and large heart d friends pulled her through. She is now convalescent.

The wife of W. S. Jones is confined to her bed by the prevailing sickness. Whole families have came down with this epidemic. The doctor says there are over fifty cases in town.

Born to the wife of Wm Ward, a girl. The little stranger came on Saturday morning but died on Monday and was buried on Tuesday,

George Green and w fe intend to pull out at an early day for their old home in Idaho.

A number of the young bloods of our town were scaring up a crowd to go down to Price to take in the masquerade. We did not learn with what success.

If any farmer in these valleys of the mountains is not satisfied with the way that the Dispenser of all good things has distributed the beautiful, he ought to come here that we may pile rocks on him. We think we have had quite enough. Any more and we are liable to gag

The many Castlegate friends of Miss Agnes Oviatt were greived to learn of her death at her home in Cleveland. It may not be too late now to tender to the bereaved parents our heart felt sympathy. She was a noble woman

County Supt. of s hools H G Webb, accompanied by the teacher from Thistle paid a visit to our district schools and found Mr. Cardall with his sleeves rolled up and right in the midst of his work. Castlegate tops all the schools in the county for rapidity in mastering the rudiments of elementary work. We do not fear that at the close of the school year but that the per cent. of the whole school will be above any school in the county. We do not boast. We have the proofs.

All the attached goods of Angus Mc Lean were auctioned off Tuesday afternoon by Sheriff Donant. Millburn, of Price, bought the butcher tools etc. John Hoon bought the house, the buggy going to H J. Nelson Each, in itself, was a bargain. Mr McLean was not seen at the sale, though his man, Friday, was on hand showing off the animals Such proceedings are to be regretted. Matters of this kind should be settled out of court.

The anniversary of the organization of the K. of P. took place on Tuesday night. A program was rendered consisting of songs and recitations followed by a dance. It was numerously attended.

Rumor has it that Charley, the organ grinder, is about to get married. The lady of his choice is Miss Rachel Griffiths.

George Washington's birthday passed off without any exercises of any kind. This day is one in history that has been accounted worthy to be set apart as a general holiday and every true patriot should remember it. In other settlements the district schools generally make the day an occasion for appropriate exercises, choosing the history of the father of his country for the main feature in order to install patriotism into the hearts of the little ones.

H. C Wardleigh, G. K. of R and S, of the K. of P. was up from Ogden taking part in the celebration on Tuesday. Other dignitaries were expected but fail to make connections.

The owner of that cow, wh ch is going around the lower part of town badly ripped in its hind parts, should shoot it in order to put the poor critter out of its misery. We were informed that it belonged to the Italian cow puncher bay, constable, take a hint.

W. Tell.

WELLINGTON.

The snow storm of Saturday deposited four inches of the beautiful.

Geo Holliday and Dose Tilwell came in from their asphaltum mine in Whitmore canyon on Saturday. They have six men at work doing developement work. They report the prospects for a paying proposition as good The gentlemen say there is more snow in Clark's valley than there has been for many years

Our schools were closed on Monday, Washington's birthday, and the occassion was fitting y celebrated by our people.

The Farnham people are replacing their dam across the river with a substantial rock and timber dam It is hoped it will withstand all floods in the future.

Railroad ties are coming in at a lively rate This industry will bring our people considerable revenue.

Miss Leonard spent Sunday with Castlegate friends.

Geo. Holliday went to Salt Lake Sunday night.

The only one making money here this winter is our genial coal dealer, S. Grundvig He has the best coal mine in Carbon county.

We had an excellant gospel sermon Sunday from Elder Wm. O Neal, of Vernal.

EMERY.

Snow, snow and still snowing Castle valley cannot complain of being slighted this winter as more than two feet of snow has fallen during the past two months. Should the snow continue to afford such pleasan. sleighing, many of the farmers will have poor teams with which to do their spring work.

The Citizens of Emery are still employed in removing the top from the tunnel. it is said that after a three dollar assessment on about 1,100 shares, it will require the same amount per share another year to finish the work. This winter's work will make the tunnel safe for next summer's water.

Prof. Giles is visiting Emery again He is determine I to place some of his beautiful organs in this vicinity. Music is elevating and refining, so, of course, we welcome his visit

The county court have granted Emery a board of health for which we feel very greatful. As good health prevails the board has little to do and we hope that while the sea is calm they will be deligent in the work of prevention.

Charles Foote and Miss Hannah Anderson were joined in the holy bonds of Wedlock, Wednesday February 17, Bishop Brinkerhoff officiating The groom displayed his liberality in the form of a delightful feast prepared at the bride's house All the guests were feeling jolly when at 4 o'clock p. m, they were seated at the table enjoying the good things of this life and when spirits or activity lagged a little rum would speedily revive them The people all wish the newly married couple long life, good health and as numerous posterity as that promised to Abraham.

The play given under the auspices of the Y. M and Y L association was a grand success, barring a slight accident on the first night of the performance, one of the actors was powder burned and was disabled for the evening

Will Emery ever be a large city' If the increase by births keep on an even pace with the last month the question will soon be settled affirmatively

Wanted: An M D, that can prescribe a medicine that will remove intemperance from the young and middleaged men. Reward The good will of the citizens of Emery and a blessing in Heaven

A PIONEER ITEM.

The commendable interest of the Pioneers of 1847 and their descendants in preserving historical items of the pioneer period for Utah is adding much to the public store of information on the subject. The NEWS trusts that this interest will not be allowed to abate, but that every name entitled to a place among the honored band of Utah's early settlers will be enrolled now, and that history will record any events through which they are deserving of special mention. The Pioneer Semi-centennial Commission is anxious to get all data attainable at the earliest possible date. Letters relating to this matter, received by the NEWS, are either turned over to the commission or published, that that body may have the information they contain. Among our letters today was the following interesting note concerning the carriage in which President Young crossed the Plains:

OGDEN CITY, Feb. 18, 1897.
To the Editor:

Learning through the NEWS that it is desirable to obtain the names of the survivors of the Pioneers of 1847, we, the daughters of Thomas J. and Rozetta Thurston, who crossed the Plains in the company of Captain J. M. Grant, in 1847, send you our names and addresses.

Our parents joined the Church in Ohio, after the martyrdom of the Prophet Joseph, and knowing that the Saints were going West they took with them to Nauvoo a nice family carriage and a span of very fine horses, which they designed for their convenience on their westward journey; but finding out that President Young was cramped for means to get an outfit for his journey, and that he intended coming with a wagon, father presented him with his carriage and horses, which he insisted on President Young's taking, telling him that the way would open up for him to fit himself out, and he would not be far behind him. President Young pronounced a blessing upon him and in a marvelous manner his blessing was fulfilled. Father was very soon on his journey with a splen-

did outfit and took with him to Winter Quarters four families besides his own.

Signed, Mrs. Sarah A. Thurston Grant, now of Oakley, Idaho; Mrs. Julia K. Thurston Arthurs, of Scofield, Emery county, Utah; Mrs. Caroline R. Thurston Fry, of Ogden City, 349 Eighteenth street; Mrs. Cordelia Thurston Smith, of Ogden City, 2385 Quincy.

WELLINGTON.

"March came in like a lion."

G. R. Hill has returned to the bosom of his family.

A number of our people attended the funeral of Father Mead at Price last Sunday.

Bassett Willson and a number of the boys have come in from the tie camp for a few days recreation

A word to the wise should be sufficient. Boys, if you do not rustle you will loose your best girl and will have to take a back seat. The same as a few did on Sunday.

Our meetings are becoming the best patronized place in town on Sundays

Supt. Webb visited our schools on Monday and was well pleased with the progress being made.

The pupils of the grammar department celebrated Longfellow day with appropriate exercises. An excellant program was rendered.

SCOFIELD.

S. Wilson and L. Jones made the rounds of the miners of Winter Quarters for the purpose of taking up a collection for the widow of the late George Martin, a miner, who was accidentally killed in the mines by falling coal. A neat little sum was realized.

Utah's best crop seems to be the most prominent feature in our Sunday school On last Sunday morning and in honor of President Woodruff's birthday a concert by the children of Winter Quarters was given under the management of Teacher Griffin The affair was an enjoyable one.

On account of the severe cold weather and exposure of the little ones attending district school a number have suffered much from coughs and colds. On this account the trustees will make a special effort to have one or two terms during the summer months.

An enjoyable concert was given by the Scofield choir on Friday last in the assembly hall for the purpose of raising funds to purchase new music books The program consisted of songs, duets, choruses and instrumental selections.

The Scofield music lovers have organized a brass band with John Hood as leader. The instruments have been ordered and are expected to arrive in a short time.

Work in the mines is rather dull and men are leaving the camp almost daily.

Like a number of others here, under the weather, we were unable to send our weekly batch of news for the last issue of the Advocate and while it is late as a news item we desire to mention the very creditable and appropriate exercises by the pupils of the Winter Quarters district school on Washington's birthday. The history of the farther of his country was the main feature. This was done in order to instil into the hearts of the little ones, patriotism and love for American institutions.

It is rumored that there will be a new demand for P. V coal on March 1st.

CLEVELAND.

Your correspondent wishes it distinctly understood that the young lady who received a mitten from Price is "unbeknown" to said correspondent All we wish is that the mitten may be fully reciprocated, or rather that the mitten so liberally given may receive a full share of reciprocity.—C.

It did us an amount of good to read the short sketch of the life of sister Agnes Oviatt. She was, indeed, a most estimable young lady and of good moral and religious qualities. Her death was mourned by the entire community.

To tell the exact truth the climatic conditions of our little berg are somewhat effected by atmospheric changes

Miss Eliza Johnson, the teacher of the primary department has been indisposed for some week or ten days and the little ones have had a lay off or rather a rest from school duties A number of the little ones are suffering from coughs and colds

We note sickness in a number of families of which we name McFarlane's, Potter's, Stoke's, Jensen's and others, none of which are seriously sick, only coughs and colds.

Thomas Farrish, who has been working in the mines at Eureka, may be seen again in our little town hale and hearty

Our friend, Charley Olson, was selling fruit trees in our neighborhood last week. Charley is now a city chap, but for all that he enjoys a visit to his country cousins.

In our next letter the Y. M. and Y. L. M. I. association will receive especial mention.

Mr. Dorius, the teacher would be glad to receive the Advocate in his school room about Friday noon that his students may select the more important news, to be used in the regular Friday afternoon service.

Sulrod.

W. J. Hill, of Wellington, was sur
prised by his family and friends on
Wednesday with a feast in honor of his
sixty-first birthday.

G. A. Willson Sr., of Wellington,
with his family and friends celebrated
that gentleman's sixty-eighth birthday
on Wednesday.

Deseret Evening News
March 9, 1897

Scofield Notes.

SCOFIELD, March 4—We had a
heavy snow fall in the latter part of
February, but a good deal of it was
melted by the March sun.

Times are very hard in this locality.
The U. P. mine only worked four and
a half days last month.

Half the men at Winter Quarters
have not worked a day yet this month.
They work this mine half one day and
half another.

Last Sunday our Sunday schools
had special exercises, to commemorate
the birthday of our Prophet.

The meeting house at Scofield has
been repainted and has a new set of
lamps.

Quite a number of people are leaving here in search of better employment.

Considerable sickness prevails at
present, especially among children.
                                    H.

Eastern Utah Advocate
March 11, 1897

SCOFIELD

This camp experienced a very heavy
snow storm on Sunday.

It is to the discredit of the leading people of Winter Quarters that they have become party to the scheme to deprive the
old miners of an equal privilege with the
younger men working in the entries. It
is, of course, well known that large
families require greater expenditures at
the company's store and on this account
the company should favor them. A
number of the large families encounter
serious hardships on this account. This
same trouble occurred about a year ago
and Supt. Sharp righted things by
equalizing the work between all miners

The night school has closed for the
season through lack of interest.

The dance at the boarding house on
Saturday was, as usual, an enjoyable
affair. John Jones of Castlegate assisted in furnishing the very excellent
music.

The sickness among the little ones
which prevailed so universally early in
the winter is rapidly disappearing.

✦ LOCAL NEWS.

Ripans Tabules: one gives relief.

Dave Evans was down from Castlegate
Tuesday.

Hy Loveless, of Huntington was a
Price visitor on Monday.

Andrew Simmons was down from
Spring Glen on Monday.

A number of Price's 400 attended the ball at Castlegate on Monday night.

W. J. Hill and W. J. Tidwell the Wellingtonites were Price visitors on Wednesday.

Abe Liddell and Geo. A. Willsou Jr were Wellingtonite visitors to the county seat on Monday.

J. E. Johnson of Huntington, brought in a bunch of fat cattle and disposed of them to Price butchers.

It is to the interest and advantage of the correspondents' own town that weekly news budgets appear in the Advocate each week.

The Jubilee commission have appointed Apostel Brigham Young director-general of the Utah Pioneer Jubilee to be held in July.

The party that left Price last week for the reservation returned a wiser party. They are also mad. They will now wait until the reservation is open.

A E Gibson and J. C Duling are camped in Fisher Canyon working their claims —Richardson correspondent of the Moab Times.

A. D. Dickson, school teacher and lawyer of Orangeville, has succeeded Albert Nageley as agent for the White sewing machine company for Emery and Carbon counties. Mr. Nagely goes to other fields

For the Corbett-Fitzsimmons contest at Carson City, Nev., March 17, the R G W., will make a rate of $46 15 from Price to Carson City and return. Tickets will be sold March 14, 15 and 16 limited for continuous passage in both directions with final limit 10 days after date of sale.

Hebe Frandsen will bring his family over from Castledale and try ranching in Carbon county this year. Lars will rustle grazing ground for the sheep.

D. H Gorley, from Cherokee county Kansas, reached Price on Monday and will in all probability locate on a ranch on Price river. He is a brother of J. H. Gorley.

Wallace Mathis and Miss Minnie Miles of Saint George were recently married at that place. Mr. Mathis will go on a mission to Europe in April accompanied by his wife.

Five foot of snow on Soldier on Sunday delayed all travel between Price and the post. The stage that should arrive here Sunday evening was compelled to turn back. It reached here twenty-four hours late.

The regular 1,000 mile books of Rio Grande Western issue, sold on and after February 13, will be valid for passage over all the lines of the R G. W., C M., R G., F & C.C., M T. and R Grade. The traveling public will appreciate the enhanced the Rio Grande Western mileage of the fact that these books used locally over the Colorado above mentioned

On Saturday night three of J. M Whitmore's horses were taken from his corral and no clue can be found of horses or thief. The sheriff, Mr. Willson and J. M. Whitmore started out Sunday and were unable to discover anything and on Monday evening returned to Price.

For the Annual Conference, L D S. and Womans Conference, L. D. S at Salt Lake the R G. W. will make the following rates from Price, Helper, Castlegate and Scofield, $5 00, Pleasant Valley Junction, $4 95. Tickets will be on sale from April 2 to 5, limited to April 13.

Late advices state that Tom Lamph who was inj red in the P. V. mine at Castlegate had his arm amputated at the shoulder and is getting along nicely while Bishop Lamph who was also in jured at the same time is in a critical condition from erysipelas having set in in the leg through which a pick was driven.

GREENRIVER.

Elgin and old Blake are just now vieing with each other in the way of substantial improvements.

Grand county commissioners have ordered finger boards at all diverging roads in Grand county pointing the way and giving distances to weary travelers They will receive the heartfelt thanks of many a weary pilgrim. Let Carbon county commissioners do the same immediately.

Sommers and Geiger received a car of lumber from Grand Junction last week. All goes to Willow Bend improvements.

Thomas Brinker, section foreman at Sunnyside, and Mrs. Rounsel of this place were joined in wedlock on March 8, at the residence of the bride's brother, Mr. Myers four miles from town.

Main street improvements are, 500 feet of picket fence extending from J. T. Farrer's store to the school house, A good sidewalk and a double row of shade trees goes with the fence. Our Mr. J. T. Farrer is spending his money in a m at praiseworthy manner.

The six month old daughter of Mr and Mrs. Chris Halverson, of San Rafael, died on March 2 and was buried here on March 5. Chris and his wife have the sympathy of their many acquaintances here.

Effie, the three-year old daughter of Mr. and Mrs. R. B. Thompson died Sunday morning from membraceous croup and was buried Monday afternoon at 3 o'clock.

County Attorney Eddy spent ten days at Greenriver and was well pleased with the growth of the place during the last two years. He took No. 2 for Salt Lake on March 4 and will return to Moab about March 9 He says Commissioner Dady Brown is the kin 1 to meet with in the line of entertainment.

Deseret Evening News
March 16, 1897

Scofield and Winter Quarters.

SCOFIELD, March 13.—We are having a great deal of sickness at Scofield and Winter Quarters just now. Nephi L. McLean lost a son on Wednesday, 9 years old, from appendicitis. George A. Green's only child, a son 18 months old, died on Wednesday; they will bury it at Springville. J. M. Beatie of Winter Quarters has been quite ill for several days; but is now improving nicely. The same may be said of Edward Dickinson of Scofield.

Dr. Smith is kept quite busy these days.

We have had a great amount of snow this week with heavy winds.

The prospect for work at the mines is not at all promising just now.

About twenty families will go from here to the Uintah country in the spring, if the reservation is opened.

H.

ORLANDO FISH MEAD.

PRICE, Carbon Co., Utah, March 3, 1897.—Another member of the Mormon Battalion has passed to the great beyond. Died at Price, Carbon Co., Utah, Feb. 26, 1897, of general debility, Orlando Fish Mead, born Jan. 10, 1823, at Wilton, Fairfield, Connecticut, U. S. A.; was the son of George and Hanna Whitlook Mead. His ancestors in America date back several generations, one of them having been born in Connecticut in 1650. His parents were of the Methodist persuasion, his father being a class leader. His mother died when he was six years of age. He was of a religious turn of mind in his youth. When sixteen years of age he first heard some vague rumors of a strange people called Mormons, and shortly afterwards had the pleasure of hearing Charles Wesley Wandle and L. S. Sparks of the New York branch of the Church of Jesus Christ of Latter-day Saints, preach in the Wilton school house. The teachings of the Elders struck a charm in his heart, and he was baptized with two others some time in January, 1838, by Charles Wesley Wandle, and joined the Norwalk branch; had to walk the six miles to meeting every week. He soon had the spirit of gathering and went to New York in 1839, arriving there too late to join the Saints bound for Nauvoo, but he followed on. He first saw the Prophet Joseph Smith in the Masonic hall early in 1840. He was ordained an Elder by Brigham Young the same year, and was instructed by him to "keep the Spirit." Went to St. Louis, Missouri, and stayed two years, returning to Nauvoo in 1843. Heard the Prophet Joseph preach in the bowery in front of the Temple. Was a member of the Nauvoo Legion and attended the parade; was deputized with others to go to Warsaw; heard the last public address made by the Prophet near the mansion; was standing by the house of John P. Green, when the Prophet with his mounted associates passed en route to Carthage; saw the wagons containing the bodies of the murdered Prophet and his brother Hyrum, brought home. On the 5th of April, 1845, he was ordained a Seventy in the Twenty-first quorum by Joseph Young, and was selected to be clerk. He was one of the artillery organization in 1846 to precede the Saints towards to setting sun; was at Sugar Creek, Pisgah and Garden Grove. On the 16th of July, 1846, was enrolled a volunteer in the Mormon Battalion. He passed through all the hardships connected with that toilsome march in the defense of his country; was discharged at Los Angeles on July 16, 1847, from which place he went to San Francisco and worked at shoemaking for a man named Francis A. Hammond. To him he unfolded the principles of the Gospel, and he afterwards became a prominent man in the Church. In 1848, when gold was first discovered, he worked in a placer digging on Mormon Island; was among the company that left for Great Salt Lake Valley in July, 1848, arriving some time in October. He had a narrow escape from being killed by an Indian near Ogden. He resided in Salt Lake City and Cottonwood for several years; was married to Lydia Aby Presley on January 27, 1853, at Salt Lake City, by Heber C. Kimball. In 1857 the threatened invasion of the Johnston army called for volunteers, and among them was O. F. Mead; he was also one of the volunteers to go out when Gov. Cummings and Thomas L. Kane came to Salt Lake City. In 1858 he moved to Lehi, and in 1861 moved to Spanish Fork. He spent some time prior to August, 1879, in a shoe shop on Market row, Salt Lake City. In 1881 his wife and children accompanied Teancum Pratt, a son-in-law, to Castle Valley, and early in 1885 went there himself, locating at a place called Helper; afterwards moved to Price, at which place he continued to reside until his demise.

He was the father of eleven children—nine girls and two boys; two of his daughters and nine of his grandchildren precede him to the spirit world. He leaves a wife, two sons and thirty-one grandchildren and a host of friends to mourn his loss.

The funeral services were held in the ward meeting house on Sunday, February 28th, at 1:30 p.m., Bishop F. S. Horsley presiding. The choir sang, Farewell all Earthly Honors. Prayer by Elder William J. Hill of Wellington. Choir sang O My Father. The speakers were O. J. Anderson of Castle Dale,

Samuel Cox Sr., president of the One Hundred and First quorum of Seventy, of which Father Mead was a member; William J. Hill, F. M. Ewell, also presidents of the quorum, E. W. McIntire, and a few closing remarks by Bishop E. S. Horsley. All spoke of Father Mead being a good man, always trying to live his religion; invoked the blessings of God upon the bereaved. The choir sang White Robes are Waiting for Thee. Benediction by Counselor A. Bryner. The remains were then viewed by all so wishing. Eighteen vehicles escorted the remains to the graveyard. The remains were lowered into the grave and the choir sang Unveil Thy Bosom, Faithful Tomb." The dedicatory prayer was offered by Elder N. L. Marsing. Brother Mead had been quite a sufferer with asthma the last few years.

E. S. HORSLEY.

Salt Lake Tribune
April 4, 1897

SHERIFF TUTTLE RECOVERING.

Hard Region Infested by the Lawless Class—Note and Personal.

Correspondence Tribune.]

Price, April 2.—Sheriff Tuttle is today said to be in a much better condition and is now on the road to speedy recovery.

A BAD NEST.

Your correspondent at Huntington, in his letter published in The Tribune this morning, shows that he is not in love with the people of Carbon county, or else is not posted regarding the recent attempts to capture outlaws which resulted so disastrously for Sheriff Tuttle of Emery county. He makes statements which are a misrepresentation of the facts, and your representative here is requested to give the public information of the true status of affairs in which official lethargy has been charged. The correspondent says "The Sheriff of Carbon county was expected to have gone with Sheriff Tuttle, but that officer did not make his appearance. The people of Emery county are not satisfied with the treatment received by Carbon county in not lending a hand toward capturing the outlaws."

These statements are erroneous in this, that Sheriff Donant with a posse put in three days down in that country vainly searching for a trace of the men wanted. On his return to Price he was unable to make the second trip just then, and deputized five men from here to assist Sheriff Tuttle. These five men were the only ones in the Sheriff's company during the seven-days' search which finally terminated in the shooting of Tuttle, and Sheriff Donant has done everything in his power to lend assistance in capturing Joe Walker, even to expending over $100 of personal funds, with no chance of ever being remunerated for it. The Sheriffs of Uintah, Carbon and Emery counties are all wanting this particular criminal, and in justice to those officers, it

should be stated that neither one of the counties, nor all three combined, is financially able to place their peace officers on a proper footing to cope with the desperate characters who infest the ravines and canyons of the country known as "robbers' roost."

Murderers, highway robbers, horse-thieves and almost every desperate criminal in the State make the San Rafael their rendezvous of safety, and probably will for years, because of its being so wild and uninviting to settlers that it must always remain a wilderness.

Criminals are comparatively safe in its wonderful natural fortresses, and to capture these defiers of the law, guides well acquainted with the country, and the exercise of a great amount of cunning will be absolutely necessary. This apparently accursed strip of country the geographics place in Emery county, one of the youngest and poorest counties in the State. Its terrible gorges and precipitous box-canyons are fast becoming the homes of gangs of outlaws who are a disgrace and menace to the life and property of every law-abiding community within the borders of Utah. The State will eventually have to take this matter in hand and give assistance in breaking up these gangs, who evidently will continue to do as they please and hold high carnival over the law, until some concerted action is taken by the State and the counties.

NOTE AND PERSONAL.

Attorney L. O. Hoffman has returned from Moab, where he has been attending court.

The County Commissioners will meet next Monday morning. This will be their second meeting this year.

J. B. Milburn has returned from Salt Lake City, where it is rumored he has been doing some political maneuvering for a "pull" to get the appointment as postmaster at Price.

Louis Lowenstein, one of our hustling business men, is in Salt Lake this week.

A number of people from Emery county are pouring into Price and taking advantage of the cheap conference rates to the metropolis.

Seven cars of gilsonite were shipped from this point by the St. Louis company during the month of March.

Postoffice Inspector Fitzgerald made Price a visit during the week.

Several carloads of wagons and farming implements have been received here recently for various points north and south of here.

County Assessor Tidwell is busy rounding up the herds of cattle and sheep, and will soon have finished that part of his labors.

Prosecuting Attorney Warf is doing good work in bringing the hotels, restaurants and peddlers to time with their licenses. This is something that was never before properly attended to, and the result of the work will net the county over $200, which is a neat increase in our revenues.

The Duchesne river is reported very high, so high was it, in fact, on Wednesday, that the mail could not be brought through that day.

Had the usual spring winds been blowing this afternoon, there might have been a disastrous conflagration in Price. A frame building, not over twenty-five yards in the rear of the R. G. W. depot, and which is occupied at present as a dwelling, was discovered to be on fire. A bucket brigade soon had the flames, which were in the roof, under control. The cause was a stovepipe, and the damage is nominal.

During the month of March Cupid Donaldson issued marriage licenses to the following couples: W. H. Babcock, aged 24, of Castle Gate, and Alice W. Thompson, aged 20, of Spring Glen; Enniar Anderson, aged 23, of Winter Quarters, and Neenie G. Bearnson, aged 20, of Spanish Fork; Jacob E. Hall, aged 18, and Martha E. Grames, aged 19, both of Minnie Maud.

Eastern Utah Advocate
April 8, 1897

SCOFIELD.

Last Friday evening, April 2, the good children of Winter Quarters did themselves proud by gathering together and surprising their school teacher W. H Griffin. Just as that gentleman was settling down to his supper, a gentle knock came on the kitchen door. The lady of the house apprised Mr. Griffin of the fact that he was wanted in his room Upon entering he was greatly surprised to meet over seventy persons filing into the house, loaded down with every conceivable kind of dainty eatables. The company then marched from the house,

to the meeting house, with picnic in hand, where, for several hours an entertainment interspersed with dancing was had. Miss Lizzie Wilson, in behalf of the school children, presented Mr. Griffin with a handsome shaving case as a token of love and esteem, and the recipient feelingly thanked those present for the honor and respect shown him. Dancing was kept up till the "wee sma' hours' when all retired fully satisfied with the success of the surprise.

Our day school closed for the season last Friday and teacher W. H Griffin took his departure for his home in Cache valley last Monday morning.

A large number of people from both Scofield and Winter Quarters have been attending conference this week.

J. M. Beatie and family spent the past few days in Zion. Mr. Beatie's many friends will be pleased to learn that he has entirely recovered from his recent severe illness.

There has been considerable sickness here lately. The mumps and "grip" seem to be going the rounds.

There is still plenty of snow in Pleasant valley, and by appearances it will be a month yet before grass will be seen Last year at this time the valley was beautifully green.

A pleasant social party in honor of Mrs. Millstead of Winter Quarters, was given on the occasion of that lady's departure for her home in Castle valley

Dr. J. W. Smith paid the county seat a visit this week.

CASTLEGATE.

Amidst the warbling of our own mountain singing birds, and the song of the Chanticleer, one of our old citizens donned his mining clothes to go to work. He had not only his clothes on, but he had a jag on too. Screwing up his courage he faced the cold morning air. Instead of cooling his heated brow and taking hold of the jag and wiping the earth with it, it only made the jag worse so that he kept on walking past the mines, Helper, Spring Glen, etc, until about 3 pm. Word came up from Sunnyside that he had got the better of that jag and for some one of his folks to come and bring him home. It is expected he will be home to-night.

The participants in the coming prize fight are in thorough training and so far as I can learn odds are in favor of the dark complexioned gent. It is to be hoped that the final stakes will not be forthcoming and the fight be declared off.

Constable Edwards was last night skirmishing around arresting and serving papers upon some of our young bloods. It appears that it is customary for them to jump on every train that comes into the yard, which gives the engineer worry and trouble. The other night they got on one and the engineer fearful that somebody would get hurt, disabled his engine by trying to pull her up out of the way. The R. G. W., are after them, hence the constable's action. At the trial before Judge Duerden the boys were each assessed $4, being merely the costs in the case, and they were given into the hands of Constable Edwards until the costs were paid. Just before the passenger train No 2 came in to-day the boys settled up and were turned loose.

The peace officers say they are determined to put a stop to this dangerous practice of making a play ground of the depot, and they should be upheld in their good work. If the youngsters are permitted to go on in their deviltry, some fatal accident may yet have to be chronicled.

An Italian residing in the lower part of town stabbed his wife this morning. Particulars are not obtainable at this writing.

Mr Joel Ricks has returned from Provo where he went as a witness in a case between the Provo Power Dam company and the R. G. W. Ry.

There has been a deal of sickness in this town, chiefly "mumps." Some grown up persons have been affected severely with them, it laying them off work for weeks.

The change in the weather has started the bicycle craze again. Last year's floods, and the spring freshets will make the stockholders of the bicycle track get down into their pockets to fix it.

Henry Holley is a little lonely just now. His better half is taking in conference and then it is expected that she will pay a visit to her parents before her return. They live in Wyoming.

When Ed Edwards was going around with head erect and shoulders braced turning his whole body when ever spoken to, and with a melancholy smile responded to interrogations, he was not drilling himself for a position on the U. N. G, no sir, it was a boil.

The railroad company have put in a new pair of scales for the weighing of coal.

D T. Evans is coaching a dramatic troupe. They intend playing "Waiting for the verdict."

The Price Dramatic troupe had their representative up here negotiating for a hall, they play "Foiled" a military drama It will be presented in the K. of P. hall.

WELLINGTON.

Wellington patrons of the Advocate are pleased to learn that the rightful manager of the paper has again taken possession, and we wish you success.

Spring, although a little late, has apparently come at last and our farmers are beginning to plow and plant.

Our primary school will probably close on the 16th. But the higher department will continue until the latter part of May.

What is thought to be whooping cough in a mild form is very prevalent among the children here.

St. Tidwell has the mumps. Girls look out for him.

Jake Liddell is still very low. Monday morning last while eating breakfast in bed, he was attacked by a severe spasm which came near being fatal.

Wm A Thayn, who has been on a mission to England, is expected to return home about the last of May.

A E McMullin and Thomas Jones are in Salt Lake attending conference and on business.

John L. Willson and family of Price spent a couple of days visiting relatives in this place.

Mrs. Amanda Taylor of Sanpete county spent a pleasant evening with her old time friends Mr. and Mrs. Geo A. Willson, on Monday last.

Eastern Utah Advocate
April 15, 1897

LOCAL NEWS.

Now is the time to plant your kitchen garden track.

H. H. Oviatt of Cleveland paid Carbon's capital a visit this week.

Dom. O. Robbins of Salt Lake City was in Price to-day and left for Huntington.

To-day being Arbor day the county Commissioners will not meet until Friday.

——mer was in Price this week. He reports things in Ferron to be on the qui vive.

The Price dramatic company will present "Forbid" in the K. P. Hall at Castlegate Saturday evening April 24.

———— Bassett will go to Ferron next week to adjust and place in position the telephone instrument at Ferron.

Mrs. A. J. Lee gave birth to a fine girl Sunday last. Mother and child doing well and the town marshall is gleeful.

Workmen will start to string the wire next week for the extension of the telephone line from Orangeville to Ferron in Emery county.

Ex-clerk, newspaperman(?), attorney(?) Braffet now threatens to sue the county for $10, salary claimed for three days services in 1897. Next!

It is thought that the disbursing of the Indian moneys at the agencies will be Col. Randlett's last official act in the capacity of acting Indian agent.

A sheep herder is confined in the Salt Lake county jail because he fails to know his own name and his mind has lost all former knowledge of himself.

Some of the soldiers from Fort Duchesne indulged in a friendly game of base ball while camped near the depot Tuesday, and they had some interested spectators.

Chris. Anderson came up from Green river Wednesday and is visiting his brothers. Chris. claims he will yet have a good farm down there if he only lives long enough.

The famous Indian band of the Teller Institute at Grand Junction, Colorado, has been engaged for the Utah Pioneer Jubilee and will be a feature of the parades and concerts.

The state auditor desires to let county auditors and treasurers know that the state is not yet liable for the salary of county collectors, and the statements sent in to the office should not contain such claims for half salaries.

"Robert Macaire," the first play produced in Utah, will be reproduced during the Utah Pioneer Jubilee, which will be held in Salt Lake City beginning July 20th and ending July 25th. Many of the original cast are still in the land of the living and will take part in the reproduction.

Major Isl y who has been in the east on a furlough for some time, passed through Price going to Salt Lake Tuesday. He will remain there but a few days when he will return to Fort Du chesne and assume the responsibilities of Indian agent, to which position he was appointed by President Cleveland ~~~~~ Ranlett upon being relieved will proceed to California where he intends making his future home.

The Holliday Coal company which was recently incorporated in Salt Lake City, and whose claims are located in this county, some nine miles from Sunnyed is working to make a shipment of four cars right away. The coal is said to be a good anthracite and brings $7 50 a ton on the Salt Lake market. Most of the incorporators are residents of Wellington and their enterprise deserves success. We understand that the company intends making another road to the mines so as as practicable to shorten the distance of hauling. As it is now the road is some fourteen miles long and that can be cut down some five miles. The seams of coal are 9½ feet and four feet thick and are separated only by a thin strain of rock.

R. G. Miller was in from his summer ranch early in the week. Mr. Miller will begin shearing sheep next week and states that 40,000 sheep will be clipped at the Price pens this coming season.

Genial William Taylor jr, of Ferron, was in Price Sunday and Monday. Mr. Taylor is manager of the Emery County Mercantile Company's branch store at that point and was up after a new stock of goods.

The Price Dramatic association will give a concert Friday evening of this week in the meeting house. An interesting program has been arranged, and the entertainment will conclude with the laughable farce "Popping the question."

Whooping cough is prevalent among the children of Price.

Louie Lowenstein is out in the Ashley country on business.

Mrs Percy Horsley's son Hugh is seriously ill from an attack of diabetis

Miss Bertrude Seely, of Castledale, is visiting her sister, Mrs. Heba Frandsen

Mrs. M. Montague has been very ill for two or three weeks but is now recovering.

Raymond Knight the cattle buyer of Payson was registered at the hotel Clarke to day.

R. G. Western carpenters have been engaged this week in repairing the corrals for shearing

Mrs Deal Hutchison is assisting her sister, Mrs. Geo. W. Bodle in the management of the Mathis hotel.

Price is just about depopulated these days The busy husbandman is preparing the ground for the seeding.

W W. Call cattle owner and farmer of Castledale, came in on No. 4 Sunday night from Zoa and left for his home on Monday.

The Castle Valley News says ' Eastern Utah is the state of Hell." We have often wondered why so many "imps" took up their residence in Price

Col J. F. Ranlett, Captain M. W. Day, Lieutenants Horne, Cavenaugh and Pritchard, Chief of the Indian police, John McAndrews were all registered at the Clarke Hotel this week. The gentlemen accompanied the company of 9th cavalry to Price.

Clerk Donaldson Tuesday issued a marriage license to McClure Wilson, aged 33, of Price and Miss Nellie Draper, aged 18, of Wellington. The couple went to Helper in the evening and were married by Justice Finch of that place. On their return by the midnight train they were met at the depot by 'Gentry's tin band" and escorted to Mr. Wilson's home.

The numerous correspondents of the Advocate are requested to please forward, no later than Tuesday of each week, their usual batch of news items. We will be pleased to give space to all news notwithstanding Brownlee's statements to the contrary. We deprecate the fact that this Brownlee should insult our correspondents, but we trust that they will consider the source and take no further notice of the wild rantings published by that individual on March 17.

The action of the court at Spring Glen last Friday in turning over all the articles which were in dispute between the Robey's and P. A. Francis, is condemned by many persons who think it was an injustice to the defendants to give the goods over before they had had a trial. Rumor has it that Mr. Robey will bring the matter up again by replevying what he claims is his and an interesting lot of facts are promised if the case comes up in the district court

Town clerk Horsley has posted notices that dog licenses will be due by May 1 and all dogs not licensed and fitted up with a collar will be decapitated after that date

Troop B 9 cavalry was in from the post to escort the Indians' cash box to the Indian agent. The escort left Price yesterday morning. The usual talk of an expected hold up was indulged in

Sheriff Tuttle's condition is gradually on the improve and he is out of danger it is hoped he may soon gain his strength and fully recover but the prospects are that he will yet have to remain in his room some four or five weeks

H. S. Loveless brought a herd of cattle over from his farm at Huntington for Ray Knight to-day.

Mrs. Kathioka Anderson has returned to her home at Castledale after a two weeks sojourn in Zion.

George McCall, foreman of the Salt Lake gilsonite mine at Castle Peak returned from the mines Monday

A. D Gash the Provo attorney came to Price last evening and went to Ferron to-day where he has a larceny case to attend to.

A number of sheep shearers are here at present and the work of shearing commenced this morning at the corrals just north of town.

W. H. Culmer superintendant of the Salt Lake Gilsonite company is in Price. Mr. Culmer says they need several more men to work at the Parlett mine.

Oscar Johnson has been brought home from Provo, and has so far recovered from the wound made in his neck by the explosion of a rifle, as to be now out of danger It was a narrow escape from instant death for the boy, and will be a lesson learned which he will not care to repeat.

Mr A E Gibson of Cleveland is in a highly elated state of mind over recent developments in some mining property in which he is interested in the La Salle mountains north and east of Moab. The latest assays received from samples secured from his property there show 25 per cent copper and nearly $500. in gold Mr Gibson claims to have a bonanza.

HELPER.

Mr. McClure Wilson of Price and Miss Nellie Draper of Wellington were quietly married here at the office of Justice J. Tom Fitch on Tuesday evening. The party arrived here on No. 8, evening passenger train, from Price and was made up of the bride and bridegroom, the latter's sister Mrs Miller, Mr. Dickson and Miss Ida Tucker. James Rooney and Attorney Warf were present and after the ceremony the party partook of a bounteous repast prepared for the occasion at the Helper restaurant after which the wedding party returned to Price by the midnight train. The happy couple have the best wishes and hearty congratulations of their many friends here.

WELLINGTON.

Bishop A. C. McMullin returned from a trip to Salt Lake and Heber City.

A number of our boys are at the Tidwell Holdaway coal mine digging coal and making a road to Sunnyside over which the coal is to be hauled. This mine will be a heavy shipper in the near future.

By reason of the light attendance in the district school the board decided to discontinue the primary department and consolidate the school. A mixed grade will continue for some time.

Our popular teacher, Miss Mary Leonard visited friends in Castlegate Saturday and Sunday.

We miss the smiling faces of Miss Mary McMullin and Miss Laura Hill who we understand are sojourning to the present in Price.

Barring a few cases of whooping cough the health of the community is good.

Farming and ditch cleaning is occupying the time and energy of most of our people.

Vernal Express. A few of the good citizens of Emery county are still camping on the trail of Walker, the outlaw who shot Sheriff Tuttle about a week ago. It is reported that there are several outlaws in the gang and that some of them hail from Vernal. It is claimed that they are in a rough, broken country and can stand off a whole regiment of men as long as provisions hold out. It is barely possible that some of the outlaws have been in, or passed through Vernal. In fact, when we come to think, Walker was here about six weeks ago— came about the time Judge Dusenberry and Rhodes did and left about the same time. This is a singular coincidence.

MINER SHOOTS HIMSELF.

Castle Gate Accident Results in Death in a Hospital.

Tomasi Saraceno, an Italian miner from Castle Gate, died yesterday morning at St. Mark's hospital, from the effects of a severe gunshot wound which he accidentally inflicted on himself at his cabin in Castle Gate on Friday. He was kneeling on the floor, endeavoring to pull a shotgun from beneath his bed, when the trigger caught in the carpet, the weapon was discharged, and Saraceno received the whole charge of powder and shot in the knee.

His leg was blown almost off and the wound was so serious that it was deemed best to bring the injured man directly to the city. When he reached St. Mark's hospital at 1 o'clock yesterday morning, he was so weak from loss of blood that the doctors decided to wait until morning before attempting an operation.

At 10 o'clock Dr. Worthington, assisted by Drs. Bascom, Critchlow and Behle, amputated the injured member, but the man was then so far gone that he did not rally from the effects of the operation, and died shortly after.

Saraceno was employed in the Castle Gate coal mines, and lived there with his brother. He had a wife and several children in Italy.

CARBON COUNTY COURT.

Justice's reports—Braffet, Donant et al. claims rejected.—Appropriations.

Last Friday, April 16, the county commissioners met pursuant to adjournment. All the selectmen were present and the following business was transacted:

On motion of Commissioner Hood, P. L. Olsen was appointed justice of the peace to fill the unexpired term of Wm. Burr.

Sheriff Donant's request for the board to appoint C. L. Maxwell deputy sheriff, was refused.

Liddell and Thayn reported that they had accepted the bridges at Wellington and Price from the contractors.

It was ordered by the board that the county clerk collect all licenses, and he was also authorized to commence action against delinquents when necessary.

The clerk was instructed to notify H. G. Webb, county superintendent of schools, to file his bonds on or before the 12th day of May 1897.

A circular letter of instructions to road supervisors was adopted and the clerk instructed to mail copies to each road supervisor in the county.

The reports of ex-Justices' Burr of Price and C. H. Cook of Spring Glen were presented and accepted.

The report of ex-Justice Howells of Winter Quarters was rejected.

M. P. Braffet's claim for $10, for three days salary in 1897, was also disallowed on the reading of the following communication:

'In the matter of M. P. Braffet's claim for salary for three days, January 1, 2 and 3, 1897, I beg to say in my opinion the county is not liable for said claim for many reasons which I do not think prudent to enumerate.

"J. W. Warf,
"County Attorney."

The following is a list of the claims allowed

A. Bryner salary treasurer	$15.00
Emery County Mercantile company	9.30
Samuel Cox bridge contract	150.00
A. K. McMullin & Son	100.00
" " "	25 00
Gus Donant expenses	18.15
" "	4.00
A. W. Horsly janitor	37.50
" " court bailiff	12.00
E. S. Horsly carpenter work	14.00
J D Smith Printing	1.25
A. J Lee, feeding Brownlee	10.00
D W. Holdaway "	7.50
Wm. Burr, justices docket	.50
M. P Braffet, Printing	15.00
J. W. Warf, expenses	7 73
Total	638.25

Court then adjourned until Monday, June 28, '97.

BOLD OUTLAWS GET $7,000 IN GOLD.

WAS DESPERATE AND DARING.

The Money Belonged to the P. V. Coal Co.

They Are Persued by Posses But Not Yet Captured.

Bold, bad highwaymen created consternation and excitement Wednesday noon at Castlegate by holding-up E. L. Carpenter the Pleasant Valley coal company's paymaster and making off with $7000 in gold.

The horsethieves, bandits and murderers infesting what is commonly known as Robbers Roost sixty miles southest of Price, on the San Rafael river in Emery county, have in the past few years committed many an autrocious deed of daring, but none so bold and audacious as this last unprecedented and nervy hold-up. This tough clique is rapidly gaining a reputation not to be envied by any except such men as composed the celebrated "James gang" and they are invariably successful in their undertakings and in evading the minions of the law.

This last daring act of theirs is supposed to have been committed by Tom Glasell and "Butch" Cassidy, and it is reasonably certain at this writing that the identity of at least Cassidy, who figured about a year ago in the Montpelier, Idaho bank robbary, can be established.

The particulars of the hold up, robbery and flight of the desperadoes is as follows: The pay rolls, money and checks for paying the coal diggers and company's employes at Castlegate was sent down Wednesday from Salt Lake City on the Rio Grande Western passenger train No. 2 which reaches Castlegate at about 12 o'clock noon. There were two sacks of silver, one of $1000 one of $960, one sack of gold containing $7000, and a satchel holding the rolls and checks for another thousand dollars, in all $9460. These were all transferred to the hands of E. L. Carpenter and a deputy clerk who were at the depot awaiting its arrival.

When No. 2 pulled out for Helper the paymaster and deputy crossed over the tracks to the Wasatch company's store, a two story rock building about fifty yards distant from the depot, and were just about to carry the treasure up the stairs, on the east side of the building, which lead up to the P. V. Coal company's offices, when a rough looking individual, evidently "Butch" Cassidy, stepped in front of Mr. Carpenter and exclaimed "drop them sacks and hold up your hands."

The request was backed up by a six-shooter being pushed into the astonished paymaster's face, and he naturally complied. T. W. Lewis the clerk, noted the situation at once and made a run into the store with the thousand dollar sack of silver. The bold highwayman then cooly stooped and picking up the other two sacks and satchel handed them to his confederate who was on horse-back near at hand. Cassidy's pal rode swiftly down the road, but the former was out of luck for a few moments as his horse got loose and started away. He however ran rapidly and caught the animal a few yards away, instantly mounted and sped after the man ahead.

While Mr. Carpenter was being relieved of the money the mounted bandit flourished a sixshooter and fired several shots promiscuously, and the only thing done toward preventing their escape, until it was too late, was the firing of three shots from the offices of the company as they flew down the road. The robbery was accomplished with so much bravado and daring, that the suddenness of the act completely paralyzed the numbers of men who were lounging about near the scene, and there were nearly a hundred of them around and in the store who witnessed the whole affair.

Passing safely through the lower part of town the robbers stopped a short distance north of the half-way house and cut the telegraph wires. They also examined the satchel and finding nothing of use to them in it, left it on the road. The sack containing $860 in silver had been dropped near the power house in town, no doubt on account of its being to heavy too carry, so their load now consisted only of the $7000 in gold. Reaching John U. Bryners ranch at the mouth of Spring creek canyon and just north of Helper, they crossed his land and went about two miles up the canyon, where they turned south over the ridge and continued on a trial which makes a perfect circuit of Helper, Spring Glen and Price, and being only distant from them about three miles.

It was 2 20 p.m. when they reached the main travelled Emery county road between Cleveland and Price, and here they cut the telephone wire, but they were too late in doing so as messages had already gone over the line to Huntington, Castledale and Cleveland where posses were being organized to intercept the men.

At 4 p.m. the mail carrier met them this side of Cleveland and they were then but four or five miles ahead of Sheriff Donant's posse which left Price at 3 p.m. The men are described as being one about 35 years of age and the other as middle aged. The younger man wore a black hat, blue coat and goggles, while the man who held Mr. Carpenter up had on a light slouch hat, denham overalls and brown coat. Both men were sun-browned and appeared more like cow boys or common hobos than desperate highwaymen. One of the men rode a grey horse with only bridle and no saddle, and the other was on a bay horse with bridle and saddle. Each carried two six-shooters and were seen loitering around Caffey's saloon during Tuesday. They had evidently laid their plans well and were there on time to prepare for the capture of the money.

Mr. Carpenter and others followed the highwaymen down the canyon on an engine, but did not see them and came on to Price where the news spread like wild-fire.

One posse left here under Sheriff Donnant, as soon as it could be organized, another scoured the hills from Castlegate to the Emery county road south of Price. Three posses started from points in Emery county and at a late hour Wednesday they were hot on the trail. Ex-Sheriff Dickinson and others were sent down from Salt Lake and were joined here by other men who proceeded to Greenriver, where they would take horses and ride the country south of there.

The affair has caused the most intense excitement all over the country, and will likely be the means of drawing the attention of state officials to the necessity of concerted action in obliterating these gangs of audacious outlaws who reign supreme in Robbers Roost.

The P. V. Coal company offered a reward of $2000 for the capture of the robbers and to-day doubled the amount. A chance for some one to earn $4000

Latest news from the seat of war as we go to press, is that the Price posse has exchanged shots with the fleeing highwaymen and two horses were killed, but the men are still at large.

GREENRIVER.

Everybody busy and things are popping.

M. H. Beardsley was in town Monday looking after his hotel interests.

A big herd of sheep are coming and Tom Farrer is happy in anticipation of a good sum for ferrying them across the river.

Nobody sick. All got well Doctor left town and every one so busy that there is no time for scandal.

Dady Brown, our popular Grand county commissioner, has just returned from Moab where he attended a session of the county court and visited friends and relatives. The broad smile makes us believe that he is glad to get back to the cabin by the river.

Miss Mary Smith and her brother Charley are in from the ranch, and are doing business with our dentist.

Somers, Geiger and R. B. Thompson are having irrigating wheels constructed for irrigating purposes. Ross Wheeler is doing the carpenter work.

A. P. Mohr has completed his irrigating wheel.

Joe Ross and Lee Valentine have their 11 by 24 foot irrigating wheel finished. It is a daisy and works splendidly.

Durant, Howland and Spicer's steam pump is doing the work for all three of them in fine style.

Mr. Valentine's one horse pump plant is a success when he is there with his whip.

J. T. Farrer's ditch is running full and the twenty ranchers below it are happy.

Mr. Atkinson has just completed a new wheel 8 by 25.

Frank Jacobs has quit railroading and will devote his entire time to farming.

Mr. Myers is in town and says he intends planting sixty acres this spring

Chris. Anderson has the piers for his irrigating wheel finished, but will not build the wheel until next winter. He is going to Price to blacksmith during the summer. Chris will be sure of a home next year.

We all rejoice with the Advocate on its being returned to its rightful owner, and hope it will have no more trouble with the B's, Brownlees, Braffet's or "Brownies," or whatever they should be called.

CASTLEGATE.

Saveedro, the Italian who was shot in the knee by the discharge of a shotgun last week, and was taken to St. Mary's hospital for treatment, died that same night. He was interred at Salt Lake City. It is a mystery who did the shooting, for when any crime is committed by any of this class of people they will not give any particulars. Some say that he did it himself while others say that another man did it. Several who were there at the time of the shooting have left town and the probability is that they will never return.

Charles Carara who got hurt a few days ago by a piece of rock falling on him, went into the city for examination as he was fearful that his shoulder bone was severely injured.

"Waiting for the Verdict" will be rendered by the Evans troupe on Saturday evening April 24.

Bp. Fullmer was a visitor to our burg yesterday, he is advance agent for the Price dramatic company.

The muddy state of the river is liable to cause a suspension of work in the mines.

The breakage of some part of the coal slack conveyor, laid the coke hands off work for a short spell. It is now repaired.

The sickness among the children has considerably abated, there being only one or two isolated cases.

It is astonishing to see the number of idle men who are soliciting charity as they make a break in their tie-pass route.

Dr. E. R. Shipp, after a brief visit of a professional nature, has gone south. It is to be regretted that she did not meet with better success while here.

Born, April 15, to the wife of W. T. Lamph a boy. Mother and child doing well.

Quite a surprise was sprung upon old lady Hansen of Helper on the occasion of her sixty-third birthday. Relatives and friends met at her house and had a good time.

Mr. T. T. Lamph has returned home from Salt Lake City, looking very well indeed after the severe ordeal he has

gone through in St. Mark's hospital. A large number of friends were at the depot to welcome him home. Mrs. W. Garbett, his sister, came with him from the city to spend a few days with her relatives here

Miss Emma Larsen of Cleveland is again an attache of the Wade hotel.

A large addition is being put on the house of F. Cameron. Rumor has it that after completion, assistant Supt. Williams will exchange residence with him.

Mike Kuzner is back again after an absence of about six months in the hospital. His leg was taken off above the knee.

HELPER.

Easter Sunday was most appropriately observed here by the church people and Sunday school children In the afternoon services were conducted in the school house under the direction of David Burnfield. Some fifty children gathered together and many of the parents were present. An interesting program was gone through, consisting of songs, musical selections and recitations. The children were made happy by the distribution among them of a number of nicely colored eggs The superintendent, Mrs C. M. Johnson, assistant superintendent, Mrs. J. Parrott, Mr. D. Burnfield and other officers of the Sabbath school are to be congratulated on the school's success.

Times are very quiet here but pay-day will rejuvenate us somewhat this week.

Our district school will close very soon for the summer.

Miss Maude Burnfield is visiting friends at Ogden and Rawlins, Wyoming. We hope that she will soon return home as her services as organist of our Sabbath school, are appreciated and it is very difficult to find a substitute.

Mrs. J. A. Parrott and son Clifford have just returned from a week's visit at Salt Lake.

Mrs. David Burnfield departed Friday for Salt Lake and Ogden where she will spend a couple of weeks visiting friends.

It is rumored that our merchant, I. Glaser, is suffering from an attack of the mumps and from the effects of being kicked by a horse, both combined has rendered his smiling countenance "a sight to behold."

Mrs. Thompson who has a stock of hardware in the New York store building, intends moving to Price where she will enter into some mercantile business.

Two of our popular young ladies will soon put in a complete stock of groceries and drygoods in the New York store building. May they prosper and have abundant success.

Mrs. James McCune has bought the restaurant business of the Kilburn sisters Mrs. McCune is perfectly familiar with this work and will assuredly meet with the success she deserves.

WELLINGTON.

Water is again turned into the Wellington canal and our townspeople are glad to stop indulging in the "passtime" of hauling water from the river, as they have been compelled to do for the past seven months.

Several of the family of W. H. Tidwell are afflicted with mumps.

Whooping cough seems to be on the increase among the children here, but no deaths have so far resulted.

People are all busy with their farm work just now, and the consequences is the town enjoys peace and quietness.

We expect by indications that work on the Wellington flood-ditch will again be postponed until the floods come down upon us again in the summer. Some of the residents will then exclaim "I knew the cow would eat the grindstone." The wrangle now on about this matter should be stopped at once, and work started on the ditch in accordance with law. It would be for the protection of the interests of all the people residing here, and they should work in harmony to complete the ditch.

LOCAL NEWS.

Ripans Tabules cure dyspepsia.

Don C. Robbins was in Price early in the week.

County Clerk Donaldson was ill early in the week.

The Miller wool-clip amounted to over 50,000 pounds.

Attorney L. O. Hoffman was out of town on legal business.

J. M. Easton, of Salt Lake, was at the Hotel Clarke this week.

Hugh Hawley is slowly convalescing and will soon be around again.

A. J. Walton of Scofield has gone to Cleveland to farm this summer.

County Attorney Warf made a trip to his ranch near Castledale late last week

Clarence Marsh of Salt Lake City came down to Price on No. 2 Wednesday.

The Emery County Mercantile company is shipping a few car loads of cedar peats.

George Nixon came over from Huntington to meet his wife who arrived here Sunday from Provo.

Joseph A. Young of Huntington is in Price. Joe is having his sheep sheared and will get a good crop of wool this year.

Jacob B. Johnson of Cleveland was here Monday for a load of freight. He has rented his farm to Mr. Bjerenson of Scofield.

Orange Seely, of Castledale was in Price early in the week receiving a lot of farm machinery from the Salt Lake Consolidated Implement company for his ranch.

Sheep are being sheared at the rate of 2000 a day at the corrals in Price, and the clip is rapidly sacked and stored in the wool warehouse which is already nearly filled.

J. W. Foote was down from Helper on Monday and in company with Price sports made a raid on the ducks in the river and vicinity and there is none left to tell the tale.

The spring winds are commencing to howl and real estate in consequence is suddenly raised above our grasp. Great clouds of desert sand are sprinkled upon the just and unjust alike, but "April showers" will soon settle the real estate boom in this part of the country.

Reports were rife this week that Joe Walker had been seen in Huntington lately, and that horses answering the description of those lost by Tobe Whitmore were also in that locality. The rumor could not be verified, but should such be true it does not speak very highly for the bravery of our Huntington friends who it is said were close enough to recognize him.

Louis Lowenstein has returned from the Ashley country.

Prof H E Giles is making a trip through Castle valley.

Callaway the barber will occupy his new shop about May 1.

Easter Sunday was fittingly observed by the younger people of the town.

Frank Wood came in from the Castle Peak gilsonite n ine Tuesday for supplies.

Postal Inspector Fitzgera'd has this week been making a tour of Emery county.

Sargeant W. W. Bessell is nursing a sprained ankle. Too much "wheel" was the cause.

W. F Culmer was in Price Monday and made a trip to the Pariett mines during the week.

The rivers in Emery county are reported as being pretty high but no damage has thus far resulted.

Sheriff Tuttle has now so far recovered as to get up and will within a couple of weeks be able to get out again.

Hebe Leonard is over from Huntington and is one among the 41 sheepshearers now employed at the Price corrals

Mabel Moore, the popular clerk of the Orangeville Co-op. went through Price Tuesday evening to Salt Lake City where she will visit with her friends for a few weeks

Thomas Wright and family, of Cedar City, Iron county, were in Price a few days ago. The gentleman is about to locate on a farm near Huntington and will in future make Castle valley his home.

R A. Shearer from Salt Lake City has taken the position at the R. G W office in Price as operator which was made vacant by Mr. Richards resignation The latter gentleman is quite sick at the Hotel Clark

Raymond Knight of Payson sold 835 head of cows and calves to J. L. McFatton of Meeker, Colorado, last Friday, and the purchaser at once shipped eight car loads east. The stock was bought up in Emery county.

The sheep shearers are kept busy and a large number of sheep have already been clipped. Miller's herds have been done and others keep coming in Shearing will probably be in progress for several weeks yet.

The state auditor desires to let county auditors and treasurers know that the state is not yet liable for the salary of county collectors, and the statements sent in to the office should not contain such claims for half salaries.

At last quite a number of men and teams are working cleaning out the town ditch The water has only been shut off for about four weeks, and if the scrapers are kept going we will possibly have water in town by time potatoes blossom.

The Price Dramatic company assisted by H. A. Southworth, will present "Foiled" in the K. of P. hall at Castlegate Saturday night. The company done very fair in this production and should be liberally patronized by our neighbors.

Carl Wilberg has sold his business at Castledale to the Emery County Mercantile company and that firm will at once assume charge of the store. They will put in a complete stock of dry goods and groceries and hereafter conduct a general merchandise business at the old stand of Mr. Wiberg.

There are apt to be some suits planted against the county, as the sheriff and his posse threaten to find out if they are not entitled to their pay for hunting Joe Walker, and Braffet needs some more salary from the county all of which the commissioners refuse to pay. The air is getting blue with sulphurous fumes and it may burst into a flame any minute.

Our county commissioners do not appear to be afraid of turning down bills which they consider exhorbitant or illegal even if the claimants do threaten law suits in consequence. Their action at the last sitting of court in disallowing the claims of Braffet, Donant, et al will probably be tested in the courts and such a test won't show whether such claims were legal or not.

The section gangs of the Rio Grande Western between Greenriver and Price are all working together for a short time. They have raised the track three feet near Lower Crossing where the floods last fall washed it out, and this week they are raising a half mile of track just east of Price. It is their intention to make the track more secure at the places where floods do damage, by building the road-bed above high water mark.

The numerous correspondents of the Advocate are requested to please forward, no later than Tuesday of each week, their usual batch of news items. We will be pleased to give space to all news notwithstanding Browning's statements to the contrary. We deprecate the fact that this Browning should insult our correspondents, but we trust that they will consider the source and take no further notice of the wild rantings published by that individual on March 17.

L. Lake passed through Price this week on his way to Ashley.

John Lott was over from Huntington with cattle for shipment late last week.

Charles McAndrews of Ogden and J R Wren of Salt Lake were registered at the hotel Clarke during the week.

Dr P C Christensen of Orangeville came to Price Tuesday. He is going through the county on professional business.

The Emery County Mercantile company's new adds are very attractive and show the enterprise of that modern business house.

County Attorney Warf has gone to Salt Lake. He will visit Loa, Wayne county, before returning home and may be absent a week or more.

Next week will close the school year for the Price district school. Nearly all the district schools in the county will close about the same time.

Mrs. O T McCormick is down from Salt Lake City making a short stay with her husband, who will go back to the city as soon as he closes school.

The Price Sunday school association concert last Friday was well patronized. There was a good program and a dance given after the entertainment concluded.

The Castle Valley News is now printed in Salt Lake City, and its columns are well filled with framed pictures and theatrical gossip, which will of course tickle its readers. Its local news, well you simply can't find any, and it is "a hot thing," we dont think, is this all patent abou't?

Major Charles S. Ilsley, Ninth cavalry, U. S. army, came to Price last Saturday and left for Fort Duchesne to assume the duties relative to his appointment by President Cleveland as agent at the Uintah and Uncompahgre reservations. Col Randlett was succeeded by Major Ilsley as commander of the post at Fort Duchesne, and he was now on his way to the post to take charge of Indian affairs there according to his instructions from the interior department. When asked for an opinion regarding the possible opening of the Uncompahgre reservation to settlers this summer, he stated that he had no more knowledge of the matter than what the press had published already. The late dispatches from Washington contained all that has so far been done, but he thought the matter would be speedily settled. During the summer some time, the major intends marching a troop of his cavalry overland to Fort Douglas simply as a practice march, and this arrangement will afford an interesting and pleasant diversion for the troopers, as the country to be thus traversed is most delightful for hunting and fishing grounds.

WEDDING BELLS

Chab Millburn and Miss Olive Branch went to Salt Lake City Wednesday morning. This fact might not be of much consequence were it not for the fact that the young couple will return home Saturday as Mr. and Mrs Millburn. Miss Olive Branch is a bright, handsome and intelligent young lady of 18 summers, and having resided in Castle valley the greater part of her life has a wide circle of friends and acquaintances. Mr. Millburn is a well known and popular young business man of Price, and the best wishes and hearty congratulations of their numerous friends will go with them in their future life

Mr and Mrs Millburn will upon returning home, temporarily make their residence with Mrs, Branch.

Eastern Utah Advocate
April 29, 1897

SPRING GLEN.

The farmers are busy getting the ditches ready for the irrigating season.

Heber J. Stowell is receiving a visit from his father who has just arrived from New Mexico.

Our district school closed last week Mr. Southworth's efforts met with good success and general satisfaction is noted among the patrons.

Justice Simmons' well is a boon to our townspeople. The water is obtained by seepage from the river and is as clear as crystal and as pure as a mountain stream.

Harrison Miller has moved his family to his ranch up Spring canyon

By the middle of June the Spring Glen canal will be completed to a point above C. B. Rhoades' place, and about 450 acres more of excellant land will be covered by this canal. A greater portion of the land to be covered by this extension is owned by H. A. Southworth and J. T. Rowly. Mr. Southworth will as soon as the canal is completed, seed about forty acres to lucern.

The Spring Glen canal company's flume just above Helper which was constructed by the railroad company has been a scource of much annoyance. The flume was constructed over the pipe line and has settled in places causing great loss of water. An effort will be made by the canal company to secure a different channel where an all earth channel can be had.

WELLINGTON.

The county road east of town is being graded, and will be a splended turnpike for a short distance, where the waters usually flood it.

Soldier and Coal creeks are both quite low at present but are very muddy.

The Tidwell ditch is being thoroughly cleaned out this week.

In several places along the road, water has broken from the Wellington canal and has flooded the country.

Our school district is to have a new school house which is a much needed improvement. It will be commenced at an early day and if possible completed this summer. The people of Wellington are to be congratulated on their progressivences.

Nearly all newspapers received by the people of Wellington are late two or three days in reaching the subscribers. The fault evidently lays with our post master, and residents are not at all pleased with getting their mail when a week old.

An accident occurred at the Big Springs ranch on April 28, that came nearly proving fatal to the six year-old son of Hyrum Ch tender, foreman of the ranch One of the men had left a team standing in the yard for a few moments, and during his absence the boy climbed into the seat and started the horses. In trying to stop them the little fellow was dragged over the dash board, and the wheels ran over his body just below the breast bone. This caused an internal hemorrhage, but medical aid arrived in time to stop it and the boy is now apparently restored to his normal condition. At last accounts he was rapidly improving.

George Holliday came down from the coal mines Monday last and reported developing work progressing nicely. At present the company is working two shifts

W. J. Tidwell made a flying trip to Sunnyside Monday, where he gathered in and assessed a few sheepherds.

All hands were thankful for the refreshing showers of Tuesday.

Our district school will continue one month or possibly a little longer.

Will Fausett has taken the Fausett cattle to the park.

Willie McMullin has started a cow-herd and will be pleased to receive all the cows in town.

John L Willson was a visitor to Wellington the first of the week.

Jacob Liddell a condition does not improve as fast as his friends would like, but they still hope for his ultimate recovery

Guy Willson has gone to Price to work.

L. M. Olsen was down from Price Sunday. He inspected the railway ties stacked at this place and was very well satisfied as to the quality.

CLEVELAND

Thomas Richards rejoices in the birth of a lovely daughter. Mother and child doing well

Mrs. E B Shipp went through Cleveland last week and delivered lectures while here. They were well attended

Miss Tina Larsen has arrived here from Ephraim, and it is rumored she will make her home here in the future. We are pleased to see her back again.

The young folks spent an enjoyable evening at the home of Miss Clara Alger Sunday. The young lady will make her home in Nine Mile this summer, and her friends are sorry to see her depart.

The relief society of Emery stake held their quarterly conference here recently, and it was well attended as was also the primary conference. Representatives from all the different wards were present, and everyone had an enjoyable time.

Steppe Johnson and Miss Emma Ward were married on the 13th instant. We wish them much joy and prosperity.

The farmers are all busy getting the canal in good condition for the summer.

Lewis Overson who attended school at Ephraim this winter, has returned home and is doing his spring work. Lewis is a successful farmer, and his cousin Henry Osterstrom came back with him and will try his luck with Castle valley soil.

One of the Listers children and two of the Rasmussen children had a narrow escape from death the other day. They had been eating a lot of dried beans and they nearly lost their lives through the consequent bloating.

EMERY.

The people are favored with a spell of warm weather, and the farmers are taking advantage of this, and planting their grain. The soil is in an excellant condition this spring, and everything goes to favor the opinion, that heavy crops will be raised this season.

The state appropriation of school funds came to the relief of the trustees just in time to prevent the closing of the school and as this appropriation exceeds the amount expected, the school board will run the school five weeks longer than per contract.

The Saints of Emery were highly entertained last Sunday by a number of young men, belonging to the deacon's quorum, who were each assigned an article of faith, as a text. These boys are under the tuition of Bishop Brinkerhoff in the Sunday school, and they have an excellant trainer.

Mr. and Mrs. Peter V. Bunderson were made to rejoice over the arrival of twin babies, a boy and a girl, each weighing 7¾ lbs. The children and mother are in good condition, and we think the little folks have come to stay The people feel to congratulate the parents, and hope they will live to see the children do them honor.

CASTLEGATE.

What might have turned out to be a serious accident occurred here Sunday evening Young Thos Williams was riding his wheel and wishing to play a joke on him, some girls put a railroad tie in his path, thinking that when he saw it he would slow up Wether he saw it or not he ran into it and was thrown very heavily to the ground, stunning him so much that he had to be helped home, and the doctor sent for Concussion of the brain was fea ed Dr Assadoorian did all in his power to restore him to consciousness but failed and the young man remained somewhat delirious until next day, when he came to himself. He is at this writing, getting along alright.

Our town has settled down to its usual quietness and everybody is now persuing the even tenor of their way It was a pleasing circumstance to note the difference of the accounts of the late robbery here as given in the two Price papers. The Advocate had a very accurate and detailed account, while the News (?) had an item that had the appearance of being sent from San Francisco.

Dr Assadoorian has been called away several times in the last few days to at tend to patients along the line. His prompt attention to the calls avert serious complications.

Black Jack has taken to riding the "bike."

There was quite a nice turnout to witness the rendition of "Waiting for the Verdict by the Evans troupe. Several of the parts were well represented.

A young folks dance was held in the K. of P. hall Monday n'ght, and a "Benlic's" dance on Tuesday night at the same place.

Ed Cox is going into training for the first road race at the metropolis.

Now is the time for a first-class butcher. There is a famine in this town for meat.

V. D. Cram of Huntington is in town with a new kind of washing machine. A lady from Denver is also showing a similar kind of cleaning apparatus.

A number of the high officials of the P. V. coal company have been here examining the workings and making a general inspection this week.

Born, to the wife of T. W. Williams, twins The mother is not so well as could be wished but it is the hope of her friends that she will soon be convalescent,

---

LOCAL NEWS.

--

Cabe Hite was in Price the other day.

E/M. Gilson Sundayed with Price friends.

H. A. Park of Nephi is registered at the Hotel Clark.

W. H. Dickson, of Denver, is the new operator at the depot.

Mrs. Hyrum Frandsen of Mt. Pleasant is visiting relatives in Price.

Agent Hunter of the Studebaker company was down on business a few days.

L. S. Dickenson stayed over in Price last Friday on his return from "Greenriver.

Mrs. M. Montague presented her husband with a fine baby boy on Thursday night.

Born to Mr and Mrs. R w Anderson on Sunday morning April 25, a boy. Mother and child are doing nicely

The Ephraim Enterprise states that Judge and Mrs. Johnson will take a pleasure trip to California in the near future.

Assessor Tidwell is staying pretty close around the sheep shearing corrals and don't intend to allow any to get away from his.

Special agent Shorrs of the Rio Grande Western was in Price this week on business connected with the Castlegate hold-up.

Sheep shearing will commence at P V. Junction about May 1, and some 75,000 or near that number, will be sheared at the corrals there.

S H. Eddy, Grand county's prosecuting attorney, was the guest of J. W. Warf on Sunday and left for Salt Lake on the evening passenger train.

Henry Blake, Denver; W. M. Elly, Ogden; T T. Young, Kingston, I. A. Green and Joseph W. Wilson, Salt Lake City were at the hotel Clark this week.

Some wag with a keen sense of the external fitness of things inscribed on the register at Hotel Clark, the following address: "Gus Donant, Afraid of Robbers Roost."

Flack and Downard have the contract for building Prosecuting Attorney Warf's residence. The building will be constructed on modern lines and rushed to completion.

Josiah Martin and J. W. Phillips returned from Emery county Thursday. They overtook the Motts and Gurrs at Price, but no stolen saddles were in their possession and Mr. Martin was free to pronounce them guiltless —Salina Press

Julian Whitmore has opened up a new store at Scofield He carries green, staple and fancy groceries, and all kinds of meats. The venture will certainly prove a success, as Julian is a rustler of the first water, and this kind of a business was needed in Scofield —Springville Independent.

There are about 25,000 head of sheep to be sheared at Sunnyside. Pace Brothers of Nephi and the Big Springs ranch company have sheared and the others will soon be through.

A committee of the state board of equalization are expected to meet with the county selectmen and assessor tonight at the county court house. The committee are returning from Grand county.

The Seventh district court was expected to have been in session here again on May 10, but word received from Judge Johnson indicates that he will not be here then, and consequently court is now set for Monday, May 17 The docket will be made up about ten days previous.

A man giving his name as Charlie Scealan was arrested on Wednesday of last week at Castlegate, on suspicion of being a pal or an accessory to McCarty and Cassidy the bold highwaymen. This was thought to be the case because Scealan was with them drinking at Caffey's saloon and seemed on intimate terms with them. He had in his possession a pair of nippers and was held in the county jail until Friday morning, when upon examination it was decided that he had nothing to do in common with the robbers, and he was turned loose. The man did not give a very clear account of his actions, but as he had just come from St. George and made the trip through Emery county. He said he had a few articles which he was peddling, and as there was no evidence to show his complicity in the hold up he could not be held

Ex Justice Wm. Burr was all smiles on Tuesday last. It was a 12 pound boy and made its debut Monday evening All well.

John R Roberts and Joseph Whitmore were visitors to Price early this week. They came up from their ranches below Farnham.

The Emery County Mercantile company this week received a car load of Studebaker wagons and carriages to be sent out to Ashley.

SPRING GLEN.

Work is still being done on the Spring Glen canal and we expect to finish it this week. The sag in the flume near the reservoir above Helper has not yet been remedied, and the water is consequently short.

Farm crops are all planted and grain begins to show up real well considering the lateness in sowing

Now that our school is closed for the season, the school house is being repaired

Arbor day was not observed here in the usual manner, but our citizens have been engaged all this week in planting shade trees around the school block. A combination wire fence has also been put up, and the square otherwise improved all of which will show that the people are finally getting a move on themselves.

HELPER.

Robert Long and Miss Rose Hammond both residents of Helper were married by Justice J. Tom Fitch Monday evening. After the ceremony was over the happy couple went to the home of the bridegroom north of Helper, where they will reside Their many friends extend congratulations.

The entertainment which was to have been given by the Union Sunday school next Sunday, has been postponed one week. The program will be prepared by next week.

There is great need of a few more dwelling houses in Helper. A number of employes could move their families here if they could get houses It seems strange that some one does not build a few more as there is plenty of idle ground

GREENRIVER.

Everything is looking up and business is on the improve is the testimony of all whom you may meet.

M. H. Beardsley, the R. G. W. railway hotel man, was in town Saturday.

Greenriver is booming. Crops are growing. Ditch full of water and irrigation wheels standing the pressure finely.

May day ball at the school house, supper at Mrs. Johnson's and everybody happy.

Our live storekeepers are happy and report a good business.

Taylor Bros are shearing sheep at Thompson's Springs. Ballard Bros. are running a hotel in connection with their store, and Harry Ballard has opened up a saloon. P. Crozier, the genial R. G. Western agent is the right man in the right place. Always on duty and a smile for all.

Our old timer, John Martin, is at the Greenriver pump once more, Frank Jacobs resigning

Fruit trees are in bloom on the ranches north of Helper, and all nature along the canyon is donning its spring attire.

Several small ranches have been taken up between here and Castlegate, and the occupants are apparently clearing every available spot upon which to plant garden truck. It is evidently their intention to knock out some of the peddlers by supplying summer vegetables.

C. P. Johnson and family have returned from Salt Lake City where they have been visiting a few weeks.

Ike Glaser's delivery team became frightened at some horses being driven through town Monday, and ran away. No one was in the wagon and the horses kept going until they ran in to the trees and willows just above Spring Glen. No serious damage was done.

WELLINGTON.

Whooping cough and mumps are rampant here. Several cases are reported.

Thomas Jones returned home from Salt Lake City last Tuesday, where he was called to the bedside of his brother who died and was buried April 23.

The R. G. W. tie inspector visited this point on Friday last, and gave the boys a pretty hard deal by rejecting many of their ties which they expected would pass as first class.

The parties who are responsible for the water flooding the county road both in town and east of it, should remedy the matter at once or they are likely to get into trouble with the county.

An excellent program is being arranged for the close of the school year which will be May 21. This date will conclude one of the most successful periods of school in our town. Much credit is due the teachers Miss Leonard and Miss McMullin for their faithful work in the school room.

SCOFIELD.

The ice business comes in as the coal business goes out.

The miners here are only working about two days a week.

Our postmaster is very indignant against Uncle Sam, and says he won't work for him any longer. He don't like post-office business anyhow. Two applications for the appointment as postmaster at Scofield have already been sent in. One is made by Superintendent Martin of the U. P. store, and the other is by J. E. Ingles. The appointment of either of these gentlemen, will take the post-office down into the town of Scofield and will consequently make it very inconvenient for the people of Winter Quarters unless an office is also established there as should certainly be done.

Our amatuer silver band, under the leadership of John Hood is improving nicely. They contemplate being in attendance at the Pioneer Jubilee at Salt Lake City in July.

Brakeman Wm Palmer is now at work again. Wm has had several sick spells this winter, with mumps, bumps, rheumatism and other complaints too numerous to mention.

Jensen the tailor has quit Scofield, and is now doing business in Eureka where his family will join him in a few days.

The new Justice of the Peace at Winter Quarters has had but one case before him since the first of the year. In that case a young gent and young lady, were sentenced to live together the remainder of their lives.

CASTLEGATE.

Jos. R. Sharp came down from Scofield Monday and visited our camp.

There has been a scarcity of money in camp since the holdup, and a number of the employes of the company are still carrying checks in their pockets.

The coke ovens were not running the first of the week, and the men were all laid off.

Owing to the muddy state of the river the feeding pumps got clogged causing a breakage in the pipes. In consequence the miners were idle Monday and Tuesday.

The Maccabees social held Saturday evening May 1, was a most enjoyable affair. Eagle Lodge No. 18, K. of P. was invited with a number of friends. Songs and other entertaining features were introduced to make up an interesting time.

The little son of John Horn who has been very ill with pneumonia, is, we are pleased to say, rapidly recovering.

Agent Dugdale of the Enquirer was rustling up subscribers for his paper. Nit!

H. J. Nelson has moved his family to Spanish Fork to reside permanently.

Assessor Tidwell was in town this week making the yearly call. Every-body this year will have the privilege of paying a little into the county treasury There has been some kicking, but the personal property assessment was made without anyone getting hurt.

Born To the wife of Richard Edwards, a girl, weight 11½ pounds. Everybody well including papa. Next?

Quite a number of improvements are being made by property owners.

Supt. Sharp is paying his regular periodical visit to Salt Lake City.

Coal mine inspector Lloyd was in town this week, and left here for the metropolis.

Mrs. Dugald Wright and family are removing to Eureka, where Mr. Wright has secured employment in the mines.

Dr. and Mrs. Assadoorian are taking in the sights at the metropolis.

The Wasatch store company is building an addition in the shape of a meat market.

Quite a number of strangers have visited Castlegate lately, and we believe the recent robbery has something to do with their presence here.

Several of the young bloods of the town have left for "pastures new." Among those departing were Andrew Young jr. and D. Henderson. Good luck boys, wherever you go.

LOCAL NEWS.

A marriage license was issued by clerk Donaldson Monday to Robert Long aged 28, and Rose Hammoud, aged 18 both of Helper.

The miners working at the Castle Peak gilsonite mine for Mr. V. LeSieur were ordered off the property last week by the military authorities.

The Emery stake conference convenes at Huntington next Saturday and Sunday. It is expected that there will be a very large attendance.

Tom Lamph of Castlegate passed through Price Sunday with his family. They will visit with his wife's relatives at Cleveland for a few days.

Charlie Allred who has been in California for some time has returned home. Mr. Allred has been under treatment by an eminent cancer specialist in San Francisco, and cancers on his lip and face were treated with apparent success. The gentleman is feeling well and thinks he has received a permanent cure.

GIANT POWDER EXPLOSION.

Two Men Seriously if Not Fatally Hurt Notes of Mines.

SCOFIELD, May 6 h, 1897—Mike Koski and Alex. Hill, natives of Finland, were very seriously if not fatally injured this morning, by a premature explosion of giant powder in No. 1 mine at Winter Quarters while doing some rock work. Hill had all the fingers and the thumb blown off the left hand. The right eye is destroyed. He also has some ribs broken and is otherwise cut and bruised. Koski is terribly cut and bruised about the head and face and has some ribs broken. Doctor Smith dressed their wounds and made them as comfortable as possible. He will take them to St. Mark's hospital tomorrow.

The streams are considerably swollen now, and there is a great amount of snow in the mountains yet.

Coal mining is very dull these days. It is expected the Oregon Short Line will take the management of the U. P. mine here, about the 10th, after which we look for better times.

Mr. Richard Howell is putting an addition to his residence.   H.

TWO MEN INJURED.

Scofield Miners Brought Here for Surgical Operations.

Mike Koski and Aleck Hill, two men employed at the Winter Quarters mine in Scofield, were brought to Salt Lake yesterday and taken to St. Mark's hospital for surgical treatment. Their injuries are the result of an accident which occurred day before yesterday at the mine. The men were engaged in throwing out some giant powder in a store, and neglected to watch it. As a result, while both were standing near the stove, the powder exploded. Hill was hurt the worst. He loses an eye and one hand, besides having his body filled with small pieces of metal. Koski suffered the amputation of a finger, and has a bad wound in his side. They were brought up to Salt Lake by Dr. J. W. Smith of Scofield. The operations were performed by Drs. Pinkerton. Critchlow. Behle, Wright and Smith. The injuries are not considered dangerous, although Koski had a very close call.

FROM CARBON AND EMERY

NEWS BITS FROM OUR MANY COR-RESPONDENTS.

The Weekly Happenings from our Neighboring Towns—How they are Progressing—Castlegate's Letter.

Assistant Superintendent H. G. Williams has been confined to his house for
several days with a severe cold.

In a short time Castlegate will equal
if not surpass any town in the county.
Householders are beautifying their
dwellings, laying out artistic flower gardens and otherwise improving the appearances of their homes.

H. C. Holly is building and addition
to his place of abode.

W. R. Ward and F. Spafford have
gone to Castle valley with the intention of
taking up homesteads, Mr Ward having sold his Woodside claim.

Young Tom Williams has tackled his
"bike" again. Keep an eye on the girls
Tommy.

Miss Florrie Evans gave a birthday
party Wednesday afternoon. Quite a
number of her young friends assembled
to extend congratulations and to partake
of the good things provided. The little
folks had a cool time. It was Miss
Evans' nineth birthday.

The mines are working but half time
and have again been idle two days this
week. This fine weather is unfavorable
to the coal business

Mr. and Mrs Shaw, of Lawrence, are
paying a visit to their daughter, Mrs
Isaac Jones.

Bishop Lamph is able to get around
on crutches Tuesday evening Allen Cox
took his buggy around to the bishop's
door and requested him to take a drive
The bishop protested saying he was
too tired but to no avail. He got into
the buggy and was driven to the bridge
at the lower end of town which, by the
way, is considerably sagged in the center. On the way home when the meeting house was being passed, Andrew
Young sr. stopped the buggy and told
the bishop that he was wanted inside
as a meeting was to be held. Wondering what meeting could be held without
his knowledge, but thinking some church-
men had just arrived, he got out of the
buggy and was assisted into the house
On entering, to his great surprise, it was
seen that a table the entire length of the
building had been spread and loaded
with the good things of life, seated
around this table were members of his
flock smiling him a glad welcome. The
members of the Relief society had planned a surprise for the bishop and there
can be no question but that it was complete When about to partake of the
food, under his plate was found a letter
of good will and a sum of money, which,
considering circumstances, they thought
to be a timely gift, and it really was.
After the repast and all was ready for
the dance the bishop in a short speech
expressed the gratitude of himself and
family for the kindness and respect
which was shown them. Then followed
a program consisting of songs, duets,
speeches and dancing Messrs Thomas
and Cox furnished the music. Much
credit is due those who had the affair in
hand for it was a genuine surprise party.

CLEVELAND.

The sickness that recently so generally prevailed among the children has disappeared.

Work on the canal was completed Monday and there is hopes of abundant water on the townsite this week, and the farmer can now devote his entire time to farm work

The brick residence of Bishop Overson is going up rapidly. It is hoped that other substantial citizens will do likewise and that all will plant shade trees.

Summer has come and with it its season's gaities. Mr. and Mrs. Potter gave a very enjoyable party celebrating anniversary of their son Joseph. In the afternoon the young people were invited to partake of ice cream and cake and in the evening all met at the hall where the merry dancers whiled away many happy hours All joined in wishing Mr. Potter many happy returns.

Our town was just about depopulated Sunday. All that could get a conveyance attended quarterly conference at Huntington

Bishop Overson has received his stock of spring goods.

Miss Tina Larsen has an elegant line of millinery. We wish her success

GREENRIVER.

Green river is booming. Eight feet rise within the last few days and raising rapidly. The ditch is broken and every available man is at work repairing the break.

Crops are looking well. Durant, Howland & Co. have put a whistle on the engine at their pumping plant. It can be heard all over the valley. Sounds like business.

Parties at Elgin are contemplating the construction of a building for school purposes and social gatherings.

Some miscreant put a spike in the electric motor of the Bennett Amalgamator plant and when the machinery was started the motor was ruined. The plant will be idle until a new one can be sent from Denver to replace the broken motor

Our hills are covered with beautiful flowers of all colors. Grass is in abundance and no cattle or sheep to eat it.

Arthur Mead's mother arrived on Sunday moning from the east. She will remain a number of weeks.

As warm weather approaches the tramp element increases and their petty thieving is becoming a nuisance. Something must be done. Can't the Advocate suggest some remedy?

[We can only recommend our correspondent to Mark Hanna of prosperity fame —Ed]

WELLINGTON.

High water in the river has been attended with considerable loss from cutting the banks and washing away some of our real estate. Some damage has also been done to the irrigating ditches.

Share holders in the Tidwell canal are busily engaged in the construction of their flume across the river and expect to complete the work this week.

A large number of our people attended quarterly conference at Huntington Saturday and Sunday, and report an enjoyable time and much good advice for future use.

County attorney, J. W. Warf was in town on Sunday.

Peace and quiet prevails. Everyone seems to be attending strictly to their own business just at present.

HELPER.

The Union Sabbath school of this place will give a free entertainment on Sunday evening, May 16, in Rooney's hall. All are cordially invited to attend. We give the program:

.—Zither solo, Paul Hunter.

2 —Words of welcome, recitation, Miss Lucy Reid.

3 —Surprise, recitation, Miss Josie McCune.

4.—Song, When the Roll is Called Up Yonder, choir.

5 —My Nellie, recitation, Miss Myrtle Baxter.

6 —A queer little toone, recitation, Nealy Johnson.

7.—Duet, Messrs. Hunten and Damon.

8 —Psalm of Life, recitation, Miss Grace Pratt.

9.—The boys we need, recitation, Alex Baxter.

10 —Recitation, Nellie McComb.

11.—Do your best, recitation, Johnnie Johnson.

12 —Song, Misses bessie, Sadie and Mr. Kilburn.

13 —A boy's complaint, recitation, Ames Miller.

14 —A boy's opinion, recitation, Geo. Van Natta.

15 —Recitation, Viola McComb.

16 —Song. There came to my window, Jonetta Checketts.

17.—Recitation, Miss Wilson.

18 —Recitation, Mary McComb.

19 —Song, Miss Burnfield and Messrs. Hunten and Damon.

20 —Reading, Nephi Pratt.

21.—Barrels of trouble, recitation, Charley Johnson.

22.— Recitation, Ames McComb.

23.—Song, God be with you, choir.

EMERY.

Dr. Shipp is in our town giving a course of lectures to the ladies. She will remain only a few days.

The Y. M. and Y. L. M. I. association will fittingly celebrate Brigham Young's birthday. A committee are now working on the program which is about completed.

About 10,000 sheep have been sheared here this spring and the wool has gone to market via. Price.

Our town has four stores and all seem to be prospering.

The water in Muddy is very high and crossing is attended with much inconvenience and serious danger. We would call the attention of the county commissioners to the great necessity of this bridge during high water.

What was thought to be a serious accident occurred near here last week. Rile and Dolph Johnson were bringing in a herd of horses when Dolph, the elder, threw a stone at horse and missed the horse and struck his brother Rile in the eye, the force of the blow producing unconciousness. A near by sheep herder gave the boys assistance in reaching home. After the soreness and swelling had somewhat abated it is probable that the optic can be saved as he can see a very little now.

Eastern Utah Advocate
May 20, 1897
Price

LOCAL NEWS.

Elder E. J. Broderick of Emery, Emery county, returned home Monday from a mission to the Southern States. He left this city March 15, 1895, and labored while away in the West Virginia and Maryland conferences. The mission, he says, is in good shape, and numbers of people are investigating the principles of the Gospel —Deseret News

Rumor had it this week that Fred Grames had been robbed of some money while staying at Downar's the other night. No one seemed to know the exact amount Fred lost, but it was claimed the sum was between a hundred and two hundred dollars. Anyhow he was robbed, and the festive burglar secured some money, probably more than two dollars and less than two thousand. The culprit has not been apprehended, but Fred is hot on the trail.

Gwylim Jones and D. L. Jones, not brothers, no relation, but both from Castlegate, came to Price Monday and appeared before Judge Johnson. They did not meet his honor face to face because they were summoned so to do, but looked upon the august court of their own accord. Both of the boys requested that the honors of United States citizenship be conferred upon them, and Judge Johnson granted their request after questioning them closely as to their records for morality, industry and their general knowledge of our form of government. They claimed they would "shoulder arms" at any time to uphold "Old Glory" in preference to the "Union Jack." Wales might be all right in its way but they wanted no more of it

Arrangements have been made by the Spring Glen canal company with the R G Western railway company, to keep the canal repaired and the flume in good order near and around the Helper reservoir.

H. G Clark was "mugged" by an artist of the Salt Lake Tribune this week and when the picture was shown him, he took two fits in so many seconds He does not, however anticipate a criminal action

There is a good opening in Price for some moneyed man to use a small amount of capital profitably, by investing in real estate and building a few tenement houses They are much needed and would go at a fair rental

CASTLEGATE

Mr. Stearns, late operator at this place, is in town doing a land office business in the life insurance line.

H Reid of Tintic stopped off here this week to visit old friends and to do business. He was enroute to Castledale, Emery county.

Born: To the wife of Charls Rougeri, a boy. Mother and child doing well.

The Wasatch store company have finished their meat market, and are now doing business. John Stagg is the festive liver carver.

The slackness of work at the mines is causing quite a number of the miners to leave here. Heber Ward and Alex Harrison have gone to seek their fortunes elsewhere. 'Great scott!' What will the poor girls do now? These two young men were the only two "eligibles" left.

Harry Duerden and Thos. E. Edwards attended the trial of McLean vs Donant et al. in Price Wednesday.

The Fourth of July, we understand will be celebrated here in grand style. A number of the citizens met Sunday and had a colloquy on the "ways and means" It was suggested that two bowries be erected, and that the bycicle track be used for the festivities Athletic games of all kinds will be indulged in, and a general invitation to all the surrounding towns will be given to participate. The fraternal brotherhood is taking a leading part in the matter, and this fact in itself inspires a successful celebration

Stockholders of the Baldy mountain mines, the Antie Laurie and Senator Stewart, are wearing a very broad smile those days Assays made of ore taken from a newly discovered vein, goes up into the hundreds of dollars per ton. As the most of those holding stock are residents of Castlegate, this news accounts for the millionaire like airs that some of the men are assuming. It is to be hoped, however, it is not without some foundation, and that the new strike will make the property a dividend payer

There will be a grand ball here Saturday night and Cox Bros, will furnish the music.

SCOFIELD.

One of our young men from Winter Quarters will next Saturday take a helpmate to aid him in the struggles along life's rugged path. Edwin Street and Miss Emma Pitman both of this place will be the happy couple, and their friends here wish them joy and success.

Born to the wife of D Rowser last week, a boy. Mother and child doing well

Arthur Anderson of Winter Quarters met with a very painful accident last Wednesday, while in the act of taking down some bad rock from the roof of the mine. A piece of coal fell and knocked the barrel, upon which he was standing out from under his feet. Mr Anderson fell and sprained his arm badly, which will lay him up for some time.

It occurred to the long headed coal miners in this state, to devise means of weighing the coal product at the mine. Accordingly the miners secured the passage of a bill in the late legislature providing for a check weigh man, to be appointed by the miners interested. A mass meeting was held by the miners of Winter Quarters last Saturday morning at 10 o'clock for the purpose of filling that position. Lewis Jones was the unanimous choice of the assembled miners, and a committee of five miners were appointed to act as an arbitration committee, and to wait upon Supt W G. Sharp when necessary to settle any grievances which may arise between them and the company's management.

Times are very quiet here and there is but little news this week.

T H. Thomas visited Price on Wednesday.

Rev Fowler the state missionary of the American Sunday school union, held services at Scofield and Winter Quarters last Sunday and Monday.

C. H. Valentine of Salt Lake came up to this camp on Saturday, and organized the endowment rank of the order K. of P.

Wm. Potter has left the Post Office store and is getting out cord wood for a Salt Lake party.

Last week the P. V Coal company moved their scales back from the shute and toward the mouth of the tunnel at at the mine. Cars can now be stopped on the scales and weighed as they come out from the mines

EMERY.

Riley Johnson the boy who had his eye hurt some time ago is improving slowly, but he has not regained the proper sight yet.

P. V Dunlerson's twins are growing nicely, and the parents are very proud of them.

The committee who are getting up a celebration here for the first of June, are taking a lively interest in it, and the prospects are that we will have a splendid time on that date.

Mrs. Brock from Huntington has been visiting her brother, Bishop Brinkerhoff but has now returned home.

It is reported that travelling by team through Salina canyon, is at a standstill at present. The creek is high enough to swim a horse.

Dr. E. R Shipp delivered some lectures here, and has now gone north in the county.

We have good weather for growing crops and the prospects for an abundant harvest is bright.

Sister Williams, the aged mother of the William boys, has been very sick for two or three weeks but we are pleased to state that she is improving.

Our canal broke above the tunnel on the 18th instant. The rushing waters made a large gap 30 feet wide and about 20 feet deep and washed the canal one hundred and fifty feet back to the depth of 20 feet on a level with the break.

The disaster caused some damage to crops through lack of water, which was shut off six days. The break is now repaired and the water again flowing in the canal, and while it was empty a few days it was repaired and cleaned out the entire length, so that it will now hold plenty of water all summer.

The Muddy river is pretty high, and is somewhat dangerous to ford. The bridge is missed very much at this time of year.

GREENRIVER.

The dam of Durant, Howland and Atkinson went out at midnight of the 18th This makes the third time in as many years and makes it quite a hardship The county of Grand spent about $100, off the work, and the three above named parties has spent nearly $500 this winter on the dam. Some of these times the cut off slough, will form the main river bed, and there will be four Grand county ranches added to Emery county

Early this week the new electric motor for the Bennett and Edwards placer camp, arrived from Denver and was loaded and sent to the scene of operations.

There is a report that there is another amalgamator ordered for work on the Greenriver placers

There are fifty invitations out for a grand gathering of friends at a birth-day party to be given at G. W. Durants residence on the eve of the 24th

The river has fallen about six inches below its highest mark, but the R G W is still building a dyke above the pump house There are reports of another rise in the river at Rawlins.

Chris Andersons new piers for his water wheel went out Tuesday, but Chris has another thousand days work in him that is aching to get out

All water wheels are safe and you can hear their sad cry for more grease above all other noises.

Our old friend Thompson who is located opposite Willow bend, has a fine crop coming on and his new wheel is a thorough success.

Mr. Allred has abandoned his lease of the Senior Farrer farm, and, will move his numerous family to Price.

Eastern Utah Advocate
May 27, 1897
Price

LOCAL NEWS.

E C Howland and wife of Helper will, on the first of June, move to Salt Lake, where Mr. Howland expects to take up other work. He has been clerk at the railroad shops in Helper for two years, and has won many friends while there. It is hoped he will meet with the success he deserves.

Born To the wife of Mr. H F Hansen, a son, on Wednesday Mother and child getting along all right.

The infant child of Herman Horsley, aged one month Wednesday, died that evening at 6 o'clock of whooping cough.

Cupid Donaldson issued a marriage license Saturday to Edwin Street aged 21 and Emma Pitman aged 75, both of Scofield. Monday a license to marry was issued to I aac Willson aged 80, and Louisa Looks aged 19, both of Price The latter couple were married Monday afternoon at the residence of the bride's sister, Mrs. John L. Willson, Justice P I, O son performing the ceremony.

GREENRIVER.

We have showers this season almost every day and the desert is covered with lovely flowers. It is a perfect garden from here to Grand Junction, and there is more grass on the desert than has been seen for five years.

There will be an immense crop of hay and we begin cutting about the 25th of the month

Joe Cunnah was in from his ranch. He reports crops on the San Rafael as O K.

Mr. Smith of the Wheeler ranch says their three wheels are all right and stand the rise in the river splendidly.

The new orchards of Frank Jacobs and Ira button are doing fine. Jacobs reports that he will not 5 per cent. which speaks highly for the home nurseries.

J. T. Farrer and the Larsen boys are visiting Salt Lake City. They are defendants in a land contest case, with the Barr family of San Rafael.

CLEVELAND.

The young people had an enjoyable time at Christmas s recently on the occasion of Miss Mathilda Christensen's birthday.

It has been very stormy here lately and considerable damage has been done by the floods, especially on what is called the south flat

Arrived: At the home of Mrs Snow, a fine baby girl. Mother and child doing well.

Last week the only child of Mr. and Mrs. Howland had a very narrow escape from drowning. The mother missed her boy from the yard stepping to the bank of the river, was just in time to see the little fellow floating off on the mad, rushing stream. She did not hesitate a moment, or it would have been too late, but plunged into the swift muddy waters at the imminent peril of her own life, and without any asistance succeeded in rescuing the boy and safely reaching the shore with her precious darling pressed closely to her breast. It was the heroic act of a woman, and the proof of a mother's anxiety and undying love for her offspring that saved the child from a watery grave. That Mrs Howland was able to reach the boy and then safely battle her way to the shore in such a raging torrent as Green river now is, must go down as next to miraculous. She is the heroine of the day and is truly admired for her brave deed. "That is love."

Thursday last Henry Farrer's babe, a little boy, escaped its mother's attention for a few moments, during which time it must have wandered off to the big ditch close by. A neighbor heard a child scream and hastened to the ditch, the little one it was found had fallen into the water. In a few moments more the child would have been drowned, but through the timely arrival of the rescuer its life was saved

WELLINGTON.

After a few mishaps the Tidwell canal flume is now a decided success.

The road through Soldier canyon is in pretty good shape, and a careful man might ride a horse through without getting off the road.

The H. J. Hill property adjoining the railway station, has been purchased by Mr. Blackburn who will move his family in the house and take possession at once

Many of our little ones are afflicted with the mumps.

Weather is fine for growing crops and lucern is ready to cut.

The Fausett boys have moved to the park for the summer, where they will try to raise a crop of potatoes and oats

A party of home-seekers from Huntington passed through here Monday last, en route to Idaho

EMERY

Elder A. J. Broderick has returned home from a mission to the north western stake, where he has labored faithfully for the past 26 months, proclaiming the doctrine of Christ. Elder Broderick informs us that there is plenty to do in the missionary field, and that while there he made many friends.

There is some fruit on the young orchard trees this spring, which is quite encouraging to the settlers

There was another small break in one canal this week, which however, was soon repaired.

We are having a beautiful spring, with mild, steady showers every few days. The crops will be abundant in consequence.

Our meeting house was filled to over flowing last Sunday. Many came who could not gain admittance and had to stand outside during the services. Elder A. J. Broderick occupied the whole time telling his experiences while in the missionary field, and explaining the plan of salvation. He was listened to through out with marked attention.

The elders and seventies quorums are going to give a public reception Friday in honor of A. J. Broderick. A committee of six has been appointed for the occasion as follows: A Smith, G T Olsen, A Overlade, Mrs Kate O'am, Mrs Marie Allen and Miss Lizzie Jorgensen. A program has been arranged and everything is progressing favorably for a general good time. Everyone has been invited to attend the reception Elder Broderick was the first missionary to be called and sent from Emery ward, and is the first to return

The Ferron band has been engaged to play at Emery on the first of June We will then have a celebration and expect a large turn out A good time is guaranteed to all who attend.

CASTLEGATE.

The P. V. Coal company is building a reservoir at the upper end of town, which when completed will be of great benefit. Pipes will connect the reservoir with the boiler tanks, so that during high water or heavy rains, when the Price river is thick enough to mould adobes from, the mine, can be worked anyhow. Every year the mines have to be idle certain days when muddy water chokes the boiler tubes. The reservoir will be large enough to hold a supply of water that will last the pumps from seven to ten days.

We are reliably informed that Andrew Young Jr , after having enough experience in the inconveniences of a tourists life, has finally concluded that it is not what it is cracked up to be. He has made up his mind to marry and settle down. For that reason he stopped off at Spanish Fork, while on the road home.

The other day the district school enjoyed their " field and picnic day" as of yore. Headed by the principal, J B. Cardall, the pupils marched in fine order through the principle streets and then took the road to Castlegate rock. On the trip, flora and fauna, rocks, shells and insects were examined through glasses, and their names and natures were explained by the professor. A rattlesnake was killed by one of the larger boys, and the teacher then gave the children a lesson on snakes. Altogether it was a splendid day of education and pleasure.

The masquerade on Saturday last was a most enjoyable affair. Quite a number assumed characters.

Rev. E. G. Fowler of the A. U. S schools held forth in the K. of P. hall Sunday.

Work at the mine is very slack, less than half time is being made now.

Miss E. Larsen has left Castlegate her home in Cleveland.

Castlegate has one specilty, i. e. that of raising rocks. We raise rocks of all sizes either by crow bar or with dynamite, and they are being raised pretty high just now, as a number of men are engaged making a trench for the reservoir pipe line.

Robert Williams is engaged in raising rock. He is building a new house, which will be all of rock, and completed it will be the tallest house in town. We are not aware how many stories he is going to build, but the stories that will be told in the course of its erection will be tall enough.

John I. Kay and W. Lund have pulled up stakes and struck out for the gold camps.

In the past six weeks over fifty miners have left camp. Many Italians have returned to their native country.

Charles Smith, John Hamel and Heber Ward have returned home again.

Alma Jones has purchased the residence of Henry Reed and is fixing up the interior before moving into it.

The Ladies Literary club will hold their meeting Tuesday at the home of Mrs Assadourian. A good time is anticipated.

Miners will be paid in checks hereafter instead of money, on account of the late hold up. This is to be regretted as it will greatly inconvenience them to get the ready cash to pay outside debts.

Mr. Hill of Wellington is a visitor at the "Gate."

The base-ball boys are practicing daily, preparatory to wiping the earth with the county clubs.

We are sorry to learn that Mrs. Wm. Blood of Cleveland, has been compelled to go to California to get treatment for cancer. She stayed here a day or two to bid good by to old friends. We trust the good lady will return to her family thoroughly cured.

Wm. H. Lawley is building a rock addition to his already comfortably home.

Manager H. A. Nelson went to Scofield this week.

When completed, the residence of Assistant Supt. Williams will be the finest in town.

The Wasatch store meat market is doing a rushing business.

Joe Bonny says he can do the mile beat the mile record. Look out, ye schorchers!

The boulevard de railroad was well patronized by pedestrs on Sunday evening. All the town families were doing the tramp act.

Dave Evans thought he had been "touched for a gun," but when he went in search of the festive hold up, the "implement of warfare was found safely at home."

Frank Stafford's home was entered by tramps Wednesday morning during the absence of Mrs. Stafford, and a six-shooter which was laying handy was carried off.

Deseret Evening News
June 1, 1897

Scofield and Winter Quarters.

SCOFIELD, May 28.—The U.P. mine here is closed down, the Oregon Short Line having turned their attention to the Diamondville mines in Wyoming. So we are left out in the cold.

Several of the miners have struck out to look for work elsewhere.

Some of the families here are in hard circumstances. Those who were a little behind in the company's store could not get their usual supply of provisions this month.

A session of the district court will be held in Scofield on June 1st, at which time applications for lots in the Scofield townsite will be considered.

Also the divorce case of Eliza Thomas vs T. H. Thomas. It will also be a good opportunity for those in the section desiring to become citizens to take out their papers.

A. W. Korki, a Finlander at Winter Quarters, has just procured a patent on a sled which runs by hand power.

Edwin Street, 23, and Amy Pitman, 18, both of Winter Quarters were married by Bishop T. J. Parmely on Tuesday evening.

There are prospects of another wedding shortly.

Peddlers coming here from the settlements find it very hard to sell their products on account of the dull times here.   H.

CASTLEGATE.

As before mentioned the following was posted up by the ball tossers of this berg: "We, the Rocky Mountain nine, wish to issue a challenge to any picked nine of Castlegate for a keg of beer or $3 60, We hope that some of you good players will take up this challenge. We wish to play on May 30th." Signed "captain." When Brownie seen that notice he exclaimed: "By the Eternal! That's enough. No keg of beer goes past this kid." He accordingly scoured the town and scared up eight more and took them down to the diamond and explained to them what bases, runs, errors, fouls, etc., meant and had them throw balls to one another. Some of them got hold of a bat and wanted to know what it was used for. Brownie instructed them as to batting and for them to 'get on" to the curves of the other fellows When the necessary information was imparted they all went home. On Monday last the Rockies and Terriers met, captained respectively, by W. Young and Al Drown and a most interesting game of ball was witnessed by a large number of interested onlookers. The Rockies with all of their practicing and gaudy costumes only came out winners by the skin of their teeth. Some good playing was done on both sides Special mention is made of Crow, Taylor, Young and Phelps of the Rockies and McVickers, T. Davis (a boy), the Larsens' and Jones of the Terriers Thos Williams, catcher for the last named club, had not played

ball before and stood behind the bat through the nine innings His hands were in a bad shape and not until the last inning did he fumble a ball Score stood 45 to 44. Umpires, J, A Harrison and Mr. Cameron. They will play again.

On Decoration day the cemetery was visited by a large number of people who decorated the graves of their departed relatives and friends.

C. R. Savage, the pioneer photographer of Salt Lake, was in town the other day taking landscape views for magazine work.

W. S. Jones had his arm injured by having a pick run into it while at work in the mines last Thursday. He is again at work the wound having healed rapidly.

The trustees of the K. of P. ball have had rail guards put on the stair leading to the lodge room which is quite an improvement.

The railroad company have put in a gravel chute at the upper end of town.

Born to the wife of Oliver Nelson, a boy. The good lady had to be attended by Dr Asadoorian at the accouchement. At last reports she was getting along very well.

Born to the wife of J, Gentry, a girl. All well.

Assistant Supt Williams is paying Winter Quarter's mines a visit.

SCOFIELD.

Sandy Wilson of Winter Quarters and John Hunter of Scofield played a game of quoits recently for points. The game was an exceedingly interesting one and the boys were closely matched They played 41 point's and Hunter came out on top, the score standing 84 to 31, and they will now play a series of games to settle the question as to which is the most scientific pitcher.

A great many trout are being taken unlawfully from the streams in this vicinity and unless it is stopped those who are governed by the fish and game laws will find that the trout have all been taken before the open season begins.

The officials of the U. P. Coal company are expected to visit Scofield this week when it will be decided as to whether the mine which has been closed some time is to be worked in the near future or whether the miners are to take out their tools

Wm H Williams, aged 21 and Miss Sheppard, aged 18, were married Saturday evening at Winter Quarters by Bp. Parmley They gave a grand ball in the boarding house at which a large number tripped the light fantastic and wished the young couple much happiness in their journey through life.

The Winter Quarters Sunday school held services Sunday evening in commemoration of the birth of Brigham Young Supt. Andrew Hood gave an interesting lecture on the life of President Young.

SPRING GLEN

The primary association enjoyed an outing at Ewells grove Tuesday in honor of the birth of Brigham Young It was an occasion long to be remembered by the little ones. Games, swings and other health giving amusements were indulged in and ice cream was in great abundance. The promoters of the p'cnic were amply paid for the time and labor expended in the pleasure given the children

Farming is progressing nicely and all crops looking well. Lucern will, in a few days, be ready for the harvester and everybody will be as busy as bees.

The children of S F Tryon are suffering greatly from the whooping cough

D R Beebe, in company with J W McIntosh, J K Bishop, and Sam Roberts, of Provo, have gone to Death Canyon, about 45 miles northwest of this camp, and will spend a few days looking over the Buckeye and prospecting in that vicinity.—Mammoth Record.

The prospects are good this season for the largest fruit crop ever grown in Ashley valley. The blossoms have fallen and the fruit is all set and in some cases a portion of it will have to be picked while green to give the trees a chance to bear their load —Vernal Express.

Mrs Phœbe Singleton was brought from Eureka Monday, suffering greatly from a broken leg. During a storm at Eureka she was trying to turn a torrent of water into another course, when a rock rolled from the hillside near and struck her, breaking the limb. Mrs Singleton has three children sick, and with this added misfortune, will have a sorry time of it for a while.—Springville Independent

WILLINGTON.

Charles Hill has returned home from his trip through the Southern country and will remain for a few weeks with his parents.

Miss Laura Hill returned from an extended stay in Price.

Mr and Mrs Frank Tidwell entertained a number of their friends at dinner on Sunday.

Bishop McMullin is on the road freighting. A scarcity of teamsters make it necessary for him to drive his own teams

Lucern is now ready to cut and it will be one of the most abundant crops for several years. Small grain, corn and other crops are looking well and from two to three weeks earlier than last year This week starts in stormy and colder and a June frost may ensue.

Eastern Utah Advocate
June 10, 1897

CASTLEGATE.

The committee on arrangements for July the Fourth are not letting the grass grow under their feet. Already a good subscription is assured. The poles and stringers are now in place for the large bowery that will be erected.

The leveling of the center of the bicycle track has commenced and is well under way.

The contract is being let for the painting of the K. P. hall.

Miss M. A. Thomas who has been attending the Logan college for several months, has returned to the gate.

Griffith Thomas and family are visiting at Lawrence, Emery county. Mr. Thomas has a farm there and while in Lawrence will make some improvements on it.

Mrs. Joseph Jones has gone to Sandy, Salt Lake county, to join her husband who is working there.

Assistant Superintendent Williams has moved into his new resident.

Born to the wife of Wm. Cowly on June 4, a girl. Everything O.K.

Born, on June 8, to the wife of Isaac Jones, a girl It took all that science in medical skill could do to bring the lady through her accouchment, and we are pleased to state that she is getting along nicely at present.

A show consisting of a talking machine and living pictures held forth, on Monday evening at the K. of P. hall. Only a few attended.

A bicycle parade in which nearly all the scorchers took part was the chief delight of the small boy on Tuesday evening. The ladies did not join in the parade. The boys are practicing for the glorious fourth. Black Joe was coach and he put them through their facings in good style.

M. Beveridge returned from Salt Lake Sunday evening where he left his family. His wife's health is poor and they thought a change would be beneficial.

Cupid is getting the bells in Castlegate in shape for a merry ringing in the near future.

The Jubilee committee have appointed men in different sections of the state to solicit and collect money with which to carry the enterprise to success. In this town W. T. Lamph was the selection but he desires us to state that the resident physician has put a veto on his getting out and regrets on this account it will be impossible for him to comply with the request of the committee.

Dr. Asadoorian made a trip to Zion the other day, business was the object.

John Ray, like the prodigal son, has returned.

Now is the time for the vegetable peddler to rake in the loose "plunks."

Miss Katie Giles, daughter of Prof. Giles, of Provo, is with us, she is staying with her young friend Miss B Santschi.

SCOFIELD.

We are having beautiful weather. This is indeed Pleasant valley for about three months in the year.

There was considerable excitement at Winter Quarters on Saturday and Sunday on account of the rumor that the mine would work night and day and employ all of the idle men on a day and night shift. The rush did not last long as the too familiar blast of the whistle on Sunday evening at 8 p. m. warned the men that the mine would not work on Monday.

Mrs. James Wallace sen., of Winter Quarters, died last Friday evening after a severe illness of several weeks. She was 57 years of age and an old resident of the place. The funeral services were held in the Winter Quarters ward at 2 p.m. Sunday, after which the remains was interred in the Scofield cemetery.

Messrs Frank Merriwether and H. H Earll have started a butcher shop

David Byrne, D. B. Laughlin and John Webber have leased the Kimball coal mine.

Many of the U. P. miners are still waiting with the hope that the mine will start up again, but the prospects are not at all encouraging.

EMERY.

The banquet and dance given in honor of the returned missionary was a success and greatly enjoyed.

Seth Allen, our school teacher, with his wife, is visiting in Sanpete. Mr. Allen had decided before leaving on this visit to make his home in Castle valley.

John B. Broderick and wife are visiting relatives in Sanpete county.

Mrs. Adelbert Petty presented her husband with a tiny baby girl. Both are doing well.

Born to the wife of Hans C. Christensen, a fine boy. All are doing well and Hans is quite happy.

The celebration of Brigham Young's birth was a success. In the forenoon an interesting program was rendered, a dance for the little ones in the afternoon and adults at night completed the day's program. Much credit is due the committee for their earnest labors to make the day one long to be remembered.

A committee to arrange for a proper observance of our nation's birth on July 4 has been selected as follows Edwin Larsen, Charles Williams, Andrew Anderson, Mrs. Cyntha Larsen, Miss Annie Anderson and Mrs Rose Doxette It is a good choice and we may expect a good time.

Crops are growing nicely and the weather is all that could be desired

A fatality occurred at the Mercur mine Thursday as a result of which Antono Cavigilo lost his life. Cavigilo was stoping in the mine above the square sets when some falling ground frightened him and he jumped through the timbers, alighting on his left side on the edge of the car below, his arm going into the car, the full force of the fall being sustained in the region of the heart Help was soon at hand, but the victim of the accident died while being carried from the mine to the hospital.

Born to the wife of Billy Floyd on Sunday a bright little baby girl All doing nicely.

CLEVELAND.

The hia'th of the community is good

The Y. M. and Y. L. M. y association held their monthly conjoint on Sunday last. An excellent program was rendered.

Arrived on June 2, at the home of W. Davis, a fine baby boy. All are doing well.

The boys are preparing their ball ground for the season's ball games They have sent for a base ball outfit and it is said will open the season by challenging the married men who we hope will win as this might influence some of our boys to become benedicts

We are glad to see Mrs. Lillie Smith in our midst 'and hope she will have a pleasant visit.

Samuel Alger and company are putting in a saw mill on Miller creek It will be a great benefit to our settlement.

Soph Olsen will move his store nearer the center of town which will be *.i.eciated by our people as then the telephone office will be in our midst.

WELLINGTON.

Wm. A. Thayn arrived home from his European mission on Monday and is happy to be back with his family again

The young men gave a dance on Monday evening Good music, good order and a good house, all contributed to a very enjoyable evening.

Haying is now on in earnest. If we can escape a storm an abundant crop of first class hay will be harvested.

A number of the boys were in from the Big Springs ranch Sunday and Monday. They report everything lovely and an abundant crop of hay jo harvest

It is reported that Bert McMullin and Will Curtis have had very valuable offers for an interest with them in their coal and wax prospects. They are all-right.

Geo B, Milner has gone to the Big Springs to help through the haying season.

Death on A Bridge.

As R. G. Western passenger train No 1 was rounding a curve near the Halfway house between Helper and Castlegate last Saturday the engineer observed a footman on the bridge The usual warnings was given but no heed of the warning was taken by the footman and before the train could be brought to a standstill the engine struck the man and instantly killed him. It was J. Gentry, father of the Gentry boys who live up Gordon creek. The old gentleman was quite deaf and with the roar of water did not hear the warnings until the train was upon him and in his enfeebled condition could not save himself. The engine struck him with great force throwing him against the bridge timbers killing him instantly. The remains were taken to Helper and an inquest was held before Justice Fitch the result of which placed no blame on the railway company.

The remains were interred at Price on Monday.

Deseret Weekly
June 12, 1897

OBITUARY NOTES.

FRANCES ALICE KEEL JOLLEY.

Jolley—At Tropic, Garfield county, Utah, May 21, 1897, at 8:30 a.m., Frances Alice Keel Jolley, beloved wife of John A. Jolley. Sister Jolley is a daughter of Thomas and Mary Keel, now residing at Emery, Emery county, Utah, and was born at Harmony, Washington county—then Kane—June 24, 1869, being nearly 28 years of age at the time of her death. She moved with her parents to Mt. Carmel, Kane county, during the year 1871; was married to Brother Jolley January 26, 1884; removed to this place with her husband and family in May, 1895; is the mother of six children, five of whom survive her, four sons and one daughter.

She passed suddenly away after giving birth to her fifth son—which was stillborn—being ill but a few hours.

Sister Jolley was of most amiable disposition, a faithful Latter-day Saint, an affectionate wife and mother, a warm friend and of a character that commanded the respect and esteem of all associated with her in life. She leaves many relatives and a circle of friends numbered only by the limit of her acquaintance, all of whom will greatly lament her early call from this stage of action. Her husband is prostrated with grief, and the entire community deeply sympathize with him and his little ones in their hour of extreme sorrow.

Eastern Utah Advocate
June 17, 1897

WELLINGTON

Ward conference was held here on Sunday, June 13. President Larsen and Counselor Seeley of the Emery stake spoke timely and cheering words to the Wellington Saints, after which the presiding priesthood were presented to the people and sustained.

At the close of the meeting on Sunday the people selected a committee of six to arrange a suitable program for the Fourth of July celebration.

A fine shower on Sunday evening cooled the air and made the growing vegetation look more beautiful.

Early garden truck is just coming in and in a short time there will be an abundance.

Bruce Willson and wife and Mrs. J. L. Willson, of Price, visited friends and relatives here on Sunday.

Mr. McNiece, of Blue valley, has purchased the portion of Alvin Thayn's farm lying north of the railroad track and west of the county road crossing. Mr. McNiece will occupy the land in the fall and start a nursery. Success to the undertaking.

A number of our young men contemplate a trip to the gilsonite mines to look for work. Boys, remember that a rolling stone gathers no moss.

CASTLEGATE.

Prof. Gunning, hypnotist, has been in town and gave an exhibition of his hypnotic power. He was billed for two nights, Friday and Saturday but on Friday night, owing to a change in the program, the show did not come off. In justice to the professor, it is only right that an explanation should be given of the failure. Several persons had promised after receiving "Comps," to act as subjects at the performance and when the professor had given an exposition of the influence and nature of hypnotism he requested volunteers to come up, which is generally the case, and of course those who got passes are invariably the volunteers. The Professor had acted in good faith and put his confidence in those who promised to do as he required. Well, they came upon the stage and when asked to put themselves in position to be hypnotized, they took no notice of what was said which action made some of the audience laugh. The request was repeated, but still no notice was taken, and again the professor got the laugh. He felt himself insulted and in truth he was. So he told them to leave the stage and they got off, but there were no strings on Mr. Gunning's tongue and he gave them such a roasting that they will never forget. Among the many things he said was, that there were only two classes of people, who could not be hypnotized, fools and idiots, and the young fellows were among that class. He hit the "nail right on the head." After breaking a rock about 230 pound's weight on the body of his partner subject and sticking a hat pin through the arm of the same person while in a cataleptic state, passes were given to those present to come Saturday night. Those who went next night enjoyed a good time, although it was some time before any one could be induced to get on the stage. Each night was but slimly attended. Should Prof. Gunning ever come to Utah again he will give the state a wide berth. Your correspondent was present and witnessed the treatment he received on the first night and was in hearty accord with the scorching he gave the hoodlums.

The annual election of the grand officers of the K of P. is being held this year in Park City. Eagle lodge No. 13 of this town has sent E J Edwards, H. Duerden and Jas A Harrison as delegates, T. T. Lamph G. O G. accompanying them.

H B Astdoorian, E Miller, H. A. Nelson and Alex McLean residents of this burg along with other directors and stockholders of the Baldy Mountain mining company, paid a visit to their properties with the view of making a general overhauling and if possible make arrangements to push the development of their properties. It being the first time some of them have visited that part of the country and with climbing hills and poor transportation are glad to get back to civilization, yet pleased with the experience they have gained fo the knowledge of the country down south.

H G. Williams took in the metropolis last week.

M B Plantz and wife had a quarrel on Saturday night and he turned both wife and child out. She went to Judge Duerden and had him fined. They divided the furniture and he gave her $50 and they agreed to call it square. She has gone to Provo to her folks. After selling the rest of the furniture and house he will decide on what he will do.

President C. G. Larsen and Orange Seely, of Emery stake, met with the people of Castlegate ward and put in order the goverment of the church There was a good turn out. Andrew Young and Joel Ricks were sustained as counselors to Bishop Lamph. A good feeling prevailed and everything was done in perfect unanimity.

Dr. H. J. Richards, of Provo, came up to look after the practice of Dr. Asadoorian while the doctor was in the Gold Mining district.

Born on June 11, to the wife of Talleeen Evans, a boy. All well.

John Stagg has been going around with a sprained wrist which is now improving.

There is a rumor that the mines will work more steadily, owing to the railroad war. We hope the rumor has good foundation.

CLEVELAND

Born, on Saturday June 12, to the wife of Henry Oviatt, a fine boy. All are doing well

A very pleasant ice cream party, was given by Mrs W. E Cowley on Sunday afternoon The genial host was much in evidence with interesting accounts of early days.

The move of Soph Olsen to near the center of town is temporarily delayed by a failure to secure a suitable location. The party went back on his trade.

Mrs Charles Clawson has taken up residence with her parents, Mr. and Mrs Thomas Davis.

Miss Sarah Lewis has returned to her parents here

H H. Oviatt, our popular postmaster and one of our first settlers is putting on a new shingle roof and otherwise improving his residence.

All crops are growing rapidly and give promise of a good yield Lucern is being cut and is an excellent yield.

HELPER.

Flowers of various varieties are in bloom, but there are few of the busy workers, the honey bee, to reap the rich harvest of honey. There has recently been great loss among the bee owners and no one can say from what cause. Some claim that it is the poison from spraying which if true the bee industry should be protected from the deadly poison

Nate Miller, our accommodating postmaster was a visitor td the county seat early in the week.

Mrs. Herbert Savage, daughter of Mr. and Mrs. Wm. Miller, was over from Castledale filing on a piece of land near Spring Glen early in the week.

The ranchers in our vicinity are very busy harvesting an unprecedently big crop of lucern.

Ward conference was held at Spring Glen on Monday. President Larsen and Counselor Seely meet with the Saints Beside the usually instructive remarks from the presidency the sustaining of the priesthood was accomplished.

SCOFIELD

Last Sunday an accident occured at Mercur, Utah, wh'ch resulted in the death of the nine year-old son of John Samuels. The little boy was playing with some more boys near a 70 foot prospect. They got hold of some giant powder and some fuse to which they applied a match. The other boys ran away while little Tommy stayed near to see the fuse spit fire, little thinking of the explosion which would follow and which terribly mangled him and threw him to the bottom of the shaft. He was taken out alive and a doctor summoned, but could do but little good, as death claimed the boy shortly after. The remains were brought to Scofield on Monday and services held in the ward meeting house, after which burial took place at 4 30 p.m. Mr. Samuels left here when the U P. mine closed down and procured work at Mercur. His family had been there less than two weeks.

Last Sunday a sheep herder came down from the mountains and called to see F W. Dickenson. He tied his horse to the fence not far from the house. Mr Dickenson's three-year-old boy was playing around with a stick and got close to the horse's heels. The result was he was kicked on the head. Doctor Smith was called and dressed the wound. The doctor found it necessary to put in thirteen stitches. The child is doing as well as would be expected, and hopes are entertained for his speedy recovery

J. R. Sharp, of Scofield and Matthew Patterson and Matthias Patterson, of Winter Quarters, have returned from Marysville district where they have been looking at some claims in which they are interested.

Mike Koekl, one of the two men who were injured in the Winter Quarters mine with giant powder, returned Tuesday from the hospital.

J. W. Lloyd has left us and gone to Diamondville, Wyoming, where he is digging dusky diamonds.

The District school will open at Winter Quarters on July 6, with the same teachers that taught the last school, viz W. H. Griffin, of Cache Junction, and Miss Hannah Johnson, of Provo.

Lars Jensen, one of the car repairers of the R. G. W., has been layed off. There are not so many cars coming this way since the U P. mine closed.

EMERY.

A number of the young boys of our town got gay Sunday night. They had things pretty much their own way until about mid night when an accident tended to check their dangerous sport. The boys got hold of a few revolvers and was amusing themselves by terrorizing the town until a carriage load of young people came along when their reckless sport was turned to occupants of the carriage. A shot too close to the horses scared the team and with much effort a runaway was avoided. This being rather tame they began shooting at each other with the result that Tommy Keel got a bullet in the fleshy part of his arm between the elbow and shoulder. He was taken to Dr. Allred who removed the bullet and dressed the wound. The boy will carry a sore arm for some time. The fact that the town is without a constable or justice of the peace probably led the boys to believe that any kind of sport could be indulged in without being recommended to the bar of justice. The citizens very generally denounce this dangerous practice and will unite in putting it down.

Sarah Jane Williams is laying very low at this time in fact her life is despaired of. Her sons and daughters are all here ministering to her every want and sadly awaiting the end which cannot be long. Her husband died very recently.

The weather is very dry and hot and the ranchers would hail a good rain with much delight. A great deal of grain has just been watered the first time. The hay harvest will begin in a few days.

Billy Bowden and wife and Mrs. Anderson all of Ephraim are here at the bedside of their sick mother, Grandma Williams.

E. A. Ireland is haying on his Quitchapaw ranch and expects to get through this week when he will begin haying at his Oak Springs ranch. During the summer he puts up several hundred tons of red top, timothy and lucern and employs a large force of men.

Price

LOCAL NEWS

Pete Francis was in from Brock late last week.

Phil McKewen, of Vernal, was in Price early in the week.

Robert Forrester, of Castlegate was in Price on Saturday.

Don Johnson was in from Minnie Maud early in the week.

George Harmon, of Ephraim, was registered at the Hotel Clarke on Sunday.

Born to to the wife of Wm. Eldredge, on Friday morning, a fine baby boy. All doing well.

Mrs. Ida McArthur and her little daughter came in from Saint George and after visiting Price friends continued her journey to Huntington where she will visit her sister, Mrs. J. W. Nixon.

No expense or effort will be spared to make the celebration of the Fourth at Castilla one long to be remembered.

Haying is in full swing and our busy ranchers are harvesting one of the best hay crops in the history of the valley.

Mrs. Parmley and her little ones came in from Cleveland on Monday's stage and departed for her home at Winter Quarters on Tuesday morning

Dave Elliott is now a resident of Price, and is camped there for keeps. Dave is in the livery business, but finds time to look after the widows.—Salina Press.

Smith and Willson, our Price blacksmiths, drew a valuable shotgun in the San Francisco Examiner's distribution of prizes to its suscribers. The gun is manufactured by one of the leading gunsmiths, and it is said to be an excellent fowling piece.

CASTLEGATE.

Unless there is a change in the life of Young By Llewelyn he will be a fit subject for the reform school. Intending to go to the Park some nine miles up Willow creek he purloined a horse of Heber Ward and after arriving at his destination he turned the animal loose to go where it may. Young Ward got wind of the affair and went after his horse, found it and brought it home, and he also brought Young Llewelyn with him and went before the Justice of the Peace who gave By some fatherly advice and admonished him as to the possible consequence of such action.

Dr. Asadoorian was called on Tuesday to attend Mrs. George Perkins, of Spring Glen who is seriously ill.

Mrs W. Demond who was recently quite ill is now convalescing.

G. Thomas came over from Lawrence with two teams and returned with his family and household goods where they will permanently reside. When his family are settled he will return to Castlegate and continue working in the mines.

Ben the painter, secured the contract for painting the K. of P. hall and is now busy at his work.

The family of E. L. Carpenter are rusticating at the Gate.

John Eden is back again presumably to seek work. He says Leadville is not what it "uster was."

Assessor Tidwell took in the town this week.

Mrs. T. W. Lewis is home again after spending a couple of weeks at Winter Quarters visiting relatives and friends. So also is Mrs. John Hol'y who has been visiting at Springville.

Mrs. Job Llewelyn is here from Cripple Creek Colo.

H A. Nelson paid Scofield a flying visit last week

Ice cream palace are becoming a clog on the market. There are no less than four such places running at the present time. This is three too many.

The Fourth of July committee have got some hard work before them to level the center of the " Bike" track. The other day there were about three dozen men and boys emptying coke slack cars with which to spread over the clayey ground. After working a full day it looked as though it will require a good many more days to make a finished job of it.

The delegates of the K. of P. society have returned fully satisfied with the results of the annual el glous and further state that they had a good time, being royally entertained by the hospitable people of Park City. While there a number went down the great Ontario and Daly Mines,

WELLINGTON.

The Western has a force of men and teams at work digging a large ditch along the track for a distance of about a mile. The ditch is to be used as a flood ditch to protect the track in case of cloud bursts Henry Rosanoe, of Springville, has charge of the work.

Now that the railroad people are at work here it would be a wise move for our people to join the railway company in the work of digging a large flood ditch that would protect both the property of the railroad and that of the townspeople. Delay is dangerous. Better do it at once.

F. C. Grundvig was awarded the contract for building the new school house at this place. The price to be paid is $1,149 The contract calls for the com pltion of the work by September 20. This new district school building will accommodate all the children in the district.

Mrs Rhoda Olsen has been very ill for the past week and is in a critical condition at this writing. Mrs. Blackburn is attending her.

Jacob Liddell is not gaining as rapidly as his relatives and friends would wish, in fact his condition is critical and may terminate fatally at any moment.

Art Birch and family, of Price, were Wellington visitors on Sunday.

On Sunday Elisha Jones, of Huntington, gave us a very plain talk on the subject of "Our duties as Saints."

Mrs Nellie Wilson and family, of Price, visited her parents on Sunday.

An excellent program is prepared for the Fourth of July celebration. A good time is looked forward to.

The citizens and voters of this school district should bear in mind that a school election will occur on the second Monday in July for the purpose of electing a trustee to take the place of the officer retiring on that date.

HUNTINGTON.

Extensive preparations are being made for the proper observance of the Fourth of July. Various committees have been appointed and the preliminary work is being rapidly pushed. A cordial invitation is extended to our sister towns to come and celebrate with us.

Haying is well under way and in a few days the first crop of lucern will be harvested. It is a good harvest and well cured. The grain is a little late but is growing rapidly and promises a good yield. The acreage is some larger than last year.

Grazing is excellent and stock is doing well.

The appropriation for the canyon road leading to Fairview is still in the state treasury or some other place equally as inaccessible. Numerous inquiries are heard as to when and who will have the matter in charge. All possible haste should be made in the matter of putting this road in the condition for travel that the outlay of this amount of money would warrant.

The mill company have concluded to dispense with the unsatisfactory water power and will sometime during the summer put in a steam plant which will be used excepting high water during the spring time. The move will surely result satisfactorily to the owners as during the winter the irregular flow of water from freezing caused much annoyance to the operation of the mill and a great inconvenience to the townspeople.

Price

LOCAL NEWS.

John Eden, the popular and successful Cleveland rancher, was a Price visitor on Tuesday.

Geo. M. Miller came over from Huntington early in the week and spent several days in Carbon's capital.

W. L. Eastman and son formerly of Omaha but now residents of Salt Lake were guests of the Clarke this week.

J. A. Parker and J. R. Kindred left Price Tuesday for Molen, Emery Co, where they will work for several weeks in the interest of the Geo. A. Lowe Implement house.

Operator Dixon who was recently sent to the hospital returned Saturday apparently convalescing Yesterday he relapsed and was again taken to the hospital seriously ill

Andrew Murcardeni the Italian with a penchant for mining picks, referred to in another column, was committed to the county calaboose Tuesday evening to serve out his sentence of $10 and costs.

Mrs. Eliza Stephens, of Ogden, was called to the bedside of her sister in law, Mrs George Perkins, of Spring Glen, who was quite sick, but is now improving. Mrs. Stephens, before returning to her home visited her sisters, Mrs. George Eldredge and Mrs. Lydia A. Mead

The little ten months-old baby of Mr. and Mrs. Geo F. Downard died Tuesday. The little one had suffered several weeks with whooping cough and a few days ago it grew worse from what is supposed to have been pneumonia and passed away Tuesday afternoon. Burrial services were held to-day.

Ephraim Dimmick, of Wellington, is making final proof on his home stead.

Bert Seaboldt came in from the post Saturday and continued his journey to Salt Lake.

J. D. Bonce has greatly improved the appearance of his residence with a neat coat of paint.

Charles Wright, postmaster at Payson, died Friday night the result of a rupture of the bowels.

Lilly Bryner returned home on Friday from a pleasant visit with her brother's family at Helper.

SCOFIELD.

Work at Winter Quarters has been better of late. The mine worked on Sunday. If the increased work continues some of the idle miners will likely be employed.

What is left of the U P. store stock is being sold out at reduced rates

The Wasatch store at Winter Quarters is busy taking stock.

Pedllers from Utah county are quite numerous these days.

An increase occurred in the family of John Webber last week. All are doing well.

The Scofield band will go up Mud creek on the fourth and have a big time among themselves.

The Webber, Barns and Laughlin company are putting considerable coal on the dump at the Kimball mine for the fall trade.

W. O. Smith, of Springville, is getting out props for the Winter Quarters mine

The U P. paid their men off Saturday night a week ago keeping only a few men to watch the mines and the balance can engage in a walk-out of town scheme

Mrs. John Cirrick presented her husband with a son recently. Although quite ow for a while she is now improving

The Winter Quarters people will celebrate at Thomas s grove.

Wm. Wilson formerly of Coalville but at present a resident of Castlegate has moved his family to Winter Quarters.

WELLINGTON.

The relatives and friends of W. A
Thayn, composing almost the entire
population of this ward celebrated his
return home from the European mis-
sion-ry field on Friday of last week
after an absence of two years. The people met at Franz Tidwell's grove and
after a speech of welcome by his venerable fath r, J J. Thayn, which was
followed by R. A. Snyder and others,
Alvin Thayn took the stand and gave an
interesting review of his work which
was given close attention. An elegant
spread on the greensward was partaken
of. An enjoyable dance in the evening
closed the event

Alvin and Brigham Thayn have gone
to Beoly's saw mill in the Simpete
mountains where they will operate the
mill during the summer.

Price's blacksmith, J. L. Willson and
his family spent several days visiting
relatives and friends last week. Mr.
Wilson has been unwell for some time
and thought a change would benefit
him.

It is reported on good authority that a
wealthy company has interested itself in
the McMullin-Carter Coal mines near
here and will in the near future do considerable d velopment work and also
ship several car loads of coal as a test
from this point. We hope it will prove
a success

A cordial invitation is extended to
everybody to come and enjoy the Fourth
of July celebration which will be held
Monday the fifth. We are going to have
a good time.

The Tidwell Haladay Coal company
are developing their mines in Whitmore
canyon and propose to do good business
this fall and winter.

After a lingering and painful illness
covering a priod of nearly one year
Jacobson of Mr. and Mrs. Peter Littell,
passed to his last rest at 7 30 p m, June
19, 1897 During this period the deceased had been afflicted with many
abcesses from which he could get no
relief having spent several weeks last
fall under the care of skilled physicians
in the hospital at Salt Lake. The funeral
occurred at Wellington to-day.

LOCAL NEWS

The wife of Operator Milton and her
two children arrived on Monday and
for lack of a suitable place to inhabit
will have to either board or live in a
tent.

Gus Anderson, the genial rustler for
the famous Three-Crown brands of
baking pow'er and flavoring extracts,
made a flying trip through Emery
county this week.

Dickson & Donant received an elegant
bar today. Work on their extension is
rapidly nearing completion and they will
have a good substantial building when
completed.

W H Dixon who was sent to the hospital at Salt Lake last week died there
on Monday. Mr. Dixon was the R G W.
operator here until seized with rheumatism which was the cause of his demise.

Hotel Clark to be Enlarged

The two hotels here have for the past four or five months been crowded to their utmost capacity and in numerous instances travellers have been compelled to sit up for want of a place to sleep

In order to keep space with the requirements of the traveling public, the genial manager of Hotel Clarke, H. G. Clark, has recently associated with him N. C. Spalding, of Payson, a hotel man of experience. They will immediately begin the construction of an addition on the west side of the hotel to be 55 by 26 feet which will be divided into 12 elegant sleeping apartments. An addition will be built on the east side which will be used for a genteel bar and large commodious sample rooms

It is to be hoped that the enterprise of those gentlemen will be rewarded with sufficient patronage to warrant the outlay. The indications now are that this increased facility for the accomodation of travelers will be heavily taxed.

Eastern Utah Advocate
July 8, 1897

WELLINGTON.

The celebration was one of the most enjoyable affairs that has been held in this place. The afternoon and evening dances participated in by the young and older was a pleasureable event. Peace and good order prevailed. There was

no boisterous or rowdy conduct. A number from the surrounding towns were in attendance and were made to feel welcome.

Miss Kitty Watson, of Springville, is spending a few days with her grand parents, Mr. and Mrs. J. B. Milner.

Strangers have been heard to express themselves very favorable toward our community and speak a desire to become one of us. We hope to ever merit the good opinion of all.

It gives us much pleasure to note the rapid advancement of our new school building. The foundation is completed and the material for its completion will be on the ground in a few days. The capacity of the building will afford ample accommodations for all of our children for some time to come. Wellington will be a desirable location for those who wish to take advantage of a good public school

CLEVELAND

All through haying season the weather was fine and the farmer has the first cutting of lucern in the stack. Both yield and quality are good.

Born to Sarah Lewis, a 9 pound baby girl. We understand that the mother and little one will hereafter make their home in Castledale.

George Oviatt returned to his house early in the week.

The band gave us good music and acquitted themselves quite creditably. We are well pleased with our band.

Mr. and Mrs. Lewis Larsen jr. came in from Castlegate and spent the Fourth visiting relatives and friends. A number of young men were here from Sco field.

Young America and the firecracker sometime prove a dangerous combination. Some scenery that was stored in the ward house caught fire from firecrackers but was discovered before much damage was done.

Soph Olsen has leveled a site on which his store will be placed in a few days. The location is a good one being about the center of town.

Joe Nielsen has again returned to Cleveland and will make this his home.

The celebration of our nation's natal day on July 5 was a success. A good program was well rendered in the morning. A dance in the afternoon and candy for the children and grand ball in the evening were the events of the day. The morning gathering was under the bowery. No unseemly conduct marred the day's event and all was joy.

SPRING GLEN,

Frank Wiseman was married to Miss Emma Hamilton by Justice Simmons on Sunday, July 4.

On Monday Columbus Gentry and Miss Rhoda Bishop both of Gordon Creek precinct were made one by our affable justice of the peace. Congratulations and wishes for their future prosperity are extended.

The first cutting of lucern is harvested and in stack and well cured. The best field yields was that of George Perkins which averaged three tons to the acre. The best single acre was grown by Andy Simmons and run four and one-half tons. The yield was unusually heavy, the lucern reaching a height of five and one-half feet

The family of George Drury are all sick from the whooping cough.

A J Simmons and family had an outing on Tuesday spent in Gentry gulch.

The Spring Glen Canal company will in a short time award a contract for strengthening and making an all dirt canal for that portion of the company's ditch along the railroad track just below the R. G. Western's lower reservoir. It is thought $600 will do the work contemplated by the board which will require

a rip rap some sixteen feet high and several feet long which will change the bed of the Price river. The railroad company will also make an all-dirt canal around their lower reservoir. The R G Western's action in crowding the canal out of its bed and constructing its track thereon and refusing to make a permanent site for the canal is censurable. Work for completing the canal to a distance of eight miles from its head will be begun soon. This will put water on the flat just above Robt Powell's place.

The talk of an extension of the Spring Glen canal to cover land north and north east of Price is going the rounds. A majority of the holders of stock would be glad to see the enterprise go through as it would necessitate the enlarging of the canal and tend to make it more permanent and give better general satisfaction.

Born—On Wednesday morning of this week to Mrs. J. M. Whitmore, a fine boy. The boy tipped the beam at 8¼. Mother and child are doing well.

Salt Lake Herald
July 14, 1897

SOME LIVING PIONEERS.

Mary Eliza Westover, who now resides at Huntington, Emery county, is a surviving pioneer. She is the daughter of Charles and Julia A. Shumway, and was born in the town of Sturbridge, Worcester county, Mass., on Oct. 27, 1835. When 2 years of age, she removed with his family to Illinois, and in the fall of 1842, went to Nauvoo. Her family was the first of the Saints to cross the Mississippi. They spent the following winter at Winter Quarters, where her mother and only sister were buried. The next spring, her father and brother started west, and Mrs. Westover followed later, arriving in the

MARY ELIZA WESTOVER.

valley in October, 1847. She went with the first company to Manti, Sanpete county, and four years later moved to Payson, where she lived during the Walker Indian war and then moved to Big Cottonwood, this county. In September, 1856,(she married Charles Westover and in the fall of 1862 they were called to go to St. George with the original settlers of that place. She then moved to Pine Valley and later to Pinto, where a flood destroyed their property.

CASTLEGATE.

The school election passed off very quickly. Nobody seemed to want the position, and as a consequence the old board will again act. W. T. Lamph was again elected to fill the 7 year term. Only a few attended the meeting in the evening to accept the annual reports. The compensation voted for the board was the same amount as voted last year, only that it was evenly divided.

The dastardly murder of John Egan in Salt Lake City has been for the last few days the talk of the town, as the genial John was well known by the majority of our townsmen when living at P. V. Junction. He always had a pleasant word and a kind welcome to all who paid him a call. It is hoped that the cowardly murderers will meet with swift justice.

Rees Job's injured shoulder is getting better.

The material for the support of the power house is expected here every day. When it comes the mine will shut down until all repairs are made.

Another electric mining machine will be put in the mine today for experiment, and if successful will be adopted.

Dr. Asadorian was called to the section house late last night to attend a severe case of sickness.

Born—On the 10th inst., to the wife of John Marlotti, a boy. All well.

Mrs Caroline Olsen's little girl, Myrtle, is improving rapidly from a mild case of typhoid fever.

The Castlegate Brass band have been engaged to take part in the Pioneer Jubilee, and are practising with a vim that is characteristic with them when their reputation is at stake. Keep it up, boys.

George Cox, of this burg, is over at Castledale for the purpose of getting spliced to a Miss Birch, and if not too premature, we extend our congratulations.

Andrew Young, Jr, and bride will soon go to housekeeping.

County Commissioner Hood has been here looking around to see what improvements can be made in roads and bridges. In company with Road Supervisor Young they made a tour of the district, and we are informed that quite a number of improvements are to be made.

The course that the commissioners propose taking to oust the derilict and useless county officers is highly commended by the voters of this district.

J. B. Cordell purposes spending a few weeks up at Winter Quarters. The high altitude has special attractions for him.

Henry Wade, after spending a few days with his family, has again gone to his coal properties at Sunnyside.

Jas. Davis, of Cleveland, has been here visiting, but has now returned home.

T. W. Williams got a severe blow in the eye by a piece of coal the other day, which caused him great pain. The physician took the piece of coal out, and treated it with eye medicine, which eased the pain and gave him relief.

Mrs. C. Carter is having a connection with the water main put in her house. This will stop water carrying. With very little expense to the company this could be done to all the company houses, and would be a boon to all householders.

The delightful evenings are causing the people to take to promenading.

"Is this hot enough for you?"

WELLINGTON.

Some of the larger children of this place at times indulge in a very dangerous pastime, that of putting the push car on the main line of the R. G. Western's track for a ride. This is dangerous sport as no one knows what moment a train may come along thus placing themselves in imminent danger of a badly disfigured anatomy and possibly a wrecked train endangering other lives and persisted in may land the parties behind the bars.

Geo A. Willson jr. has been appointed justice of the peace for Wellington precinct and will qualify this week. This matter should have been attended to long ago.

The annual meeting of the Wellington precinct school board occurred Monday morning. A good showing was made All debts paid and money in the treasury. The vote for trustee in the afternoon resulted in the election of Mrs Eva Tidwell for the three-year term as school trustee.

A committee of ladies and gentleman have been appointed to arrange for a Pioneer day celebration on July 24, and who will report to the people at the close of services Sunday afternoon

We are experiencing very hot weather just now. All crops are growing rapidly.

SCOFIELD

District school at Winter Quarters began this week. The trustees decided to begin early in order that the little ones may get the advantage of almost the entire school year, as during the winter months they are unable to attend, owing to the excessive cold and deep snows.

John Biddoe's family have returned from Cleveland, and will remain here during the summer.

William Howells has moved his family back to Spanish Fork.

Mother Gordon is improving from a third stroke of paralysis.

A number of the idle men here have been employed at the Winter Quarters mine.

The hay crop in Pleasant Valley is very backward this summer, by reason of the unusually cold nights, frosts occurring almost every night.

While running a race on the Fourth, Alex Wilson fell, receiving injuries from which he has suffered considerably, and has been unable to work.

Deseret Evening News
July 17, 1897

Scofield Notes.

SCOFIELD, July 14, 1897.

To the Editor:

A petition is being circulated for signatures asking the county court to appoint J. L. Price of Scofield as sheriff of Carbon county vice G. Donant resigned.

Wm. Pugh and George Wilson were tried before Justice of the peace J. B. Thomas at Winter Quarters yesterday on a charge of disturbing the peace of D. Rosser and family. They were fined $5 and $4.50 costs each. Wilson paid his fine, but Pugh preferred to go to jail. County Attorney Warf appeared for the State.

It has made it quite inconvenient for the employes of the P. V. Coal company, now that they are paid in checks, but the Union Pacific has done still worse at Scofield, they have quit paying altogether.

Some of the Scofield miners have been put on at Winter Quarters.

There was born to the wife of Frank Merewether yesterday, a girl. Mother and child are doing well and the father wears a bright smile.

We have had frosts every night until last night, and the hay crop in Pleasant Valley is quite backward.

WELLINGTON.

A large number of our citizens left on Monday to attend the Pioneer Jubilee.

Joseph Draper and family have gone to Salt Lake country for a visit with friends. They will be away a month.

Bishop McMullin is confined to his bed with a lame back. He received the injury while loading gilsonite at the mines It is thought that he will be around again in a few days.

CASTLEGATE

While a chronic kicker is an object of condemnation, and one who causes a feeling of fatigue to come over the body of politic, yet a well regulated kick is often beneficial, and we are kicking right now for good roads. Some parts of the county road between here and Helper is just now in a deplorable condition and if not soon repaired the county is liable to have a damage suit on hand. We are informed that there is no road supervisor in that district to look after the road. It is high time some one was appointed. There should be a place for surplus water to run off and we think that proper conduits should be made for that purpose and not let it cut all the road bed which is the case below Jone's farm. Verbum sap.

It is evident that by Friday that the town will be almost depopulated It is the Jubilee and nothing but the Jubilee. Some few are going to Emery county to visit friends while some will stay at home and curse the fates or else go up the canyon picnicing

Little Evans, the son of Rowe Lewis, came near putting his eye out with a pick the other day. He was playing with it and it was too heavy for him to swing over his head it only got to a level with his forehead. The point went into the corner of his left eye cutting the eyelid and causing the blood to flow freely. After examination and treatment the little man felt better and is now running around. It was a close shave.

Geo. B. Milner has taken the bull by the horns and has started the construction of a flood water ditch across his arm Becoming aweary of action by the people and the approaching rainy season behooved him to take steps to protect himself. He shows good judgment.

Thos Farish and wife with Mrs L P Overson of Cleveland came up to Castlegate to see friends before going to Salt Lake Lake J W. Lewis is also here from the same town. He came purposely to take back some relatives to spend the holidays. The mines having shut down for a week or more to make repairs hence the exodus

Blake McLaughlin a tourist from California enroute to Colora lo stopped off here with a view to find suitable employment if possible, but after finding his efforts vain, he was informed that in Price he might get something in his line of business and we understand that he has located there.

Dr Asadoorian was called away on a special Sunday night to go to Sphinx as there had been a bad accident near that place in which General Road Master Lee lost his life and an engineer and fireman seriously if not fatally injured when the doctor got there he found that the injured men had been taken to Grand Junction The accident was caused by sand on the road, the sand having been blown there by a heavy wind storm. It took the wrecking gang several hours before they could extricate Mr. Lee from under the debris. He was mangled in a fearful manner. Mr. Lee was well liked by all the railroad men

SCOFIELD.

George Wilson and Henry Pugh were taken before Justice of the Peace Joseph S. Thomas last week on a complaint of disturbing the peace. Each received a fine of of $3 0) and costs amounting to $1 5) in each case. Wilson paid his fine and Pugh went to the county jail. Attorney Warf deserves much credit for the fair and impartial manner in which he presented each side of the case to the court.

The people of Scofield and Winter Quarters signified their good will to J L Price by signing his petition to the board of county commissioners for the appointment of sheriff. As marshall and constable Mr Price proved himself worthy

Last Saturday evening Fred Kurtz, of Eureka, and Miss Lena Gorden of Winter Quarters were united in wedlock by Justice John E Ingles, of Scofield.

It has become a disgraceful habit in this vicinity for a crowd of boys ranging from twelve to twenty years of age to gather at weddings with all manner of noise-making instruments for the purpose of raising such a hullabaloo that to get rid of the noise the parties are compelled to make the boys a present of money or beer when a carousal begins that must make his Satanic majesty hug himself with delight. This should not be allowed. For the good of the child the parent should see that he is in bed in proper time.

CLEVELAND.

The big reservoir of the Cleveland Canal and Irrigation company up Huntington canyon has just been opened and Cleveland water owners will soon have a considerable increase in flow of water. The river is getting low and the Huntington canals was taking most of the water. The reservoir will furnish plenty water until the close of the irrigating season.

The ice cream party at Mrs W E Cowley's was an enjoyable affair as was also that at Bishop Oversen's

Miss Helga Frickson is visiting her sister, Mrs. H C Smith at Price.

H. H Oviatt and his estimable lady have started for the Jubilee by team. This worthy couple are long residents of Utah and the reunion of old friends at Salt Lake will be a keen joy to them.

The school election resulted in the election of John Potter for a three year term to succeed H. H. Oviatt jr.

A mistake occurred in the Advocate's last Cleveland correspondence regarding Sarah Lewis. The item stated that mother and child would make their home in Castledale which was incorrect as only the child will live in Castledale with Mrs. Nichols while Miss Lewis will remain in Cleveland

The brick work on Bishop Overson's residence is completed and will probably be ready for occupancy in the near future.

The Advocate is a welcome visitor to the many Cleveland homes. Even the little ones are disappointed when it fails to come on Friday.

The New Sheriff.

Pursuant to call the county commissioners met in special session on Monday and after a long-drawn-out session appointed C W Allred, of Price, to fill the unexpired term of sheriff made vacant by the resignation of Gus Donant and which resignation was by request of the county commissioners as previously stated in these columns

Of the candidates there were varied and many who were anxious to do valient service for the county. Petitions galore was in evidence. Those who were in the race to win were, H G Clark, and Ras Anderson, of Price, Joseph Durch and J R Roberts, of Wellington, Nephi L McLean, Game Warden Metcalf and J L Price, of Scofield Ras Anderson did a manly act in withdrawing and putting up a good talk for his neighbor which probably elected Mr. Allred.

The choice appears to give very general satisfaction and the commissioners are to be congratulated on the selection. Mr. Allred was formerly from Beaver where his father held the position of marshall for some time and Charley was frequently pressed into service and is not without experience He has lived in Carbon county a number of years and his interests are closely identified with that of the county. All lawabiding citizens should, and we think will, give the new sheriff hearty support. It becomes Mr. Allred's very plain duty to go vigorously after the lawlessly inclined and make the strong arm of the law be felt.

The minutes show Commissioner Liddell as voting in the negative.

Price

LOCAL NEWS.

S. M. Brown, of Vernal, was stopping in Price several days this week.

A. D. Dickson transacted business in this part of the valley this week.

J. T. Fitch was down from Helper on Tuesday trading with Price merchants.

Mr. and Mrs. John Martin returned from Provo where John had been under the doctor's care from a very badly lacerated thumb caused by being penetrated by an ugly sliver.

Sergeant Bissell made a flying trip to Sunnyside on Monday to repair the private telephone of the Big Springs ranch company. The line extends from the ranch to the Sunnyside depot.

Mrs. E. Miller, of Castlegate, was visiting relatives and friends in Price on Sunday.

Robert McKune spent several days in Zion last week and returned to Price Sunday.

A large number of Vernal and Ft. Duchesne parties went to Salt Lake through Wasatch county.

Miss May Pace returned from New Harmony yesterday, where she has been visiting friends and relatives. Miss Maggie Pace, sister of Mrs. Albert Bryner, accompanied her, and will remain in Price for some time.

When her front wheel struck a gully with a startled cry of 'Holly Gee' she hit this mundane sphere a vicious spat. To a drug store they bore her, and an hour they labored o'er her ere she opened her eyes and asked. "Where be I at?"— Denver Post.

Information reached us yesterday of the marriage of two of Price's most popular ladies in Salt Lake early this week. The contracting parties were James Roomy the well known Hyper saloon man, to Deesie Warren, o'Shit place, and who has a host of Price friends, JohnW. Foote, who has recently purchased the Senate saloon, to Mrs. Deal Hutchison, of this place, and sister of Meadows Whitmore and Belle. We join with their many friends in wishing them long and happy lives.

Eastern Utah Advocate
August 5, 1897

EMERY.

Fully one-fourth of our citizens attended the great Jubilee and all are well pleased with their visit and feel that it was time and money well spent.

A neat little tithing office is just about completed. It is situated on the north west corner of the tithing lot. The structure is of wood and quite ornamental. The worthy bishop is doing a good work.

A number of brick residences will go up in Emery during the fall months. Johnny Burk, of Castledale, is here and will burn 80,000 brick all of which have been contracted for.

Miss Keller, of Manti, is in our town for the purpose of securing classes in both vocal and instrumental music. We wish her much success.

The grain crop is looking fairly well and is a heavy increase in acreage over last year. Harvesting will begin next week and owing to the increased acreage more binders were necessary and a number of our people have gone to Price to secure binders and twine.

Wheat is being injured by a bug that is new to this county. The bug is quite large and with a long bill bores to the heart of the kernel. It is called the Finch bug.

Ed. Tergerson is trying an experiment which may be the nucleus of another "infant industry" for Emery county. He has planted a piece of ground to the great american staple—peanuts. Ed. says they are doing well.

The following were Emery's quota of visitors to the great Jubilee—E. H Duzette, Mr and Mrs. Nephi Williams, Mr. and Mrs. S. M. Williams, Mr. and Mis G. T. Olson, Mr. and Mrs Hans Casper, Mr. and Mrs. John Williams, Mr. and Mrs Tom Williams, El. Tergason and Stine Williams.

SCOFIELD.

District school opened on Monday We have a very large school population when compared to the size of the place Utah's beet crop is in a flourishing condition.

Most of the Scofield miners are now working at Winter Quarters which have worked steadily of late. The mines are very much crowded by reason of the development work being behind the requirements of the output.

Your correspondent is informed by a prominent Springville Citizen that a sugar factory for that town is assured and will be built in the near future.

Eastern capital has been secured for the erection of the plant and the farmers surrounding that town will take stock in the company to be paid for out of their beet yield. The people of Springville and surrounding town will receive great benefits from the enterprise.

Barney Magnuson an old employer of the P. V. Coal company at Winter Quarters, started for Alaska last Monday to try his fortune with the gold seekers.

O. K. Stoney and P. W. Wood, of Provo, were here for a day or two the first part of the week.

WELLINGTON.

At the meeting of the citizens held on Monday night the question of a flood ditch was, we are pleased to say, settled. It was decided to cut a ditch along the east side of town connect with the flood ditch constructed by the railroad company which it is thought will protect the town from the largest flood. While some of the people are kicking because the ditch will pass alongside their property, a big majority are of the opinion that the proposed ditch is properly located and will begin construction at once.

The new school house is fast taking on the appearance of a building. The contractor has a competent force of men employed.

~Notwithstanding the occasional showers the work of harvesting the second crop of lucern goes on apace and will soon be in the stack.

Jehu Blackburn, wife and sons, Fred and Lesley have left for Loa, Wayne county, to attend a session of district court. They will be gone two weeks.

Some little sickness is reported which is occasioned by the sudden change of weather.

CASTLEGATE.

Young Charl's Flew met with a severe accident Tuesday morning. He was swinging on one of the ropes left over from the 4th of July, and in getting off the swing to allow some one else to use it, h's coat or some other portion of his clothing got tangled up with the rope causing him to loose his equilibrium and he fell heavily upon his left arm from which he sustained a compound fracture of the arm. It was broken just below the elbow. Doctor Asadoorian set the injured limb and at present writing the boy is resting easily.

We call the attention of the people of this town to the above accident as a warning. It is a suprise that there has not been more boys and girls hurt by this very same swing. The young folks will get a plank and balancing it upon the rope they will then go as high as possible making it a 'angerous pastime for any one to come within reach of that plank.

Sylvester Deroski, an employe of the R.G.W. came nearly pass'ng in his checks the other evening. He tried to make a running leap for No.J as she pulled out of the yard, miscalculating the distance and the speed of the train. He was thrown violently against the car, and just managing to keep his hold on the guards. He got aboard alright but it was a close call.

Young George Shultz has not yet fully recovered from the powder burns caused by shooting firecrackers during the late holidays, but he is around and playing.

Mrs. M. A. Taylor who left here a couple of weeks ago to reside in Salt Lake City is reported to be dying. Her children who are here have been sent for. We regret to hear this sad news.

People who own chickens must see to it that they do not annoy and destroy other people's property. Householders have rights and one among the many is, that they shall not be disturbed in the even tenor of their way; but waen a chicken has the chance to make neighbors quarrel, we call a halt and proclaim, to all who keep chickens, to fence them in gentleman, fence them in.

There is some talk of organizing the old white caps vigilance committee. The movement is to be deprecated as we were under the impression that the moral code was in the ascendency in this town, but the way the people are talking about the actions of some persons here justify rigid methods to be taken to straighten out a few of the kinks in loose morals. We have, so far, refrained from writing on this matter, but the time has come when to keep silent is almost a crime in itself. Something ought to be done to try and bring these wayward persons to a sense of their degradation. If persuasion 'ails then let the law be enforced.

Criticisms of our last article have been both long and loud. If a newspaper is not an educator, what is it? It is a mirror in which the puposes, desires, actions and aims of all that is good and true is held up to view and it is a medium where crime, casualties and other kindred topics are exposed and discussed, where science, art and genius portray their research and practicability and the advertiser with the long purse gets the dead cinch on space; there are many other purposes for which a newspaper is used, for which, you have not space to give me to enumerate. Hence, we court criticism in exposing that which is a blot upon the fair history of any town or people. We feel justified in so doing.

The family of Engineer Knight are here from Colorado and have gone to housekeeping.

A kindergarten school is opened up for a few weeks, Mrs. J. E. Cardon, of Logan, is teacher. The lady is a relative of Agent Ricks. She intends to stay here for a short time.

Mr. Mercer is now operator in place of Roy Gibson.

LOCAL NEWS.

B. F. Caffey is down from Castlegate to-day.

J. W. McCarlin, of Vernal, was registered at Hotel Clarke last week.

Quarterly conference convenes at Cleveland on Saturday of this week.

Joseph and Charlie Vacher were down from the sheep herd early in the week.

A. E. Gibson, of Cleveland, was registered at the Mathis hotel early in the week.

Wm. Howard came in from Salt Lake and left this morning for his home in Huntington.

L. R. Rhodes passed through Price enroute to Vernal where he will attend a session of the district court.

Geo. H. Eldridge, of the United States geological survey arrived in Price last evening and left on this morning's stage for the reservation.

Wm. Lamph and family of Castlegate, passed through Price to-day enroute for Cleveland. Mr. Lamph will look after his Cleveland property and also attend conference which convenes on Saturday.

Randolph Seely, at one time a resident of this place, and one of the Seely families, is here on a visit. He is now a resident of San Bernardino county, Cal., and came to Utah to attend the the Jubilee as one of the pioneers. Mr. Seely owns one of the finest orchards in the county in which he lives, and has premiums at the caterstate fair

Lieut. Horne with his troop, B, will start early this week for a practice march by way of Ogden to Carter station and from there by the old Bridger Military road back to Ft. Duchesne.

If the friends of John L. Day, the well known traveling man, have missed him on his accustomed round, they need not worry. John is all right John is a papa. The new arrival is a fine boy and was born last evening.—Tuesday's Herald.

A. E. Edwards, who has been teaching school at Ferron for two years, and our regular correspondent from that place, was in town on Tuesday, returning from the Jubilee. Mr. Edwards is thinking of permanently settling down at Emery. He has been engaged to teach there for the coming season.—Manti Messenger.

Judge Dusenberry sitting at Provo on Friday granted a new trial in the Vernal Water suit holding that Judge King, who had formerly heard it, erred in the admission of certain testimony. The case is that of E. G. De Freeze et al. against H. D. Calton et al. and involves a greater portion of the water in ashley river.

John Martin and wife on Sunday morning left for Provo where they will make their future home. Mrs. Lavina Loek, mother of Mrs. Martin and of Mrs. John L. Willson who has been visiting her daughters for some time accompanied them to Thistle where they separated Mrs. Loek going to her home in Mt. Pleasant.

The McKee boys who were recently arrested near Vernal for killing and running off a herd of bucks, had their preliminary examination last week and were bound to the district court. Sufficient evidence was brought out in the hearing to make conviction almost certain.

Mrs. Geo W. Bodle and her daughters Clara and Maud left Price on Monday for Salt Lake where they will make their home. Mrs. Bodle has long been engaged in the hotel business in Price and by her strict attention to the comfort of

We are informed that several head of cattle belonging to Oscar Anderson and John Carter have been found dead in Straight fork of Pleasant creek, and the carcases indicate that the animals had been killed by bears. The bears must have been unusually savage and ferocious to have attacked cattle. Sheep losses from depredations of bruin are numerous but this is the first attack upon the cattle.—Ephraim Enterprise.

Court at Price.

Court at Price opened Monday with a large docket. Following are the names of the jurors drawn and notified to appear at Price on Tuesday, August 10, at 2 p.m.:

G. A. Wilson, Peter Liddell, Wellington; William Ward, John Hern, Allen Cox Castle Gate; Thomas Gatherin, Scofield; W. A. Faucett, Shillings; Charles Peterson, Price; A. S. Wilson, Joseph Wallace, Jr., Winter Quarters; James Metcalf, Scofield; John Babcock, Minnie Maud; L. A. Warren, Price; H. D. Allred, Wellington; S. A. Henrichsen, Scofield; Thomas Rhodes, Helper; H. F. Hanson, Wellington; J. H. Lloyd, Scofield; George Frandsen, Erastus Anderson, P. J. Olson, Price; John Strong, Scofield.

C W. Allred, recently appointed sheriff of Carbon county, to succeed Gus Donant, resigned, qualified on Monday as such, and furnished bonds in the amount of $6 000, with George Frandsen, Charles H. Taylor, L Lowenstein and Wyatt Bryan as bondsmen. The new sheriff will assume the duties of his office in a day or two.

KILLED IN A COAL MINE.

John Bishop Crushed By Falling Rock at Winter Quarters.

A dispatch to the News from Scofield says: John Bishop, son of Mr. Robert Bishop, met his death today in the P. V. Coal company's mine at Winter Quarters. The father and son were working together in a room, and were in the act of loading a car, when a large rock gave way directly over the young man, striking him on the head and killing him instantly. His brains were knocked out. Deceased was 22 years of age and was a great assistance to his father in helping to support a large family.

Electric machines are being introduced in the mines here for undermining the coal, and are working successfully.

A larger fan than the one now doing service is to be placed in the near future for the better ventilation of the workings of the mine, which is very much needed.

WELLINGTON.

John R. Roberts had a narrow escape from death last week by the mad rush of a vicious bull while he and others were engaged in rounding up cattle in what is known as the little park. Rob erts started a bunch containing a vicious bull, which most of the boys had been warned to look out for. Roberts had not heard of his fighting proclivities. The animal did not want to go the way he was wanted to and when Roberts attempted to turn him he made a sudden and vicious rush for man and horse. Roberts attempted to draw his gun but was to slow. The bull caught the horse back of the fore leg with his horns killing him instantly and throwing the rider into a cedar close by. Roberts soon scrambled up into the top of the tree from another onslaught, but before he recovered his presence of mind and obtained his gun, the bull had made his escape into the cedars. When Roberts told the others of his adventure they decided to go in a posse and kill the bruto which they and the next day.

Mrs. Sidney Thayn, wife of J. J. Thayn, at this writing is laying very sick from something like ague, accompanied by great pain in the stomach.

Barett Willson and mother have returned from their visit with friends in Utah county, and report having a good time. Also has Joseph Draper and family returned and they say this place is as good for a home as any they seen while gone. So we think they will stay a while with us.

Several of the old veterans have gone from this place to be present at the Black Hawk reunion to be held in Spanish Fork this week.

We are informed on good authority that some of the people of Utah county are constructing a ditch to convey some of the water from the head of White river across the mountains into Spanish Fork canyon, and that the ditch is nearly finished. Can this be done lawfully? If not our water commissioners should look this matter up at once. We also understand that there is a ditch, conveying a part or all, of the water from Gooseberry creek into Spanish Fork river now, and that that is the reason of the low water in Price river at this time. There are serious matters which our farmers should look into at once.

SCOFIELD.

John Bishop, a miner, was instantly killed in the Winter Quarters mine on Monday at about 2 45 p m. by a piece of rock falling from the roof. Deceased was about 23 years of age and unmarried. He was working in a room with his father, Robert Bishop, and was the main assistance in helping his father support a large family. Mrs. Bishop and the other children except one girl were on their ranch between Scofield and Price at the time but were sent for immediately.

The work at the P. V. mine has been very good of late.

Last Wednesday night cars of coal ran away from the elevator. Two of them ran off at the switch one of which was very badly broken.

Game Warden Metcalf yesterday wired Indian Agent Beck at Whiterocks that a number of Indians were off the reservation and killing deer on Willow creek. This is the second time since July 21 that Game Warden Metcalf has made complaint to the Indian agent of the slaughter of deer off the reservation by the Indians.

Price

LOCAL NEWS.

Mrs. H. G. Clark and child left Price last Monday morning for Kentucky.

The Mathis hotel has had a big business to care for the past week or two.

C. W. Spalding, of Payson, visited his brother, N.U. Spalding, of Hotel Clarke, for a few days.

Mrs. B. R. McDonald visited her sister, Mrs. H. A. Nelson at Castlegate, several days returning on Saturday.

Mrs. L Glaser spent several days last week visiting the family of L Lowenstein who are stopping at the Mathis hotel.

Mrs. Elizabeth Staker, once a resident of this place, but now of Huntington, is here on a visit.—Mt. Pleasant Pyramid.

Sem Thurman left on Sunday's stage for Vernal where he will take a hand in the now famous McKee sheep killing case.

Louis Baron, a well to do sheep owner registered at the Mathis hotel Sunday evening Mr. Baron was en route to Huntington on business.

The Mathis hotel under its new management is rapidly coming into popular favor with the general public. Last week there was an unprecedented large number of guests.

The complimentary ball given in honor of the marriage of Mr. and Mrs. Johnnie Foote at the town hall Friday evening was an enjoyable affair for lovers of terpsichore.

There is a wedding ceremony on the tapis in the near future in Price. Rumor has it that the ceremony will be performed not a thousand miles from the Mathis hotel on next Sunday.

On Saturday morning last the Fort Duchesne and Vernal stage line took as passengers nine attorneys enroute to district court session at Vernal. Two stages were necessary to accommodate the numerous passengers

G. W. Allred recently appointed sheriff of Carbon county by the county commissioners to succeed Gus Donant, resigned, qualified last Monday afternoon with George Frandsen, C. H. Taylor, L. Lowenstein and Wyatt Bryan as his bondsmen.

Mrs. Mariah Olsen, wife of Bp. Olsen, of Castledale returned by Saturday's stage to her home in Castledale after several months visit with friends and relatives in Sanpete. Mrs. Olsen returned home to make preparations and to be present at the wedding of her son, Victor, to Miss Mariah Hanson in the near future.

Mrs. William McIntosh died last week at the age of 73 years, after a long period of failing health. She was born in Canada and there married Mr McIntosh, and with him came to Utah upwards of forty years ago, residing most of the time in Tooele county. About six years ago they came to Mt. Pleasant. Her husband and six grown children survive her.—Mount Pleasant Pyramid.

"Colonel" E. M. Smith, returned from Salt Lake City a day or two ago, to which city the genial "Colonel" was compelled to return to obtain medical treatment for a sev re case of lumbago which attacked him in the lower portion of the spine at Fort Duchesne about a month ago. Mr Smith is advised by his physicians not to attempt the long stage journey until he has fully recovered.

Mrs. E. C. Lee, and Mrs. Tom Taylor, of Fort Duchesne with their children, who have been visiting relatives left on the north bound stage last Monday morning for their respective homes

Price seems to be a most attractive place for our neighbors. There is not a day which passes but what visitors from neighboring towns are perambulating our streets. Come again early and often.

Andrew Oyard and O C. Anderson, of Fountain Green, were before the Scofield justice of the peace last Friday, charged with defiling the waters of Mud crIk. They were assessed forty dollars fine and the costs of prosecution,

Dave Holdaway opened up his new saloon near Hotel Clarke on Saturday.

Sheriff Tuttle, of Orangeville, was in Price this week and was a court visitor.

W H Sills, of the Mercantile Protective agency Salt Lake, was in Price in the interest of the above firm.

Yesterday the McKee case came up at Verual and the entire day was consumed by the usual legal preliminaries.

Lars Thompson, of Ferron, was a Price visitor early in the week and left on Wednesday's train for Provo on business.

Louis Goldsmith, of St. Joe, Mo., was in Price Tuesday. Mr. Goldsmith represents a St. Joe wholesale house with whom L. Lowenstein deals.

Attorney Rhea, of Earll and Rhea Salt Lake attorneys, was interested in a number of cases coming up for trail at the present sitting of district court.

Governor Wells has appointed H G. Mathis agent to supervise the expenditure of $1000 appropriated by the state for a road between Price and Scofield.

Wm. Burr raised a beet of the common garden variety that tipped the beam at 9 pounds. This is a fair sample of the productiveness of our valley.

Fred E. Grames, one of the early settlers of Price, died at his home near Brock at 10 30 last night from strangulated hernia. It is reported that burial will take place at Price.

Game Commissioner Metcalf, Alex Wilson, S A Henrichsen, Thomas Guiherms, John Strang, Davel Burns and John X. Lloyd were down from Scofield attending court.

Two Italians, G. Capo and Charles Paltiene, were arrested near Castlegate Monday evening charged with killing fish in Price river with dynamite. They are now in the Price jail awaiting trial. The officers are on the trail of other dynamiters and further arrests are expected.

Eastern Utah Advocate
August 19, 1897

WELLINGTON.

Work on the new school house goes steadily on, nearly all the outside work being finished and the building will be ready when school opens When the building is completed we will have the largest and best school building in the county.

The flood which swept through town last week did little damage in town, but did considerable damage to Tom Gale's crop just below town. It is thought that 200 or 800 bushels of wheat was lost. All this might have been avoided, but the flood settled the controversy and the people went to work with a will locating the ditch along the track of the flood and when completed no further damage to town property is expected.

Mrs. Thayn was quite ill, but is now said to be convalescing.

Alvin Thayn's lucern was cut and raked two or three weeks ago and after bleaching for some time has just been placed in the stack. What will happen next? (We give it up.—Ed)

CASTLEDALE.

As an instance of the prolificuess of Emery county soil and its peculiar adaptability to the cultivation of sugar beets it may be noted that in two rows but eleven rods in length, Mr. John Peterson raised five bushels of the saccharine bearing vegetable. If more had been planted and the same ratio had held out, it would b a yeild of 500 bushels to the acre

When Castle valley gets a railroad it will rival the famous Southern California belt as the home of sugar beet factories.

E C Jorgensen of Mexico is paying a visit to his father in law, Neils Christensen, and other friends. Mr. Jorgensen has resided in the state of Chihuahua where he has an extensive farm, for seven years. Chihuahua is one of the richest mining districts in the Southern Republic. Mr. Jorgensen states that while the recent depression in the price of silver somewhat effected them, generally speaking, the people of Mexico are in a most prosperous condition.

On Tuesday last two of Castledale's most popular young people were joined in lymineal bonds. The contracting parties were V L Olsen and Miss Marla Hansen. Many of their friends from Sanpete county and other places were present at the ceremony. The bride is one of our fairest and favorite daughters. Mr. Olsen, or "Vick" as his hosts of friends call him, is a genial and enterprising young business man. All Castledale join in wishing them a happy and prosperous voyage on the pleasant sea of matrimony.

Ole O'sen has been visiting friends in Mt. Pleasant the past week.

On Friday evening last John Giddings and bride, nee Miss Mable Potter, gave a wedding dance at Social Hall which was attended from far and near. All went merry as a marriage bell and the young people thoroughly enjoyed themselves till "jocund morn stood tiptoe on the misty mountain tops"

Genial Soren Hansen will matriculate as a student at B Y. Academy, Provo, on the opening of the fall term.

Seymour Olsen is again a happy, happy father.

There is a ditch close to P U Harresson's blacksmithing shop, which the road supervisor of the precinct should see to It is a menace to life and property and unsafe to cross by any save the stoutest conveyance. If we mistake not there is an ordinance which requires all persons taking water across streets to bridge or rock the ditch so it will be passible If so, it should be enforced The ditch referred to is a standing invitation for a law suit.

On Tuesday Sheriff Tuttle arrested and delivered into custody, Edw Olsen, of Ferron, on a charge of grand larceny. Complaint alleges that Olsen ran off the range a cow belonging to Leyman S. Beach, of Molen, and sold same to parties passing through the country. Examination is set for Wednesday, August 23 at 2 p m.

The telephone company should take cognizance of the condition of the telephone wires between Castledale and Orangeville Two poles are down in the bed of Cottonwood creek and the wire has been sagging lower for several days until at present it nearly touches the ground

SCOFIELD

The funeral of J an Martin, the young man woo was killed in the mines, occurred on Wednesday of last week. Services were held in the Scofil l ward house. The employes of the mine laid off for the occasion. Mrs Bis op who was at the ranch confined to her bed when the sad news reached her managed to get to Scofiel l and attended the funeral. The funeral was largely attended. The family have the sympathy of the entire communit y in their breavement.

The P V Coal company are moving the fan from No 4 mine to No 1 mine.

Officials of the Oregon Short Line were examining the U. P. mines last week with a view to leasing them. It appears the high figure at which the company holds the mines is the only bar to the deal. The people here are very anxious for some reliable company to lease or purchase the mine and work it.

Peddlers are making regular trips from Sanpete and Utah valleys with produce and the Utah county peddlers load back with coal.

The Scofiel l miners who are at work at the Winter Quarters mines have petitioned the R G Western to run a train to carry them to work. It is hoped that the company will run the train.

LOCAL NEWS

J R Sharp and wife were down from Scofield late last week.

Mrs. A. J. Lee left Price on Saturday for Springville to visit her parents.

W.H. Leonard, of Huntington, is paying the highest cash price for wheat.

Sheriff Jack Cottrell and Omer White, of Hanksville, were in Price on Monday.

The remains of Fred L. Grames was interred in the Price cemetery on Saturday last. A large concourse of friends and neighbors paying their last respects to the departed pioneer.

H G Webb, our genial county superintenden , returned from Salt Lake last week. Mr Webb has been taking his usual summer vacation and resumes his work much invigorated.

Mrs Julia Arthurs, Cleveland's pioneer, returned to her home on Saturday morning. Mrs Arthurs has been visiting in the other valley since the Jubilee festivities in Salt Lake on July 24.

County examination of teachers begins at Castlegate on Monday next.

Detective Shores of the D &R G was a Price visitor on Monday.

W.H Leonard, of Huntington, is paying the highest cash price for wheat.

St V LeS eur, of Provo, was attend ing court the latter part of the week.

State Mine Inspector Lloyd was circulating among Price friends early in the week.

Robert McKune returned to Price Monday after a week's absence in the other valley.

Married on August 14, 1897 by Bishop Horsley, L Roy Gilson to Miss Annie Ryan. Both Mr. Gilson and his accomplished bride are well known in Price, Mr. Gilson having resided here for a number of years. Mrs. Gilson has taught school at various places throughout the state, giving evidence of marked ability. The Advocate joins their many friends in wishing them much happiness and success through life.

The little 6-year-old son of G W Mc-
Call fell from a bench at his home
on Thursday last and dislocated his arm
Mrs Warren was called and with the as
sistance of Mr McCall the injured arm
was soon set. The little fellow will
suffer very little from the injury.

Eastern Utah Advocate
August 26, 1897

WELLINGTON.

The new concrete house of W. J. Hill
is nearing completion and is going to be
a daisy.

Now that the flood ditch has become
an assured fact, the people generally
have a feeling to make many improvements, that have heretofore been held
back.

R. A. Snyder has purchased a new
self binder and is doing fine work
Grain is ripening so fast that all the
machines in the place are kept very
busy.

Miss Josephine Grundvig is suffering
from something like dropsy. The disease
attacked her about a month ago,
through local medicines she appeared to
be getting better. Monday last she
began to grow worse and is now in a
very critical condition.

John Blackburn and family have returned from their visit to Loa and report having a good time while there, but
the going and coming was very disagree-
ably by reason of the dust and heat.

SCOFIELD.

John Strang of this place was seriously injured last week in the Winter
Quarters mine. About 1900 pounds of
rock fell on him, but he was close up to
it when it gave way so that it did not
have the force it would have had if he
had been on the floor. He fell down
between some large pieces of coal which
saved him from being instantly killed
It was a miraculous escape From
present indications John will be at work
again in a few weeks.

Roderick Davis has just started to
work again after a ten days lay off from
the effects of a kick from one of the
mules in the mine

The Reverends De Graff and Fowler
of the American Sunday School union
preached at Winter Quarters last Saturday evening and at Scofield on Sunday
evening

The P. V Coal company distributed
the "velvet" to their employes on Monday.

O O. Kimball has been to Salt Lake
City several days on business

Our district schools are closed down
for one week The teachers are not
out on a strike, but are in attendance
upon the institute which is being held at
Castlegate.

CLEVELAND

A greater part of the second cutting
of lucern is in the stack and harvesting
is well under way.

The work on Bp Overson a new residence is progressing rapidly.

The popular Castlegate bishop, W. T.
Lamph, is still with us.

Mrs S. J. Cowley, our popular president of the Primary association is engaged in putting a play on the boards

for the benefit of the association.

The Sunday school was reorganized
last Sunday, the stake presidency Brother
Jameson and his assistants Brothers
Washburn and Reynolds being in attendance for this purpose Brother Erickson,
the former superintendent, and his
assistants were released and Brother
John Potter was elected superintendent
with Brothers John Eden and Joseph
Dorins as assistants Good results is
anticipated.

GREENRIVER.

(Jr)

County Commissioner Brown returned to Moab to-day (Thursday) with Messrs Durant, Mohr, Atkinson and Spicer for the purpose of building the ferry boat which construction will consume about two weeks.

Doctor Howland is visiting his son Harry. He will return to Denver next Monday.

The weather has been and is now extremely hot and very dry. All crops are suffering for the want of water. Farmer ditch is dry. The top of the dam has washed out and the main ditch has filled two feet deep with sand. Mr. Sutton says he will lose ninety per cent of his bees. All crops are suffering from the hot and dry weather.

Fruit is in abundance. No market.

The river is now fordable and water wheels at a stand-still. Even Farmer Brown's "old faithful" is quiet.

A. D Farnsworth will sell his home, resign the postmastership and go to pumping for the Rio Grande Western.

Our new spring arrivals from Idaho are preparing to return to their old homes. Greenriver is to tough for them.

The Bennett Amalgamator has closed down. Nobody knows who owns it. Grand county has $500 worth of taxes against it.

The R. G. W. Ry has a large grading outfit between here and Thompson's, and a large force of masons are putting in fine stone culverts at all big washes. Trains pass hourly and the R. G. W, is a real live railroad and has as fine a set of trainmen as can be found anywhere. The road bed is A 1

The health of the people in this valley is splendid. There is another consolation(?)money is as plenty as wild cats at the north pole.

Eastern Utah Advocate
September 2, 1897

WELLINGTON.

Joseph Birch and wife and Mrs. Thos. Gale have gone on a visit to Moab. They intend to be gone five or six weeks visiting friends and drying fruit.

Born to the wife of Albert O McMullin, on Saturday morning a girl. Mother and child doing well.

Grain is ripening so fast now that the machines are unable to keep up with the work of harvesting and in consequence some grain will be lost from shattering.

The new school house is now ready for the plastering and it is expected that it will be ready for use by the time school begins.

Bishop McMullin is again suffering from a pain in the back caused by a wrench received some time ago.

Some corn is now ripe and being cut and is a good yield. This is as fine a section for corn growing as any in eastern Utah.

We are pleased to note the gradual convalescence of Mrs J. J. Thayn. She has suffered severely for some time, but is now on the road to recovery.

S. H Grundvig will start his coal mine next week and says he will be ready to supply all his customers with a superior quality of coal as cheap as the cheapest.

CLEVELAND.

Thursday last Hans Jacobson sold his farm east of town for $1100 mostly cash. The purchaser was an eastern party who will locate here and is well pleased with his bargain, as is also Mr. Jacobson.

Will E. Alger has his new store well stocked and is enjoying the usual run of custom attendant upon fair and courteous treatment.

Mr. and Mrs. A. E. Gibson tendered a few of their friends an ice-cream social on Tuesday evening It was a very enjoyable function. Duets, artistically rendered, were sung by Bishop and Mrs. Wm. Lamph, recitations given by Prof. Dorius and Mrs. Bryson and solos by the hostess and others Those present were Bishop and Mrs. Wm. Lamph, Mrs. L. P. Overson, Mr. and Mrs. J. F. Dorius, Mr. and Mrs. Thos. Farish, Mr. and Mrs. W. E. Cowley, Mr and Mrs Scott Blackburn, Mr. and Mrs W. E Alger, Mrs. Ollie Bryson, Mrs. M. L. Snow, Mrs. Christensen, Messers Don Cowley, Geo. Hales and the Advocate representative.

Mrs. Annie Blood of this town died at Provo Monday and was buried here Wednesday 1 st. Deceased was a most popular lady and her funeral was largely attended, She had recently been treated at Provo for Cancer but efforts to stay the disease proved unavailing.

Hans Jacobson, who recently sold his farm to an eastern purchaser, will take up his residence at Powell, below Desert Lake, where he has contracted for eighty acres of land.

There is talk around Cleveland of getting up a company to bore for artesian water. The expense would be but slight, and if the effort meets with success, as there is every indication that it would, it would be a great boon to this portion of the county and a source of profit to the projectors.

The orchards in this vicinity are only from three to four years old, but for "youngsters" are blooming, healthy and fertile. Mr. J. G. Timothy's looks especially well. His four-year-old pear and cherry trees are low with luscious fruit.

LOCAL NEWS.

Price

Mrs Mamie Fausett, who has been visiting her brothers at Price for several weeks, left for her home at Provo last Saturday afternoon.

Judge Dusenbury, of Provo, reached Price Saturday afternoon from Vernal, where for three weeks he has been holding court, and took the 4 p.m., train for his home at Provo.

For some days the law firm of Baum & Braffet of Price were engaged consulting with their clients, the lessees of the Castle Peak Gilsonite Mining company evidently upon some important matter. It transpires that last Saturday complaint was lodged by the above named attorneys charging St. V. LeSieur charging him with grand larceny. The alleged larceny was of a recent date, and alleged that LeSieur took and carried away, or caused to be carried away a car load of gilsonite ore in the possession of the Emery County Mercantile company.

Another Snake Story.

Salina Press. We often hear of snake stories. Here is a true one. While Ben Travis and Edgar White of Emery county were cutting posts in the mountains east of Ireland's ranch, last week, they found and killed forty rattlesnakes, the largest one measuring six feet in length and having eighteen rattles. Another party killed ten snakes near the same place the week before. It seems to be a great year for snakes and snake stories.

CLEVELAND.

Friday last Bishop and Mrs. L. P. Overson left for Ephraim via Huntington canyon, to attend the funeral of Mrs. Otterstrom, Mrs Overson's mother.

Hyrum Dorius, of Ephraim, arrived in Cleveland Friday. He is thinking seriously of locating here.

Bishop William T. Lamph is making necessary arrangements to abide in Cleveland. His recently burned down house is about to be rebuilt. The people are interested and will give a helping hand.

The entertainment given by the Primary association passed off in a most creditable manner, so far as the children were a factor. Some help from the older ones was more of a damper than anything else.

At a meeting of the Cleveland district school board, held September 1, it was decided to retain Joseph F. Dorius as principal, with Miss Tina Larson, formerly of Ephraim, as his assistant. The district is in excellent shape, and it will be only a matter of time when the school will run four terms. The board also decided upon Mrs. C. N Christensen to act as janitor for the coming school year.

Miss Tilda Christensen and Miss Helga Erickson departed Tuesday for the land known as Sanpete county. It is hard to say just what particular spot they will visit. Some say Ephraim is to be their objective point, while rumor has it that perhaps Manti will be a place of interest. At any rate they are in good hands, and if Hyrum had a say so perhaps Manti would be the objective point. They go through Huntington canyon.

We are informed that Professor Hardy of Huntington his organized a class in music and singing A fine thing—but why not our own Professor Richards?

Louis, Aurilla and Nora Overson, son and daughters of our bishop, will leave for Ephraim this week to be on hand Monday, the beginning of the Sanpete stake academy for the year.

The Misses Larson, Tina and Eliza, who have been visiting with their sister, Mrs Joseph F. Dorius, are on their way to their Sanpete county home.

UNIO.

WELLINGTON.

District school begins September 13 at this place, with Miss Mary Leonard as principle teacher. Parents should realize the advantage to children of every day cf school and get them there promptly.

Born, to the wife cf Henry D. Allred, a daughter, on September 2. All doing nicely.

Miss May Jones departed for Grand Junction on Tuesday last, where she intends to remain for some time with the family of Dr. Ball.

The last flood down the river cut the Farnham canal dam clean to the bed rock. It will cost two or three hundred dollars to repair the damage. The stockholders say it will be done this fall and winter.

The railway company is putting in some fine substantial stone abutments at the ends of the bridges along here. It realizes that an ounce of prevention is worth a pound of cure, and is fixing up to avoid a possible washout.

The complaint of assault with intent to kill, preferred against Walter M. and John W. Mortens, the boys who assaulted Wm. Nisonger at Soldier Summit, has been changed to assault with intent to do bodily harm. Both waived examination before Justice Booth and are held in $3,00 bonds to appear in the district court.—Provo Enquirer.

SCOFIELD.

Mrs Hector Evans died last Sunday morning of child birth, aged about 22 years Dr. Smith, after doing all he could for her, gave her up. Dr. Asadoorian of Castlegate, was then sent for, and the two doctors made another effort to save her but without success Mr. Evans has the sympathy of all the people of Scofield and Winter Quarters, where he has lived for several years He was married about three years ago at Manti. He has had the misfortune to lose his entire family, wife and two children.

On last Friday evening the wife of Samuel J. Padfield presented him with a fine boy, and on Saturday one of the gentler sex came to the home of Thomas Phipps.

Little Tommy, the son of Henry Wilson, fell from a fence last Saturday and broke his arm. He had a very narrow escape from death two days previously. He was playing among some cars on a sidetrack when the engine was coupled on to take them out. Just as the train started one of the brakemen saw the boy hanging on to a brakebeam with his feet dragging over the ties. The train was immediately stopped and the boy taken out unharmed. It was, however, a very close call.

William Palmer, one of Scofield's oldest and most respected citizens, has left us and moved to his former home at Springville. Mr. Palmer ran the first train to Scofield over the narrow gauge road which was built from Springville, known as the Calico road He then took a position with the Rio Grande Western when that company purchased the road and has been with them ever since.

Last week Attorney Warf had some peddlers from Sanpete up before Justice Thomas at Winter Quarters, and they were fined for selling produce without a license. The sympathy of the people in this case is with the peddlers.

EMERY.

The second crop of alfalfa is gathered in and harvesting is receiving the attention of every farmer.

John Bert, of Castledale, is preparing a kiln of 100,000 bricks to be burned in October.

We now support four stores, a pool hall and barber shop. Though the youngest place in the county, Emery is fast becoming an equal of her sister towns of the valley. There is room here for many more settlers, and if some inducement could be offered to bring settlers in, this would be a thriving place.

There is a large amount of uncultivated ground here, and if the waters were used with economy all tillable land could be brought under cultivation, but the selfishness of man in this as well as all other places prevents the distribution of water, thereby retarding the growth of the place. It requires a large population to make good times for the merchant, the clothier, the farmer, the tradesman, even if the butcher has no one to sell his meat to his business is a poor one. The demand for the products of my business is what makes it a success, and this can only be done by an increased population.

The district school of Emery opened Monday, September 6, with A. E. Edwards as teacher.

The stake superintendency of Sabbath schools was in Emery Sunday last, viz: Messrs. Jameson, Jewks and Washburn. A lot of good advice was given to superintendent and teachers for conducting the Sunday schools. P. V. Bunderson's resignation as superintendent was accepted with a vote of thanks for his past services, and A. J. Broderick was elected to succeed him. Brother Bunderson has been connected with Sunday school work here for five or six years, was well liked and has given good satisfaction. The Sunday school is one credit to Emery and of which every Emeryite may be proud.

EASTERN UTAH ADVOCATE.

PRICE, CARBON COUNTY, UTAH, SEPTEMBER 9, 1897.　　　No. 32.

LOCAL NEWS.

Wheat at Chicago, yesterday, 93½.

Wm. Miller of Spring Glen was a Price visitor on Saturday.

W. R. Leonard, of Huntington, is paying the highest cash price for wheat.

The Western's depot and other station buildings are receiving a new coat of paint.

Wyatt Bryan made a flying trip to Ferron on Sunday, returning by Monday's stage.

Jesse Knight, of Provo, came in Friday night and left on Saturday's stage for the Vernal country to look after his mining interests.

J. H. and L. K. Coxy representing Peet Brothers' Soap company of Kansas City, were calling on Price merchants early in the week.

W. H. Donaldson left on Saturday's No. 1 train for Scofield where he spent Sunday and Monday visiting friends and returned to Price Tuesday.

Deseret Evening News
September 9, 1897

Scofield and Winter Quarters.

Scofield, Sept. 6, 1897.

To the Editor:

Sister Catherine D. Evans, wife of Brother Hector Evans, died at Winter Quarters Sunday morning at 8 o'clock, after intense suffering for four days. She was 22 years of age. A baby was born to her on Friday, which is also dead. She was an active worker in the Relief Society and the Primary association, and was a faithful Latter-day Saint, beloved by all who knew her. Brother Evans is our ward clerk and is one of our best citizens. He has the sympathy of the entire community.

Mr. Henry Wilson's son, Tommy, about 8 years old got his arm broken on Saturday by falling off a fence while playing.

Attorney Warf of Carbon county, entered a complaint in Justice Thomas's court at Winter Quarters last week, against three peddlers from Sanpete, for peddling without a license. They were fined $7.50 each, which they paid. They then took out a county license.

Mr. Frank Merriweether, a butcher of this place, has gone to Utah county to bring in a bunch of beeves. H.

Eastern Utah Advocate
September 16, 1897

CASTLEDALE.

Charles Swasey has been seen about home and town the last few days.

Hyrum and Rastus Larsen left home for a sojourn in Price and the gilsonite mines.

Mr. and Mrs. Bonnie of Mount Pleasant spent a few days with us.

Mrs. A. E. Miner of Fairview has been visiting old friends here and attended the Day family reunion at Lawrence.

Miss McMullin of Wellington has been about town the past week.

The district school is under full sway, with an attendance of 60 in primary department and 45 in the advanced.

The choir is busy rehearsing songs for the November conference. Brother Jameson is doing his best to get them in proper trim.

Several new dwellings are going up and others are soon to follow. James H Wilcox's is of solid brick, James Peterson's and the Evans' being frame. Seth Allen is repairing and adding to his new home.

Hector Evans spent a fortnight among us and returned to his home in Scofield Monday.

Elder Bonnie of Mount Pleasant, a newly returned missionary, gave an excellent discourse at the meeting Sunday.

Joe Lund and family are giving Sanpete a visit.

Preparations are being made for a self-supporting flume over Grime's wash The Mammoth Canal company find it a great expense to put in a new flume after every flood. They will now try a plan which they think will be a success.

Mr. and Mrs Larsen feel jubilant over the arrival of a new girl at their home All doing well.

WELLINGTON.

Eugene Branch with his two sons and daughter Rosey have gone on a visit to friends in Summit county and expect to bring back two of Mr. Branch's nieces who will remain here this winter

Nearly all the boys have returned from laboring at the saw mills in the Park country.

Hassett Wilson and Dan Tidwell took a short trip in the mountains last week in search of the precious metal, but they are very close mouthed as to any find.

The latter part of last week was very rainy and considerable damage has been done to crops, but the climax was reached on Monday morning last when there came another aw'nl flood down the river. It reached its highest point about noon. The river was out of its banks and swept everything before it. Although the county bridge was supposed to be entirely above the reach of the highest flood, people were surprised to see the flood steadily rise until it ran over the bridge. It was then that the people began to think of fastening it to the bank, which was done with chains, and the bridge was saved.

On account of the heavy rain Monday the district school did not commence until Tuesday morning when it began its usual course for the ensuing year Miss Mary Leonard, our popular teacher of last year has charge

Three families from Greenriver have bought themselves homes and located here within the past week We extend a welcome to them as to all good citizens.

SCOFIELD.

The railroad company has made a proposition to the miners to carry them to Winter Quarters to their work for five cents each per day. Orders have been given strictly prohibiting people from riding either up or down on the freight cars If the company's offer is accepted the passenger car will be run between Scofield and Winter Quarters

Hector Evans has gone to Castledale to visit his parents.

The P V mines are still working very good, the Oregon Short Line having renewed its order for coal.

Mr. and Mrs. Moon of Almy, Wyoming, have been at Winter Quarters for a few days

William Potter, who has been at the postoffice store for some time, has gone to Price. Andrew Wilson is in his place

WINTER QUARTERS, Sept. 11
Editor Advocate

Mr. Hector Evans of Winter Quarters wishes to express through the columns of the Advocate his heartfelt thanks and gratitude to all those who helped him by their kind words and acts in his late bereavement, and especially the Y. L M I A. for their kind acts and the beautiful wreath of flowers presented by them, and also to thank the neighbors and many kind friends who came to his relief. Very respectfully,

EVAN S. THOMAS

EMERY.

It has been raining since Friday morning stopping occasionally to get a fresh start, and roads and pathways are almost impassable with mud ankle deep. It is feared that much damage has been done to wheat, as a great deal of that cereal is yet in the field. It is reported that the United States will have a surplus this year of one hundred and eighty million bushels of wheat, and at the present outlook it means about that many dollars to the poor, down trodden American farmer.

Some washouts are reported along the county road but no serious damage has yet been done.

On the 6th instant was decided the question of bonding the school district for building purposes by a vote of 18 noes and 7 yeas. Although a school building is needed the taxpayers determined not to bequeath indebtedness to their posterity.

A party was given on Monday, the 14th, under the auspices of the Y. L. M. I. A., all participating in a general good time.

Anderson is in town doing photographic work.

The pool hall is the most frequented place in town. Boys and men will find nickels and dimes for this when they can be found for nothing else.

John Edwards received a powerful kick Sunday while in the mountains. The pack on his pack animal becoming loose, he passed behind his saddle horse to tighten it when the animal kicked with both feet, striking him fairly in the short ribs and knocked him senseless for some minutes. He recovered sufficiently to ride to Emery. The next morning developed no internal injury. He thinks perhaps a rib or two may be broken.

CLEVELAND

Our crops are greatly damaged on account of the heavy rain storms which were followed by destructive floods.

On account of the Sunday school conference being held at Huntington, the Cleveland Sunday school was dismissed to give teachers a chance to attend. The attendance was limited. Cause, bad roads.

Professor Hardy has a good class of students, considering the time of year. This is probably the busiest season of the year for our Cleveland people, most of them being farmers.

The Cleveland canal has made another bad break. Particulars in our next write up.

Lewis Larsen, who obtained the contract to build a fence around the Cleveland district school property, is busily engaged hauling the necessary timber, etc. This is a desired improvement and will add beauty to the appearance of the property.

Our public school opens to all school children Monday, the 20th.

The wife of Henry Oviatt, Jr, is very sick.

Samuel Alger & Co are getting their planing machine in running order. They expect to have all the work they can attend to.   URIO.

CASTLEGATE.

Pietro Franot and Theresa Aristotari of Salt Lake were united in marriage by Bishop Scanlon of Salt Lake on Wednesday evening. Every one had a good time and all wished them a long and happy life.

Attorney Warf spent Tuesday in town looking up points in regard to the case of Levina McCombs, which it is said will be brought to the notice of Judge Johnson at the next sitting of district court.

Superintendent H. G. Webb has started a night school with 33 members. The charge is one dollar per month and three evenings each week is devoted to the work. It is a snap for the boys.

Bishop Scanlon is down from Salt Lake making preparations to build a Catholic church. We wish him success.

Mrs. Henry Wade went to Salt Lake on Monday, accompanied by her daughter Annie, who will attend school in Zion the coming winter. Mrs. Eugene Santschi went to the city the same day with her son who will also attend school in Salt Lake.

LOCAL NEWS.

County Clerk Havercamp of Provo has issued a marriage license to N. M. Keel of Emery and Martha Boyack of Spanish Fork.

The material for ceiling the school building just north of the Huntington river at Huntington went out yesterday.

The Frandsens loaded seven cars of sheep at P. V. Junction on Tuesday for the eastern markets. Lars and Orson accompanied the shipment.

H. M. Fugate and family of Ferron have spent a few days in Manti this week and last visiting relatives and friends.—Manti Messenger.

A married lady of Price induced benedict Bob McKune of that town to wheel her baby buggy along the street, and when he met his best girl and she clasped her hands and rolled her pretty eyes heavenward and said "O! how sweet," he blushed so fiercely that the fire engine had to run out to extinguish him.—Denver Post

Geo. M. Miller, of Huntington, points out vacant land on township plats.

W. H. Leonard, of Huntington, is paying the highest cash price for wheat.

A. D. Dickson was up from Castledale and spent a few days in Price this week.

A. Tuttle came in from Emery accompanied by Lars and Henry Thompson and left on Monday's train for Salt Lake where Lars Thompson's case will be tried in the supreme court.

P. L. Flannigan of Reno, Nevada, came in late last week with 12,000 lambs for the eastern market and grazed them a day in the vicinity of Price and reloaded in 21 double-deck cars.

John Van Kervis, Post Stewart, arrived in Price from the post on Tuesday evening. Mr. Van Kervis came out to meet his family, who reached here this morning from Texas. They will leave for the post at once.

Mrs. Helen Beemer, who the Price ladies will remember was here a short time ago with an elegant line of ladies' hats, has returned from Provo accompanied by Miss Book. The ladies have secured rooms at the Mathis hotel and have opened up a stylish line of fall and winter hats. They also do dress making.

Geo. M. Miller, of Huntington, has for sale several good farms on easy terms.

G. L. Forrester, the traveling auditor for the R. G. W. railway, was in Price yesterday.

LOCAL NEWS

Mrs. D. R. Beebe of Proyo is visiting Mrs. A. Ballinger.

Arthur G Johnson and wife of Vernal were in Price Saturday

Miss Della Nixon of Saint George is visiting her sister, Mrs. J. M. Whitmore

Born, to Mrs. W H. Kelsey on September 21, a fine baby girl. All doing nicely.

Frank C irroll of Orangeville spent a few days in Price, returning to his home on Tuesday.

Mr. and Mrs. Robert A. Powell, who live up Price river, buried their eighteen-month old child last week.

Johnny McIntire left for Greenriver on Saturday where he will take charge of a section on the R. G W.

Bil'y Potter came down from Scofield last week and will make Price his home. Mr. Potter is employed by D. W. Holdaway.

George A. Eldredge has sold his Price property to Lou Johnson and will move to Spring Glen where he has purchased property.

Earnest Lee came in from Price Monday night for a week's visit with his parents and friends. Earn has been carrying the mail from Price to the Wells for the last year.—Springville Independent.

Mrs. Louise Hale of Grantsville came in last week and was met at Price by her nephew, John H. Halgate of Vernal, to which latter point they left early in the week, where Mrs. Hale will visit friends and relatives.

Tom Fitzgerald is a very happy man to d iy. It's a bright eyed little girl, and bo'h mother and child are doing nicely

Dean Holdaway left for Logan early in the week where he will attend school He was accompanied by his father as far as Ogden.

There will be a grand ball at Price town hall to-morrow night, September 24. Evans Bros. will furnish the music. A good time is guaranteed.

Labbie Walton, who has been employed by the Emery County Mercantile company for several months, left for her home in South Id last week.

James H. Heath returned a few days ago from Idaho points where he has visited since the pioneer festivities at Salt Lake on July 24.

N. L. Marsing and family left Price this week for a two or three months pleasure trip through a number of the southwest counties.

School opened last week with a good attendance, with W. H. Allen as principle, and on Monday the intermediate grade opened with Miss May Pace teacher

Mrs. J. Maginn with her two little daughters reached Price last week and rested a few days before continuing her journey to Vernal, where her husband is employed.

William Palmer of Scofield has moved his family down to Springville and th y are residing in a tent until Mr. Palmer finishes the brick residence which he is erecting on his property out by Cook's — Springville Independent

G. B. Pritchard, Henry H Wright, captain of the 9th Cavalry at Fort Duchesne, and Miss Lenora Wright came in Tuesday and left for the east. Miss Wright is a niece of Captain Wright, whom she had been visiting at the post.

C H Winders, who resides at Desert Lake, was a heavy loser by the recent floods. Mr. Winders had a load of melons which he was taking to Helper and Castle-gate to sell, and while crossing Miller creek the flood came down and struck the wagon just as he was pulling out of the bed of the creek, carrying wagon and me out with it. The team was not hurt. His loss was about $50

C. P. Melton, who was until recently operator at the depot and resigned to take a position with the S. P. railroad, has returned to Price and is holding down the night shift. We are informed that the Western will keep the office here open day and night.

Eastern Utah Advocate
September 30, 1897

LOCAL NEWS.

A flea bitten old gray horse was the innocent means of a considerable amount of trouble between Castle valley citizens.

A. C. Davis reached Price last night with a large train of Indian freighters The Indians will return loaded with Indian freight.

The first wheat of the new crop came in last Thursday and was purchased by Mr Crandall, who is buying for Wm. Roylance of Springville.

Emery County Mercantile company had in another car of sugar the other day. Their box is not empty, and 15 pounds of sugar for a silver dollar. Go there and get it.

The many patrons of the Mathis house throughout the valley will be pleased to learn that this now popular hostelry has stable and feed conveniences in connection with the hotel.

Everyone desires to keep informed on Yukon, the Klondyke and Alaskan gold fields. Send 10c. for large Compendium of vast information and big color map to Hamilton Pub Co., Indianapolis, Ind.

The roads between Price and Helper are said to be in a deplorable condition. Water in many places standing in the road, and which by constant travel soon becomes a perfect quagmire and a menace to life and property.

Klondyke is all right, but how few they are that get there. It is otherwise with local interests and judicious household management, they can and must be attended to at home. It is wrong to pay a high price for an article when a moderate one can buy it. You get child's pants at Emery County Mercantile company for 25 cents, and child's suits for $1 75. Other clothing in proportion This is better to you than Klondyke.

Dr. W. C. Richman, who practiced medicine and surgery in the state of Tennessee for the past ten years, has located in Price for the practice of his profession The doctor comes well recommended, having passed a most rigid examination before the state board of physicians. The people of Price and vicinity have long felt the great need of a physician, as the charges made by doctors from Provo and Salt Lake have always been looked upon as exorbitant.

Springville Independent. The wedding bells have again given forth their merry music, this time in honor of the marriage of E. J. Edwards of Castlegate and Miss Ella Whitmore of this city, last Thursday night. The ceremony was performed at the home of Mrs. Johnson, in the Third ward by Bishop Loynd. This accounts for Mr. Edwards' pre-occupied air, spoken of in last week's paper. The happy couple will make their home in Castlegate for a time. The Independent extends its congratulations.

CLEVELAND

The Cleveland Canal company has levied a 5 per cent. tax on the capital stock of the company in order to repair and make good the canal 'or the coming season.

She has come—a nice blue-eyed beauty, only a few days old. Mr. and Mrs. W E Alger are content to keep the little one. However, all is well.

Two of Ephraim's popular young men are in Cleveland for a while—Messrs Hyrum and Orson Dorius. They are making their headquarters with our school teacher, who is their brother.

John R Tilby, one of Cleveland's early settlers, has sold out his farm and farm belongings to a gentleman from Castlegate for the sum of $1,250. Tilby will go back to Chester, Sanpete county.

Cleveland now boasts of a young nimrod—Noah Potter—who has been cutting timber up in the canyon near by our saw mil s, and who succeeded in killing a large mountain lion, measuring nine feet from tip to tip Noah was in close quarters and had to make good use of his shooting iron The lion was bounding straight for him when he (Noah) lowered himself on his knee and took deadly aim—the lion was shot between the eyes It made a jump in the air and came down dead.

Last Sunday Brother Erick Larsen was called to fill a vacancy in our bishopric—that of H. H. Oviatt, jr , who resigned Brother Larsen is a good man and, we believe, will prove to be a wise counselor.

Bishop W. T. Lamph of Castlegate was the principal speaker at the Tabernacle last Sunday.

At this writing we have been visited by most all the rain in Castle va ley.

CASTLEGATE.

Mrs. T. W. Lewis is visiting her mother in Scofield.

The Josher is all right.

Ed Edwards and his bride returned to the gate on Tuesday. They were serenaded by the brass band and the tin-can brigade. May success crown their married life.

Mrs. Richard Olsen is moving her household goods to Provo, where she will make her home. Poor Dick is going to bach it

Joe Boney, one of our good citizens, has bought a farm over in Castle valley, where he will move his family. May he prosper.

A wave of prosperity is passing over Eag'e Lodge No. 14, Knights of Pythias The boys, expect to clear the indebtedness by the 1st of January.

The boys are going to give the Oriental Degree to all comers about the 1st of October. Price boys are especially invited

WELLINGTON.

Never before in the history of this valley has so much heavy rain fell at this time of year, and it is a source of much satisfaction to the farmer and stockman.

The hum of the thrasher is heard in our midst from daylight until dark.

There seems to be a flour famine in Price and Wellington just now. In fact there is none to be had at any price

Our new school house is now completed, with the exception of a few days more painting, when we will have a house that every taxpayer in this district can be proud of. F. C Grundvig, the contractor, is as fine a workman as is to be found in the county, and as was expected has done a splendid job The house is built from the finest of material and the work on the building from the ground to the top indicates skilled workmanship.

W. J Hill's new residence is nearing completion and will be a fine residence.

Bishop McMullin has completed two of the rooms in his new house and contemplates finishing it this fall.

Quite a number of our people are either building new houses or putting on new additions to their present buildings.

SCOFIELD.

A grand wedding took place at Winter Quarters last Saturday evening David John Rowe, the son of Lewis Rowe, and Miss Hannah Jeanette Edwards, daughter of Wm Edwards, were the contracting parties. The ceremony was performed by Bishop T. J. Parmley. A supper and ball was given in the boarding house, and everything was so lively around there that even the driest old bachelor in town was induced to put on his dancing pumps and join in the sport just like he used to in ye olden times.

Scofield and Winter Quarters have been quite lively since the boys got their pay. Some of them kept the gin shops pretty warm for a few days

The large fan in the P. V. company's mine was started last Sunday, since which time the ventilation has been much improved The smaller fan is to be placed at No. 3 mine, where a few men will be put to work, as No. 1 mine is unable to supply the increased demand.

Frank Sturges, boiler inspector for the Harvard Insurance company, was here on Saturday

Mrs. Andrew Gilbert returned Monday from a two weeks' visit to Richfield.

Some important improvements are under way at the Winter Quarters meeting house.

J. M. Loveridge bought a fine bearskin a few days ago Bruin was killed by some saw mill hands between here and San Pete.

Mrs. Mary Johnston returned by Monday's train from a visit to relatives at Spanish Fork.

GREENRIVER.

J. T. Farrer is in Moab.

Crops are all safe in the stacks and barns. There is an abundance of each kind.

More rain this season than in the past 10 years. The hills are well covered with feed, but there is no sheep nor cattle in the country this fall to eat it.

Our district school will open on the 1st, with Miss Benson as teacher She taught in Little Castle one year, Moab one year and comes well recommended by County Superintendent Muienaux.

The river is now fordable for teams. The ford this year is not changed from last year, and is O K.

Wagon roads between Lower Crossing and Thompson Springs are washed out considerable, but are passable.

Commissioner John F. Brown and Mrs Cecil Brown of Elgin were married by Justice Durrant on September 10th. The latch string is on the outside to their many friends in the two counties.

SCOFIELD.

No. 3 mine at Winter Quarters is to start this week. The fan was started Monday, and preparation is being made to put about 50 men in the mine at once. Wm. Parmley of Coalville is to be assistant foreman. The coal trade has been on the improve for the last three months, and our merchants and all others in business are doing much better than they have for several years.

The train crew here is in need of help They are working almost night and day.

In a private letter to a party at Winter Quarters from a friend at Diamondville, Wyo., a few days ago, it was stated that the miners there were still on a strike

Well, yes, we have had rain too this fall. They say more rain more rest, but with us this time it is more rain and more work.

Mrs Robert Wilstead gave birth to a fine baby boy last week. Mother and child doing nicely.

But few of our people are attending the conference this fall on account of the busy times.

Our commissioner, Mr. Andrew Hood, went to the county seat on horse back last Monday to attend court and to make an examination of the roads in his district.

The Wasatch Store company at Winter Quarters is very much in need of a new store building The one now occupied by them is leaning over so badly and is so rickety that it may fall over some of these days and do considerable damage to both life and property. The building was pushed to its leaning position by a snow slide.

EMERY.

The sky cleared up on Saturday and Sunday morning bid fair for a continuation of good weather, and accordingly a hopeful smile was noticeable on the faces of those anxious farmers whose crops are yet in the field exposed to the rain and wet, but after "old whiner" had passed the meridian the welkin became cloudy and the smiles of our populace turned to looks of despondency. However, the clouds passed over and the people emerged from church looking jovial and bright. A large amount of the wheat crop in this vicinity has already started to grow during the continued humility of the weather, and a few days more rain would almost entirely ruin the crops.

The Muddy creek on Friday was so swollen by rain in the upper regions that the mail driver was unable to cross until evening; thus our mail came about six o'clock instead of at noon.

The Advocate always comes a welcome visitor to our village and is eagerly perused by its subscribers and others. Always having an abundance of local news, it is a paper of interest to Emery county and should have a larger circulation here. There are many advantages afforded by a county paper not appreciated by a good many of our citizens.

For lively times and large crowds go to the pool hall either day or night.

Casper Christensen will soon open up his coal mine for the fall trade. Mr. Christensen says coal will be $1 per ton at the mine.

Mr. Bert, the brick burner, had several thousand adobes ruined by rain.

An enjoyable time was had at the conjoint session Sunday evening.

CASTLEGATE.

An axident happened last Thursday evening to Mrs. Wm. Decker and son. Mr. Decker was moving his family to Castle valley, when botwoen Castlegate and the half way house Mrs. Decker and her 3 year-old son wero pitched out of the wagon, which resulted in Mrs Decker receiving a badly sprained ankle and the son having his arm broken.

We notice John Horn and family have returned to Castlegate. We hope that he will pitch his tent and stay with us.

Thomas Edwards is running the saw mill at Castlegate.

B. F. Caffey has gone to state conference.

Robert Forrester has returned to the gate for a brief stay.

Wm Forrester is moving his household goods back to Scofield.

by some of his family and his nieces who will return to their home.

We are informed that the higher grade of school will open on Monday next.

Wm A and Brig Thayn returned from a summers work at Seely's saw mill in Sanpete mountains. They look hale and hearty.

The Robert's threshing machine is again in the field under the management of O. B Milner, who says it can do as good work as any machine in the country.

The suspension flome across Price river at this place is a decided success, as t has withstood the ravages of all the floods this season. Companies contemplating the erection of suspension flumes should see this one.

The last flood in Price river was a big one and did considerable damage to the fields along its banks.

WELLINGTON.

E. F. Branch, accompanied by two of his nieces, arrived home on Thursday last from the St. George country in southern Utah. He reports the roads as being in a terrible condition, yet he is not satisfied, for h e contemplates another trip to St. George, starting about the 1st of November, and will be accompanied

Famous Caleb Rhoades' Discovery

A council of the Uintahs was held last week relative to the leasing of m'neral lands on the Uintah reservation to F. W. C. Hathenbruck and a company of Salt Lake men

Hathenbruck proposes to lease certain mineral lands for ten years at $83,000 for the full term.

Captain Beck told the Indians that he thought it to their interest to give the grant and it is thought that those who opposed the leasing of mineral lands will come into line at a later council

The land proposed to be leased covers certain rich gold mining claims, believed by some to be the famous Caleb Rhoades' discovery that caused such excitement many years ago According to an old story Rhoades took out several pounds of pure gold from this mine and gave it to Brigham Young and afterwards secured enough to keep him in comfort At the time of his death his son, who lives near Price, was the only man who knew the location of the mine, and this son is now associated with Mr. Hathenbruck. It is said that several men have been killed by the Indians while searching for this property. If the Indians grant the lease it must receive the approval of the Indian department.

The County Commissioners.

The commissioners met on Monday, all members present. Allowing claims and auditing justices' reports took up the time of the commissioners during Monday and a greater part of Tuesday.

The reports of the various justices from the different precincts were gone over, and barring a few minor changes were accepted.

Henry Flack was appointed registration officer for Price precinct and S. J. Harkness was on September 4 appointed registration agent for Scofield precinct.

As the office of county quarantine physician was by law abolished March 1st, 1897, and the board in error had appropriated a sum to cover the regular salary of the county quarantine physician the board appointed Commissioner Hood to call on quarantine physician D. J. W. Smith, and by reason of the office being abolished ask him to return salary warrant to county treasurer for cancelation

James L. Smith, special agent of the Pleasant Valley Coal company, was appointed deputy sheriff to serve without salary. The object in appointing Mr Smith was that when the occasion might arise he would be able to enforce the law without being compelled to call on the sheriff.

A claim of James Nagles for $20 was disallowed.

The following claims were allowed

Fred W M Iverton		$ 24 83
Do Do		8 00
A D Gash and S A King		20 00
James Hamilton		34 50
A J Lee		8 75
Do		8 00
Do		2 00
Do		6 00
Do		3 00

C O Bratot	1 20
Geo Dickerson	3 50
G C Johnston	30 00
C W Allred	4 25
Gus Donant	3 00
Do	5 40
H D Elliott	4 00
Matthias Pattinson	13 00
Price town	90 00
J W Warf	18 45
Do	8 50
W H Donaldson	14 00
C W Allred	5 70
C P Johnson	2 00
P A Smith	6 80
I Glaser	2 00
Wm Burrows	1 00
W H Stinson	1 00
J N Miller	2 00
J Ketchum	1 00
Sadie Kilburn	1 80
Mabel Nelson	1 80
Ethel Fulmer	2 80
H B Horsley	2 20
Thos Fitzgerald	2 50
E S Horsley	2 20
A W Horsley	49 50
Wm Robinson, jr	25 50
F D Lang	43 00
Wm Miller	2 00
John Tryon	2 25
Martha E Hamilton	4 00
Paul Hunter	1 00
Henry Flack	2 20
F M Uwell	2 40
Andrew Wallace	2 40
Andrew Gilbert	2 40
B E Lewis	2 40
J W Metcalf	75 10
Willard Hitchcock	4 50
Charles Torkelsen	2 00

L O Hoffmann	40 00
Albert Bryner	10 80
Do Do	130 00
J W Warf	130 00
C W Allred	85 00
W H Donaldson	231 25
J S Thomas	4 80
Matthias Pattinson	8 90
George Callaway	1 80
Byron Loveless	1 80
J W Davis	2 30
John Moore	2 00
James McCune	25 40
Charles Goldberg	1 40

A Liddell	$1 55
Do	45 00
Do	8 00
Edgar Thayn	25 13
Do Do	45 00
Andrew Hood	25 55
Do Do	45 00
D O McIntire	18 25
P V Coal company	7 85
Wasatch Store company	13 06
J D Smith	21 70
M H Beardsley	2 00
Robert Bishop	1 00
E A Wedgewood	25 00
John Street	21 00
Edwin Street	18 00
M Pitman	21 00
Walter Donaldson	1 20
Lars Frandsen	2 20
J Tom Fitch	19 85

F B Lang	71 30
E Van Wagner	22 50
Wm Robertson	22 25
Enoch Gurr	9 00
Wm Curtis	4 50
John Swanson	22 25
John Fausett	50 00
James Hamilton	25 50
D Van Wagner	27 00
Robert Forrester	25 00
W J Tidwell	150 00
John Duerden	2 00
J B Thomas	2 70
Price Trading company	19 22
Do Do	61 44
P I Olsen	27 25
J W Warf	17 60
Henry Duerden	13 55
Wellington Co-op	20 00
J H Van Natta	5 00
G G Milner	4 30
Total	$1,272 73

Price

LOCAL NEWS.

Wheat at Chicago, yesterday, 91¼.

James Rooney was down from Helper on Tuesday.

E. R. Gibson is quite sick from an attack of bilious fever.

The picture man Porter was in Price this week making deliveries.

Miss Adelha Avrett came in from Castledale and left for Cisco.

—A meeting of the Price cornet band is called for Friday evening at 8 p. m. in the school building. Lars Frandsen president.

F. M. Ewan left for Salt Lake on Tuesday where he will remain until the sitting of district court the first Monday in November.

Levi Jones, who has been mining gilsonite at the mines, came in Tuesday and left on Wednesday's train for his home in Scofield.

The finest lot of English, white figured and decorated semi porcelain ware just in. Come and examine the goods. Emery County Mercantile company.

R. Veltman, a prominent Vernal attorney, was in Price early in the week.

The Mathis hotel has feed and stable conveniences in connection with the hotel.

E. G. Webb, the popular superintendent of schools, was in attendance on county court.

A. C. Davis loaded the Indian teams out Friday and Saturday and followed them Sunday.

Mrs. Ida Jacoby of Castledale returned from Salt Lake last week, where she had been visiting for some time past and left on Saturday's stage for her home.

The many patrons of the Mathis house throughout the valley will be pleased to learn that this new popular hostelry has stable and feed conveniences in connection with the hotel.

State land appraiser Reese and local appraisers L. M. Olson and H G. Mathis appraised school lands at Wellington last week. It is not known when the Price school lands will be appraised.

CASTLEGATE.

A rear end collision occurred on Wednesday evening at Castlegate Rock, one and one-half miles from Castlegate, between two freight trains, which resulted in David Ogleby of Goshen being instantly killed and David Morgan of the same place seriously injured. It appears the two men had several carloads of sheep which they were taking east to market, and as is customary they were riding in the caboose, and when opposite the section house, without any warning whatever, the engine of the second section telescoped the caboose. Everything was upside down, sheep and fruit being scattered in all directions.

L. O Hoffmann was a visitor at Eagle Lodge No, 13 last Friday evening

The Wasatch Store company will not have much call for prunes the next five months

The coroner's jury returned a verdict of accidental death at the inquest on David Ogleby.

Mike Helland contributed $100 toward the Catholic church, now in course of erection

David Jones has gone to Salt Lake City to have an operation performed on his knee.

WELLINGTON.

At a meeting of taxpayers it was decided to empower the school board to finish the second story of the new school house and levy a tax next year to pay for the work.

On Friday last the school board formally opened the new school house by giving a dance for the children in the afternoon and for the adults in the evening. A fine time was had by everybody.

A surprise party was arranged on Monday evening for Miss Belinda Hill, it being her twentieth birthday. It was a complete surprise and a fine time was had by all present. Instrumental and vocal music enlivened the occasion.

Born, to the wife of Hans Hansen, a son, on Friday, October 8th. All doing well.

John Blackburn, accompanied by his son Manassey and daughter Kate, have gone to Ephraim, Sanpete county. Massi and Kate will attend school there this winter.

We are sorry to learn of a serious accident which happened to our townsman Ed. Curtis. While engaged working on a threshing machine at Brock's he got his hand caught in the machinery and was badly lacerated. He was immediately taken to Fort Duchesne to get medical aid. It is thought the hand will have to be amputated.

GREENRIVER

Harry Howland and wife have returned from a week's outing in Book cliffs. Caught no fish and killed no deer.

Reports from parties coming over on horseback from Moab say the mud is shoulder deep to the horses and all washes nearly impassable. Anyone contemplating a trip to Moab or Thompsons should surely have a shovel along.

The San Rafael will be abandoned as a farming district, as the dams and ditches are completely washed away. The people are discouraged, as they have spent all they have raised for years trying to make the dams hold.

There is a report here that the Bennett

amalg mator will start up soon under new management.

Surveyors will be here Monday to commence their work on the big high line canal.

The 10th of October and no frost yet

The fourth crop of alfalfa is 15 inches high. Pumpkins and squash vines are blooming the second time and have made new runners. It has been raining five days and Greenriv r is booming

J. T. Farrer departed for Pueblo on the 8th to look after a shipment that he sent east last Monday, about which there is a question of law to be decided. The point is whether a contract will hold over a bill of sale. There was $100 paid upon contract by Mr. Castor of Red Cloud, Neb. Mr Farrer then sold the cattle to Mr. Noab, who shipped them east. Castor started after them and found them in the stock yards at Pueblo and he immediately commenced proceedings for possession

Your correspondent was made to say that our school would be taught by Miss Mabel Benson, but word has been received from her that she has accepted a school at Ridgeway, Colo. Mr. A. P. Mohr of Elgin will now have charge

Harry Farrer, Bert Allred and Wilson Allred have returned from Moab.

In Happy Wedlock.

J W Warf, Carbon county's popular attorney, and Miss Celesta Mangum were quietly married Tuesday afternoon, Bishop Horsley officiating Mr Warf has been a resident of Price since his election last fall and in that time he has proven himself capable and has looked well to the interests of the county Miss Mangum has been in Price only a short time, having formerly lived in Wayne county. The many friends of the happy pair wish them a long and prosperous life.

LOCAL NEWS.

Wheat at Chicago, yesterday, 99½

The first snow of the season may be seen on the mountains.

Call at Lowenstein's and get highest cash prices for your grain and hides

The Mathis hotel has feed and stable conveniences in connection with the hotel.

Tuesday, October 26, is the last and only day voters may be registered for the city election.

You are cordially invited to inspect my goods and prices You can save from 25 to 20 per cent. No trouble to show goods or price them for you. My stock is now complete in every line. L. Lowenstein, Price.

John F Brown, one of Grand county's popular commissioners and an old time friend of the editor, paid us a pleasant visit early in the week Mr. Brown was surprised and pleased with the growth of Price within the last two years

GREENRIVER.

Our school opened Monday, with A. P. Mohr as teacher.

Ed Atkinson has leased the Mohr ranch for one year.

Mrs. Farnsworth is getting along in the postoffice in fine shape, while her husband is working a gang of men at Soldier Summit in the water service of the Western.

Mrs. Frank Jacobs runs the home ranch while her good husband visits the Western paycar at Helper once a month and promptly forwards the cash to his amiable wife.

Harry Green of Moab arrived Monday eve and stopped with Commissioner Brown. Mr. Green will go westward and meet Henry Goodman, who is coming from P. V. Junction with 5,000 sheep. These sheep will be grazed on lands from Book cliffs to the Blue mountains.

Mr. Carlisle has bought 10,000 sheep which are to arrive soon for his ranch. We have room for 250,000 to take the place of cattle.

On Sunday the weather cleared up and at night a heavy frost nipped the tender vegetation.

The river is still too high to ford.

J. T. Farrer has arrived home from Pueblo.

Mr. Smith and family have removed from Wheeler Bro's ranch to their old home at Moab.

SCOFIELD.

We have about three inches of snow and a considerable amount of frost, but the weather agent here has sent for a few weeks of good weather.

Richard T. Evans, who has been a resident of Winter Quarters for many years, has moved with his family to Spanish Fork. They leave many friends and take with them the best wishes of the community for their future welfare.

Mr. and Mrs. Archibald Anderson's child died last Saturday night.

News comes from Diamondville, Wyo., that the strike is ended. The price for digging coal agreed upon is 44 cents per ton, the coal to be weighed on top.

James Staples, one of the miners who came here from Coalville, made up his mind last Friday that it was not all sugar and honey in this part of the country, and on Saturday morning he could be seen making his way to the train at a brisk rate whistling "Home, Sweet Home."

A coal train was wrecked between Scofield and P. V. Junction on Sunday. Six loaded cars were derailed. Fortunately no one was hurt.

EMERY.

Samuel Williams, one of our teachers, is recovering from the injury to his foot some time ago caused by jumping from a shed upon a spike, which entered his foot just in front of his heel, penetrating to the ankle joint and inflicting a severe wound.

J. P. Nielson and Annie Christensen were, on Wednesday, the 13th inst., united in the holy bonds of matrimony, many people being present at the ceremony. May theirs be a pleasant journey through life.

Five or six inches of snow covered the ground Sunday morning, and the farmers are more despondent than ever.

It has been decided to build a school house by taxation. The district will not bond and a contract will be let accordingly.

A heavy frost came Sunday night, the first of any consequence this season.

CASTLEGATE.

Wm. L Jones has gone to Zion for a few days.

Mrs. Henry Duerden returned home last Saturday, having been away three months visiting her parents in Nebraska.

The members of Eagle Lodge will give a ball on the 23rd.

There are quite a few stray sheep on the hills since the wreck and the boys have a great time.

I have heard it said that T T. Lamph, as leader of the team in the K. P.'s, can hold his own in Carbon county. It is also said that the team will compete with any other team in the county for an oyster supper.

The boys have made arrangements to wipe out the debt on the hall by the 1st of November. They will then have paid out about $3,000 in a little over two years, which shows what grit and energy there is among the pit laddies.

Rally 'round Saturday, boys, and we will give you a welcome.

Price

LOCAL NEWS.

Hank Stewart of Nine Mile and Miss Nerva Van Wagner were married on Saturday, October 16, Bishop Horsley officiating. The many friends of Miss Wagner wish her much happiness.

Mrs. Harlet Wild, mother of Mrs. Sam Singleton, returned from Ferron where she has been visiting friends and relatives, and yesterday morning took No. 1 for her home in American Fork.

Fern, the 14-months old daughter of Mr. and Mrs. Soren Olsen, passed to the great beyond about 11 o'clock Tuesday evening, after a short illness from a complication of brain fever and pneumonia. Funeral ceremonies occurred to-day.

C. P. Melton and family left for Fruita, Colo, on Sunday night, where Mr. Melton was transferred by the Western. Mr. and Mrs. Melton are a very affable couple and during their short residence at Price made many friends.

Everyone desires to keep informed on Yukon, the Klondyke and Alaskan gold fields. Send 10c. for large Compendium of vast information and big color map to Hamilton Pub. Co., Indianapolis, Ind.

Herald: J. R. Letcher, clerk of the federal court, left on Sunday for Marshall, Mo., upon receiving news of the precarious condition of his father's health. Mr. Letcher, sr., has been ailing for quite a long time, although not dangerously so until recently.

Coalville Times. Harry Wycherley writes us from Scofield that all those who went down there are at work and that there is plenty of work there for many more men. A. Stokes arrived there the other day and went to work next morning

Tribune: A personal letter received Saturday announced the fact that Thomas Lloyd and "Doc" Norrell had finished the construction of their boats and were ready to start on the trip down Lake Bennett, on their way to Dawson City. The latter was dated September 30th.

PRICE TOWN DEMOCRATS.

A STRONG TICKET PUT UP FOR THE LOCAL OFFICES.

Popular Sentiment for a Change in Municipal Government Will Elect the Ticket Hands Down—The Ring Rushes a Slate Through at the Republican Caucus.

For President of the Town Board:
ALBERT BRYNER.

For Members of the Town Board:
SOREN OLSEN,
O. G. FRANDSEN,
ERASTUS ANDERSON,
JOE JONES.

Pursuant to call the Price town democrats assembled at the meeting house on Friday evening, October 15, and placed in nomination for the coming municipal election the above ticket.

The following platform was unanimously adopted:

1st—We the democrats of Price town, in convention assembled, adopt the Rooster, the common emblem of democracy, as our emblem.

2d—We believe in a rigid enforcement of the town ordinances, to the end that law and order may be maintained, and that a marshall be paid a stipulated salary for attending to the police duty of the town.

3d—We believe in a just and economical administration of municipal affairs, but not at the expense of the peace, welfare and safety of the citizens of Price.

The chair was empowered to appoint a campaign committee of three and he named the following: L. O. Hoffmann, H C. Smith and Thomas Fitzgerald.

The follow'ng committee of three was named to fill any vacancies on the ticket that might occur: Albert Bryner, Thomas Fitzgerald and P. I. Olsen.

The above candidates need no introduction to the taxpayers and voters of Price. They are old residents of the valley. They have seen Price grow from the little settlement to the thrifty town and strategetic business center of eastern Utah. Their every interest is closely identified with the growth of our town They have proven themselves capable of providing a competency of this world's necessities. Then why cannot they intelligently and economically administer the affairs of our municipality? We think they can. The taxpayers think they can.

The citizens of Price, above all things, desire a change in municipal affairs. While personally they are not belligerently inclined toward the crowd which worked the republican caucus to a finish on Thursday night last, no argument will convince the people that to elect the last year's bolters and office seekers will effect the desired change of administration in town affairs.

The ticket heading this article is a pea warmer from the ground up

A vote for the democratic nominees is a vote for good municipal government

Mark an X by the Rooster and let 'er slide.

Eastern Utah Advocate
October 28, 1897

CASTLEGATE.

W H Donaldson of Price was a visitor at the ball on Saturday night.

It is thought the new Catholic church will be completed and dedicated on Sunday next.

The ball last Saturday night was a financial success but the music was a complete failure

Quite an improvement could be made in the next dance if the committee would keep the stairs and hallway clear so the people could pass out without unnecessary annoyance

Messrs Tidwell and Seely are guests at the Wade hotel

We notice Harry Jacobs back at his old stand

SCOFIELD.

The ward conference was largely attended. Among those present were Reed Smoot of Provo second counselor of Utah county stake and N L. H Bliday of Salt Lake These gentle men delivered instructive addresses on the conservation of morals.

The coming town election will be warmly contested The republican ticket is as follows President of the town board, H H Earll, trustees, S J. Harkness, John Hunter, Andrew Smith and David Burns, The citizens ticket is President of the town board, John E Ingle, trustees, Andrew Smith John Hunter, Thos S. Rees and John Hood

The miners were idle on Tuesday morning last by reason of a lack of cars

Anderson, the photographer, has left Scofield for Price

WELLINGTON

Henry D Allred has purchased a half interest in the S H Grundvig coal mine, and they are making big improvements on the road to the mine and in a short time will be able to supply all comers with a superior grade of coal and a good road to haul over

Taylor & Glazier shipped a car of hay and grain from this place this week.

The man with his crops in says "this is fine," but the other fellow can't see it that way.

Considerable sickness is reported among our people just now The most serious are several cases of typhoid fever.

Winter seems to be upon us in earnest and as usual has caught most people out in the cold without either wood or coal being hauled. However we have a great quantity of both close in the town, so we guess no one will suffer much.

—It looks as if dame nature had engaged herself to water Castle valley this fall, and the consequence is that much grain and hay has been too wet to haul and is yet in the field and some of it may stay there all winter

GREENRIVER.

A. D Farnsworth came in early in the week to visit his wife and baby.

Cox & Carroll of Orangeville shipped ten cars of cattle from this place early in the week

Henry Goodman, Crispin Taylor and Harry Green arrived on Sunday with 8,000 sheep and crossed the river on J T Farrer's ferry. A rate of three fourths of a cent per head was given which was conceded by all to be quite reasonable.

Miller & Hughes of Ouray Colo, arrived early in the week, they were bound for Southern Nevada where they will spend the winter. They had an elegant outfit and are well prepared for a winter's camp.

Mr Frank McIntyre, the Advocate rustler, was in town last Saturday and secured good contracts for the forthcoming mammoth edition of the Advocate Frank takes well and is quite a smasher and a good boatman but no good walking bridges or keeping off dogs.

The weather is settled and very pleasant, only one slight frost.

Surveyors have arrived and will commence work Monday on the big ditch Your correspondent has not been able to see these gentlemen so far, but will give particulars in next issue.

THESE ARE THE WINNERS

BRIEF BIOGRAPHICAL SKETCHES OF THE DEMOCRATIC CANDIDATES.

All Are Native Sons and All Are Pioneer Residents of Price—They Will Give the Town a Clean, Capable, Business Like Administration—Tuesday Tells the Tale

It is fitting and proper that the people should know something of the lives and character of the men who cater for their suffrage as aspirants for public office. Below we give brief biographical sketches of the candidates of the democratic party, a clean, capable body of men, whom the consensus of opinion already declare elected.

ALBERT BRYNER.

The selection made for the head of the ticket by the Jeffersonian disciples was an exceedingly apt and judicious one. Among all the business men of Price it is doubtful if a one more competent to preside over and direct the city government could be chosen.

Mr. Bryner was born at St. George, Washington county, February 3, 1863, and is therefore in the prime of virile and vigorous manhood. After a common school education he engaged, at the early age of sixteen years, in the stock-raising business, a pursuit which he soon thoroughly mastered and which he has ever since successfully followed. He located at Price in 1884 and, with the exception of 28 months when he was on a mission to Germany and Switzerland, has since been a permanent resident of our thriving town. In 1890 Mr. Bryner was a candidate for county treasurer on the democratic ticket and was triumphantly elected, being the first democrat ever chosen for this important office in Carbon county. The wisdom of the selection has been manifested in the reforms inaugurated in the treasurer's office, the thorough system of book keeping adopted and the courtesy extended to all having business with the office. Mr. Bryner will make an excellent president of our incoming administration.

SEREN OLSEN.

Genial Seren comes of the hardy stock who settled Sanpete county, dug the ditches in its then barren soil and by patient industry and toil brought it to "blossom as the rose" and become famous as one of the richest counties in the state. He was born at Manti, September 21, 1866, where he received a common school education. In early youth Mr. Olsen was a farmer boy and subsequently learned the carpentering trade, serving an apprenticeship of seven years, which latter calling he followed for some time. On coming to Price he engaged as clerk with the Price Trading company, and the seven years passed in this capacity with both our leading mercantile establishments give him an experience which will be invaluable in the management of town affairs. He is not a stranger to public life, having been a member of the town board in 1894. Mr. Olsen is an extensive property owner having a large ranch near the city on which he this year raised 1,200 bushels of grain. His residence in the northern part of town is one of the prettiest in the neighborhood. He has ever been a consistent democrat.

Mr. Olsen was also one of the pioneers and upbuilders of the Dixie country.

J. G. FRANDSEN.

The above named gentleman was not an aspirant for any place on the municipal ticket. He only accepted the nomination as a candidate for member of the town board on the democratic ticket at the solicitation of friends and in the interest of good government and the fair fame of Price

Like his associates on the ticket Mr Frandsen is a native son of Utah. He was born at Mount Pleasant, Sanpete county, November 5, 1861, and educated in the common schools of that city, subsequently taking a course at the B. Y. academy at Provo.

Mr. Frandsen has been successively and successfully engaged in the farming, stock raising, saw mill business and sheep raising, the latter being his principal business. He now has a herd of 2,100 head near Price

Two years ago he selected Price as his permanent home, moved into the residence he now occupies adjoining the court house and purchased a well developed 50 acre farm about two miles from town. Although a young man he is the head of a family of three.

Politically Mr Frandsen has ever been a consistent republican, and as heretofore stated allows the use of his name at this time simply in the interest of a clean administration of town affairs

Mr. Frandsen adds great strength to the good government ticket.

F. ANDERSON,

our popular blacksmith, who, by hard knocks and hardy toil, has acquired a competence and achieved an exceptional standing in the community, is also a Sanpete boy, having first seen the light of day at Ephraim, July 13, 1850. His education has been self acquired and in what he has attained Mr. Anderson is self made. He tilled the fruitful Sanpete soil until eighteen years of age when he learned the blacksmithing trade, a business which he has since steadily followed

In 1889 Mr. Anderson removed to Price, purchased property and built the shop and residence where he is at present located. Nor has scarcely a day elapsed since that time that the merry ring of his anvil has not sung an industrious song in the ears of our people.

Since his residence in Price Mr. Anderson has rendered the town faithful service as constable, marshal and deputy sheriff. He will prove an efficient member of the town board

JOSEPH JONES.

Like all his confreres on the democratic ticket Mr Jones claims Utah as his native heath. He was born at Provo May 10, 1854 and educated in the common schools of that city. His first vocation was logging and farming which he followed for some years

Mr Jones was in Price when there were but two houses in the town—in the fall of 1881. At that time he located in Huntington, where he was engaged in the produce business for ten years. Coming to Price six years ago, Mr Jones opened one of the first meat markets in the town, a business which he successfully conducted till the spring of 1896. Since that time, while diligently at work at all times, he has followed no settled vocation

Joe Jones' name is a synonym all over Carbon county for honesty and integrity and if elected, as he undoubtedly will be, will be a faithful, hard-working and useful member of the town board

LOCAL NEWS

Arthur Lee will convey the 16 handsome Studebaker farm wagons now in this city to the Ashley Co-op company at Vernal the first of the week. Mr. Lee states that travel Vernal way is first class, but that the roads are still in a deplorable condition.

Roy Gibson, the old time operator, who has been ill with fever for some time, has accepted a position as brakeman with the R G W His run will be between Grand Junction and Helper.

Marina Lambert, Joseph Houguler, W. M. Edwards and J. M Bush, a quartette of P. V. sheepmen, were at the Clark Tuesday.

Eastern Utah Advocate
November 4, 1897

CLEVELAND.

Our crops are nearly gathered. Some cattle are to be found in Cleveland, this brings in a little ready cash to pay taxes, store bills, etc.

The primary fair held in our town was a success and pleased the fancy of the children. Prizes were given for best exhibits.

Bishop Overson reports a good time at the Castledale quarterly conference held last Saturday and Sunday.

Our genial merchant S Olsen, is building upon the town site He believes in being in the whirl of business, his present business location is inconveniently located.

It is rumored round about that a first class millinery store is soon to be established in Cleveland

The Y L. M. I A. will give a ball in the new hall the coming Friday.

SCOFIELD.

The mines worked about half time last week. The coal trade is not as good as it has been

A fine girl was born to the wife of Joseph Muhlestein last Friday. Mother and child doing well.

Mrs C. H. Peterson, our milliner, has gone to Castlegate for a few days on business.

H. C. Burrows is spending a few days at the county seat.

The Finland population at Winter Quarters has been greatly increased this fall, and they are buying up every available house in the camp.

Several of the miners who came here from Coalville have just got their families here. Some of them wished they had left them at home since the prospects for steady work are not so bright.

LOCAL NEWS.

Coalville Times Born, Sunday morning, to the wife of Thomas Lee, a son. Thomas is at Scofield, but we understand he has not felt so young for eleven years, as that was the date of his last born before the new arrival. Mother and babe doing nicely.

A FATAL ACCIDENT.

Death as the Sequence of a Hunting Trip in Castledale.

Spring Glen, Carbon Co., Utah,
November 7, 1897.

To the Editor:

A sad accident happened to Wm. Savage, son of Herbert and R. J Savage, at Castledale. As he and his younger brother was out hunting with a single-barrel breach-loading shotgun, he came up behind his little brother, who was swinging a wiping-stick around, and set the gun down and leaned his left armpit over the muzzle of the gun. His brother did not know that he was there, and the stick struck the hammer of the gun and knocked it off. The load went up through the shoulder and shot off one of the arteries of the heart, said the doctor. This happened on Oct. 24th. He lingered till the 29th and passed away. He said he would like to live but if the Lord wanted him he was willing to go. As they were about to move back to their former home in Spring Glen, they brought the remains here for interment. He was laid away on Nov. 1st. He would have been 17 years old in February next. The accident has caused a gloom over the place as the deceased was beloved by all that knew him.

WM. MILLER.

SPRING GLEN,

Harry Keepers and family have moved to Price, where they will make their home.

The families of J. T. Rowley and Harry Keepers have had the fever and ague for some time and find it hard to stamp out the disease.

John T. Rowley has moved his residence from the lower kilns to a lot recently purchased near the upper kilns where he will be closer to his work.

The upper kilns have been repaired and are now being loaded preparatory to burning. It is thought that these kilns will run a greater part of the winter. The lower kilns have been abandoned and the switch taken up.

George Perkins loaded two cars of wood and shipped them to the Co-op Wagon and Machine company, Salt Lake.

The Spring Glenites finished threshing on Saturday. While the yield is less than was expected the quality is O. K. The only loss was from floods, and that not very great, little loss occurred from sprouted grain.

H. A. Southworth is teaching the young mind and is getting good results The attendance is fair

The burial of William Savage, who died at Castledale from a gun shot wound, occurred on Monday of last week. The funeral was largely attended Willie was a bright and promising young man and had many friends in Carbon and Emery counties who were shocked to hear of his untimely demise Mr and Mrs. Savage have the sympathy of the community.

GREENRIVER

Grand county commissioners met on the 1st to attend to some extra business in regard to the ferry boat contingent fund and other matters. Commissioner Brown left for the county seat on the 9 h.

Mrs. Adda Hart, the late lessee of the Maxwell house at Moab, is visiting with J. F. Brown at Greenriver.

Mrs. Clayton has returned from her visit to Salt Lake and is at home at the Palmer hotel.

Mr. and Mrs. Howland will leave on the 18th for a winter visit to Denver.

About 80 cars of sheep and cattle have been shipped to the eastern markets from Greenriver yards the past 10 days.

Mr. Barr and family moved in from the San Rafael this week and will stay here all winter.

Early in the week J. T. Farrer shipped 1000 pounds of his peaches to Mr. Beardsley of the Rio Grande eating house at Helper. John F. Brown also shipped to Mr. Beardsley at Helper 500 pounds of his now famous Eden musk melons. The Eden musk melon is a new growth in this country and is for winter use. At the end of the growing season the melons are gathered and put in cellar or buried and will keep in excellent condition until spring The flavor is generally conceded superior to that of the cantaloupe

WELLINGTON.

Mrs. W. J. Tidwell, who has been quite ill with typhoid fever, is rapidly improving.

Old Father Allred is in a very critical condition. About a week ago his feet began swelling and at present the swelling has extended to the body and limbs. The patient also has smothering spells. Mr. Allred is nearly 73 years of age and there is grave fears as to his recovery.

F. C. Grundvig has had almost continual sickness in his family for the past four months. Various members of his family have been seriously sick. Joseph Ine, who has suffered continuously for three months, passed away Saturday, aged 17 years. The sympathy of the entire community is with the bereaved family.

George A. Wilson, sr, has exchanged part of his Wellington property for property in Salem, Idaho, where he will remove in the spring. His son Basset will accompany him.

The thresher is again at work and will soon have finished for the season.

E. E. Branch with his daughter and two sons started for St. George on Tuesday of last week and will probably be gone six weeks. Mr. Branch's two nieces who have been visiting his family of Miss Jennie Branch of Price were

and her able assistant, Miss Marshall, are conducting a very excellent school. There is a good attendance and rapid progress is being made.

H. Chittenden's wife of Big Springs ranch presented him with a lusty son on November 2d.

Our new school building has just been furnished with new and modern desks There is also a good supply of slate blackboards. The building is one of the best equipped school buildings in the valley.

Miss Mattie Jones accompanied her sister and brother in law, Mrs and Mr. J. W. Davis, to their new home in Arizona.

Wm. Jones, who has been quite sick with typhoid fever, is recovering.

LOCAL NEWS.

Elwin Caldwell was on November 9 commissioned postmaster at Molen

Treasurer Bryner is a very busy man these days. The tax money is just pouring into the county treasury

Attorney G P. Rhea, of Rhea & Earl, Salt Lake, was early on the scene taking part in a number of cases.

Thomas R. Williams, of Scofield, aged 38, and Mrs. Ann E. Evans aged 55 of Spanish Fork, received license to wed from the clerk of Salt Lake county.

B. P. Nevius, general agent for the D. & R. G., was in Price in the interest of his road securing shipments of cattle and sheep.

H. Wade of the Wade house, Castle gate, was excused from jury service by Judge Johnson on account of pressing business at home.

Joe Davis and family left Price Saturday night for Salt River valley, Arizona, where they will make their future home. Mr. Davis disposed of his Price property to the Price Trading company, from whom he purchased it a few years ago. Mr. Davis will go into the drug business.

Eastern Utah Advocate
November 18, 1897

Joe Davis and family left Price Saturday night for Salt River valley, Arizona, where they will make their future home. Mr. Davis disposed of his Price property to the Price Trading company, from whom he purchased it a few years ago. Mr. Davis will go into the drug business.

NOTES.

There are various straws floating about which would seem to indicate that the U. P. coal miners will soon be at work again. This would be a great boon to Scofield and would make it the banner town of Carbon county.

The railroad boys on the Scofield branch are the hardest worked in the state, but withal are the most courteous and obliging.

Notwithstanding the fact that the U P. coal mine is shut down Mrs Thomas, the winsome and popular hostess of the Depot hotel, reports a flourishing trade

A wanderer by the wayside who was taken in and cared for by some Scofield boys for a week, repaid their generoslly by making off with a fine suit of clothes and "hiking" for P. V. A wire to the latter place failed to wing him.

Mrs. Mary Trevaur of the French hotel, will leave ere long for a visit to her native lowlands of Belgium to recruit her health.

J. V. Williams was up from Castlegate overlooking things in general, on Friday last.

Joe Whitemore, formerly of Farnham, and well known in Price, is now conducting a meat market at Scofield.

Price

LOCAL NEWS.

Wheat at Chicago, yesterday, 91.

I. Glaser of Helper was a Price visitor Tuesday.

R. Forrester was a county seat visitor on Saturday.

A. H. Johnson of Vernal was a Mathis house guest on Saturday.

The highest price allowed at Lowenstein's store for grain and hides

J. B. Milford sell shoes things to Simon Brothers at $2 00 per head.

S. S. Chipman, an American Fork Cattle man, was a Price visitor Friday last?

Don't forget that Friday is the day our fresh fish arrives Emery County Mercantile company.

D. W. Wipple, of Denver, a well known Colorado contractor was a Price visitor early in the week.

Salina Press: Mr. and Mrs. Goodrichson and little son, of Helper, are visiting relatives and friends in Salina.

J. L. Boulden P. V. Coal company's blacksmith at Winter Quarters, visited his family in Orangeville this week.

Mrs. Mary Shafer returned last week from Cisco, where she had been keeping house for her brother, John McIntire.

Mrs. Mary Shafer returned last week from Cisco, where she had been keeping house for her brother, John McIntire.

St. V. LeSieur came in from Provo early in the week and made a quick trip to the reservation returning yesterday.

Pyramid's Spring City Correspondent. Attorney Kofford left for Castle Valley this week where he will resume his practice.

Provo Enquirer: A marriage license has been issued to Joseph W. Jackson, aged 22, of Castledale, and Ida May Van Leuven, aged 18, of Mapleton.

There will be an apron and cap dance at the ward house on Thanksgiving evening under the auspices of the Y. L. M. I. association. The following committee on arrangements bespeak a delightful entertainment Misses Mary Rasmussen, Lilly Bryner, Mae Pace, Rose Bryner and Mame Robb. The receipts will go to the association.

H. C. Hansen of Molen was a Price visitor of late last week and did not forget to call and arrange for the continued visits of The Advocate to his home.

D. C. Woodward and J. E. Johnson came in Sunday to meet the attorneys, Messrs. Judge and S. K. King, in the Huntington injunction case. The party left for Castledale Sunday evening

Thomas and R. Singleton of American Fork, brothers of the popular superintendent of the Ferron Co-op, passed through Price on Monday on their way to Castledale to attend to some court matters.

A grand musical and dramatic entertainment will be given Saturday evening, November 27, at Castlegate under the auspices of Eagle Lodge No 13 K. of P. Of the participants Castlegate's best artists are pressed into service and a rare treat will be given lovers of music and the drama. The indications are that this will be a record breaker for Castlegate.

EMERY.

Friday was the closing day for our first term of school which has been completed without interruption. Something should be done in the near future for a more commodious school building There is a sufficient number of children of school age to employ three teachers and a good attendance for each. Many children will have to be refused admittance to our schools for lack of seating capacity The two departments are already crowded, and from 60 to 80 are yet out of school and intend starting soon The trustees are doing all in their power to provide more room for next year, but they get little encouragement from the people from whom aid should come.

A new pool hall is in course of erection and the proprietor, H C Petley, Jr, says he intends giving a free dance before the pool table is put in.

The hum of the thresher is still heard, but it is expected that this week's threshing will finish all.

The monotony of the town of Emery was broken on Saturday morning, when the Messrs. Rol and Sid Swasey were brought in charged with cattle stealing and arraigned before P. V. Bunderson, but through some error in the warrants they were liberated.

There seems to be a good deal of cattle and sheep hustling in this region at present. Some parties passing through a few days ago with a small flock of sheep having their ears recently marked and some brands shorn off caused sheep owners to look suspiciously on and inquire into the matter, but as nothing could be identified they were not molested There should be something done to stop such work and the guilty parties, whoever they may be, brought to justice. The employes of the Salina Cattle company are considerably worked up over the present state of things, as that company seems to be the main loser, their losses in cattle being up in the thousands.

We got pretty thirsty here for a drink (of water) last week, the canal undergoing repairs.

SCOFIELD

Last week the mines worked nearly full time but they are now so far ahead of the orders, that the prospects for steady work are not so good.

John Strang met with a very painful accident last Thursday. As he was going to his work in the mine he fell and the point of a large pick which he was carrying under his arm entered the back of his left hand. The weight of his body falling upon the handle drove the pick through his hand pinning him to the ground, making a very bad wound and in consequence of which John will not be able to work for some time.

A grand ball was held in the Winter Quarters hall last Friday night and they tripped the light fantastic quite gaily until some of the boys thought they would try a set of five couples, but it would not work. The consequence was a little disturbance and some arrests. His honor, Judge Thomas, held a midnight session of court and soon made things right by imposing a nominal fine upon the guilty parties.

W. W. Thompson has gone to Spanish Fork on a visit.

A traveling concert troupe, consisting of two men and two women, appeared in our town last week and gave an entertainment. Those who attended are kicking themselves for wasting their time and money. They hitched up their outfit at 8 a. m. and tried to jump their board bill, but Mrs. T. M. Thomas, the hotel keeper, being on the alert, prevented them going until they paid their bill. We think the public should be warned through your valuable paper against such frauds.

---

additional Scofield Correspondence.

We are having a cold spell just now to remind us of what is coming.

A conjoint meeting of the Y. M. and Y. L. associations was held at the Winter Quarters meeting house last Sunday evening A very nice program was rendered to a crowded house, after which the Young Men's association was organized and vacancies were filled in the Young Ladies' association.

The infant child of Mr. and Mrs. J. J. Carrick died very suddenly on Monday. It appeared to be well and hearty when all at once it was taken with convulsions and died in a few minutes.

Alexander Wilson has a little boy sick with typhoid fever.

HELPER.

William Morgan will in the very near future begin the erection of two cottages on his Helper town property recently purchased from Levi Simmons.

Ike Glaser is widening his already commodious store building in order to give room for the increased stock made necessary by his growing business

P. A. Smith is building a residence just north of James Rooney's residence.

Helper was almost depopulated Friday and Saturday by reason of the great number of our leading citizens attending court at the county seat. The sentiment here was in favor of Mrs Hoge in her suit with the Price Trading company

WELLINGTON.

O d Father Allred gradually grows worse. He now remains constantly in a litting position and at times it is almost impossible for him to breath.

Mrs. Wm J. Tidwell and her brother Wm. Jones are now on a fair road to recovery from the typhoid fever and we are glad to state that there is no new cases reported.

William and John Fawcett and Frank Lang were in town Tuesday and report everything O K on the range and stock in fine shape.

Professor Hardy is conducting a class in music and singing and apparently is having good success.

R. W. Avery is preparing to put up a fine substantial frame dwelling this fall and winter.

Lehi Jensen is on a short visit to friends in Sanpete this week.

Geo. Milner is prepared to do all kinds of black smithing and wagon work. Give him a call.

The interests of the Holladay Tidwell coal mine held by the Tidwells was sold to Castlegate parties last week for the sum of seventeen hundred dollars.

GREENRIVER.

Harry Howland and wife left on Saturday evening for Denver where they will visit Mr. Howland's father.

Commissioner Brown returned on Saturday from Moab where he attended a special session of the county court. Dady Brown says the roads are good and Grand river fordable.

Messrs. Howland, Durant, Spicer and Atkinson are making extensive preparations for putting in a large acreage of crops next spring. They have rich bottom land which by reason of the climatic conditions is very productive.

Messrs Sommers and Geiger have sold their Willow Bend property to Mr. Bennett, of Leadville, who will occupy and farm the ranch.

J. T Farrer is again at home, having recently returned from a trip to Moab.

THOMPSON SPRINGS.

Ballard Bros., the popular caterers, have enlarged and fitted up their hotel in elegant style and are prepared to pleasantly entertain the traveling public.

Arthur Taylor came in from Salt Lake on Wednesday of last week with a car load of material for the construction of a dipping vat. Material alone cost over $1,000 and is owned by Henry Goodman and the Taylor Brothers. The Western transported the lumber free of charge. The capacity of the vat when completed will be 5,000 head of sheep per day. Sheep dip will be kept on hand and sold to those desiring to use the vats at actual cost.

Mr Cerlslo has received a carload of fine bucks, he has 10,000 sheep which are feeding toward his ranch near Blue mountains.

Ballard Brothers will contract for digging 100 tons of coal at their mine near this place.

Goodman and Green are driving their sheep this way and expect to dip here when the vat is completed.

WELLINGTON.

Orange Tidwell returned home from Colorado last week, where he has been working since July last.

The Misses Minerva and Bertha Ellis came home for a few days' visit to their parents. They have had charge of the culinary department on one of the R. G. W. work trains this summer.

W. J. Tidwell made a flying trip to Castledale this week on business.

Bert McMullin has sold his house and lot to his brother Bryant, and has moved his family to Price where he expects to make his home in the future.

Joseph Draper has returned from his trip to the Colorado river where he went with a load of freight. He reports a good trip barring the loss of one of his horses.

The general health of our people is good just at present, and everything is quiet and peaceable.

SCOFIELD.

O. G. Kimball is going into the butcher business again.

S. A. Hendrichsen has returned from Salt Lake where he purchased a large stock of merchandise for the holiday trade.

The Grand Lodge officers of the Knights of Pythias made an official visit to the local lodge last Thursday and went to Castlegate Friday.

The P. V. Coal company delayed their pay-day this month until the 23d

A grand calico ball will take place in the Scofield school house on Thanksgiving.

On account of the unusually heavy rains this fall the roads have been so bad that teams could not bring so much produce to Pleasant valley. The merchants are not sorry, but the people are.

CASTLEGATE.

Charley Smith, who met with a sad accident a few months ago in which he had both legs broken and was sent to the hospital at Salt Lake City, is again with us and is able to get around slowly on crutches.

William Davis and Joseph Pringle of Cleveland were Castlegate visitors the first of the week.

Invitations have been given to a few people of this burg to attend an entertainment which will be given at the Catholic church Sunday night.

John Horn is now clerking in the Wasatch store. Mr. Horn takes the place made vacant by the resignation of John Holly, who left for the east where he will travel as drummer for an eastern firm.

Everybody was happy in town Monday, the event being pay-day.

The mine was idle on Monday on account of repairs being made on some of the machinery inside the mine.

Misses Rosie and Lilly Bryner were visitors at Castlegate Sunday.

Dave Evans, Thomas Phelps and Dave Jones went down to Price Saturday night to attend the K. of P. lodge at that place and returned home Sunday evening.

John Hamel had his finger badly mashed between the cars on Thursday morning.

Joe Dumayne of Cleveland is visiting friends and relatives in town this week.

GREENRIVER.

Mr. Ed Graves paid us a visit Sunday. Mr. Graves will invest $500 in cattle and stock his old range when he can find some one with cattle who covets his golden ducats.

Mr. and Miss Smith are up from Box B ranch and are stopping with Atkinson.

Greenriver people are all at work on the Farrer ditch dam.

About 2,000 bushels of grain were threshed out by the Farrer & Hartman threshing machine.

There will be about 25 head of fat hogs slaughtered this winter.

Greenriver raised her own winter apples and potatoes this year.

When the court of county commissioners was asked to put the road in repair from Greenriver to Little Grand their reply was, "Let them (the travelers) carry a shovel as they have done for ten years." Is this progress? Will Moab always remain Grand county?

LOCAL NEWS.

Dave Holladay has moved his family into the new postoffice building.

The highest price allowed at Lowenstein's store for grain and hides.

Wm. Potter with his family will occupy the rooms in the Holdaway property recently vacated by Dave Holdaway's family.

Of the Castlegate Pythians who visited the Price Knights of Pythias on Saturday night were James A. Harrison, T. T. Lamph, T. Phelps, D. D. Evans and David L. Jones.

E. B. Reynolds, Indian inspector, left for the reservation Friday morning, where he will investigate the recent unpleasantness between the Indians and Colorado game wardens.

H. J Harkness, an old resident of Scofield, has been appointed postmaster at that place, vice A. H. Earll, resigned

Edward Jones' family who have resided in Price for some time removed to Castlegate Sunday where Mr. Jones is employed in the P. V. Coal company's mine.

Miss Nettie Shipp, who for the past two months has been assistant postmaster at Price, returned to her home at Castledale Wednesday morning. By her careful attention to the duties of the office Miss Shipp made many friends among the patrons of the office.

Sergeant Bessell and County Clerk Donaldson made a trip through Emery inspecting the telephone line and on pleasur bent.

Mrs. World left for Salt Lake this morning with her little son who has been suffering from the effects of a severe attack of typhoid fever. She will get expert medical aid for the little sufferer

Cleveland s New Millinery Store.

We have just opened up an elegant lot of millinery goods in Cleveland. For variety and price our goods cannot be equaled We are anxious to serve the people. Place of business with J. F. Dorius, the school teacher.

Miss Tena Larsen.

Eastern Utah Advocate
December 2, 1897

GREENRIVER.

Sheriff D B Willson and Deputy Boughton returned to Greenriver on the night of November the 25th, having made the trip from this point south to the lower crossing of the Robbers' Roost trail, thence east to Court house, thence north to Cisco, then back to Greenriver, a total of nearly 200 miles in less than forty hours The sheriff has made this circuit twice since the evening of November 20th, and on the 26th left for Price on the noon train, leaving five good men mounted in the V between the rivers. Every sheep camp and every ranchman in the county is on the lookout to get the reward of $50, but no track of man or horse since they left Court House on the morning of November 20th, can be found The sheriff is a no-surrender man, and if pluck and endurance can win these thieves will get landed in the Utah penitentiary.

A rain and snow storm visited this valley on November 23 and 24

The health of the settlement is O K.

We celebrated Thanksgiving with a dance and roast pig

Agent Allison is well liked by the patrons of the road.

All the sheep men are smiling and are getting out onto the mesa's since the snow, Goodman finished dipping at Thompson on the 24th. Gordon took the trail south on the 23th with 7,000 sheep.

Mr. Gosling of Salt Lake arrived Friday with a car load of registered high-grade bucks and is feeding them at J. T. Farrars Mr. Gosling will put 18,000 sheep on San Rafael.

The last issue of The Advocate shows good work. News from three counties and all well written, with editorials that show there is some one that thinks and is working to make The Advocate a blessing to Eastern Utah An advertisement in this up to date paper is what every merchant needs. The attention of one of Greenriver's business men was attracted to the ad of William Howard of Huntington and was heard to remark "that ad would bring Howard at least $50 per month that would not otherwise have reached him."

CASTLEGATE.

This seems to be an unlucky month at the mine by reason of the numerous accidents that have occurred. Sandy Harrison had his foot injured last Thursday morning.

Born, on Nov. 26, to the wife of Ed. Edwards, a baby boy. Mother and child doing nicely.

Some of our young folks tripped the light fantastic in Helper last Thursday night. They report having spent an enjoyable time. The dance was given in Rooney's hall. Jones' orchestra furnished the music.

Joseph Jones of Price was a Castlegate visitor last Saturday night.

The whistle blew last Saturday night to give warning to the miners that there would not be any work Monday.

It is reported that Eagle Lodge No 18, Knights of Pythias, will give a concert, supper and dance on December 4, at the K. of P. hall.

The Catholics held a mass meeting last Sunday morning and a large crowd attended.

The battle ax man was much in evidence last Tuesday. He treated all the miners with ' Battle Ax" tobacco and also made a fine display in our town with his bills.

The Wasatch store was kept pretty busy this week sending out the m s' supply of groceries and flour.

SCOFIELD.

Times have been quite lively here since pay-day.

A man attempted to go into the mine last Friday under the influence of liquor, and when the boss, Wm Parmley, told him he could not go in he struck at him so hard that he jerked his shoulder out of joint. He struck Parmley in the mouth, and to save himself from further punishment the latter picked up a piece of iron and hit the big fellow on the head which knocked some of the spirits and a little blood out of him. This bully, who calls himself Purdie, is from every place but here, and has been fighting his way through the world in this manner ever since he was twelve years old.

Everybody seemed to enjoy the holiday on Thanksgiving the mines having closed down for the day.

Evan Williams has built a nice addition to his residence. Mr Williams has good faith in the future of Scofield.

Miss Libbie Walton has gone out to Smith's Well for the winter, where she will be governess in the Smith family.

J. S. Patterson, who is looking after the U. P. property here, has had orders to have the mules ready to send to Rock Springs about December 1st.

WELLINGTON.

Old Father Green Allred died on Nov. 24, after an illness of about four weeks. He was aged 72 years and was formerly a resident of Spring City, Sanpete county. He removed to Price about thirteen years ago and to Wellington about three years ago, where he resided until his death. The sympathy of the community is extended to the family.

There is considerable sickness here just now, but we hope nothing of a serious nature.

G. B. Milner has been down to Farnham with his threshing machine cleaning up the odd jobs down that way this week.

Considerable fall plowing has been done here this fall and the farmers expect a fine crop the coming season

LOCAL NEWS.

No. 15, the through freight, went into the ditch near Nolen on Friday and delayed train No. 1 for several hours

Frila West and John O Brit came in from Mercur on Monday and will prospect in the vicinity of Lower Crossing.

County Clerk Donaldson on November 20 issued a license to wed to Solomon Bowngren and Maggie Allan, both of Helper.

While Alf Grames was away from home this week his wife set fire to their cabins and burned them to the ground. A party passing near the place saw Mrs. Grames piling sticks and rubbish on the fire to hurry the work along Warrant for her arrest was issued on Tuesday and preliminary hearing will be had Friday. No reason or excuse is given by Mrs Grames for the wanton destruction In all probability her mental condition will be looked into at the coming term of the district court in February

I M. Deline of Helper and Mrs Emily Perkins of the same place were married at the residence of Mrs Mead, east of town, on Tuesday. Bishop Horsley officiated.

Gus Anderson, salesman for the Hewlett Bros. company, returned from Uintah county last evening and as usual reports a good business. The broad minded policy of this company and its up to-date methods is pushing it rapidly forward

Ephraim Enterprise There are three weddings billed for to day in this city, and three couples of our prominent young people will be united in wedlock They are James Frost and Annie C Peterson, Ephraim Peterson and Hannah E Nielsen, and Charles L Despain and Lorinda Anderson They are all well known in this city and their friends, who are legion, wish them unbounded happiness in their new relations

Deseret Evening News
December 2, 1897

Pleasant Valley News.

Scofield, Dec. 1.—The mines have been working pretty steadily of late, the P. V. company's output being about sixty flats per day's work. They have to lay off part of the time for want of cars. The coal trade has been better this fall than for several years.

We have had considerable snowfall here, but most of it has disappeared. We have had frost, too, the mercury having reached 6 degrees below zero.

It has been rumored here that Thomas Lloyd has lost his life in the attempt to reach Klondike. We hope it is not true, however, as the gentleman has many friends here.

William Farthman and family leave this week for England. He sold his residence to Lee Gordon.

S. J. Harkness has been appointed postmaster vice A. H. Earll, resigned.

The health of the people is good. We have good district schools both at Scofield and Winter Quarters. The Sunday schools as also the other Church organizations are in a flourishing condition in the Pleasant Valley ward.
H.

Salt Lake Herald
December 3, 1897

DRUNKEN MINER SUBDUED.

Foreman Parmley Did It With a Bar of Iron.

Scofield, Dec. 2.—A drunken miner at the Winter Quarters mine attacked Mine Boss Parmley, who had denied him admittance to the mine on account of the miner being intoxicated. Mr. Parmley received a very heavy blow in the face, and to save himself further punishment, felled the man with a bar of iron. Although inflicting a painful wound, it had the effect of sobering the miner, and stopped further trouble.

WELLINGTON.

The Fawcett Bros have bought the Frank Lang place in Soldier canyon and will make it headquarters for their large stock interests.

F. C. Grundvig has completed his new residence and will shortly occupy it with his family.

Work on R. W. Avery's new house is progressing nicely and he expects to have it completed soon.

The school board had to take in hand the procuring of the new school books, and all kinds of books can now be had at the secretary's office.

As per advertisement, some of the stock in the Wellington canal was sold on Monday to pay for the water master service this year.

Cold winter has come considerable earlier than usual and the ground is covered with about three inches of "the beautiful" and the air is as cold as an iceberg.

We understand that the Chittenden town property is for sale cheap. This would be a desirable home for some one wishing to locate here.

Sleighing parties were quite numerous the early part of the week, but the roads are again bare and the sleighing cut short until another snow.

CASTLEGATE.

The Wasatch Store company is building an addition to its butcher shop which it will use as an ice house.

E. Miller made a trip to Scofield last Thursday and returned Friday.

It snowed Wednesday night and Thursday last, and we have had about a foot of snow ever since.

An Italian by the name of Frank Passetio, who was track walker above Kyuno, had his leg cut off by a train about a mile above Kyuno. He was being taken to Castlegate when he expired. It is thought he was intoxicated and went to sleep on the track.

Tally Evans, who has made Castlegate his home for some time, has moved his family to Scofield, where he will work in the P. V. Coal company's mine at Winter Quarters.

Robert Howard, who has been attending the Agricultural college at Logan, is again back with us and will resume work in the mine.

It is rumored that the mine will slow down and not work more than three days a week. This is bad news for the miners, from the fact that most of them wish to put in full time in the winter and spend the summer on their ranches in the valley.

Mrs. J. H. McMillan went to Salt Lake Monday.

Mr. H G. Williams, assistant superintendent, has posted notice stating that the mine time will hereafter be a half hour behind railroad time.

Morgan Thomas, a book agent from Spanish Fork, was around town Saturday delivering books to his numerous customers.

A masquerade ball will be given in the K. P. hall Christmas eve. A prize will be given for the best masked character and after the dancers have unmasked a prize will be given for the best waltzers.

In the case of the state of Utah vs. James Rooney for selling liquor on Sunday, defendant was found guilty by Judge Duerden, who imposed a fine of $45 and cost. M. P. Braffet was attorney for defendant and J. W. Warf prosecuted.

H. G. Clark was a visitor in this town Monday.

Something like two years ago Eagle lodge No. 13, Knights of Pythias, was organized at this place. Since the organization the lodge has had an unprecedented growth and has built an elegant hall. A short time ago the last obligation against the building was paid, and in honor of this event the members and their friends, on December 4, enjoyed a very pleasant evening in felicitous speech making and social intercourse James Harri on made the opening address and covered the growth of the lodge briefly, the payment of the last obligation and remarked that all present should throw dull care aside and join in making the evening one long to be remembered. He stated that after the long season of work in which the hall was built and paid for, the lodge would now devote its energies to social entertainments. After the dance an elegant lunch was served at 11 30, after which Dr. Asadsorian, H. J. Schultz and B F. Caffey spoke briefly and entertainingly of the lodge and the high esteem in which it was held by the people.

GREENRIVER.

John Peak and his father have a contract with J. T. Farrer & Company owners of the Black Diamond coal mine for mining coal. They are putting a fine grade of coal on the dump.

Green river is full of ice and the weater is cold. There was a light fall of snow on Wednesday.

Mrs. Robert Hatrick has arrived and Bob is happy. The Western can now depend upon the pump running steadily.

Mrs. Laura Lang has returned from the Big Springs ranch and will reside with her mother this winter.

Harry Farrer came up from Moab on a visit to his Greenriver home.

Born, on the morning of December 2, to the wife of Alf Farrer, a liney girl. The mother and babe are doing well

There are four families of Thompsons living at at Greenriver none of whom are related.

Major Stanton is locating and buying placer claims on the Colorado river and, it is said, will form a company and put in an extensive placer mining plant.

W. P. Durkee purchased the last of J. B. Buhr's cattle and shipped about ten cars east on Saturday.

SCOFIELD.

Gus Gordon and Miss Allwin Jones of Winter Quarters were married last Friday evening by Judge Thomas.

John Hood is training the children in an operatta for the holidays.

The mines worked four days last week.

We have about a foot of snow and it is very cold

Robert Wilson is doing the butcher act for O G Kimball, whose market is again open for business.

Everybody seems to be quietly attending to their own business and nothing of a sensational character occurred during the week.

Eastern Utah Advocate
December 16, 1897

WELLINGTON.

It is rumored that there will be at least two weddings about Christmas time in this place. It is easy to guess their names

Mr. Fowler of Huntington is here for a short time doing the plastering on W. J. Hill's new house.

Henry Hill is rushing work on his new house and expects to have it ready to occupy some time next week.

E. E. Branch, sons and daughter are expected home the end of this week from their trip to the St. George country.

SCOFIELD.

The greatest snow storm of the season occurred Saturday night. It was a regular blizzard.

Superintendent Welby has issued an order forbidding the train crew to allow miners to ride on empty cars between Scofield and Winter Quarters. This action on the part of the superintendent resulted from a letter written the railroad company by some evil-minded person anxious to curry favor with Mr. Welby. The action of the company works a great hardship on the miners.

A viciously disposed person a few days ago shot and killed one of Mr. Campbell's Shetland ponies. The pony was a highly prized pet of Mr. Campbell's children. He has offered a reward for the arrest and conviction of the guilty party.

A grand social will be given by the Knights of Pythias on Friday, the 17th.

Bills are out announcing a concert at the Winter Quarters ward house for the benefit of the church.

A concert will be given by the silver cornet band on Christmas eve. The boys are hard at work on the program and a musical treat is anticipated.

J. M. Brattie, the genial manager of the Wasatch store, is in Salt Lake purchasing a stock of Christmas goods.

Born, to the wife of David J. Reece, a fine boy. Mother and child doing well.

EMERY.

The cold days of the past week were keenly felt, and on Sunday a cold north-westerly wind came off the snow capped mountains which caused the inhabitants to seek warm fires.

William Edwards and Chris Link are doing good work for the sheep owners who anticipate lambing their herds in the mountains of this vicinity next spring. They will put out three or four hundred bottles of strychnine, and the carcasses of some twenty horses will furnish baits for the carnivora of this section. They have taken the skins of quite a number of coyotes, wild cats and one mountain lion, and the boys state that they find only a small portion of the poisoned animals.

G. T. Olsen is enlarging his store room and a display of Xmas goods may be seen there in a few days.

It is rumored that H. C. Pettey is at Castledale with the view of taking out a liquor license.

George Peacock and wife of Manti are visitors here. Mr. Peacock is looking after the interests of his sheep herds.

W. G. Pettey went up to the county seat to make final proof on his homestead.

Delinquent Tax List.

Office of Treasurer, Carbon County, Utah.

Public notice is hereby given that I will, according to law, offer at public sale at the front door of the county court house in Price, Carbon county, state of Utah, and sell to the highest responsible bidder, for cash, on Monday, the 9th day of December, A. D. 1897, and succeeding days, commencing said sale at the hour of 10 o'clock a. m. of said days so much of the following described real estate and personal property situated in said county and state, on which the taxes for the year 1897 have not been paid, as shall be necessary to pay said taxes, interest and penalties, to-wit:

WINTER QUARTERS.

William Miller, 1 house, amt due $1 74.

William Boweter, 1 house, amt due $1 74.

William Personner, 1 house, amt due $1 86.

J W Kissel, 1 house, amt due $1 53.

George Reese Estate, 9 houses, amt due $10 09.

Roderick Davis, imp, amt due $1 53.

Jacob Koehl, imp, amt due 93c.

David Reese, imp, amt due $1 53

Thomas Llewelyn, imp, amt due 93c.

John Everson, 1 house, amt due $1 53.

SCOFIELD TOWN.

S J Harkness, e½ nw¼ sec 5 tp 13 s r 7, e 80 acres, amt due $30 10

Adam Hunter, imp, amt due $2 33.

C A Robinson, personal property, amt due $1 17.

W C Burrows, imp, amt due $2 70.

William Douglas, imp, amt due $1 17

Roderick Davis, imp, amt due $4 23.

W L Burrows, imp, amt due $1 41.

Frank Strang, Jr., pers'l property, amt due 94c.

A H Sturgis, imp, amt due $3 03.

Mrs John Arthur, imp, amt due $1.17.

Thomas S Reese, imp, amt due $2 84.

William Forrester, pers'l property, amt due $1.17.

J W Vale, pers'l property, amt due 70c.

George R Decker, personal property, amt due 91c.

Union Pacific Coal company, net proceeds of mines, amt due $519 14.

SCOFIELD PRECINCT.

William Burrows, e hf nw qr sw qr of the nw qr, nw qr of the sw qr, sec 17 tp 13 s r 7 e, 160 acres, amt due $11 29.

W L Burrows, se qr sec 17 tp 13 s r 7 e, 160 acres, amt due $19 34.

D C Burrows, e hf sw qr, sw qr sw qr, sec 17 tp 12 s r 7 e, 120 acres, amt due $7 03.

Ira D Gardner, e hf of the ne qr, n hf of the se qr, sec 9 tp 12 s r 7 e, 155 acres, amt due $13 10.

Joseph Cattle, se qr nw qr, e hf sw qr, sw qr sw qr, sec 9 tp 13 s r 7 e, 165 acres, amt due $9 75.

S J Harkness, sw qr ne qr, nw qr se qr, sec 5 tp 13 s r 7 e, 80 acres, amt due $7 52.

William Burrows, ne qr ne qr sec 18 tp 14 s r 7 e, 40 acres, amt due $1 88.

Christena Hunter, mortgage on David Wilson, Carbon county, amt due $8 65.

Christena Hunter, mortgage on William Vruggrink, amt due $11 75.

CASTLEGATE PRECINCT.

John O Nelson, pers'l property, amt due 47c.

Robert Williams, Jr, pers'l property, amt due 93c.

Joseph T Jones, personal property, amt due 19c.

J J Cronner, personal property, amt due $1 85

W H Duke, personal property, amt due $1 02.

Castlegate Coal and Coke Company, lots 6 and 7 and e hf of sw qr sec 6 tp 13 s r 10 e, 158 acres, amt due $50 61.

Ed Caison, imp, amt due 93c.

Robert Howard, mortgage Jos. Whiteley, amt due $9 25.

J X Ferguson, sw qr, n hf se qr, sec 12 tp 13, s r 9 e, 240 acres, amt due $20

P A Smith, lot 1 block 4, amt due $7 10.

J X Ferguson, lot 2 block 4, amt due 50c; lot 10 block 8, amt due $1 50, lot 1 block 4, amt due 50c.

L M McComb, lot 1 in block 1, amt due $7 60.

J T Reid, lots 3, 4, 17 and 18 block 1, amt due $6 90

Don C Corbett, lot 9 block 8, Pratt's survey, amt due $1 50.

Heber Goodmanson, imp, amt due $1.10.

W M Reister, imp, amt due 40c.

D Banfield, personal property, amt due $2 50

Guy Angle, personal property, amt due $1 50.

E C Howland, personal property, amt due 80c.

T Pratt, part of e hf of w hf of nw qr sec 19 tp 13 s r 10 e, 48 acres amt due $7 70, lots 4 and 10 block 7, Pratt's survey, Welby townsite, amt due $1; all of block 8, Pratt's survey, Welby townsite, amt due 90c.

Heber Thompson, part of se qr of nw qr sec 31 tp 14, s r 10 e, 25 acres, amt due $14 06, special school tax Spring Glen precinct.

Mrs. Thompson Estate, lot 1 block 4, Spring Glen townsite, amt due $3 90.

E D Fullmer, part of nw qr of se qr sec 25, tp 14, s r 9 e, 10 acres, amt due $6 80.

J F Crowley, lots 10 and 11, block 2, Welby townsite, amt due $12.

PRICE TOWN.

Henry Flack, lot 2 block 20, Price town, amt due $6 80.

Price Drug Co, 1 house, amt due $1.03.

S S Jones part of lot 1 block 43, amt due $3 68.

Clarence Marsh, part of the se qr of se qr sec 17 tp 14, s r 10 e, 32½ acres, amt due $18 91.

Gilson Asphaltum Co, warehouse, amt due $17 06.

G H Jewett, warehouse, amt due $10 50.

John J Martin, personal property, amt due $1 93.

Isaac Kimball, personal property, amt due $6 15.

Castle Valley News Co, personal property, amt due $1 90.

Wilson & Davis, personal property, amt due $3 00.

PRICE PRECINCT.

Clarence Marsh, ne qr se qr, sec 17 tp 14 s r 10 e, 40 acres, amt due $3.70.

WELLINGTON PRECINCT.

Newton Hill, part of the se qr of the sw qr and part of the sw qr of the se qr sec 1 tp 15 s r 10 e, 26 acres, amt due $6 65.

Roberts Brothers, part of the w hf of nw qr and part of the ne qr of sw qr sec 26 tp 15 s r 11 e, 88 acres, amt due $9 97; and part of the sw qr of the ne qr, and part of the nw qr of se qr of sec 35 tp 15 s r 11 e, 25 acres, amt due $3 97.

Joseph Whitmore, s hf of the se qr and part of the nw qr of se qr of sec 35 tp 15 s r 11 e, 110 acres, amt due $10 44.

John C Vance, s hf of sw qr and s hf of se qr sec 5 tp 15 s r 10 e, 160 acres, amt due $12 00

E A McMullin, lots 1 and 4 block 3 Wellington townsite survey, amt due $21.64, also lot 4 in block 9, amt due 80c.

William Curtis, lot 1 block 5, amt due $4 83.

Ed Curtis, imp amt due $6.82.

B R McMullin, 1 lot in Thayn addition, Wellington townsite, amt due $7.15.

Big Spring Ranch Co, nw qr sw qr, sec 18, tp 15, s r 13 e, 40 acres, s hf and s hf of the ne qr and s hf of nw qr of sec 9, tp 15, s r 13 e, 440 acres; s hf of sec 7, 340 acres, w hf sw qr and sw qr of nw qr, sec 10, 120 acres; ne qr and n hf of se qr and ne qr of sw qr and e hf of nw qr and nw qr of nw qr, sec 17, 400 acres, n hf ne qr n hf nw qr, sec 15, 160 acres, s hf sw qr, sec 11, 80 acres; ne qr ne qr, sec 15, 40 acres; nw qr nw qr, sec 14, 40 acres, s hf of sec 8, 230 acres, tp 15, s r 13 e, amt due $450 83.

Big Spring Telephone Co, imp, amt due $6 24.

George C Whitmore, imp, amt due $64 05, special school tax

Eva Whitmore, mortgage Alex K Reid, amt tax due $4 62.

John A Powell, Jr, lots 2 and 3 block 11 Wellington townsite survey, amt tax due $6 49.

GORDON CREEK PRECINCT.

V Rambaud & Vacher Bros, personal property, amt due $68 64.

S J Hall and I Trimbril, ne qr of sec 12 tp 14 s r 8 e, 160 acres, amt due $6 97

H Wilson, personal property, amt due $1 60.

R J Wright, house, amt tax due 60c.

MINNIE MAUD PRECINCT.

E L Harmon, 1 house and personal property, amt due $34 45.
Charles Hall, 1 house and personal property, amt due $3 40.
D W Russell, house, amt due $9 90.
A J Russell, house, amt due $10 98.
J W Russell, personal property, amt due $4 51.
J D Boyd, personal property, amt due $8 55.
Lunt & Miner, personal property, amt tax due $115 67.
Clark Elmer, personal property, amt tax due $15 40.
M M Montague, 1 house, amt due $2 45.

STATE OF UTAH, } ss.
COUNTY OF CARBON }

I, Albert Bryner, treasurer in and for the county of Carbon, state of Utah, do hereby certify that the foregoing statement of delinquent taxes in and for said county and state is true and correct as appears of record in my office.

ALBERT BRYNER,
Treasurer of Carbon County, Utah.

To the Public.

The undersigned having purchased the stock of drugs and medicines of the Price drug store from Mr. McWilson, begs to solicit at the hands of all old patrons their continued patronage, and to assure all customers of prompt and satisfactory dealing The stock of drugs will be immediately increased and everything usually found in a strictly first-class drug store will be kept constantly in stock.   DR. W. C. RICHMAN.

Price, Utah, Dec. 15, 1897.

Eastern Utah Advocate
December 23, 1897

CASTLEGATE.

The first drill of the uniformed rank of the Knights of Pythias, was held at the K. P. hall Wednesday night, December 15.

D. O. Robbins was visiting this burg last Friday.

W. W. Wimmer of Huntington was in town last week taking orders for clothing.

Christmas vacation for the district schools will begin on December 21 and instructions will not be resumed until January 10.

Saturday was pay day for the coal miners here.

E. Miller made a trip to Scofield Friday morning to do some repairing on the P. V. Coal company s machinery at Winter Quarters. He returned home Tuesday.

A card party was given at Assistant Superintendent Williams' last Friday night to which only a few were invited A prize was given to the best gentleman and lady players.

WELLINGTON.

Born, to the wife of Peter Liddell, December 20, a fine healthy girl. The same morning the young wife of Brigham Thayn presented him with a little girl also. All parties are doing nicely at present.

Brother Eugene Branch returned home from the south Monday evening, and is glad to be home again.

Glazier and Taylor shipped another car load of hay west this week.

John Blackburn arrived home late last week from Wayne county, where he has been to collect his stock and bring them to this place. He has some fine animals in his herd.

The weather is extremely cold here just now and little work is being done in consequence.

Joseph Birch and Thomas Gale came in on Friday last from the Moab country where they had been with a load of flour which they sold at a fair price. They brought back a little of the wine of that country, and some of the boys having been enjoying a good time since their return.

The health of Mrs George A Wilson, et, has been very poor this winter, and she is confined to her bed just now, but we hope she may soon recover and be around again.

GREENRIVER.

Mrs. Herman Dahling presented her husband with a fine pair of twins, a boy and a girl. All are doing nicely.

Lock and Sanders of Salt Lake crossed 11,000 sheep on Farrer's ferry, Monday

Mr. Gwelin is holding 18,000 sheep in the San Rafael reefs waiting for the river to freeze, which from present appearances will be at an early day. They will cross near the amalgamator.

J. T. Farrer is rapidly putting his coal mine in shape to be a revenue earner. Before spring opens he will have two tunnels from the intersection of which he will continue further developments.

A. P. Mohr, who has so successfully conducted our district school, with the help of some of our liberal people, is preparing an elegant treat for the pupils on Christmas. There will be an exhibition and Christmas tree on Christmas evening, from which every child in the settlement will receive a present.

There will be an all night dance at the school house on Christmas eve.

Joe Fyss was called to Helper last week by the R G W, where he will be employed as machinist.

LOCAL NEWS

G. T. Olsen came in from Emery on Monday with a car of Emery wheat for the market and four or five carloads of cattle which he shipped to the east on Tuesday. Mr. Olsen is one of Emery's live and rustling merchants.

William Wayman, an employe of the Whiterocks agency, passed through Price late last week en route to Salt Lake Mr. Wayman was called to give testimony in the federal court against John Egan, charged with selling whisky to the Indians.

James G. Callaway and Tom Burton will give a ball in the Price town hall Friday evening. Evans Bros' complete orchestra will furnish the music, and McKune and Cotner of the Clarke Hotel will serve refreshments at the hall Callaway and Burton's dances are always a success.

Wm. Burr and Rus. Peterson are taking out of the Neighbor mine, eight miles north of Price, a very fine quality of soft coal. The coal is free from sulphur and contains only 10 per cent ash. The Price blacksmiths use this coal exclusively and it keeps the owners busy to supply the local demand. They have had orders from Provo and the post and by reason of the high transportation charges it is impracticable to ship. The Provo party offered $5 a ton on track at that point. They are now in about 120 feet and the vein is about 5 feet thick.

Early Monday morning while Arthur Birch was riding one of the stage horses to water the horse fell on the ice, catching Arthur's leg and breaking it just above the ankle joint. Dr Richman was called and attended to the injured limb. The doctor stated that only the large bone was broken and that the fracture would probably heal quickly. Although Arthur has been driving the stage for about a year, and the work is known to be arduous, he has been unable, after supporting his family, to lay by a sum for a rain, day and the enforced idleness will work great hardship on himself and family

Eastern Utah Advocate
December 30, 1897

CASTLEGATE.

A very enjoyable Christmas was spent by the people of this place The masquerade ball at the K. of P. Lall on Christmas eve was a grand success The prizes for the best masked characters were taken by Thomas Davis and Carle Halvcrsen, dressed as butterflies and Richard Haycock, dressed as a Catholic priest. The prize waltz took place at 12 o'clock and Reese Lewis and Miss Lizzie Young took the prize given for the best waltzers. The Latter-day Saints gave a dance for the little folks in the ward house Christmas morning, and also treated them to a goodly supply of candy and nuts. A splendid program was rendered in the ward house in the afternoon The American Sunday School Union distributed presents from a Christmas tree to the members of their Sunday school in the morning and gave a dance in the afternoon

Born, to the wife of Charlie Smith, a fine boy. Mother and child are doing nicely. Charlie's face is wreathed in smiles.

Jones' string band was around serenading the people of this town Christmas eve.

Griffith Thomas and Dan Lewis left here last Friday to spend Christmas in Emery county with their families.

T. Phelps, Tom Featherstone and Dave Llewellyn spent Christmas at Scofield.

A large number of our boys attended the masquerade ball at Price Christmas night and returned home Sunday morning

Jones' string band went to Helper Christmas night to play at the ball given in Rooney's hall

The Italians held a dance at the K. of P. hall Christmas night.

The Wasatch Store company gave its customers at Castlegate a nice turkey for Christmas.

A ball was given at the K. of P. hall in honor of the wedding of Joe Cox to Miss Alice Griffiths, who were married on Christmas day. A number of Price young folks attended the dance.

Miss Rosy Bryner of Price was a visitor at Castlegate early in the week.

GREENRIVER.

The school exhibition, followed by a dance on Christmas eve, was a brilliant success. The pupils, under the able training of A. P. Mohr, acquitted themselves creditally, and at the close of the exercises the dance began and lasted until nearly 5 o'clock. Fifty-one couples sat down to an elegant supper shortly after midnight. The music was furnished by Mrs J F. Brown and A. A. Farrer. It was conceded by all to be the most enjoyable entertainment Greenriver has had for many years. Genial J. T. Farrer was master of ceremonies.

R D Smith came in from "Box B" ranch and enjoyed the Christmas festivities with Greenriver friends. Mr. Smith has removed his family from "Box B" ranch to his ranch 9 miles south of Moab. He reports 12 inches of snow on the divide.

The contract has been let to Messrs Smith and Brocks to furnish poles for the proposed new telephone line between Moab and Thompsons. The poles are to be in position by February 20. Mr. Maddy has charge of the construction work.

Mrs J. T. Farrer and her mother, Mrs Larsen of Moab, left on Christmas for Dixie land, where they will visit friends and relatives.

Miss Rena Larsen and her brother Tom came up from Moab and spent the holidays with friends and relatives.

N C Spalding of Payson will ferry 2,500 head of sheep this week and will graze them in the V.

Benjamin Trapp, the 17 year-old son of Mr. and Mrs W. W. Trapp, while repairing an implement, was struck in the eye by a piece of a nail, causing the loss of an eye.

WELLINGTON.

The marriage of Bryan McMullin to Miss Laura Hill was a pleasurable Christmas event. Mr. McMullin gave the usual free dance, which was well attended.

A number of our young folks attended the wedding dance at Price on Monday evening.

A grand ball was given last night for the benefit of the primary department.

Hallis Haladay and Charles Zerley left on Tuesday for the Haladay coal mines.

The health of the people of our little settlement is good.

Price

LOCAL NEWS.

Robert Powell, son of John A. Powell, was married last week to Miss Emma Ingle.

Miss Carrie Boyd of Brock visited Price friends during the Christmas festivities.

Mrs. John M. Deline and her 'amily, of Helper, will remove to Ogden th s week, where they will make their future home.

J. T. McConnell, Vernal s most popular attorney, came in Christmas day and left for Salt Lake.

On Monday Lou Johnson was married to Miss Ida Tucker of Cleveland, Bishop Horsley officiating.

George A. Willson, jr., and George A. Willson, sr , of Wellington, with the'r families, spent Christmas with Mr. and Mrs. John L. Willson.

J. B. Cardell, the popular Castlegate pedagog, and Miss Johnson of Scofield attended the grand masquerade ball at the town hall Christmas night.

John R. Beck, son of ex Indian Agent Beck of Whiterocks, passed through Price early in the week en route to Whiterocks on a visit to his parents.

Abe Powell, son of John Powell, met with quite a painful accident on Tuesday by the explosion of a cartridge. The young fellow was reloading shells when one exploded, bursting the shell. Pieces of the shell badly lacerated the index finger, while his hand was powder burned. Dr. Richman dressed the wound, and no serious results are anticipated.

Hubble Warren was arrested on Monday and pleaded guilty to indecent exposure at the town hall dance on Friday last and was fined $10 and costs by Justice Olsen. The maximum fine for so contemptible an offense is not to exceed $300, but by Warren's whining entreaties to the justice to be easy on him, the justice placed the fine as above, which, to say the least, is very low.

Salt Lake Herald
January 1, 1898

CARBON COUNTY'S WEALTH.

Total Assessment of a Million and a Half.

Price Advocate: Below we give the value of Carbon county's real and personal property, subject to taxes for the year 1897, excepting railroad and property, viz:

23,258 acres, valued at	$ 232,987 00
Improvements	141,289 00
1,075 horses and mules, value	17,918 00
2,699 cattle, value	23,784 00
62,125 sheep, value	93,286 00
291 swine, value	526 00
268 stands of bees, value	362 00
Merchandise and trade fixtures, value	63,131 00
Machinery, tools, imp., etc., value	56,787 00
Money, solvent credits, etc., value	9,619 00
Personal property not otherwise enumerated, value	26,929 00
Total value of personal property	286,882 00

Total value of all property assessed	662,200 00
Total value of taxes assessed	1,475,320 00

There is an increase in acreage over 1896 of 1,065 acres, and an increase of $5,692 in real estate values. Personal property shows an increase in value over last year of $14,162. There is a slight gain in number and value of mules and horses, cattle and swine, and a falling off of over 2,600 head of sheep, representing a value of $4,114, which apparent falling off is accounted for in transitory herds. The total value of personal property shows a gain of over $20,000, and the total amount of taxes assessed shows an increase of over $434,000.

The year for the Pleasant Valley Coal company, working mines at both Castle Gate and Winter Quarters, shows very heavy gains, both as to the number of men working and the product of the mines. The total output of this company's mines for the year will be about 442,000 tons of coal, and 24,000 tons of coke.

CASTLEGATE.

Ed Jones met with a painful accident on Tuesday afternoon in the P. V. Coal company's mine at this place. He was in the act of raising a rail with a spike-bar when a large rock fell, striking him on the hip and back. The injured man was taken to his home, where he was attended by Dr. H. B. Assadoorian. It is thought that the accident will not prove serious.

The miners worked on New Year's day and the day passed off very quietly.

A free dance was given by the Knights of Maccabees last Friday night.

The Knights of Pythias are not to be outdone in the way of free dances and entertainments. They will give a free ball at the K. P. hall next Saturday.

SCOFIELD.

A happy New Year to you, Mr. Editor, and to all your readers.

These have been the most prosperous holiday times the people of Scofield and Winter Quarters have had for many years.

Quite a number of our people went to their homes in the various settlements all over the state to spend the holidays. Those who wished to work could do so as the mines ran both Christmas and New Year's.

Mr. and Mrs. James W. Gatherum had the misfortune to lose their baby boy, 18 months old. He died December 29 and was buried at Provo on the 31st. The parents have the sympathy of the community in their sad bereavement.

A number of Castlegate people spent New Year here.

WELLINGTON.

Bryant McMullin and wife have gone on a visit to Salt Lake and expect to stay a couple of weeks.

The dance on New Year's night was one of the best conducted and most enjoyable of any in the past year, for which we are under obligations to the able manager, R. L. Smith.

Mrs John Blackburn has been very sick for the past week, but at present is slowly recovering.

Some of our people are preparing to put up ice. Now is a good time, as there is plenty of fine ice in the river.

Miss Minerva Ellis spent New Year with her parents and friends.

Skating is fine and the young people are having great sport on the ice.

The Tidwell Canal company held their annual meeting on January 3, and after hearing and accepting the report of the directors for the past year, elected the following officers and directors for the ensuing year: H. P. Hanson, president, R W. Avery, vice-president, George A. Willson, secretary, Lehi Lisson, treasurer, Thomas Zoudle.

The Wellington Canal company failed to hold its meeting on the 3d for lack of a quorum.

A COSTLY WEDDING.

Colorado Couple Married Last Week at Price.

Emery County Pioneer: On Tuesday of last week there occurred at the Clark House, Price, a wedding which was somewhat out of the ordinary. The bride was Mrs. Alice Shinneman of Saw Pit, Colo., and the groom Mr. C. W. King of the same place. The ceremony was performed by Justice Olsen, in the presence of a number of the guests of the hotel, the gentlemanly proprietors, Messrs. Cotner and McKune, and the housekeeper, Mrs. Miller, also gracing the occasion with their presence. It cost the couple $80 in railroad fare to reach Price and return, which, together with their other expenses, made the ceremony cost them about $150. It appears the bride had only recently secured a divorce from her former husband, and, according to the laws of Colorado, she could not marry again within a year. But love laughs at locksmiths and lawmakers, and Utah is not as particular in regard to these matters as her sister state. Therefore, a wedding in Utah usually follows a divorce in Colorado, and the coin of the realm is kept in circulation.

WELLINGTON.

Snow fell to the depth of eight inches on Sunday last and sleighing parties are flying in all directions.

It is reported that Jesse Jessen and Miss Anna Hill were married on Monday, the 10th inst., and skipped directly for Sanpete. Now this is very unfair, as they have enjoyed all the wedding dances for a number of years, and the young people naturally expected that Jesse would give a dance on the occasion of his marriage.

Ed Curtis, the young man who had his fingers taken off by a thresher at Brock last fall, was in town this week and reports his hand almost well again.

The Farnham Canal company will soon begin the construction of their dam. This is the third time the dam has to be rebuilt, and will cost about $150 or $200.

The Wellington Canal company held its annual meeting on Monday. The annual report was read and accepted, and the following officers elected H. D. Allred, president, T Gale, vice-president, Edgar Thayn, secretary. B Thayn, treasurer, and W. A. Thayn.

EMERY.

The holidays were fittingly celebrated here, all participating in a general good time

The ball of the season, a prize ball, was given on New Year's eve. Everything went off nicely. The Misses Zina Williams and Maggie Pettey and Messrs. Thomas Williams and Lewis Edwards took first and second prizes, respectively.

The Johnson and Houtz Dramatic company played here two nights last week, having a full house both evenings It being the first play of the season, the people were very desirous for something in that line Why can't our home dramatists do something?

Professor H. E Giles and Mr. Taylor were welcome guests of our burg the fore part of the week.

Several wagon trains of wheat have left here recently for the eastern markets.

It seems that the recent act of the Emery county commissioners in placing a $10 a month license on pool tables has had the effect of closing Emery's pool hall

George Pettey has returned from looking after the lambs on account of ill health from the effect of an injury sustained by a fall nearly a year ago.

H. C. Pettey, jr, made a trip to Salina with a load of passengers.

A fall of about ten inches of snow occurred during Sunday afternoon and night.

SCOFIELD.

D Trevier was seriously hurt last week in No 1 mine. One of the timbers where he was working fell on him, breaking four of his ribs. Dr. Smith attended the injured man and made him as comfortable as possible. He is now getting along as well as could be expected.

The miners are doing better than last month. So far there has not been so much stoppage on account of storms, lack of cars, etc.

David T. Evans, the Castledale comedian, and his brother Harry came here last week and are now digging dusty diamonds in No 1 mine.

Thomas and William Cox have left the Castlegate mines and are working at Winter Quarters.

S J. Harkness, our new postmaster, is building a new office near the site of the present one The people of Scofield and Winter Quarters have a long way to go for their mail

William Palmer, who was formerly brakeman on the branch, has returned and is again twisting brakes.

John H. Sinister, a former branch conductor, is again on the branch run. His many friends here are pleased to welcome his return

The double line between Soldier's Summit and Clear Creek has been completed, and the R G. W. is now operating seven miles of double track.

Deseret Weekly
January 15, 1898

Scofield, Jan. 4th.—After spending a merry Christmas and a happy New Year, every body is settling down to work again. The mines here are working full time, and the company is being crowded to fill its orders. There are plenty of miners but it is impossible to handle the coal fast enough. Two trains are kept busy in the coal service between the mines and P. V. Junction.

Brakeman Wm. Palmer, who has been away for several months, is again with us. Conductor John H. Simater is also back on this branch again. Times change, and so do we railroaders.

The R. G. W. have completed their double line of railroad between Soldier Summit and Clear Creek, a distance of 7 miles, which is a great improvement, and enables them to handle their great traffic much better as well as making it safer.

Nearly two hundred turkeys were distributed by the Wasatch store company to their patrons at Scofield and Winter Quarters, free.

Brother and Sister James W. Gatherun lost their 13-months-old baby boy last week. The little one was buried at Provo. They have the sympathy of the community in their sad bereavement.   H.

WELLINGTON.

Ward conference was held here on Sunday last. Orange Seeley of the stake presidency attended. After a good and timely sermon, the local church authorities were presented to the people and sustained in their several positions.

An enjoyable time was had at the ward house on Friday last, the occasion being an entertainment gotten up in honor of the birthday of Mat Sumr ns and Miss Minerva Ellis.

The past week has been the coldest of the season.

Putting up ice is a great industry just now.

SCOFIELD.

An accident occurred at Winter Quarters last week by which Willie, the son of Mr. and Mrs. William Ayre, had three fingers of his left hand badly crushed The boy was switching mine cars on the outside of No. 1 mine, and in spragging a loaded car he fell, the wheels passing over his hand. Dr. Smith found it necessary to amputate the fingers at the second joint. The boy is between 14 and 15 years of age. He stood the operation like a little man, and is getting along as well as could be expected.

Mr Trevier, the French hotel keeper, who was hurt in No. 1 mine, as stated in last weeks Advocate, is getting along nicely.

The mines are not so busy as they have been, but they are still doing a good business.

It seems that the great rush for coal is over for the season.

Rathbone lodge No. 9, K. of P. of Scofield, installed officers for the ensuing term as follows. J. Sneddon, C. C.; William Forester, V. C; William Palmer, prelate, Lewis Jones, M. of W.; T. Brown, K. of R. V. S; J. S. Patterson, M of F; J. M. Beattie, M of E; W. C. Rees, M. at A.; T. Edwards, O G; M. Pitman, I. G.

CASTLEGATE.

The wife of Robert Williams, sr., has been quite ill for the last two weeks, but is now on the high road to recovery.

The Johnson & Houtz Dramatic company played "Queen's Evidence" and "Lynwood" Monday and Tuesday nights respectively. A large crowd attended both performances.

A few of Spring Glen's young folks attended the theatre here Monday night.

A free dance was given Saturday night in honor of the wedding of Robert How and.

H. A. Nelson, the genial manager of the Wasatch store, made a business trip to Scofield the latter part of last week.

G. Bickle, R. G. W. car repairer, has been transferred to Helper.

George Ipson was in town last week for the purpose of securing capital to help perfect patent and manufacture his new rotary grain sickle.

A number of Cleveland's young men have been in town looking for work.

Castlegate is experiencing the coldest weather since its settlement.

Last Thursday night all the members of Eagle lodge No. 18, K. of P., attended a meeting for the purpose of instituting and mustering in of a uniform rank. About 80 of the 150 members of the lodge signed the application for a charter. The roll for charter members will be closed on the 26th inst., when all officers will be elected. There exists quite a rivalry for the position of captain. B. F. Caffey now leads the van for the honors.

GREENRIVER.

The ice in the river is about twelve inches thick; there is about ten inches of snow, and the thermometer is constantly in the neighborhood of zero.

While crossing the river on the ice recently Chris Anderson had a narrow escape from drowning. When some way out from land the ice under him gave way, dropping him into the icy water. He threw out his hands and caught the edges of the ice, and a battle for life followed. For fifty feet he broke the ice in an attempt to get out, finally he found ice sufficiently strong to bear his weight, when he crawled out. Drenched to the skin and almost exhausted, he made his way to his cabin, a mile distant, where he found warmth and a change of raiment.

All available teams are busily engaged hauling coal from J. T. Farrer's mine.

John R. Thompson and W. E. Cassiday have secured a five-year lease on the "Box B" ranch from Wheeler and Company.

Matt Hartman and several other Greenriver citizens visited Lower Crossing recently and engaged in one of the old time dances for which that place is noted.

Amasa Larsen and his sister Rena returned to their home in Moab on Saturday, after a pleasant visit with Greenriver friends and relatives.

Ben Trapp has returned from Salt Lake, where he had his injured eye taken out.

EMERY.

- A light fall of snow occurred on Saturday evening

- The weather is cold, making it exceedingly pleasant to stay close around the fire.

Two coal mines are in operation here, making fuel cheap as well as plentiful Coal is delivered at $2 a ton.

Professor H E Giles, Mr. Taylor and Mr. Stewart have been with us a couple of evenings, and enjoyable times were had at U. T. Olsen's on Saturday evening and at George Mortensen's. They are good entertainers and all enjoyed their hospitality.

Professor Giles and Mr. Taylor departed for Salina Monday, and Mr Stewart goes north in the interest of the International Book company.

G. T. Olsen is confined to his house with rheumatism.

The Y. M. M. I A. gave a ball Tuesday evening, which was an enjoyable affair.

Born, to the wife of Newel Beal, a son. All are getting along nicely.

WELLINGTON.

Bishop McMullin and his council went out to Nine Mile on Saturday for the purpose of establishing church organizations at that place A meeting was held at Brother Charles Smith's place on Sunday, and the following business was attended to (1) The organization of a branch of the Church of Jesus Christ of Latter day Saints, with Brother Charles Smith as presiding elder and the necessary council, (2) organization of a relief society, with appropriate officers, (3) organization of a Sunday school, with necessary officers. After a very enthusiastic meeting, in which the spirit of the Lord was felt to be present, the meeting was dismissed and left in the hands of the local officers of the several organizations.

Bishop McMullin and party report having a very cold and difficult trip The snow is about 18 inches deep in the Park and drifted pretty badly

On Saturday last Jesse Jessen and wife arrived home from their visit to Sanpete, and we expect that Jesse will now give the young folks a dance in consequence of his having been permitted to pluck one of the fair flowers of the place for a wife We wish them both much pleasure and a houseful of little joys

Born, to the wife of Ephraim Dimmick, a fine daughter, on Monday morning, 24th inst. Mother and child all right.

We understand that the county commissioners have removed John C. Vance to the Clarke hotel at Price, to be cared for at the expense of the county. This is a proceeding that should be looked after, as he is amply able to pay his own way.

CASTLEGATE

H. A. Nelson, the genial manager of the Wasatch Store company, left here Thursday morning for Scofield, where he was to meet E. L. Carpenter, P. V. Coal company's paymaster. After paying the miners at Scofield they returned to Castlegate and paid off the men Saturday evening

A large number of peddlers from Emery county were here last week until after pay-day to take in some of the miners' earnings.

Ephraim Davis returned home from Cleveland Friday evening Mr. Davis has been making some improvements on his farm at Cleveland and contemplates moving his family there in the spring

Superintendent W. G. Sharp was a visitor at Castlegate the first of the week.

Born, to the wife of John Jones, a bouncing baby boy. Mother and child getting along nicely.

Castlegate is experiencing some of the coldest weather she has had for a long time.

Ed Jones, who was injured a few weeks ago, is now able to get around and will soon be at work again.

A miner named Farizo was severely injured on Tuesday by a mass of coal falling on him. He was removed from beneath the coal and taken to his home, where Dr. Asadoorian attended his injuries, which consisted of a bad cut on his head and many bruises on his body.

Mrs. John Williams of Cleveland passed through this place on Tuesday en route to Spanish Fork, where she was called by the serious illness of a brother

Charles Johnson, the R. G. W. conductor, met with a painful accident while switching in the yards on Monday by severely straining his back He will have to lay off a few days.

SCOFIELD.

We have been having extremely cold weather of late, the mercury having gone to 40 below. The snowfall has been light so far this winter hereabouts.

The Johnson-Houx Dramatic company has had a good harvest here during the past week. They played at Scofield four nights and at Winter Quarters two nights They left Wednesday for their homes, where they will take a few days rest and then strike out again The people here as a rule were well pleased.

A home dramatic company is being organized at Winter Quarters Bolding ton Lewis, William E Hagford and others are the promoters.

Times have been quite lively since pay day. Great guns, little pistols, knives and razors were flourished, but fortunately no one was hurt Some of the boys are to be called to account for disturbing the peace The officers have resolved that hereafter no such thing shall be allowed, and any person found carrying concealed weapons will be prosecuted to the full extent of the law.

Winter Quarters News.

Special correspondence to the "News."

Scofield, Jan. 28th, 1898.—Four accidents have occurred at No. 1 mine, Winter Quarters, this month. The first two were H. Trevier, with four ribs broken, and Willie Ayre, three fingers crushed, as stated in the "News." Last Tuesday a Finlander had a leg broken and was taken to the hospital; and today James Neilson was the unfortunate being taken out of the mine in a very critical condition. Doctor Smith did not make a thorough examination, as he thought it best to send him to the hospital at once. It is thought that one leg is broken near the hip. The patient was taken on a special train this evening. Brother Neilson is from Richfield, where he has a large family. Most of the accidents are caused by bad roof in the mine. As the coal is taken out, the rock becomes broken and is very dangerous.

The district school at Winter Quarters closed today with an entertainment. The children were treated to nuts and candy, and a dance, given by the trustees and the teachers. The closing is only temporary and school will be taken up again about April 1st. This is a wise plan, as these two months of vacation are the ones in which we have the most inclement weather.

Wm. H. Griffin will return with his bride to his home in Cache Junction, and Miss Hannah S. Johnson, the assistant teacher, to her home in Provo. Both teachers have become very popular with the people as well as the children of Winter Quarters.

Mr. John Hood gave an entertainment with the children of Scofield on Friday night in the school house, entitled King Winter.   H.

LOCAL NEWS.

Ripans Tabules cure dyspepsia.

Wheat at Chicago, yesterday, $1

P. H. Murphy of Manti was registered at the Mathis hotel on Monday.

W. Hammond and Marcus Lambert of Moab were Price visitors Sunday.

Charles James of American Fork was a Mathis house guest on Friday last.

E. D. Cooley and Henry Thompson of Ferron were Price visitors yesterday

A. D. Ferron, the surveyor, was a guest of the Hotel Clarke on Friday last

William McGuire, the butcher, will hereafter have fresh fish on Friday of each week.

Commissioner Edgar Thayn was up from Wellington on Monday transacting county business.

St. V LeSieor came in from his gilsonite property on Monday and left for his home in Provo.

Don't forget that Friday is the day our fresh fish arrives. Emery County Mercantile company.

There will be a dance at the town hall on Friday evening, February 11. Good music will be in attendance

Night Operator Peyton has taken a vacation and O. H. Kafton, recently from the Northern Pacific, is relief operator.

G. W. Kone, wife and little son came in from Lamy, N. M , on Monday and took Tuesday's stage for Vernal, where they will visit relatives.

The finest lot of English white figured and decorated semi porcelain ware just in. Come and examine the goods. Emery County Mercantile company.

Springville Independent: D. R. Beebe, recently manager of the Mammoth Mercantile company, has assumed the management of the Smoot Lumber company at Provo.

Mrs. Amanda G. Rollo of Cedar City died at her home Saturday last. She was the mother of Stenographer Rollo, who last year visited Price with Judge McCarty.

George Bodle, who has for some time been employed by the R. G. W., as freight conductor, has taken a lay off and is spending the vacation with his family in Price.

Harry L. Bartlett of Cherryfield, Me., representing J. C. Ayer & Son, Lowell, Mass., one of the best proprietary medicine manufacturers in the country, was a Price visitor late last week.

As appears elsewhere in this print, bids for the construction of a wagon bridge across the Price river at Castle gate will be opened on February 19, at 10 a. m., at the court house, Price.

W. Fred Culmer came in from the Salt Lake Gilsonite company's mine on Saturday and left for Salt Lake. Rumor has it that Mr. Culmer's visit to Zion is for the purpose of taking unto himself a wife.

P. H. Nienkamp, editor of the Washington, Mo., Journal, was a Price visitor on Sunday. Mr. Nienkamp is looking for a location and was on his way to Emery county with a view to the establishment of a paper at Castledale, but learning that one had already been started there, changed his plans and will look elsewhere. The gentleman is seeking a change with the hope that his and his wife's health will be improved.

W. C. Patrick, with the L. C. M. I, made a trip through Emery in the interest of that popular mercantile institution.

Late last week County Clerk Donaldson issued a marriage license to William L Miller, aged 19, and Bertha Ellen Jones, aged 14, both of Helper. Justice Olsen performed the marriage ceremony

On Saturday the supreme court granted the motion to advance the case of Lars Thompson vs the state of Utah, and set February 21 for the hearing Senator Rawlins made the motion for Thompson's attorney

J C Weeter of Park City is in Price today looking for a business location. Mr. Weeter has interested with him a number of Salt Lake gentlemen who appear to appreciate the fact that Price will be the town of eastern Utah

Salina Press: The young lady we used to know as May Whiting writes us that her new name is Mrs. T. M Milligan, Milligan is a young Danishman and a brakeman on the Rio Grande Western He and his wife will make their home in Salt Lake City

Herald: James Neilsen, the Scofield miner who was severely injured in a coal mine accident a few days ago, is lying at St. Mark's hospital in a very precarious condition. It is impossible yet to predict with any degree of certainty what the outcome will be.

Herald: Preston Nuttar, one of the leading cattle men of the state, is registered at the Cullen, from Clear Creek. Mr. Nuttar is wintering about 8,000 head of cattle on the reservation at the forks of the Duchesne and near the mouth of the Strawberry, and he states that they were doing well and that he had suffered but little loss on account of the recent cold snap

An item in our Wellington correspondence last week stated that J C. Vance, who is being cared for at the expense of the county, was amply able to take care of himself. On investigating we learn that what little property the man has is tied up in a divorce proceeding and that he is unable physically to do manual labor. Hence he must have help or suffer for the bare necessaries. We make this statement in behalf of the commissioners, who are endeavoring to perform their duties.

CASTLEGATE.

The outlook for work is good, and the boys are pleased

No 6 hoist has been moved in the mine, and the output has greatly increased the past few days

W G. Sharp, our popular superintendent, paid the camp a visit on Saturday and also visited the Winter Quarters mine before his return to Salt Lake.

Mrs. McMillan's musical entertainment was a very creditable one and is much talked of by our people. She is deserving of much commendation for painstaking work among her pupils.

Three cars broke loose from the trip in main entry a few days ago and kicked up quite a bit of dust Fortunately no one was injured, but L. Tyler, who was working near the incline when the cars shot past, was so frightened that he threw up the sponge. He has moved his working place away from the incline.

WELLINGTON.

Several of the old Indian war veterans from this place will be in attendance at the reunion to be held in Huntington the last of this week, and our best wishes will go with them, as it was largely through their efforts that it was made possible to settle this beautiful country. May they enjoy themselves to their heart's content.

The church goers of this place were well paid for their attendance last Sunday by an excellent sermon on the first principles of the gospel, by a visiting brother from Spring Glen—namely, Teancum Pratt.

A theatre troupe from Spring Glen will play here Saturday night, Feb 5

On Wednesday morning, January 26, the wife of William Curtis presented him with a bouncing baby girl, and, although the weather is very cold for such tender emigrants, we are pleased to say all parties are doing well.

We are pleased to hear at this writing that old father William Faucett of this place is a little better and, for almost the first time in weeks, is resting easily. He has been affected with a severe pain in the left side, and has been in a helpless condition for the last four or five weeks.

The general health of this place is good, no contagious disease having appeared so far this winter, for which we are very thankful.

The snow is about eight inches deep on the level, and the air has been cold for this country. Stockmen report cattle on the range as holding their own very well, so far.

H. C. Smith, agent for the Pioneer Nurseries company, has been canvassing our town and done fairly well. Our wide-awake people believe in getting an orchard started as soon as possible.

GREENRIVER.

Colonel George W. Durant and Frank Spicer will begin at once extensive improvements on their pumping plant, and will double their acreage of last year.

Mr. Darlington has returned from Raton, N. M., and is making his headquarters at Joseph Gammage's.

Joseph Gammage was taken suddenly ill on Saturday evening, but his strong constitution will undoubtedly wear out the disease, as it has in the many similar battles of his 72 years.

The owners of 90,000 sheep and 10,000 cattle say that a bridge across the Green river at this place will be a problem for the next legislature to solve.

At Little Grand wash, 15 miles south east of Greenriver, there is great need of a bridge. The bad condition of this place spoils the good road from Castledale to Moab. The many broken pieces of wagons are silent witnesses to the loss of the teamster and probable wrath he expressed toward the county officers.

Of the sheep that have entered Grand county during the last four months, Goodman & Green have 7,000, Mr. Gordon 6,000, Mr. Saunders 13,500, N.

C. Spaulding 2,500, Goslin & Co. 18 000 Taylor, Pace & Rockhill 9 000, E. J Nash 5,000, making in all 56,000, which, added to the sheep owned by Grand county residents, will swell the number to nearly 85,000

A P Mohr has been retained by the school trustees to complete the school term County Superintendent Scott was well pleased with his work.

Our merchant, J T Farrer, says business is improving, but thinks he made a mistake when he purchased ice from the R. G. W.

It looks now as though ice will be in the river all the summer, as Mr. Atkinson is cutting 28 inch ice below the canal dam

Mrs. M E. Peysert left for Salt Lake on Monday.

All the sports of Greenriver have home-made cutters, and are enjoying themselves with their best girls.

Commissioner Brown has filled his ice-house with 15 inch ice of excellent quality.

William Foy left on Saturday for a short visit to Moab.

By reason of the Chinamen celebrating their New Year, Section Foreman Gibson now makes daily trips over the line with his velocipede.

Frank Spicer has returned from Cisco, where he was employed by the R. G. W.

The weather has, to the great delight of sheepmen, moderated, and the thermometer now ranges from 30 to 40 degrees above zero. The snow is rapidly settling, which exposes the feed, and it is now thought that the danger which recently threatened the sheep is passed

Work on the telephone line from Moab to Thompsons is progressing rapidly The line is completed beyond Court House, and ten days more will see it almost finished.

Juror List For 1899.

Following are the jurors selected by the jury commissioners, Messrs. Ingles and Taylor, to serve in the Seventh judicial district court for Carbon county during the year 1899, viz

WINTER QUARTERS

Daniel Pittman,	J. M. Loveridge,
John Pittman,	B K Lewis,
Lewis Jones,	Andrew Gibert,
Samuel Harrison,	J. W. Kisel.
John P. Johnson,	

SCOFIELD.

James S. Robertson,	Wm C. Burrows,
N L McLean,	Thomas Jenkins,
John Webber,	Henry Wilson,
David Burns,	John Hool,
William Murphy,	William Ramsey,
Robert Bishop,	S. A Henrichsen

CASTLEGATE.

W. K. Ingles,	William Lund,
Thomas Cox, sr,	B. F Caffey,
Andrew Young, sr,	John Forrester,
Wm Fetherstone,	Wm. S Jones,
John Holly,	Henry Wade,
John Horn,	Eugene Santschi,
Michael Beveridge,	Allen Cox.
James A. Harrison,	

HELPER

Thomas Rhoades,	John U Bryner,
P A. Smith,	Edwin T Jones.
James Hansen,	

SPRING GLEN.

H J. Stowell,	C H Cook,
E. D Fulmer,	John T. Rowley,
L. H Ewell,	George M. Perkins
Joshua Wireman,	

PRICE.

Lars Frandsen,	Herman C. Bryner,
Seren Olsen,	A W Horsley,
H G Mathis,	E W McIntire,
C. H Empey,	R. G Miller,
George Fausett,	Jacob Kofford,
L. A. Warren,	I. D Lytmall,
Thomas Fitzgerald,	George W McCall,
Chris Peterson,	George Robb

MINNIE MAUD.

E L Harmon,	G C Johnston.
A. J. Russell,	

WELLINGTON

Thomas Gale,	R A. Snyder,
Alvin Thayn,	Joseph S. Birch,
Lehi Jensen,	E E. Branch,
W. A Fausett, jr,	Frank Tidwell.

LIST OF PETIT JURORS

For January Term of the District Court to sit February 14

Below are the names of petit jurors selected to serve at the January term of the district court, which will convene at Price on Monday morning, February 14

Winter Quarters—Daniel Pittman, John P. Johnson.

Spring Glen—John T Rawley, C. H Cook Joshua Wiseman

Scofield—Robert Bishop, Wm C. Borrows, Thomas Jenkins, James B, Roberts, David Burns, William Murphy.

Castlegate—D..F. Caffey, John Forrester, Eugene Santschi, William S, Jones

Price—Thomas Fitzgerald, George Fausett, George W. McCall.

Minnie Maud—G. C. Johnston, E L. Harmon. A. J. Russell

Wellington—E. E. Branch, Frank Tidwell.

Helper—P. A. Smith.

Eastern Utah Advocate
February 10, 1898

CASTLEGATE

The outlook for work is good, and the boys are pleased

No 6 hoist has been moved in the mine, and the output has greatly increased the past few days.

W G. Sharp, our popular superintendent, paid the camp a visit on Saturday and also visited the Winter Quarters mine before his return to Salt Lake.

Mrs McMillan's musical entertainment was a very creditable one and is much talked of by our people. She is deserving of much commendation for painstaking work among her pupils.

Three cars broke loose from the trip in main entry a few days ago and kicked up quite a bit of dust. Fortunately no one was injured, but L. Tyler, who was working near the incline when the cars shot past, was so frightened that he threw up the sponge. He has moved his working place away from the incline.

GREENRIVER.

Colonel George W. Durant and Ike Spicer will begin at once extensive improvements on their pumping plant, will double their acreage of last year

Mr. Darlington has returned from Raton, N. M , and is making his headquarters at Joseph Gammage's

Joseph Gammage was taken suddenly ill on Saturday evening but his strong constitution will undoubtedly wear off the disease, as it has in the many similar battles of his 72 years.

The owners of 90,000 sheep and 10,000 cattle say that a bridge across the Green river at this place will be a problem for the next legislature to solve.

At Little Grand wash, 15 miles south east of Greenriver, there is great need of a bridge. The bad condition of this place spoils the good road from Castledale to Moab. The many broken pieces of wagons are silent witnesses to the loss of the teamster and probable wrath expressed toward the county officers.

WELLINGTON.

Several of the old Indian war veterans from this place will in attendance at the reunion to be held in Huntington the last of this week, and our best wishes will go with them, as it was largely through their efforts that it was made possible to settle this beautiful country. May they enjoy themselves to their heart's content.

The church goers of this place were well paid for their attendance last Sunday by an excellent sermon the first principles of the gospel, by a visiting brother from Spring Glen—namely, Teancum Pratt.

A theatre troupe from Spring Glen will play here Saturday night Feb. 5

On Wednesday morning, January 26, the wife of William Curt presented him with a bouncing baby girl, and, although the weather is very cold for such tender emigrants, we are pleased to say all parties are doing well

We are pleased to hear at the writing that old father William Feuct of this place is a little better and, for most the first time in weeks, is resting easily. He has been affected with a sore pain in the left side, and has been a helpless condition for the last four or five weeks.

The general health of this place is good, no contagious disease being appeared so far this winter, for which we are very thankful.

The snow is about eight inch deep on the level, and the air has been cold for this country. Stockmen report little on the range as holding their own very well, so far.

H. C. Smith, agent for the Pheer Nurseries company, has been canvasing our town and done fairly well Our wide-awake people believe in getting an orchard started as soon as possible.

Eastern Utah Advocate
February 17, 1898

EMERY STAKE CONFERENCE

TWO DAYS' INTERESTING SESSION HELD AT ORANGEVILLE.

The Different Organizations Are in a Thriving Condition—Good Increase in Membership—Extended Report of the Proceedings.

The quarterly conference of the Emery stake convened at Orangeville, Saturday and Sunday, February 5 and 6 A goodly number from both north and south was in attendance. The weather was clear and cold

All wards were represented, with the exception of Castlegate, Spring Glen and Price.

The stake and local officers of the different organizations were present and reported on the condition of their respective fields of labor. Orangeville choir, under the management of its able and energetic leader, Alma G Jewkes, made the meetings interesting by its excellent music. The hospitality of the wives and mothers of Orangeville made every visitor glad and comfortable, and there were enough loaves and fishes left for another two days' gathering of a similar kind.

President C. G. Larson and his two counselors, Orange Seely and William Howard, were on the stand, as were also many of the bishops and other officers of the stake.

President Larsen called the conference to order at 10 o'clock, when the choir sang on page 766.

Prayer was offered by Andrew Van Buren.

Singing by the choir, page 291

The president welcomed the Saints and was happy to see so many old people present, notwithstanding the very cold weather. Many of the Saints were, no doubt, disappointed by reason of the non attendance of the apostles, which was due to engagements at other points. The president stated that it had previously been announced at the quarterly conference at Price that hereafter the stakes should not look for apostles at their conferences, as other duties would keep them employed much of the time. The bishops for their wards and presidency for the stakes should look after their own affairs and settle their own difficulties, if any arose. As for himself, he had not, neither by word or action, wished to hurt any one since last he met the people in conference The stake counselors and himself were in full accord in all work pertaining to the welfare of the Saints in the stake. God is at the helm of the ship Zion, and he will take care of his own work, and will raise up men who will be equal to the occasion. The Lord's name will be honored and his purposes filled to the utmost.

Since last conference the stake presidency had visited the wards in half of the stake and found things in fair condition. The missionary committee at headquarters had sent in a demand for fifteen missionaries from this stake and the names had been selected by the several bishops and will be forwarded to Salt Lake. The president counseled the young elders to be prepared when the call came to at once take up their work and not ask for six months in which to prepare for the same

Counselor Orange Seely was the next speaker. He heartily endorsed what had been said, and hoped everyone present would be benefited by it He rejoiced over the changed condition of things among the people Only a few years ago some of our brethren were hunted, persecuted and prosecuted, and the leaders of the church were compelled to hide and to go into exile Some of them died in exile and some returned after many years of hardship and suffering. Under the present happy conditions no one need fear, and they could enjoy the society of friends and loved ones. For this we owe gratitude to Him who rules on high. The young men and women should make every possible effort toward acquiring an education No reasonable excuse could now be given for failure. The rough foundation for our Zion has been laid deep and solid and a structure of learning and intelligence has been reared upon it and the young men and women are invited and urged to enter its portals ,

Counselor William Howard said we have the principals of salvation with us and if we live up to them we cannot help but be blessed. We are different in our church organization to that of all other denominations. We invite the whole people to our conference Many of the creeds of today are counseled and governed through the priests' and preachers' meetings and the members have little to say. They must accept conditions as they find them. In this church the governing priesthood lays all matters before the people at public gatherings called conferences, and are there made acquainted with the plans and can reject or accept them as they choose. In this manner the people become co-partners in and responsible for the results. The success of this mode of organization and government is visible all through our church.

The Lord has blessed Castle valley this winter with a good depth of snow, and the wise and prudent farmer will have no time to loiter away. He should now prepare his seed grain and repair his farming tools, so that he may be ready to put the seeds in the ground as soon as the conditions will permit. We can then be prepared to answer the call on our time and talents to promulgate the truth with better results and greater personal satisfaction

Bishop Jasper Robertson of Orangeville gave a report of his ward, and it was gratifying to hear that the people were united and that all organizations were filling their mission satisfactorily in the ward There was no sickness of any alarming nature, and no widows or fatherless children suffered for lack of food, clothing or shelter.

Meeting adjourned by singing on page 66

Benediction by Peter R. Pedersen

THE AFTERNOON SESSION
was called to order at 2 o'clock

Singing, 'Joy to the World"

Prayer by Peter Frandsen.

Singing, on page 216

The following bishops reported the condition of their wards A Nelsen, Ferron Frank B Reynolds Castledale Counselor Dan C Woolward, Huntington, Counselor L B Reynolds, Lawrence, A E McMullin, Wellington These brethren reported their various wards in most instances in good condition. Bishop McMullin reported that a branch had been organized in the Wellington ward, called Nine Mile branch, with Charles L Smith as presiding elder A Sabbath school was also organized there.

William Taylor, senior, president of the high priests in the stake, gave a very good report of that quorum He dwelt a short time upon the changes which had been wrought in the nineteen winters he had lived in Castle valley and said that Apostle Erastus Snow's dedicatory prayer at the first meeting at Ferron had been followed by abundant blessings

Peter R. Petersen reported the 81st Quorum of Seventies and said everything was favorable, but recommended the moving of several old members to the high priests.

Joseph E Johnson reported the 81st Quorum of Seventies, with headquarters at Huntington, as doing good work in interesting and instructive meetings, and that there are now three missionaries in the field from that quorum

Brother Johnson and his counselor, D C. Woodward, reported the Young Men's Improvement association in a thriving condition The Improvement Era the Y. M. magazine, was highly recommended by Mr Johnson to the young men and also to the families, as it treated subjects of much interest to the Saints in general He laid especial weight upon the importance of honoring old age, which the light minded and thoughtless young man and maiden so often overlook.

Alexander Jameson, superintendent of Sabbath schools and religious class work reported progress in these organizations. Two Sunday schools, Greenriver and Helper, have been discontinued on account of lack of population and interest in the cause He urged upon the superintendents the necessity of furnishing a true and correct report of their respective schools.

Religious class work was yet in its infancy and had not met with that interest and success for which it was intended, but most of the wards have made a fair start, and Mr. Jameson urged the parents, bishops and instructors to pool interests and efforts in its development.

Conference adjourned by singing on page 61.

Benediction by George A. Willson

SUNDAY MORNING
Meeting called to order at 10.30 o'clock

Choir sang on page 417.

Prayer by Albert Collar

Choir sang on page 67

The next speaker was the old blind Father Jewkes, who was led to the stand. He testified to the goodness of

God to him and the truth of the everlasting principles revealed to Joseph Smith. Although he was nearly blind and very feeble, he was always glad to meet with the Saints in their gatherings.

The next speaker was old Father Noah T. Guymon. He had been identified with the church as far back as 1836, when his father, by a very queer incident, happened to get acquainted with some Mormons, of whom there were only a few at that early date. The speaker had been Joseph Smith's bodyguard and related many interesting happenings from the prophet's remarkable life and work. He had been associated with him under circumstances of both joy and sorrow, and had never met a mortal in whom he found so much true manhood and so great perfection. He was present when Joseph was taken prisoner by Colonel Hinkly, and he had to lay down his firearms with the rest of the company of militia to which he belonged. He felt the end of his earthly career was approaching, but he was always glad for having been faithful to the Priesthood of God and for the many occasions granted him to help along in its defense.

Meeting adjourned by singing an anthem.

Benediction by John Petersen.

AFTERNOON SESSION.

Meeting called to order at 1 30 o'clock, and choir sang on page 64.

Prayer by Andrew Anderson.

Singing on page 44.

The sacrament was administered, after which the general and stake authorities were presented and unanimously sustained.

Christopher Wilcock of Huntington was the first speaker. He has only lately returned from a mission to England, and related several of his experiences. He

admonished the young men to use well their time in reading and informing themselves on the principles of our religion so that when called to the missionary field they may be prepared to present the gospel and church doctrines ably and forcefully.

The next speaker was David Prior superintendent of the Huntington seminary, who reviewed God's work among the different nations, from the birth of Christ until Joseph Smith's declaration in 1830 that the Church of Jesus Christ was organized to be no more broken down.

Alexander Jameson made a few additional remarks regarding religious class work, and said that where the bishops themselves could not superintend the work, they were at liberty to appoint some one else under their supervision.

President Larsen made the closing remarks, and urged upon the Saints to be charitable in their feelings towards the erring ones, and to foster a spirit of peace in our midst, and if any controversy arose to try and settle it among themselves without troubling the Priesthood. He charged the bishops in all the ward to not accept of any complaints for investigation before the parties concerned had done all that the law of God requires. He lifted his voice in warning to young and old against the saloons and pool tables, as that vice is greatly increasing in our midst, and if persevered in, destruction, unhappiness and death are sure to follow.

The conference adjourned for three months, when it will meet at Ferron.

Choir sang an anthem.

Benediction by O J. Anderson.

SCOFIELD.

The weather has been very pleasant in our valley the past week.

The Winter Quarters mines are still working quite briskly.

Recently a loaded box car ran away from the chute to the switch on the main track and turned on its side, a total wreck. It was caused by a broken chain Fortunately no one was hurt, but the man on the car was pretty badly frightened.

The latest news from the hospital of the miner Neilson, who was injured in No 1 mine some time ago, is that he is rapidly improving

Several of our citizens contemplate a trip to the Klondike gold fields in the near future

Mrs. J. M Loveridge of Winter Quarters gave birth to a fine son Mother and baby are doing nicely, and papa— well, he's away up now.

The local Knights of Pythias will give an entertainment on February 19 to celebrate the 35th anniversary of the birth of the order.

GREENRIVER.

A snow fall of about five inches occurred here last week. On the desert east the snow is about 12 inches deep John F. Brown says the ice is 20 inches thick in front of his residence. The weather is moderating rapidly.

Harry Howland and wife returned from Denver last week, where they have for some time past been visiting Dr Howland

Uncle John Rockbill and E Nash came in last week from their herds, ten miles southeast of this place, and report the sheep as doing well.

B. W Valentine has a crew of men putting in three piers to protect his land from being cut away by the high waters which will soon be here.

Sleighing parties are numerous and all are enjoying the new born climate, with no regrets for the departure of the Italian.

Commissioner Brown left on Sunday for Moab, where he will attend a session of the county court.

James Stark of Moab, assessor for Grand county, was calling on the citizens of the west end of the county last week in regard to tax matters. He was accompanied by Carlos Wilcox, who acted as guide to Mr. Stark, this being the latter's first visit to this part of the county.

E. J. Nash is in from his sheep camp, and reports the herds doing well, although the snow is heavily crusted.

R Pace, foreman for Goslin & Co, is in town and says the sheep are doing all right They are now ranging between Box B ranch and Ten Mile.

William Liddell, driver for Goslin & Co., went out Monday with a load of provisions for their supply camp.

T L Fuller and E O Day of Lawrence came in Sunday to work for Goslin & Co.

John Rockbill is visiting his home in Spanish Fork.

The "bal masque" given by the boys of this place on the 14th, St. Valentine's eve, was a marked success. The hall was crowded with merry makers There was the usual array of clowns, kings, queens friars and monks. At 1 o'clock a. m. an elegant supper was served by Mrs R P Johnson at her residence. After supper dancing was resumed, a program of 16 numbers being gone through, and it was daylight before the last was finished. The dance was pronounced the finest of the season. Music by the popular Greenriver orchestra.

The new dog tax law which goes into effect in Grand county this spring is causing considerable comment among sheep men and others, although there don't seem to be any disposition to try and evade it

WELLINGTON.

Two deaths occurred in our settlement this week—that of William J. Fawcett, sr., who died at 10 o'clock Sunday morning, and that of Mrs Allred, widow of the late Green Allred, who passed away, after a short illness, on Monday morning about 1 a m. Both are aged people and we e respecte l by all who knew them, and their families have the sympathy of the entire community. Father Fawcett came with his family to this valley in its early settlement and located in Clark's valley, where they lived until two years ago, since which time they have resided in this town. Mother Allred's family also came here in the early days and settled near Price, where they lived until the last few years, when they moved to Wellington.

The snow is beginning to disappear, and it looks as though the hardest part of winter was over.

We did not realize the place gained in the homes of the people by The Advocate until last week s issue failed to arrive on time. The numerous inquiries as to what was the matter showed the esteem in which it is held by its readers.

BLACKHAWK WAR VETERANS

Held a Pleasant Reunion at Huntington. List of Names on the Roll.

The reunion of the Blackhawk war veterans, held at Huntington on February 3 and 4 was a rousing success and everybody enjoyed themselves The first meeting was opened by the singing of America." Prayer by J F Wakefield, sr Speech of welcome by William Howard, responded to by Jasper Robertson of Orangeville The balance of the meeting was taken up by speeches, songs, recitations and dances.

At 7 p m the meeting was continued with dancing, songs, speeches, etc, until 2 p m

On the 4th, at 10 a. m the veterans again assembled J K Reid of Orangeville read a short history of the Black hawk war from the ninth volume of the Contributor Then an organization for the counties of Carbon and Emery was perfected, as follows M E Johnson, captain Albert Collard secretary, and a lieutenant from each town, as follows F M Ewell, Spring Glen, George Franden, Price A E McMullin, Wellington, Henry Oviatt, Cleveland, Alma Staker, Lawrence; Orange Seely, Castle dale, J K. Reid, Orangeville, John Hitchcock, Ferron, L. S. Beach, Molen, Thomas Williams, Emery

In the afternoon the public were invited to meet with the veterans in the large brick meeting house, and a large crowd assembled One pleasing feature of the occasion was that the teachers of the district schools and the principal of the Huntington seminary marched their pupils into the house and took seats assigned to them William Howard had all the veterans sign a roll, and he presented each one with a neat badge, on which was inscribed:

"BLACKHAWK WAR VETERAN,
Huntington, Feb. 3-4, 1898"

Those who were ten years old and over at the time of the war and who took part in guarding, herding stock or helping in the defense of their fathers' homes or property were allowed to sign the roll All ladies who took part or are the wives of veterans were also permitted to sign. The committee, out of the proceeds of a unique voting contest, bought ribbon, out of which Brother Howard made badges and presented one to each lady on the roll

Altogether it was a very pleasant time and we all look forward to another reunion, which we hope will be in the summer time, when more people can atten1

Following are the names on the roll

Emery—Heber C Petty, T. A Williams, John Williams, Mrs Eunice Petty Stena Williams.

Ferron—John Hitchcock, J. S. Stevens, Frederick Olsen, Ezra Funk, Mesdames A M Stevens, Mary A Funk, Deatha Stringham, Jane Williams.

Molen—Hans Hansen, L. S. Beach, Seth Wareham, Joseph Callwell

Orangeville—T F Housekeeper, Robert Johnson, A C Van Buren, J K Reid, Jasper Robertson, Edwin M. Cox, James S. Killian. Mesdames Lavina Van Buren Rachel Killian, Jane R. Cox, Anna Johnson, Lizabeth Reid, Rhoda Ella Robertson

Castledale—John Petersen, Jane O. Petersen.

Huntington—Albert Collard A P Johnson, A L Sherman, M E. Johnson, J F Wakefield, Peter Johnson, T. G. Wakefield, Joseph B. Meeks, D H Leonard, R Gordon, J. E. Johnson, Samuel Rowley, Thomas B Wright, Joseph Hunt, Leander Lemmon, E E. Dodge, H S. Loveless, W. A Guymon, William Howard, Mesdames Mary J

Woodward, Mary J Wright, Esther Grange, Louisa Dodge, May C. Sherman M J Wakefield, E J Loveless, Lybea Collard, Julia Wakefield, Sophia Wall, Margaret Guymon, Adelia Mackleprang, Anne Rowley. Julia S McKee, Hannah E. Johnsen, Effie Nixon Elizabeth Leonard, Catherine R. Blackburn, Bessie Johnsen, Eliza Howard

Lawrence—W. A Staker, Andrew Mortensen Abraham N. Day, Alma Staker, Elizabeth Staker

Wellington—George A. Wilson, John Blackburn, A E. McMullin, Thomas Zundell, Jefferson Tidwell, Wm. J Hill, June Blackburn, Sanch Tidwell, Ephraim Dimmic.

Cleveland—Lewis Larsen, H H. Oviatt, L P Overson, H H Oviatt, jr, Mesdames Louisa Overson, Sally R Oviatt C A Oviatt

LOCAL NEWS.

A valentine ball will be given at the town hall on Washington's birthday, February 22.

There is considerable sickness in Price this week, resulting from the change in the weather.

Born, February 11, to Mrs. A. Ball inger, a little girl. Mother and chill are doing nicely.

Bert Seaboldt came in from the Gilson Asphaltum mine Saturday and left for the east on Sunday.

The infant child of Mr. and Mrs Ephraim Allred died at Ferron Monday night. This makes the fourth chill Mr Allred has lost since his arrival in Ferron some three or four years ago, and he and his family have the sympathy of the entire community.

H W. Varnon of Sedalia, Mo , who has secured the contract for carrying the mail from Price into Emery county, has been in town several days trying to sub let the contract to local parties. By reason of the low price at which Mr Varnon secured the contract, the sub-contractor ought by right to have a subsidy beside the entire amount of the contract.

James Seely a Victim of Diphtheria.

Mt Pleasant, Feb. 3 —The case of diphtheria recently reported has proven fatal The physician pronounced it ton-sillitis until last Friday, when it was declared diphtheria, and the case quarantined. The victim is James Seely, son of Wink Seely of Castle valley He was 23 years of age and was in Mt. Pleasant for the purpose of attending school

Deseret Evening News
March 3, 1898

March Mention.

Scofield, March 1st.—The "News" was correct in the statement that we would not have spring yet, for March is coming in like a lion, and it looks like we are going to have considerable rough weather here before seed time.

The miners are working about five days a week, most of the coal going to the Central Pacific company.

The Winter Quarters school district will build a school house in the near future, to cost about $1,500.

It is to be regretted that the home missionaries who did such a great work among the young men in Utah Stake this winter could not make it convenient to visit this isolated quarter of the Stake. We had our Mutual Improvement Association organized last fall, but for lack of interest the meetings were discontinued. The other organizations are in a pretty good condition.

Mr. John Hood, who has been a resident of this place for several years, is leaving, and expects to reach the Klondike region during the early summer. Mr. Hood was leader of the band, and also did a good work in training the children of this place to sing. Mr. Hood will be missed, especially by the musically inclined. We wish him success in h tufsiruiga2n gwoibuetah hw

Mrs. B. E. Lewis has been very ill for several days past. H.

LOCAL NEWS.

George Ristine was up from Farnham early in the week.

T. T. Fitch of Helper was a county seat visitor on Tuesday.

Miss Nellie Holly is visiting her sister Mrs. B. R. McDonald.

Harry Goss, son of Geo. Goss former chief engineer of the R. G. W. railway, is visiting Price.

W. S. Ashton of Vernal was a Price visitor late last week.

Clarence Marsh spent several days in Salt Lake this and last week.

Born—March 5, 1898, to the wife of Lehi Jensen of Wellington a boy. Mother and child are doing nicely.

Miss Clara Mitbis and Miss Della Nixon returned from Provo today where they have been attending the academy.

The snow is about all gone and frost is rapidly leaving the ground. The roads for some little time will be very muddy.

R. S. Collett, who was in Salt Lake for a week or ten days returned Saturday night, and Sunday left for his home in Vernal.

Those who have been waiting for lumber to build can now begin the construction of residences, of which many will be erected in the near future.

The dance at the town Hall on Monday night, given by Messrs Callaway and Gentry was an enjoyable affair. A number of the young folks from Helper were down.

J. O. Wester has every available man in town at work on his buildings which are going up rapidly. The buildings when completed will add much to the business portion of town.

Clarence Marsh spent several days in Salt Lake this and last week.

William McGuire, the butcher, will hereafter have fresh fish on Friday.

M. P. Braffet made a business trip to Salt Lake late last week returning on Tuesday.

Mark P. Braffett was on Monday admitted to practice in the state supreme court.

Frank Carroll of Orangeville and Dr. W. P. Winters of Castledale were Hotel Clarke guests on Friday.

Miss Maggie Morehead of Smithfield and Miss Claire Stringham of Salt Lake left on Sunday's stage for Vernal.

John Forrester, who was arrested and fined by the Helper justice some time ago for gambling and appealed his case to the district court and allowed his case to default is now serving his term in the county jail. He will, unless fine is paid serve four months and ten days.

The stirring western drama, 'Nevada' or "The Lost Mine," will be played on Saturday evening by the Price Dramatic company and Elocution lass. The members are working hard and a good performance is looked for. Johnson Brothers will have charge

J. B. Millburn and party left on No. 3 on Thursday for the Klondike country. They stopped over in Salt Lake until Saturday. The party consists of Mr Millburn, Parley Warren and J. D. Boyd. Their many friends in Carbon wish them a pleasant trip and hope they may return m'llionaires.

CASTLEGATE.

A serious accident occurred in the mines Thursday afternoon to Chris Halverson, a driver. It appears that he was bringing a loaded car out to the switch, the mule made a swerve to one side, throwing the car off the track. The young man's left leg was caught between the "gun" and the car, receiving such injuries that it is feared he has sustained a fracture just above the knee joint, besides the leg being badly lacerated. He was taken to the hospital Friday morning. Great sympathy is shown to the mother of the young man. He had the same leg broken some time ago.

GREENRIVER.

Mr. Litsea of Santaquin has been engaged by the R. G. W. company to take charge of Thompson's Springs shearing corral for the coming season. It is estimated that the clip at this point will reach 40,000 sheep.

Sanders & Company are negotiating for the purchase of the West ranch near Cisco. They will, in the event of a purchase, use the ranch for a shearing and feed station.

Rockhill's pack outfit of three horses were struck by a train east of here on Sunday night and killed.

S. E. Peak has signed a contract with J. T. Farrer the owner of the Black Baby coal mine for another 100 foot drift.

John Rockhill of Spanish Fork, who has a large number of sheep on the desert east of here came in from the range and reports his sheep as doing well.

Mr. Badygaured who has had charge of the Rockhill sheep herds came in a few days ago with his feet badly frosted. He left for his home on Monday.

The snow is all gone and the mud is too deep for pleasant travel. The ice in the river is breaking up and the river will soon be clear.

Elders Childester, Tolman, Crawford, Young, Madsen and Hubbard held meetings in the L. D. S. meeting house Thursday evening. There was a good turnout, and as they are all to be released to return home the good people of this ward intend to give them a good sendoff. A great awakening has been accomplished through the untiring efforts of these missionaries.

SCOFIELD.

More miners have arrived from Coalville, and the mines are working every day including Sundays. And the train crew—well, they work all the time.

The Castle valley people are likely to be short on their water supply this summer, as there is very little snow in the mountains this season.

Utah's best crop is doing well here. A bouncing baby girl arrived at the home of Mr. and Mrs. William H. Williams and another at Thurber Johnson's. All concerned are doing well.

in charge of the French Hotel

Mr. William Palmer has gone to his home in Springville.

Mr. John Hood has left us. He has gone to Klondike.

Thomas Cox, Jr, has been chosen as leader of the Scofield silver band.

The many friends of Miss Maggie Strange will be pained to learn that she is very ill at the hospital at Salt Lake City.

Mr. Harkness has moved the postoffice into his new building. Part of the building is being used for a barber shop.

SCOFIELD.

Winter weather has returned and is felt very keenly after having nice weather for the past two months

Times are quite brisk at Scofield and Winter Quarters. The mines are working full time and there are a great many people. Every house and stable is full.

Alfred Newren, a driver in No. 1 mine had his hand badly crushed between two cars last week.

Mrs G. Halverson gave birth to a fine baby girl last week, mother and child are doing well.

Mr and Mrs J. M Beatie have returned from their visit to Salt Lake.

There will be a grand Lall in the Scofield school house on St. Patrick's day in the evening

Ouina Anderson and family started for Iceland on the 14th, inst.

Mother Douglas is still quite ill.

John W. Loyd has returned from Diamondville and has resumed business in his confectionery store.

EMERY.

Temperate spring weather with Castle Valley zephyrs prevail the last few days

Some of the more energetic farmers have sown some seed.

We wonder if the increase of posterity in our community can be attributed to the benign influences of the Dingley bill as is the prosperity among our farmers and sheep owners During the past three or four weeks there have arrived at the home of Newel Beal, a boy, Nephi Williams, a son, Martin M. Olsen, a male child, A. E Edwards, a son, Ray Real a Ray Jr, Jacob Minchey, a daughter, J. Killian, a girl, Dixon Keel, a son. Who says the population of Emery is not increasing and that we don't need a more spacious school building?

The Emery Dramatic company presented the drama "Grandfather's Mistake or Chimney Corner" last Saturday evening concluding with the comic farce, the "Lium Pedler" to a small but appreciative audience. The acting was fair, considering that nearly all were beginners.

A complete reorganization in the Y. M. M. I. association was accomplished a few Sundays ago and it is hoped that the young will put forth more energy and go in with a new determination to win in mutual improvement work. If the real good of these associations could be grasped by the young and weighed thoroughly the meetings would not be such drags as they sometimes are.

WELLINGTON.

The spring building boom has struck this town and already four new buildings are under construction.

It is now time for cleaning the canals, and everyone interested should be ready to do his assessment work when called upon, so that there may be no lack of water this spring

The people of Price river valley should heed the note of warning that comes from E field in regard to the snow in the mountains and get their crops in early.

It is reported that a vein of gilsonite has been found about three miles east of Wellington in the foothills, and considerable development work is being done on the claim.

The wide-awake farmer is already getting his ground ready to plant. Considerable land in the Sandy river bottom is ready for the plow, and the upland will be dry enough in a few days. It is said that the conditions here has never been better for a good crop the coming season.

Most all the range cattle of this place have already been started for the summer range, and the prospect for early beef is very good.

The health of our people is very good for this time of the year.

Through the influence and foresight of G. T. Olsen a number of heards of sheep will be shorn of their fleece at the Emery corral this season. This means employment for a good many of our boys and others from adjoining towns, also the distribution of a number of dollars among our merchants. The shearing will commence early in April.

R. E. PORTER.

Glaser a Branch Store.

On April 1, I. Glaser, the Helper merchant will open a branch store at Pleasant Valley Junction where he will carry a complete line of general merchandise and sheep-men's supplies.

Salt Lake Herald
March 19, 1898

OUTRAGE AT CASTLE GATE.

Man's House Wrecked By a Charivari Crowd.

Castlegate, March 17.—John Bardisoni got married last evening, and there was an accompaniment to the ceremonies that was not down on the programme. After Judge Duerdon had tied the knot, there arose from the outside of the house such a pandemonium that has not been heard in this burg. A charivari took place that will cost dear to those participating. Mr. Bardisoni is a poor man and could not afford to gratify the wants of the thirsty gang outside, and in revenge, large rocks were hurled at the house, and the windows were broke. One large rock was hurled with such force that it was bedded in the shingles, and still remains in that position. One rock was thrown through the bedroom window and struck the bridegroom on the leg. The yard around the house was literally strewn with rocks of all sizes and tinware of all kinds.

To make matters worse a neighbor's wife, who has lately been confined, and was just able to get around, received such a bad scare that the doctor had to be summoned to attend her. As a climax to the whole affair, when it became known that Mr. Bardisoni was going to prefer a charge of willful destruction to property, some one of the scoundrels saw him and threatened that if he prosecuted them they would "fix" him. Your correspondent went down to the house this morning when made aware of the fact, and saw such a state of affairs that he feels justified in asking you to publish this article with the added comment that he hopes that whoever tries this case, should it come to trial, that a salutary lesson will be given to those who have done such dastardly work.

Assistant Superintendent Williams went to Winter Quarters mine this morning.

Chief Engineer Miller is also up at the P. V. mines inspecting the motors and electric plant. The new motor is being taken into the mines here. A large force of men are retained to clear the way for it after the mine has finished tonight.

LOCAL NEWS.

MARRIED—At Helper March 17, 1898, at the residence of the groom's mother, Mrs. Emily Dunton, Mr Morris Dunton and Kathrine Leck, both of Helper, Justice Fitch officiating. After the wedding the happy couple received the well wishes of their many friends, which was folowed by a sumptuous repast prepared by the generous mother in honor of the occasion Mr. and Mrs. Dunton will aide in Helper.

L. Lowenstien will open a branch store in the Leiter building at Pleasant Valley Junction in a few days. He will carry groceries and a full line of sheepmen's supplies.

County Clerk Donaldson issued license to wed on Monday to R S. Thompson and Miss Frankie Miller, both of Helper and they were united in marriage later in the day by Justice Olsen.

CASTLEGATE.

Chief Engineer Miller was at Winter Quarters mines late last week inspecting the motors and the electric plant.

Assistant superintendent made a trip to Winter Quarters late last week.

John Bardisoni, an Italian, got married recently, and being a poor man had not the means to treat the boys, who in revenge began a fusillade with rocks and other missels, windows were broken. One large rock was hurled with such force that it is bedded in the shingles, and still remains in that position One rock was thrown through the bedroom window and struck the bridegroom on the leg. The yard around the house was litterally covered with rocks of all sizes and tinware of all kinds Mr. Bardisonl, it is said, will prefer charges of wilful destruction of property and have the gang roughly handled It is hoped that an example will be made of those who participated in the savage attack.

CLEVELAND.

Mr. and Mrs Neils Christianson returned from Manti Tuesday of last week and on Wednesday gave a wedd ng dinner at 5 p m. and a dance at night. About sixty were present at the dinner. Among those present were, Bishop L. P. Overson and wife, Henry Oviatt and wife, John P. Johnson and wife, J. N Davis and wife, Robert Whitehead and wife, John J. Thordarson, A. Jenson and wife, E, M, Martensen, Mr. and Mrs. E. Johnson, Mr. and Mrs N. C. Christensen parents of the bride and groom, Erick Larsen and wife, Emma Larson, H. C. Smith and wife, and Rose and Lillie Bryner, and Lofter Bjearnsen of Spanish Fork. The presents given were twenty acres of land by the bride's father, cow and calf by her mother, large lamp, set dishes and numerous other useful articles. There were about 200 at the dance, several coming from Huntington, Lawrence and Desert Lake. The happy couple will reside at Cleveland.

GREENRIVER.

J. T. Farrer is pushing work on the Greenriver canal. A large force of men are employed.

Lee Valentine is expected home on a visit the latter part of the week

Three hundred head of cattle are on the range between Thompson's and Greenriver. They are said to belong to Mr. Chipman at American Fork.

Goelln Bros received 2,000 head of sheep at Elgin on Wednesday which they purchased from White & Co, of Salt Lake.

Mrs. Valentine has received the appointment as postmaster for Elgin postoffice and has sent her bond to Washington for approval.

County Clerk Elliott is visiting the west end of the county and is making his headquarters at Commissioner Brown's.

Shearing will begin at Thompson's on April 10 and Uncle John Rockhill is the first on the list.

The river can be easily forded and is free from ice. Road Supervisor R. W. Valentine has put the road east of the river in good condition. Bridges are found where needed.

SCOFIELD

Mrs. Mary E. Waller the mother of Wm. Ayer, was found dead in her room last Saturday morning She was living in part of the house occupied by Mrs. Kearnon. When her daughter in-law, Mrs. Ayer went to get the old lady her breakfast as usual, she was horror-stricken to find her dead. Deceased was a native of England and was seventy-six years of age. She leaves two sons and a daughter. The remains were taken to Draper for interrment, where she has a son, Robert Ayer.

The mines are working night and day, and all the good miners that come along are given employment.

The farmers that have been here from Castle valley during the winter are beginning to leave for the summer to attend to their farms. They return each fall with hayseed in their hair

Mr. John Hood and Miss Magg's Strang were married at Salt Lake City last Tuesday.

WELLINGTON.

We understand that Charles Bill of this place has been called to the missionary field and will probaby leave early next month. The field to which he has been called is not definitely known at present. This will make two missionaries from this place this spring. "Pretty good for us!"

F. C, and S. H. Grundrig have the contract of building the new house of W. J. Tidwell, and the work is progressing nicely.

The Tidwell Canal Co have levied a 10 per cent assessment on all capital stock for the purpose of repairing the canal, and work will begin at once under the supervision of R. W. Avery and rushed to completion.

Tom Lords has charge of all the work

n the new residence of John J. Thayn.

G. R. Bill has returned from a winter spent on Elliott mountain and will remain at home for an indefinite time.

The early part of this week was as cold and windy as it is in Klondike.

HELPER

The ranchers are busy these days making preparations for the spring work

The benefit ball on Saturday night was an enjoyable affair, quite a number being present.

Our popular townsman and postmaster J. N. Miller will soon leave on a mission to the southern states. He will be gone probably two years.

J. H. Van Natta visited Price on Wednesday.

J. A. Parrott, who has for several years been station agent for the Western at this place has resigned and will leave the service of the road and probably embark in business for himself. His plans for the future are not fully matured His acknowledged ability and uniform courtesy has made him hosts of friends both among citizens and railroad men who are sorry to see him leave our little town

The railroad company is making extensive preparations for added improvements. A steam shovel is leveling ground for additional track facilities and a large cinder pit from which cinders will be loaded in cars by mechanical appliance Not of the least importance is the plans now under way for the construction of six or eight company cottages for employees at once and others later on when the demand will justify. The cottages will contain four rooms and water and light will be furnished for the nominal sum of $6 per month.

SPRING GLEN.

John T. Rowley leveled his yard early in the week which adds much to the appearance of his handsome residence.

H A. Southworth left last week for Woodside to look after property interests there He will be gone several days.

Mr Elllrodge is leveling a garden spot this week.

School closed last week until the fall term. The teacher, Mr Southworth, met with good success and a rapid advancement of the pupils is shown.

Mr. Keefer and family have returned to Spring Glen to reside during the summer. They are living on the Thompson property.

GREENRIVER.

Saunders will trail back west with his heard of 1800 sheep and will shear at Price. He crossed Greenriver yesterday

R E. Went and Ira Chipman went to Castledale this week to get a bunch of cattle they bought last fall

The river is raising rapidly and is above the fording point

The shearers are rushing work at Thompson's, there being fifty men at work.

Ballard Bros at Thompson's have taken out a saloon license and a man can get his whistle wet if he has the price.

Moab is in torch with the outside world since the completion of the telephone line A message was sent from Greenriver and an answer received in one hour.

C. J Flliott, county clerk spent a few days here last week returning to Moab on Sunday.

J. W Stark, county assessor was in Thompson on business a couple of days this week.

Commissioner Brown goes to Moab Sunday to attend the regular monthly meeting of the county commissioners.

WELLINGTON.

Mrs. Geo Milner has been quite sick but is now slowly improving

Assessor Tidwell is pushing work on his new residence which, when completed, will be another handsome residence of which Wellington now has not a few.

The benefit ball given on Friday night was quite a success financially. It was given for E. E. Branch, our popular superintendent of the Wellington Co-op. who will depart for the north west in a short time.

Parties from Farnham ran up on the hand car on Friday night to attend the benefit ball and during the dance parties unknown took the car and made a trip to Price and on reaching Price they turned the car loose after giving it a

start back to Wellington. The car kept going as long as the grade was in its favor, when it stopped a couple of miles above town and was struck by No. 4 and demolished. No serious damage was received by No. 4 s engine. It is not yet learned who took the car from Wellington, but if found out they may possibly have a chance to board with the county for some time.

Born to the wife of Geo. A. Wilson, Jr., on Saturday evening last a fine son. Mother and child doing well.

Mother Fawcett and sons have gone to their ranch at the mouth of the soldier for the summer. Charley Hall has rented their town property and took possession on Monday.

Everyone is busy now, plowing, sowing and cleaning ditches, and otherwise getting ready for summer.

Eastern Utah Advocate

April 14, 1898

Price

Rye, the eight-year-old daughter of Thomas Gatherum, of Scofield died late last week of diphtheria. This is the third death in Mr. Gatherum's family in as many years.

A noticable feature of street work this spring is that all streets are being worked. This is a decided improvement over former years as a greater part of the work was confined to one street.

GREENRIVER.

Dr. W. C. Richman and Attorney M. P. Braffet of Price visited Commissioner and Mrs. J. F. Brown of Elgin on Sunday. The doctor gave his hosts much anxiety by his sudden disappearance during the evening. However their fears were dispelled when word reached them at a late hour that the doctor had spent a pleasant evening worshiping at beauty's shrine.

W. M. Doren and W. H. Wiscarver crossed Greenriver with 219 head of cattle that they had been buying in Emery county. They will range in Willow creek, at the Graves & Chapman place.

Mrs. Addie Hart of the Mathis house, Price, is visiting with her father, Commissioner Brown.

J. T. Farrer & Co. are pushing repairs on their canal and will soon have the water turned on.

The Greenriver school closes Friday for the term. Everyone has a good word for Mr. Mohr, the teacher. The pupils have made better progress this term than has been noticed before.

Mr. W. L. G Trapp has disposed of his farm and will leave the River in a few days. He has not decided where he will locate.

WELLINGTON.

[From our regular correspondent.]

Ike Roberts and family have returned from their long stay in Provo. Mr. Roberts will cultivate his farm here this summer. He has been attending the B. Y. academy for the past year and a half and says he has had a very enjoyable time besides learning a few things.

Geo N. Hill came in from the Vernal country on Friday last and started back on Tuesday, where he is canvassing for and delivering enlarged pictures and frames. He reports everything in that country in a flourishing condition.

Bp. McMullin's freight teams started on the road again on Saturday morning last, headed for the Post and intermediate points.

W. J. Tidwell spent several days in the Nine Mile country assessing the residents of that locality.

[Additional Wellington correspondence]

F. C. Grundvig while at work on the new residence of W. J. Tidwell last week fell several feet, striking a projecting timber and received very painful injuries He was confined to his room for several days but is now much improved and will resume work in a short time.

The residences of J. J. Thayn and W. J. Tidwell will soon be completed Commissioner Liddell, Thos. Gale and probably two or three other residents will in a short time begin the erection of dwellings.

Mr. and Mrs. J. J. Thayn returned from conference bringing with them a very elegant top buggy and single harness, which will be a great comfort to the old people in their declining years

Salt Lake Herald
April 14, 1898

SCRAP AT CASTLE GATE.

Bartender Quells a Disturbance With a Club.

Castle Gate, April 12.—A row occurred in the Magnolia hall this afternoon, between two young fellows named Young and Jones. One of the bartenders took a good sized club and whacked Young over the head, inflicting an ugly gash, about four inches long, laying open his scalp. Then Reeseman turned his attention to Jones, and gave him a rap, but the blow failed to do any great damage.

Young was taken to the surgery, where Dr. Asadoorian treated him and dressed the wound. No serious complications are feared.

Bishop Ed Fulmer of Spring Glen was in town tonight.

Mrs. Reese Lewis is very sick.

The sociable given the other evening by Mrs. John H. McMillan, was a most delightful affair, and a musical treat. We regret to record that a disturbance took place, which may end in the justice's court.

The work in the mines has dropped off considerably. The crusher broke yesterday morning, which caused the mine to lay idle.

Mr. John Sneddon, Scofield's pedagogue, was a visitor today.

There is some talk of trying to have the L. D. S. authorities have Carbon county made into a separate ecclesiastical stake. As it is, it is yet a part of Emery stake. Your correspondent is credibly informed that an effort will be made at the next stake conference to have this done.

Eastern Utah Advocate
April 21, 1898

CASTLEGATE.

John Sneddon, Scofield's pedagogue, was in Castlegate last week. His mission, it is thought, was for the purpose of building a few pannels of political fence. John would not hesitate to take the nomination for superintendent if offered by his party's convention.

Work in the mines has dropped off considerable of late.

There is a strong feeling here in both political parties to do their own nominating for superintendent of schools. Castlegate may have more than one candidate for nomination

Friday being Arbor Day the band was out serenading

Joseph Jones, a miner, while working in his place Saturday morning was struck by a fall of coal and rock. He was brought out and examined by Dr. Asadoorian, who reported that there was no bones broken and that no serious complications would result from his injuries The young man is slowly recovering

John D Llewelyn, of Scofield, was a Castlegate visitor last week.

Mrs Reese Lewis has been very sick but is now slowly improving.

A notice was given to the miners on he 15th to the effect beginning April 18th, only one half of the mines would work on every alternate day until further notice.

The Castlegate band has been organized again. The boys are practicing every idle day and are getting along nicely.

H. B Asadoorian and wife spent a couple of days in Zion last week

Road Supervisor Young has men out making some much needed repairs on our roads.

WELLINGTON.

Over 100 of our people visited Price on Saturday last for the purpose of viewing the military movements and also assisting in the program gotten up for the entertainment of the departing troops. It was a pleasing sight to see the school children at the head of the procession as the soldiers were escorted to the Price town hall for dinner.

Bishop McMullin returned from the post the other day with the ordinary freighter's luck—wagon broke and the load left on the road for another trip

Mrs. Blackburn and family returned Monday evening from a visit to Wayne county, also Monasen and Miss Katie Blackburn returned with their mother, they have been attending school in Ephraim the past winter. We welcome them all home.

SCOFIELD

On Saturday evening Apr" 23 Henry Wecherly, late of Coalville and Miss Margaret Ann Edwards daughter of Wm. Edwards, the genial company boarding house keeper were united in wedlock at the home of the bride A free dance was given at the boarding house and a good time was had.

Mrs. Mary Lewis, the beloved wife of Mr David Lewis, died Friday evening, April 22 The burial took place Monday, the 25th.

Born to Mrs. Edwin Street a fine daughter, mother and child doing well.

Mr. Wm Howells has left this locality and has gone to seek a homestead in the southern part of Utah

Our school commenced again last Tuesday with the same efficient teachers, Mr. W, H. Griffin and Miss A. S. Johnson.

ITEMS FROM SCOFIELD.

A Volunteer Company Organized—The Coal Mines—Death of Mary Lewis.

Scofield, Carbon County, Utah,
April 26, 1898.

To the Editor:

The people of Scofield are showing their patriotism in a substantial manner. A company of thirty have volunteered its services to aid in giving Cuba its independence.

The coal mines at Winter Quarters continue to work about half time with no better prospects for the future in view.

Sister Mary E. Lewis, wife of David W. Lewis, died on the 22nd inst. She was one of the oldest residents in Winter Quarters, having resided here for fourteen years. She died as she had lived, a faithful Latter-day Saint.

P. H. Wychley and Margaret Ann Edwards were married at the home of the bride's parents Saturday evening, April 23rd.

Brother William Howells, an old resident here, has just left us, intending to make his home in southern Utah. He had not decided just where he would locate.

We are having very good weather here. The snow has almost disappeared and vegetation begins to show the return of spring.   A. G.

Deseret Evening News
April 30, 1898

Emery Stake.

President: C G Larsen, Castle Dale,
    Emery county.

Counselors: Orange Seeley, Castle Dale
    Emery county; Wm Howard, Hunt-
    ington, Emery county.

Stake Tithing Clerk: D C Woodward,
    Huntington, Emery county.

Emery County, Utah.

WARDS.	BISHOPS.
Castle Dale	Frank M Hermansen, P E
Cleveland	L P Ovesen
Emery	Alonzo Brinkerhoff
Ferron	Hirum Nelson
Huntington	Peter Johnson
Lawrence	
Molen	Hans P Rasmussen
Orangeville	Jasper Robertson

Carbon County, Utah.

Castle Gate	William T Lamph
Price	Earnest Horse
Spring Glen	Edwin Fullmer
Wellington	A E McMullin

Salt Lake Herald
April 30, 1898

SCOFIELD RETURNS.

Ten Miners Enlisted By Captain Caine Yesterday.

(Special to The Herald.)

Scofield, Utah, April 29.—Captain
Joseph E. Caine, recruiting officer, to-
day enlisted ten stalwart miners at the
Winter Quarters coal mine. Captain
Caine will go to Pleasant Valley Junc-
tion to-morrow morning and to Castle
Gate in the afternoon. Following are
the names of those enlisted today:

John Erickson, Samuel Auforth, John
Price, William Miller, David Podfield,
George Taylor, Edward Hardee, Hamil
King, John Phillips, Richard Pack.

Died—Monday evening, May 2, 1898, Minnie, the daughter of Mr and Mrs A. M. Allred. The deceased had been an invalid for a number of years, and hopes for her final recovery had been abandoned some time ago. Funeral services occurred Wednesday.

W. G Smith, J H. Doyle and Doc. Mead who attempted a hold up at Sunnyside and were arrested and taken to Castledale for trial were found guilty and bound over to the district court, the bonds of Smith and Doyle were fixed at $1,500 and Doc. Mead at $1,000 The trio were taken to Provo for safe keeping as it was thought unwise to let them remain in the Castledale jail.

Mrs Hart, who has for some months had charge of the Mathis house dining room retired and Mrs. Emma Bodle took charge. Mrs Hart will occupy the Jones cottage for the present.

Of the nine who enlisted from Price four were chosen by letter and on the eve of their departure the governor telegraphed the boys to delay their departure until further advised The boys were badly disappointed.

WELLINGTON.

Saturday afternoon, Luiz, the little 8-year-old son of W. H. Tidwell fell from a wagon standing in the yard and broke his arm. Local help was soon at hand and the arm set all right and the little one is resting quietly.

The young men gave a picnic dance Monday evening which was well attended, and an enjoyable time was had as is usual.

There has been almost a continual rain since Friday morning last, and at this time, Tuesday noon gives no sign of abatement. We like plenty of all good things but enough is enough, and some of us have had plenty of this.

Born, on April 27, a fine daughter to the wife of Carl Johnson. All parties concerned doing well.

Scofield, Carbon County, Utah,
April 26, 1898.
To the Editor:
The people of Scofield are showing their patriotism in a substantial manner. A company of thirty have volunteered its services to aid in giving Cuba its independence.
The coal mines at Winter Quarters continue to work about half time with no better prospects for the future in view.
Sister Mary E. Lewis, wife of David W. Lewis, died on the 22nd inst. She was one of the oldest residents in Winter Quarters, having resided here for fourteen years. She died as she had lived, a faithful Latter-day Saint.

P. H. Wychley and Margaret Ann Edwards were married at the home of the bride's parents Saturday evening, April 23rd.
Brother William Howells, an old resident here, has just left us, intending to make his home in southern Utah. He had not decided just where he would locate.
We are having very good weather here. The snow has almost disappeared and vegetation begins to show the return of spring.   A. G.

WELLINGTON NOTES.

Beautiful weather since Saturday last.

Mrs. Mae Wilson of Price visited her mother on Sunday

The little baby of Mr and Mrs. Thomas Lord died suddenly on Tuesday. The cause of death is unknown.

The recent rains caused a break in the Wellington canal, just north of town, which left the people in the east end high and dry for a few days until the flume was rebuilt.

Friday, the 6th inst , was the closing day for the grammar department of the district school. The exercises consisted of songs, recitations, etc., and a very enjoyable time was had. There were many expressions of regret at the departure of our amiable and competent teacher, Miss Mary Leonard, who has gone to Castlegate for a few days, from whence she will go to Kansas, where her parents reside. We extend to her our best wishes and earnestly hope for her return and engagement for another season.

Last Friday evening William the 17-year old son of John Blackburn, was kicked by a horse, receiving a badly fractured skull from which he may not recover. Mr. Blackburn and his son were covering a small bridge with gravel, the boy driving and his father holding the scraper. When close to the crossing the team stopped, William struck the near horse with the end of the lines and immediately turned to his father who had addressed him. At this moment the near horse kicked, striking the boy on the left side of the head which knocked him to the ground. Help was summoned and restoratives applied, and it was 15 minutes before consciousness was restored. A messenger was hurried to Price for Dr. Richman, and Dr Allen of Provo was also summoned by wire Dr Richman on his arrival learned that Dr. Allen would be here about midnight, and after an examination concluded to await his arrival. A portion of the skull, about three inches long and an inch and a half wide, was forced in against the brain This part of the skull was removed on Dr. Allen's arrival, and it was found that the impact had caused a slight hemorrhage of the brain. The boy is still unconscious, and one of his sides is partially paralyzed

LATER —William Sheridan Blackburn died early Wednesday morning as a result of his injuries John and Ephraim Blackburn and Mrs. Nellie Robertson, brothers and sister of the deceased with Mrs Robertson's husband, arrived just before the boy died. They will remain with their parents a few days

Price

DIED

Grace Edith, the five-months old child of Mr. and Mrs. J. C. Burgland, died on Tuesday night of measles.

BUTCH CASSADY KILLED.

Surrounded by a Posse and Shot Down While Resisting Arrest.

Salt Lake, May 14 —Butch Cassady, the master spirit of innumerable depradations and a leading spirit among the desperadoes in Robbers Roost, was killed yesterday in a fight with a posse while resisting arrest. Joe Walker, another of the gang, was also killed and Lay and Thompson were captured About a week ago these desperadoes forcibly drove off 25 head of cattle belonging to the Whitmore boys of Price Whitmore followed them but was held up and relieved of his horse and compelled to walk to Price, Carbon county, where a posse was raised which started in pursuit They traveled night and day and surprised the bandits while asleep A call to surrender was met with a shot from Cassady A battle then begun which lasted about five minutes, during which Cassady and Walker were killed The other then surrendered

Both the dead men had rewards hanging on them of $500 each, offered by Governor Wells some months since Cassady was the leader in the Montpelier, Idaho, bank robbery two years ago, and also of the robbery of the P V. Coal Company last summer The two raids netted $14 000 He and Walker robbed a store at Green River about a month since

PRICE'S PIONEER PASSES AWAY

George Frandsen Died at His Home in This City on Saturday Last.

George Frandsen died at his home in this city on Saturday, May 21, at 5 p m., after a little less than a week's illness, from pneumonia During his illness and up to a few minutes before his death his family felt no serious alarm—In fact, the deceased after eating his breakfast on Saturday morning expressed the hope that he would be able to leave his sick bed within a day or so At about fifteen minutes to five he began to sink, and at 5 o'clock he passed peacefully to the great beyond and was at rest. Owing to his unexpected death only a few members of his family were present.

A brother and sister of the deceased who live at Mount Pleasant were telegraphed for, and owing to train accommodations were unable to reach Price until Monday night This delayed the funeral until 2 p m. Tuesday Long before the appointed hour for the services the town hall was crowded with friends of the deceased to pay their last respects to him.

Promptly at 2 o'clock the body, accompanied by the family and relatives, arrived, and after singing and prayer by N. L. Marsing, Counselor Orange Seely spoke feelingly of the faithful work the deceased had performed in the building up of the Price ward. Mr. Seely was followed by E. W. McIntire, who was a counselor during the time the deceased was bishop of the Price ward. L. M. Olson spoke of the many sterling traits of character of the deceased, comforting the bereaved ones with the thought that the separation was only of short duration. Apostle Lyman, who had been notified of the death, reached Price on the noon train, and followed Mr. Olson, dwelling on the work the deceased had accomplished and the high esteem in which he was held by the church authorities.

The remains were followed to the cemetery by a large concourse of people, where Apostle Lyman performed the burial services, thus laying to rest all that was mortal of George Frandsen.

"[T]he deceased was born on the isle of Lenz land, a province of Denmark, on May 4), 1834, and was the eldest of a family of three. His father, Francis Jorgensen, was a tiller of the soil, and amid the peaceful surroundings of a pastoral life George grew to manhood When just attaining his majority his father died. Having previously embraced the Mormon religion, the deceased, with his mother and brother and sister, emigrated to the United States and crossed the plains with ox teams, arriving in Salt Lake City September 1?, 1856. During January, 1857, he was united in wedlock to Miss Karen Nielsen and the same year moved to Ephraim, where he resided until 1859, when he removed to Mt. Pleasant. In 1878 he was called on a mission to his fatherland, returning to his home and family in 1880. In 1882 the church authorities sent him to preside over the then newly settled Price valley as ward bishop, and he has since resided here.

He was one of Sanpete county's pioneers, and with the other settlers endured many hardships, struggling for an existence and fighting Indians. He participated in the Black Hawk war, and in an engagement between the settlers and redskins at Fish Creek was wounded.

George Frandsen can justly be called the father of Price. When he reached this valley in 1882 there were only a few ranchers along the Price river, and his work of organizing the ward and constructing canals for irrigation purposes was entered into with a firm belief in the rapid growth of the ward. During the fourteen years that he diligently labored for the advancement of his people, the little settlement has grown to a populous community. In the early history of the settlement and in later years many of the poor received substantial aid from the generous bishop and, strange as it may seem, few others than those receiving the needed help would know of it.

A wife and family of eight children in Price and a second wife and four children in Mount Pleasant survive him The names of the children here are Peter, Joseph (deceased), George, Hyrum, Heber Rasmus and Lena (twins), Larsen and Annie, all of whom, with the exception of Rasmus, Lena and Annie, are married.

The deceased leaves considerable property, thus providing well for his family. He was a kind husband, a loving parent and a good neighbor.

The deceased's mother, Mrs Mariah Jorgensen, died in 1881. His brother, Rasmus Frandsen, and his sister, Mrs. Peter Madsen, reside with their families in Mount Pleasant and were present at the funeral services here.

Eastern Utah Advocate
June 2, 1898
Price

Deputy County Clerk L. O. Hoffmann issued a marriage license last week to Heber Ward of Castlegate and Miss Via Riley of Huntington. The couple were united in marriage by Bishop Lamph of Castlegate.

Hon. O. G. Kimball, John X Lloyd and I. Llewellyn of Scofield were county seat visitors this week.

Miss Maggie Snow and Miss Addie Page of Orangeville; Miss Bertrude Seely, Miss Sybil Seely, Seren Hansen and Lon Seely of Castledale, who have been attending the B Y. academy at Provo, passed through Price last week en route home.

Dave Jones of Castlegate was a Price visitor Sunday.

For the May term of the district court which will sit at Price on Monday, June 13, the following list of petit jurors has been drawn

Thomas Cox, sr , Castlegate
W. K logle,   "
Chris Peterson, Price.
H J. Stowell, Spring Glen.
Wm. Ramsey, Scofield.
Michael Beveridge, Castlegate.
Joseph S. Birch, Wellington.
L A Warren, Price.
Thomas Rhoades, Helper.
James A Harrison, Castlegate.
Wm. Featherstone,   "
L. H. Ewell, Spring Glen
R. A. Henrichsen Scofield
J. M. Loveridge, Winter Quarters

Alvin Thayn, Wellington.
Lehi Jessen,   "
A. W. Horsley, Price.
H. C. Bryner,   "
C. H. Empey,   "
John Webber, Scofield
W A. Fausett, jr , Wellington.
L D Lyman, Price
N. L. McLean, Scofield.
B. E. Lewis, Winter Quarters.

No grand jury has so far been called for this term of court.

Owing to the case of L. M. Olson vs Price Water company coming up at this term of court, and as Judge Johnson is disqualified by reason of his having been the plaintiff's attorney prior to his election as district judge, it is probable he will ask some other district judge to sit here.

A SERIOUS RUNAWAY

While returning from Price yesterday with his wife and family Joseph Lord of Wellington had a runaway. Mrs. Lord was thrown out of the wagon, falling under the wheels and receiving a compound fracture of the ankle joint.

Mr. Lord and his family had finished their trading at Price, and when within a short distance from their home, which is across the river south of Wellington, a clevis gave way, letting down the single tree on the heels of one of the horses, which became frightened and began to plunge. The tongue dropped out of the neck yoke and swayed to one side, the tongue and front wheel striking fence posts which threw the occupants to the ground and a wheel passed over Mrs Lord's leg, resulting in a compound fracture of the ankle joint. Besides a shaking up no other member of the family was injured.

Mrs. Lord was taken to her home and Dr. Richman of Price summoned The bones were badly splintered and protruding through the flesh. Being a heavy woman the joint may not after healing have sufficient strength to bear Mrs. Lord's weight.

Funeral of Billy Davis.

Billy Davis, who was killed in the mines at Castlegate last Saturday, was buried at Cleveland, where his family resided, on Monday. A large number of the deceased's friends and relatives assembled at the meeting house and after the funeral obsequies accompanied the remains to the cemetery The deceased leaves a wife and four small children and a host of friends to mourn his sad den and untimely death. Mrs. Davis nine months ago buried her mother, Mrs Blood, and shortly afterwards her father passed to the great beyond The sympathy of the Cleveland people go out to the bereaved wife.

CASTLEGATE CULLINGS.

John Stagg, the butcher at this place, left for Provo where he will become a benedict.

* * *

A party was given last week at the home of Allen Cox in honor of William Hartley, who will leave shortly for Alberta, Canada.

* * *

A Franciscan priest was here last week from Denver holding meetings among the Austrians.

* * *

Miss Minnie Halverson left on Tuesday for Price, where she will visit friends for several days

* * *

A large attendance of teachers is expected here next Monday at the examination for certificates.

* * *

Mrs Robert Williams, who has been at Provo under medical treatment, was reported seriously ill and her husband was telegraphed for.

Superintendent H. G Webb and State Superintendent Parks returned to this place late last week after a trip through the county visiting the various schools.

* * *

Our taxpayers have voted $2,000 for the construction of a district school building. Work will begin soon, and it is thought the building will be ready for occupancy when school opens in the fall

* * *

W. C. Davis was struck and instantly killed in the mines here on Saturday by falling coal The man and a younger brother were working together, but the latter was unhurt. The unfortunate miner's skull was found to be crushed and death resulted almost immediately. He lived in Cleveland and leaves a wife and four children The body was taken to his home for interment.

Many old soldiers now feel the effects of the hard service they endured during the war. Mr Geo S Anderson, of Roseville, New York county, Penn, who saw the hardest kind of service at the front, is now frequently troubled with rheumatism. 'I had a severe attack lately," he says, 'and procured a bottle of Chamberlain's Pain Balm It did me so much good that I would like to know what you would charge me for one dozen bottles " Mr. Anderson wanted it both for his own use and to supply it to his friends and neighbors, as every family should have a bottle in their home, not only for rheumatism, but lame back, sprains, swellings, cuts, bruises and burns, for which it is un

ROBBERS' ROOST IN HARD LUCK

Another of the Famous Gang Gets Killed.

C. L. Maxwell, Late of Price, Was Captured.

They Robbed the Springville Bank of $3,000.

The Springville bank was robbed of $1,070 early Saturday morning by members of the Robbers' Roost gang. One of the robbers was killed by a pursuing posse and the other surrendered. A member of the posse, J. W. Allen, was shot through the thigh and has since had his leg amputated

Two men entered the bank about 10 o'clock and presented an order for $200 to the bookkeeper, as the cashier had just stepped out. While conversing in regard to the order the bookkeeper had turned away busying himself with office work. While he was doing this one of the men said "Look here, young man!" He turned at once, and the two had their guns on him and ordered him to throw up his hands The robber that was killed stayed at the teller's window, where they were standing, and kept the bookkeeper covered with his gun, while the other walked around into the teller's quarters and proceeded at once to put all

the visible money in a handkerchief While doing so he dropped a stack of $20 gold pieces, and while picking them up the bookkeeper lowered his right hand to an alarm button and touched it The alarm is connected with Mr Reynolds's store across the street Mr Reynolds heard the alarm but thinking it might have been discharged accidentally he went to the telephone and called up the bank. Receiving no reply he grabbed two Winchesters and rushed out of the store, but the robbers had just gone and he saw them turn the corner to the east, one block south

After securing all the loose money, which amounted to $8,920, they backed out of the bank, still holding their guns on the bookkeeper. They jumped in a buggy that they had left near by and drove east for Hobble Creek canyon Mr. Reynolds leaped into a lumber wagon that was standing at the bank corner and started in pursuit. The news soon spread, and in a short time nearly half the town was out after the robbers. The desperadoes near the edge of town met a man riding a fine horse and compelled him to dismount, threw $16 down in front of the man and rode the horse away, while the other continued with the buggy. The delay in getting the horse brought Mr. Reynolds within about 150 yards of the fugitives, and he fired two shots at them without effect. By this time a number of horsemen caught up with Mr. Reynolds, and the robbers seeing their pursuers gaining upon them and their buggy horse nearly exhausted, they leaped from the horse and buggy and took to the brush, they being in the mouth of Hobble Creek canyon. The brush is very thick and very difficult to get through, so that further pursuit was at once checked for the time. In less than twenty minutes over 100 horsemen were on the ground, and the patch of brush was surrounded so completely that escape was impossible.

At this time Joseph W. Allen proposed that a line of men be formed and march through the brush. In a short time the plan was being carried into effect, and after repeatedly passing through the brush one of the party while crawling on his hands and knees saw one of the robbers within a few feet covered with leaves and rubbish, and a request to surrender was immediately obeyed by the robber. The other desperado was found pretty soon and he commenced firing as soon as he saw that he was surrounded. One shot from his revolver struck J. W. Allen just above the knee, knocking him to the ground, and in this position Mr. Allen took deliberate aim, fired and killed the robber instantly.

The robber taken alive was none other than C. L. Maxwell, who formerly resided here, and took much pleasure in terrorizing Price people. Maxwell had $2,085 30 on his person. About $500 was picked up in the brush, leaving $600 unaccounted for. Maxwell was lodged in the Provo jail, where he now languishes. The other bandit so far has not been recognized.

Eastern Utah Advocate
June 9, 1898
Price

L. Lowenstein came in Sunday with his wife and family and will make this his home, having moved into the Foote residence.

Dick Cotrer, one of our soldier boys, was honored on decoration day at San Francisco by being appointed orderly to General Otis.

The R. G. W. Railway company has changed the name of the station P. V Junction to Colton to conform to the name of the postoffice.

Mrs. Lord of Wellington, who received a compound fracture of the ankle joint last, and which was reported in these columns, is getting along very well.

Mrs. J. W. Loughborough and children reached Price last week and will reside here during the summer

R. G. Miller has disposed of his entire clip of wool, about 70,000 pounds, at a little better than 18 cents

Assessor Tidwell met with the county board of equalization this week and assisted the board in its laborious work

Ike Glaser's family came out from Salt Lake this week and will make Helper their home during the summer.

Seph Pace of Spanish Fork and Miss Lydia Gammage of Greenriver, Emery county, were married in this city last Friday by Justice Olsen. Mr Pace is a well to do sheep man and the bride is the daughter of Mr. and Mrs. Joseph Gammage, who were the first residents of Greenriver. The bride's many friends in Carbon and Emery will be glad to learn of the happy event.

On Saturday afternoon Mrs George W. Bodle walked into an open cellar and received very painful injuries from the fall. On entering the dining room she failed to notice the open cellar and plunged about 7 feet to the bottom Although badly bruised she was soon about, attending to the wants of her guests

BRUTAL ATTACK.

John Watson Terribly Beaten by County Attorney Warf, Aided and Abetted By Alpha Ballinger.

On last Thursday, the 9th inst., John Watson, 59 years of age, was the victim of a cowardly and brutal attack.

The facts are as follows: About half-past six in the evening Clarence Marsh and John Watson, his employee, went up to the water canal to turn on the water with which to irrigate. Marsh was confronted with a shotgun in the hands of a cowardly fellow by the name of Youngberg, who pointed and held his gun on Marsh for the space of three to five minutes, and threatened to shoot, and shoot to kill, if he attempted to raise the headgate or in any way interfere with the water in the ditch. Despite the threats of Youngberg, however, Marsh did raise the headgate and turned on the water, believing then, as he believes now, that he had a perfect right to the use of a portion that courses through the Price water ditch.

At this point Mrs. Marsh, fearing trouble, appeared upon the scene with a babe in her arms, and succeeded in persuading her husband to accompany her home.

At this time Watson was sitting on the embankment. Warf and Ballinger came up, armed with rifles. B immediately covered Watson with his gun, while Warf approached from behind, pulled his six shooter and without warning dealt Watson a vicious blow on the side of the head. This was followed up by others, until the poor man fell insensible from the beating.

Next day when Watson pulled himself together sufficiently to count the cost, he found himself carrying around a badly split ear; the right side of the upper part of the occipital bone was laid bare. while a glance at his forehead would suggest that he must be a member of the Red Cross Society. He was badly bruised about the ribs and body, and for several days his stomach as an assimilater and digester of food was a complete failure, the result of a well placed vicious kick by one of the assailants. Dr. Richman was called and dressed his wounds, and in doing so found it necessary to put several stitches in his head and ear. Jack is slowly convalescing.

The parties have been arrested and will have their examination next Saturday before Justice Fitch of Helper, on a charge of assault with a deadly weapon with intent to commit murder.

LOCAL NEWS

Price

Ike Glaser and family of Helper visited L. Lowenstein on Sunday.

Peter Liddell of Wellington was a county seat visitor, Friday last.

Mrs. Hy Herriman presented her husband with a fine baby girl on Friday last. This is the cause of the broad grin seen on Hy's face the past week.

Sophus Olsen, the new postmaster at Cleveland, was a Price visitor late last week.

J. B. Cordell, the popular Castlegate pedagog, was a county seat visitor on Monday.

John Hamel and Miss Elizabeth Young were married at Castle Gate on Tuesday by Bishop Lamph.

Miss Stella Barton of Salt Lake is visiting her brother, Thomas Barton, and other Price friends.

Born, June 1?, 18??, to the wife of Wm. Miller, an employe of the R. G. W. at Helper, a fine baby girl.

Mrs. Lewis Larsen of Cleveland, who has had a very painful attack of the rheumatism, is slowly recovering.

The citizens of Price and vicinity are cordially invited to visit my ice cream parlor at the Jones cottage, on Saturday evenings and Sundays, where ice cream and cake will be served.—Mrs. Ada Hart.

WELLINGTON NOTES

A complaint, entitled the State of Utah vs. R. A. Kirker for assault with a deadly weapon with intent to commit murder, was filed in the justice's court here on Monday and a warrant issued for his arrest. Defendant appeared on Tuesday evening, and after giving bond for his appearance asked for a continuance of the case that he might prepare for examination. The request was granted, and Friday, June 17, at 2 p. m., was set for the hearing

* * *

Monday last Dr. Richman came to the conclusion that it might become necessary to amputate the foot of Mrs. Thos. Lord, which was so badly smashed some time ago, and for that purpose called in Dr. Winters of Castle Dale. After making a careful examination of the injury, however, it was thought possible to save the limb.

* * *

The three-year-old son of William H. Tidwell fell and broke his arm just below the elbow, on Monday last. The fracture was reduced by Dr. Sarah Tidwell, and the little one is resting easy.

* * *

Crops look better this year than for many years past, and the prospects are good for an abundant harvest.

* * *

The general health of the people is first-class just now.

* * *

Haying will start here in about ten days.

GREEN RIVER NOTES.

Commissioner Brown returns to Moab next week, as the county commissioners meet as a board of equalization on the 25th.

* * *

The first crop of lucern is about all cut and put in the stack. The crop is generally light as the water was not turned on until too late to do much good.

* * *

The river has apparently reached its highest point and is now falling. It did not reach last year's mark by 5 feet.

* * *

A. P. Mohr and Sam Peysert have left for the La Sal mountains, where they will put in the summer prospecting.

* * *

The ladies of Green River are making preparations for a Fourth of July celebration.

LOCAL BRIEFS.

Price

Clarence Marsh having sold his house will proceed at once to build a new residence, just west and adjoining the one he sold. This will be followed by two more residences on the same street. It looks as though the west side was on the eve of a substantial boom.

The Price shoemaker has moved to Helper and it is rumored that the butcher will follow suit. We confess that this does not bode any good for Price, yet so long as Providence, or some other power, influence or agency, vouchsafe to us our worthy bishop, we will always "feel to say" that the judgments of the Lord are just and righteous altogether.

COME ONE! COME ALL!

And Help Celebrate the Glorious Fourth. Price Afire with Patriotism.

A glance at the following program is suggestive of the grand celebration by our citizens on the Fourth. The day will be ushered in by the booming of cannon and will end in "the wee sma' hours" of the following morning to the sweet strains of "Home, Sweet Home."

A cordial invitation to all the people of Carbon county and surrounding country is extended and a grand time is promised.

Read the program following

Hoisting the flag.
Salute of 13 guns at daybreak.
Music by the band.
Parade at 9 o'clock. Signal guns will be fired at 9 o'clock for assembly at town hall. Parade will be under the supervision of the marshal of the day, H. G. Mathis
Reassemble at hall at 11 o'clock
Assembly called to order by marshal of the day.
Singing "America" by choir and congregation.
Prayer by chaplain, E. W. McIntire
Singing 'Star Spangled Banner" by Henry Flack and choir.
Reading Declaration of Independence by E. S. Horsley.

Music by the band.
Oration by A. Ballinger.
Song by P. Anderson.
Recitation by Miss Maggie Jones.
Song, 'Remember the Maine," by H. Flack.
Music by the band.
Stump speech by Seren Olsen.
Toasts and sentiments.
Singing by choir.
Benediction by chaplain.
Committee on artillery—Henry Flack, Peter Anderson.
Standard bearer—James Burges.
Committee on Goddess of Liberty—Mrs. Empey, Misses May Pace, Lilly Bryner and Annie Fraudsen.
Finance committee—Dave Holdaway, Peter Anderson, E. S. Horsley
Committee on fireworks and sports—H. G. Mathis, Doll Fausett, George Fausett, C. H. Empey
Committee on decoration—A. Bryner, Joseph Jones, Jas. Bunce, Misses Pauline Pace, Rosie Bryner and Ella Branch
Committee on band wagon—Herman Bryner
Committee on Goddess of Liberty wagon—James Bunce.

If I'm designed yon lordling's slave,
By nature's law designed,
Why was an independent wish
E'er planted in my mind?
If not, why am I subject to
His cruelty and scorn?
Or why has man the will and power
To make his fellow mourn?
—Robert Burns.

A notable wedding took place in Price on Saturday night, when the genial Will Robinson of Nine Mile was united in the holy bonds of matrimony to Miss Orinla Petersen. The ceremony was performed by Hon P. I. Olsen in his characteristically solemn manner, in the presence of several friends of the happy pair. The young couple start off in life with the best wishes of a host of admirers for their future happiness and prosperity.

Wm. Hill, boss on section No. 83, east of town, was transferred to Saltda, Colo, and last Sunday the vacancy was filled by John Gall, an experienced railroad man

James Rooney, the big hearted, has removed with his family to Helper, where he will reside permanently. His business in Price is in charge of Tom Barton.

PIONEER DAY.

Interesting Program for the Celebration at Price on July 25.

On account of the 24th of July (pioneer day) falling on Sunday, the day will be celebrated in Price on Monday, July 25, when the following interesting program will be carried out.

Flag hoisted at sunrise.

Salute of artillery by Henry Frack.

Music by the band.

Salute of artillery at 9 30 a. m. for starting of parade.

Order of Parade.

Marshal of the day—Albert Bryner.

Band wagon

Float—Utah and her maids.

Utah—Miss Maggie Jones.

Maids—Misses Jennie Branch, Edith Pace, Gertrude Miller, Edith Bryner, Florence Kelsey, Stena Jensen, Mary Empey, Preal Anderson, Mary Warf, Dora Barlow, Pearl Bryner, Ada Bryner.

Pioneers, representing Utah as it was

Indians lead by chief.

Sunday school.

Citizens

Meet at town hall at 11 a. m.

Singing "America" by the choir.

Prayer by chaplain, N. L. Marsing.

Singing "Star Spangled Banner" by the choir.

Oration

Music by the band.

Song by George Adair, sr.

Recitation by Miss Maggie Jones.

Instrumental music by Hubbard Warren

Song by Miss Mamie Robb and company.

Recitation by Miss May Pace.

Step dance—A. W. Horsley.

Song by Rosy Bryner and company.

Recitation by Percy Horsley.

Toasts and sentiments

Music by the band

Singing by the choir.

Prayer by the chaplain.

2 p. m.—Dance and sports for children.

Dance in the evening; tickets 50c

Committee on finance—Edith McIntire, Jennie Branch, Dean Holdaway.

Committee for pioneers—Ras Anderson, George Fausett, Doll Fausett, Enoch Bryner.

Committee on sports—Herman Horsley, Henry Empey, Mrs. H. Empey, Mrs. J. H. Pace, Mrs. C. W. Allred, John Burgess, George Mead.

THOS. COX SEN.

Thos Cox Sen. died at Castledale, Emery county, Utah, on the 4th of July, 1898, of dropsy. Deceased was born in Wiltshire, England, in the year 1834. He joined the Church of Jesus Christ of Latter-day Saints when a young man. Moved from Wiltshire to Durham, where he presided over the South Church branch of the Church in the Newcastle conference. Leaving South Church, he went to Stanley where, through his efforts, a branch of the Church was organized over which he presided for several years; emigrated to this country about 14 years ago; settled in Rock Springs, where he worked in the coal mines, that being his occupation. After being there some time, he was associated with Bishop Salisbury as one of his counselors. He located at Winter Quarters, Emery county, Utah. Ten years ago he removed from there to Castlegate, where he was presiding Elder for a short time; then as first counselor to Bishop W. T. Lamph, when a ward organization was effected. Getting too old to follow such hard work as coal mining, he took up a farm in Castledale, where he removed some 18 months ago. He took sick shortly after getting settled down, from which he never fully recovered, and which turned into dropsy. He suffered very much, and it was a glad release when death came. He died as he had lived, full of faith. He was the father of a large family, ten of whom, with his aged wife, survive him. He was of a patient and retiring nature, and always desired to do good to every one. W. T. L.

Millennial Star, please copy.

JOHN WATSON KILLED.

About 3 o'clock on Saturday evening, July 23, a shooting occurred in the street between the Price Trading company's store and the Senate saloon, in which John Watson lost his life. It appears that for some time past bitter feeling has existed between County Attorney J W. Warf and Mr. Watson, and, the parties meeting on Saturday night, so some words passed between them, when both pulled a six shooter and a number of shots were fired. Little can be determined as to the immediate origin of the difficulty, as witnesses were scarce at the time the fracas began, but it has been known for a long time that differences existed which would ultimately be settled with guns, and the tragedy was not a great surprise to those acquainted with the parties. Some six or seven weeks ago Watson was beaten over the head with a gun and club in the hands of Mr. Warf, and after the latter was acquitted of the offense by the Helper magistrate, Watson is said to have expressed a determination to secure private satisfaction. A number of shots were fired by each of the men, but Mr. Watson was twice struck, one ball entering the right groin and crushing the hip, the other entering the lower part of the body and taking an upward course through the intestines and being found above the second rib on the left side. The latter shot was fatal, and two hours later, after Dr. Richman had extracted the two bullets and everything possible for the man's comfort had been done, Watson expired.

A coroner's inquest was held on Sunday, and the jury found that death had been produced by gunshot wounds inflicted by J. W. Warf.

Warf was later arrested charged with the homicide, and took a change of venue to Helper precinct, where on Wednesday he was tried before Justice J. T Fitch, who dismissed the case, it appearing to him that sufficient justification existed for the act.

Attorney S. R. Thurman defended and D. D Houtz was appointed by the attorney general to prosecute.

Mr. Watson was 59 years of age, had been around Price one year, and among those acquainted with him was highly regarded. His relatives in his former home in Tennessee were wired soon after the tragedy, and at their request the body was buried at Price.

PERSONAL MENTION.

— J. Grames of Oak Spring Bench was in Price on Tuesday.

—Mrs. J. G. Callaway visited friends at Helper last Sunday.

—Dr Richman was in Helper, Tuesday, looking after his patients.

—Miss Violet Grange of Huntington was visiting friends in Price the first of the week.

—Special Agent Ketchum of the Rio Grande Western was in town the first of the week.

—Geo. Frandsen was up to P. V Junction the first of the week on business, returning to Price on Tuesday.

—Capt. Smith, who is connected with the Rio Grande Western, came down from Salt Lake Tuesday night.

—Mrs G. W. Bodle leaves Saturday for St. George, Utah, to visit with her mother who resides near there.

—Mrs. Warren was up to Helper Sunday visiting her daughter, Mrs. James Rooney, and her son, Hub Warren.

—Mike Halloran, who has a big bunch of sheep in Utah county, was in town the first of the week looking after business matters.

—H G. Clark, formerly of Clark's Hotel, came down from Salt Lake, Monday, where he has been for some time on business and pleasure.

—E F. Cassidy, special agent of the Home Fire Insurance company of New York, was in town Tuesday and is now in Vernal He will be back in Price next week.

—Miss Stena Jensen has returned to Price from a week's visit to her parents at Helper.

—Wesley K. Walton, secretary of the Board of Land Commissioners, was in town Wednesday.

—Mrs. C L Davis, wife of Section Foreman Davis, came in Tuesday night from Salt Lake

—Sheriff Allred is back from Beaver and Sevier counties, where he has been on private business

—Mr. and Mrs Wm. Potter returned home last evening after a week's visit with friends at Scofield.

—Miss Lina Garber, who has been the guest of Mrs. L M. Olsen for several months, leaves next Monday for her home at Golden City, Mo, where she will teach school this year. She taught in Idaho last year.

—S. M. Whitmore is down from Salt Lake City looking after his interests in Carbon and Emery counties During the week he made a trip to Huntington neighborhood, where he has a big bunch of cattle.

—Mrs. R M Carey, who has conducted a restaurant at Vernal for about two years, has been in Price for a couple of weeks and has taken a lease on the Jones cottage. She will go to Salt Lake and buy her furniture and fixtures She will conduct a firstclass boarding house.

THE LOCAL NEWS OF PRICE

The town board meets in regular session the first Monday in September.

There has been an immense amount of hay put up hereabouts during the past few days.

Photographer Thompson is nursing a badly battered up thumb since the ball game of Sunday.

Thompson, the photographer, will go to Salt Lake the latter part of the month, probably next week.

There were light showers in this section Sunday and Monday, which cooled off the atmosphere considerably.

Impure baking powders injure the stomach. Use the pure brand named "Perfect," and have no indigestion.

Messrs. Gentry and Warf have opened a meat market in Price and will in future keep everything in the meat and poultry line.

There will be a wedding in Price next week. The contracting parties have sworn the editor to secrecy, however, for the present.

E. L. Harmon and Josephine Babcock of Nine Mile have been licensed to wed.

George Fausett is back in Price and at work after undergoing medical treatment at Provo.

The Maxwell reward has been divided at Provo. Joseph Allen gets $50 and the others $150 between them.

L. Lowenstein reports that business at his store is good for this season, and he is well satisfied with the outlook for the future. He has bought heavily for the fall and winter trade.

Fitzgerald & Co now write their letters on stationary printed at THE ADVOCATE office. The man who patronizes Fitzgerald & Co, gets his printing here and reads this journal is not far off the right track.

Robert McKune, proprietor of Hotel Clark, has taken a long lease on the property and will repaint and repaper it in the near future. The house is one of best conducted in Eastern Utah and enjoys a splendid trade.

Don't pay fictitious prices for oats any more. You can get good Utah oats, sacked, at $1 50 per 100 pounds at Emery County Mercantile Company.

J. H. Cooper, who has been at the Rio Grande Western depot for several weeks under Agent McDonald, has been given the station agency at Thompson.

Only a short time now and the schools will open and the voice of the street urchin will warble its merry notes of laughter as he goes to and from school.

The stomach is our best friend and the next best is the "Perfect" Baking Powder. It is chemically pure and assists digestion.—Emery County Mercantile Co.

E. N. Peyton is back from Salt Lake and again at the key on the daylight job at the Rio Grande Western, while his brother, W. T. Peyton, goes on again at nights.

Advertising won't make you rich in a week, but if persistently followed and scrupulously lived up to in one's store, will do much to make one's business profitable.

We this week turned out a fine lot of job printing for the Senate Saloon, but the work and stock, though the best to be had, is no finer than the good old whiskia kept in stock and sold over the bar by this popular firm, Messrs Nichols & Egan.

The editor of this paper this week had the pleasure of meeting Mr R. G. Miller, one of the oldest residents of this valley who came here some fifteen years ago, and has been a resident and prominent in the affairs of Carbon county and Eastern Utah ever since. He is one of the largest owners of sheep in this section of the state. THE ADVOCATE will henceforth go into his home.

N. J. Thomas, representing Schillings Best, was in town Saturday, calling on merchants. Saturday afternoon he went down to Wellington, taking the editor of this "great moral and religious journal" along in the buggy with him. He sold a nice bill of nice goods there. The newspaper man had the pleasure of meeting a number of people there and adding several new subscribers to our already growing list.

George Frandson, who was up to Colton this week, says that J. M. Miller has finished his sheep dipping corral at that place, and can handle 200,000 head during the balance of the season.

There have been quite a number of traveling men at the Hotel Mathis the past week. The house is very popular and is well and favorably known from one end of the state to the other.

The Western on Friday last carried through Price nearly two hundred excursionists from the San Juan towns in Colorado on their way to Salt Lake. Their tickets are good for fifteen days

Lieutenant Powers with a detachment of eleven soldiers came in Sunday from Fort Duchesne and left Monday morning with about $4,000 which came in from Salt Lake by express to pay the soldiers stationed there.

Don't have your letters sent to the dead letter office, when you can get one hundred envelopes with name and post-office address neatly printed on the corner for $1 25, or five hundred of them for two-fifty.

R. Veltman was here recently from the La Sal Mountain country. He says there are over three hundred prospectors scattered through the hills there. He thinks the camp will become one of the biggest and best in Utah, not excepting any of them.

The east bound passenger train due at Price at 1 o'clock in the afternoon was over five hours late, Tuesday, due to a couple of cars of a freight train getting off the track in the small tunnel about twenty mile above Price. The cars were derailed by a rock slide. No one was hurt.

Prof. McCormick, well and favorably known to most of the people of Carbon and Emery counties, has been up to Salt Lake and was in Price the forepart of the week. The professor will teach school at Tooele the coming term, and we understand will receive a good salary for his work.

J. G. Callaway, the tonsorial artist, had a nice lot of envelopes printed at this office this week. Callaway is doing a nice business and believes in helping to sustain home institutions. Such men as he deserve to prosper.

George Haverstick, representing the Symns-Utah Grocery company, came in from the Fort Duchesne country, Monday, and later left for Orangeville and Castle Dale. Times are very dull with the merchants in the Indian country he says.

The Thomas company ordered a lot of letter heads and envelopes from this office last week, and are now using the same. They believe in keeping money for such work at home, which is good business policy and deserves to be emulated. The firm is doing its share of the business of this section

Large consignments of freight are being received at the depot here for merchants of outlying towns, which would go to show that they are preparing for a heavy trade this fall. On an average of about 25,000 pounds is being handled here daily.

H G Clark, who opened the Clark Hotel in Price and conducted the same until it came under the present management, returned to Price the first of the week and has taken the management of the Mathis House. Mr. Clark is an experienced hotel man, has a large circle of friends and acquaintances all over the country and will no doubt add much to the popularity of this long established and well conducted hostelry.

E L Harmon came in from the Nine Mile country on Tuesday and was a welcome caller at this office. He has lately leased his ranch to Contractor Bartholomew of the stage line, who has taken a four year's lease and will maintain a stage station there. Mr. Harmon says they have had plenty of rain all along and the country never looked better. Everybody is busy in the harvest field and a great deal of hay is being put up. The health of the neighborhood is good There are a great many newcomers going in there

Few people have any idea of the vast outlay of money and the capital invested in conducting first class stages lines, and of which Price is headquarters for two, one running east to the Indian country and the other south as far as Emery. Mr Bartholomew, the owner of the first mentioned line, has a payroll and feed bill that will foot up nearly $40 a day, to say nothing of the capital invested and his own time. He buys most of his supplies in Price and Carbon county and during the course of a year puts many thousands of dollars in circulation. The line is a daily one, well equipped with good stock and vehicles, and is popular with the traveling public. G. T. Olsen, the owner of the line south lives at Emery, where he conducts a general merchandising business. His stages run every day except Sunday and are liberally patronized by those coming from and going to the south. Both lines carry express matter, and are liberal in the fares and charges exacted.

This office was this week the recipient of large bouquet of beautiful flowers plucked from the garden of Mrs. L. M Olson, whose home by the way is one of the most delightful spots in all Eastern Utah. Though the name of the generous and thoughtful donor was not attached to the delicate white ribbon that held the flowers in its gentle embrace, we suspect that the gift is from Miss Lina Garber, whose home is not far from that of the editor's back in Old Missouri, the land of beautiful women, noble manhood and countless resources, every girl from babyhood to maternity as lovely as a sculptor's dream, where flowers of every hue and clime freshen in the evening dews till the green ivy of the north and the fragrant magnolia of the south meet each other in a common home and rebuking sectional hate entwine their arms in tenderest love. It is such little remembrances as this that call back pleasant recollections of home and friends and loved ones, and make one's pathway the smoother. Miss Garber departs for her home at Golden City, Mo., next week. The many friends she has made during her visit in Price wish her bon voyage.

WELLINGTON WAIFS.

At Wellington last Saturday the editor of THE ADVOCATE had the pleasure of meeting Mr. Jefferson Tidwell, one of the oldest residents of that settlement. He informed us that the supply of water there is very short, and what is left is unfit for use. As a result of this, some twenty five or thirty persons, mostly women and children, have moved up to Whitmore Canyon, where they will remain until there is a change for the better. The water there is good and there is an abundance of it. At Wellington there are any number of horses and cattle sick, due to the impurity of the water. Along down the valley several head have died, and if those remaining are not driven out to the canyon there will be a heavy loss to come. There has been considerable sickness among children, due no doubt to drinking milk from sick cows

GLEANED AT SCOFIELD.

Schofild, Emery County,
August 8th, 1898.

While waiting at the station called Colton (but known as Pleasant Valley Junction) for the train to take us up to Schofield, some twenty-three double decked cars passed us loaded with sheep, 220 in each car, making a total of 5,060 Utah sheep, bought in the neighborhood by a Mr. Walt Gosling, and being shipped by him to Colorado, their fine condition being evidence of the splendid feed which abounds in the mountains, caused by the fine rains of the spring and early summer.

On account of the rush of the coal business the railway company's train from Pleasant Valley Junction to Schofield has been making two or more trips per day, and therefore has not been running on schedule time; but the great monster engine with its long train of cars, loaded with coal, soon came in; pulling its cars on to the side track—then coupling on to a long row of empty cattle and coal cars, with the passenger car as the switch end to its long tail, the iron horse pulled us up the winding way over the road that follows the course of the creek, that runs down from the meadows of Pleasant Valley. Sometimes the train would form the letter S, and how the cars kept the track with the motive power on the curves so far ahead was a wonder, but as we passed on, now rounding sharp curves, then over bridges, in safety, our confidence became strong that the men in charge knew how to control the powerful steed that was snorting and puffing around the curves hidden from our sight, but whose black breath was seen over the hill around the curve to the right.

J. E. Ingles met us at the station, and after a good supper in his comfortable home, we walked on up to Winter Quarters, some two and a quarter miles distant, and held a meeting with the Priesthood of the place. President Partridge gave some valuable instruction, and judging from the interest manifested by those present, was appreciated by them.

The Sabbath dawned upon a day of rest for the miners—no whistle called them to their accustomed toil—and save the hammering of a few house builders, and the work of the railroad hands in replacing some three coal-laden cars on the track, which had run off the day before, all was quiet at the big coal mining camp.

Big coal mining camp it is; from T. J. Parmley, who occupies the dual position of foreman of the mine, and Bishop of the ward, I learned that in the month of March last the output of the mine was forty-two thousand tons—an enormous amount, showing that the work must have been conducted with ability and skill; in the year 1897 the output was two hundred and twenty-four thousand tons; the average output per month now is twenty thousand tons, with an expenditure of fourteen thousand dollars per month for the mining of the product alone.

The coal is used on the Southern Pacific Railroad system, for their locomotives; a small amount is marketed in the state; some three hundred men and boys work in and about the mine; twenty to twenty-five mules and horses are used in the inner workings of the mine hauling the coal from the different chambers on tracks to a station about one thousand eight hundred feet from the mouth of the mine, where the electrical appliance brings out a

long train of trucks to the shoot at the rate of twelve miles per hour, where it is shot down the screens into the cars below.

The rattling, banging, jawing noise of the truck combined with the rushing, grinding noise of the falling coal—the quick movement of men and boys at the mouth of the mine, in managing the heavily loaded trucks, releasing the loaded, hitching on the empties—makes a scene of confusion to the uninitiated; but to those who watch awhile, see that everything moves with precision and order; otherwise loss of life and limb would be frequent, if the transportation of the coal by the powerful electric force at the rate of twelve miles per hour, was not governed and controlled by some masterly and powerful hand.

Sitting in our comfortable parlor, enjoying the genial warmth of our fires, we seldom think of the lone miner, grimey with sweat and black dust, in his chamber far down in the depths of the earth, who by the light of the candle stuck in his cap, is hewing out the coal, or lighting the fire and hurrying to some barrier in the dark chamber for safety, while the shot shall take effect—then reaching with a long rod of iron, pulling down the partly detached wall of coal, and with quick spring backwards avoiding the fall of the diamonds we burn—then shoveling it into his truck, and calling the boy to hitch on, and away with it, for another empty. And thus they toil in danger of their lives beneath the earth in darkness, save the flickering light of their small oil lamp.

To enter and remain for a few hours in the mine, say a mile from its mouth, passing away from the main line, lit up by electricity, to the chamber of the miner with his small oil lamp, gives one an idea of the brightness produced by the superior light of electricity—but then to pass on out to the mouth of the mine and behold the light of the sun—how glorious it is! One does not know what sun light is, or fully realize its brilliancy and magnificence, until being deprived of it, and then returning to its light, while the powerful king of day is shining with its noon day strength, as was the experience of the writer at a prior visit to the mine.

The business of the company is increasing yearly, new side tracks will be put in this season, and a new chute, which will make four in use, to enable the company to supply the orders which are increasing every day. A new company store is contemplated. Thomas Roylance of Springville has the contract for the excavation, 32x76 and has it nearly completed. A district school house for the Winter Quarters district with capacity for 150 pupils, will be finished in about two weeks at a cost of $1,500. Mr. Margaards of Spanish Fork and T. T. Davis of Provo are the contractors. The money is on hand for its payment. Andrew Hord, D. E. Lewis and W. T. Evans are the trustees.

The ward conference on Sunday was well attended. The choir, under the leadership of Andrew Hord, are deserving of the thanks of the community there for the fine singing which they rendered on the occasion. "They be Welsh, do you see;" and their powerful, rich voices maintain the fame of the old Welsh bards, their fathers. President Partridge and other speakers were listened to with great attention.

The Sunday school cause is well supported. Brother Andrew Hord again coming to the front as superintendent of the Winter Quarters branch, and J. E. Ingels of the Schofield branch. Good order was maintained by the children, and a strong corpse of teachers were on hand to support their superintendents in their labor of love.

Going up stairs—nearly 2,000 feet—the difference in the altitude between Provo and Schofield makes quite a difference in the temperature—and we realized that a "duster" makes a poor substitute for an overcoat in the slight frost which was experienced this morning. Bishop T. J. Parmley may well be proud of his ward, and we think that the Saints and people up there generally appreciate the Bishop and his labors in their behalf.

ALBAL JONES.

PRICE AND VICINITY.

Tom Nichols Offers to Donate Ground For a New Hotel—Comings and Goings of the People Hereabouts —Personal and Otherwise.

Several new dwellings are going up about the city.

Shoes and hats marked down to cost at the Price Trading company's

The Si Perkins Dramatic company is coming to Price on September 1st.

Insurance that insures. For rates, etc., see R. W. Crockett at THE ADVOCATE.

The Price Trading company are selling dress goods below Salt Lake City prices.

Insure your home or stock of goods with R. W. Crockett, who represents companies that pay their losses promptly.

Every woman, in justice to health and pocket book, should try the "Perfect" Baking Powder. Once used always used.

John Donnelly, late section foreman here for the Rio Grande Western, now has a job with the Oregon Short Line at Salt Lake.

The curfew law is a good thing and if enforced will keep many children in after 9 o'clock that might otherwise get into mischief.

School books and school supplies at the Price Trading company's.

When a girl wears red, white and blue stockings does she show her patriotism?

Take your produce to the Price Trading company and get the highest price.

Note the prices on staple articles quoted in this issue by the Price Trading company.

Fire insurance written in the best companies doing business in Utah —R. W. Crockett, at THE ADVOCATE office.

Paul Hanten's new home in the southeast part of the city will be ready for occupancy about the first of the month

Ball programs, and in fact all kinds of fancy stationery printed at THE ADVOCATE office New stock to select from.

F. J. Thomas has been up to Helper the greater part of the week doing painting and paper hanging for residents there.

You cannot better your condition by buying goods in Salt Lake and paying freight when you can buy as cheaply of Price Trading company.

It pleases everybody to know that they can buy the pure baking powder named "Perfect" so reasonably.—Emery County Mercantile Co.

The Price Trading company are determined to sell goods now in stock and make room for the mammoth lot to arrive in September.

Freight receipts at the office of the Rio Grande Western are on the increase. Hundreds of freight wagons are, in consequence, in and out of Price now every week.

Several of our citizens will go up to Castle Gate on the 5th of September to attend the republican county convention. The work of the convention will be done in one day.

The democratic county convention will be held at Price on September 8th, the precinct primaries on the 3d of September and the senatorial convention on the 12th of September.

Under the management of H. G. Clark, the Hotel Mathis becomes more popular with the traveling men who make Price. They are "at home," as it were, under his hospitable roof.

The young ladies of Price will probably play the married women a game of baseball on Sunday afternoon The stakes will be ice cream and the expenses of giving a dance in the near future.

The examination of applicants for state teachers' certificates has closed, and as soon as the examining board reports its findings to the state board of education the names of the successful candidates will be announced.

J. W. Warf was up to Helper the first of the week looking after business matters in which he is interested there. The new store which carries a stock of general merchandise has opened up for business and is doing a fairly good trade for a starter.

By using the baking powder named "Perfect" you will show appreciation of pure food. Always use the "Perfect."—Emery County Mercantile Co

Five stalls are being added to the round house at Helper, and a new machine shop is also under construction there by the Rio Grande Western.

Dr. Richman was in Helper this week several times to see Mrs Catherine Dunton and Mrs. Van Natta, patients of his, and who are now beyond the danger line.

During the week there were several commercial men at the Hotel Clark. Mr. McKune sets a good table, keeps a clean house and in consequence catches his share of both the local and transient trade.

The Chinese paymaster of the Rio Grande Western was here Saturday and left the monthly salaries of the section hands. He also took orders from them for such Chinese goods, rice and so forth, as they use.

Mrs. R. M. Carey has purchased the furniture of the Jones cottage from Mrs. Hart and will conduct the place as a first-class boarding house hereafter. Mrs. Carey comes from Vernal and is said to have conducted the best house in that part of the country.

Says the Salt Herald of the 24th. "Hon. H. P. Myton of the Uncompahgre and Uintah Indian commission was in the city yesterday, en route to Washington, having been summoned there for consultation with the department officials on matters relative to the opening of the reservation."

Z. L. Harmon and Josephine Babcock, both of the Nine Mile country, were married in this city last Thursday by P. I. Olsen, and left for home the latter end of the week with the best wishes of a large number of friends. Mr. Harmon is one of Carbon county's best citizens and a host of people will wish him and his bride all that is good in life.

Mrs. L. M. Olson invited in a number of friends to her cozy home on Sunday evening to meet Miss Lina Garbor, who has been her guest for several months and who left for her home at Golden City, Mo., the following day. Music and pleasant conversation made the evening pass quickly and pleasantly. Choice refreshments were served by the hostess before the guests departed.

Sheriff Storrs of Utah county is smoking a box of cigars at the expense of Captain Ballinger of the Price Trading company, the same being won on a bet when the sheriff was down here a few weeks ago. O. W. Warner, the sheriff's attorney, first tried one, and he having survived the experience the sheriff felt safe in sampling the remainder. At last accounts Sheriff Storrs was in good health and spirits.

Tom Nichols, of the firm of Nichols & Egan, is nothing if not liberal. For some time he has had under consideration the building of a hotel on the lot which adjoins his place of business, but finding a better investment for his surplus money and knowing nothing of the hotel business, he has given up the project. However, he still wants to see a hotel near him, and says he will give the ground mentioned above to anybody who will erect the house and furnish it up. This piece of ground is worth considerable money as it now is without any improvement on it, is enhancing in value and is just the place for a hotel of twenty to thirty rooms. The offer is liberal and will no doubt be snapped up by some one soon.

Messrs. Elliott & Lee, the popular liverymen, have just put on an addition to their already large barn in the rear of the Clark Hotel, which gives them a great deal more room and makes their stable one of the best in all Eastern Utah. They now have about twenty-five head of first class livery stock and any number of good buggies, road wagons and the like. Everything is modern and of the best with them.

Tom Nichols received the sad news the first of the week of the death of a brother at the family home in Austin, Texas. Mr. Nichols had expected to be at his bedside, but a delay somewhere in the transmission of a telegram delayed his departure until after the demise of the brother. The mother and sister of Mr. Nichols, who reside at Austin, are expected to arrive here soon on a visit and will remain for some time if the climate agrees with the mother, who is quite aged and feeble.

Mark P. Braffet, Clarence Marsh and Judge Lochrie were arrested here last Thursday on the charge of criminal libel preferred against them by A. J. Simmons, justice of the peace at Spring Glen, and taken before Justice Fitch at Helper, where the case was dismissed. The alleged libel grew out of an article published in The Advocate at the time the defendants were connected with it, in which serious reflections were made against Simmons in the conduct of the affairs of his office. It is understood that the case may again come up in another form.

CASTLE GATE GLEANINGS.

CASTLE GATE, Aug 28 — A road to the cemetery is being quite generally talked of, and it is thought the P. V. Coal company will materially assist in building it.

* * *

About the unluckiest man in town is Lert Pesetto. He had just gotten over his injuries received in the mine a few weeks ago and started in to work again, when after a few hours' work he unfortunately had both arms pretty badly burned.

* * *

Two little boys of B. F. Caffey are down with the measles. This disease is prevalent among the Italians.

* * *

There are several cases of sickness in town right now. Among the families afflicted is that of H. J. Schultz who has two children suffering from typhoid fever, the youngest child being dangerously ill.

* * *

Mrs. John Aarmodt, who has been sick for some time, is improving.

* * *

* * *

Mrs. Jeanette Ferguson, sister of Superintendent Sharp, arrived here late last week.

* * *

Friends from Cripple Creek are making a pleasant visit with Mr. and Mrs. H. G. Williams

* * *

The uniform rank of K. P. will give an entertainment here Saturday evening, which promises to be a success.

William J. Hill of the Wellington neighborhood was in town on Tuesday. Mr. Hill has burned about 600 tons of lime so far this year and has disposed of all of it but about 100 tons. The water in that section continues very bad, and there are some eight or ten families still up Whitmore canyon, where the water is better and where they will remain until there is a change for the better. There is still considerable sickness among the horned live stock in that part of the county, he says, due no doubt to the bad water.

Price

PERSONAL MENTION.

—Charles Sorrells of Crescent was in Price on Tuesday.

—L. Johnson of Vernal passed through town the first of the week for Salt Lake.

—Mrs. J. Whitmore has been in Salt Lake ten days on a visit to relatives and friends.

—Miss Ida Whitmore will attend St. Mary's Academy at Salt Lake as soon as that school opens.

—Miss Belva Ballinger will attend school in Salt Lake this winter, probably St. Mary's Academy.

—Dr. Richman's mother and sister came down from Salt Lake, Tuesday, to pay him a short visit.

—Mrs. H. P. Myton and son of Fort Duchesne are registered at the Manitou Hotel, Salt Lake City.

—Postmaster Holdaway was out of town Tuesday looking after his interests in other parts of the county.

—Joseph E. Mauquni, who left here to locate at Thurber, Idaho, will return to Price and make his home here.

—Prosecuting Attorney William Howard of Emery county, whose home is at Huntington, was in Price on Sunday.

—L. Robbins of Orangeville was in the city on Tuesday and put his autograph on the register at Hotel Mathis.

—Among several other guests at the Hotel Mathis this week was H. E. Jones of Deseret, who was in town for a few hours.

—Editor Jamieson of the Pioneer of Castle Dale was a visitor to Price on Sunday and left for home by the stage Monday forenoon.

—Says the Manti Messenger: "B. F. Luke, superintendent of schools of Emery county, has been in our midst this week. He has been in Salt Lake on business pertaining to his office and returned to his home in Emery county this morning."

—Charles Goldberg, of the Utah Dry Goods and Grocery Store, is back home again after an absence of several weeks in Salt Lake, where he has been on business and pleasure combined. His many friends are glad to see him home and looking so well.

—Mrs. Bodle of the Hotel Mathis left Friday for St. George on a visit to her mother. She was accompanied by her daughters, Misses Clara and Maud, and will be absent several weeks. Her many friends here wish her a pleasant visit and a safe return home.

—Mrs. L. O. Hoffmann, wife of Acting County Clerk Hoffmann, with the children returned to Price the first of the week, after an extended visit with relatives in Oregon. Mr. and Mrs. Hoffmann are at the Hotel Mathis until they go to housekeeping.

—J. M. Easton, one of the stockholders in the Emery County Mercantile company, was here several days the first of the week and made this office a pleasant and welcome call. Mr. Easton is largely interested here and in Emery county and takes a great deal of interest in our affairs.

Pioneer Woman Passes Away

The Emery correspondent of the Salt Lake Herald makes this reference to the death there last week of a good woman: "The remains of Rachel Miller, one of Utah's pioneers, were peacefully laid away in the Emery cemetery, Thursday afternoon, after an impressive funeral service was held in the meeting house, which was appropriately decorated for the occasion. The speakers were W. R. Allred, W. G. Pettey, Peter Hanson, Thomas A. Williams, P. V. Bunderson and Bishop Brinkerhoff, all of Emery, who spoke in terms of great praise of the deceased.

"Sister Miller, as she was called, was born in Little Britain, Lancashire county, Pa., May 4, 1829. Her husband, Miles Miller, was called to serve in the Mexican war as one of the battalion boys. They came to Utah in 1847. They were among the first to settle at Nephi, Utah. From there they removed to Emery, where Mrs. Miller resided until her death. She was the mother of eleven children—nine boys and two daughters."

NOTICE FOR PUBLICATION.

No 3523.
Land Office at Salt Lake City, Utah, August 13, 1896.

Notice is hereby given that the following named settler has filed notice of his intention to make final proof in support of his claim and that said proof will be made before the county clerk of Carbon county Utah at Price, Utah, on September 24 1896, viz: Harrison A Miller, H R. No. 9005, for the N ½ NE¼ Sec 23, N½ NW¼ Sec 24 Tp 13 S R. 9 E.

He names the following witnesses to prove his continuous residence upon and cultivation of said land, viz Thomas Rhodes, James Hansen, Heber J Stowell and Joshua Wiseman, all of Helper, Utah

FRANK D HOBBS Register
First pub Aug 13, last pub Sept 21.

PRICE AND VICINITY.

Two Old Forty-Niners Meet Unexpectedly in Price—Democratic Primaries and Precinct Nominations— Personal and Otherwise.

School books and school supplies at the Price Trading company's.

Shoes and hats marked down to cost at the Price Trading company's.

Take your produce to the Price Trading company and get the highest price.

Several persons went up to Helper, Sunday, by wagon to see the ball game there.

Insurance that insures. For rates, etc., see R. W. Crockett at THE ADVOCATE.

The Price Trading company are selling dress goods below Salt Lake City prices.

Note the prices on staple articles quoted in this issue by the Price Trading company.

Impure baking powders injure the stomach. Use the pure brand named "Perfect," and have no indigestion.

Fire insurance written in the best companies doing business in Utah.—R. W. Crockett, at THE ADVOCATE office.

Insure your home or stock of goods with R. W. Crockett, who represents companies that pay their losses promptly.

Ball programs, and in fact all kinds of fancy stationery printed at THE ADVOCATE office. New stock to select from.

Every woman, in justice to health and pocket book, should try the "Perfect" Baking Powder. Once used always used.

All of our merchants are getting in exceptionally large fall stocks, which would indicate that a big trade is expected.

AFTER FORTY SIX YEARS

Meeting of Two Old Forty-Niners in Price Last Saturday.

C. E. Colton and William J. Johnstone, two old Forty-Niners who had not seen each other in forty-six years, met unexpectedly in the office of the Price Trading company last Saturday. They went across the plains together from Leavenworth to California. Mr. Johnstone lifted the first shovel of dirt from the foundation of Sutter's mill containing the first gold taken out in California. He now lives at Raymer, N. M, and is well known here in Utah as one of the four survivors of the California pioneers who later made that state famous by its stream of golden wealth. Mr. Johnstone left for home Monday night.

Mr Colton is an old friend of Captain Ballinger and his home is at Los Angeles He is an old Indian fighter and tells many interesting yarns of the early days on the plains when he was freighting, carrying the mails and soldiering and scouting. He has been in Vernal looking up the estate of a relative who recently died there, and left Sunday morning for his home, but will stop en route at Provo, Salt Lake and Ogden, where he has hundreds of friends, made in early days

Saturday evening the two old pioneers were the guests of Mr and Mrs Ballinger, who made the evening pass pleasantly for them, and where they were photographed together, and parted for probably the last time, as both are feeling the weight of years that has passed over each. Mr. Colton is 6. and Mr Johnstone 74 years of age

James Fedasco and Ross Caruson, both of Castle Gate, were licensed to wed, Tuesday, by County Clerk Hoffmann.

The purity of the Baking Powder named "Perfect" is a guarantee against sallow complexion, caused by indigestion.

It pleases everybody to know that they can buy the pure baking powder named "Perfect" so reasonably.—Emery County Mercantile Co.

The Price Trading company are determined to sell goods now in stock and make room for the mammoth lot to arrive in September.

You cannot better your condition by buying goods in Salt Lake and paying freight when you can buy as cheaply of Price Trading company.

By using the baking powder named "Perfect" you will show appreciation of pure food. Always use the "Perfect."—Emery County Mercantile Co.

The stomach is our best friend and the next best is the "Perfect" Baking Powder. It is chemically pure and assists digestion.—Emery County Mercantile Co.

Considerable Indian freight arrived at the depot here during the week and more is to come soon. The freighters are expected in soon to take it to its destination.

In the ball game at Helper Sunday afternoon the Price nine came out victorious by a score of thirty nine to twenty-two The Helper fellows were not in it from the start.

Tur Advocate has received a large

Asking for Donaldson's Release

The friends of County Clerk W. H Donaldson have telegraphed him offering him the republican nomination for county clerk this fall, and if he will accept his name will be placed on the ticket He is now at Yosemite Park in California, and it is expected word will be received from him before the convention meets on the 5th of September. Mr. Donaldson is popular with the people and will make a strong race if he will allow his name to be used. It is more than likely that Governor Wells will release him from the army so that he may become a candidate.

Since the above was put in type word has been received from Mr. Donaldson saying he will be a candidate His friends claim his election is certain and that the democrats will not put up a candidate against him

The Democratic Primaries.

The democrats of Price precinct met at the meeting house Wednesday night and named delegates to the county convention They are Thomas Fitzgerald, Mrs. Percy Horsley, Mrs L O Hoffmann, J D Smith, J. L. Willson, Albert Bryner and C. W. Allred. Alternates are Joe Jones, P. I Olsen, Bruce Willson, William Burr and W. Durfur Albert Bryner was elected precinct chairman and F. J. Thomas, secretary. John L Willson was nominated for justice of the peace for this precinct and W, Durfur, constable There was a big crowd out and much enthusiasm shown on all sides The democrats are confident of victory, so the leaders declare, this fall.

Elliott & Lee have bought the livery business of Mr. Bartholomew, who gives up livery and will devote his entire time to the stage line, business over which is increasing perceptibly.

The young ladies and the boys played a game of base ball on the grounds here Sunday afternoon, in which the boys came out second best in the game. The girls defeated them by two runs.

The little child of Mr. and Mrs. A. J. Van Natta of Spring Glen died on Tuesday night of this week. The bereaved parents have the sympathies of a large number of people in their affliction.

Some half a dozen tourists were put off a Green Line sleeper here Sunday. The railroad is just now rushed with this class of travel, and there is not a day but what several hobos are sidetracked here.

County Commissioners Thryn and Liddell and County Attorney Warf went up to Scofield this morning to investigate the condition of the river there and the supply of water. It is charged that the stream is polluted through filth at Helper being allowed to run into the Price river. They were joined at Scofield by Commissioner Hood.

United States Attorney Whittemore and United States Marshal Miller are at the Uncompahgre reservation on business connected with the litigation arising over the location of the western boundary line, which affects gilsonite claims in the vicinity. They are accompanied by W. L. Maginnis, who is associated with Mr. Whittemore in the litigation.

CASTLE GATE GLEANINGS.

CASTLE GATE, Aug. 31—The contract has been let for the building of the new school house here, and it will be ready for occupancy in the near future.

* * *

The entertainment given by the Uniform Rank, Knights of Pythias, last Saturday night was a most pleasant affair and was well attended Ice cream and cake were passed around and a ball concluded the entertainment.

* * *

Professor Thomas Hardy and family of Huntington visited Castle Gate last week. His daughter, who has been living here for some time, accompanied him home.

* * *

Several new settlers have arrived here lately and are well pleased with the country.

* * *

The contract for building the road up Willow creek to the cemetery has been given to Hansen & Bryner

* * *

The republican caucus to select delegates to the county convention was held Tuesday night, when the following were chosen E. Santschi, J. H. McMillan, T. L. Reese, Joel Ricks, F. Cameron, D. Jenkins, James Young, Chris Davis and M Beveridge. Although a number of ladies were present not one was chosen delegate.

* * *

The teachers' institute convened Tuesday afternoon, and among those present were Professors Roylance and Cummings, Dr. Howard and Miss Kimball A great majority of the county teachers were in attendance

The Cat Was Killed.

Last Tuesday evening lightning struck the house of Mrs Jane Babcock at Spring Glen. The family was assembled at the time, but it was their good luck to escape injury A cat was killed by the electric fluid, which ran up and down the weather boarding inside the sitting room

There has been quite a deal of rain up and down the this week, accompanied by thunder storms, but this is the only one where life was endangered that has been reported There was a heavy shower of rain in Price this morning

Parties in from the south say rains have been frequent as far south as the town of Emery.

PRICE AND VICINITY.

Democrats and Republicans Each Make Nominations For the Various County Offices to Be Filled— Personal and Otherwise.

William B. Boweter and Violet Gardner of Scofield took out a marriage license Tuesday afternoon.

Impure baking powders injure the stomach. Use the pure brand named "Perfect," and have no indigestion

Fire insurance written in the best companies doing business in Utah.—R. W. Crockett, at THE ADVOCATE office.

The Price public schools open next Monday. The attendance this year will be the largest in the history of the city.

Every woman, in justice to health and pocket book, should try the "Perfect" Baking Powder. Once used always used

Quite a number of persons who were not delegates went up to Castle Gate Monday to attend the republican county convention.

It pleases everybody to know that they can buy the pure baking powder named "Perfect" so reasonably.—Emery County Mercantile Co.

You cannot better your condition by buying goods in Salt Lake and paying freight when you can buy as cheaply of Price . . . . ng company.

By using the baking powder named "Perfect" you will show appreciation of pure food. Always use the "Perfect"—Emery County Mercantile Co.

The stomach is our best friend and the next best is the "Perfect" Baking Powder. It is chemically pure and assists digestion.—Emery County Mercantile Co.

From the large number of cattle cars that are going west we are led to believe that extra large shipments of live stock are to be made east in the near future

THE ADVOCATE has received a large stock of stationery and new print papers and is prepared to furnish anything in the job printing line on short notice and at Salt Lake prices

The Rio Grande Western company has declared a dividend of 2 per cent on its common stock, payable at its office, New York City, on September 30th, in preferred stock at par to common stockholders of record September 20th.

Low Johnson's Comedy company played at Town Hall last Friday night to a good-sized audience and after the show gave a dance which was highly enjoyed. The Missouri fiddler was the best that has been along this way in a long, long time. They are assured of a big house the next time they come.

Until the editor of this "great independent, moral and religious weekly" finds some girl who will so far overlook her best interests as to take him "for better or for wuss," no turnips, cabbage, fodder, alfalfa or potatoes will go on subscription. However, a few loads of coal will be the same as cash. Our back yard is large and there will be room for all that is brought in. Drive up early and avoid the rush.

The county commissioners were at Helper last Thursday looking into the condition of the water supply there and will no doubt take action against the Rio Grande Western hotel and others there and at places farther up the Price river, on the grounds that they are polluting the stream. County Attorney Warf accompanied the commissioners and will advise them in the matter.

Prosecuting Attorney Howard came up from Huntington Wednesday and tells us that the democrats of that precinct met on Tuesday night and nominated delegates to the county convention to be held at Huntington on Saturday, September 10th. They are S. P. Sweet, Chris Johnson, M. E. Johnson, W. A. Guymon, D C. Woodward, Levi Harmon and A. N. Truman. Mr. Howard says the party down his way is united, reports to the contrary notwithstanding, and that they will clean up the county. Mr. Howard was too modest to tell us, but we know it to be a fact, that the democrats of Emery are talking of him for the state senate. He would make a strong candidate and a competent one if elected

PERSONAL MENTION.

—Judge Lochrie has been in Salt Lake for several days.

—Clarence Marsh was in Salt Lake the first of the week on business.

—Dr. Richman was in Helper Tuesday where he visited several patients.

—J. W. Warf was in Helper on Tuesday looking after business matters

—Hon Orange Seely of Castle Dale was in town on Tuesday on his way to Salt Lake

—A. B Thompson has sold his photographic outfit and will spend the winter on the Pacific coast.

—Mrs Mary Sperry of Fort Duchesne was registered at the Manitou Hotel in Salt Lake last week.

—James Rooney was down from Helper, Tuesday, on business and remained a few hours in town

—Game Warden Swan of Colorado passed through the city the first of the week from Denver to Salt Lake

—L Lowenstein, who has been down with a fever for a week, was able to be at his store today for a short time.

—E. Santschi of Castle Gate was in town yesterday looking after business affairs and incidentally talking politics.

—Orson Bubbies of Huntington passed through town today for Salt Lake, where he goes as a delegate to the republican state convention.

—M. H Beardsley has gone east with his wife. The hotel at Helper is now conducted by his son, who lately came out from the east.

—J. M Whitmore went to Salt Lake today to see about putting his daughter, Miss Ida, in school there He will be absent several days

—C T. Harte, news editor of the Salt Lake Herald, with his wife and babies, has been spending the past week at Helper on a vacation.

—Mr Pease, who is interested in the stage line here with Mr. Bartholomew, was in town Saturday, leaving in the evening for Salt Lake

—Mrs. A. Ballinger will go to Salt Lake and Ogden in a few days to arrange for the schooling of her sister in-law, Miss Belva Ballinger.

—Mrs J W. Loufbarrow left the first of the week for Salt Lake, where she will reside during the winter in order that the children may attend school

—Prosecuting Attorney Howard of Emery county was in town Wednesday on his way to Salt Lake to attend the funeral of the late President Woodruff.

—Mrs H G. Clark and bright baby boy came down from Salt Lake Friday night. Mamma and baby being here, Manager Clark's happiness is now complete.

—L O Hoffmann is pushing his residence to an early completion. He and his family are stopping at the Clarke Hotel until they go to housekeeping again.

—R G Miller went up to Salt Lake Tuesday afternoon and will attend the funeral of the late President Woodruff today and remain over to the republican state convention.

Deseret Evening News
September 19, 1898

MARGARET ELEN VAN NOTTA.

Helper, Sept. 16, 1898.—This evening at 7:25, my wife passed on to another condition of life. She had given birth to her seventh son on August 15th, and he passed away on the 30th. Her maiden name was Margaret Elen Partington. She was born in Lancashire, England, May 23, 1864; was married to J. H. Van Notta October 17, 1884.

J. H. VAN NOTTA.

Eastern Utah Advocate
September 22, 1898

AROUND THE TOWN.

Price

Wren & Killpack are preparing to erect a new store building at Ferron, their business having outgrown the present quarters.

It pleases everybody to know that they can buy the pure baking powder named "Perfect" so reasonably.—Emery County Mercantile Co

The Price Trading company are determined to sell goods now in stock and make room for the mammoth lot to arrive in September

Mrs. D. W. Holloway will have in a fine line of millinery in the near future. All the latest styles will be shown direct from the Eastern markets

You cannot better your condition by buying goods in Salt Lake and paying freight when you can buy as cheaply of Price Trading company.

By using the baking powder named "Perfect" you will show appreciation of pure food. Always use the "Perfect."—Emery County Mercantile Co

The stomach is our best friend and the next best is the "Perfect" Baking Powder. It is chemically pure and assists digestion —Emery County Mercantile Co.

Thirty seven cents a bushel for wheat is enough to make the farmer look down his nose. In store pay the cereal brings a trifle more a bushel, says the Sanpete Democrat.

The first days of registration will be on October 11th and 14th. The next will be October 18th and the last November 1st. Voters should bear these dates in mind.

The cool weather at night the past week has driven the cattle from the mountains. Judging from their sleek appearance they have fared very well this summer.

THE ADVOCATE has received a large stock of stationery and new print papers and is prepared to furnish anything in the job printing line on short notice and at Salt Lake prices.

Quite a number of lots owned by Emery county in the townsites of Ferron and Emery will be sold at the front door of the court house at Castle Dale on October 29th, pursuant to an order of the board of county commissioners.

The Rio Grande Western announces a rate on the Sanpete and Sevier branches for a Scandinavian reunion at Richfield on the 24th and 25th at a rate of one fare for the round trip to Richfield from points on both branches.

By direction of the assistant secretary of war, Private Charles E. Fitzgerald, Troop A, Seventh cavalry, now at Fort Duchesne, will be discharged without honor from the service of the government by the commanding officer of the station. He will not be entitled to travel pay.

Last Saturday was the festival of Rosh Hashanah, or the Jewish New Year, and marks the beginning of the year 5659, according to the Jewish calendar. The holiday began at sunset Friday evening and concluded at sunset Saturday. It was observed by the Jewish population of Price.

B. F. Luke on Saturday last purchased the residence property of Frank Carroll at Orangeville, and on Wednesday sold the property to J. F. Dorius, who is now a bona fide resident there. Frank Carroll has removed his family from Orangeville to Payson, where he has engaged in business, says the Pioneer of Castle Dale

Ike Glaser, the Helper merchant, has not paid his merchant's license since last October, and, failing to do so upon being requested, Prosecuting Attorney Warf caused him to be arrested. The trial comes up at Helper tomorrow.

The wheat crop in the vicinity of Orangeville is the best that has been raised there for several years. J. B Crawford took ninety bushels to the mill last week, in the cleaning of which only about one bushel of screenings was taken.

Attorney General Bishop, in answer to an inquiry from County Treasurer Lynch of Salt Lake, says the only safe plan is to heed the notice from the postal inspector and mail the tax notices instead of delivering them to property owners wherever practicable as has been the custom heretofore.

Charles LeComte, a member of the Stutts Dramatic company, was sent to the asylum for the insane at Provo the other day from Manti. The fact that he was out on the road with an outfit like the Stutts combination is proof conclusive that he was sent where he properly belongs.

The Emery County Mercantile company has bought an exceptionally large stock of fall and winter goods, many of which have already arrived. The firm is thoroughly cognizant of the wants of the people in this section and can suit the most fastidious taste.

T. L. Wallace of Salt Lake, who has been out along the south line of the Price Trading company's telephone, came in last night after making extensive repairs as far south as Ferron. New receivers and transmitters have been put in and the line now is in excellent condition.

Utah towns are being pretty well worked this year by jim crow dramatic companies. Price has so far escaped all but two of them. The Stuttz outfit and the Lindsays, two of the toughest, from a dramatic point of view, that ever came down the pike, are drawing dreadfully close and may inflict themselves upon the good people here at any time.

The Reid Sisters conduct one of the best, cleanest and neatest restaurants at Helper to be found anywhere in the West. They have a splendid trade and are deserving of all the patronage they receive. One evening this week when the editor of "the great moral and religious" was up there they fed fifty two people for supper.

Nichols & Egan will build a large ice house in the rear of their saloon this fall and put up a sufficient quantity of ice to last them the year round. They will also erect a big warehouse and buy their beer in car load lots, which will make Price a distributing point for a considerable area of country.

Attention is directed to the advertisement of the Oasis saloon in this issue of THE ADVOCATE. The proprietor of this house, popular "Chub" Millburn, handles only the best line of goods to be had and is never happier than when making it pleasant for his numerous patrons. It is headquarters for those who enjoy a good cigar, a game of pool or "a little something for the stomach's sake."

J. C. Weeter of the Weeter Lumber company, came down from Park City Tuesday night and is looking after business matters in Price and vicinity. Mr. Weeter says Park City is being rapidly built up since the fire and already some fifty substantial business houses and many fine residences have gone up. The camp is fairly prosperous, considering the low price of silver.

Colonel D C Dodge, president of the Rio Grande Western, is to be married in Denver soon. The engagement of Superintendent A. E Welby is also announced. Night Operator Peyton is going to Salt Lake in a few days. The old saying that accidents, murders and marriages all come in threes may hold good this time.

Edgar Thayn was in from Wellington the first of the week and made this office a pleasant call. He left one dollar poorer in purse, for he ordered THE ADVOCATE sent to his address and planked down one plunk for the same, which pays him up one year in advance. He reports the health of the neighborhood good and the people down there happy, prosperous and contented.

Spring Glen Neighborhood

A. J. Simmons, justice of the peace of Spring Glen precinct, was in town Tuesday. Though he did not say so in so many words, we suspect that the judge was here to brush up a little on the marriage ritual, for he incidentally remarked that on or about the 13th day of September, A. D. 1898, he expected to unite in marriage C. J. Gentry and Agnes Frances Bishop, two popular young people of the Garden Creek neighborhood, license for the nuptials being issued by the county clerk on the day Judge Simmons was in town. The wife of Judge Simmons has been quite ill of typhoid fever and is just recovering. C H Cook and wife and four children have lately been ill of malaria and typhoid, all six of them being in bed at one and the same time.

PERSONAL MENTION.

—R. A. Kirker went up to Salt Lake Tuesday

—R. G. Miller went out to his ranch yesterday.

—L. C. Caldwell of Vernal was here Monday on business.

—Chauncey Cook of Spring Glen is reported seriously ill.

—Thomas Brasher of Huntington was in Price the first of the week.

—J. Swarts, the San Francisco liquor salesman, was in the city Tuesday.

—Captain Smith was down Sunday from Salt Lake, returning Monday.

—A. R. Howard, representing Dwight's soda, was here Tuesday on business.

—George A. Lounsbury of Denver was registered at the Clarke Monday last.

—L O Hoffmann went out to Whitmore Canyon Sunday on legal business.

—Ike Blaser came down from Helper Monday afternoon, returning in the evening.

—George C Forstner of Fort Duchesne was a guest of the Clarke the first of the week

—H A. Ballard of Thompsons, Utah, was in town Monday on his way to Salt Lake

—Jack Gentry was up to Helper the first of the week and sold a lot of beef while there.

—Louis Goldstein of St. Joseph, Mo., was calling on Price merchants the first of the week.

—W. T Ratcliffe of Detroit spread his autograph on the register at the Clarke Hotel Monday.

—H. Eckstein of Helper, who has lately opened up a cigar store there, was in town on Monday.

—Night Operator Peyton will get a lay off about the first of the month and will visit in Salt Lake.

—H. P. Myton passed through town Monday night on his way to Fort Duchesne from Salt Lake.

—Miss Mary Warf, who has been quite ill with typhoid fever for some time, is reported as much better.

—Doc Shores, the detective of the Rio Grande Western, was here Sunday and left for the East Monday.

—H. G Clark, manager of the Mathis Hotel, left Wednesday morning on a business trip to Salt Lake.

—John Good of Richfield was in the city yesterday and spread his autograph on the register at the Clarke.

—R. H Kirker went out to his coal mines in Whitmore Canyon, Sunday, and left for Salt Lake Tuesday.

—Miss Annie Larsen visited her parents at Cleveland on Saturday and Sunday, returning home Sunday evening

—John Olson, a nephew of L. M. Olson, recently arrived here from Salt Lake and will make his home in Price.

—C. H McMahon of St. Louis, selling cutlery and hardware, was here Monday and sold big bills of goods to our merchants

—Mrs H. A Chase, M. C. Bryan, Mrs J King and Mrs J Hitcock, all of Ferron, were registered at the Clarke Hotel last Saturday.

—Miss Olive Boyd of Minnie Maud was visiting friends in the city the first of the week, and left for her home Wednesday morning on the stage.

—W. W. Old, the life insurance agitator from Salt Lake, is in town. Mr. Old has the reputation of being the best single handed talker in Utah.

—Lieutenant Littlebrandt of Fort Duchesne left Monday night for Fort Grant, Arizona, where he has been appointed regimental quartermaster.

—G T. Olsen, proprietor of the stage line to the south, came in from Emery the first of the week, and after transacting some business here left for home.

—Mark P. Braffet went up to Provo last Monday and was present at the trial of Maxwell, whose case came up before Judge Dusenberry the first of the week.

—Ed Taylor, who recently put in a stock of general merchandise at Vernal, was in the city Tuesday on his way to Southern Utah, where he has large business interests.

—Manager Fox of the Ferron store of the Emery County Mercantile company was in Price yesterday. He reports business fairly good in his section of the Kingdom of Emery.

—Miss Belle Boyd will resign her position with the Emery County Mercantile company the first of the month. She will return to her home at Minnie Maud. Her many friends will regret to see her leave Price

—Thomas Murphy, of the firm of Fitzgerald & Co., has been quite ill for a week past, but is improving and has been out a few days His many friends missed him from his haunts and hope for a speedy recovery.

—Mr. and Mrs Kie Oldham of Little Rock, Ark., were here Sunday on their way home from Fort Duchesne Mr Oldham is the attorney for the Uintah Indians and represents them in the depredations claims litigation He had been to the agency on this business.

—Mr. and Mrs. L O Hoffmann, who have been living at the hotels since Mrs Hoffmann's return from Oregon, will move into their new home near the school house next week, probably on Tuesday. It will be, when completed, one of the coziest homes in town.

Death of Mrs. Van Natta.

Mrs. Margaret Van Natta, wife of J. H. Van Natta, a prominent citizen of Helper, died at the family home on Friday night. The funeral was held at Helper Sunday and was largely attended by friends of the family. The bereaved husband and family have the sympathy of the entire community. Mrs. Van Natta was a good Christian woman, respectful and beloved by all who knew her.

Her Right Foot Amputated.

Dr. Allen of Provo came in Sunday night and was met at the Price depot by a buggy and conveyed to Wellington, where he later amputated the right foot of Mrs. Thomas Lord. It will be remembered that Mr. and Mrs. Lord were thrown from a wagon in a runaway several months ago, at which time Mrs. Lord's foot was crushed. Mortification set in and an amputation was necessary. The patient is getting along as well as could be expected, but it is feared she will not survive the operation.

Salt Lake Herald
September 24, 1898

CASTLEGATE NEWS.

"Alfalfa Choir" at Huntington Will Sing In Salt Lake Soon.

Castlegate, Sept. 23.—Professor Alex Jameson of Castledale is in town and lectured in the Latter-day Saints meeting house. He is interesting the people in the stake academy now in course of erection at Castledale.

Judge H. Savage and wife of Spring Glen made a friendly call.

The new school house is going up rapidly, and will be the best looking building in town when completed.

John H. Lloyd of Scofield stopped off here on his road home, he has been to Huntington practicing with Professor Hardee's choir. He thinks that when the "Alfalfa" choir sings at the Eisteddfod, at conference time, there will be a surprise in store for the Salt Lake musical people.

Dominic Pesseto and wife have returned from Sterling, Sanpete county. They prefer the rocks to the meadows. Messrs. Hansen and Bryner, who took the contract for the cemetery road have completed their work.

Eastern Utah Advocate
September 29, 1898

Petit Jurors Drawn.

The following petit jurors have been drawn for district court on October 10th

E. D. Follmer, Spring Glen, Wm Lund, Castle Gate, Ed F Jones, Helper, Henry Wade, Castle Gate, John Pittman, Winter Quarters, R. A Snyder, Wellington, Henry Wilson, Scofield, George Robb, Price, J. W. Russell, Winter Quarters, John Horn, Castle Gate, James Hansen, Helper, Thomas Gale, Wellington, George Faucett, Price, H. J. Stowell, Spring Glen, John P Johnson, Winter Quarters, Chris Petersen, Price, Frank Tidwell, Wellington, J M. Leveridge, Winter Quarters, Thos Fitzgerald, Price, Wm. Ramsey, Scofield, Robert Bishop, Scofield, R. L. Lewis, Winter Quarters, G. C Johnson, Minnie Maud, John T. Rawley, Spring Glen, Wm C. Burrows, Scofield, P. A Smith, Helper, W A. Faucett, Jr, Wellington, A. W. Horsley, Price, Herman C Bryner, Price, Thomas Jenkins, Scofield

Wedding Bells.

Invitations have been issued announcing the marriage on the fifth of October of Miss Henrietta Barlow and John William Gentry, both of this city, at the home of the bride's parents. Both are popular young people and their many friends will wish them many years of wedded bliss. THE ADVOCATE with their friends extends congratulations. They will go to Salt Lake next week, and will give a free dance at the town hall on October 7th, in honor of their marriage, to which everybody is invited.

The following grand jurors have been drawn for the district court which convened on October 10th

John U. Bryner, Helper; Louis Jones, Winter Quarters; R. G. Miller, Price; Andrew Gilbert, Winter Quarters, E. W. McIntyre, Price, Allen Cox, Castle Gate; H G Mathis, Price, Soren Olsen, Price; Jacob Kofford, Price; Samuel Harrison, Winter Quarters.

Marriage Licenses Issued.

Peter Longo and Margaret Jene Locke, both of Castle Gate.

Ingansxio Falchone and Pasqualina Marxulola, both of Helper.

CASTLE GATE NEWS.

Alex Jameson of Castle Dale was in town last week and lectured in the meeting house. He is interesting the people in the stake academy now being built at Castle Dale.

Judge H. Savage and wife of Spring Glen were here recently.

The new school house is going up rapidly, and will be the best looking building in town when completed.

John H. Lloyd of So. Gold stopped off here the other day on his way home from Huntington, where he had been practicing with the Emery stake choir. He thinks that when the choir sings at the Eisteddfod there will be a big surprise in store for the Salt Lake musical people.

The new road to the cemetery has been completed.

William R Ward's infant child was buried last Friday.

Eugene Santschi and B. Knight went to Logan last Saturday to put their sons in the Agricultural college.

The wife of Allan Cox is very sick.

W H Hawley has been sick for several days.

This town has been flooded with visitors the past few days.

Isaac Jones and family left Saturday to make their home at Lawrence, Emery county.

The reason for so much sickness hereabouts is that good drinking water is so scarce. Price river is polluted, and unless a change is effected there will be a great deal more sickness.

The mines are turning out about 1,600 tons of coal per day.

H. Wade has returned from a prospecting trip up at Soldier Summit. He, with a number of others, has located some fine gilsonite claims.

The social hop given by the Saturday Night Club was not very largely attended. The reason given is that there are few young ladies here and the boys dislike to go alone.

The Pleasant Valley Coal company's payroll is now about $17,000 a month, with some 400 men working in all departments. The company will put 100 more men to work as soon as they can be had. The greater part of the output of the mines finds a market in Nevada and California.

The new school house is nearing completion and will be ready for occupancy about the middle of October. J B Cardall is principal of the schools this year, with Miss Nellie Bell and Miss Minnie Knight, assistants. There are about 125 pupils enrolled. A levy of 2½ mills on property has been made and this sum, it is expected, will pay off the expense of building the new school house.

HELPER NEWS NOTES.

I Glaser, the Helper merchant, was fined five dollars for contempt of court the other day before Justice Fitch. Glaser was before the court on the charge of failing to pay his license for doing business as a merchant. The jury disagreed. Mr. Glaser used words more impolite than elegant to the justice and he was assessed five dollars.

Business men report that this pay day has been one of the best they have had in months.

The railroad library is a popular place for both residents and strangers in the city.

Manager Beardsley of the Rio Grande eating house was a visitor to Salt Lake a few days ago.

Felice Santolini has opened a first class store here and carries a full line of groceries, candies, cigars, fruits and tobaccos. He comes from Salt Lake, where he also has a store.

H. Eckstein has opened a cigar and tobacco store in the building next to James McCune's saloon and is doing a good business. Soft drinks are served in the pleasant card rooms. Billiard and pool tables will be added in the near future.

The Red Sisters are having about all the patronage they can take care of at their restaurant. It is one of the neatest and cleanest in the country.

Several parties from here took in the dance at Price last Friday night.

The railroad company has about finished the last of its twenty houses being built here for the accommodation of employes.

Mrs. James Harrison lies very low with typhoid fever. This is a sympathetic case, the lady losing a child the other day while sick in bed. The husband enlisted with the volunteers and is now in Cuba.

Eastern Utah Advocate
October 6, 1898

Marriage Licenses Issued.

Ignazio Falchono and Pasqualina Marzzuia, both of Helper.

Oto Waitula and Selma Waitula, both of Winter Quarters.

J. W. Gentry and Henrietta Barlow, both of Price.

Mrs Jane Babcock and E. J. Tolan both of Spring Glen, were married in this city by Justice Olsen last Thursday Both are popular and well known in Carbon county and a host of friends will wish them happiness and prosperity.

Were Married On Monday.

Miss Henrietta Barlow and Jack Gentry were married at the home of the bride's parents in this city last Monday afternoon, and later left for Salt Lake City where they attended the Eisteddfod. Mr. and Mrs. Gentry will be home tomorrow and will give a dance to their friends at Town Hall tomorrow evening. Their many friends are prepared to give a hearty reception.

Peter Longo and Miss Margaret Locke were married at Castle Gate Saturday night. Quite a number of the friends of this young couple were invited to witness the ceremony.

PERSONAL MENTION.

- William Young of Castle Gate was in town Sunday.

—William Howard of Emery county went with the choir to Salt Lake.

—Misses Belle and Olive Boyd left for their home in Nine Mile last Saturday.

—Friends of Thomas Murray will regret to hear that he is again confined to his bed.

—Editor Jamieson of the Castle Dale Pioneer was here Sunday en route to Salt Lake.

—Mrs. Mark P. Braffet and children left Tuesday morning for a visit to Salt Lake friends.

—William H. Allen of Provo was here during the week and was accompanied by his wife.

—Will O Hurst of St. Louis was registered at the Clarke Hotel the first of the week.

—W W. Olds, the insurance man, came in from the south Monday and left Wednesday for Vernal, where he will be for several days.

—Mrs. G. T. Olsen of Emery was at the Hotel Clarke, Wednesday, on her way to Salt Lake.

—George F Timms of Washington, D C., was a guest of the Mathis House several days during the week.

—A J. Donnan, Indian inspector, was at the Mathis Hotel, yesterday, he having been on a visit to the agencies.

—E B Torrey of St. Louis and Thomas Wise of Kansas City were guests of Hotel Mathis the first of the week.

—S. M Miller and E. R Harper, both of the Uintah commission, were at the Hotel Clarke Sunday en route to Salt Lake.

—George W. Bodle was down from Helper the first of the week. He heard the Emery stake choir sing Monday evening.

—Ike Glaser, James Rooney, James McKune and Justice Fitch, all of Helper, were visitors to Price during the week.

—Hon Moos Peterson of Moab and republican candidate for the state senate, is expected to be in Price the fore part of next week

—M E Crandall, Jr , of Springville, was here the first of the week and shipped a carload of honey for William H Roylance. It went east.

—Sheriff Wilson of Grand county passed through the city today enroute to Salt Lake. He will get requisition papers while there for some bad men down in Arizona

—Mary D Carter of Washington, D C , passed through the city Sunday en route home from Fort Duchesne, where she visited relatives. The lady is employed in the interior department.

—F S. Luetol and wife of Vernal were guests of Hotel Clarke last Sunday and were accompanied by Miss Rowena Sutherland of Boulder, Colo , who has been their guest for several weeks and was en route home.

—Samuel A King of Provo was here Sunday en route home from Orangeville, where he attended the democratic county convention in the interest of his brother, William H. King, who is an aspirant for United States senator

Eastern Utah Advocate
October 13, 1898

ELECTION JUDGES NAMED.

County Commissioners Take Action In An Important Matter

The county chairmen of the republican and democratic parties having neglected to designate members of their respective parties to act as judges of election, the board of commissioners named Albert Bryner for the democrats and D W Holdaway for the republicans, who filed a list of names. The first two are democrats and the third republican in each precinct:

Winter Quarters—T. J Parmley, T. H Thomas, J H Schloers

Scofield—William Ruff, James McKinley, H H Earll

Castle Gate—William T Lamph, Joseph A. Young, C W. Lewis.

Helper—Thomas Rhoads, James Harrison, P. A Smith

Spring Glen—Herbert Savage, H. A. Miller, G W Aldredge.

Price—F. J. Thomas, Seren Olsen, H. O. Mathis.

Minnie Maud—E. L Harmon, A. J. Russell, E. C. Lee

Wellington—Peter Liddell, Lehi Jessen, J. S. Birch.

Wellington News Notes

There was a grand reception given in the new school house under the direction of Miss Mattie Caffey, Miss May Smith and Miss Agnes Liddell in honor of Bernard Liddell, who is going to attend college in Salt Lake City. A good time was had and everybody voted it a most enjoyable affair.

J. B Roberts has moved to town so his children may attend school.

Peter Liddell, it is said, is going to try city life

About everybody is busy digging and putting away potatoes

AROUND THE TOWN.

Price

The Price people who went up to the conference and Eisteddfod have about all returned home.

Born, to Mr. and Mrs. L. M. Olson, on Thursday, October 6th, a girl. Mother and baby doing nicely.

There was a rumor in circulation on Tuesday that ten horses belonging to A Ballinger had been stolen from his pasture. The horses had broken out and were found before noon Tuesday not far from town

Mr. and Mrs Jack Gentry returned from their wedding trip to Salt Lake on Friday last, and in the evening gave a dance to their friends at Town Hall A most enjoyable time was had by everybody present.

Charles P Lind, one of the substantial citizens of Castle Gate, was in Price on Monday, looking after business affairs He says the coal company at Castle Gate is working all the men it can get, nights and days and Sundays, and still wants more good miners. The payroll there runs from seventeen to twenty-five thousand dollars per month and there is no complaint of hard times whatever. Very little interest centers in politics.

S. H Miller has lately opened up at Helper a firstclass butcher shop and market and is said to be doing a splendid trade, which is the best indication that the stuff he handles is all right. A lady down from there this week told the Advocate man that she could get just as good a steak or a roast from Miller's shop as she could in Salt Lake and that hereafter she proposed patronizing home people

PERSONAL MENTION.

—John M. Zane attended court here this week.

—D F. Luke and wife of Orangeville were here this week.

—E. W Tatlock of Manti was at the Mathis Hotel this week.

—Ike Glaser came in from Vernal the last of the week where he has a branch store.

—George W. Bodle came in Monday night from Helper, and went back again Tuesday.

—Nora Christensen and her mother of Cottonwood were guests at Hotel Clarke on Tuesday.

—Judge Henderson was among the prominent attorneys in attendance upon district court.

—Mrs. A. H. Hart has returned to the city and was registered at the Clarke on Wednesday.

—C. T Holladay, one of the owners of the Clarke Hotel, is in town this week on court business.

—Mrs J O. Fausett was among the visitors to the Eisteddfod from Price at Salt Lake City last week.

—S. H. Miller, the Helper butcher, was down Tuesday on business and went back home in the evening

—Tom Nichols went up to Salt Lake Saturday morning on business and returned the first of the week.

—Attorney Hoffmann of Richfield, a brother of L O. Hoffmann, was in attendance upon district court here this week.

—Dave Elliott was among the Price fellows to take in the conference and other attractions at Salt Lake City last week.

—Judge Jacob Johnson stopped at the Mathis Hotel during his stay in Price this week He will open court at Castle Dale next Monday.

—J. T. Richards, L. R. Rhoads and George P. Costigan, Salt Lake attorneys, were all three guests of the Mathis Hotel during the week.

—John Costigan, who rolls cigars for himself, was here Monday and went out on the stage Tuesday morning for Vernal and other points.

—Doc Shorts and Special Agent Ketchum of the Rio Grande Western attended district court as witnesses during the fore part of the week

—Thomas P. Murphy's friends are pleased to see him out again and to know that he is feeling like "a two time winner at Sheep's Head Bay."

—J. T. Farrar, the Green River merchant and candidate on the republican ticket for county commissioner, came up to Price last Saturday on business, and left for home Wednesday.

—George Haverstic came in from the south Saturday, where he had been for the Symns Grocery company. He left for Vernal Sunday morning.

—S. M Miller and E. R Harper went through town on Sunday bound for Fort Duchesne from Washington. They were guests of the Hotel Clarke while in the city.

—Mrs A Ballinger has been at Salt Lake and Ogden for several days visiting friends, and also placing her sister-in-law, Miss Belva Ballinger, in school at St. Mary's.

—James McCune was down from Helper Monday shaking hands with his host of friends here and congratulating himself that he had not been caught on one of the juries.

—Manager Loufbarrow of the Weeter Lumber company attended conference at Salt Lake this week and visited Mrs Loufbarrow and the babies. He came down Tuesday.

—Claud Maxwell, W. C. Brooker and Sam Glaser and Mrs. Miller from Helper were down Friday night and attended the dance given by Jack Gentry and his bride at Town Hall.

—John P Johnson, Sam Harrison, B. E. Lewis, J M Leveridge, W. B. Burrows and Lewis Jones, all of Scofield, were at the Clarke Hotel on Tuesday. They were here on a jury.

—Mrs B R McDonald, who was visiting relatives at Springville this week, was called to Evanston, Wyo, to attend the funeral of a brother, Henry C. Holley, who died suddenly at Anaconda, Montana.

—Captain Cornish, Indian agent at the Uintah agency until relieved a few days ago, passed through the city Sunday enroute to Huntsville, Alabama, where he goes to join his regiment, the Seventh

—Senator Rawlins and Bishop Iliff, of the Methodist church, passed through here Wednesday on their way to the reservation, supposedly on business in connection with the opening of the reservation, which Congressman King thinks will occur about January 1st.

—Elder J. W. Nixon, who has just returned from a two years mission in California, will teach school at Wellington this winter. Asked why he did not teach at Huntington, he stated that the Huntington teachers were all employed before he knew of his release from missionary work hence his application was too late. He says his mission has been a source of great satisfaction to him.

—The Rt. Hon. Michael Hickey, the member from Cork, who for more than a year has materially assisted in the production of "the great moral and religious," departed Sunday night for the East and will spend the winter among orange groves of Florida or the oleanders of the Lone Star State. May his shadow never grow less, nor the "squares" come less than three times a day.

CASTLE GATE NEWS.

David Howells, who works in the mines here, had his foot badly mashed last Monday. He was rothing a fractious mule which turned out of the track and pinioned him against a post. His right foot was forced down on the track, two loaded cars passing over it, fracturing all the small toes.

Deonard Carroll, a boy of 7 years, fell on his right arm the other day, causing a compound fracture at the elbow joint.

James Rutherford, who has been the car repairer here for some time, has been relieved by a Mr. Dunlap.

Samuel Bowley, an old timer in Castle Gate but now of the Iowa soldiers' home, is visiting his daughter, the wife of Judge Duerdon.

O. Cupo is going about with his head bandaged. He sustained a blow from a chunk of coal falling on him, and also complains of being hurt internally.

The filthy case before mentioned in the newspapers in dispatches from here came up again Saturday morning, when County Attorney Warf and Sheriff Allred came up from Price and consulted with the justice of this precinct. It was decided to send young Scalzo to the reform school at Ogden. It is hoped that nothing will come up to change the decision, as the town can well spare such a brute.

WELLINGTON WAIFS.

The young ladies of Wellington gave a grand ball in the upper room of the new school house on Monday evening. Everybody had a good time.

Some of the young folks had a surprise party on Miss Belinda Hill the other evening (Tuesday). It was her twenty-first birthday.

Eugene E. Branch has left here to be gone for a couple of months.

Eastern Utah Advocate
October 20, 1898
Price

PERSONAL MENTION.

—Hon. Orange Seeley of Emery county was in Price Monday.

—Billy Potter and wife are at home from their trip to Salt Lake City.

—Judge Reid was at the Mathis Hotel Sunday on his way to court over at Castle Dale.

—County Attorney Warf and Sheriff Allred were up to Helper Monday on legal business.

—Mrs. A. Ballinger is at home from a visit to friends and relatives at Ogden and Salt Lake.

—J. W. Warf was among the guests of the Walker House at Salt Lake City last Tuesday.

—Mrs. A. McLean of Castle Gate visited friends in Salt Lake City the fore part of the week.

—James McKune of Helper was in Salt Lake City the greater portion of last week on business.

—W. W. Ott the insurance man, came in from Verual on Sunday and left later for Salt Lake City.

—Captain Smith came down from Salt Lake Wednesday night and left for the West the morning.

—D T Thompson and Alex Jameson, two of Emery county's prominent citizens, were in Price this week. Both attended court here.

—Bishop Iliff of the Methodist church did not come in with Senator Rawlins from the reservation. He will probably be here Saturday on his way to Salt Lake City.

—Dr Richman returned on Saturday from Salt Lake City, where he visited relatives during conference and listedded His mother and sister reside in the capital city

—Prosecuting Attorney Howard of the " kingdom of Emery" was here Saturday on business and returned home the next day, in company with Judge Johnson and others

—R. A. Kirker attended court here last week and left Sunday for his camp in Whitmore Canyon, where he says he will hibernate until about the middle of November or the first of December

—M. C Bryan, assessor of Emery county, was here over Sunday. He has just completed his new store building at Ferron and will open up now in a few days one of the nicest liquor stocks in Eastern Utah

—Fred W Milverton, official reporter of Judge Johnson's court, was here yesterday on his way from Castle Dale to Sanpete county, where an extra term of district court will be held next week at Manti.

—Mrs. B R McDonald has returned from Evanston, Wyoming, where she was called last week to attend the funeral of a brother who died suddenly at Anaconda, Montana She stopped off at Springville on her way home.

—Judge Jacob Johnson cleaned up the district court docket on Saturday and left Sunday by private conveyance for Castle Dale, where court was opened on Monday. Judge Rhoads and one or two other attorneys were in the party.

—Messrs F. T. Knox and J. F. Stone, two coal barons from Columbus, Ohio, were in Price Wednesday and left yesterday across country for Southern Utah and Arizona, where they go to look after copper properties with a view of buying

—Dave Elliott, our do n to date liveryman, was one of the last to return from conference and the Eisteddfod. He had a Lelluvagood time he says and will not miss any of these attractions in the future. He looks ten years younger after his outing

—Mike Hickey, who left here some two weeks ago, his nose pointed to the east, has landed at Glenwood Springs, Colorado, where he is living at a three-dollar-a day hotel and holding down a steady situation on the Daily Avalanche of that city.

—W. H Cassday of Salt Lake passed through here Sunday on his way to Emery county, where he will make several speeches under the direction of the democratic state central committee. At no distant date other speakers will follow the gentleman up.

—M. Tuttle of Orangeville was registered at the Clarke Hotel last Monday with his sister, Mrs Mabel Moore. The general store they are to open at Orangeville will soon be ready for business. They will carry one of the best and the largest stocks in Emery county.

—H. C. Myton of White Rocks and John S. Abbott of Fort Duchesne, two me ibers of the Uintah commission, were in town this week on their way to Salt Lake City. They had no information to impart concerning the progress of negotiations with the In ians relative to the allo m nt of lands

—Hon. Mons Peterson of Moab, candidate for state senator on the republican ticket, came to town Tuesday and is here to get better acquainted with the people of the town and county. Mr. Peterson has a host of good friends in Carbon, and it goes without saying he will make many more in time for them to vote for hi n fo senator in November.

AROUND THE TOWN.

Hardin Benion, democratic nominee for state senator, and Sam A. King will make a tour of Carbon, Emery, Grand and San Juan counties. Benion spoke at Moab yesterday.

There was a big crowd up from "the kingdom of Emery" on Sunday and Monday to attend quarterly conference here and which was in session two days, adjourning Monday.

According to the new law, each set of judges of election selects its own presiding judge and the board of county commissioners in appointing the judges have nothing to do with designating the judge of each respective district to preside at the polls on election day

Michael M Beveridge writes the Salt Lake Tribune from Castle Gate as follows 'Your paper reported today, October 14, 1898, that the nominee for the republican party for assessor and treasurer of Carbon county had resigned It is false, and not true The nominee for the said office is the writer of this note "

J. P. Gardner, the Salt Lake clothier, J. W. Smith, of the Utah Steam Laundry, and R C Dustan, the grocery salesman, went out from here in a rig last Monday for the northeast looking for deer, or bear, or any old thing that will stand in one place long enough to be shot at. They expect to be gone ten days or two weeks.

Mr. and Mrs Jack Gentry have taken Herman Bryner's house and are now at home to their friends Jack tells the bachelors there is nothing in the world so nice as to stretch one's legs out under his own table at meal time. "Go thou and do likewise," is his advice to the fellows who have not been landed in the matrimonial net.

The Brimhall brothers, who are lately up from the Sanpete country, gave a dance at Town Hall, last Friday night. One of them tickles a fiddle to the queen's taste, while the other can make old man Steinway ashamed of himself when it comes to rounding a piano, and give him cards and spades The boys will give these dances about once a week during the winter

As will be seen by a card published in another portion of this paper one of the members of the firm of Tatlock & Livingston of Manti will be in Price at each term of the district court, and will look after any litigation intrusted to the firm Messrs Tatlock & Livingston are numbered among the representative lawyers practicing before the Utah courts and make a specialty of mining and irrigation cases The Advocate can recommend the firm as worthy and thoroughly reliable.

Onward Lodge No. 15, Knight of Pythias, will give a grand ball at Town Hall one week from tomorrow (Friday) night. Two hundred invitations are being printed at The Advocate office, and these will be sent out over Eastern Utah and other portions of the state. The committee on reception is composed of D W Holdaway, J O Faucett, John L Wilson, A. J. Lee, Robert McKune and Thomas Fitzgerald. A good time is in store for all who attend The best music obtainable will be engaged for the occasion.

Work of the Grand Jury.

The grand jury which was in session five days last week returned five indictments and ignored a number of cases that were reported to that body The county records were examined and the report says they were found properly kept The condition of the county jail is condemned because of its being dirty and filthy, in bad condition generally and unsafe

M P. Johnson and Miss Eliza V Lovelace, prominent young people of Emery county, were married at the residence of the bride's parents at Huntington last Saturday, Bishop Peter Johnson making them man and wife. There were some 150 guests present who partook of a big dinner after the ceremony. They were the recipients of some valuable and useful presents At night there was a dance given at the Huntington hall by the popular young couple.

Professor Hardy and members of the Emery stake choir have been receiving praise and congratulations ever since the return of the choir home for the splendid showing made at the Eisteddfod Regardless of the fact that the trip to Salt Lake cost close on to two thousand dollars the choir members are pleased with their trip.

Thirty five thousand pounds of honey arrived here this week from the apiary of James Hacking of Uintah county for shipment to Chicago About a carload of the sweet product came in also from Emery county and was shipped out direct to Boston by the agent of William Roylance of Springville.

For the first annual Sunday school convention of the Mormon church at Salt Lake City, November 27th to 27th, a rate of one fare for the round trip has been authorized. Tickets will be good returning with final limit of December 1st Eastern Utah will no doubt be largely represented

It will be to the interest of anyone who desires good underclothing for grown people or children to come and examine our remnant outing flannels. We have just received a whole case. It costs nothing to examine, but you will surely buy. Emery County Mercantile company

Mrs. D W. Holdaway, at the post office, has got in one of the very nicest lines of millinery ever shown in Price. New and stylish hats 85c and up. Children's hoods and caps, ladies gloves, etc. Everything new and the latest patterns,

PERSONAL MENTION.

—"Miss Nellie Holley, an accomplished young lady of Springville, is the guest of her sister, Mrs B R McDonald, and will remain here several weeks

—Junius F Wells, a bright young republican and a brother of the governor, was here this week on his way home from Emery county, where he made a number of speeches

—Guy King and M C Bryan were in from Ferron last Sunday.

—Orange Seely and A. Tuttle, two prominent citizens of "the kingdom of Emery, were registered at the Clarke this week.

—C W. Stansel of Salt Lake City was in town this week.

—Indian Agent Myton was here yesterday on his way to the reservation from Salt Lake City.

—James McKune came down yesterday from Helper and was here for an hour or so in the afternoon

—Hardin Bennion, democratic nominee for the state senate, was at Hotel Mathis several days this week.

—Mr. McAllister of St. Joseph will take charge of this territory for the firm which the late John M. Easton represented.

—Arthur J Lee went out to Fort Duchesne last Sunday on business.

—Agent Smith of the Consolidated Implement company, of Salt Lake, was at the Mathis this week. His firm will open a branch house here next spring

—Steve Chipman, the sheep prince, was at the Clarke this week

—H G. Byer of Springville was a guest of the Mathis Hotel this week.

—The wives of Lieutenant Walker and Indian Agent Myton have been expected to arrive here for the last day or two and accompany their husbands on the present trip to Fort Duchesne.

—Mrs. Louis Lowenstein is still at the hospital at Salt Lake City, but is recovering rapidly so her husband states.

Hardin Bennion spoke to a small audience at Wellington on Wednesday night and then left for Grand county, the home of his opponent, Mons Peterson. Yesterday Mr. Peterson took the stage for Uintah county, the home of Mr. Bennion. Each candidate it is said, will make a speech at the home of the other.

CASTLE GATE NOTES

CASTLE GATE, Nov 1—Mesdames Stevenson and Alder of Salt Lake City who have been touring Emery stake in the interests of the relief societies of the Latter day Saints stopped here last week and gave some very good talks on the business of their mission There was a splendid turn-out at both meetings to hear the eloquent ladies.

An epidemic of measles is raging and in consequence many children are debarred from attending district school

Mrs M Beveridge was brought from the city to her home here but the change has not been as beneficial as was desired She has had a severe siege of sickness and is no better

The town is full of strangers presumably after work. There is plenty of work for miners

The Republicans are disgruntled over the way the campaign expenses are handled There has been only one rally here and as yet the biggest part of the expenses remain unpaid The bosses propose to go after the protectionists with a sharp stick if they do not put up soon and it is determined by the party leaders not to hire the Knights of Pythias hall again.

DEMOCRATIC TICKET.

FOR REPRESENTATIVE IN CONGRESS
B H ROBERTS

FOR JUSTICE OF THE SUPREME COURT
R N BASKIN.

FOR STATE SENATOR
HARDIN BENNION

FOR REPRESENTATIVE.
J W DILLEY.

FOR COUNTY COMMISSIONERS
EDGAR THAYN

WILLIAM WARD

ISAIAH LLEWLYN.

FOR SHERIFF
CHARLES W ALLRED

FOR CLERK
ROBERT HOWARD

FOR ATTORNEY
L O HOFFMANN

FOR TREASURER
ALBERT BRYNER

FOR ASSESSOR
ALBERT BRYNER

FOR RECORDER
ROBERT HOWARD

FOR SURVEYOR
ALVIN THAYN

FOR JUSTICE OF THE PEACE.

FOR CONSTABLE

REPUBLICAN TICKET.

FOR REPRESENTATIVE IN CONGRESS
ALMA ELDREDGE

FOR JUSTICE OF THE SUPREME COURT
CHARLES S ZANE

FOR STATE SENATOR
MONS PETERSON

FOR REPRESENTATIVE.
R G MILLER.

FOR COUNTY COMMISSIONERS
HARRY A NELSON.

JOHN JAMES

GEORGE G FRANDSEN

FOR SHERIFF,
JOHN L PRICE.

FOR CLERK
WILLIAM J TIDWELL.

FOR ATTORNEY
SUMNER J HARKNESS

FOR TREASURER
MICHAEL BEVERIDGE.

FOR ASSESSOR,
MICHAEL BEVERIDGE.

FOR RECORDER
WILLIAM J TIDWELL.

FOR SURVEYOR

FOR JUSTICE OF THE PEACE.

FOR CONSTABLE.

	DEMOCRATIC.	REPUBLICAN
PRECINCT NO 1		
For Justice of the Peace .		John P Johnson
For Constable		T Bearnson
PRECINCT NO 2.		
For Justice of the Peace	W E Dickerson.	James Curtain
For Constable	George Green	William Ramsay
PRECINCT NO 3		
For Justice of the Peace	William Featherstone	Henry Duerden.
For Constable	Rooser Davis.	James Young

Salt Lake Herald
November 7, 1898

CARBON COUNTY FIGHT.

Democrats Concede Election of Republican Representative.

(Special to The Herald.)

Price, Utah, Nov. 6.—The election in Carbon county is going to be very close and neither side is over confident of all its ticket or any considerable portion of it. County Chairman Albert Bryner of the Democratic committee concedes the election of R. G. Miller, the Republican candidate for the legislature, but says the balance of the Democratic ticket will pull through by 50 to 100 majority. He thinks the vote of the county will be 950 to 1,000. The Price vote will be 200, and the odds, if any, Democratic. The Republicans will carry Winter Quarters, where the vote is about 175. Wellington casts 125 votes, and will be overwhelmingly Democratic. Minnie Maud went Republican two years ago, but will give the Democrats 25 majority on Tuesday next. Spring Glen is Republican, with 45 votes. At Castle Gate there are 150 votes, about evenly divided. Helper is doubtful, with 40 votes, nearly all of whom are railroad men. Scofield casts 175 votes and is claimed by Chairman Bryner.

The registration on Tuesday was very large throughout the county and is believed to have been beneficial to the Democrats. The county ticket on the whole is safe, according to the estimates of Chairman Bryner. He is also chairman of the Democratic senatorial committee and figures a majority in Carbon county of 100 for Hardin Bennion and 400 in the district. R. G. Miller, according to Chairman Bryner, will have 100 over J. W. Dilley.

REPUBLICANS IN DOUBT.

(Special to The Herald.)

Castle Gate, Nov. 6.—The Republicans, through their county chairman, Mr. H. Knight, claim that the state ticket of their party will receive 100 majority over Roberts and Baskin. The county, they claim, will go about 75 in some of the offices. Others they do not claim at all.

CARBON COUNTY RETURNS.

The returns from the several precincts in Carbon county were slow in coming in. Up to this time (Thursday night) nothing has been heard from Minnie Maud, Scofield and Winter Quarters, while the vote at Castle Gate and Helper as sent down is confusing in some instances. Enough is known, however, to be safe in saying that Roberts carried Carbon county by 30 majority, Zane by 25, Peterson 20. R. G. Miller is elected representative by 100 majority. Not a democrat will sit on the board of county commissioners. Robert Howard is chosen county clerk by 130, Allred, sheriff, 75, Hoffmann, prosecuting attorney, 130, Bryner, treasurer, 10. Thayn had no opposition for county surveyor and is therefore elected. Harry A. Nelson, John James and George O. Frandsen, all republicans, will constitute the incoming board of commissioners.

In Price precinct W. T. Dufer, democrat, and D. W. Holdaway, republican, are the successful ones for constable and justice of the peace, respectively, by majorities of about 100. Hardin Bennion is elected state senator over Peterson by about 200.

The official count will be made next Monday. The complete returns in tabulated form will be published next week.

PERSONAL MENTION.

—J. A. Young, of Castle Gate was a visitor in Price yesterday.

—Ike Glaser was down from Helper the first of the week

—James Rooney and wife were down from Helper yesterday.

—J. M. Whitmore will feed 200 head of fine cattle this winter

—George Haverstick was here election day from a trip to Vernal and left yesterday for Salt Lake.

—Captain Gilfoile was here the latter part of the week on his way to Salt Lake City, where he went on private business

—J. C Weeter came down from Park City Sunday last and after spending several days in the city left for home on Tuesday.

—George T. Holladay came down from Salt Lake the first of the week and is looking after his interests in this part of the country.

—H C Smith has moved his family in from Brocks and will make Price his home Mr. Smith is engaged in the freighting business from here to Vernal

—Will E Mease, of Fort Duchesne, was in town yesterday on his way to the East, and will while away visit his old home in Virginia He will be absent several weeks.

—Agent McDonald is already looking ahead to the time and making preparations for sheep shearing next spring He figures that there will be 75000 head of sheep sheared here

—Miss Nellie Holley, a sister of Mrs. B R. McDonald, and whose home is at Springville, with several musically inclined friends and acquaintances, entertained a party of friends and several guests of the house at Hotel Clarke last Sunday evening The young lady is an exceptionally fine musician and has a voice of rare sweetness It was a treat that will not soon be forgotten by those who were fortunate enough to be present The editor of "the great moral and religious" was there through the thoughtfulness of Mr McDonald It was one of the most pleasant evenings in our recollection

—N. Bartholomew, of the Price and Vernal stage line, came in Sunday night from Idaho and has been out over the line during the week. Mr Bartholomew has lately added new stock and equipment to his already heavy investment and can give the traveling public their money's worth wherever they may want to go This line makes, perhaps, the best time on any route in the West, appreciation of which is shown by the large and increasing travel There is now a system of eating stations that is second to none other and the traveler who embarks on one of Mr Bartholomew's elegant four horse coaches travels in the next finest thing to a Pullman buffet. B R. McDonald, agent for the line, has also helped to bring this increased growing business

Capta'n and Mrs. Ballinger, the other day celebrated the eleventh anniversary of their marriage. They were wedded at Ogden and some two years later came to Price, where they have since resided, and are numbered among the city's best people The host of friends of this estimable couple wish them many happy returns.

The town board met Monday night in regular session Very little business was transacted The piano in use at Town Hall and belonging to Robert McKune was purchased for $95.00 and a warrant ordered issued for it.

F J. Thomas has sold his store building and ground to the Price Trading Company and will move to Wellington He has bought a corner lot there and will put up a store building twenty by forty feet He will move his stock down there from here and add a line of general merchandise

GREEN RIVER IS LOW.
Victor Rambo, who owns a herd of about eight thousand sheep now ranging in the neighborhood of Green River, was in town to-day and will leave to-morrow for home. Mr Rambo says the range in his section is in fine condition, but that the water in Green river is low —in fact

J. H. Eccles has opened up a planing mill and turning shop at Scofield, near the depot. The place can and will turn out any work in this line in as good shape as any like institution in Utah and at the right prices. Mr Eccles is an experienced man at the business and should in a short time work up a good trade.

DYER TAKES HIS DEPARTURE.
Charles J Dyer, who was brought here from Castle Gate and lodged in jail on the charge of breaking into the Wade Hotel there and appropriating a pair of pants, some money and other articles belonging to a guest, was discharged on this count and committed on the charge of petit larceny for which he paid a fine of $8.00 and took his departure at once If he took Sheriff Allred's advice he has placed many of the hills and valleys of Utah between him and Price by this time

County Treasurer Bryner says taxes are coming in very slowly, only about $2000 having been paid in so far this year The taxes this year will foot up over $24,000, and become delinquent after November 15th when a penalty will be added.

the lowest for many years. Unless there is a rain soon he may have to get out. There is no sale for sheep in his section, outside buyers not going in there of late. If present conditions hold out another year Mr Rambo thinks the sheep men will get even on losses for the past few years

CASTLE GATE NEWS

There is a factional rumpus among the different sections of the Italian element, which has been the cause of a couple of trials before Judge Duerton. The first, that of Bert Pessets and Domonic Melano, who were charged with threatening the life of Cupio Giverin, was dismissed, but the second, that of Vincento Jacinto was more interesting. The last case was one of assault with intent to commit bodily injury. Jacinto met Baptisto between Castle Gate and Helper and took hold of him and fired a revolver at him, which fortunately missed him and then beat him over the head with the butt of the weapon, inflicting several scalp wounds and left him insensible on the ground. Jacinto was fined $30 or a day in jail for each "plank." There are two more cases to come out of this one.

The dance in honor of D D Evans in the Knights of Pythias Hall last Thursday evening was well attended. Mr Evans is going to leave Castle Gate

Another batch of Italian miners with their families arrived here.

A little boy came to the home of Thomas T. Camph Friday afternoon, it being the first boy in the family.

The road from town to the cemetery has been completed for the sum of over $200, and is a credit to the road contractors

GETS FORTY FOUR DAYS.

Vinsengo Jaquinto was brought to Price Saturday night by Constable James Young, of Castle Gate and placed in the county jail. He was tried in the justice's court at Castle Gate and found guilty of assault and battery on another Italian there, and was fined $30 and costs, in all about $44, and as he would not produce that amount he was brought here and given over to the tender care of Sheriff Allred. It will take him forty four days to repeat if he don't produce the ducats before then

In many former cases of like character these Italians have been dealt with very leniently, but Sheriff Allred will make an example of this one by working him on the streets until the court has been satisfied.

Salt Lake Herald
November 18, 1898

FOUND DEAD IN BED.

John Patterson, One of the Old Residents of Castle Gate.

(Special Correspondence.)

Castle Gate, Nov. 16.—John Patterson, an old and esteemed citizen of this vicinity, passed away very peacefully this morning. He went to bed as was his wont very early last evening, making no complaint to his aged spouse, only that he was tired. On the old lady awakening this morning she found that her husband was dead. He was well liked and was somewhat of a celebrity. A somewhat remarkable circumstance is connected with this case. One of the daughters, Mrs. M. Pitman of Winter Quarters left home on a visit to her parents here, and did not hear of her father's death until she went into the room where he was lying dead, which gave her a severe shock.

Mat Cowley and Ren Bryson of Price, Emery County, are visiting relatives here.

Salt Lake Herald
November 27, 1898

PIGEON DIED ON MONDAY

VICTIM OF LEE'S GUN IN BROWN'S PARK SHOOTING.

Latter Said to Have Had Previous Experience—Sheriff Will Leave Today to Investigate.

(Special to The Herald.)

Price, Utah, Nov. 26.—News was received here tonight of the death of the sheepman Pigeon, who was shot on the Davenport ranch in the Browns Park, one week ago today, by Ike Lee. After the shooting Lee went to Vernal to give himself up, but the sheriff, William Preece, was in Salt Lake with a prisoner for the penitentiary, and Lee waited for his return until today. Lee claims that the shooting was in self defense. Sheriff Preece will leave tomorrow for the scene of the killing, which is sixty miles from Vernal. Pigeon, after being shot on Saturday, lingered until about Monday noon. Lee is a most handy man with a gun, and has been in several shooting scrapes before, it is said. He has a brother in the Wyoming penitentiary for robbing the postoffice at Fort Bridger, Wyo., about eighteen months ago. Another brother served a year in the Wyoming pen for shooting and wounding William Meeks at Fort Bridger some two or three years ago.

Eastern Utah Advocate
December 1, 1898
Price

AROUND THE TOWN.

S H Miller, the Helper butcher, was in town on Tuesday

Two tons of fine candies for the holidays. Price Trading company

Business is good with the merchants of Price There are no complaints from any of them

Railroad trains and battleships, and every novelty going for the babies, at Price Trading company s.

Dolls in one hundred different makeups for the girls at Christmas Price Trading company

The board of trustees of the city will meet next Monday evening

Clerk and Recorder Hoffmann says the marriage license market has been extremely dull for weeks

Price Trading company has in the swellest line of toys and holiday goods ever brought to Eastern Utah See the stock and get prices

J S Barclay got in seventeen Home Comfort ranges the other day which he had previously and more to come in the near future.

Mrs G W Bodle returned Sunday night from a weeks visit with relatives at Salt Lake City

Full line of celluloid goods low prices and best values. Price Trading company

Oats are now scarcer in Carbon county than at any time in years

Never was there a stock to compare with the holiday goods now in at Price Trading company s

Mr and Mrs W H Beardsley, late of Helper and who are now visiting in Ohio, will make an European trip in the early spring They are now at or near Findlay, Ohio

Full line of celluloid goods for the holidays Other articles too numerous to mention Price Trading Company.

One of the Finch boys, writing back from Dawson City, Alaska says John Millburn father of Club Millburn of Price has some fine prospects and a good show to come out of that country with a tight lot of money

G T Holladay has assumed the management of Hotel Clarke Mr McKune says he is going to rest awhile

It will be to the interest of anyone who desires good underclothing for grown people or children to come and examine our remnant outing flannels We have just received a whole case It costs nothing to examine, but you will surely buy. Emery County Mercantile company

Juvenile books, the finest line ever seen in Price for the little ones at Christmas time. Price Trading company

S P Barron of St Louis, manager of the Gilson Asphaltum company, was in town Monday, talking over the asphaltum campaign with his local manager and resident agent of the company, Arthur J Lee

Smoking sets for your husband or best fellow, cheapest to the best, at Price Trading company s

The Rough Rider lady s hats at $1 00 are just the thing All who see them admire them Don t wait but get them before they are gone Emery County Mercantile company

Mrs Lowenstein is expected home in about ten days from Salt Lake.

Trains are nearer on time again than has been the case for some time.

The babies and the grown folks will find two tons of candies to fill Christmas stockings at Price Trading company s. Prices are lower than ever this year.

Charley Goldberg returned from Salt Lake Monday night

Tom Barton went up to Salt Lake last Sunday on business and pleasure combined

Price Trading company have in $5000 worth of toys and candies for Christmas Their prices are such they can wholesale to other dealers

Delinquent Tax List

OFFICE OF TREASURER CARBON COUNTY, UTAH —Public notice is hereby given that I will, according to law, offer at public sale at the front door of the county court house in Price, Carbon county, State of Utah, and sell to the highest responsible bidder, for cash on MONDAY DECEMBER 19 1898, and succeeding days, commencing said sale at the hour of 10 o'clock a. m of said days, so much of the following described real estate and personal property, situated in said county and state, on which the taxes for the year 1898 have not been paid, as shall be necessary to pay said taxes, interest and penalties, to wit

WINTER QUARTERS.

David R Reese, bldgs and imp, amt $. 77

B E Lewis, bldgs and imp, amount $1 55

Henry Hjalberg, bldg and imp, amt 89 cents

Hector Evans, bld and imp, amt $1 12

Elias Thomas, bldg and imp $3 00.

Wm Street, bldg and imp, amt 89c.

E Bearnson, bldg and imp, amt 89c.

Thos Williams, bld and imp, amt 57c.

Ami Armason, bldg and imp, amt $1 33

Wm Pesola bldg and imp, amt $1 89

T H Thomas, sw qr nw qr, sec 5 tp 18, range 7, 40 acres amt $6 62

Marley & Nichols, mdse and fixtures, amt $1 12

Kali Happi, personal property, amt 44 cents.

Kosta Nitolo, bldgs and imp, amount $1 45

John Koski, personal property, amt 40 cents

C E Koski, bldg and imp, amt 87c.

Thos Riley, bld and imp, amt $1 12

Alex Wilson, bldg and imp, $1 33.

Edwin Street, bldg and imp, amt $1 12

L Donelson, bldg and imp, amt $1 12

Thomas Brown, two houses, amt $3 09

J A Jones, bldg and imp, amt 89 cents

SCOFIELD

W D McLean, lot 4 blk 16, amt $3 18

D D Green Estate, lot 1, blk 9, amt $3 19

David Burns, lot 8, blk 4, amt $2 57

John D Llewellyn, lot 1, blk 2, amt $15 84

Henry Davis, lot 10 blk 1, amt 92c

Julia Arthur, lot 8, block 5, amt 59c.

M P Braffett, lot 5 blk 5, amt 26c

J W Lloyd, lot 4, blk 4, amt $3 10.

J S Robinson, lot 1, blk 1, amt $2 19.

Frank Mereweather, lot 11, blk 1, amt $3 77

C C Olsen lot 14 blk 1, amt $1 03

Nephi L McLean, lot 8, blk 5, amt $ 68

John T Karsard, bldg and imp, amt $1 32

Thos Gatherum, lot 5, blk 17, amount $1 76

Thos S Reese, lot 17, block 2, amount $2 10

T H Thomas, w half sw qr nw qr nw qr, sec 5, tp 13, range 7, 120 acres, amt $6 00,

Thos Lloyd, sw qr se qr se qr sw qr, sec 5, tp 13, range 7, 70 acres, amt $1 13 —e half nw qr nw qr, sec 8, tp 13, range 7, 120 acres, amt $5 04—sw qr ne qr, sec 8, tp 13, range 7, 40 acres, amt $1 64—ne qr nw qr nw qr ne qr, sec 8, tp 13, range 7 80 acres, amt $3 01

Daniel D Green, w half ne qr e half se qr sec 8, tp 13, range 7, 160 acres, amt $6 7.

Etber Pratt bldg and imp, amt 43c.

Joseph Kengier, personal property, amount $101 45

CASTLE GATE

Mike Paernal, house, amt 98 cents
Battel Prebel, house, amt 98 cents,
Carlo Pricce, house, amt 98 cents.
Jas Nini house, amt 9¼ cents
Frank Edginton, personal property, amt 21 cents
Griff Thomas, personal property, amt 98 cents
O W Nelson personal property, amt 99 cents.
Peter McLan pers l property, amt 38c.
John B Cardall, personal property, amt 98c
Roht Williams, Jr, personal property, amt 98c
Wm S Jones, personal property, amt 21 cents
J R Ward 4 houses, amt $3 7?
W W Paire, pers l propty, amt 98c.
Alex Henderson, pers l propty, amt 19c
Castle Gate Coal and Coke Company, lots 6 and 7 and e half sw qr s e 6, tp 14 range 10, 153 acres, amt $59 43
H Wade, hotel, amt $6 00.
Dominic Milano, house, amt $6 61.
John Ourmiller, house, amt 50c.
Anthon Olegente, house, amt 59c
Yng Gonrienti, house, amt 59c.
Joseph Milano, house, amt 78c.
Chris Jenson, house, amt 98c.
Berul Peffer, house, amt 98c.
John Batisto, house, amt 98c.
Pace Bros, house and personal propty, amt $62 54
U Gentry, house and personal propty, amt 98 cents

HELPER

L H Ewell, pt nw qr se qr, sec 24, tp range 9, 40 acres, amt $5 03
L H Ewell sw qr sw qr, sec 24, tp 13, range 8, amt $5 03
Zoriah Hoge, lot 1, blk 2, plat A, amt 78
Maggie A King, lot 5, blk 2, plat W, amt 61c.
Jas McCune, pt se qr ne qr sec 24, tp

18 range 9, 3 acres, amt $8 80
Bridget Hoge, lots 5 and 16, blk 7, plat H, amt $5 80
Bridget Hoge, lots 5 and 6, blk 8, plat W, amt 52c.
Francis Trimbrel, bldg and imp, amt 85 cents
J X Ferguson, sw qr n¼ se qr, sec 12, tp 13, range 9, 24 acres, amt $21 00.
Barlow Ferguson lot 2 blk 3, amt 52c.
J X Ferguson, lot 2 blk 4 amt 57c
J X Ferguson, lot 10 blk 3 amt $1 45
J X Ferguson, lot 1 blk 4, amt 52c.
J F Crowley, lots 16 and 11, blk 4, amt $12 60
T Pratt, e ½ nw qr e ½ sw qr, sec 19, tp 13, range 9, 40 acres, amt $12 24
P A Smith, one lot, amount $6 40.

SPRING GLEN.

H J Stowell, pt nw qr nw qr, sec 31, tp 13 range 10, 37 acres, amt $17 71
A J Simmons, n half r e qr se qr, sec 6 tp 13, range 9, 150 acres, amt $15 63
L H Ewell, pt sw qr nw qr, sec 30, tp 13 range 10, 5 acres, $3 41.
L H Ewell, pt nw qr sw qr, sec 23, tp 14 range 9 16 acres, $3 41.
Frank Ewell, nw qr sw qr, sec 30, tp 13 range 8, 85 acres, amt $11 94
Frank Ewell, sw qr nw qr, sec 30, tp 13, range 9, 11 1 2, amt $1 74
Harry Thompson, lots 1 and 2, blk 1, amt $3 72
Chris Sandborg, per propty, amt $2 41
Thos H Jones, bldg and imp, amt $1 96
Mary Ann Ward, all blk 10, amt $5 26
John Y Bigelow, lots 3 and 8, blk 12, amt $3 45
Thompson & Bean, personal property, amt $59 08

PRICE TOWN.

H Flack, lot 2, blk 30, amt $5 83
Castle Valley News Co, per propty, amt $1 94
Jennie Peterson, lot 1, blk 30, amt $1 17
W C Richman, per propty amt $12 14
McClure Wilson, bldg and imp, amt $3 70
McClure Wilson, mortgage, amt $1 54

PRICE PRECINCT.

Lynn Valentine, sw qr ne qr, sec 7, tp 14 range 10, 40 acres amt $1 94
Jenson Bros, per propty, amt $145 73
R W Avery, lots 3 an 4 s half ne qr, sec 3 tp 13, range 10, 137 acres, amt $9 19
O W Adair, per propty, amt $1 94.

MINNIE MAUD

E L Harmon, per propty, amt $9 76
Clark Elmer, per propty, amt $3 25
Mike Holleran, per propty, amt $74 34
J H Olsen, per propty, amt $5 56
A J Young, per propty, amt $1 52
Frank Warren, per propty, amt $3 6?
Wm Hamilton, per propty, amt $3 64
Daniels & Holdaway, per propty, amt $1 04

ASSESSMENTS BY STATE BOARD OF EQUAL-IZATION

American Refrigerator Transit Co	$1 43
Burton Stock Car Company	2 91
Canda Cattle Car Company	86
California Fruit & Transport'n Co	6 17
Continental Fruit & Express Co	7 54
C H Havens & Co	7 97
Goodell Refrigerator Line Co	58
Libby, McNeil & Libby Rfg L Co	1 15
Lipton Refrigerator Line Co	58
Merchants Dispatch Transpt'n Co	1 11
National Rolling Stock Co	89
Provision Dealers Dispatch Line Co	35
Pabst Refrigerator Line Co	1 75
Santa Fe Fruit & Rfg Line Co	2 09
Swift s Refrgr and Transp'n Co	6 81
Street s Western Stable Car Line Co	79
Union Refrigerator Transit Co	1 47
St Louis Refrigerator Car Co	1 15
Western Refrigerator Transit Co	80
Western Refrigerator Car Line Co	81

WELLINGTON.

Jefferson Tidwell pt s half ne qr se qr sec 7, tp 15, rang 11, 1 3acres, amt $11 40

John F Tipwell, pt n half ne qr, sec 7, tp 15, range 11, 65 acres, amt $11 30

Roberts Bros, pt s qr ww qr and pt ne qr sw qr, sec 26, tp 14, range 11, 28 acres, amt $17 34

Roberts Bros, ne qr se qr, sec 35, tp 14 range 11, 23 acres, amt $3 94

Joseph Whitmore, s half ne qr and nw qr se qr, sec 35, tp 14, range 11, 110 acres, amt $9 54

Joseph Roberts, s half ne qr nw qr sw qr ne qr, sec 26, tp 14, range 11, 160 acres, amt $4 40.

Wm Curtis, per propty, amt $3 40

John A Powell, Jr, lots 2 and 1, blk 8, amt $7 44

John Morgan, pt sw qr, sec 30, tp 15, range 11, 80 acres, amt $9 97.

Wm T Reid, one lot, Thayn add, amt $1 70.

Lars Christensen, lot 1, block 6, amt $1 37.

W J Tidwell, part nw qr nw qr, sec 7, tp 15, range 11, 6, 100 acres, amt $1 6...

STATE OF UTAH, COUNTY OF CARBON ss.—I, Albert Bryner, treasurer Carbon county, State of Utah, do hereby certify that the foregoing ement of delinquent taxes in and for said county and state is true and ct as appears of record in my office. ALBERT BRYNER, Treasurer of Carbon County, Utah.

H W Damon, clerk at Price for the quartermaster's department at Fort Duchesne, was married last Saturday to Miss Agnes Olga Hunten at the home of the bride's parents Justice Olsen officiated A host of friends of the young couple will wish them all that is calculated to make life pleasant. Only a few friends and immediate relatives witnessed the ceremony

G W Walson, the fellow who posed here a few weeks ago as a sheep and cattle buyer, and who was later arrested at Thompson's by Sheriff Allred, got four years in the penitentiary at Provo last week He had worked his game there previous to landing in Price He is known in Price and Eastern and Southern Utah to the extent of several hundred dollars He will with good behavior get out in something like two years

---

HOME MISSIONARIES

Through the courtesy of D. T Thomander The Advocate is enabled to give names of the following home missionaries, who have been appointed to visit before next quarterly conference the following wards

Emery—George W Stevens.

Ferron—W A Guymon and D. D Cranfall.

Molen—Warren S Peacock and Parker A Childs.

Orangeville—Samuel N Alger and Joseph Pringle

Castle Dale—Elias Cox and John P Wakefield

Lawrence—Charles T Black and John P Pearson

Huntington—Sylvester H. Cox and Joseph H Taylor

Cleveland—C O Larsen, Jr, and Boyd P Peterson

Price—Oscar A Wood and W A Guymon, Jr

Wellington—John H Pace and A. W. Horsley

Castle Gate—John H Pace and A. W Horsley

Spring Glen—Joseph Draper and Jefferson Tidwell

Meetings will be held in the various wards at 2 o'clock in the afternoon.

D T Thomander at Castle Dale is clerk of Emery stake

CASTLE GATE NEWS.

There was a most delightful entertainment given here last Wednesday night by the district school pupils. The little folks were thoroughly drilled in marches, dumb bell exercise and hoop drills, and their songs and recitations were excellent. The entertainment was given in honor of the opening of the new school, and was under the direction of Professor Crandall and his aides, Misses Belle and Knight, assisted by Mrs. J H McMillan. The Knights of Pythias ball was full to overflowing. The parents of the children turned out to see their little ones render the exercises, and after the concert was over the new school house was opened for inspection of the audience. Great credit is due to the indefatigable labors of the teachers for the success of the concert, which was free. A night school is soon to be started with Professor Sardall as teacher.

Eagle Lodge No. 13, Knights of Pythias will give a grand masquerade ball on the evening of December 24th. There will be a number of prizes for the best dancers, costumes and the like.

Eastern Utah Advocate
December 8, 1898
Price

Emery County Mercantile company is showing a handsome line of up to date holiday goods

A Ballinger is confined to his home with inflammation of the stomach. His many friends hope to see him out soon

The town board met in regular session last Monday night. Nothing out of the ordinary routine of business transpired

Arthur J Lee has built on an office at his implement house that is handy and will be as warm this winter as a pocket stove

The Advocate wants a young lady that desires to learn typesetting, one that has had a fair school education Liberal wages will be paid the right party.

County Treasurer Bryner says that this year's taxes will pay all of the outstanding warrants of the county There will be money left in the treasury at the beginning of the year of 1899

There was an unusually large number of freighters in town this week and camped near the gilsonite warehouse

Tom Nichols received a barrel of apples last week a present from his friend Sheriff Wilson of Moab, Grand county They are beauties and are finely flavored

The Houtz Johnson Theatre company will be at Town Hall tonight, tomorrow night and Saturday night. The company is very well spoken of wherever it has appeared

Mrs. Louis Lowenstein has decided to remain at the Manitou Hotel at Salt Lake until her health is entirely regained She will remain there until after Christmas at any rate

I write fire insurance and buy and sell real estate in fact trade and traffic in most any old thing Come and see me and have your property listed or your home insured in some good company. R. W. Crockett.

Local boarders are paying $1.20 per

Mr and Mrs J G Callaway are the parents of a bright baby girl that came on Tuesday to gladden their home. Dr Taylor of Provo was the attending physician. Mother and baby are getting along nicely

There is a report in circulation to the effect that G T Olsen the Emery merchant and owner of the south stage line contemplates building an hotel and livery stable in Price to cost several thousand dollars

Any postmaster in Emery, Uintah, Grand or Carbon county has authority to receipt for subscriptions to The Advocate. Are you a subscriber? At a dollar a year you should be ashamed to borrow your neighbor's copy

To subscribers to The Advocate paying up one year in advance before the first of January one dollar, we will send free for one year the Twice a Week St Louis Republic, one of the very best newspapers in America. This offer will not be good after the first of the year

Hon Reuben G. Miller and Joseph Jones attended the state Sunday school convention of the church at Salt Lake City as delegates from Price. They report the convention as having been most satisfactory and a great deal of work in the interest of the Sunday schools of the state accomplished

For the holidays a rate of one single fare for the round trip between any two stations on the Rio Grande Western railroad system. Tickets will be sold December 24th, 25th 26th and 31st. Also on January 1st and 2d. Final limit January 4th 1899. B R McDonald, agent Price, Utah

Local buyers are paying $1 20 per hundred for oats in cash and $1 per hundred for wheat. There are people who predict that oats will retail for $2 before spring and will have to be shipped into Price from Kansas and elsewhere

R G Miller has been designated by the first presidency of the church as the successor to C G Larsen who has tendered his resignation as president of Emery stake. The stake conference meets at Huntington on the 15th of next month

Prof J W Nixon rode up from Wellington Tuesday night and hitched his horse in front of the Mathis Hotel. When the professor came out horse, saddle and bridle had all disappeared and at last accounts had not been heard from. The animal was securely tied

There will be a grand ball given at Wellington on Friday evening, December 23d. Suitable prizes will be awarded. Good music and a fine time is assured everyone attending. Everybody cordially invited to help swell the crowd which will undoubtedly be a select one

Deputy United States Marshal Wyman passed through here Sunday from the reservation with sixteen Indians. They were headed for Salt Lake to testify in the liquor selling cases against Eckstein, Davis and Noe that come up before the federal grand jury this week

Miss Snow the leading lady of the Houtz-Johnson company playing at Town Hall this week, is a daughter of President Snow of the Mormon church. She is an actress of more than ordinary ability and in private life a most charming young woman. The company plays the principal towns of Emery county the coming week

The case of the state against Allen Cox charged with the theft of some hay and in which Matt Plautz was the complaining witness, was dismissed before Justice Fitch at Helper on Monday by Prosecuting Attorney J W Warf, it appearing that the taking of the hay was more of a mistake than intention at wrong doing Cox paid for the hay

The several saloons will have the usual variety of drinks at Christmas time. The Senate has ordered a quantity of champagne and Tom Nichols says if the stuff isn't sold he'll call in the sporting editor of the Advocate, who has guaranteed that none of it shall be allowed to spoil Fitzgerald & Co. Chub Millburn and Billy Potter will have wine also and various other things that grow in bottles out west, to say nothing about egg nog, Tom and Jerry and relatives of the latter

C W Spalding, the Payson sheep man was here Sunday last and met by appointment W. T Goslen of Salt Lake Goslen agreed to pay Spalding four dollars per head for a bunch of twenty five hundred head of sheep if they come up to representations Both gentlemen left Monday for the vicinity of Castle Dale where the sheep are running There is little doubt of the deal going through as Mr Spalding is known as a man of his word This will be the highest price paid in many years in Eastern Utah for stock sheep

William Beddig, who is always on the lookout for an asphaltum proposition, was here last week and took by purchase several good things to the northeast of Price and which he will make public in the near future He left for his home at Denver Sunday night but will return to Price soon

The Gibson Asphalt company has stopped hauling in its product, owing to the fact that the warehouse here is filled to the utmost capacity When hauling is resumed the company will pay the freighters in cash The payroll, says Arthur J Lee, amounts to about a thousand dollars a month at the present time

The professional card of Dr C E Pearson of Huntington appears elsewhere in this issue of The Advocate The doctor makes a specialty of diseases of the ear, nose and throat We are not personally acquainted with the doctor but have heard him very highly spoken of both as a gentleman and a physician

Miss Mary Warf of Price and Claude Maxwell, late of Helper were married at Colorado Springs, Colorado last Monday week Mr Maxwell is now in the livery business at Cripple Creek and is said to be prospering The many friends of these young people here extend hearty congratulations.

Indian Agent Myton and the five head men of the Uintah Utes who have been in Washington on Gilsonite lease matters, passed through here Friday on the way to White Rocks agency. The lease was signed up and the Indians and all concerned are well pleased. It embraces some two hundred and thirty thousand acres of lands south of the Strawberry river.

R. A. Kirker, a mining expert of recognized ability and who is well and favorably known all over Utah, Colorado and the West, has decided to locate in Price, as will be seen by his professional card that appears in another portion of The Advocate. Mr Kirker has had twenty five years practical experience in his profession, in which he stands at the head and can furnish the best of references to anyone interested. He is thoroughly reliable and worthy of any man's confidence.

The Tribune of last Monday says J A Gogarty, in charge of Ouray agency, is in town. Mr Gogarty has charge in the absence of Agent Myton, and is in the city to testify in the cases of the government against the Winns of Vernal, father and son for breaking into the commissary at Ouray on June 2d last. These men were released by Commissioner O Connell of the reservation under a sufficient bond and their cases are to come up before the federal grand jury this week. Mr Gogarty has as one of his chief witnesses Wichits, captain of the Uncompahgre reservation, who came in last evening with Wonrodes and the other Indians who are to testify in the whisky selling cases. To this Indian, Mr Gogarty says, is due the credit of the capture of the Winns.

Eastern Utah Advocate
December 15, 1898

CASTLE GATE NEWS.

CASTLE GATE, Dec. 13 — Mrs John Broglio has a very bad attack of erysipelas.

The Knights of Pythias are preparing to entertain a big crowd at their masquerade ball on the evening of the 24th. A good time is assured everyone attending.

Tuesday night, while returning to Castle Gate from Price in a buggy, John Molock, Mark Petrick and another man were thrown from the vehicle near the half way house. Two of them received bruises that necessitated the calling in of a physician. The buggy was pretty well wrecked by coming in contact with a stone in the road.

William Phelps had his hand very badly hurt in the mines yesterday by a piece of falling rock.

Martin Resick of Castle Gate, who has been working in the mines of the Price Trading company, some eight miles north of Price, had his leg broken last Sunday and was brought here tonight.

Mrs Joseph Pringle, who has been ill for over two months, died Sunday morning at 9 o'clock. She came here on a visit to her sister, Mrs John Locke, and was taken down ill. The remains were shipped to Cleveland, Utah, for interment at her former home. She was about 48 years of age and leaves a husband, but no children.

There was a family row down at Helper Saturday night It appears that a man named Miller and his wife have not been living in anything like domestic felicity They had a spat and the wife came near killing the husband, so the story goes. She is reported to have struck him in the neck with a butcher knife, severing an artery. Had not Dr Asadoorain gotten there in the nick of time, the fellow would have died from the loss of blood This woman, or rather girl, for she is only 15 years of age, had a man named Matthews up for criminal assault the other day, but he got off, and the family jar was the aftermath of the trial.

Price

PERSONAL MENTION.

R. L. Woodward of Verdal was in town this week.

George W. Bodle was down from Helper the first of the week

Prosecuting Attorney Warf was up to Helper Wednesday on official business

Lieutenant White of Fort Duchesne was among the guests at the Hotel Clarke this week.

Bob Kirker went to Mercur the other day to examine and report on some mining property

Arthur J Lee went up to Salt Lake yesterday morning and came back at night. A flying trip, as it were

Mark P. Braffett came down from Salt Lake Wednesday night, having been called there on professional business

Steve Chipman came in Wednesday night from Salt Lake, where he had been on a sheep deal for a week or ten days

Mrs. Gilfoille, wife of Captain Gilfoille, passed through the city en route to Fort Duchesne this morning from Salt Lake City

Dr Tolhurst of Salt Lake was in town this week on one of his periodical professional trips He had been down in Emery county.

Sheriff Wilson of Grand county passed through town Saturday on his way to Salt Lake and will stop over in Price on the return trip

Dr H Inman came in Wednesday evening from Salt Lake City, where he visited his mother and sister and also looked after business matters

S R Thurman of Provo Doc Shores of Salt Lake and Special Agent Ketcbem of the Rio Grande Western were all three registered at the Hotel Clarke yesterday

Mrs. J. M Easton was here from Salt Lake this week. She is administratrix of the estate of her late husband and has large interests in this and Emery county

LeGrande Young of Vernal was here Sunday on his way home from Salt Lake City where he had been as a witness before the federal court in the whisky selling cases against Eckstein and others.

N E Gibson of Cleveland was in town this week on a visit to his brother, Roy Gibson, operator at the Rio Grande Western depot He is an old operator, but gave up the key to live on a fine ranch which he has in Emery county

F. E Woods, the Castle Dale attorney, was here this week on his way to Denver, where he goes on legal business He has been in the kingdom of Emery only a few months, but in that time has built up a practice second to none other in that part of the country.

C J Elliott, county clerk of Grand county will be in Price next week. It is suspected his mission is to get a certain canine of the feminine gender, which one McDonald at divers and various times is supposed to have expressed to the aforesaid Elliott, but which has never as yet arrived at its destination

AGAIN COME TOGETHER

Robert McKune and George T. Holladay got into an altercation on Tuesday evening over business matters in connection with the Hotel Clarke, and the second coming together by the way. Who the aggressor was "the great moral and religious does not pretend to say. The result of this meeting is that McKune has a badly beaten up head, which shows the skin of the scalp broken in two places, a badly bruised wrist and several other punctures about the face and head, which he alleges were inflicted with a sixshooter of the regulation size. Holladay has a bad looking bruise in the left groin that he says was made by McKune's boot, as well as several more or less painful scratches. Holladay alleges that McKune's wounds were received in falling against a trunk, while McKune denies that he kicked Holladay. In the absence of a surgeon, the editor of "the great moral and and religious," who has "done everything from the noble art of acting to the work of dealing kings," dressed McKune's wounds, which will be to say the least painful for several days to come. Holladay and his father were arrested, charged with an assault with a deadly weapon. The facts leading up to the trouble will be aired in the courts.

The case will come up for hearing before Justice Willson at Wellington one day next week.

Salt Lake Herald
December 24, 1898

SALT LAKER DEAD.

F. C. Trapp Stricken By Heart Failure at Price.

(Special to The Herald.)

Price, Utah, Dec. 23.—F. C. Trapp of Green River, died here this morning of heart failure. Trapp came here last Monday to have a foot dressed, through which he had run a pitchfork, while working at Green River, Utah, for a man named J. T. Farrer. His parents reside at Salt Lake City, and the remains will be shipped there tomorrow for interment.

ABOUT TOWN.

James Rooney is down from Helper today

Bert Friel spent Christmas in Salt Lake City

Hector Evans of Scofield was in town this week.

G T Holladay will go up to Salt Lake tomorrow.

Dave Elliott was among the visitors to Zion during the week

The town trustees meet in regular session next Monday night

Thomas Pratt of Spring Glen was a guest of the Clarke Hotel during the week.

Bob Forrester was here Monday and returned to Castle Gate the following day.

Will Peyton is down from Salt Lake and is among the guests at the Hotel Mathis

County Surveyor Fox of Emery county was here Monday He went on to Salt Lake

W. H Donaldson went to Castle Gate Wednesday to go to work for the coal company

William Howard and wife came in from Huntington on Monday on the way to Salt Lake.

W. C Brocker came down from Helper Wednesday and autographed at the Hotel Mathis.

J B. Cardell and Miss Johnson of Castle Gate were here Monday evening and attended the dance.

Sam King, the Provo attorney, was in town during the week on business of a professional nature

W. W Trapp of Salt Lake City was here Sunday, looking after the funeral of his brother who died at the Hotel Clarke

Miss Nellie Holley and Mrs B. R McDonald were up to Castle Gate on Tuesday, where they spent the day with relatives

Mr and Mrs W H Beardsley of Helper sailed from New York for Jamaica recently. They will spend the winter on the island for their health.

Orange Seeley and wife of Castle Dale were here Saturday, Mrs Seeley being on her way to Salt Lake and Provo to visit the children who are at school

A W Horsley enacted the role of Santa Claus last Friday evening instead of John Pace, as stated in the article from the Salt Lake Herald published in another part of The Advocate.

William Cox of Orangeville was a visitor to Price last Friday having come over to meet some relatives and friends from the state schools who were going home to Emery for the holidays.

Hon R G Miller and wife are at home from Salt Lake City, where they went to have their little boy operated upon He stood the ordeal well and is getting along as well as could be expected.

TWO WEDDINGS

Justice Olsen on last Saturday, at his home in this city united in marriage William M Smith and Miss Kittie M Gingery, both of Ruedi, Eagle County Colorado After the ceremony the newly-wedded couple left for their home in the Centennial State where they are prominent in society circles

Miss Bertha J Olsen and Hulbert Warren, both of Price were also made one by the judge on the same day They have the best wishes of a large circle of friends and acquaintances here where they have grown up from childhood

Lot Powell and Miss Mary Burgess were united in marriage on the 24th by Bishop Horsley These young people have a host of friends who wish them unbounded prosperity and happiness.

The case of I. M. Olsen against the Price Water company was heard before J M Whitecotton, presiding by stipulation, last Monday Judge Johnson was at one time an attorney in the case. A decision will be rendered some time during the month of January

I. W Metcalf, superintendent of the state school for the deaf dumb and blind, made a visit to Price this week He took back with him the little six year old daughter of Mr and Mrs E H Cox of Huntington for instruction at the institution, which is considered among the best in the West. Mr Metcalf has had no small part in making the school what it is.

DEATH OF YOUNG TRAPP

F C Trapp who ran a pitchfork into his foot while working for J O Farrar at Green River, about two weeks ago died at the Hotel Clarke in this city and was buried on Sunday a brother having come down from Salt Lake, where deceased s parents reside, to arrange for and look after the funeral Dr Richman who was the medical attendant gives heart failure as the direct cause of Trapp s death he being not strong enough to stand the administering of strong medicines, such as are necessary in such cases

FIRST CHRISTMAS IN PRICE.

The Christmas number of the Salt Salt Lake Herald contains this account of the first celebration in Price from its correspondent here

"Carbon county was not in existence when the first Christmas celebration occurred at Price. This territory was held a part of Emery county, with Castle Dale as the county seat. The year was 1892. There were few people then in Castle valley, as compared with the number today. The business interests of Price were confined at that time to two mercantile institutions The volume of business done then was perhaps, one-tenth of what it is now The vast irrigating ditches that have brought thousands upon thousands of acres of fertile land under cultivation had not gotten well under way The vast coal interests of the county had not been dreamed of In fact a thousand enterprises and industries that are today flourishing were not to be dignified as yet even in their infancy And that but six years ago"

"The idea of a celebration of the world's most sacred day originated with the Primary association of the Price ward. The carriers of all the children were interested, and ever since has there been anything, it is said, that is looked back to with so much pride on the part of those who participated, the greater number of whom are today living A fine pinion pine tree was cut in the hills to the east of the town, and this taken to the old log meeting house which is still in existence and in use for church purposes. Here it was erected upon the platform used by the church speakers and daintily decorated by the women folks. At night candles that had been brought down from Salt Lake City were brought into use upon the tree and about the old building Bunting and red fire lent an enchantment to an already pretty scene George Frandsen then bishop of the ward and since deceased, opened the exercises the evening with a prayer These were of sort and of a literary and religious character. The prayer concluded, A W Horsley, a brother of the present bishop, P H Horsley made his appearance upon the stage, and, after a few remarks of a humorous nature to the assembled crowd, the presents were gathered from the tree by Santa Claus (Mr Horsley) and distributed among the crowd.

"There was something for each and every one both old and young, big and small The crowd there that Christmas night was the largest ever seen before or since, and it is said, with more or less pride that not a single person was forgotten There were 150 children there besides almost as many old folks The crowd was so great that those getting presents first were asked to make way for the ones who could not gain admittance to the house

Mr Horsley, who has the distinction of being the first Santa Claus in Carbon county came here from Iron county, Utah, in 1886, and has since made his home in Price He is an Englishman and a prominent worker in the cause of religion. He has an interesting family of children, and yuletide time is always an event in his household.

'This year the Christmas tree was at the city hall, where the presents were given out on Friday night by Mr John Lac a high school boy who had been chosen by the principal of the city schools, Miss Mary Leonard, to enact the role of Santa Claus The celebration was fathered by the school children of the district, assisted by the teachers and their parents, and was in every way a success But for novelty and hearty appreciation of the event it is most doubtful if it surpassed the first one of 1892. In the language of an old timer who was there Friday night with several of his grandchildren Christmas now ain't what it used to be '"

Scene of Price's First Celebration.

Salt Lake Tribune
December 31, 1898

CLEVELAND NOTES.

CLEVELAND, Utah Jan 2 —Stock men will buy up all the hay for sale in this neighborhood between now and spring at a good figure, which is another evidence of prosperous times Cattle and sheep being worth some thing it pays to feed them hay, benefitting the farmer as well as the stockman

The coyotes robbed several hereabouts of their Christmas turkeys and chickens Everyone will be glad when this nuisance can be dispensed with

The new hall which the ladies of the relief society are building was completed last week, and on Friday night occurred the grand opening The programme was dinner at noon, followed by singing, recitations, select reading and dancing for the children In the evening there was a play by home artists, more singing, speaking and dancing The entertainment was gotten up especially for those who have helped to build the hall, which has been erected entirely by donation, and is a structure which any town of the valley could be proud of The dimensions are twenty eight by sixty, while the floor is of hard wood, making it A1 for dancing purposes

S N Alger is making a fine lot of shingles these days. Although turning out sixteen thousand a day, it is impossible for him to supply the demand Charley Johnson of Price is the " head push" at the chopping block *

The board of county commissioners of the county of Carbon ordains as follows

The regular stated meetings of the board of county commissioners shall be as follows

Second Monday of April, second Monday of July, third Monday of October, and 29 th day of December
(Signed)   H A NELSON,
Attest   Chairman
ROBERT HOWARD, Clerk

HOME MISSIONARIES

Through the courtesy of D T, Thomander The Advocate is enabled to give names of the following home missionaries, who have been appointed to visit before next quarterly conference the following wards:

Emery—George W Stevens

Ferron—W A Guymon and D. D. Crandall

Molen—Warren S Peacock and Parker A Childs

Orangeville—Samuel N Alger and Joseph Pringle

Castle Dale—Elias Cox and John P Wakefield

Lawrence—Charles T. Black and John P. Pearson

Huntington—Sylvester H Cox and Joseph H Taylor.

Cleveland—C G Larsen, Jr, and Boyd P Peterson

Price—Oscar A Wood and W. A. Guymon, Jr

Wellington—John H Pace and A. W Horsley

Castle Gate—John H Pace and A. W Horsley

Spring Glen—Joseph Draper and Jefferson Tidwell

Meetings will be held in the various wards at 2 o'clock in the afternoon

D T Thomander at Castle Dale is clerk of Emery stake

Eastern Utah Advocate
January 12, 1899

CLEVELAND NOTES

CLEVELAND, Utah, Jan 2.—The new hall erected by the ladies of the relief society has already become very popular as a dancing resort The grand opening ball was given on Friday evening the 30th ult, by the ladies The next night, New Year's eve, another was given under the auspices of the Young Ladies Mutual Improvement association Monday evening the relief society ladies gave another, and Friday night a concert was held by the Young Ladies Mutual Improvement association As this is the best hall in this end of the county the young people come from neighboring towns when wishing to enjoy a good dance

Water is again in the canal for the benefit of those who have run short Reservoirs will now be replenished to last until spring

Professor Anderson, one of the teachers has been on the sick list. His room was closed in consequence last week

Adelbert Oviatt has returned from Price with his family, who have been spending the holidays with relatives at Ephraim

PERSONAL.

Robert Forrester was down from Castle Gate today and registered at the Mathis House

Miss Maggie McIntyre departed a few days ago for Thompson's to remain some time.

C. W. Spalding, the Payson sheep man, is at the Hotel Clarke.

Mrs Roy Gibson and baby are in Salt Lake City, Mrs Gibson for her health.

Tom Nichols and Ike Glaser went out to Fort Duchesne and Vernal the forepart of the week.

J. W. Curry of Ouray was in town during the week.

Mrs. James Rooney returned to Helper the first of the week Mrs Warren, her mother, went up with her, and will remain with her daughter until her health has somewhat improved.

E. A. Wild and wife of Salt Lake were guests at the Hotel Clarke this forenoon.

Miss Ida Whitmore has returned to school at Salt Lake City after spending the holidays with her parents in Price

Sam Whitmore has returned to Salt Lake. He was here helping the boys at Price Trading company take stock.

Charles Goldberg came in today from Salt Lake City, where he was during the holidays He is looking much the better for his vacation and says he is feeling the better for the outing

A Tuttle of Orangeville was here a few days ago on his way to the state capital.

Hon R G Miller will be here tomorrow or next day on his way to Huntington to attend the Emery stake conference which convenes on Sunday

W W Old was in town Sunday and left on Monday morning for the state capital

George B Haverstick was among the visitors of the week in Price. He says business in the towns of Utah are good since the first of the year, that is in his line, wholesale groceries

Gus Anderson, representing the firm of Hewlett Bros, Salt Lake City, was in town during the week on his way to Vernal.

Bishop Horsley will leave tomorrow for Huntington to attend conference on Sunday and Monday.

J. C. Weeter is expected in Price about the first of month He has been at Williamsport, Massachusetts, for several weeks

Lieutenant White of Ft Duchesne and Indian Agent Myton were here the latter part of the week en route to the reservation with the annual money for the Indians and the pay for the Ninth cavalry, amounting in all to something like twenty two thousand five hundred dollars The money came down from Salt Lake by express and was mostly in silver The package weighed eight hundred pounds

John Hite came up a few days ago from the Colorado river on his way to St. Louis This is his first trip back to his old home in more than ten years

Victor Rambaud is up from the Green River country. He says sheep in that section are wintering nicely and the losses of late have been light.

J. W. Warf went up to Castle Gate last night on legal business.

George T Holladay was over in Emery county last week.

Dick Cotner goes up to Castle Gate tomorrow. He expects to go to work for the coal company.

Dr. Richman was up to Helper Wednesday on profussional business

J Dexter Smith has been heard from at Pocatello, Idaho.

Pete Francis was in from Brocks during the week and left for home Wednesday.

Dr Asadoorain was down from Castle Gate a few days ago to attend Master Holley McDonald, who was a sufferer from la grippe, but he is up and around now

Dr. Allen was here from Provo yesterday looking after several of his patients, among them Mrs. J G Callaway.

J. S. Barclay, who has been sick at Hotel Clarke, is able to talk about Home Comfort ranges again

The coal company at Castle Gate is working at full capacity and can use a few more good miners there and at Scofield.

The west bound mail leaving here at 4.36 o'clock in the morning now closes at 9 30 o'clock the previous evening

The great moral and religious can use a few silver dollars on subscription. Gold and paper doesn't go

Eastern Utah Advocate
January 19, 1899
Price

PERSONEL.

Miss Annie Larsen visited friends at Castle Gate last week

Hon R G Miller was here a few hours this week on his way to Salt Lake from Huntington

Mrs H P Miton passed through the city the first of the week on her way to White Rocks from Salt Lake City

Thomas Murphy is confined to his home with an attack of the la grippe which threatens to develop into pneumonia

Miss Clara Mathis is back in Price after an absence of five months in Dixie where she visited friends and relatives

Miss Nellie Holley went up to Castle Gate last Friday and after visiting her sister Mrs H A Nelson, will go to Springville

Mrs Jane Gentry died at Spring Glen last Sunday from pneumonia which came on during child birth and was buried in Price cemetery on Monday, the funeral being largely attended Deceased was an aunt of Jack Gentry of this city She leaves a husband, five children and a large circle of friends and acquaintances to mourn her

Price Trading company is making cleaning out prices on everything in the house since stock taking Many bargains are offered in every department In order to turn goods into money before the lines for spring and summer are here to further crowd the already well stocked shelves Call and look over the goods and get prices There is something to interest everybody.

The local paper published a long obituary of a man who had died in the community, closing with the statement that "a long procession of people followed the remains to the last roasting place." The family discovered the supposed error and asked the editor to make the correction in the world "roasting," but he said he could not do it until the seven years back subscription which deceased owed had been paid.

J. M. Whitmore and A. Ballinger of Price Trading company have both had slight attacks of the la grippe during the week. There have been many others similarly afflicted. The malady seems to be prevalent generally and few have thus far escaped.

News was received here last night that two children of Ed Lee were not expected to live. One has the pneumonia and the other la grippe in an aggravated form.

CLEVELAND NOTES

CLEVELAND, Utah, Jan 15 - The Cleveland Dramatic company is preparing to put on a drama, entitled "Strife," representing a conflict between capital and labor interspersed with wit and humor making it a very interesting play. It will be given Friday evening, January 27th.

Sampson Potter has gone to Scofield to work for the coal company as a miner.

We have about four inches of the beautiful on the ground. Sheepmen who have been holding their

William L. Miller was brought to Price on Sunday night and placed in charge of Sheriff Allred by Special Agent Ketchem of the Rio Grande Western railway, who arrested the man at Grand Junction, Colorado. Miller is accused of breaking into the half way house, between Castle Gate and Helper, on the 28th of last October and taking some clothing and other articles from a peddler, commonly known as "Frenchy," and who alleges that the property taken is worth twenty dollars. Miller was taken before Judge Holdaway on Monday, and was bound over to the district court, which convenes next month. He is in jail.

Bishop Horsley, John H. Pace and H. G. Mathis returned Monday evening from Huntington where they attended conference. The great moral and religious is under obligations to the bishop for an account of the proceedings.

Bob Kirker was in yesterday from Whitmore Canyon and looks much the worse from an attack of the la grippe that has had him in bed some ten days or two weeks.

herds close around here, are now able to get out on the desert.

Quite a number of our citizens attended conference at Huntington on Sunday and Monday.

The married ladies will give a ball in the new hall next Friday evening. Visitors are expected from adjoining towns, and a general good time is anticipated.

Mrs. Ollie Rowan is painting some new scenery for the dramatic company.

CASTLE GATE NOTES

CASTLE GATE, Jan. 17 — W G Sharp, superintendent of the Pleasant Valley Coal company's mines, and bride passed through here tonight on the Rio Grande Western train returning from an extended wedding tour to the East. They were met at the station by the Knights of Pythias band and a large number of the employes of the coal company, and given a rousing welcome. Mr and Mrs Sharp acknowledged the greeting from the car platform and the train pulled out amidst the martial strains, the cheers of the crowd and the deafening discharges of giant powder on the hills in and around the town.

Mrs John Embroglio presented her husband with a fine girl a few days ago.

Mr. and Mrs Vincent Marta are the parents of a fine boy that came to further gladden their home on last Thursday.

An Italian whose name could not be learned got badly hurt last Saturday afternoon by a chunk of coal falling on him. His head and chest were badly bruised.

Eastern Utah Advocate
January 26, 1899
Price

PERSONAL.

J L Brasher of Huntington was in town this week

Miss Annie Larsen is visiting her parents at Cleveland.

Ike Glaser was down from Helper the forepart of the week.

Bil'y Forle will go up to Salt Lake the latter part of the week

J M Crnci of Spanish Fork was here several days this week

James McCune went through from the east to Helper Monday afternoon

Robert McKune spent Wednesday at Provo and neighboring towns of Utah Valley.

Hon R G Miller came down from Salt Lake City Saturday night and remained over Sunday.

Dr Richman made a trip down to Grand Junction last night and will return this evening

George B Haverstic was here the first of the week in the interest of the Symmns Grocery company.

Miss Nellie Holley, who has been visiting Mrs H A Nelson at Castle Gate, has returned to her home at Springville

J G Callaway will leave in the morning with his wife for Salt Lake. Mrs Callaway will go to one of the hospitals

County Commissioner Nelson and wife of Castle Gate were registered at the Kenyon in Salt Lake City on Tuesday last.

A D Hudnell, live stock agent of the Colorado Midland, was here last Friday, working up a crowd for the live stock convention at Denver

Among the visitors from Salt Lake in town this week were F W Penfield, W L Woodruff, G W Patrick, J L Poole and P N Bishop.

J M Lynch, editor of the Pioneer at Castle Dale was in Price Tuesday on his way to Salt Lake. He is putting in a new newspaper plant at the Emery county seat

Mr and Mrs G H Yack, who have until recently lived in South American countries, passed through Price this week on their way to Orangeville, where they own a farm and will remain for some time.

B F Lake, the Orangeville merchant and county superintendent of schools, was here Tuesday on his way home from Salt Lake. He says the schools of Emery county are in excellent condition and good results are being attained in each and every district.

Eastern Utah Advocate
February 2, 1899

CASTLE GATE NOTES.

CASTLE GATE, Jan. 25 —The wife of Domin.c Pereto died last night of pneumonia.

Mrs I Plastino, wife of the section boss at Clear Creek, is in town, the guest of E Sautachi. She brought her family down here to avoid scarlet fever, which is somewhat prevalent in her town.

Castle Gate is full of the grip. It would take a whole column of space to write the names of those affected

Willard Snyder, the mining man of Salt Lake City, has been in town a few days in confab with B. F Coffey, rustler for the Bald Mountain Mining company

W H Lawley is getting around all right, but is not entirely free from his injuries received from falling over a switch handle in the mines and cracking his jaw and forcing the blood through his ears This was a lucky escape, as it was feared that he had internal hemorrhage

CLEVELAND NOTES.

CLEVELAND, Ut., Jan 31.—"Strife" was played to large audiences by the Cleveland Dramatic company Friday and Saturday nights Such general satisfaction was given that the company was requested to repeat the performance next Saturday evening, Feb 4, for the benefit of those wishing to attend from adjoining towns Characters have been cast for a new play entitled "Foiled," which will probably be played in a couple of weeks

J. M. Thomas of Price passed through here Saturday with a bunch of stock which he was taking to Orangeville to have fed.

The snow has just about disappeared and sheep men are again getting back into the foothills with their herds

A surprise party was sprung upon J B Cardall, principle of the district schools, by his pupils.

Mrs H. G Williams has gone to take in the metropolis.

The new experimental coke oven is about completed and a test will be made in a few days as to whether it is better for this coal or not.

Born—To the wife of S Tedesco, on the 23d, a fine boy.

A most serious accident occurred this morning to a miner by the name of Archibald Black. He was in his place when a large piece of rock fell upon him, breaking his left arm between the elbow and the shoulder. The injured miner was taken home and the resident physician was in immediate attendance and set the broken arm. Mr Black has just been here a few weeks, having come from California with his family.

Quite a number of men are here from the surrounding settlements purposely to seek work at the gilsonite mines, some miles from here. Our correspondent is informed that about thirty men are required

Price

PERSONAL.

C. W Spalding went up to Salt Lake Tuesday on business.

Mrs Roy Gibson and baby are home from Salt Lake, where they have been for several weeks.

Master Holley McDonald visited at Castle Gate the latter part of the week.

George T Holladay was among the visitors at Salt Lake this week

Mrs C. W Spalding have arrived from Payson

Bob Kirker was here from Whitmore Canyon Tuesday.

Mr. and Mrs. James Rooney were down from Helper Tuesday last.

Claude Maxwell and wife, formerly Miss Mary Warf, came in the first of the week from Cripple Creek, Colo.

Frank Carroll and family were at Hotel Clarke Friday, en route to Orangeville from Payson.

Misses Rosie Anderson and Lottie Borrenson of Castle Dale were guests of Hotel Clarke last week

E. E Cassaday, the insurance man, was here the other day, going to Vernal from Salt Lake.

O C Olson was a Castle Dale visitor to Price last Friday.

J C Wexler has arrived at Park City, from the East, and will be in Price during the next week or ten days

William Howard of Huntington was at the Mathis House the latter part of the week.

Dr. H C Keamer of White Rocks was in town the first of the week and registered at the Mathis

W. S Woodruff and John Day of Vernal were here the other day, en route from Salt Lake.

St V Le Sieur, the Provo mining man, was here yesterday and went out to his properties on the reservation.

J. G. Callaway went up to Salt Lake Tuesday to see Mrs Callaway, who is in a hospital there. She is reported considerably improved

Joseph Christianson, a prominent merchant of Castle Dale, was in town today on his way to Salt Lake, and will return the first of the week. He reports business good in his part of Castle Valley.

Deseret Evening News
February 6, 1899

PRICE.

Special Correspondence.

Price, Feb. 4, 1899.—The weather the last 24 hours has turned to a bitter blast, blowing from the north. The snow is falling heavily along the mountain ranges.

The sheepmen say their flocks will do well on the desert east of here, providing the snow does not crust too hard.

Discharged soldiers from the Ninth cavalry, at Fort Duchesne, are coming in every day, most of them going East.

The two-year-old child of Erastus Petersen died after a severe attack of scarletena. The health of the people in general is fair.

Hon. R. G. Miller came in on No. 2 today from Utah's capital. He was accompanied by Mrs. Miller and their little boy, who has been very sick for sometime. The poor little fellow has suffered untold pain in the last six months.

The Price Trading Co. has agreed to finish the government freight contract between here and Fort Duchesne, Utah, for a consideration of some eight hundred dollars, besides receiving the regular contract price. The original contractor, Mr. Travis, did not succeed in finishing it.

Deseret Evening News
February 8, 1899

PRICE.

Special correspondence.

Price, Carbon Co., Feb. 6th.—The weather is still very cold. A discharged soldier coming in on the stage from Fort Duchesne had his feet and legs badly frozen.

Freight seems to be coming in quite briskly in the last few days, quite a number of teams are loading up.

Carbon county's popular representative, Hon. R. G. Miller, took a flying trip today to his large stock ranch west of this place. He will leave here in the morning (Feb. 7, 1899) on No. 1 for "Utah's Capital."

The program rendered at the conjoint session of the young men and young ladies "Improvement Associations" Sunday evening was a marked success. Both associations are talking of getting up an entertainment with a view to procuring a new organ for the meeting house.

Price is blessed with three of the most successful public school teachers ever known in these parts. The three schools combined will give an entertainment in the near future for the purpose of establishing a library.

The health of the older people is fair, but there is more or less sickness among children, mostly bad colds.

Elder Wm. Dixon, from Huntington, lately returned from a mission in California and now teaching school in Wellington, was a welcome visitor in our midst, both in Sunday school and in meetings on Sunday last.

Eastern Utah Advocate
February 9, 1899

PETIT JURYMEN

Following is a list of petit jurymen for the January term of district court, which convenes on the 13th of the month, next Monday:

B O McIntire, Price.
William Bowater, Winter Quarters.
Brigham Thayn, Wellington.
J B Shimer, Winter Quarters.
O G Kimball, Scofield.
J M Thomas, Price.
John E Ingles, Scofield.
J O Faucett, Price.
H D Allred, Wellington.
W E Dickinson, Scofield.
William T. Evans, Winter Quarters.
William Gogarty, Castle Gate.

Harrison Miller, Spring Glen.
John H Pace, Price.
W. H. Babcock, Castle Gate.
Erastus Anderson, Price.
C P Johnson, Price.
Alexander Wilson, Sr, Winter Q rtrs.
J. H Eccles, Scofield.
F. N. Cameron, Castle Gate.
Joseph Young, Castle Gate.
C H McKenrick, Price.
George W Eldredge, Spring Glen.
H P Hanson, Wellington.
T J Parmley, Winter Quarters.
J M Beatle, Winter Quarters.
Samuel Padfield, Winter Quarters.
Frank Merriweather, Scofield.
Henry Finch, Price.
C H Taylor, Price

CASTLE GATE February 6.—T Ramsey, an old time mine foreman, both at Almy, Wyo, and in Utah, was in town last week. He is now hustling up business for a mining machinery firm. He met with many friends among the workmen who had formerly been in his employ

E Sintschi, foreman of the coke ovens, has been down with the grippe, but of a mild nature.

Mrs. John McLean is down with a mild attack of pneumonia

Isaiah Llewellyn and Lewis Jones of Scofield were visiting friends here last week

Joseph A Young is down from the gilsonite mines to attend district court which convenes on the 13th inst He is summoned as a juror He states that the new mines will, as soon as the snow disappears put on a good force of men

Castle Gate and surrounding country is all right on the ground hog theory He could not have seen his shadow if he had had an arc light behind him, and since it has been about the same though not much snow has fallen

The concert given Saturday night by the Y M I A was first class There was quite a nice turnout and a dance finished the evening's entertainment A good sum was realized, which is for library purposes

Saturday night some visitors from Spring Glen were returning home when the buggy containing a woman and little girl went to pieces, throwing both occupants out, but fortunately without serious injury

The change in the mail service is a snide affair This morning a mail was left. Another change would be highly appreciated by the inhabitants of this burg The morning's mail going west must all be in before

8 15 o'clock the night before. This keeps the postmaster tied up till late at night and the mail carrier up nearly all night

Salt Lake Herald
February 7, 1899

Castlegate Notes.

(Special Correspondence.)

Castlegate, Feb. 5.—The concert given last night by the Y. M. I. A. was first-class in every respect. There was quite a nice turnout and a dance finished the evening's entertainment. A good sum was realized, which is for library purposes.

Last night some visitors from Spring Glen were returning home, when just opposite the writer's house, the buggy, containing a woman and a little girl, went to pieces, throwing both occupants out, but fortunately without any serious injury.

The change in the mail service is a snide affair. This morning the mail was left. Another change would be highly appreciated by the inhabitants of this burg. The morning's mail going west must all be in before 8.15 the night before. This keeps the postmaster tied up until late at night and the mail carrier up nearly all night.

PRICE.

Price, Emery County, Utah,
February 8, 1899.

Special Correspondence.

The district court will convene here on the 15th inst. About thirteen cases are to be tried this session.

The weather has moderated, it is cloudy and apparently getting ready for a snowstorm.

Report has it that there will be no gilsonite hauled for some time.

EARTHQUAKE SHOCK.

An earthquake shook the country west and northwest from here last night about half past eight. A large flash of light was seen here at Price which seemed to cover the mountains in a semi-circle running from west to northwest for miles, and was immediately followed by a muffled, rolling noise like the sound of distant thunder. People living up at Miller's ranch, west from here, and also up along Gordon creek, northwest from here, report the earth shaking violently for a few seconds.

Castlegate Notes.

(Special Correspondence.)

Castlegate, Feb. 7.—William Cowley came home tonight with one of his eyes tied up. He had been struck with a piece of coal while working in the boxcars.

The weather is much milder today.

Assistant Superintendent H. T. William and Civil Engineer H. B. Williams went up to Scofield this evening.

Hy Loveless of Huntington, Emery county, was in town today. Business connected with his property in Cleveland was the cause of his presence here.

Wesley Jolly's Home Burned.

(Special Correspondence.)

Emery, Feb. 6.—The house of Wesley Jolley was consumed by fire this morning. Mr. Jolley moved here from Washington, Utah, last summer, and had barely got his house completed when it burned down. The fire was caused by the stovepipe running through the roof. A subscription was got up to help Mr. Jolley rebuild.

PRICE.

Special Correspondence.

Price, Carbon County, Feb. 15.—The weather is pleasant and warm the last few days. The ground is dry and dusty. Snow is reported very deep in the mountains, consequently the farmers are rejoicing.

Apostle A. O. Woodruff held meeting here on Tuesday evening which was fairly well attended. His instructions were timely and were highly appreciated. He referred among other things, to the anti-"Mormon" crusade now being waged, and in forcible language showed the folly thereof.

COURT NOTES.

The district court convened here Monday morning, February 13th, at 10 o'clock, Judge Jacob Johnson presiding.

The case of the State against Peacock for befouling water supposed to be running into Fish creek, was dismissed on demurrer.

The case of the State against Faussett Bros., for unlawfully branding a cow, supposed to belong to George A. Whitmore, was brought before a jury, but the jury returned a verdict of not guilty, and defendants discharged.

The case of the State against William Miller from Helper, for housebreaking, was brought before his honor. Defendant pleaded guilty and was sentenced to one year in the State prison.

The case of the State against E. T. Jones, from Helper, for being implicated in the same crime that Miller from Helper was sentenced for, was brought before the jury. The jury, after being out nearly all night, returned a verdict of guilty. Sentence will be passed February 16th. Defendant's attorney made a motion for a new trial. Court is still in session and will last all week.

CASTLE GATE NOTES.

CASTLE GATE, February 9 —The preliminary trial of Frank Puchi for assault and battery with intent to do bodily harm upon the person of Antonio Fazio, was held before Justice Duerdon last evening. Prosecuting Attorney Hoffmann came up from Price in behalf of the state The complaining witness stated his case very clearly, indicating the defendant had made a vicious and unprovoked assault. He was corroborated in part by Mrs. W W. Paire and Miss Jennie Paire, her daughter. Dr Assadoorain described the nature of the wounds. The weapon was produced—an iron pipe about two feet long, having on one end a coke fork tine—a murderous looking implement surely.

After sufficient evidence was introduced to justify the judge in holding him over to the district court, the defendant was bound over in $250 bonds to await the action of the grand jury. The defendant was not represented by any counsel, and it required the aid of an interpreter to make things plain.

Batisto Oberto, an Italian, is lying dangerously sick with pneumonia.

Dr. Assadoorain was called up to Colton this morning, the word being sent down that the section foreman had met with an accident. It appears that the section hands were replacing a frog, when somehow the foreman got one of his hands badly bruised

Sickness is very prevalent in town, quite a number being down with both pneumonia and grippe

Born, to the wife of Chris Hansen, a girl. Mother and child doing well. The little stranger came early Monday morning.

Messrs. Draper of Wellington and A W. Horsley of Price, visited this place yesterday as home missionaries.

HELPER NEWS.

An important change has been made in the Rio Grande Western's mechanical department. Helper has been established as division headquarters for the line from Castle Gate to Grand Junction, and Richard English has been appointed division master mechanic.

Owing to the increasing traffic and growing importance of the main line it was deemed best to establish a new division for locomotive and car work Helper was the most advantageous point for such a shop and headquarters. The plant there is small, but very complete and fitted up for all kinds of light repairs. The shop will be enlarged and modernized as traffic demands it, and in time will be made the most extensive plant of the mechanical department outside of Salt Lake.

Mr. English will have charge of all the engineers and firemen on the division, besides the mechanical force at Helper. He is an old time mechanic, a man of great experience, and will no doubt be a valuable addition to the force. He has long been with Western roads, having lately come from the Santa Fe Pacific. He and his family will reside at Helper.

BATISTO OBERTO BURIED.

Funeral Services Were Impressive and Largely Attended.

(Special Correspondence.)

Castlegate, Feb. 18.—The funeral of Batisto Oberto was conducted by the Societi de Napoli. The lodge, headed by the band, proceeded to the K. of P. hall, where the ritual was read and remarks were made by President John Babroglio and Erculo Longi. A large number of friends and sympathizers went to the cemetery. The deceased was a member of the I. O. O. F. and a Forester.

It is payday at the mines today, consequently everybody is feeling good.

The wife of John Broggins is quite sick and in grave danger.

The 10-days'-old infant of F. Edgington died, and was buried today.

Death of a Mormon Missionary.

(Special to The Herald.)

Price, Utah, Feb. 21.—News was received here today of the death of Louis L. Warren of this city at Chattanooga, Tenn. Deceased was 25 years of age and had been on a mission to the southern states about twelve months. The body will be brought here for burial, where deceased was raised and was at one time assistant postmaster and identified with the Price Trading copany.

PRICE.

E. T. Jones Sentenced to Six Months' Imprisonment for Housebreaking.

Special Correspondence.

Price, Carbon Co., Feb. 20.—For changing weather, Carbon county beats the records. From a beautiful spring day yesterday, it has turned to a regular hurricane today, blowing from the northwest.

Hon. Reuben G. Miller came in on No. 4 from Salt Lake Sunday morning. With his counselors he went to Wellington and held a well-attended afternoon service.

B. F. Cummings, representing the Deseret News, and who is now on his way East, in its interests, stopped over at Price, Sunday, Feb. 19, 1899, and attended Sunday school and afternoon services.

The organization of the Price Sunday school was completed yesterday, by the appointment of Albert Bryner as first and Robert Howard as second assistant superintendents. Brother Joseph Jones has carried the burden of superintending alone for some time.

DISTRICT COURT NOTES.

E. T. Jones of Helper, who was found guilty of housebreaking, appeared before his honor this morning, his attorney made application for a new trial, but the motion was denied. His honor then imposed a sentence of six months in the State prison.

The case of Scott Elliott vs G. C. Whitmore, a dispute over certain water rights, in Whitmore canyon, came up before the court this morning.

PROBATE MATTERS.

In the matter of the estate of Geo. Frandsen, deceased, all property was ordered to be sold, except real estate and water stock.

CLEVELAND NEWS NOTES.

CLEVELAND, Feb 22 —The three year old daughter of B Erickson died of scarlitina Sunday morning and was buried Tuesday

The elders and seventies held their reunion Monday at Social Hall After an elaborate program, consisting of singing, recitations, speeches and the like, a lunch was served and an enjoyable time was had by all who attended

— The farmers of this section may be seen nowadays following the plow and harrow, preparatory to putting in their crops.

W E Cowley, Jr, has accepted the position of watermaster for the Cleveland canal during the coming season

The Oviatt boys, J P Johnson, B Erickson, Rudolph Cramer, Niels Nielson and William Pilling have returned from DeLamar, where they have been getting out wood for the mining companies.

CASTLE GATE NOTES.

CASTLE GATE, Feb 22 —The anniversary ball of the Knights of Pythias tomorrow night promises to be the social event of the season

Batisto Oberto died here Wednesday night and was buried Thursday. He leaves a wife and five small children He was a member of the Italian and Knights of Pythias orders, and the funeral was under their direction

Gabriel Stringari was quite badly burned in the mines by a flash of coal damp last week Last November this same man was burned in the same place and in the same manner, only more severely.

Funeral services over the infant of Mr and Mrs Appedoile were held Wednesday.

B P Caffey has gone to Alabama to see his mother he having received word that she is very ill

About fifty pounds of baling wire taken from the company stables was found in the wagon of a peddler by the name of Shoemaker one day last week He will be prosecuted

Saturday was payday with the coal company, and the usual amount was distributed

The wife of John Broggins has been dangerously ill for several days past, and slight hopes are entertained for her recovery.

The ten days' old infant of P Edgington died, and was buried Saturday last.

Price, February 26—L. P. Larson and Samuel Alger

Cleveland, March 12—A. W. Horsley and James Draper

Orongeville, March 12—J P Pearson and Delos Crandall.

Lawrence, March 12—Oscar A Wood and Albert Guyman

Huntington March 12—Uriah E Curtis and Joseph H Taylor

Emery, March 12—C G Larson Jr and F M Reynolds.

Molen, March 12—Abinadi Olson and John J Thurston

Castle Gate, March 13—L P Larson and Samuel Alger.

Wellington, March 19—Elias Cox and John F Wakefield

Ferron March 19—Peter Nielson and J Fleming Wakefield

Castle Dale, March 26—Elias Cox and John F. Wakefield

Emery, March 26—J D Killpack, Jr. and William Taylor.

DEATH OF LOUIS A. WARREN.

A cloud of sorrow was cast over the city Tuesday last when a telegram was received from Ben E Rich in charge of the Southern States mission at Nashville, Tennessee, announcing the death of Louis A. Warren, which occurred at Alpha, Louisiana, last Monday.

The young man was 32 years of age and had been on a mission since last June. He was in poor health when he left, and it is supposed the damp climate of the South brought on pneumonia. His lungs were not strong.

The remains are expected to arrive here Sunday and are accompanied by one of the elders laboring in that field The funeral will be held next Monday or Tuesday.

Deceased was an exemplary young man, and was not only held in high esteem, but was universally loved by everybody with whom he came in contact. The bereaved mother and relatives have the heartfelt sympathy of the entire community in their deep sorrow.

Price

PERSONANALITIES.

Abe Liddell was up from Wellington Monday.

Ike Glaser was down from Helper last Saturday.

L M White, the Salt Lake packer, was here Tuesday

Robert Forrester was here Tuesday from Castle Gate

Chub Milburn thinks of going to Klondike in the spring

George T. Holladay went up to Salt Lake the fore part of the week.

Attorney Zane and Judge Hender son have been here this week attending court.

Miss Ella Lewenstein will return to Salt Lake City to school Sunday evening

Mrs. James Rooney of Helper visited relatives here the first part of the week.

J. C. Giles of Woodside, Utah, was a guest of the Hotel Clark on Tuesday.

L M Olson has returned from a business trip of several days to Salt Lake City.

R A Kirker has gone to Mercur to look after his mining interests on the West Dip

George C. Whitmore and Sam Whitmore have been here this week attending court.

Hon R. G. Miller came down from Salt Lake Saturday night and spent Sunday with his family.

Judge Jacob Johnson goes to Castle Dale Saturday and will open court there next Monday.

Mrs Roy Gibson and baby are at home from a visit to Mr and Mrs A E Gibson at Cleveland

F. J Gehringer and wife of Randlette, Utah, were guests of the Hotel Mathis the first of the week.

Miss Belle Boyd of Nine Mile was visiting friends here during the week. Her elder sister was with her.

Mrs C. W. Spalding will go to Salt Lake tomorrow to pick out new furniture and carpets for the Hotel Clarke.

C. M. Owen, an expert on irrigation, was here attending court this week and was a guest of the Hotel Mathis

J C. Wester left Monday evening for Park City, after being here a week or more looking after business interests.

Mrs B R. McDonald returned on Saturday from a visit to her sister, Mrs H. A. Nelson at Castle Gate for several days

B F. Cummings, Jr, of Salt Lake and agent of the Williams estate, was at the Hotel Clarke the latter part of the week.

Charley Goldberg went to Lower Crossing on Tuesday He has an eye on some fine copper prospects in the Cedar mountains

Mrs J. A. Gogarty was registered at the Hotel Mathis the latter part of the week from White Rocks She was en route home from Salt Lake City.

O P. Gable, one of the representative business men of the Ashley Valley, was at Hotel Mathis the first of the week, going home from Salt Lake City.

Mike Hickey, formerly an employe of "the great moral and religious," is now located at Leadville, Colorado, working on one of the newspapers of the Cloud City.

John M Zane, who has been here this week attending court, will locate in Chicago for the practice of his profession, says the Salt Lake Herald of Tuesday.

County Commissioner Gibson was over from Emery county Saturday. He doesn't think much of the fabulously rich finds of copper reported from the Cedar mountains.

Hon. R G Miller was a guest on Monday evening at a dinner at the Alta Club, given by ex Senator and Mrs Arthur Brown, to the republican members of the legislature.

Miss Nellie Holley was visiting her sister, Mrs B R. McDonald, during the week, returning to Castle Gate in time for the Knights of Pythias ball there this evening. •

Mrs Warren has been confined to her home for several days with an attack of the grippe, and was much better until the news of the death of her son reached her. In her condition the shock was most severe.

Miss Isabella Brown, a most accomplished and charming young lady from Salt Lake City, was the guest of B. R. McDonald and wife last week, returning to Castle Gate on Sunday, where she will visit Mrs. H. A. Nelson.

Mrs J. G. Callaway has been discharged from the hospital at Salt Lake, but will remain there several weeks at the home of friends until her strength is more fully recovered. Mrs Allred and the baby arrived home Sunday night.

The high wind of Monday demolished the big tent used as an annex to Hotel Clarke.

Coyotes are becoming more numerous in Eastern Utah. Their serenades are frequent.

The Rio Grande Western has reduced its station force at Price by laying off one man, Arthur Hunten.

The soldiers at Fort Ducheane are being paid by checks this month, sent out from the quartermaster's department.

The wool clip at Price this spring will be the largest ever known. The railroad company calculates that 75,000 head will be sheared here.

There is to be a big new pump of improved pattern put in at Smith's Wells. It came from Salt Lake and was sent towards its destination last Monday.

Dick Cotner has accepted a position with Hotel Clarke, and he looks very much at home there to the old timers who frequent that popular and well conducted hostelry.

Several loads of lumber for government use at Fort Ducheane, and which has been tied up in the snow blockade for weeks, was loaded out last Monday, and more is soon to follow.

Reports from the Cedar mountains and the Green river country are to the effect that sheep are doing most excellently. There have been few losses from any cause for the last six weeks.

The Hotel Clarke has a new register, upon the advertising pages of which are cards of the leading business houses and professional men. It was gotten out by "the great moral and religious."

Lieutenant Walker and Lieutenant Hickok were here yesterday on their way from Fort Ducheane to Salt Lake, where they will be examined for promotion. Mrs. Hickok accompanied her husband.

The snow is reported to be piling up very deep at the head of Price river, and high waters are looked for this spring. The warm weather of the past few days is breaking up the ice in the irrigating ditches.

The laundry building at the Hotel Clarke caught fire for the second time Saturday night from a defective flue, and had it not been discovered in time there would have been a conflagration of no small proportions.

Charley Taylor was in town yesterday and bought fifteen head of calves from about as many different parties. He also sold a fine Durham bull to H. B Horsley, the price being in the neighborhood of one hundred dollars

Elder W. P. Camp of Idaho, who is traveling as a missionary in the interest of the Young Men's Mutual Improvement associations in Emery Stake, held a well attended meeting here Thursday evening. His remarks were good and timely and were listened to by a good sized audience.

Dr Richman and Attorney Braffett were out looking for chickens Sunday. They covered the ground from here to Helper pretty thoroughly and got—what the small boy shot at. Tom Fitzgerald and Louis Smith did better. They brought back two ducks —tame, or otherwise, deponents sayeth not.

L. Lowenstein will leave the first of the week for Vernal, where he will open a store about April 1st. He will carry a twenty five thousand dollar line, all of which has been bought, he says, but the groceries. He has made an offer for a building, and if this is not accepted he will erect one.

A. Ballinger and Sam Whitmore leave in a few days for the Colorado river, where they are interested in the Good Hopes placer bars. They will be joined there by Bert Seaboldt, manager for the company, and a thorough examination made. They will be absent three weeks to one month.

The twenty third anniversary of the Knights of Pythias order will be celebrated at Castle Gate tonight by Eagle Lodge. There will be a big dance, and quite a number from Price have signified an intention of attending, going up on the train this evening and returning home at midnight.

Deseret Evening News
March 1, 1899

PRICE.

Too Dry to Plow—Building at Fort Duchesne—Funeral of Elder Warren.

Special Correspondence.

Price, Carbon Co., Feb. 26.—The weather is cold and windy. The ground is getting very dry, and will have to be irrigated before spring-plowing can be done, unless we have a heavy snowstorm soon.

CARPENTERS WANTED.

Considerable lumber is being hauled from here to Fort Duchesne. Lieutenant Walker, post quartermaster, was in town the fore part of the week looking for carpenters to put up some buildings at the fort this season.

FUNERAL OF ELDER WARREN.

Elder Cornwall, in charge of the body of Louis A. Warren, who lately died while on a mission in the Southern States, arrived here safely on No. 1 this morning. Funeral services were held in the city hall at 2 o'clock this afternoon, where one of the largest congregations ever assembled in this place, was gathered, to pay their last respects to their departed brother. The floral decorations were beautiful.

Hon. Reuben G. Miller came in on No. 4 this morning, and attended funeral services this afternoon.

The Relief Society is making preparations to give the old folks a regular good time shortly.

PERSONAL MENTION.

Leslie Ashton of Vernal was here last Friday.

L O Hoffmann went up to Castle Gate yesterday.

Miss Nellie Holley has returned from Springville.

W H Donaldson was down from Castle Gate Sunday.

Mrs. McClure Wilson went up to Castle Gate yesterday.

William Howard of Huntington was in town last Friday.

Robert Forrester was here during the week from Castle Gate.

Mrs Peter Martin of Helper visited friends here Tuesday.

Jack Gentry went over to Emery county the first of the week.

Mrs B. R. McDonald has been on the sick list for several days.

Jack Egan and Chub Millburn were in Helper during the week.

Mrs Claude Maxwell of Helper visited friends in Price during the week.

Mrs. James McCune was among the visitors from Helper during the week.

Mrs George W Nephew has gone to Salt Lake City to remain permanently.

Mrs Jesse Bryan of Ferron was a guest at the Hotel Mathis on Monday last.

Mrs George W. Bodle visited relatives and friends at Wellington on Tuesday.

Miss Belle Boyd has returned home after a short visit with friends in Price

Professor Nixon of the Wellington schools was visiting relatives in Price last Sunday.

Billy Earle, for some time at the Hotel Clarke, returned to Salt Lake Monday last.

Mrs James Rooney has returned to Helper, accompanied by Mrs Warren, her mother

R A Kirker was registered at the Cullen Hotel in Salt Lake City the first of the week.

Pete Anderson is down in the Cedar mountains this week prospecting for copper

R S. Collett of Vernal was here the latter part of the week on his way to Salt Lake.

John D. Boyd was in from Brocks on Monday. He is just up from an attack of the grippe.

Mrs Jane Arnold and Miss Bessie Lewis of Scofield were guests of the Hotel Mathis today.

J W Seeley and wife are among those from Castle Dale registered at the Hotel Mathis today.

J C Weeter is expected here from Park City next Saturday or Sunday to remain several days

B Jorgerson and wife of Castle Dale were in the city yesterday and registered at the Ma'is

C. Anderson of Nepan and Colonel Tatlock of Manti were visitors to the city the first of the week

H E Taylor of Richfield and J C Reynolds of Springville were at the Mathis during the week.

J A Robey of Colton and N S Madsen of Maroni were guests at the Hotel Mathis on Monday.

Mrs J. G Callaway is expected home next Monday from Salt Lake City, after an absence of several weeks.

Louis Lowenstein went out on the stage Tuesday morning to Vernal, where he is to open a big store in the near future

James H Mease and Lieutenant Kinzie W. Walker were here Sunday on the way to Fort Duchesne from Salt Lake City.

Doc Shores and Special Agent Ketchem were here the forepart of the week on business for the Rio Grande Western

O Harmon of Huntington and P C. Borenson of Castle Dale were among the Emery county people in Price during the week.

Judge Johnson, Stenographer Fred Milverton and several attorneys left here Sunday by private conveyances for Castle Dale, where district court opened on Monday.

~ Charley Taylor came in from Provo today where he has been visiting Mrs Taylor and the babies He says the weather there is not to be compared with the Italian climate of Carbon county.

Miss Effie Hardin of Gallatin, Mo, arrived here last Saturday morning en route to White Rocks agency to accept the position of teacher in the Indian school. Before she had taken the stage she received a telegram announcing the serious illness of a near relative, and returned on the first train.

~ W T. Goslen, who has some seven thousand head of sheep down in the Green river country, was here Monday. He says his flocks have wintered well, and out of his entire herd he has not lost to exceed one hundred and twenty five head He will shear at Thompson's along about the first of April

CLEVELAND NEWS NOTES.

CLEVELAND Feb 28 —A very enjoyable time was had at the dance last Friday night.

'Foiled' will be played by the Cleveland Dramatic company, Friday and Saturday evenings, March 3d and 4th, at Social Hall New scenery has been painted, and judging from rehearsals the play will be pulled off in good shape.

A mass meeting was held by the people of Cleveland last Friday for the purpose of remonstrating against the passage of House Bill No 14, by Mansfield, providing for the changing of county boundaries. There was a large turnout and strong resolutions were adopted, which were forwarded to our representative in the legislature, Hon Joseph Robertson

The building of another new hall is under consideration by some of the young men of our town, and subscription papers have been circulated to see what amount could be raised for the purpose, with very favorable results. Let the good work go on

A. Alexson will leave next week for Ferron, where he is to erect a large brick business block for A Worthen.

Sergeant Thornton and Dick Cotner of Price and Corporal Donaldson of Castle Gate very kindly lent their uniforms to the Cleveland Dramatic company, to be used in the play next Friday and Saturday nights This was a great help to the company and the favor is highly appreciated

J. A Cornwall, who has been la boring as a missionary in Louisiana for several months, accompanied the remains of the late Louis A Warren to Price. His eulogy of the deceased at the funeral services last Sunday was among the best that has ever been heard here. Mr. Cornwall's home is at Murray, Utah, whith r he went after the funeral.

If there is such a place as hell — and there are those who hope there is — about a half dozen old women gossips here in Price will wake up some morning in hot lava up to their garters

Deseret Evening News
March 6, 1899

PRICE.

Mining Boom—Thieves Apprehended.

Special Correspondence.

Price, Carbon County, March 5 — For the last week high winds have been blowing all over Castle Valley, Thursday night a slight fall of snow covered the ground, but all melted away before noon the next day. Today is the only pleasant day we have had for some time.

The health of the people is fair considering the changeable weather we are having.

Copper prospecting is all the go now. Some very good prospects have been found along the Cedar mountains.

The Price Dramatic company played the original drama, "Tempest Tossed," to a well filled house Thursday night. The play was rendered in splendid style. Those who took part in rendering it deserves great credit. The company has been requested to repeat it here in Price on the 24th inst., and at Castle Gate on the 25th inst. All proceeds will go to the Sunday school.

Charles K. Bradt, the rape fiend, has been safely lodged in the county jail at Price, to await a trial in the district court at its next session.

Several arrests have been made at Castle Gate for stealing.

Eastern Utah Advocate
March 9, 1899

CLEVELAND NEWS NOTES.

CLEVELAND March 8 — Foiled was played last Friday night by the home dramatic company to a very large house, and would have been repeated Saturday night, but one of the caste, Miss Ollie Bryson, was taken very ill, and the play had to be postponed until next Friday night to the disappointment of a large crowd from both Cleveland and adjoining settlements

B M V Gould has returned from Scofield, where he has been engaged in coal mining during the winter months

The relief society is getting up an entertainment for March 17th n celebration of the anniversary of their organization A general good time is expected

CASTLE GATE NOTES.

CASTLE GATE, March 5. —Dominic Williams "Italian terror," was brought up before the justice of the peace of this precinct Saturday for disturbing the peace. He pleaded guilty and was fined $25 and costs, amounting in all to $36 This man, for the last eight or nine years, has been the ringleader in nearly all the Italian rows and the judge, in passing sentence, told him that the last time he was up before him he had let him off easily, but this time he must pay the fine and costs or go to jail a day for each dollar

John Ward, an old time resident of

this town, but now of Cleveland, Emery county, has been visiting relatives and shaking hands with old friends

Price

PERSONAL.

Mrs. C W Spalding returned today from Salt Lake City

Miss Nellie McMullin spent Sunday with friends at Spring Glen

Miss Mattie Caffey of Wellington was the guest of friends here the first of the week

J C. Weeter came in Sunday from Park City, and will be hereabouts for several days.

Ike Glaser was down from Helper on Tuesday on his way to the reservation country.

George T. Holladay came in from Salt Lake City Tuesday night and returned yesterday

Miss Stella Box of the Ashley Valley was in town yesterday on her way to Salt Lake City

Hy Lovelace, the Emery county cattle buyer, has been in Price a week. He goes home Saturday.

R A. Kirker came in the last of the week from Mercur, where he was looking after his mining interests on the West Dip

Judge McConnell passed through Price yesterday going to Salt Lake City, where he will be on business for several days.

Mrs J. G Callaway returned on Monday after an absence of several weeks at Salt Lake City, and much improved in health.

Robert Forrester of Castle Gate was in town yesterday on his way to Whitmore Canyon, where he is looking after mining properties for several parties

C N. Campbell and George E. Forrester, auditor respectively of the Wells Fargo express and Rio Grande Western railway, were here Monday checking up accounts with Agent McDonald.

Indian Agent Myton was in town yesterday on his way to Salt Lake City He was accompanied by Mrs. Myton, who will visit friends there for a short time. The Advocate acknowledges a very pleasant call, and is indebted to Mrs Myton for some excellent kodak pictures of the crazy Indian on the reservation.

Deseret Evening News
March 13, 1899

PRICE.

Interesting Carbon County News.

Special Correspondence.

Price, Carbon Co., March 10.—The weather the last week has been pleasant and spring-like. Garden planting has begun on a small scale. Everybody is wishing for storms to moisten the ground, which is very dry and dusty.

The program rendered by the young folks in conjoint session Sunday evening was a decided success.

Peter Francis from Brock, who was charged with selling whisky without license, was fined $40 and cost of court, by Justice Holdaway.

A couple of drunken Indians were seen on our streets a few days ago. Where they get their fire water, most people of Price would like to know.

CONTEMPTIBLE WORK.

Some freighters undertook to haul some Gilsonite from the Gilsonite mines to Price, at the old rate of $6c per cwt. They got as far as the Duchesne bridge, when the next morning they discovered the burrs gone from the wheels of their wagons, and consequently found themselves unable to proceed any further. The owners of the different outfits swear bitter vengeance.

Deseret Evening News
March 16, 1899

HELPER.

A Daring Robbery—The Bandit Captured After Brisk Battle, with Fractured Arm.

A special to the Tribune from Helper, Carbon county, gives the particulars of a bold robbery which occurred at that place at 10:30 yesterday morning, March 15. A stranger walked into Ike Glaser's store, and said he wanted a suit of clothes, underclothes and a pair of shoes. After he got what he wanted he took up the parcel and walked out; when questioned about paying the bill he drew a large 44-caliber gun, and started away with the parcel.

Mr. Glaser secured a gun and followed him, ordering him to halt, upon which he turned and began firing. Glaser returned the fire, both emptying their guns, the bandit making his escape for the time being.

A posse headed by Glaser and others was quickly formed and soon were in pursuit and overtook the freebooter about two miles out of town, he being on foot. In the meantime he had reloaded his gun and met his pursuers with hot resistance, emptying his gun again, but while he was reloading he was shot in the arm, fracturing it badly, and was unable to finish loading.

The posse then thought they had an easy victim, but when they drew near he still made a vicious fight with a dagger he had in his possession, and was not taken until he was knocked senseless with the butt of a gun.

He said his name is Antonio Carro, a Mexican, and that he was from Rawlins, Wyoming, where he had been herding sheep. The stolen property was recovered.

The wounded robber was placed on a train and taken to Price. An examination of his arm by Dr. Richman at Price showed that the bone between the elbow and shoulder is a mass of splinters caused by the bullet fired by one of the posse and that amputation would be necessary. He was placed in charge of Sheriff Allred, who brought him last night to Salt Lake, when he was placed in St. Mark's hospital, where his arm was amputated this afternoon.

Eastern Utah Advocate
March 16, 1899

SHOT IN THE ARM

Wednesday morning a stranger walked into the store of Ike Glaser at Helper and after getting on the inside of a good suit of clothes, underclothes, shoes and the like, started on his way, remarking to the clerk that he might charge them. Glaser in the meantime went up to the new customer and informed him he did not do business in that fashion. The stranger drew a gun and backed him out of the house. Glaser got a gun and followed when the fellow opened fire upon his followers who by this time had become a formidable posse. The robber fired on the crowd but was himself shot in the left arm above the elbow. When he had shot the second round from his revolver he made a vicious attack upon the crowd with a dagger. He was finally knocked senseless with the butt end of a gun.

The man was brought here and in the evening taken to a hospital at Salt Lake by Sheriff Allred. The arm, says Dr. Richman, will have to be amputated. The fellow who is a Mexican sheepherder, gives his name as Antonio Faorroo.

VERY SAD ACCIDENT

There was a most distressing accident near Cleveland Tuesday night, which resulted in the death of one of the most popular young men in all Emery county. Roy Oviatt, son of County Commissioner H H Oviatt. Four or five young men of his age were out riding, and in some manner the lines became loose and were dragging. Young Oviatt leaned over the front endgate of the wagon to regain possession of them, when the endgate gave way letting out on his head. Two of the wheels ran over him. He was taken to R O Rasmussen's house where he died about an hour later. He was conscious up to the last and would not allow his friends to send for a doctor or any of his folks saying he would be all right in a short time. It is feared it will go very hard with his mother, who was confined on the 9th instant. The deceased was about 21 years of age and a most excellent young gentleman.

CLEVELAND NEWS NOTES.

CLEVELAND March 11 — A baby boy made its appearance at the home of County Commissioner Oviatt on the 9th instant.

Mrs Roy Cowley presented her husband with an eight pound girl on the 10th

Bishop Oveson has been sick in bed for the past week with grippe. Nearly everyone in town has had a slight touch of this malady

Mrs Jane Alger of Nine Mile is spending a few days with relatives and friends at Cleveland

The mask is off and the true nature of Castle Valley now asserts itself. Cold, dry winds from now until the first of July

Assessor Killpack says the assessed valuation of Emery county will be increased over 25 per cent this year over last years showing

On account of the abundance of work at the coal camps, a great many of our citizens will remain away all summer, instead of coming home and farming as has been the custom heretofore

Price

PERSONAL.

I Alldredge came up from Ferron Monday

Illie Lovejoy returned to Huntington Sunday

J D Killpack and wife of Ferron were in Price this week

James Rooney and wife from Helper were here this week

Thomas Pratt of Spring Glen was registered at the Hotel Clarke during the week

R S Collett of Vernal was registered at the Mathis House during the week.

W G Matherly was among the Castle Gate visitors in Price during the week.

Miss Zady Burton of Castle Dale was a guest of Hotel Clarke during the week

J W Nixon and wife of Wellington visited Mrs O W Bodle the first of the week

Bishop Lamph of Castle Gate was here Monday and autographed at the Hotel Clarke.

Mrs William Thornton went out to Fort Duchesne today to visit with friends awhile

Cyrus Seeley and wife registered at Hotel Clarke from Castle Dale the first of the week

Judge McConnell returned from Salt Lake Tuesday and departed yesterday for Vernal

Frank Carroll of Orangeville was shaking hands with Price friends the fore part of the week

Miss Lena Myers of Preston, Ida was at the Mathis House this week en route to White Rocks

Mr and Mrs H P Myton were here the first of the week returning to White Rocks from Salt Lake

C P Crawford, an expert from Denver, was here yesterday on his way to the Blue Mountains gold mining district.

Mrs S E Warren has returned from Helper where she visited her daughter, Mrs James Rooney, for several days

---

Joseph Hoge aged 38 years died at Helper Sunday evening after a short illness of typhoid pneumonia Deceased was born in Ireland, but came to America when a young man and was one of the pioneer residents of Utah He was a member of the Knights of Pythias lodge at Provo A brother and sister survive him his mother having passed away but a few months ago

---

Someone shot and killed the St Bernard pup belonging to Station Agent McDonald this week It had the making of a fine dog

---

Miss Olive Boyd of Nine Mile visited friends in Price last week and attended the fancy dress ball on last Friday evening

Mr and Mrs J M Link of Fairplay, Colorado are visiting their son J M Link, at Helper, and will remain during the summer

Mrs Narkervis wife of Steward Nankervis at Fort Duchesne, arrived here yesterday from San Antonio Texas, where she has been visiting for some time

Mrs. Clara Chotau of the Indian Territory and a teacher in the Indian schools, arrived here Tuesday and departed on the first stage for the reservation

---

Victor Rambaud came up Friday from the Green river country where his sheep have been ranging during the winter Mr Rambaud says the losses in that section have been very light. A three inch fall of snow occurred last Thursday night, putting the range in fine condition He will shear at Price next month

---

The March that came in like a mutton may fool the oldest inhabitant and refuse to go out like a howling St Bernard, mourning for her first born

---

G T. Olsen of Emery was here on Tuesday He bought three hundred head of young cattle from Matt Thomas, which will be driven into Emery county and fed until ready for the market.

Deseret Evening News
March 18, 1899

PRICE.

The Welcome Snow—Dull Times—Old Folks Remembered.

Special Correspondence.

Price, Carbon Co., March 17—The long-hoped-for snowstorm has come at last. Six inches of snow covers the ground today and plenty more in sight.

The town commissioners purchased a number of chemical fire extinguishers to be kept in the town hall.

Price is duller at present than it has been for years. Everybody is crying, "Hard times, come again no more."

The old folks are having a good time today, in the shape of a good dinner, and a program and dance tonight.

The bandit who robbed Ike Glasier at Helper on Wednesday is said to be an Italian and not a Mexican, as he claimed. The Italian element at Castle Gate has ever been a source of considerable trouble and expense to Carbon county.

Eastern Utah Advocate
March 23, 1899

CLEVELAND NEWS NOTES.

CLEVELAND March 22—The funeral of Roy Oviatt, which was held last Friday, was about the largest in the history of Cleveland

The entertainment which the relief society was to have given on the 17th was postponed until the 22d. A general good time is expected

"Foiled" will be played again by the Cleveland Dramatic company, Friday night, the 24th

By an appropriation of the legislature, the county commissioners will be enabled to improve the roads of the county to a considerable extent, and also to build a road from Cleveland to Green River by the way of Lower Crossing When this road is completed the people of Lower Crossing will be able to reach the county seat or the mill in about one day's travel.

Joe Potter has returned from Scofield, where he has been engaged during the winter by the Pleasant Valley Coal company

Water will be turned out of the Cleveland canal next Monday for the purpose of cleaning out the canal

Roy Johnson, one of our popular school teachers, has returned to his home in Sanpete his department having been consolidated with that of the other teachers.

CASTLE GATE NOTES.

CASTLE GATE, March 21—John Phillits, working on the section here, got a bad cut on the head this week by a large rock falling on him. The injury is painful

The grand ball Thursday evening next at Helper promises to be well attended by the people of Castle Gate and vicinity

There was a fight here the other day between Mrs John Brogio, Mrs John Bonometta and Mrs Vincent Merta, all Italian women, in which the former got the worst of it. Mrs Bonometta had her face badly scratched up, but the others escaped with but few marks The case is to be reviewed by Justice Duenlou

The postoffice is having a general overhauling and several additions are being made that will facilitate the delivery of mail The hotel is also being renovated.

B F Caffey is in Salt Lake City this week on a mining deal.

Professor Hanly of Huntington is in town. He has two sons and a daughter residing here.

Uriah Bryner is the guest of E. Santschi and family.

The wife of William Gogarty is very ill She gave birth to a child this morning which did not live

The remains of the infant child of Mr and Mrs. Dominic Bardisoni was laid away this afternoon It died on Sunday

PERSONAL.

Mr and Mrs. H A Nelson of Castle Gate were here Sunday, visiting B R McDonald and wife.

Miss Stena Jensen visited relatives at Helper Sunday.

Mrs J M Gogarty passed through Price Tuesday on her return to White Rocks agency from a short visit to Salt Lake friends.

W C Broeker and Sam Glaser of Helper attended the dance here last Friday night.

R S. Collett and S R Bennion of Vernal were here the first of the week on their way home from a business trip to Salt Lake City.

B F Lake, county superintendent of schools of Emery county, was in Price Sunday on his way home from Salt Lake and Provo where he had gone to arrange for the summer school to be held at Huntington He thinks Dr Park will act in the capacity of instructor.

Colonel Tatlock of Manti was in town Tuesday.

Major Illsley of Fort Duchesne was at the Hotel Clarke the first of the week on his way to Salt Lake City, where he goes for rest and recreation for a few weeks

Miss Stina Jensen of Castle Dale was registered at Hotel Clarke last week.

Mrs L. H. Mitchell, wife of the farmer at the White Rocks Indian agency, arrived here Saturday from Pueblo, Colo, on her way to the reservation

Robert McKune was in Helper and Castle Gate yesterday.

Miss Kimball, teacher in the public schools, will probably attend the meeting of the National Educational Association, which convenes at Los Angeles this summer.

S M. Miller, who was a member of the late Indian allotment commission, was at Hotel Clarke yesterday

W. H Goss of Salt Lake, who owns valuable gilsonite deposits near Colton, was in Price Saturday on business matters

Mrs Mary M Thurman of Vernal passed through Price Saturday returning home from a visit to relatives at Provo.

Mayor Brown and Hardin and Owen Bennion were three Vernall es who registered at the Hotel Clarke last Friday, on their way home from Salt Lake City

Mrs S. M Browne of Vernal registered at Hotel Clarke last Friday She was returning from a short visit at Salt Lake City.

Miss Mary Beers and her brother, Frank, of Vernal, who have been attending school at Provo, were the guests of the family of A Ballinger this week.

Jack Egan went out to his ranch in the Nine Mile country on Wednesday's stage.

N. Bartholomew went out over the stage line yesterday morning.

Louis Lowenstein is expected back tonight from Salt Lake City.

Miss Mary Leonard, principal of the public schools, expects to spend her vacation in California, and will attend the N E A convention at Los Angeles.

Judge Dusenberry of Provo and Attorney Rhodes of Salt Lake City were at the Hotel Clarke Friday on their way to Vernal, where court is in session this week.

George G Frandsen went up to Salt Lake City the first of the week, on his way from the reservation to Salt Lake City.

Victor Rambaud has returned to Green River to bring his sheep up to Price for shearing

Miss Lillie Bryner is visiting relatives at Helper.

Gus Anderson was in town yesterday, talking cigars and other things to local merchants

Deseret Evening News
March 24, 1899

LITTLE BOY BADLY HURT.

A special to the Herald from Price states under date of last evening: Vernal Whitmore, the 6-year-old son of J. M. Whitmore, manager of the Price Trading company, was run over by the trailer of a freight wagon this evening. He was taken home in an unconscious condition, with blood oozing from his nose and ears. Dr. Isgreen of Helper was summoned and came down on a special train. Little hopes are entertained for the boy's life.

Deseret Evening News
March 27, 1899

PRICE.

Will Shear 150,000 Sheep—Failed to Capture Robbers' Roost Gang.

Special Correspondence.

Price, Carbon Co., March 26.—Rain has been falling down in good shape for the last four days, doing a great deal of good to the farmers, who are rejoicing.

The Imperial Dramatic Co. played here Friday and Saturday nights, to well filled houses.

The railroad carpenters are working west of town fixing up the extensive shearing pens, belonging to the railroad company, which will be used very extensively from now on, and for some time to come. Sheep are coming in every day. It is estimated that about 150,000 sheep will be sheared here this season.

Business is beginning to pick up. Mechanics are beginning to go to work, the merry song of the saw and the hammer can be heard from daylight till dark.

MUTUAL MEETINGS TO CONTINUE.

The president of the Young Men's Improvement association has decided to hold the Young Men's meetings on Sunday evenings in place of Tuesday evenings, and keep the meetings up all summer.

Sheriff Allred and posse made a trip down to the Robbers' Roost country the other day, to help capture some outlaws down there, but the attempt proved a failure. No robbers were seen or heard from. Sheriff Allred has a method of his own to capture outlaws, and he is convinced that unless his ideas are carried out, the robbers will be left at liberty for some time to come.

PRICE.

Freighters' Strike Ended—Prospectors Busy—Fine School Program.

Special Correspondence.

Price, Carbon Co., March 22.—The weather continues cloudy and windy, with an occasional sprinkle of snow, in the valley; considerable snow is still piling up in the mountains.

The program rendered Tuesday night, by the public schools of Price, under the supervision of Miss Leonard, was a decided success. The singing was excellent. The house was filled. The proceeds will be used to start a school library.

Considerable gilsonite is now being hauled to Price, at the old rate of 50 cents per 100 pounds. The strike for higher rates is completely knocked in the head.

Prospecting is still the go in Price. Parties are coming and going all the time. Everybody's pockets are loaded with samples of ore being discovered southeast of Price.

A GOOD MAN IS NO MORE.

James N Link died at Helper on Wednesday, aged 82 years For a period of several years he had resided at Fairplay, Colorado, but he went to Helper about two weeks ago to make his home there with his two sons who have lately engaged in business there Mr. Link was born in Kentucky, but at an early age removed to Missouri, where he married and raised a family. Later in life he and one of the sons, J. M Link, a resident of Helper, enlisted in the Confederate Army joining at Troy, Mo, a company commanded by Colonel Tom Carter, and fighting for nearly four years as privates for the lost cause After the war deceased made a new home in the West, engaging in mining in Colorado and elsewhere. Between him and R A. Kirker, of this city, who fought on the union side, there was the most profound friendship Deceased had been a member of the Masonic order for forty five years, and the remains will be laid to rest at Provo tomorrow with Masonic honors The wife with whom he lived for fifty-five years, survives this good old man who has "passed beyond our horizon, beyond the twilight's purple hills, to that ast realm of silence or of joy, where the innumerable dwell He has left with us his wealth of thought and deed, the memory of a brave, imperious, honest man, who bowed alone to death'

Marriage licenses were this week issued to Ell Pace of Provo and Miss Minnie Brown of Price.

CLEVELAND March 27 —On last Thursday Jacob Johnson's correl, sheds and stockyards were burned, the loss a total one, together with seven head of sheep, one calf, several chickens, ten tons of hay, a new set of harness, and numerous smaller articles The fire was started by one of his children playing with matches under the shed. There was no insurance on the property. The people of Cleveland will turn out and help Mr. Johnson rebuild, which is always the custom here in cases of this kind

Another very sad accident occurred here Saturday. Willie Pulsipher, aged 13 years, and Sanford Scofield were playing with or repairing a dilapidated shotgun on the front porch of the former's home, when the gun was accidentally discharged, hitting him just above the right eye, scattering part of his brain out over the side of the house He lived about four hours after the accident. The deceased was a son of Bishop Charles Pulsipher of Huntington, who was sent for and arrived a short time before the boy expired The funeral occurred today at 10 o'clock at Huntington

President Miller and his two counsellors of Emery Stake, spoke to the people of Cleveland ward yesterday. This is the first visit the new presidency has made to this ward, but it is hoped it will not be the last. The discourses were very instructive and were listened to attentively by a large congregation

Price

SHORT STORIES.

Considerable new farming machinery is being sold these days by Price merchants and dealers.

Mrs. Holdaway is showing some pretty things for the ladies in new millinery and flowers.

Tom Nichols is going over to Mercur in a few days to look into a business proposition that has presented itself there.

Several loads of dirt thrown on the ground between town and the the depot are the starter for a sidewalk that is to be laid.

Arthur Hunton has again entered the employ of the Rio Grande Western at Price, and looks very much at home around the depot.

Verne Whitmore, who was run over by a wagon last week, is getting along nicely and will be out in a few days. He was sitting up this afternoon.

Judge Dusenberry had so far recovered from his indisposition that he hopes to proceed this evening to Provo, where court matters demand his attention

The president of the Young Men's Improvement association has decided to hold the Young Men's meetings on Sunday evenings in place of Tuesday evenings, and keep the meetings up all summer.

Mudslides in Colorado have again caused some delay in the movement of trains. The mails in consequence have been more or less delayed for a week, and in one or two instances trains were abandoned

So far no wool buyers have appeared in this market, and it looks as if owners of wool are to have to hold or else go onto a most uncertain market. Buyers and consumers of wool, it is said, do not know where hey're at

Carbon county is sure to get some mines from the many prospects that have been staked off the past few weeks There is plenty of ore within our borders and we believe it only a matter of time when the output will astonish people.

Huntington is soon to have a new mercantile establishment that carries the name of the People's Co Op It will be doing business by May 1st in the Elias Cox building, recently purchased in preferer to the erection of a new one.

Bert Seaboldt came in the other day from the Good Hopes placers on the Colorado river. He did not remain long, but went on to Salt Lake to arrange for some machinery to work the property on a big scale the coming summer.

Sylvester Tedesco and William Boren got into a personal encounter Tuesday and were taken before his honor, Judge Holdaway, who gave the former a fine of $3 for the first offense and $5 for a second one Boren was levied $5 for fighting.

J. M. Healy, who was here some two weeks ago on his way to Vernal to examine certain mining properties on the gold and copper belt, is said to have been sent there by Colonel De Lamar, whom it is believed has a desire to get a foothold in those diggings, and will invest if his experts find anything that looks good to the mining world.

Sheep shearing began in earnest here Tuesday, the first shorn being those of Hon R G. Miller, which will take about a week The next on the list are the flocks of the Frandsen Bros, about ten thousand head, to be followed by smaller owners, in all about seventy thousand head There are some seventy men employed in shearing

The Helper correspondent of the Deseret News says: "Helper is certainly going to be a thriving town, judging from present indications. The railroad company is putting in a new line of nine-inch pipe from the reservoir system, also planting many shade trees, and expects to begin the erection of a commodious chapel soon, as well as building many more dwelling houses. Every house in town is occupied and there is pressing demand for more. The fruit prospects are very fair. This is a good place for fruit, with a first-class market. There are some lands to be had here yet on easy terms."

TIMBER CULTURE, FINAL PR OF —NOTICE FOR PUBLICATION.
No. 11,072

United States Land Office, Salt Lake City, Utah, March 14, 1899 Notice is hereby given that James Larsen has filed notice of intention to make final proof before William Howard, United States commissioner, at his office in Cleveland, Utah, on the 5th day of May, 1899, on timber culture application No. 1097, for the W½, SE 1-4 and W½, NE 1-4 of Sec. 13, In Twp. 17, S Range No 9 He names as witnesses Hans Jensen, John M Cowley, Rasmus O. Rasmussen, Joseph Dumayne, all of Cleveland, Utah.
FRANK D. HOBBS, Register.

DESERT LAND, FINAL PROOF— NOTICE FOR PUBLICATION.
No. 4071.

United States Land Office, Salt Lake City, Utah, March 13, 1899 —Notice is hereby given that John A. Aiken of Castle Dale, Utah, has filed notice of intention to make proof on his desert land claim No. 869, for the SW 1 4 and W 1 J, SE 1-4 S c. 23, Twp. 18, S. R. 8 E., before the County Clerk of Emery county at Castle Dale, Utah, on the 4 th day of May, 1899. He names the following witnesses to prove the complete irrigation and reclamation of said land E. A. Jones, D F. Thomander, A. Oman, Joseph Lund, all of Castle Dale, Utah
FRANK D HOBBS, Regis et.

Eastern Utah Advocate
April 6, 1899

FIFTEEN MILES OF WATER.

Ten Thousand or More Acres of Land Reclaimed by the Hill's Canal Through Which Water Now Runs.

After ten years of hard work and with great expense, the Hill a Canal and Irrigation company has brought the waters of the Price river out onto the arid desert to the west and south of Price, and within the next few weeks, if all goes well, the last flume will have been constructed and the ditch completed to Miller Creek It has been a big undertaking and one that many men with ability to carry out large enterprises would have hesitated over But not so with the men who lately took up this work where others left off for want of capital They have brought to a successful termination a proposition that means much to Price, much to Carbon county—much to all of Eastern Utah in fact

But something of the magnitude of the enterprise may be seen in the fact that the ditch when completed will reclaim in the neighborhood of ten thousand acres of the most fertile soil in existence Sixteen thousand dollars has so far been expended and it is now estimated that some two thousand more will complete the last flume and finish the canal construction as originally planned by the incorporators of the company

The Hill a Canal and Irrigation company has a capitalization of $20 000 divided into shares of the par value of $5 each so that according to the estimates above given, the company will own about two thousand shares of stock in its treasury after the canal is finished The greater portion of the stock issued has been in exchange for labor employed in construction by persons having land filings under the canal from the mouth of Gordon Creek on the Price river where the canal is started, to the end at present contemplated, is a distance of about fifteen miles, and it is estimated that there are some ten thousand acres of land which will be reclaimed by the waters diverted by this company

Some of this land is yet open to entry, but it is not thought that with a general knowledge of the recent accomplishments of the company it will long remain open. There is a vast quantity of water yearly permitted to flow into the Gulf of California by way of the Price river which this enterprise will arrest and employ in the upbuilding of Castle Valley.

The capabilities of the Castle Valley soil are attested by every ranch on Price river. Castle Valley fruit is the finest in this or any other state and the productiveness of the soil is simply marvelous. All sorts of fruits, vegetables and grains are raised and a ready local market is

land for everything. With such an environment why should not the ranchers succeed here?

Lucern is selling at $8 the ton, and the average yield is three tons to the acre in this valley. With the extensive freighting and stock raising interests of Price the demand for lucerne has annually increased until in recent years our merchants have found it necessary to ship in hay to supply their custom. With the addition of the rich farms created by this new canal, the local supply of lucerne hay should be sufficient and importation become a thing of the past.

There is ample water in the Price river for the reclamation of ten thousand acres of land in addition to that which at present is cultivated. Water has never been known to be scarce until well into July, after the first crop of lucerne is harvested, and with water sufficient until that

time, two crops of hay are assured. It is estimated that the cost of sowing lucerne and the irrigation for one year is $7.50 an acre, so the profits are apparent to those who take up the lands under this canal, when it is seen that lucerne land is not to be purchased for less than $60 an acre in this vicinity.

Mr L M Olson of Price is the president of the Hill's Canal and Ir-

rigation company, and to his indefatigible disposition must be attributed the success of the enterprise. Other officers of the company are Mark P Braffet, vice president, Paul Hunton, secretary and treasurer, and Frank C Bryner and Jesse Jensen, directors. Frank C Bryner is water master. All have aided materially in the building of the canal. The articles of incorporation have in all respects protected the stockholders, and have provided that immovable, self regulating gates of distribution shall be annually fixed by the watermaster of the company and so arranged that there shall be a continuous flow of water from the canal to the stockholder of the quantity of water to which his stock entitles him, and the stockholder may do as he pleases with the water, it being his property and he may either use it or divert it to a neighbor if desired. This principle of water distribution is equitable and just, and its advantages over other systems will be readily seen. All expenses for the maintenance of the company's canal are provided to be annually paid by assessment, opportunity being afforded able bodied stockholders to pay their assessments in labor if desired.

Work was first begun on this canal by Mr W J Hill, now living Wellington, and his two sons in July of 1887, when the first survey was made ten miles from the head of Miller Creek, but for the lack of sufficient capital they were never able to carry the project to a successful termination

After the water had been turned in a few days ago it was the pleasure of the Advocate young man to go over the greater portion of the canal with an officer of the company. Everywhere the work done is of the most substantial character, and it does also show there has not been a single dollar wasted in construction. The fluming is of the best and heaviest of timbers and the dirt and rock fillings of the kind that will remain for ages

With the exception of about three flumes and some little scraping on level land the canal is now completed

---

CASTLE GATE NOTES

CASTLE GATE, April 4 —Yesterday the wife of David Llewelyn gave birth to a boy. The mother is very low and the infant is not expected to live

William Lund and bride have returned from Provo, bringing back with them the aged father of Mrs Lund.

B F Caffey went down to Spring Glen yesterday to look after the business affairs of Alex McLean, who is at present in Marysvale. Mrs John McLean is soon to leave for Diamondville, Wyoming.

J Tom Fitch was up from Helper yesterday.

Mrs C Santolini, wife of the Italian merchant at Helper, was thrown from a buggy about two miles south of town Sunday afternoon, the vehicle colliding with a protruding rock. The baby she carried in her arms was with the mother pretty badly scratched up. The driver was not hurt, but the buggy was considerably damaged in the mixup

Peter Gabardi, a coal miner, had an arm crushed and a leg broken today by falling coal. He was sent to the hospital at Salt Lake by the company surgeon after his injuries had been treated

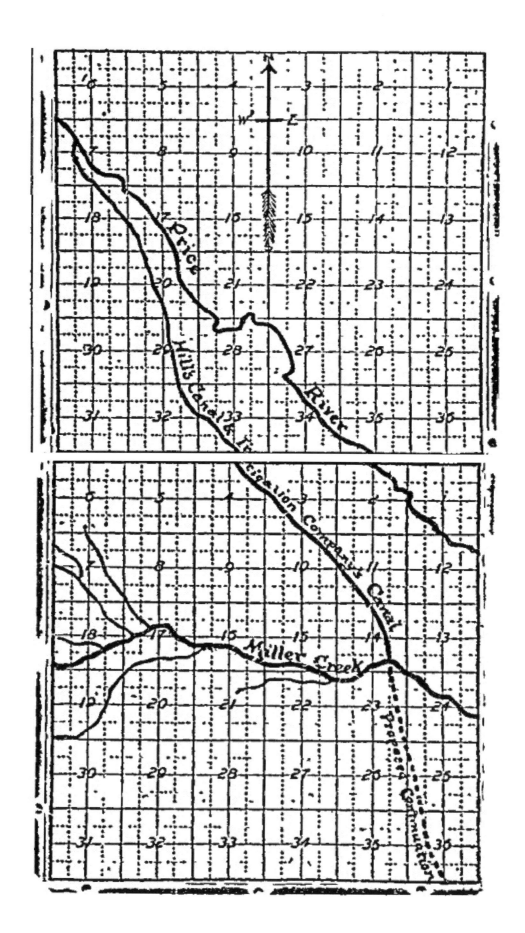

Washington County News
April 8, 1899

THE NEWS is informed that Tobe Whitmore's little son, who was dangerously hurt recently at Price, Emery county, is now considered out of danger.

Eastern Utah Advocate
April 13, 1899
Price

PERSONAL.

Tom Nichols came in from Mercur and Salt Lake last night.

Lee Seagmear came in the first of the week and is shoeing his flocks at Price.

W T Gowien the sheep man was here yesterday He will harvest his wool at Thompson's next week

Mrs I Stevens of Fort Duchesne was a guest of Hotel Mathis during the week, en route to Salt Lake City.

John P Walsh of Vernal was in town during the week

Frank McCarthy, manager of the north stage line, went in to Salt Lake last night.

St V Le Sieur was here yesterday looking after the shipment of the car of copper ore from his Copper Globe mine below Ferron

Jack Egan came in last week from a short trip to his ranch in the Nine mile country

Mrs B R McDonald is expected home from Springville some time next week

Mrs R M Carey returned yesterday from a week's sojourn in Salt Lake City

O c e Chipman came in today from the Nine Mile country to make arrangements for shearing his sheep

Bishop Horsley has returned from conference

Mr and Mrs E I Stewart returned today from Salt Lake, accompanied by Mrs John H Pace

Bert Seaboldt was here Tuesday and left in the evening for the Good Hopes placers on the Colorado river, where he will remain during the summer months

Mr Liddell of Wellington will leave next week for Idaho with the view of locating He is a good citizen and his many friends and acquaintances will regret to see him leave Carbon county

Mrs Noah Bartholomew and children have returned to Price after an extended visit to California, Idaho and Salt Lake City

Miss Sadie Kimball returned on Sunday evening from Salt Lake City

Miss Mary Leonard is at home from a visit to the public schools of Salt Lake City

Mrs J A Gilfoyle and her little daughter were here Tuesday on their way to Fort Duchesne They have been visiting friends at Denver for two weeks or more

Mrs George W Bodle went up to Zion the latter part of the week to visit her mother who lives at St. George and was in attending conference

Mrs J O Faucett left the latter part of the week for Provo, where she goes to have her baby treated for eczema

W W Oln came up from Emery county the first of the week He and Arthur J Lee local representative of Mr Old's company, wrote up several life insurance policies, and Old went on his way rejoicing

Robert Howard and wife returned Sunday from Salt Lake City

Joseph P Donus a prominent educator of Emery county, was a visitor in Price on Monday

Len Huntington of Emery county was here Monday to meet his mother who has been visiting relatives and friends for several weeks at Springville

L M Olson has returned from a business trip of several days to Salt Lake City

Mrs Louis Lowenstein, Miss Ella and Master Sherman departed Saturday evening for a short visit with relatives in Zion

B R McDonald spent the Sabbath with his wife at Springville.

Sam Glaser and W C Brooker attended the play and dance here Tuesday evening returning to Helper yesterday morning

John Forrester was down from Colton Tuesday, mingling with Price friends for the day

Thomas Murphy came in Sunday night from Salt Lake City

H A Nelson of Castle Gate and John James of Scofield were here Monday and Tuesday in attendance upon the meeting of the board of county commissioners

Mrs A. E Gibson of Cleveland visited Roy Gibson and wife several days last week

Dr. Assadoorain was down from Castle Gate Tuesday to attend the meeting of the board of health, returning in the evening

Sheriff Leamaster, J E Wools and J W Seeley of Castle Dale were at Hotel Clarke Monday on the way home from conference

G W Feakins, representing the Rock Island railroad, was here the forepart of the week looking out for wool shipments

Sheriff Preece of Vernal was here Tuesday, going home from Salt Lake City, where he had been on official business

D C Woodward and wife from Huntington were registered at the Clarke during the week

Ike Glaser of Helper was in town during the week

C M Humphrey of Springville was here the other day and loaded out a carload of honey for William Boylance that came in from Uintah county.

J R Wren of Ferron was in town Monday

N C Spalding of Payson is in town and is the guest of Mr and Mrs C W. Spalding at the Hotel Clarke

J F Pennington and wife of Elko, Nev have been guests of the Hotel Clarke for several days Mr Pennington is here looking up a business location

Mrs W H Hutchison of the Imperial Dramatic company returned to Salt Lake yesterday, while Mr Hutchison and his brother William, went up to Castle Gate to finish the painting of the scenery at Knights of Pythias Hall there

Dr. Assadoorain was down from Castle Gate Tuesday to attend the meeting of the board of health, returning in the evening

William Howard and Levi N Harmon of Huntington were here Monday on their way home from conference at Salt Lake

R. A. Kirker came in yesterday from Whitmore Canyon.

Professor Nixon was among the Wellington people attending conference returning from Salt Lake City Sunday evening

Dr Isegreen of Helper passed through Price Saturday from Whitmore Canyon where he had been to see one of the Thayn boys, who was quite ill

M P Braffet came in Tuesday night from Salt Lake City

Manager Loofbarrow of the Weeter Lumber company returned Sunday evening from a short visit with his family in Salt Lake City Mrs Loofbarrow and the children will be in Price to remain during the summer after the Salt Lake schools have closed

COUNTY COMMISSIONERS.

The board of county commissioners met on Monday and continued in session until Tuesday, when they act as a board of health for a short time County Clerk Howard was instructed to make requisitions on Emery and Utah counties for Carbon county's share from assessed sheep, which has not been paid by them

An order was made permitting County Superintendent of Schools Webb to remove his desk to Castle Gate, the same, however, to be at his own risk

The resignation of John P Johnson as justice of the peace of Winter Quarters precinct was accepted and Lewis Jones appointed Leon Gourdon was named as constable in the same precinct, F Burnasor having resigned James Young sent in his resignation as constable of Castle Gate precinct.

B O McIntire was named as road supervisor of Price district and T H Auphand for Helper

Constable Deufur was appointed to collect peddlars' licenses for Price precinct, and J L Price for Castle Gate precinct.

The usual number of accounts were allowed

The board adjourned to the next regular meeting, the 10th of July, but will meet as a board of equalization the first Monday in June

WE HAVE NO TENDERLOIN

Says the Castle Dale Record "It is reported that two or three of the fair damsels from the tenderloin district of Price are negotiating for a location in Castle Dale About the first step that should be taken by the people of Castle Dale if they should decide to locate here is to run them out of the country Castle Dale, at present, enjoys the distinction of a good moral record and that class of society should not be tolerated It is the solemn duty of every mother, father and taxpayer to attend to this and see that the officers of the law do their duty, and see that such places of disrepute are not allowed to exist We cannot afford to have our young men go to destruction by our neglect to do our duty There are plenty of existing means by which a young man can spend his time and money without frequenting such places of disrepute We think that the county can arrange to meet the current expenses without any revenue from that source

Deseret Evening News
April 17, 1899

PRICE.

Spring Work—Early Irrigating—Fine Reservoir Site.

Special Correspondence,

Price, Carbon Co., Utah, April 14.—Warm spring has come, the apricots are out in bloom; sheep shearing has been going on for some time. Great piles of sacked wool are staked in different places. It is estimated that at least seventy thousand sheep will be sheared at this point this season. As the sheep are sheared they are moved toward the summer range in the mountains.

A great amount of gilsonite is being delivered here for shipment.

The extremely dry weather has made it necessary to begin irrigating earlier than usual and all have begun to use the water on their gardens and farms. The great rush of water down the Price river makes the thoughtful begin to talk about water storage so that there may be irrigation water later in the season. There is an excellent site for a reservoir that would supply water for all the available land in Carbon county if it were utilized—that is, Pleasant Valley. If this were utilized for a reservoir it would no doubt be the means of redeeming this part of the country, which is now subject to drouth.

Apostle Lund, Elder Rulon S. Wells of the First Presidency of the Seventies and Elder Andrew Jenson were taken from here to Cleveland to attend the Emery Stake conference by President R. G. Miller yesterday.

PRICE.

Government Freight Contract—Sheep in Good Condition—Fine Crops of Wool.

Special Correspondence.

Price, Carbon Co., Utah, April 14.— The weather the last week has been warm and pleasant. Crops are growing nicely. Price river is beginning to boom with high waters.

The Western rDama of The Goblen Giant Mine, was rendered at the Price town hall, Monday and Tuesday evenings, to fairly good sized houses. The play was presented by some members of the Imperial Dramatic company, assisted by local talent. Those of the local caste did well, and deserve great credit, for the part they took, considering that they are only amateurs, and that they rendered their part of it for the benefit of the Price Sunday school.

Some copper ore is being shipped from the copper mines, 2 miles south of Ferron, Emery county, to the Taylor & Brunton sampling mills at Salt Lake City, Utah. The property is owned by St. V. Le Sieur and company. Considerable ore is reported in sight, and more shipping will be done in the future.

Rumor has it that A. J. Lee of Price succeeded in getting the government freight contract at much higher figures this year than they were last year. The freighters are rejoicing at the prospect of higher wages and cash at that.

Sheep shearing is still in full blast, and fetches quite an amount of money to our merchants. Sheep men report good fleeces and their flocks doing well.

Quite a number of our people went over to Cleveland, Emery county, to attend quarterly conference hedr there on the 16th and 17th inst.

CASTLE GATE NOTES.

CASTLE GATE, April 17.—Yesterday a high wind struck this town The partly built house of Michael Beveridge was blown down and the outhouses of other residences turned over and damaged

Heber Ward and wife have a new girl baby at their home that came into the world Sunday.

Pat Ryan, the mining man, has been here several days in consultation with the directors of the Bald Mountain company.

Preparations are being made for a new crossing over the river, as it is feared the old foot bridge trestle will not longer stand the pressure of the high water.

Thomas Williams and family are here from Scofield visiting their parents and friends.

W. H. Donaldson spent the Sabbath in Helper.

McClure Wilson has retired from the Hotel Wade and H. G. Webb is continue the business.

Price

PERSONAL.

Major Sam Q Robinson of Fort Duchesne has gone to Washington on official business.

Mrs. B. R. McDonald and Master Holley have returned from a visit to Springville.

Miss Nellie Holley returned Sunday evening from a two weeks visit to relatives and friends at Springville and Salt Lake City.

Mrs George W. Bodle returned the latter part of the week from a short visit to her mother at Salt Lake City.

E. R. Harper, special agent of the Indian department, came in Tuesday evening from White Rocks agency He left at midnight for Washington, where he was called by urgent business,

Sheriff Allred came in Sunday evening from a short trip to Salt Lake City.

Robert Skelton, manager of the Skelton company at Provo, was in town Tuesday and made "the great moral and religious" an appreciated call during his stay.

Mr. and Mrs. M. H. Beardsley of Helper, who are spending some time at Los Angeles, expect in a short while to leave for the Hiwaaian Islands, and will be accompanied by a son who is now at college in the East.

Mrs. H. A. Nelson and babies came in today from Castle Gate on a short visit to the family of Station Agent McDonald.

Mrs. A. Senate of Salt Lake City came in on today's train on a visit to her sisters, Mrs. McDonald and Miss Nellie Holley. Mrs. Senate is the mother of Miss Belle Brown, who recently visited here.

County Superintendent Webb of Castle Gate was in Price yesterday arranging for the teachers examination to be held next month.

Manager McCarty, of the Price and Vernal stage line, has returned from Zion.

Mrs. Louis Lowenstein, Miss Ella and Master Sherman have returned from a visit of two weeks with relatives and friends at Salt Lake City.

A. E. Gibson came over Sunday from Cleveland on his way to the La Salle mountains, where he has some copper prospects that are promising to elevate him from a ranchman to a millionaire.

Miss Stena Jensen will probably to go to Springville to reside in the near future, her parents having lately gone there from Helper to make that place their home.

Mrs. Mabel Moore was in Price on Monday en route home to Orangeville from Salt Lake City.

J. M. Lynch, late editor of the Pioneer at Castle Dale, went through here Sunday with his family, going to Ogden, where he intends to locate.

Shea & Assad have moved their lunch room at Helper from the saloon of James Rooney to more commodious quarters a few doors north and where they have a neat and attractive place. They are the only people there that keep open all night. The boys are enjoying a good business, as they well deserve to. Price people visiting Helper will find this lunch counter and restaurant an excellent place to entertain the inner man.

Price Trading company is making cleaning out prices on everything in the house since stock taking. Many bargains are offered in every department in order to turn goods into money before the lines for spring and summer are here to further crowd the already well stocked shelves. Call and look over the goods and get prices on the same.

Vernal merchants are giving 70 cents store pay for the hauling of wool to Price.

Price merchants all say business is good for this time of year, and they have no kicks to register.

"Woman Against Woman" Friday and Saturday evenings at Town Hall. Matinee Saturday afternoon for the children.

Tom Nichols didn't fall in love with Mercur as a business town. He thinks Price is worth half a dozen such places.

Bartholomew and Herriman sent a wagon load of copper ore to the sampling works this week from their prospect in the Cedar mountains.

Mudslides in Colorado and Nevada have caused frequent delays of trains this week on the Rio Grande Western road. Few passenger trains have been on time.

Misses Mary Leonard and Sadie Kimball and Professor H G Webb will conduct the examination for teachers at Castle Gate next month—May 24th to 26th, inclusive.

James Rooney has in contemplation some extensive improvements in his place of business at Helper, which will make his saloon one of the most attractive in all Eastern Utah

The Old Dyer mine has several teams on the road to Price with copper ore enough to make up a carload with that is already on storage here It goes to a smelter just ouside of Chicago

Thirty five teams are on the road from the Indian Canyon mines of the Raven Mining company with claterite ore, five cars of which will be shipped from Price to Chicago in a few days

Price Trading company will take half the stock if any man or set of men will build and furnish a twenty to twenty five thousand dollar hotel in this man's town of Price. The Advocate is authorized to make this statement.

Shaw & Redding, who recently engaged in the butcher business here, report that they are having a good trade, and that their business is steadily increasing They run a wagon that makes daily trips up to Helper and Castle Gate. The boys are conducting a neat, n'ce place and are deserving of a most liberal and substantial patronage.

Quite a number of Eastern Utah wool owners will ship their clip to Salt Lake City, where it can be put in warehouses at a cheap storage and insurance rate, and where money can be easily borrowed upon it in case such is necessary

Hill's Canal and Irrigation company has instituted an action for damages against Jensen Bros of Emery county by reason of their driving sheep across the ditch of the company, after which extensive repairs, it is alleged, had to be made. Attorney Braffet represents the canal company.

Letters have been lately forwarded to the higher officials of the Rio Grande Western railroad concerning the building of the Whitmore Canyon branch out from Price. Very favorable replies have been received General Dodge and Manager Palmer have had the matter referred to them by Superintendent Welby.

Eleven thousand pounds of wool was unloaded here Monday at the Rio Grande Western wool sheds. It came from Vernal and belongs to J. H. Mease and George Goodman and is the first delivered here this season from the north Other clips are on the road, and the sheds will soon be full

Over four thousand acres of school land will be sold at auction at the court house at Castle Dale on May 9—next month Terms are one tenth cash at time of sale and remainder of purchase price in ten equal annual payments, with interest at 3 per cent per annum in advance on deferred payments The sale is made under order of the state land board.

A. J. Mead, who owns a mine of lusterite seven miles from Colton and four miles from the railroad spur, was here the first of the week. He will begin work on the property in about two weeks, when the snow will all be gone. He has a shaft down 100 feet, with a vein of ore twenty six inches in width The shaft will be sunk to a still greater depth. The product of this mine goes direct to Chicago, where it is used in the manufacture of fine paints and varnishes.

The board of county commissioners meet again in regular session on the 10th of July.

C F. Jensen and family have gone from Helper to Springville to make their home there.

The boys giving the dance last Friday night at Town Hall came out about five dollars behind.

Hotel Clarke has lately built a cistern, that will afford patrons the best water the house has ever had.

Some good work is being done on the streets under the direction of Frank Bryner, who is giving every detail his personal attention.

H G. Clark, who conducts a store and the stage station at the Wells, was here Monday on his way to Salt Lake to purchase a large stock of merchandise

---

The swell dance of the year will take place at Town Hall on the evening of Monday, May 1st. The affair is being gotten up by about a half dozen young gentlemen who have engaged the orchestra of Professor Dalton of Provo, said by those who have heard it to be one of the best in the state. During the evening refreshments, such as sherbets, ices, punches, coffee and sandwiches will be served. Everybody attending is assured of a good time.

There was a big crowd from here to the Emery Stake conference which was in session at Cleveland Sunday and Monday.

The Price Sunday school benefits by it if you cough up a half dollar and go to the play tonight or tomorrow night.

Up to date no wool buyers have appeared in this market. Owners do not expect to get the prices they did last year for their clip.

Attend the play Saturday night and help the Sunday school people pay for the new scenery now being painted for Town Hall.

The high wind of last Sunday was the worst in the recollection of the oldest inhabitant For about three hours it was next to impossible to get around out of doors

---

Judge McConnell has been here several days looking after a shipment of elaterite from the mines of the Raven company in Indian Canyon, which goes to Chicago.

Deseret Evening News
April 22, 1899

PRICE.

Fruit Destroyed by Frost—Gigantic Irrigation Enterprise.

Special Correspondence.

Price, Carbon Co., April 20.— High winds in the day time and heavy frosts at night, have destroyed all the early fruit in this part of Eastern Utah.

Quite a number of people around Price are suffering from severe attacks of rheumatism this spring.

The reported trouble among the Utes out on the reservation does not amount to anything. Your correspondent interviewed Sergt. Thornton, government signal officer here at Price, who expressed himself to the effect, that there was no trouble of any kind on either reservation, and if there was the government had not been informed of the matter. All he knew was that the Indians expressed a desire to go back on their old reservation in Colorado.

The Price people will meet on the 29th inst. to consider the advisability of erecting a new school house this summer, which the town is badly in need of. The proposition should be encouraged.

The Hill canal west of Price is just about completed. Great credit is due those who worked so hard for years to accomplish this great work. The ditch covers between eight and ten thousand acres of land. The next thing that ought to be done now, is to build a large reservoir at the head of Price river, in order to insure all the ditches leaving the river, full flow of water during the irrigating season.

Deseret Evening News
April 25, 1899

PRICE.

Real Estate Going Skywards—Interest in Branch R. R. to New Coal Beds.

Special Correspondence.

Price, Carbon Co., April 24.—Castle Valley real estate in the shape of dust, has been on the move at the rate of about forty miles per hour the last two days.

Sergeant Thornton, government signal officer at Price, reports everything quiet on the agencies.

There is considerable talk around Price about the Rio Grande Railroad company building a branch road from Price to the Whitmore Canyon coal beds. No doubt the officials of that road expect some inducement from our people. The Price people are wide awake, enterprising and have the interest of their town at heart. They are willing to meet the company on any kind of a fair proposition. Let the railroad people say what they expect of us and we will then say what we can and will do for them.

Salt Lake Herald
April 25, 1899

CASTLEGATE NOTES.

Several Interesting Happenings In the Little Coal City.

(Special Correspondence.)

Castlegate, April 22.—E. Santchi and wife leave here tonight for a journey to Salt Lake City to visit two of their children, who are in St. Mary's academy. From the city they will go to the Agricultural college, Logan. Their eldest son is a student in that institution. After a short stay in the granary of Utah they intend to take in some parts of Wyoming, including Diamondville and Kemmerer, as they have many friends in that region of country.

The district schools will be given a vacation of one week commencing Monday. The principal, John R. Cardall, intends to take the opportunity of visiting friends in Salt Lake and other points in the state.

Bishop Scanlan is here from the city. A new bell is to put on the Catholic church.

Last evening several maids from Italy were expected in camp. The advent of these damsels justifies the writer in stating that there will be several weddings in town this coming week.

The Italian element is preparing to celebrate its annual festivities. A selection of the ground has been made and a large bowery will be erected and a dancing pavilion put up and other conveniences will also be added to make the time a hummer.

Bernard Seidal leaves this evening for his home in Germany.

Pay day at the mines yesterday.

Salt Lake Tribune
April 25, 1899

George M. Fitzsimmons's Funeral.

Correspondence Tribune.]

Scofield, Utah, April 20.—One of the largest and most imposing funerals that Scofield ever held occurred yesterday when the Odd Fellows of Scofield lodge No. 22 and the Knights of Pythias of Rathbone lodge No. 9 gathered to pay their last sad respects to Brother George M. Fitzsimmons.

He was an active member of Scofield lodge No. 22, I. O. O. F., and was much respected by the community at large as well as by the brothers, who will miss his hearty greetings as he extended the hand of fellowship.

His death occurred here Sunday evening, after an illness of seven hours. He leaves a wife and three children to mourn.

The Pleasant Valley Coal company, out of respect to his memory and respect to the fraternal societies which desired to attend the funeral, closed the mine at 1 o'clock and gave everyone the privilege of attending.

Eastern Utah Advocate
April 27, 1899
Price

There are a number of good reservoir sites above Price that should be taken up by home people before outside corporations get hold of them. It is a matter of only a short time until they are utilized. This valley is rapidly settling up and the water now going to waste will be saved

Week before last Mr Shaw, of the firm of Shaw & Redding lost his pocketbook containing valuable papers between Helper and Price. He left a notice to be printed in the great moral and religious but before the paper had gone to press the pocketbook was returned to him. It pays to advertise

SHORT STORIES.

Tickets to the ball Monday evening next are one dollar

Hotel Clarke will serve refreshments during the evening for the dancers at the May Day ball

There will be several couples from Helper in attendance upon the May Day ball next Monday evening

Water will be turned out of the ditches of the Price Water company next week for the annual spring and summer cleanup

There will be an election Saturday to vote on the proposition of building a new school house this summer, which the district has badly needed for some time.

The railroad company is getting ready to build nine more cottages at Helper. Some of them will be put up south of and across the street from the depot.

Several Indians who are prominent on the reservation will be here in a few days on their way to Salt Lake City, where they are to appear in the Winn case as witnesses

Remarks the Emery County Record of last week "Price has no tenderloin Good for Price. This is an example of the benign influence a 'great moral and religious newspaper' has on a community."

Hyte Loveless of Huntington has been down on the San Rafael prospecting for several weeks and thinks he has some claims staked off that will pan out well The assays show good values in copper and gold. The country is swarming with prospectors

W. L White shipped a train load of twelve cars or about 700 head of yearling steers from here to Denver on Wednesday They were raised in Eastern Utah and are a fine bunch of youngsters He has as many more on his ranch in this county that are being made ready for market.

Arthur J Lee has so far this season handled three cars of wagons, one car of farming implements, one car of rock salt and is now unloading a car of twine Mr Lee says this, however, is only a starter of what he expects to do later on in the season Gilsonite shipments out are something over three hundred tons a month with the probability of steady increases from month to month.

Inquiries are coming in to the Hill's Canal and Irrigation company from many people who express themselves as being anxious to locate in Castle Valley if land and water can be secured. H L Bowen of the Utah Immigration Bureau was here the other day looking up the matter with a view to locating a colony. He read a description of the canal in a late issue of "the great moral and religious"

Denver and Chicago capitalists have their eyes on a reservoir site about twelve miles above Price and near Castle Gate, and if they build the dam as they hope to, it will create a dam some fifty feet deep, half a mile wide and about a mile and a half long. The melting snow in the mountains will feed the reservoir. The company is believed to be after control of the stock of one of the canal companies.

W. J. Burgess came up from the southern country the other day after a prospecting trip of two months. He has located four claims on the Dirty Devil and upon which there is, he says, a four and a half foot vein of copper that runs high in the red metal, besides ten ounces in silver and over $5 in gold. Sheriff Allred is interested with him, and they will work the property together. It is about one mile east of Thurber in Wayne county.

There will be but two weeks more of school, and it is said, one week of the time will be occupied in examination of pupils.

Arthur J. Lee is looking after the wool coming in from Verual for the consignors there. It is being stored in the Rio Grande Western railway warehouse.

Wool owners here, at least some of them, have been offered an advance of eight and a half cents for this year's clip. We have heard of none accepting the proffer.

The Thirteenth infantry in two sections of an extra train, passed passed through here Monday from Fort Porter, N. Y., en route to the Phillippine Islands. General Shafter was in command.

There was a traveling fakir along here last Saturday who worked the business community for one thousand cards each, ten thousand cards in all. He raked in $4 50 each, or $45 for his day's work. The printing he has done at Provo, not owning himself a line of type, an ounce of paper nor a drop of ink. The work in Provo costs this fellow $15, for we know whereof we speak, and the express charges to Price, leaving him a profit of about $20 for one day's work. Any time the people who went up against the game want the job duplicated—same paper, identically the same faces of type, the same ink and printed off on the same press—The Advocate will furnish the work for $25 and donate $5 of the amount to any worthy charity, church or Sunday school in Carbon county. The offer holds good for one year from this date.

The long distance telephone box recently put in at the Rio Grande Western depot works to perfection. It connects with all the towns on the line of the Price Trading company to the south and the east.

Charles Russell, a young man and aged 21 years, who was taken from Scofield to Salt Lake City last Friday for treatment for neuralgia of the heart, died Monday. The remains were taken to Ogden on Tuesday for burial.

Stages for the north have been crowded for a week, many of the passengers being mining men on their way to the Blue mountains. The snow has about disappeared and prospecting can now be done to some advantage.

One of the most severe dust and wind storms of the season raged here the first three days of the week The continuous dry weather allows the dust to come along in clouds that are blinding to persons traveling on country roads

The Imperial and the Price Dramatic companies play "The Golden Giant Mine" at Castle Gate tomorrow night and "Woman Against Woman" Saturday evening Those attending may rest assured of getting their money's worth

There was a fire at the home of C M Allred Tuesday that did considerable damage A shed in the rear of the residence was destroyed with a quantity of baled hay, and a horse more or less scorched The fire is said to have caught from a spark from the chimney.

Richard Sparrow and Terisa Sparrow took out license to wed at Salt Lake City the first of the week. The bride was the widow of her husband's deceased brother by whom she has had a batch of several little Sparrows, and if everything goes well the usual number may be looked for next spring

There arrived here one day this week a machine for making brick. Emery County Mercantile company has ordered 250,000 for their new two-story building, and most likely will use half as many more. The foundation was put in last fall, and when completed the building will be the best and most substantial of any in Carbon county.

The death of George M. Fitzsimmons, a highly respected citizen, occurred at Scofield last Sunday week, after an illness of only seven hours. He leaves a wife and three children The funeral was held last Wednesday under the auspices of the Knights of Pythias and Odd Fellows' lodges, and of both of which he was a prominent member.

Special Officer Ketchem arrested one G. W. Clayton at Helper Sunday night, and took his prisoner to Grand Junction, where he is wanted for the larceny of surgical instruments from the offices of doctors. The fellow has worked about every town from Pueblo to Salt Lake. He was in Price Sunday and walked up to Helper where he was nailed to the cross the minute he landed on the depot platform.

CASTLE GATE NOTES.

CASTLE GATE, April 25.—There was not much work done at the mine today, the main hoist being out of repair.

David Howells and Tom Phelps have left here to locate at Diamondville, Wyo.

The local dramatic company will soon appear in "Down the Black Canyon."

D. F. Thomas of Wellington has been here for several days, doing a lot of painting.

William Crow and Miss Maggie Jenkins are to be married here on tomorrow evening.

E. Santschi and wife are in Salt Lake visiting two of their children, who are attending the St. Mary's Academy.

The district schools will have one week's vacation. Professor Cardall is in Salt Lake.

Bishop Scanlan was down from Salt Lake the other day. A new bell is soon to be put on the Catholic church.

There are soon to be several weddings in Italiandom.

Bernard Seidal has gone on a trip to Germany.

The advent of warm weather has caused a collapse in the coal company's output. For the last few days the miners have worked half time only.

A new mine will most probably be opened up by the company near Sunnyside the coming summer.

W. H. Donaldson spent the day in Price Sunday.

For the annual convention of the Travelers Protective Association at Louisville, Ky., May 16th to 19th, a rate of one lowest first-class regular fare plus $2, is authorized from all points on the Rio Grande Western railway to Louisville and return. Tickets will be sold for trains No. 2 and No. 4 of May 12th and 13th only, and will be limited to three days in both directions. Going passage must commence with date of execution. Regular iron clad signature and witness form of ticket, including exchange order on Chicago or St. Louis will be used on this occasion. The final limit will be May 24th, and will be honored for return leaving Louisville up to and including May 20. B. R. McDonald, agent, Price, Utah.

HOME MISSIONARIES

Following is the list of missionaries of the Emery Stake of Zion who were appointed to visit the wards of the stake on the dates named

J W Nixon and William A Thayn—Castle Gate, April 30, Price, May 28, Spring Glen, June 25

B M Y Goold and John Thordarson—Spring Glen, April 30 Lawrence May 28 Orangeville, June 25

Andrew Nielson and L P Larson—Wellington April 30, Castle Dale, May 28, Price, June 25

John P Pearson and Peter Nielson—Castle Dale, May 14, Cleveland, May 28, Castle Dale, June 25

Joseph E Johnson and J Fleming Wakefield—Price April 30, Wellington, May 28 Molen June 25

John Oliphant and Joseph H Taylor—Cleveland April 30, Huntington, May 28 Ferron June 25

Uriah E Curtis and F M Reynolds—Huntington April 30

Alma G Jewkes and Uriah E Curtis—Emery, May 28, and Cleveland, June 25

Samuel Williams Jr and Peter Christensen—Orangeville, April 30, Molen, May 28, Lawrence, June 25

George W Stephens and J D Killpack, Jr—Emery, April 30 Orangeville, May 28, and Huntington, June 25

J W Seely and John Peterson—Molen, April 30, Ferron, May 28, Wellington, June 25

Abmrali Olsen and C G Larson, Jr—Ferron, April 30, Desert Lake, May 28 Emery, June 25

A W Horsley and Chris Peterson—Spring Glen, May 28, Desert Lake June 25

Deseret Evening News
May 2, 1899

PRICE.

Two Men Killed in a Quarrel Over a Woman and Two Others Wounded.

Special Correspondence.

Price, Carbon Co., May 1.—Three negro soldiers of the Ninth cavalry and a white man named Jack Thomas, got into a row in a saloon or house of ill repute on what is known as the "strip," a piece of ground lying between the Uintah and Uncompahgre reservation, last night, and Thomas was shot and killed, and one of the negroes mortally wounded.

The quarrel was on account of a woman known as Sarah Allred, all of them being jealous of her. The report is that the other two soldiers are badly wounded. Two of the negroes and the woman are the ones who stopped and held up the Price and Vernal stage a few months ago. Thomas owned a ranch near-by, and has long been regarded as a tough character generally.

Eastern Utah Advocate
May 4, 1899
Price

PERSONAL.

C. F Warren, general agent of the Santa Fe Route, was here today looking after wool shipments.

Walter H. Graves, superintendent of irrigation on Indian reservations, was a guest at the Mathis Hotel yesterday.

Superintendent Ferron of the Raven Mining company was a guest of Hotel Clarke today

R. A Kirker went through here today from Salt Lake to Whitmore Canyon.

Mrs R G Miller has returned from a visit with relatives at Murray and Salt Lake.

Mrs James Rooney of Helper attended the ball here Monday evening.

Sam Glaser and W. C. Brocker from Helper were here Monday.

Dick Cotner was in town Sunday from Whitmore Canyon, where he is working in the mines. He says considerable development is being carried on in the properties of that section of the county.

Hon. Orange Seeley was here yesterday from Castle Gate on his way to Salt Lake.

Mrs Noah Bartholomew departed Tuesday for Salt Lake City and will be absent some time.

Mrs. L. O. Hoffmann and the children returned Sunday from a short visit at Sunnyside.

Misses Sadie Kimball and Mary Leonard were visitors to Castle Gate last Saturday.

Charley Taylor went up to Provo Sunday evening to visit with his wife and babies, and to have a black bass out of Utah Lake.

Judge McConnell left here Sunday night for Chicago, where he expects to close up a mining deal of considerable importance.

Manager Lonsberry of the Old Dyer mine was here Monday on his way to the property from Boston, where he has been for a month or six weeks.

CASTLE GATE NOTES.

CASTLE GATE, May 3.—Paul Veillard will move his family to a ranch near Marysvale, he being employed in the mines there.

E. Santschi and wife have returned from Logan.

Ed Cox has sold out and will go to Scofield to live.

Yesterday Old Glory was flying to the breeze in honor of the anniversary of Dewey's victory.

We are having some splendid winter weather.

Cold weather has killed much of the early fruit around Moab, Grand county.

Considerable freight is coming in these days for merchants and others of Emery county.

There have been several buyers of wool in town the past week, but no sales have been reported.

Castle Dale claims to have more pretty homes, the population of the town considered, than any other place in Eastern Utah.

The number of shade and ornamental trees planted this spring will prove surprising to anyone who takes the time to walk about town.

The Chinese section men here are no more. They were let out on the first of May and their places taken by white men and Italians.

Dun's Review says of the state of business in Salt Lake: "Trade is steady and collections fair, with local stocks active and money easy."

Flock owners of Emery county are somewhat discouraged at the low price of wool. Great lots of it are stacked up waiting for the market to advance.

The bad weather has delayed the shearing of sheep at Colton about a week. Considerable loss has been suffered among those already shorn of their wool.

Tem Nichols expects to leave before a great while for his placer holdings on the Colorado river in Wayne county. He will be gone about a month, he thinks.

Coal that very much resembles anthracite and in well defined and large veins, has been discovered not far from Castle Dale and the owners have what they think is quite a big thing.

Bids for the transportation of government freight from Price to Fort Duchesne will be opened at Denver next Thursday, May 11th, by the quartermaster of the Department of the Missouri.

This appears to be one of the springs when the young man's fancy has not run along the old lines with consequent results. The marriage license market has been extremely dull for weeks.

Water was not turned out of the ditches the first of May as announced in The Advocate on account of so many fruit trees arriving that had not been counted upon, and for which those planting want water.

President Miller and his counsellors, John H. Pace and H. G. Mathis, and Stake Clerk Arthur W. Horsley were at Castle Dale last Sunday afternoon, Orangeville in the evening and at Lawrence on Monday, where well attended ward conferences were held.

Emery Stake Academy will be finished this year and in time for the regular school term. The money is to be raised by popular subscription. When completed the building, which is located at Castle Dale, will have cost near five thousand dollars. It is now about ready for the roof. All the branches will be taught.

The funeral services over the remains of the little 4 year old child, a daughter, of Mr and Mrs William Hamilton of the Nine Mile settlement was held at the residence of Mother Warren Tuesday afternoon, the body being interred here. Death occurred Monday last from pneumonia. Elder John H Pace officiated at the funeral.

Attorney General Bishop, replying to the prosecuting attorney of Uintah county states as his opinion that a person other than a member of the board of pharmacy may make a complaint for a violation of the provisions of the law relating to the practice of pharmacy which will justify the county attorney in prosecuting such a case.

Frank Caffey has repainted and redecorated his Magnolia Hall at Castle Gate. The work was done by the Hutchinsons and is an artistic throughout.

Several teamsters loaded down with wool have been in this week from the Vernal country. The stuff was stored in the Rio Grande Western warehouses.

Several wagons loaded with rich copper ore from the Oil Dyer mine are expected in this week for shipment out over the Rio Grande Western to the smelter.

There was a killing at the saloon on the Strip Sunday night. Jack Thomas, a white man and a gambler, got into a row with three negro soldiers, Sergeant Henderson, Private Carter and another whose name is unknown, over a woman named Sarah Allred. The party with Red Mary and Jessie Robinson were in the saloon drinking. Thomas, who is said to have fired the first shot, was killed almost instantly. Six shots took effect. Carter was mortally wounded, so report has it, and will not recover, while Henderson has a troublesome wound. Al Baxter, the bartender, and the women were put in the guard house during the coroner's inquest, and the sergeant reduced in rank The body of Thomas was taken to Vernal for burial, deceased owning a ranch near there.

Bishop Horsley has gone over to Emery county with a consignment of fruit trees for delivery in the valley. He will be absent several days on the trip.

James Rooney will put in a new floor, repaint and otherwise improve his saloon building at Helper, his intention being to make the place a model of neatness and comfort and nothing finer this side of Salt Lake City or Denver.

The dance given at Town Hall on Monday evening was not so well attended as might have been expected. The music as furnished by Professor Darton's orchestra from Provo was the best ever heard here. The boys giving it came out about thirty dollars behind

Harvey Hardy will be down from Salt Lake this week on the way to his sulphur deposits in Sulphur Gulch, Emery county, where work is to be inaugurated on a big scale. The group of claims taken in an immense deposit that can be traced on the surface for about eight hundred feet, while the deposit is fully four hundred feet wide, the ore running from 20 to 85 per cent sulphur. He will before a great while install a mill on the ground for the reduction and refining of this product.

Deseret Evening News
May 5, 1899

PRICE.

Ward Conferences—To Push Stake Academy—New School Building at Price.

Special Correspondence.

Price, Carbon Co., Utah, May 2.—The weather is still windy and cold in the day time, freezes ice at night, fruit is destroyed and vegetation is at a standstill. Snow is still falling in the mountains.

WARD CONFERENCES.

Ward conferences were held in the following places, President H. G. Miller, his counselors, J. H. Pace, H. G. Mathis, and Stake Clerk A. M. Hersley being present: Castle Dale, April 30, 1899; Orangeville, 7:30 p.m., same day; and Lawrence, Monday, May 1, 1899, at 7:30 p.m. Good feeling prevailed; all Stake and ward officers were unanimously sustained.

STAKE ACADEMY.

The Stake board of education met at Castle Dale May 1, 1899, at 10 o'clock a.m., quite a number of the higher Priesthood were present. A number of reports were read; among other things it was decided to complete the Academy building at Castle Dale at once, and start school not later than October next.

Elders Joseph Johnson and Hyrum Harmon visited Price ward in the capacity of home missionaries last Sunday; the remarks they made were timely and highly appreciated.

PRICES OF WOOL.

Some of our sheep men have been offered as high as 10 cents per pound for this year's wool. Sheep shearing is

over with here at Price; there must at least be $100,000 worth in sight.

Some copper mines south of Ferron, Emery county, Utah, will be worked steady this summer; the ore will be shipped from Price to its destination. The property is owned by Huntington men.

Some Price people hold claims 11 miles west from here, that carry 16 ounces of silver and a trace of gold to the ton.

NEW SCHOOL BUILDING.

The majority of Price people voted for a new school house, which is to be a modern one; but there is a great deal to be done yet, before its erection will be commenced.

The public schools of Price will close about the 15th inst.

Dewey Day was celebrated by the young people of Price in the shape of fancy ball and supper in the evening; everybody had a good time.

CLEVELAND.

Golden Wedding of Patriarch Charles Pulsipher.

Special Correspondence.

Cleveland, Emery County, May 1.—Relatives and friends of Patriarch Charles Pulsipher and his wife Ann met at the social hall at 11 o'clock a.m. today in honor of and to celebrate the fiftieth anniversary of their wedding day which occurred April 29th, but the date coming on Sunday the entertainment was postponed until today. At 12 o'clock tables were spread to accommodate 125 guests. A program was carefully prepared, after singing and prayer Brother Charles Pulsipher Sr. gave a brief history of his life in Utah. Being one of the pilgrims his narrative was very interesting.

A very happy day was spent. Appropriate songs, recitations, speeches, etc., were given and the honored couple received many very nice presents and mementoes. A social ball in the evening wound up the anniversary.

Salt Lake Herald
May 5, 1899

Post Trader Kennedy Dead.

(Special to The Herald.)

Price, Utah, May 4.—Thomas Kennedy, manager of the post trading store at Ouray Indian agency, is dead of paralysis. He was about 48 years of age and has been associated with J. H. Mease, post trader, for a number of years. He has a family at Higginsville, Mo., where the body will be shipped.

EMERY COUNTY STRIKES.

Several Copper Discoveries Reported —Copper Globe Shipment.

General Manager Le Sieur of the Copper Globe mine reached the city last night and states that the property is looking better every day. He says that as depth is gained the quality of the ore improves. He is in the city to arrange for another shipment of ore to Denver, which will be sent on in a few days. He states that he has put fourteen men to work on the mine, and expects to increase the force to sixty before the season is over.

In speaking of the district, he says that new copper strikes are made every day, and that the country is beginning to boom. Among those who have made discoveries are several parties from Ferron. Jesse Brown of Ferron has uncovered a ledge of ore about six miles south of the Globe, which gives an average assay of 9 per cent copper across the vein. Burton, Nelson and Swasey, also from Ferron, uncovered a six-foot vein of copper that assays 5 per cent on the surface. A man by the name of Lovelace, whose home is in Castle Dale, has come in and reports having made a strike on the San Rafael river, which has a good showing of high-grade copper ore.

Salt Lake Tribune
May 6, 1899

MAURITZ C. JENSEN.

Soldier from Castle Gate who Recently Died in the Philippines.
[From a photograph taken in San Francisco.]

PRICE.

At Last, Spring—Large Shipments of Copper Ore—Freight Business Booming.

Special Correspondence.

Price, Carbon Co., May 8.—The cold and windy weather has at last changed to spring, sweet, gentle spring, and if we have no more cold snaps now, there will yet be a chance for a good fruit crop this year.

Isaac McFarland from St. George, southern Utah, is a welcome visitor among the Price people.

Charles Pulsipher from Huntington, one of the Patriarchs of Emery Stake, was among our people Sunday, pronouncing Patriarchal blessings upon the heads of those who had a desire to obtain them.

The program rendered at the conjoint session Sunday evening was interesting, well attended, and a credit to those who took part.

President R. G. Miller reports good feelings and prosperity in Emery Stake.

The infant child of Erastus and Pharon Petersen, died Sunday morning after a very short illness. Price people feel to sympathize with the bereaved parents, as this is their second loss within a few months.

Considerable copper ore will be shipped from Price this week. It comes from the mines in the southern part of Emery county.

Wool buyers are coming in lately, but as yet no sales of wool have been made in Price this year.

Freighting is quite lively these days, and quite a large amount of Gilsonite and other freights are coming in daily. Business has picked up considerably; our merchants, mechanics, etc., have plenty to do, and our little town looks like a bee-hive as usual. For enterprise and push, Price is hard to beat.

PERSONAL.

Judge McConnell left by private conveyance this morning for the Vernal country.

John P Hite was here Sunday having come through from Chicago and St. Louis, where he has been for several months.

A E Elliott and Theodore Davis, Boston wool buyers, have been in town several days.

George T. Holladay was in Price Monday.

Gus Anderson and George Haverstick registered from Zion at Hotel Clarke during the week.

L M Olson was down in Emery county this week, looking after his interests there.

E W Davis, a prominent citizen and one of the leading merchants of Vernal, was in town yesterday, going to Evanston, Wyo., to attend a session of the grand lodge of the United Workmen.

Hon Orange Seeley and District Attorney Woods were at the Hotel Clarke today, en route home to Castle Dale from Salt Lake.

George Peacock, the Manti sheepman, was at Hotel Clarke on Monday last.

Miss Annie Forrest of Washington, D C, arrived here the first of week en route to Vernal, where she will spend the summer with her sister, Mrs George Adams. Miss Forrest is a charming and highly accomplished Southern girl, and is greatly pleased with what she has seen of the West, especially Utah.

Major and Mrs. S M Browne of Vernal were here Tuesday going to Salt Lake City, where they will be for several days.

Mr and Mrs J H Mease of White Rocks passed through here Monday on their way to Zion.

Miss Nellie Holley returned Monday from Castle Gate.

Mrs. B R McDonald visited her sister, Mrs H. A Nelson at Castle Gate during the week.

Miss Nellie McMullin visited at Wellington the latter part of the week.

Miss Maggie McIntire is expected to return from Thompsons about the first of July.

Miss Annie Larson is visiting at Cleveland

Robert Forrester was here from Castle Gate Saturday and stopped at the Hotel Mathis

Lieutenant White of Fort Duchesne was registered at Hotel Mathis during the week.

M J. Thomas (Schilling's Best) was in town yesterday.

B F. Luke was over from Orangeville Saturday, a guest of the Hotel Mathis while here

SHORT STORIES.

A pretty young girl of DuChesne
Was caught one day in the rene;
    Her hat was a mess,
    And she cried in distress:
"Now, wouldn't that give you a pense!"
Her tears her plump cheeklets did streme
Till her fellow said. "Darling, refrene!
    I'll buy you another
    Much prettier than t'other,"
And that made her happy agrene.

Ras Anderson is this week working the road in Soldier Canyon

Great quantities of farming machinery continue to arrive here for Emery county

Victor Rambaud has driven a big bunch of his sheep into the hills near Colton for summer range.

Lieutenant White and an escort of troopers were here Tuesday for the pay of the soldiers, which came in by express

Some wool has lately been sold in the Sanpete country at eleven cents Buyers in the Price market offer to advance nine cents.

Somebody's mule is in the city pound, and unless claimed by the owner will be sold on the 20th of the month by Marshal Anderson.

The Price Dramatic company has been asked to go to Castle Gate on or about the 20th, and repeat the drama, "The Golden Giant Mine." The matter is under consideration.

Judge McConnell has a new buggy and harnesses which he was showing off about town Tuesday. The vehicle is of the latest style and one of the finest that ever came to Eastern Utah.

The bids for forwarding government freight are to be opened at Denver today and the contract for the year to come awarded George W McCall is one of the freighters to put in a bid

Commencement exercises of the Huntington Seminary are to be held on May 17th and 18th, at which time an excellent program will be rendered Several of the church authorities will attend.

Victor Rambaud has sold his wool clip to Zimmerman Bros of Chicago It is said Mr. Rambaud's flock this year averaged more pounds of wool to the head than any herd of sheep in Carbon county.

The Winn brothers were cleared of the charge of stealing goods from the government on the reservation in the federal court at Salt Lake City last week The case of J. W. Burgess was postponed for a month.

The Old Dyer mine has ordered a smelting plant with a capacity for treating forty five tons of ore daily. The contract for a telephone line to the mine from Vernal has been let. The distance is twenty-eight miles.

Emery County Mercantile company brought an action before Judge Holdaway last week against C. M. Smith on a note, obtaining judgment against defendant. A like action against Joseph E Nielson will be decided on the 16th.

Conductor Little and crew of the Rio Grande Western have a dog that makes the trip regularly from Helper to Grand Junction He goes over the top of a freight train in motion the same as a man Affidavits go with this story if there are any who doubt it.

Duck shooting in front of the office of "the great moral and religious" has been fairly good for two weeks or more. The frog crop in the same locality will be good this spring—that is, judging from the number of gentlemen frogs that are very much in evidence during the early hours of the evening

St. V. LeSieur has taken up the bond on the Copper Globe property which he held from George Havercamp, George Allman and others of Provo He was here Tuesday with H. D. Edwards of Salt Lake and Edgar G. Tuttle of Tacoma, who are to report on the mine. They will return about Monday.

Sheriff Chappell of Wayne county came in Tuesday night from Vernal with Pete Nielson, arrested a few days ago on the reservation and wanted in Wayne county for grand larceny. Sheriff and prisoner left here for the south yesterday. Sheriff Preece gets $300 reward for the capture of the man, Nielson.

Anderson Bros are doing the best blacksmithing, repairing and horse-shoeing of any shop in this part of Utah. The report that they were out of the business is entirely without foundation. Ras is out working the roads, but Pete is doing business at the old stand, and also doing all work right that is left at the shop. Read their advertisement in this issue of The Advocate.

Deseret Evening News
May 15, 1899

PRICE.

Loss Among the Flocks—Jail Breakers Captured—Ward Conferences.

Special Correspondence.

Price, Carbon Co., Utah, May 14.—The weather is somewhat windy, but warm; everything is growing nicely.

Sheepmen report considerable loss among their flocks, during the late cold spell, especially so up at Cotton and higher ranges. Wool has been sold at 10 cents per pound at Cotton, but Price men demand 12½ or no sale.

Pete Sheridan and Charles E. Brandt, who broke jail here at Price yesterday, were captured by Sheriff Allred and his deputy, Pete Andrews, down Price river, in a place known as Box Canyon. Sheriff Allred is positive that the two men were assisted by someone in making their escape from the steel cages in which they were kept.

President R. G. Miller, his counselors, J. H. Pace and H. G. Mathis, and State Clerk A. D. Horsley, went over to the south end of the Stake, to hold ward conferences, at Emery today, Ferron Monday morning, and Molen Monday night.

The Primary of Price ward have announced a good program, to be rendered at the Price town hall June 1st, in honor of Brigham Young's birthday.

Eastern Utah Advocate
May 18, 1899

CASTLE GATE NOTES.

CASTLE GATE, May 13.—Paul Crispo was married today to the last remaining single of the girls who recently came from Italy.

Invitations will be issued soon for the marriage of Miss Bertha Wright and James Hencley, which is to occur at the home of Mrs. Halverson aunt of the groom, on the evening of the 24th

County Commissioners Nelson and Young, together with Road Supervisor Young, today viewed the bridges of the Price river to see if they will withstand the pressure of the high water. They also viewed the roads o see what improvements are necessary the coming summer.

Father Zupan, an Austrian Catholic priest, has been in town for several days, holding services for his countrymen

W H Lawler has gone to Cleveland, Emery county. His oldest daughter lately arrived from England, and he has taken her to the rest of the family.

The new foot bridge crossing the river has been completed.

Price

PERSONAL.

Mrs. Arthur J. Lee is visiting at Springville this week.

Miss Clara Mathis was a visitor to friends at Helper Sunday.

District Attorney Woods was here Tuesday, going to Salt Lake.

C H Pennington was among the visitors to Zion during the week.

Morley McIntire went with Tom Nichols on his Colorado river trip.

Ole Olson of Castle Dale was registered at Hotel Clarke on Monday last.

L R Long of Montrose, Colo, was a guest of Hotel Clarke during the week

Frank Carroll and Dr. Winters of Castle Dale were here yesterday on business

James Peterson, the photographer has gone to Fairview, Utah, and will be absent some time.

Bert Myton, son of Indian Agent Myton, came in the other day from Denver, where he has been attending school.

Dr Richman went through here yesterday evening, going from Moab Helper. He returned to Price in the evening.

Miss Stena Jensen will depart in about ten days for Springville, where her parents lately went from Helper to reside permanently.

Mrs. J. M Whitmore and Mrs G W Bodle went up to Salt Lake City Sunday evening to see Mrs Foote their sister, who was not at that time expected to live.

Miss Mattie Wimmer, one of Parson's many most winsome young ladies, is this week the guest of her sister, Mrs C. W. Spalding at Hotel Clarke. She will make an extended visit.

S S Jones, a prominent business man of Provo, was here this week on his way to and from some copper prospects in which he is an owner and which adjoins the Copper Globe, south of Ferron

While Mrs. James Rooney was out visiting a neighbor Friday evening last several dozens of her friends invaded the home of her mother, Mrs S J Warren, bringing with them baskets well filled with everything imaginable that was good to eat. The evening was most pleasantly spent by all present at cards, music social conversation, and at a seasonable hour refreshments were served Among those present were Misses Clara Mathis, Lillie and Rose Bryner Susie Kirkman, Smith, Nellie Holley Nellie McMullin, Messrs Ernest Peyton, G B Friel, Thomas Nichols Ben Stein, McKInnie, Master Sherman Lowenstein, and Mr and Mrs Thos Murphy, Mr and Mrs L Lowenstein Mr and Mrs J G Callaway, Mr and Mrs G. W. Bodle, Mr and Mrs Hul Warren, Mr and Mrs Olsen, Mr and Mrs. Victor Rambaud, Mrs R M Carey, and Mrs Morrison and son, and Mother Warren. The occasion was the birthday of Mrs Rooney, who was—but then it isn't the proper thing to discuss a woman's age, especially in a newspaper The evening was one that will long be remembered by everyone participating

Charles D. Bradt, the Wellington rape fiend, and Pete Sheridan, who is awaiting trial for attempted criminal assault upon Annie Gathurum at Scofield, broke jail last Friday night by two and, it is thought of friends on the outside. One of the men was on the inside of the cage, while the other had the privilege of the corridor. They got possession of a monkey wrench, and by removing some plates, liberated the fellow inside the cell. They then climbed to the ventilation window at the south end of the building, jumped to the ground and—were off Sheriff Allred tracked them to the railroad, which they followed about seven miles, and then went down the river. He and Town Marshal Anderson came upon the men in a canyon about thirty miles east of here Saturday They are again behind the bars, but no longer enjoy the freedom and fresh air of the corridor

Deseret Evening News
May 20, 1899

PRICE.

Reported Heavy Loss Among the Flocks of Eastern Utah.

Price, May 18.—There are thousands of head of dead sheep strewn along the hills and in the gulches leading into the canyons of the Price river in eastern Utah. Flock owners have been out since the cold snap of two weeks ago getting their flocks together and find the worst condition of affairs that has existed for many years. The 20,000 head or more sheared at Price and 35,000 to 40,000 at Colton were sent into the hills, where there was snow at the time and where the grazing was good. The shearing season was too early and in some instances as high as twenty-five per cent is the loss. Out of 40,000 head owned in Price there is a loss already accounted for of over 3,500. Herds further back in the hills will have heavier losses.—Denver Field and Farm.

Deseret Evening News
May 22, 1899

PRICE.

Destructive Frost—Big Wool Shipments—School Closing.

Special Correspondence.

Price, Utah, May 21.—The frost last night completely destroyed all late fruit, besides all garden plants such as potatoes, tomatoes, etc. So far this has been the most destructive spring ever known in eastern Utah.

JUNE COURT CASES.

District court will convene on the 12th of June, quite a number of cases are set for trial, among them are two rape cases, and several divorce cases. Some of the best legal talent of Utah will be here this setting of court.

BIG WOOL SHIPMENT.

A shipment of twenty carloads of wool went east today. The heaviest owners of wool today sold for 12 cents, About fifty wagon loads of wool were stored away in Price this week, all coming from Emery county, Utah. Baled hay is coming in daily from that section in large quantities, and brings a very good price, on account of the scarcity of hay, and brisk freighting.

CLOSING EXERCISES.

The public schools closed Friday, May, 19, 1899. Quite a number of people were present to enjoy the closing program rendered by the schools, which was an excellent one. Much can be said in praise of of Miss Mary Leonard the principal and her two assistants, Miss Nellie McMullin and Miss Sadie Kimball. The people of Price feel grateful to them for the good work they performed among the young of Price, and the excellent example they set before all. People who are interested in school work and the welfare of their children, earnestly hope that it will be their good fortune to have them amongst us again, when the schools open next fall.

Eastern Utah Advocate
May 25, 1899
Price

Judge Holdaway tied his first nuptial knot Tuesday, when he married Daniel Skervis and Elizabeth Shneferhoff, both of Colorado. He omitted that part of the ceremony, however, where the officiating officer should kiss the blushing bride, but whether this was on account of the size of the groom or the presence of Mrs. Holdaway, or both, the judge declines to say. Otherwise, the affair was done up in the highest style of the art.

Says the Salt Lake Tribune of Tuesday last "Huber Frandsen, a citizen of Price, yesterday underwent a very delicate operation at the Holy Cross hospital. It was thought that he was afflicted with appendicitis, but an examination revealed the fact that this was not his affliction, but that portions of the intestines were in a fearful condition, caused by inflammation. Dr Richards attended Frandsen and it was reported last night that he was doing nicely, although it is not known whether or not he will recover."

SHORT STORIES.

Price Trading company offers for sale a quantity of cedar posts

The hotels of Price have had an exceptionally good run of business for the past two weeks

Castle Gate young men will most likely get up a dance for the teachers who will be there this week

Examinations for teachers certificates will begin at Castle Gate today and continue up to and including Saturday

There is but one stack of wool to be seen in Price now, where a few days ago there were many dozens to be shipped out.

President Miller and his counselors, H G Mathis and John H. Pace, was at Huntington, Sunday, where interesting ward meetings were conducted

J H. Pennington, the barber, has opened a shop at Colton, and says he already has a nice business started He bought everything new from Salt Lake City

Several young gentlemen came down from Helper Tuesday evening to attend the dance and the alleged theatrical entertainment, both being a disappointment.

Considerable excitement exists in Emery county over reported new finds of copper about twenty miles south of Ferron, where many locations have been made.

Antonio Fierro, who tried to hold up the store of Ike Glaser at Helper, and was shot through the arm in trying to escape, was brought back here from the hospital at Salt Lake on Friday by Sheriff Allred He is minus an arm from his adventure. He was taken to Helper Wednesday and had his preliminary hearing before J. Tom Fitch, justice of the peace there, and was bound over to await the action of the district court which convenes next month

Three parties caught rolling the bones one evening last week by City Marshal Anderson were assessed five and costs each when taken before his honor, Judge Holdaway

The north stage line is to establish another station at Anderson's or Russell's, about two miles beyond what is known as Whitmore Summit, and twenty six miles from Price.

Steve Chipman went out to his lands in the Nine Mile country the first of the week, after selling his wool. He is said to have received the highest price paid here this year for his clip

About fifteen men are now doing development work for the P. V Coal company in Whitmore Canyon This force is soon to be increased, it understood, to some forty or fifty additional men

Tom Nichols, who left by wagon a few days ago for the Colorado river country, wrote from Lower Crossing the other day that that section is full of prospectors looking for copper and wax properties

Mrs. D. W. Holdaway went up to Helper on Tuesday with a stock of fine millinery which she offers for sale at retail. She will visit other towns of the county from time to time with a complete line of goods

Those having the affair in charge are preparing an excellent program for the Brigham Young anniversary entertainment to be held at Town Hall, Thursday evening, June 1st There will be dancing and refreshments.

Marriage licenses have lately been issued to James Hensley and Bertha Wright of Castle Gate, J. E. Arthur and Jesse Cunningham and John Koski and Ida Asha of Scofield, and Daniel Skersis of Scofield and Elizabeth Schaferhoff of Colorado

John Gaul contributed eight dollars to the city treasury the other day for disturbing the peace about the Rio Grande depot. He has since departed for the north, where he says he'll take a section on the Oregon Short Line.

Sheriff Allred has brought back from the hospital at Salt Lake the Mexican who was shot at Helper in an attempt to rob Ike Glaser's store a short time ago, and who had an arm amputated as a result of a wound inflicted at the time.

Utah railroads will give a rate of one fare from all points in the state for the Young Men's Mutual Improvement association conference to be held at Salt Lake City, May 28th to 30th. Tickets on sale the 27th, good to return until June 3d.

Wool buyers and railroad men looking after wool shipments have about finished up in Price for this year. The Vernal clip remains to be disposed of yet, as well as some small lots at railroad points east of here in Emery, Grand and Uintah counties.

B. R. McDonald has sent out some samples of stuff for analysis from Whitmore Canyon, which everybody calls "chewing gum" for the want of a better name. It occurs in big bodies and is much softer than elaterite or gilsonite. It makes an excellent chewing gum.

The Advocate has purchased and will in future carry in stock a complete line of justices blanks, blank deeds and in fact everything in the legal blank line. Prices no higher than Provo or Salt Lake City. Good stock and the best forms in use in Utah. Orders by mail will receive prompt attention.

Miss Stella Barton, sister of Thos Barton, and well known here in Price where she has visited, will be married next Thursday at Salt Lake City to Orvin Morris, at the home of the bride's mother. Several relatives of the young lady from here will likely attend the wedding. Mr Morris is an employe of the Oregon Short Line and holds a responsible position with the company.

REMEMBER THEIR TEACHER.

Some forty pupils of Miss Mary Leonard went to her home last Thursday night and presented her with a handkerchief box and glove case as tokens of their appreciation of her as a teacher. After the presentation the evening was spent in social conversation and Miss Leonard treated her callers to refreshments. Those present were Misses Rosa Bryner, Isa McIntire, Anna McIntire, Edith McIntire, Florence Kelsey, Dell Burgess, Maud Powell, Mitb'e McIntire, Ada Bryner, Mattie Holdaway, Celia Downard, Mary Olson, Sarah Horsley, Hazel Frandsen, Mary Empey, Nellie Roth, Edith Pace, Gertrude Miller, Edith Bryner and Della McIntire, John Burgess, Frank McIntire, Ed Beutler, Dean Holdaway, Verne Carey, Abe Powell, Will Robb, Alexander Pace, Frank Branch, James Peterson, Will McIntire, James Jones, Tom Kelsey, Almy Bryner, Will Perkins, Roy Allred, Will Powell, Penn Olson, Milton Miller, and Rex Miller. Misses Nellie McMullin and Sadie Kimball assisted Miss Leonard in entertaining her guests during the evening.

PERSONAL.

William Howard of Huntington was in town today

Miss Nellie McMullin went to Castle Gate Tuesday evening

Mrs. George W Bodle has returned from Salt Lake City.

Hon. Orange Seeley was in town from Emery county yesterday.

Charley Gollberg was a visitor to Salt Lake the first of the week.

Miss Stena Jensen departed yesterday morning for Springville.

Miss Anna Anderson has returned to her home in Emery county.

Miss Annie Larsen is back from visiting her parents at Cleveland.

George W Bodle has gone to Salt Lake and will be absent some time.

Mrs. E. E. Hoffmann of Richfield is visiting Mr. and Mrs. L. O Hoffmann of this city

Miss Nellie Holley has gone to Castle Gate to be with her sister, Mrs. H A Nelson, who is ill

Mrs. J. M. Whitmore has returned from Zion, accompanied by her daughter, Miss Ida, who returns for the summer vacation.

Misses Mary Leonard and Sadie Kimball are at Castle Gate this week, helping to conduct the examination for county teachers

Sam Glaser, W. C. Broeker and Rio Grande Western Operator Johnson of Helper were in town Tuesday evening on pleasure bent.

David Prior principal of Huntington Seminary, was here the first of the week on his way to Spanish Fork. He will move his family next week to Emery county

Mrs. C W Spalding departed this morning for Payson, where she will visit with relatives for a few weeks. Her sister, Miss Mattie Wimmer, returned with her.

General Agent Nevins of the Rio Grande railroad came in Monday night from Salt Lake City to look after wool shipments over his popular line to the East

Mr and Mrs. E Santschi, accompanied by Mas Davis, were down from Castle Gate on Monday, and called on The Advocate. The editor very much regrets the fact that he was that day out of town

HOME MISSIONARIES.

Following is the list of missionaries of the Emery Stake of Zion, who were appointed to visit the wards of the stake on the dates named.

J W Nixon and William A Thayn—Castle Gate, April 30, Price, May 28, Spring Glen, June 25

H M V Goold and John Thorlason—Spring Glen April 30, Lawrence, May 28 Orangeville, June 25.

Andrew Nelson and L P Larson—Wellington April 30 Castle Dale, May 28, Price, June 25

John P Pearson and Peter Nelson—Castle Dale, May 14 Cleveland, May 28 Castle Dale June 25

Joseph E Johnson and J Fleming Wakefield—Price, April 30 Wellington, May 28, Molen June 25

John Oliphant and Joseph H Taylor—Cleveland, April 30, Huntington, May 28, Ferron, June 25

Uriah E Curtis and F M Reynolds—Huntington, April 30.

Alma G Jewkes and Uriah E Curtis—Emery, May 28, and Cleveland, June 25

Samuel Williams, Jr, and Peter Christensen—Orangeville, April 30, Molen, May 28, Lawrence, June 25

George W Stephens and J D Killpack, Jr.—Emery, April 30, Orangeville, May 28, and Huntington, June 25

J W Seely and John Peterson—Molen, April 30 Ferron, May 28, Wellington, June 25

Abinadi Olsen and O G Larson, Jr—Ferron, April 30 Desert Lake, May 28, Emery, June 25

A W Horsley and Chris Peterson—Spring Glen, May 28, Desert Lake, June 25

PRICE.

Primary Celebration—Teachers' Examinations—Big Wool Shipments.

Special Correspondence.

Price, Utah, May 25.—The Primary association is making elaborate preparations for the celebration of Brigham Young's anniversary next Thursday evening, June 1st, for which an excellent program is being arranged. There will be a dance in the evening at Town Hall with choice refreshments to be served by the ladies. Appropriate literary and musical programs will be rendered.

Miss Bertha Wright and James Hensley, two popular young people of Castle Gate, this county, were married at the home of the groom's aunt, Mrs. Henrotten, last evening.

Miss Nellie Bailey, of Springville, who has been visiting her sister, Mrs. B. R. McDonald of Price for some time, was called to Castle Gate yesterday by a telegram announcing the illness of her sister, the wife of Hon. H. A. Nelson, manager of the Wasatch store there.

TEACHERS' EXAMINATION.

Some twenty-five teachers will appear for examination for certificates to teach next year in the Carbon county schools at Castle Gate this week. The board this year is composed of Professor Webb, county superintendent of schools, Miss Mary Leonard, the principal of the Price schools, and Miss Sadie Kimball, assistant to Miss Leonard, and whose home is at Scofield. The examinations began yesterday and will continue up to and including Saturday.

BIG WOOL SHIPMENTS.

This week has seen a clean-up of the wool clip in Price, and there now remains here to be sold only the wool from Uintah county, which is on storage at the warehouses of the Rio Grande Western. The owners are expected in next Monday when this will be disposed of to the highest bidder. A big crowd of wool buyers and railroad men are expected here Monday and for whom about every room in the two hotels of the town is already engaged. The amount of wool shipped out from Price station this year will foot up something over a million pounds, for which an average of eleven to twelve cents was paid.

SCARCITY OF FARM PRODUCTS.

There is a scarcity of all products of the farm and ranch in the markets of eastern Utah and for two months everything consumed here, Fort Duchesne, the Indian agencies and towns nearby, has been shipped in. Oats cannot be had at any price, and the same may be said of beef, mutton, potatoes, poultry, butter and eggs, for all of which there is a steady and reliable market.

Three hundred and fifty thousand brick are being burned for new buildings to be erected in Price this year.

Dr. W. C. Richards thinks of locating at Moab, Grand County, and if he does Dr. W. P. Winters of Castle Dale, who has lately sold out there, will come here and open a drug store in connection with his practice.

The Rio Grande Western railway has begun work on six new dwelling houses for employes at Helper. Work on the new chapel to cost about $3,000 will begin in the near future. Plans have been submitted to the officials by the company's architect.

Death of Thomas Cunningham.

[TRIBUNE SPECIAL.]

Price, May 25.—Thomas Cunningham of Ferron, Utah, died there last night. The remains were brought here today, accompanied by the wife and five children, who are left to mourn the loss of a kind, loving husband and father. The sad party left on a train over the Rio Grande Western for American Fork, where Mr. and Mrs. Cunningham formerly resided and where his father and mother live. Mr. Cunningham was about 35 years of age. Death was caused by complication of lung and heart trouble.

PRICE.

Building Boom—No Drinks on Sunday—Ward Conferences.

Special Correspondence.

Price, Utah, May 28.—This year promises to see more building in Price than any year previously in the history of the town. Among the buildings to be erected and already under construction is that of the Emery county Mercantile, company to be of brick, plate glass front and two stories high, to be used for banking and mercantile purposes. Louis Lowenstein, general merchant, has let the contract for a two-story brick building, 78x40 feet, the second floor to be fitted up for an opera house and public hall. As soon as the architect can make ready the plans, a new school building will go skyward. This will most likely be also of brick, of such proportions as to allow the growth of the town to go to it for four or five years to come. Present school facilities are such that there are two hundred children with a seating capacity in the present building of about one hundred. The Price Trading company has for some time been consider-

ing the construction of a modern twenty-five room hotel and this is apt to take definite shape ere the brick making season has gone by, to say nothing of numerous modern dwelling houses and other substantial buildings.

District court convenes here on the 12th of June. There are no new civil cases, but three or four criminal cases that have come up since the last term, chief among which is that of Charles Bradt and Peter Sheridan, who will answer to the additional charge of jail breaking. Both are being held on charges of criminal assault. Bradt has already served one term in the Utah penitentiary for the same offense.

DRY SUNDAY.

City Marshal Anderson is rigidly enforcing the city ordinances against gambling and Sunday closing of saloons. Drinks were not obtainable in Price last Sunday and it is believed will not be for many Sundays to come.

President Miller and counselors, John H. Pace and H. C. Mathis, and Secretary A. W. Horsley, go to Emery county tomorrow where ward conferences will be held in several towns Sunday and Monday, returning to Price Monday evening.

CASTLE GATE.

Prominent Visitors to K. of P.—Testing a New Heating Apparatus.

Special Correspondence.

Castle Gate, Carbon Co., May 26.—The Knights of Pythias tonight will have the pleasure of having with them some of the Grand Lodge officers. H. C. Wardleigh of Ogden, G. R. S., and others are here to meet in session with the lodge members. Castle Gate has the esteemed honor of being one of the most progressive lodges in the inter-mountain region. The Castle Hall has been of late under great improvements and is a credit to the energy and enterprise of its members. The upper hall has been remodeled and the lower part has been in the hands of the Hutchinson brothers of Mount Pleasant, decorators, who have done quite a large amount of work in scene painting, etc.

TESTING NEW HEATING APPARATUS.

Paymaster Carpenter of the P. V. Coal Co., with several other gentlemen, came in on No. 2 yesterday for the purpose of examining the operations of the "American Stoker," which has lately been put under one of the boilers in the power house. After making a thorough tour of the works they returned on No. 3 last evening to the city.

The Fighting Sixteenth regiment went through here this morning, but when they came to the berg they had to be held for a short time to allow another train to pass. This delay gave the inhabitants an opportunity of conversing with some of the heroes of Cuba and among the number we shook hands with was the mascot of the company, a little coon as black as the ace of spades, who we were told was born in the South. He told us of his exploits in Cuba and what he was expecting of the regiment when they got among the Filipinos.

PRICE.

Whitmore Canyon Coal Mines—Counterfeit Quarters—Teachers' Examinations.

Price, Utah, May 29.—Second Class Private Brown, who has been in charge of the government telegraph office at Fort Duchesne, will be in Price in a few days on his way to Cuba, where he is assigned for duty in the signal corps service. He has been raised to a second class sergeant with double his present pay. Corporal Brown will be most likely succeeded by Sergeant Thornton of the Price station, who has been in the service for thirty-four years.

PROSPECTING FOR COAL.

The Pleasant Valley Coal company has some fifteen men at work developing the coal mines in Whitmore Canyon, and which are to be opened up the present season. This force will be increased from time to time as development progresses. A tunnel is now being driven on the main vein in the hope that when the fault is reached at a point about a hundred feet further a body of water, already encountered, will have been reached sufficient to serve for the purposes of the town that will be built up. As things are now George C. Whitmore, the Nephi banker, owns a big ranch south of the proposed townsite and has a right to all the water of the gulch. If none is to be had from the mines the company will have to pay him a big sum to get him out of the way. The general land office at Salt Lake has ordered a survey of two sections of land, where the development is now going on and upon completion of this survey, the Pleasant Valley company will come into title of the lands, some 5,000 acres, where the finest grade of coking coal in all this western country is known to exist. A town of several thousand inhabitants will be built up there and the principal output of the P. V. company for years will come from there. The coke ovens at Castle Gate will be abandoned, it is said, and new improvements never before seen in coal mining inaugurated at this new camp. The Rio Grande Western railroad has a party of surveyors on the ground and it is believed a branch line of railroad will be constructed to the new camp by the 1st of October. The proposed line will be twelve miles in length, and will run out from the station put down on the map as Farnham or the Mounds. This property has long been in litigation between R. A. Kirker and George T. Halliday and the Halliday Coal company. Halliday, not long since sold out to the Pleasant Valley company and it is expected that a deal will take place between Kirker and the company, whereby the company will gain possession of the property. The new camp, when fairly well developed will make homes for some four or five hundred miners, and at the same time afford the farmers, fruit growers and others of the little Castle Valley a market for all their products. At the present time these people have their best market at Castle Gate.

County Attorney Hoffmann is back from Scofield, where he was called to look into a case of counterfeiting but failed from the evidence at hand to make out a case against an Italian coal miner, who has an unpronounceable name. Merchants there and the peddlers of produce in the town have lately had passed upon them a large amount of spurious counterfeit quarters, and considerable loss has resulted. They are of a good imitation and hard to detect from the genuine.

County Superintendent of Schools Lake of Emery county announces that an examination for teachers will be held at Orangeville, June 26th and 27th. While the examination is not compulsory, those who take it will be given the preference when teachers are hired, over those who do not. The Carbon county examination was concluded at Castle Gate, Saturday last. There were but ten teachers to appear.

The Sunday school teachers of Emery county have arranged an entertainment in honor of Brigham Young's birthday at Castle Dale. There will be recitation, addresses, speechmaking, with a picnic at John Lemon's grove.

The Price Sunday school will this week complete the stage and several pieces of scenery being put in the town hall, and from which they will derive considerable revenue. The work is done by the Hutchinson Bros. lately connected with the Salt Lake Theater. The expense has been several hundred dollars.

ADVERTISED LETTER LIST.

The following letters remain uncalled for in the postoffice at Price. Parties calling for the same will please say "advertised"

Cooper, John H.
Fanx, John
Kilpack, J. W.
Pickup, Frary
Creason, N. L.
Vorden, S. H.
Legg, Samuel
Prettirch, Wm.
Schultz, Wm.

Price

PERSONAL.

L. M. Olson went up to Salt Lake the first of the week on business.

Mrs. Arthur J. Lee and the babies returned home Sunday noon from a visit to Springville.

Master Holley McDonald went up to Provo Monday evening and attended the Ringling circus, which exhibited there on Tuesday.

Miss Mary Leonard returned Sunday from Castle Gate.

Miss Sadie Kimball and Miss Nellie McMullin returned from the teachers' examination held at Castle Gate last week on Saturday.

Miss Nellie Holley was a visitor to Springville the first of the week.

Ben Nevins, general agent of "The Scenic Line of the World," was down from Salt Lake Tuesday looking after wool shipments.

J. W. Trewhela, contracting agent of the Great Rock Island Route and a popular and bright young railroad man, was in town during the week, routing wool consignments.

W. H. Donaldson of Castle Gate Sundayed in Price.

Dick Cotner came in Friday from Whitmore Canyon and remained over Sunday.

Charley Goldberg has returned after a week's sojourn in Zion.

A. E. Jamieson was over from Castle Dale Tuesday.

Dr. Richman has decided to locate in the La Salle mountain country and grow up with the new town to be built there, as it were.

Attorney Braffet was in Salt Lake the first three days of the week.

County Attorney Hoffmann was at Scofield last week on business in connection with his duties.

Ernest M. Peyton, late manager of the Western Union telegraph office here, has gone to Ohio to visit relatives. He will not return to Price.

G. S. Collins from Kyune is now night operator at the depot, succeeding Roy Gibson, who has been given the daylight job.

Sergeant Brown of Fort Duchesne is expected here in a few days on his way to Cuba, where he has been assigned to duty in the signal corps service.

R. A. Kirker has gone to Salt Lake City on a mining deal.

Colonel Dodge, manager of the Rio Grande Western, passed through Price last Friday on his way to Salt Lake City from Whitmore Canyon, where he had been with W. G. Sharp, manager of the Pleasant Valley Coal company.

L. M. Link was down from Helper Tuesday and made "the great moral and ⸱⸱⸱ associated call while in ⸱⸱⸱ Provo City.

Mrs. C. W. Spalding is visiting Salt Lake friends this week.

C. F. Warren was looking after the Santa Fe's wool shipments at Price on Tuesday last.

President Miller visited Castle Gate last Sunday.

Tom Barton left this morning for Salt Lake to attend his sister's wedding this evening

Mrs. A. L. Welch came in Tuesday evening from Sunnyside to visit Mrs. L. O. Hoffmann.

Mrs. E O. Whitehead of St. George is visiting her sisters, Mrs. Whitmore and Mrs. Bodle and other relatives here this week.

Miss May Perry of Provo was a guest of the Mathis House Tuesday.

Mrs. R. L. Woodward of Ashley was registered at the Hotel Clarke the first of the week.

A. C. Patterson of Fort Duchesne and H. D Nebeker of Vernal autographed at Hotel Clarke during the week.

J. W. Pierrenot and family, registering from Salt Lake, were at the Hotel Clarke this week.

Mrs. Ella LaFavor was at the Mathis House Tuesday on her way home to Provo from Orangeville.

W. P. Colthorp of Vernal registered at the Mathis House Monday

Edward Pike, George R. Stoney and H. C. Wardleigh, officers of the grand lodge, Knights of Pythias, visited Price lodge Saturday night.

George W. Bodle came in Tuesday evening after a ten days' trip through Texas, going as far south as El Paso. The country he saw is badly dried up for want of rain.

J. W. Nixon was over from Huntington Sunday and spoke at the meeting house in the afternoon.

G. T. Olsen, the Emery merchant, came in yesterday to look after the sale of his wool clip, some fifty thousand pounds.

S. P. Snow and E. R. Cox of Orangeville were at Hotel Clarke the first of the week on their way to Zion.

P. C. Christensen and L. Jeffs of Castle Dale were at Hotel Clarke the forepart of the week.

Mrs. John A. Mease of White Rocks was registered at Hotel Clarke on Tuesday last.

———

L. M. Olson, manager of the Emery County Mercantile company of Price, is registered at the Kenyon "Some improvements are being made in Price, and the town is enjoying a good local trade,' said Mr. Olson. "As we do a large freighting business for the surrounding settlements, trade with us is naturally lively. There is yet a considerable supply of the wool clip in Price, and there are quite a number of buyers in town, and I understand others will arrive at Price within the next few days"— Salt Lake Herald, 31st.

Salt Lake Tribune
June 6, 1899

Death of Mrs. Emma Eden.

Correspondence Tribune]

Castle Gate, June 4.—Mrs. Emma Eden, an aged resident of Cleveland, Emery county, died here at 2 p. m. today. The lady came here two or three weeks ago to visit her granddaughters, Mrs. T. T. Lamph and Mrs. Homer Lewis. Several days ago she took a chill which developed into pneumonia, which caused her death. Mrs.

Eden came to Utah about twenty years ago from the East and for several years has resided at Cleveland, where her son, John Eden, still resides. Had she lived four months longer she would have passed her eightieth milestone. The body will be taken to Cleveland for interment.

PRICE.

Fitting Observance of Birthday of Brigham Young—News Notes.

Special Correspondence.

Price, Utah, June 2.—The 98th birthday anniversary of Brigham Young, prophet, statesman and leader of his people was fittingly and appropriately observed in Price yesterday under the auspices of the societies of the Church. The exercises which were literary and musical were begun at 10 o'clock in the forenoon and continued well into the evening. The lecture upon the life of Brigham Young, by Bishop E. W. Horsley, of Price ward, was instructive, original and most appropriate to the occasion, and was one of the best and ablest efforts of the speaker, whose remarks are at all times and on all occasions able, logical and learned. There was a big attendance from the surrounding towns, the house being packed to the doors, extra seats being brought in and many forced to remain standing. There were many children out, the day being most pleasant—in fact an ideal one. In the afternoon they were served with the delicacies of the season, of which there was an abundance for all present.

The program was an excellent one in all of its numbers.

GROWTH OF PRICE.

Some idea of the growth of Price may be had from the fact that there are close to ten thousand pieces of mail matter handled weekly, to say nothing of the through pouches and packages that go through this office to Vernal and the towns to the south in Emery county. Postmaster Holdaway has been notified by the department that after July 1st next his allowance for clerk hire will be $800 per year, more than double what it is at the present time.

Though bids were opened on the 12th day of May at Denver by the quartermaster of the department of the Colorado nothing has been heard here yet as to the awarding of the government forwarding contract for freight from here to Fort Duchesne and the Indian agencies at White Rocks and Ouray. There were bids put in here and at towns throughout Emery county as well as by a number of responsible teamsters.

President R. G. Miller and his counselors, H. G. Mathis and John H. Page, with Arthur W. Horsley, the Stake clerk, go to Castle Dale next Sunday week, the 11th of June, where ward conferences are at that time to be held.

Mrs. E. E. Horsley has gone to Parowan, where she has been called by the serious illness of her father, Mr. John Topham, a highly respected citizen of that section. Should his condition become worse Bishop Horsley will follow his wife.

E. E. Jones of Castle Dale has secured a contract here for burning 125,000 brick to be used in new buildings here the present summer.

H. T. Olsen is here from Emery with 40,000 pounds of wool for which there are five or six buyers on the ground dickering. The Uintah county clip was all closed out with the exception of one lot the first of the week.

Castle Valley ranchmen are getting $2 per hundred for home grown potatoes and are offered $1.50 for their oats. There is little of either in the country at present.

PRICE.

To Bond County—Equalizing Taxes—Bounteous Rain—"Varmints" Destroy Sheep.

Special Correspondence.

Price, Carbon county, June 7.—The board of county commissioners will meet on the 10th of July, at which time proper steps will be taken to bond the county to pay off the indebtedness of about $4,000 that existed when the Territory was admitted to Statehood. This indebtedness is drawing 7 per cent, while the bonds would draw only 5 per cent, or less.

INDEPENDENCE DAY.

There will be a big mass meeting of business men and others here on Saturday night next at the old meeting house to arrange for a Fourth of July program.

EQUALIZING TAXES.

The county board of equalization has concluded its session. The principal work done was the getting on to the assessment rolls people who have heretofore never been caught by the assessor and tax dodgers generally, of whom there appears to have been a good many in the coal camps and railroad towns of the county. As a result of this alertness on the part of the board and the increase of population of late, taxes this year will be materially reduced in the county.

SUMMER SCHOOL.

B. P. Luke, superintendent of schools of Emery county, went to Salt Lake yesterday to arrange for the summer school for teachers of Emery county, which is to be held this year at Huntington, June 12th. State Superintendent Dr. Park, Prof. J. M. Tanner, Prof. Roylance and Mrs. L. H. Cannon, all well known State educators, have been engaged under salary for lectures and have promised to be present. The examination for teachers is to be held at Orangeville, June 27th to 29th inclusive, and longer if the work in hand de-

mands it. Prof. Webb, superintendent of the Carbon county schools, will
attend both meetings.

Harry Wade has again assumed the
management of the Wade hotel at
Castle Gate, succeeding H. G. Webb,
who went there from here a few
months ago.

District court convenes here next
Monday with Judge Jacob Johnson
presiding. There are four new criminal cases, two civil suits and the re-

mainder of the docket comes over from
last term.

BOUNTEOUS RAIN.

The rain of last Saturday night
which was general throughout Castle
Valley is worth many thousands of
dollars to the farmers and stock growers of this part of Utah.

"VARMINTS" DESTROYING SHEEP.

Sheep men report heavy losses of
lambs in the mountains where their
flocks were driven for lambing, from
coyotes and mountain lions. Poison
does not seem to diminish the beasts
which have been increasing at an
alarming rate for two years past and
seem to follow up the flocks from desert to mountain and mountain to
desert.

William McCaslin, a prominent citizen of Vernal, left here in the night
Monday to reach the bedside of a sick
child. He was in Salt Lake and traveled from Price by special relays arranged for in advance.

Eastern Utah Advocate
June 8, 1899

EMERY COUNTY.

The Emery county board of commissioners met last Monday. Nothing out of the routine was transacted,
such as the allowance of accounts,
receiving reports, etc.

An examination for teachers will
be held at Orangeville, June 26th
and 27th.

Hon Orange Seeley is a candidate
for road supervisor, which the governor is soon to appoint, for Emery
county. He would be a good man
for the place.

Frank Carroll has completed the
invoice of the Dr Winters stock and
is now in possession as manager of
the new company. O. J. Anderson
is assisting Mr Carroll.

Farmers are feeling good over the
recent copious rain.

Mrs Emma Eden an aged resident
of Cleveland, Utah, died at Castle
Gate, Sunday. The lady went there
three weeks ago to visit her grand
daughters, Mrs T. T. Lamph and Mrs
Gomer Lewis. Several days ago she
took a chill which developed into
pneumonia, which caused her death.
Mrs. Eden came to Utah about twenty
years ago from the East and for several years has resided at Cleveland,
where her son, John Eden, still re-

sides. Had she lived four months
longer she would have passed her
eightieth milestone. The body has
been taken to Cleveland for interment.

Green River is endeavoring to
secure a State experimental farm,
and petitions are being circulated and
signed for that purpose.

A home dramatic company is being
formed in Castle Dale, with Mr Tom
son of Salt Lake City as director.
They are rehearsing now preparatory
to putting on the stage 'Comrades'

Decoration day dawned bright and
clear at Castle Dale, and was most
appropriately celebrated. The public
buildings were decorated with flags
and flags were flying from the flag
poles. Many were in attendance
from the adjoining settlements.
The entire population of Castle Dale
turned out to honor the noble dead.

It is reported from pretty good authority that James Jeffs has been offered $5000 for his claims in the San
Rafael country and that he now has
the matter under consideration.

The Copper Globe is working steadily, and prospectors are arriving daily,
and parties from all the settlements
around are starting out to prospect.

PRETTY JUNE WEDDING.

Mrs ORVIN MORRIS
NEE BARTON

Mr ORVIN MORRIS

The marriage of Miss Estella Barton and Mr Orvin Morris was solemnized in the Temple at Salt Lake City last Thursday at high noon

In the evening a large reception was held at the home of the bride on West Second South street. The parlors were attractively decorated with palms, roses, carnations and smilax The bay window, where the bridal party received the congratulations of their many friends, was converted into a great bower of early summer flowers.

The bride wore a dainty gown of white organdie over taffeta, with trimmings of lace and ribbon, and carried a shower bouquet of bride roses Her maid of honor, Miss May Barton, was gowned in white Swiss with trimmings of orange ribbon, and carried yellow roses

During the evening refreshments were served in the dining room from a table artistically arranged with La France roses and ferns

The bride is well known in Price, where she has visited, and has several relatives She is a sister of Thomas Barton, who was present at the wedding Mr and Mrs Morris will be at home after June 21st at 129 O street, Salt Lake City.

SHORT STORIES.

The front of the Price Trading company's store building is wearing a coat of new paint.

Miss Belle Ballinger and Miss Ida Whitmore are now both behind the counters at Price Trading company's store.

The new stage, scenery and the like for Town Hall has cost so far something like $150. The money will come back from rents.

Jacob Lilington and Miss Susie Mallcoat, both of Scofield, were given license to wed by County Clerk and Recorder Howard Tuesday.

More new wagons and buggies have been unloaded at the depot in Price this spring than in any two previous seasons heretofore.

John MacMillan is filing the position of weighmaster for the coal company at Castle Gate during the absence of W. H. Donaldson in the East.

The first rain of the season fell in this section Saturday night and was quite general throughout the valley. Though it was light an immense good will result.

Attend the meeting Saturday evening next at the old log meeting house and help along with the Fourth of July celebration. The various committees will at that time be named.

The big new scales of the railroad company are now completed and in use. They save the reweighing by the piece of hundreds of tons of incoming and outgoing freight every month

F. Lockhart, Frank Hadlock and Charley Guiwitz outfitted here last week and left for the country south of Moab to prospect. They said they had a good thing in sight before pulling out.

Last Tuesday was the fourth birthday of little Wilma, daughter of Mr. and Mrs. H A Nelson of Castle Gate, who spent the day in Price and gave the children an outing in honor of the occasion.

Mrs. K S Horsley has been absent at Paragoonah for several weeks at the bedside of her father, John Topham, an old and respected citizen of that section, who has been quite ill for some time.

Silver Tip, alias Hawkins, the alleged Hoobers' Rooster, whom Joe Bush captured down in Southern Utah near the Arizona line last Saturday, was taken to Provo Monday afternoon and will be kept in jail there for safe keeping.

Tom Barton enjoys the distinction of being the first citizen of Price to take a meal on one of the new dining cars of the Rio Grande Western last Thursday on his way to Zion. He doesn't like the waiters—presumably because they do not wear any petticoats.

County Clerk Howard received a voluminous mortgage for record this week It is given by the Rio Grande Western railroad company to the State Trust company of New York, and is for $16,000,000, running fifty years and to April 1, 1949. The recording fee is $27 50

Deseret Evening News
June 13, 1899

PRICE.

Emery County Summer School at Huntington—Ward Conference.

Special Correspondence.

Price, June 12.—The presidency of Emery Stake were at Spring Glen yesterday and held ward conference and returned in the evening.

SUMMER SCHOOL.

The Emery county summer school under the direction of County Superintendent B. F. Luke, began at 10 o'clock today at Huntington, and will continue in session from June 12th to June 23rd. The work will include lectures, discussions and practical illustrative work on the subjects taught in the public schools. Professor William O. Roylance of the State University will conduct the work in psychology and pedagogy and Mrs. Lillian H. Cannon of Brigham Young academy, that of teaching the methods of drawing. Public evening lectures will be given in Castle Dale, Tuesday evening, June 13; Cleveland, Wednesday evening, June 14; Orangeville, Thursday evening June 15; Ferron, Friday evening, June 16.

Joe Nacglear is down from his herds which are ranging in the hills to the west and north of Price, and reports the losses of lambs heavy from coyotes and wolves, which in one night recently got away with some twenty lambs in his flock alone. Other owners report like losses.

Miss Mary Wride of Provo, was here yesterday, the guest of friends for the day, returning home from Minnie Maud, where she has just closed a successful term of school.

Eastern Utah Advocate
June 15, 1899

SHORT STORIES.

Al Baxter has opened a lunch counter in Rooney's saloon at Helper

Mrs. D W Holdaway has returned from a visit of a week at Salt Lake.

Mrs. Sam Whitmore of Salt Lake is visiting friends and relatives at Huntington

Miss Lou Thomas of Scofield visited her aunt Mrs. B. R. McDonald, during the week.

James Rooney is back from Glenwood Springs, Colo. where he took the baths for several weeks. He says he is now a new man.

Mr and Mrs. Ed Lee have returned from Provo, where they went a few days ago to have their boy operated upon by Dr Allen.

Dr Field will locate in Price, returning here in about a month He has rented for an office the building lately occupied by Dr Richman.

State Auditor Richards has drawn warrants for $196 and $1,000, the amounts of the claims of Wayne and Kane counties respectively, for criminal prosecutions The claims were allowed by the last legislature

Emery County.

Dr Winters has taken the contract to build the school house at Lawrence, which is to cost about a thousand dollars

Frank Carroll has moved his family from Orangeville to Castle Dale, where he will reside.

Potatoes are worth $2 a bushel at Castle Dale, and few in the country at that price

Miss Susan Day of Lawrence visited her aunt Mrs Smith, at Castle Dale last week

Mrs. Jennie Winters of Castle Dale is visiting with friends and relatives in Salt Lake.

Chris Madsen and H. Nielson of Sanpete are prospecting in the copper belt in the southern part of Emery county.

Mrs. H. P Ottoson of Castle Dale has returned home from a visit to Salt Lake.

Joseph F. Davies of the Emery County Mercantile company was in Price several days last week on business matters

Castle Dale now has a home dramatic company. "Comrades," the first play attempted, was presented last Monday evening.

R. W. Crockett at The Advocate office buys county warrants, school warrants, etc. Highest cash prices paid for those of Carbon, Uintah Grand and Emery counties.

A F Nielson and Bruce Barton were in Castle Dale last week from Mt. Pleasant, visiting with relatives and friends.

Miss Emer J. Day was tendered a pleasant surprise at her home in Lawrence Monday evening of last week, the occasion being a farewell party in honor of the young lady, who has resigned as president of the Mutual Improvement association and is going away. A dance was given at the hall and dainty refreshments dispensed. Miss Day was the recipient of several useful and most valuable presents.

Crops throughout Emery county are doing nicely, the late rain followed by warm weather being most beneficial

Ira R. Browning and A. D Dixon were down at Green River the other day trying to get hold of some fruit lands.

Some new and promising finds are being made on the copper belt west of Green River.

Alfalfa is in full bloom around Green River and haying will begin this week.

Ira R Browning of Castle Dale wants to buy some good copper prospects for Eastern people

William H. McArthur of Lawrence has gone to Oregon to look over the country, and he may decide to make his home there.

Mr. and Mrs. John U Bryner, of Helper, have a new girl baby at their home, which arrived on the 10th inst. Mother Warren reports mother and baby doing nicely.

T. E. Norton and the Price boys have located thirty-eight claims in Cottonwood Wash. The ore is high grade copper, and is about twenty miles southwest of the LeSieur mine. They have also taken up a millsite on the Muddy.

Bruce Wilson of Price thinks of starting a blacksmith shop at Castle Dale. He thinks favorably of the location

The Hinckln and Scultz coal mine, about seven miles south of Castle Dale, has started up

A Tuttle and E W. Fox of Orangeville and Tom Hudson and L. Jeffs of Castle Dale have gone into the San Rafael country to prospect and work their copper claims the coming summer

Report has it that James Jeffs has been offered $5000 for his copper claim, located down in the San Rafael country.

Sheriff Leamaster has assays from his San Rafael claims showing $3 in gold, small values in silver and 20 per cent copper

O J Sitterud has some excellent copper prospects on the San Rafael river, and out of which he expects to make a good thing

The institute and summer school for Emery county teachers convened at Huntington last Monday. It will be of two weeks duration. Some of the best educators in Utah have been engaged as instructors and to deliver lectures

"Our mining industries are fast coming to the front," says the Emery County Record. "The excitement is increasing, and many who a year ago would rather whittle sticks than take any stock in mining excitement have gone out and located some promising claims."

Dr. Pierson will move from Huntington to Castle Dale.

Emery county today offers as good inducements as any county in the state for capital seeking investment in mining

Hyte Loveless and Postmaster and Attorney Miller of Huntington were over to Price the first of the week on a mining deal.

Mr and Mrs. Ed Lee have returned from Provo, where they went a few days ago to have their boy operated upon by Dr Allen.

Dr Field will locate in Price, returning here in about a month He has rented for as office the building lately occupied by Dr Richman.

State Auditor Richards has drawn warrants for $195 and $1,000, the amounts of the claims of Wayne and Kane counties respectively, for criminal prosecutions The claims were allowed by the last legislature

Neph Scofield has sold his bunch of wethers to Walter Goslin, who will ship them to his range near Leadville, Colo. There are about 1000 in the bunch, and the price is $2.25 per head. They will be loaded at Colton, Utah.

A representative of the Kemmerer Coal company was at Castle Gate last week with a carload of coal, to make a thorough test of its coking qualities. If the tests are satisfactory, it will mean much for that already thriving camp.

CARBON COUNTY'S SCHOOLS.

The Salt Lake Herald of last Monday has this article on the schools of Carbon county, by Professor H O Webb:

"From the time of the separation of Carbon from Emery about five years ago education has slowly but steadily advanced all along the line. The school population has increased from 800 to 1001, and the pupils are beginning to feel the importance of education and to show that interest in their work that makes the school more the home of knowledge.

"The number of districts in the county remains the same as when first organized, but the number of teachers employed has more than doubled. There are now employed sixteen teachers with a promise of nineteen for the next school year. Of these ten are teachers of experience, and are doing very good work. It is expected to keep up this improvement in the status of the teachers, so that the advancement of our pupils may not be stopped. Last year for the first time in the history of the county three pupils from the Castle Gate district passed the eighth grade examination receiving diplomas for the same, which were recognized by the authorities of the higher institutions to which they went, one to the University and two to the Agricultural college. This is a good beginning and, although the locality is unfavorable for higher education, yet we hope to have some graduates every year.

All the districts excepting the two smallest Spring Glen and Minnie Maud, now possess their own school houses. Winter Quarters and Castle Gate have good new houses, and used them for the first time this school year. Price will build, to be ready for use in September a good modern house of four or five rooms. This promises to be the finest in the county.

"Great interest is taken by the county in education, as may be seen in the steady increase of the county tax. In the school year of 1895-96 the tax distribution was $1,100, while for the year 1897-98 the same was $2,195.75, an amount nearly equal to the state apportionment. This amount is supplemented by district and special taxes. Then again the schools have been kept open a much longer period, the average now being 3 4 terms for the year. The money received for the teachers' fund from all quarters was $6,429.73, which gave an average of nearly $40 to each teacher."

PRICE WILL CELEBRATE.

Following is the programme decided upon for the Fourth of July celebration in Price this year

Firing of artillery at daybreak Henry Flack

Hoisting of colors at sunrise, Joseph Jones.

Salute of thirteen guns, Henry Flack.

Music by the band.

Signal gun at 10 o'clock to assemble at hill

Assembly called to order by the marshal of the day, R. G. Miller

Singing "America," by choir and congregation.

Prayer by chaplain, Bishop Horsley

Singing "Star Spangled Banner," by Miss Nellie Holley

Reading of the "Declaration of Independence" by H W Damon.

Oration by the orator of the day, L M Olsen

Instrumental music, by Gertrude Miller

Recitation, by Mrs. L O Hoffmann.

Song Mrs Birdie P Olsen.

Stump speech, by R. W. Crockett.

Comic song by Herman Horsley

Dialogue, by Violet and Della Flack

Song, by Robert McKune

Instrumental music, by the Hobson lodge

Sentiments and toasts

Singing by choir

Benediction by chaplain,

Dance for children at 2:30 to 4 o'clock.

Dance in the evening for adults

Following are the several committees appointed at Wednesday night's meeting

Committee on Finance—Bishop Horsley, George Fausett and R. W. Crockett

Committee on Decoration—E. S. Horsley, Mrs Dora Fausett and Mrs. Olive Millburn

Committee on Sports — Miss Rose Bryner, Henry Flack, Soren Olsen and Mrs. Olive Millburn,

CASTLE GATE NEWS.

Castle Gate Utah, June 15.—The first shipment of mining cars tools and supplies for the miners were loaded up today for Sunnyside. Harry Parmlee will leave here today to take charge of the Sunnyside mine as foreman. For some time he has been assistant foreman in the Castle Gate mines. He is well qualified. A short time ago he took the prize for the best method of ventilating mines, having among his competitors some of the most practical miners and foremen in the district.

Mark Petric an Austrian while unloading mine rails out of a box car last evening got a painful and severe cut on the head by a rail striking him. He says that it was done thoughtlessly by those throwing them out of the car Dr Asadoorian dressed the wound and Petric will be at work again in a day or so.

Joseph Senaigl a miner got a blow in the eye from a piece of coal flying from the end of his pick.

Joseph Thomas and Andrew Wallace, two of Scofield's respected citizens were Castle Gate visitors yesterday

Mr Evan Thomas of Cleveland is here, and will return home today, taking with him his daughter, Mrs John Jones. Mrs. Jones will stay for several days in Castle Valley, visiting relatives and friends.

A few friends of Mr and Mrs E bintschi met at their home last evening and spent a very agreeable time Mr and Mrs. Ricks were among the number. Mrs. Ricks came down from Logan some days ago

Only one half of the mine is working on account of the motors in the other part being out of order

The Castle Gate band has been again resurrected and an effort made to keep the members together until after the July holidays

Alfred Olsen is still confined to his house through having his left foot injured by a piece of coal falling on it while at work in the yard

The large bowery and dancing pavillion is rapidly nearing completion.

A large number of Italians are every day working upon the structure in the lower end of town.

John Jones, sr., is erecting a fine frame residence at the upper part of town.

Shot a Mountain Lion.

Hyrum Wilcox, watchman for the Pleasant Valley Coal company, killed a large mountain lion near Castle Gate last Wednesday. Two of these animals have been committing depredations on stock in that vicinity for some time and killed several horses belonging to the coal company. Wilcox has been on the lookout for them, and while burying a horse one of them came within range and he shot it. The animal measured seven feet from tip of nose to end of tail, and stood two feet and a half high.

Salt Lake Herald
June 21, 1899

Castlegate News.

(Special Correspondence.)

Castle Gate, June 20.—Dr. Paul Caffey is here from Ann Arbor, Mich., and is installed as assistant to Dr. Asadoorian.

A complimentary concert will be given Saturday evening as a token of appreciation to Prof. Stefano Bartol.

Mrs. F. N. Cameron leaves today for a few days' visit to her folks.

H. Duerdon has sold his fine residence to W. Flew, the consideration being $300.

Judge Duerdon will leave in a short time and join his family, who are now in the state of Washington.

CASTLE GATE NEWS.

Mrs F N Cannon has gone for a few days' visit to her folks.

H Duerden has sold his fine residence to W. Flew, the consideration being $300

Dr. Paul Caffey is here from Ann Arbor, Mich , and is installed as assistant to Dr Asadoorian

Men are excavating the foundation where the bed of the new engine will be laid for the power house.

Eugene Santschl, John H Knight and Chris Halvorson are home from the Agricultural college at Logan

Judge Duerden will leave in a short time and join his family, who are now in the state of Washington

Charles Young, manager of the company boarding house at Scofield, was in town Friday His purpose here was to perfect arrangements to go to Sunnyside to take charge of the new boarding house there.

Signor Stefano Bartot, a musician of rare ability, is in town to conduct the musical part of the festivities on the 2d, 3d and 4th of July He plays the harp, clarionet, guitar, mandolin, violin, organ and piano. He gave a splendid organ recital in the Catholic church Thursday afternoon, and in the evening entertained a large number of musically inclined on the piano

The concert to be given on Saturday evening has been greatly augmented by adding to the performers the name of Mrs. J. M. McMillan, a pianist of exceptional ability Mrs McMillan has been the originator of several splendid concerts of late, and with Professor Bartot will demonstrate that Castle Gate possesses musical talent that cannot be duplicated outside of Salt Lake City The promoters of the concert are to be complimented on securing the services of the talented lady.

Since the opening of the fishing season the boys have been busy along the creeks trying to catch the sport ive trout.

There has been a great deal of sickness here of late, probably on account of the exceptionally cold weather

There was a daring robbery here some time Monday night or Tuesday morning The store of S A Hendrickson was broken into and about $200 worth of jewelry and about the same amount of clothing and other goods taken. The robbers entered the store by cutting a panel out of the back door They took a section trolley car to get away with their booty.

The Pleasant Valley Coal company here has never been so busy at this time of year as at present. Twelve hundred to 1,400 tons of coal are loaded every day and it is still behind in its orders The company is excavating for an addition to the power plant, which, when completed, will more than double its present capacity There is some talk of the Union Pacific mine starting up again so that present prospects are that this will become one of the largest if not the largest coal mining camp in the West in the near future.

Emery County.

Born, to Mr and Mrs John Leamaster, on June 13th, an 11 pound boy. All doing nicely.

Rumor has it that St. V. LeSieur has refused an offer of $95,000 for the Copper Globe mine, at Devil's Canyon.

Dave Price had fifty pounds of ore brought into Castle Dale last week to show some parties who think of investing

Hort Tuttle, brother of A Tuttle of Orangeville, is lying seriously ill at his home with an attack of heart disease. Dr Ray is attending the sufferer

Clara Seely and Soren Hansen and Lizzie Borreson and Fred Anderson left for Salt Lake City last week, where they were married and went through the temple.

Castle Dale is going to celebrate the Fourth Arrangements are being made and committees appointed A brass band is being organized which will consist of twelve pieces and will be composed of good musicians

It has come to our notice, says the Emery County Record, that there is much rivalry and uncalled for prejudice existing between the different towns in the county. Now this is altogether wrong, and will do more to injure and retard the growth and prosperity of a community than anything else It stands as a barrier, and the sooner it is thrown down the better

A special to the Salt Lake Herald from Provo says "Word comes to Provo that another rich copper strike has been made in Emery county The strike is near the Copper Globe grant and was made by Will

lam Price and his brother, two men
from Ferron The report received
here is that the find is a big ledge,
easy of access, with an abundance of
rich ore in sight. An assay on this
rock, made by R J Kroupa of this
city, shows 19 71 per cent copper,
twenty two ounces silver and four
ounces gold

Deseret Evening News
June 28, 1899

PRICE.

**Railroad Buildings — "Sunnyside" Coal
Mines—Fine Market for Farmers.**

Special Correspondence.

Price, Carbon Co. Utah, June 28.—
One-half a mile of grading for the
new railroad up Whitemore canyon
from Mounds station is now completed
and the three camps have been moved
a couple of miles up towards the canyon from where they were last week.
Bishop A. E. McMullin of Wellington
has completed his first grading contract and will take another half mile.
There are some twenty-five to thirty-
five men at work developing the mines
where the output of coal is to come
from, and by the time the grading is
all done it is expected there will be
all done it is expected there will be
miners at work. The new camp, to be
known as

SUNNYSIDE COAL MINES

will give the ranchmen of Emery and
Carbon county the best market they
have ever had for their products, a
thing long needed in Castle Valley, as
the drive to Helper, Castle Dale and
elsewhere has been too great for profit.

President Miller and his counselors,
John H. Pace and H. G. Mathis, and
Secretary A. W. Horsley of the Emery
Stake, will leave here Saturday to at-
tend conference at Salt Lake on Sun-
day next. There will be a generally
good attendance from eastern Utah, so
Secretary Horsley says.

Price ward has been asked to raise
$137 for the completion of Emery Stake
Academy at Castle Dale. Bishop
Horsley has been out with a subscription paper and has met with a generous response from the public in general.

THE FOURTH.

Wellington and Price and Castle Dale
will all celebrate the Fourth of July,
and have arranged good programs, literary, musical and pyrotechnical. At
the latter place the Italian portion of
the population will indulge in a three
days' celebration, from the 2nd to the
4th inclusive. Helper people will go
there and come to Price.

There are many inquiries received
here for copper and gilsonite and elaterite properties, and it begins to look
as if there was a boom in store for all
eastern Utah this year.

Emery County

At the May term of the Seventh district court, held last week at Castle Dale, the following cases were brought up for trial before Judge Johnson and disposed of

M Goold and Thomas Hardy of Cleveland were admitted to citizenship.

Mabel Potter Gittings vs C R Crandall, suit to quiet title, decree granted

Margaret Rowley vs J E Rowberg, judgment of no cause for action and plaintiff given ten days in which to file answer

Mary Hammaker vs Emery County Mercantile company, money claim, demurrer overruled, defendant given twenty days to answer

Michael Halloran vs William Floyd and John H Scott, executors, default denied and defendants given ten days to file a demurrer

A divorce was granted to Mary Nansen from her husband, Ben Dix Nansen, and one to Katharina Schulthis from her husband, John Schulthis

Letters of administration were issued to William Grimes in the matter of the estate of David Griffith deceased, and to Joseph A Lake in the matter of Christian Paulsen deceased

H H Averill Jr, vs J C Alger et al, default entered, judgment for plaintiff in the sum of $71 19 on the first cause of action and the same against the second cause, together with costs

Golding & Co vs A H Jamison and J M Lynch, no cause of action against Lynch found, Jamison in default and judgment against him for $1 00 damages, for the property prayed for in plaintiff's complaint and for the costs

Eva Campell vs Rio Grande Western railway, motion for change of venue denied by the court and case set for the term beginning October 2d, 1899 Plaintiff sues for damages for the death of her husband, who was killed in an explosion at Lower Crossing

The large blacksmith shop is getting near completion

Mrs Ed Kimber last Thursday morning gave birth to a baby girl.

The Knights of Pythias held their memorial services Sunday afternoon Great preparations had been made and the occasion was an impressive one

George Dauber is busy dressing rock for the foundation of the new ventilating fan for the mines which will be laid on the spot vacated by the old blacksmith shop

Miss Bessie Henderson and Toomas Phelps were married last Wednesday evening by Judge Duerdon A large number of the friends of the young couple met to do them honor and to offer congratulations

The complimentary concert to Professor Stephen o Bartot, held in Knights of Pythias hall last Saturday evening was a magnificent success in every way The hall was filled The music, songs and other features were of the highest order of merit The concert was followed by a ball.

For several days past a large number of tramps have been passing through town headed for Salt Lake A night or two ago one of them reported that he had been held up by two or three others in a box car and relieved of his loose change Wednesday night of last week a man entered an out kitchen adjoining the residence of S H Pierce and helped himself to the eatables in sight and also tried to effect an entrance into the main building, but found all the windows securely fastened He visited the residences of H G Williams J A Harrison, S H Pierce B P Caffey Chris Davis and others with like results Later on he entered the house of David Crow and was inspecting the room in which Mr Crow was sleeping when that gentleman was awakened by the noise and the burglar took to his heels Several other houses were visited and attempts made to get in without success Nothing of value was taken No arrests have been made It is thought the gang left at daylight for the west.

Price

SHORT STORIES.

Ward conferences will be held in Price July 9th

Town trustees meeting next Monday evening, July 3rd

Attend the play tomorrow night. Your money's worth

County commissioners meet on the 10th of July, next Monday week.

"The Battle of Santiago" at Town Hall tomorrow night will be a good play

Orangeville is to have the next conference of Emery Stake, July 16th and 17th.

John J Craner has been appointed postmaster at Colton, vice John V Smith deceased

Special scenery has been painted for 'The Battle of Santiago' at Town Hall tomorrow evening.

Dell Fausett has been out repairing the telephone line to the south this week It is now in good working order

Several of the new houses under construction at Helper by the rail road company will soon be ready for occupancy

Ground is being broken for the new brick building of Louis Lowenstein He will occupy it in about two months

Since the interior was overhauled James Rooney's saloon at Helper is one of the most attractive places in all Eastern Utah

Dr Allen of Provo was here last week, called in consultation with Dr Fisk of Helper, who is attending Mrs J C Berglund

The Gilson Asphaltum company will assume charge of the government forwarding contract the first of July—next Saturday.

The waters of the Duchesne river have receded and the stage line is now booking passengers and express through to the end of the route

The plans for the new chapel to be built by the Rio Grande Western at Helper have been completed and are now in the hands of the builders

There will be several special prizes for pony races here on the Fourth The program has not yet been arranged, but the purses will be liberal ones

E T Borgenhagen has resigned his position with Ike Glaser at Helper, and will engage in business there for himself — most likely a meat market.

The Utah boys should arrive in San Francisco from Manila within thirty days It is not unlikely that numerous Utah relatives will welcome them at the Golden Gate

Sheriff Alred, County Clerk Howard and County Attorney Hoffmann are feeling good over tests made of coking coal just located by them nine miles from Price They say there is a great body of it and it is easy of access, and all conditions necessary for the successful working of the proposition are presented there.

Dr W P Winters was over from Castle Dale the other day He says he will most likely locate here with a drug store when he winds up his business affairs in Emery county

Price Trading company has put on a wagon for the Helper trade Genial Doll Fausett looks after the business up there. Goods are delivered promptly and trips made regularly.

W C Brocker the Helper tonsorial artist, is able to be at work again He has been knocked out for two weeks nursing a bruised leg While riding a horse fell on him

On account of the meeting of the Mormon church authorities at Salt Lake City, next Sunday, July 2d, a rate of one single fare for the round trip will be made by the Rio Grande Western railway

St V LeSieur went up to Provo yesterday from his Devil's Canyon mine in Emery county He says a load of ore from the property will be in Price inside of a few days for shipment to the smelters

The estimated earnings of the Rio Grande Western for the third week in June are $72,800 This estimate shows an increase of $1,700 over the corresponding week of last year The increase is due chiefly to the excellent passenger business

President Miller and his counselors John H Pace and H G Mathis, and Bishop Horsley and others will go to Salt Lake, Saturday next, to be present at the special conference of the church authorities to be held in the Temple on Sunday There will be a general attendance of bishops and church officers generally from the wards of Eastern Utah

PERSONAL.

James Jones of Huntington was in town yesterday.

Mrs. Chauce Maxwell of Helper visited friends in Price yesterday.

William W. R has gone to Kaysville to visit friends there for a short while.

Miss Hattie Canning of East Jordan was registered at Hotel Clarke yesterday.

Miss Nellie Holley is the guest of her sister, Mrs. T. H Thomas, at Scofield

Arthur J Lee made a short business trip to Z on the latter part of the week.

Attorney Louthel of Vernal was at Hotel Clarke yesterday on his way to Zion.

Frank Carrell of Castle Dale came in yesterday and is registered at Hotel Clarke.

Miss Annie Lister of Springville is visiting her sister, Mrs Arthur J Lee of this city.

J Meyer was in town yesterday looking after the trade of F A Keisel & Co. of Ogden.

E V Cox of Scofield was looking after business here yesterday, and stopped at Hotel Clarke.

Dr. W P Winters came over from Castle Dale yesterday and is autographed at Hotel Clarke

Miss Ella Lowenstein is expected home tomorrow from Salt Lake, where she has been attending school

Mrs. D R McDonald and her sister-in law, Mrs. John Holley, went to Castle Gate Monday to visit Mrs H A Nelson

Captain Guilfoyle came in Tuesday from Denver, and went out to the post at Fort Duchesne yesterday accompanied by Mrs Guilfoyle, who came in to meet him

Mrs Cottrell, who has for some time visited her sister, Mrs H P Myton at White Rocks agency, arrived here Tuesday and left at night for her home at Guthrie, Okla.

Sergeant Thornton and wife left this morning for Fort Duchesne, where the sergeant will be stationed with the signal corps Their many friends regret to see them leave Price.

United States Signal Sergeant Myers, who was at one time stationed at Price, came in last week from San Francisco, where he had been on a leave of absence, and after visiting old friends a few days departed for his station at Wilcox, Arizona.

Captain Guilfoyle of the Ninth cavalry arrived here Tuesday from Fort Logan, accompanied by Mrs Guilfoyle's mother, Mrs Law They were met here by Mrs Guilfoyle, and the party left for Fort Duchesne by ambulance yesterday morning

Bert Seabohlt and G B Rhoades of Denver are in town on their way to the Vernal country, where they have a deal on in some mining property Mr Seabohlt has lately made a big deal in Colorado river placer property with Eastern people, whereby some $300,000 changes hands

Mrs J H Mease, wife of the post trader at Fort Duchesne, is rapidly recovering from the serious illness which made necessary her removal to a hospital in this city, and Mr Mease is much gratified at the prospect of a speedy return home with Mrs Mease entirely recovered —Salt Lake Tribune

Levi N Harmon and J H Killpack of Huntington went up to Salt Lake last week on a big mining deal and returned on Saturday They made a sale of several claims on the San Rafael ledge to a party of Denver people who will begin work at once developing the same, and will put a number of men to work at once

PRICE.

Special Correspondence.

No Place Like Home—The Fourth—Good
Crops—Dramatic—Boom at Ferron.

Price, Carbon County, July 1.—Ex-
County Commissioner Abe Liddell,
who sold out in Carbon county several
months ago and went north in search
of a better country, has returned to his
old home at Wellington, this county,
having failed to locate anything that
suited him better than Castle val-
He went over the best part of Oregon
and Washington in a wagon with his
family, taking his time and viewing
the country thoroughly. Before leaving he sold out his ranch and stock
and machinery, and since returning has
tried to buy back the old place, but
as the present owner got it at a bargain he does not care to part with it.

H. G. Clark, who opened the Hotel
Clark, here several years ago and who
later conducted the stage station at
Smith's Wells, has gone to Duchesne
bridge, to take charge of the stage
station and hotel there, and which was
but recently opened.

Arthur J. Lee, for the Gilson Asphaltum company, today began the moving
of freight for the government under
the contract recently awarded for one
year. Should the railroad now being
built up Whitmore canyon be extended
on over the pass to the Duchesne river
this freight will most likely be hauled
to the fort and Indian agencies from
the end of the line. If the railroad is
not at once extended on to the Duchesne, it is believed here a wagon road
will be constructed from the coal
camp, to be known hereafter as Sunnyside, that will considerably shorten
the distance to the Vernal country and
at the same time divert a large portion of the freighting business from
Price.

THE FOURTH.

An excellent program of sports has
been arranged for the Fourth in Price,
consisting of foot races, literary and
musical exercises, baseball, pony races
and the like. The children will be
given a dance at town hall in the afternoon and served with refreshments by
a committee of ladies who were appointed to take the matter in hand.

GOOD CROP PROSPECTS.

Crops never looked better or gave
greater promise in this section of Castle Valley. Haying time is here and
there is plenty of work for those so inclined in the fields at good wages. What
the farmers lost on their fruit by the
frosts early in the spring they will
make up with good interest in other
directions.

This has been an unusually healthy
season throughout Castle Valley, though
there are two or three cases of scarlet
fever in Price at the present time. Mrs.
J. C. Berglund, who has been at the
point of death for several days from
pneumonia, preceded by childbirth, is
now considered out of danger.

DRAMATIC.

The Price Dramatic company, assisted by the Hutchinsons, late of the Salt
Lake Theater, presented the war drama,
The Battle of Santiago, at town hall
last night to a crowded house. The
play was for the benefit of the Price
ward Sunday schools, and netted a
very handsome sum. The piece will
most likely be presented at Castle
Gate and possibly at Scofield in the near
future.

FERRON BOOMING.

Ferron, in Emery county, since the
recent copper discoveries in that section, has become an important point,
and has promise of great growth, so
much so that a Mr. Thomas of Salt
Lake, it is said, will put in a newspaper there in the very near future.

BUILDING UP HELPER.

The plans for the new chapel at Helper are now in the hands of the railroad
company's builders, and work is soon
to begin on the same. The railroad
company is now constructing six new
cottages there, besides making various
other improvements of a substantial
nature.

PRICE.

Battle of Santiago"—Showers Insure Fine Crops in Eastern Utah.

Special Correspondence.

Price, Utah, July 4.—By special request the war drama, "The Battle of Santiago," was repeated at Town Hall last night, for the benefit of the Price ward Sunday school by the home dramatic company, assisted by the Hutchinsons, late of the Salt Lake Theater. The play was first rendered on Friday night last and there was a packed house out to witness it. In addition to being good actors and directors of theatrical events, the Hutchinson brothers are exceptionally fine scenic artists and have painted a number of good pieces for the stage and thoroughly redecorated and overhauled the house, which is now one of the best appointed opera houses along the Rio Grande railroad, with a seating capacity of 500.

Willis T. Beardsley has sold out the eating house system of the Rio Grande Western to a Mr. Russell, who has assumed charge and will hereafter conduct the same. The dining room at Helper will be open in the future for railroad employes, trains no longer stopping there for meals since the advent of the dining car system. The lunch counter at Helper and Thistle Junction will be enlarged and a better service arranged. Where trains have heretofore stopped twenty minutes for meals there will henceforth be a stop of but ten minutes. Mr. Beardsley goes to Colorado.

BENIFICENT RAINS.

Good rains have fallen throughout Castle Valley the past week, and although the showers have been light, they have been frequent and good crops all along the line will be the result. The outlook for a bountiful harvest throughout eastern Utah at this time was never better.

Mrs. J. C. Bergland, who has been at the point of death for a week or ten days, is much improved and hopes for her recovery are now bright. The infant child of H. W. Millburn is also considered beyond the danger point after a severe spell of scarlet fever.

Mrs. H. C. Smith, who is being attended by Dr. Fisk of Helper, is now convalescent, as is also Miss Tucker.

The next convening of the Emery Stake conference will be at Orangeville, and the date is July 16th and 17th. Ward conference will be held in Price the 9th of this month.

PRICE.

Progress at Sunnyside—County Bonds— Price Paper at Par.

Special Correspondence.

Price, Carbon Co., July 6.—The few horse races here on the Fourth of July so interested the owners and admirers of good horse flesh that several races have been matched for a later date, and it is exected that several matches will be made for the 24th, which is always a big day in Price.

SUNNYSIDE COAL MINE.

Richard Cotner is in from the new coal camp in Whitmore canyon and says everything is moving along there in a business like shape. The coal company is now working about forty men in the development of the coal mines there and is calculating to put on very many more as soon as houses can be erected for the accommodation of the men.

Next Monday the annual election of school trustees for Price district will be voted for, and it is more than likely that the present board will be retained in office. It has managed the business of the district in a business-like manner and the people generally believe it to be the proper thing to keep the old board in power.

COUNTY BONDS.

The board of county commissioners meets Monday, at which time the question of bonding the county will come up for final action. This indebtedness is to pay off the warrants that were outstanding at the time the territory became a State and will amount to something like $4,000. All together this will make the debt of Carbon county less than five thousand dollars, one-third of which can be paid off with the taxes that are to come in this fall.

The town trustees meet next Saturday evening to consider the revision and adoption of a new set of town ordinances. The semi annual report of the town treasurer, Albert Bryner, shows that the city has something over $800 in the treasury and is on a cash basis for the first time in a long while.

CASTLE GATE.

Italians and Other Citizens Celebrate the Day—The Aftermath.

Special Correspondence.

Castle Gate, Carbon Co., Utah, July 5.—The Fourth was spent gloriously in this town. In the grove, K. of P. hall and in the Italian bowery were gathered together the whole of the town to celebrate the country's natal day. Patriotic speeches, songs, etc., were rendered, while games and sports of various kinds were indulged in, and amid all this the boom of the explosion of the heavy charges of powder caused the canyons to reverberate with echoes.

The Stars and Stripes were unfurled at 9 o'clock a. m., while the Castle Gate band played the Star Spangled Banner. A most delightful day so far as patriotism was concerned, was spent by all the people of Castle Gate and the evening of the Fourth wound up the Italian festival.

The music of the band was an inspiring feature in yesterday's celebration.

THE AFTERMATH.

Jas. Hensley and David Howells look as though they had been through a threshing machine; "booze" caused the row. There were a good many swelled heads this morning.

THE SCOFIELD BURGLARY.

The Salt Lake Herald of today contains this special telegram from Provo, bearing on the Policeman Strong murder case and the burglary of Hendrichsen's store at Scofield a few weeks ago "Frank Morris has confessed to being one of the men who robbed Hendrichsen's store at Scofield on June 19 He is the man who was arrested between Provo and Springvile on the morning William Strong was murdered He was held in Springville three days and then brought to Provo He denied ever having been in Provo, denied that he knew Frank Connors, the man who confessed to the Scofield burglary, and also denied knowing anything about that crime or the murder Now he has changed his story. He knows Connors and says they were pals in the burglary On confessing this he took the officers to the Rio Grande Western depot and showed where they had hid their grip, afterwards found by the officers Then he took them down the track and pointed out the way he went when leaving for Springville

"When asked why they separated and tried to get out of town, leaving their plunder behind them, he said they heard of the murder and knew that the officers were out and that they were afraid of being found with the plunder in their possession Still the officers believe these burglars, with another who is still at large committed the murder, but as far as can be ascertained at present they have no evidence that will fasten the crime upon them. Morris has been in jail for eight days and yet no charge has been preferred against him '

THE FOURTH IN PRICE.

The Fourth of July celebration in Price this year was the most successful one ever held here. The crowd was a big one, good natured, and as one fellow expressed it, everybody had a 'bully good time.'

The program, literary and musical was carried out substantially as published in The Advocate last week In the afternoon the hall was packed from front door to stage with children and their parents, who accompanied them. Lemonade, sandwiches and refreshments were served the little ones, preceding and following the dance, the latter being for their sole amusement

The races for the boys and the girls also was a pleasant and entertaining feature for the youth and a great deal of friendly rivalry was shown in the various sports.

In addition to this there was horse racing and a ball game, both of which were well attended The ball game was between two home nines, the Helper boys having failed to put in an appearance, they going to Salt Lake to play the Rio Grande Western nine.

There were three good horse races in the afternoon and in which ponies belonging to Tom Nichols, Tobe Whitmore, Ike Glaser, Matt Thomas and others were entered.

There was no drunkenness to speak of and everybody appeared to be in a good humor and out for the fun and sport that was to be had during the day. A better behaved crowd at all times was to have been seen nowhere

At Castle Gate there was a good celebration, as also at Wellington A great many young people were down from Helper, where there was nothing but a dance in the evening

The ball at Price Town Hall at night was well attended.

CASTLE GATE CELEBRATION

The Festa de Societe de Napole commenced in good earnest at Castle Gate Sunday afternoon. The parade traversed the main thoroughfares, headed by the band, finishing up at the bowery. The society was called to order by the president of the festa, E Sintschi, who made a speech of welcome. Joseph Barbroglio fol lowed with a few words to the mem bers on the duties and obligations that would be required of them, and to see to it that every visitor be made a welcome guest. The festa was then declared open, and a royal good time was had for three days. All work at the mines was suspended for the occasion.

Price

SHORT STORIES.

Work will in a few days begin on the foundation for Lowenstein's new brick building

The town trustees meet Saturday night to consider the matter of the revision of the town ordinances.

The recent improvements at Town Hall make it one of the neatest public buildings in the state.

Harry Heyman has opened a general store at Helper, but will make a specialty of cigars and groceries.

Chub Millburn has finished repainting his place of business, and it is now one of the coolest houses in this part of the country

There is a new boy baby at the home of Mr and Mrs H. C. Smith which ar rived last week. Mrs. Smith is getting along nicely

Considerable material is going through here every day for use at the coal mine in Whitmore Canyon and upon the rail road grade turrets.

Price merchants and those we have talked with from towns of Emery and Uintah counties say business generally is better than at any time for several years previously.

The depot building at Sunnyside will be moved to the new town in Whitmore Canyon, which is to be known as Sun nyside. The old station of Sunnyside is to be abandoned.

Alf Ballinger and Tobe Whitmore cleaned up about $150 between them on the horse races on the Fourth, the for mer about $50, and the latter in the neighborhood of $100.

The horse races here on the 24th will no doubt draw a big crowd to Price from the surrounding country There will be plenty of fun and amusement for all who come here on that date.

Travel of all kinds has been light since the Fourth Traveling men and those who are considered travelents as a gen eral thing went into the city, and have not as yet gotten around again

Abe Liddell will go to Sunnyside to work for the coal company in the capac ity of contractor and builder. His fam ily will remain at Wellington until such time as women are allowed to live in the camp

The board of county commissioners will meet next Monday. The most im portant matter to be considered is the bonding of the county to pay off out s anding warrants existing at the time s atehood was granted

The Advocate has in stock over 150 different forms of legal blanks, and sup plies anything in this line at Salt Lake and Provo prices All kinds of blank d eds and location notices Mail orders given prompt attention

The dance given at Town Hall on the night of the Fourth was quite largely at tended and netted the Sunday school a neat sum The dances after the play Friday and Monday evenings also brought out big crowds

There will be no women allowed in the new town in Whitmore Canyon for a year, or at least until the titles to the coal lands are perfected The intention of the company is to prevent any trouble like that it went through at Castle Gate

The town tru tou met in regular session last Friday night. The evening was taken up with routine business The report of the city treasurer showed that there is about $5 0 in the city treasury. The report was for the six months ending June 50th.

The Pennsylvania, Rock Island, Denver & Rio Grande and Rio Grande Western have secured the contract for hauling the whole of the Nineteenth regiment, United States infantry It means 1500 men and a train of baggage to pass through Price.

Of the crop prospects in the Ashley Valley the Vernal correspondent of Salt Lake's Herald says ' Haying has commenced in some parts of the valley. The fine weather of the last week is beginning to have its effect, as crops of all kinds are now growing nicely."

Dick Cotner came in Saturday from Whitmore Canyon and went down to Cleveland to remain over the Fourth He says the force of men employed in the mines is being steadily increased and there are now some thirty five to forty miners employed doing development work.

M M Riley of Moab, Utah, well known here in Price, was arrested in Salt Lake the other day on the charge of assault and battery upon one of the numerous Jenson family, whom the newspapers state was badly beaten up. The row occurred in a saloon over a game of cards.

The Railway Age states that the Rio Grande Western is in the market for 150 to 500 forty ton ore cars These are the 80,000 pound capacity cars of which so much has been said of late, and are no doubt calculated to be put in use in handling the output of coal in the near future from the Whitmore Canyon mines

Superintendent Rock Pope, of the Old Dyer mine in the Vernal country, passed through Price the other day on his way to Castle Gate with samples of a very fine quality of coal which he was taking to Castle Gate to have tested for its coking qualities The coal comes from a large vein located some twelve miles east of Vernal

The rumor is out that the Southern Pacific is tired of paying the Short Line and Western for hauling its freight from Ogden to Salt Lake and that the company intends to build into Salt Lake in the near future Although this may will be made sometime, Salt Lake railroad men do not regard it as an event of the near future.

Deseret Evening News
July 8, 1899

PRICE.

Building Boom—Stage Accident—Fine Honey Crop—Fine Wool Clip.

Special Correspondence.

Price, July 7.—The third car of copper ore from the Copper Globe property of St. V. LeSieur, located some seventy miles south of Ferron, is expected in here at any time now for shipment to the sampling works at Salt Lake City. It is said this ore will go 20 to 30 per cent copper, with some five or six dollars in gold and silver to the ton. There will be no more work at the mine until the litigation over the property has been settled. The parties to the litigation are all residents of Provo. Some twenty to fifty men employed directly and indirectly at the mine have been thrown out of work, and the report is that there is much bad feeling towards Mr. LeSieur in consequence of money that is due them for work as miners and for hauling.

About four miles of the track of the Rio Grande Western is finished from Mounds station up towards Whitmore canyon, and it is expected that track laying will begin next week some time.

BUILDING BOOM.

Price has a genuine building boom and if nothing unforeseen happens this year will witness more improvements than any like period in the history of the town. The Emery County Mercantile company is burning brick for a large two-story building for mercantile and banking purposes that will be by far the largest as well as the best building in Carbon county, 60x80, two stories high, with basement, vaults, granery, etc.; Louis Lowenstein has started work on his two-story brick business house, with basement, warehouse, granery and the like. Besides these, a number of new residences are building. Mrs. R. J. Armstrong of Provo has lately located here with a stock of millinery goods, which gives the town another good business house.

News comes in from the agency at White Rocks that the Indians are through with their "harvest dance" and have gone back to their homes. At last accounts the dissatisfied White River Utes were still talking of going back to their reservation in Colorado, which move they declare they will make as soon as the water in the Green river has subsided.

STAGE ACCIDENT.

What came near being a bad accident occurred to the incoming Price and Vernal stage on Thursday evening some ten miles to the east of this city. The vehicle went into a rut and turned over on the side. A woman who registered at one of the hotels as Mrs. H. Hempstead of Little Rock, Arkansas, was thrown under the vehicle and pretty badly scratched up, though her injuries are not serious. Only the presence of mind of the driver prevented the horses' running away.

The road is generally in bad condition, though the full appropriation of the county has been most judiciously expended.

LARGE HONEY CROP.

The honey crop of Emery and Uintah counties will this year break all previous records; that is judging by the large shipments of five gallon tin cans that are going out from here in both directions by wagons and which come to Price by railroad. There has been nothing to equal the quantity heretofore.

FINE WOOL SHIPMENT.

Charles Crouse of the Brown's Park country is somewhere on the road between Price and Vernal with 25,— pounds of wool, which he will ship to Boston from this station. It is of a very fine grade and is understood to have been sold at a figure around 16 cents.

Deseret Evening News
July 10, 1899

PRICE.

Ward Conference—Will Celebrate the 24th—Scarlet Fever—Vandalism.

Special Correspondence.

Price, Utah, July 9.—There was a large attendance at the ward conference held here yesterday afternoon. Addresses were made by the presidency of Emery Stake, Reuben G. Miller, and counselors, Elders John H. Pace and Henry G. Mathias, and Secretary Arthur W. Horsley. Bishop Horsley of Price ward was also a speaker. The officials were unanimously sustained.

The city council has decided that there shall be no horse racing inside the city limits on the 24th. Pioneer day, and if the races already arranged for are run at that time, it will be outside the town. The committee on Pioneer day sports and program will meet on Wednesday evening next and arrange for the celebration, which it is expected will eclipse anything ever before attempted in Price.

The infant child of Mr. and Mrs. H. C. Smith died on Sunday morning and the remains will be taken to Emery county, the former home of the parents, for burial.

SCARLET FEVER.

There is considerable scarlet fever in town at the present time, but so far there have been no deaths from the disease. All cases so far reported are under the control of a physician, and it is believed there is no danger of an epidemic.

DASTARDLY VANDALISM.

Considerable damage was done by some vandals here on the night of the 4th of July. A number of half-grown trees in front of the meeting house were "barked" by someone, evidently a grown person, with the result that the trees will die, and it will be necessary to plant others for shade purposes.

Henry G. Mathias, who was appointed by Governor Wells to expend the money on the roads in Carbon county between here and Vernal, has filed his bond with the secretary of State and will begin work now in a few days, acting in conjunction with the appointee from Uintah county. It is believed the two counties will thus have the best roads they have ever had.

Light showers fell throughout Castle valley today. There is much hay lying in the fields, but as the showers were light, it is not thought any serious damage will result.

CONNORS IS HELD.

Frank Connors was held at Provo Tuesday without bail to stand trial for the murder of Policeman Strong He is the man who a few weeks ago robbed Hendrichsen,s store at Scofield. Monday the grip that was hidden by Connors the night of the Strong murder was found by two boys, Everett Mackentosh and Leroy Hollaway. A reward of $25 had been offered for the grip. The bag was full of things that had been stolen from the store of Mr. Hendri hsen of Scofield. There were four pair of pants, two pair of shoes and jewelry, such as diamond pins, earrings, etc., that would amount to about $100. There was also in the grip an old slouch hat that he wore on the night of the murder. When he was found the next night he wore another hat, a better one. One of the witnesses who saw him that fatal night says he wore an old hat that was worn at the points where it had been dented. This one is old and worn at the points mentioned But all that the finding of the hat in the grip goes to show is that he changed here that night.

An individual from Castle Gate has been down to Price several times of late, and it is said makes himself very annoying to a number of young girls here. The father of one of the girls whom this fellow has insulted called at this office this week, and during the conversation that took place on another subject, incidentally remarked that the Castle Ga e fiend was very apt to go away from here some evening with a load of buckshot in the regi n of his hip pocket. It is said the fellow has a wife and two or three children back "where the meadow grass is blue." He may consider himself is mighty lucky if he doesn't get into serious trouble in this man's town.

The board of county commissioners met in regular session on Monday, all members being present.

The report of County Superintendent of Schools Welb, estimating that the funds required for the school year 1899-1900 would amount to $1,175, was received, and the sum of $675 was set aside for the salary of the superintendent and for institute and contingent expenses, the same to be taken out of the school fund

A communication from the clerk of Emery county, regarding the assessment and collection of taxes on transitory herds of sheep, was referred to the treasurer of Carbon county, who will ask the Emery county official to give the names of the owners of the sheep on which that county desires to collect taxes. It seems that the Emery and Utah county officers are after the same stock.

Henry Knight, who was elected justice of the peace of Castle Gate precinct, did not desire to qualify and W H. Donaldson was named to fill out the unexpired term.

The bond of Hyrum Wilcox, as constable of Castle Gate precinct, was approved, with Joel Ricks and Richard White as sureties.

County Clerk Howard was given permission to appoint a deputy to assist him at the meetings of the district court.

The tax levy was fixed at 5 mills for county purposes and 3 1 2 mills for school purposes, and it was so ordered.

Bonds in the sum of $3,500 were authorized to pay off outstanding warrants issued up to January 1, 1896 Chairman Nelson and County Attorney Hoffmann were appointed a committee to negotiate the sale of the bonds.

The reports of J. P. Curtin and J Tom Fitch, justices of the peace at Scofield and Helper, respectively, were read and approved.

The saloon men of the county were ordered to file new bonds in the office of the county clerk

An ordinance regulating the licenses of merchants, peddlers, hotel keepers, etc, was passed. It appears in its entirety in another column of The Advocate

Erastus Anderson filed his report on the damages to the road in Soldier Canyon by reason of the driving of herds of sheep through there. He had been recommended for the place by Commissioner Frandsen, but when the report came in that the damage by some herds was $1, Frandsen thought the figure too high. The matter was discussed at considerable length and much good time was consumed in arguing the case, with the result that Frandsen withdrew from the controversy and the other members settled the fracas by agreeing on $2 as about the proper thing Frandsen's sheep had been driven over the canyon road. It was proposed to tax his herd $1. Frandsen insisted that $2 was quite enough.

Some sixty five to seventy bills, ranging from one dollar to one hundred, were then allowed and the commissioners met as a board of health. By virtue of his office as chairman of the board of county commissioners, Nelson became chairman of the board of health. The first business was the election of a secretary. Frandsen and James each put the other in nomination for secretary, and according to Clerk Howard, each of the gentlemen admitted his incompetency to act in the capacity of secretary. The result

was that after much solicitation on the part of the board, Mr. Howard consented to act as secretary. When the labors of the board had been finished, Howard put in a bill of six simoleans, coins of the realm, shekels of the vintage of William Jennings Bryan. This caused as much consternation as a bomb thrower in the office of Russell Sage. There

were sulphur fumes for a period of many minutes, with the result that Mr. Howard carried his point with a big P. When the board had cooled off, the matter of the adoption of a health ordinance was discussed. Nothing was done, however, and the lion and the lamb, so to speak, laid down side by side.

Emery County.

D. C. Woodward of Huntington is expecting a call to the missionary field.

Miss Stella Johnson of Huntington, is visiting friends and relatives in Sanpete county.

Eugene Maxwell has returned to Huntington after an absence of six or eight months.

A. E. Smith came up from Gold Mountain to spend the Fourth with his family at Castle Dale.

Robert Howard, son of Attorney Howard, has returned to Huntington after an absence of over a year.

Mrs Shipp is employed in taking the school census of Emery county and has about completed her work

Miss Sarah Larsen and Miss Stena Peterson visited friends and relatives at Castle Dale the Fourth, and will soon return to Price.

Miss Hettie Guyman and Retta Wakefield of Huntington are both improving in health, the warm weather seeming to be beneficial for rheumatism.

Floyd & Co. at Huntington have removed from their old stand to the store room formerly occupied by Jesse Penny.

Charles Aiken and Val Acord of Castle Dale came in from the copper diggings last week and report everything booming out there.

Mrs. Lansen Aldridge of Mt. Pleasant has been spending the past week with her parents, Mr. and Mrs. Barton, of Castle Dale.

Peter Anderson and Ras Nickleson of Mt. Pleasant were in Castle Dale on the Fourth spinning their best girls around and having a good time generally.

George Collingham has gone to the state of Washington, where he will remain during the summer, having employment with a railroad contracting firm.

During the parade at Orangeville on the Fourth, A. G. Jewkes was overcome by the heat and fell from his wagon which was in the parade. The wheels passed over his body, rendering him unconscious for the day. His injuries were not serious.

The trustees of Ferron have engaged an eastern professor for principal of the Ferron school for the ensuing year. The gentleman is Professor B. P. Alexander of Prairie Creek, Ind.

The Fourth of July was celebrated in a glorious manner at Orangeville, says the Castle Dale Record. The floats used in the parade were all elegantly decorated, and those who took part spared no expense to make the day one of the grandest Orangeville has ever witnessed

Ephraim Clausen of Ephraim arrived at Castle Dale last week from Sanpete, and accompanying him were Marinus Peterson, Silas Shiner and Mr. and Mrs. Carl Olsen of Castle Dale. The boys expect to go to Wyoming in a few days Mrs. Olsen, who has been visiting in Ephraim for several weeks, will remain in Castle Dale with her parents while Carl is in Wyoming.

Editor Allard of the Emery County Record throws this "hot one" at an enemy. "Our readers will not be interested in any newspaper controversy, and we do not care to enter into any We are compelled to say a few words, however. Two weeks ago we published an article referring to some underhanded work going on in order to injure this paper. Our surmises were correct, and this man has been delving further into the affairs of this office—he is well adapted for such an occupation—and we will take the advice of people who are of some consequence, among whom are a score of worthy citizens of his own town, and pay no attention on to his mutterings The people are with us and we care not for the vituperations of this party. Do your worst, mister, he who laughs last laughs best."

SHORT STORIES.

There was not a marriage license issued this week by the county clerk.

The infant child of Mr. and Mrs. C. H. Millburn has entirely recovered from an attack of scarlet fever.

Rolling ladders have been put in at the Price Trading company. They are a great convenience to the clerks.

Blank notes and blank receipts, bound in books of 100, kept in stock and for sale at The Advocate office.

Hyrum Frandsen went up to the hills to the east of Colton the other day to look after his sheep which are ranging in that vicinity.

There will be a large number of horses here on the 24th, Pioneer Day, to enter the races. Some estimate the number at twenty five, more or less.

Lieutenant White, it is said, will be made recruiting officer at Fort Douglas for the volunteers that are to be raised in Utah for the Phillppines.

Blank school district warrants found in books of one hundred and suitable for any school district, kept in stock and for sale at The Advocate office.

New linoleum has been put down on the office floor of the Mathis Hotel, which adds much to the comfort of the guests of this always popular house

Arthur J. Lee shipped out a car of gilsonite on Tuesday to the East from the mines of the Gilson Asphaltum company on the strip near Fort Duchesne.

There was not a Fourth of July accident in Carbon county so far as we have heard, due no doubt to the absence of powder, fire crackers and explosives generally.

Little Pearl Holdaway has been indisposed for several days with something like tonsolitis. The report that she had scarlet fever is without the slightest foundation.

The county commissioners met as a board of health on Tuesday and adjourned after considering the health ordinance. Nothing was done in the matter, however.

Dr. Fisk reports that Mrs. J. C. Berglund is entirely out of danger and will be up and around again within a few days. This will be good news to the lady's many friends.

There was a big crowd out to the ward conference on Sunday. Interesting talks were made by President Miller, Counselors Pace and Mathis, Stake Clerk Horsley and also Bishop Horsley.

The fees taken in by County Clerk Howard for the month of June amounted to $158 45, one of the largest months in the history of the office. The receipts for the same time last year were $45 60.

The Advocate has in stock over 150 different forms of legal blanks, and supplies anything in this line at Salt Lake and Provo prices. All kinds of blank deeds and location notices. Mail orders given prompt attention.

The infant child of Mr. and Mrs. C. H. Smith died Saturday night of fever. The father was away from home, freighting on the road to Vernal at the time, and did not know of the little one's illness, which makes the case an additionally sad one. The remains were taken to Emery county, the former home, for burial. The bereaved parents have the sympathy of many friends in their affliction.

There is a big boy baby at the home of Mr. and Mrs. J. W. Gentry that came on Tuesday night. Dr. Fisk of Helper and Dr. Field were both in attendance. Mother and child are doing well, but Jack's friends are more or less worried about him

---

William Fitt and A. J. Hawks of Orangeville have the contract for the brick and stone work on the Lowenstein building, and have already begun work on the stone end of the contract. It will be rushed through and the building made ready for early occupancy.

Coal from the new Sunnyside mines will be brought to the ovens at Castle Gate to be coked for some time after the line is built. It will greatly add to the tonnage of coke as well as of coal by the opening of these new mines, which are said to produce a very fine grade of coal.

Charley Goldberg was up in the vicinity of Colton on Sunday and says he came back with plenty of fish, but nobody believes him, notwithstanding his heretofore good record for truth and veracity. But then—there are so many people in this part of Utah who hail from "Old Mizzouree."

E A. Beers has returned to Vernal from a trip to Chicago with a carload of Uintah county honey, and is enthusiastic over the success of his venture. The honey was pronounced the finest ever placed on the Chicago market, and brought a premium of a cent per pound over all other shipments

---

The district attorneys appointed by the governor are likely to have to provide their own traveling expenses. State Auditor Richards has discovered that the legislature made no provision in the appropriation bill for expenses for these officers. He will ask an opinion from the attorney general, however.

Work began yesterday on the race track to be used on the 24th. The events are to come off to the northeast of town and across the ditch. Graders and scrapers were brought into use all day yesterday and at night the work had advanced to a considerable extent. The track will be sprinkled to do away with the dust.

Friday evening, July 31st, the Price Home Dramatic company, assisted by the Hutchinson Brothers, will play that greatest of Charles Frohman's comedies, "Confusion." The piece is now being rehearsed and some of the best local talent will be cast for the play. There will be Castle Gate music and a free dance after the play.

This is the way the Price correspondent of Salt Lake's Tribune puts it: "A spasm of virtue struck Price today in the shape of the enforcement of the town ordinance as to Sunday closing of saloons. The saloon men made a vigorous kick, for the Sunday business has helped largely to pay the heavy license demanded here."

PERSONAL.

Mrs Belle Hudson has returned from Salt Lake City.

John Forrester of Colton was a visitor to Price on Monday.

Louis Lowenstein went up to Salt Lake Tuesday evening

William O Neill of Vernal was at the Mathis House the first of the week.

Mr and Mrs James Rooney of Helper were here the latter part of the week for a day.

Joseph Sanders of White Rocks was in Price the first of the week going to Salt Lake City.

Mr. and Mrs. David Prior of Huntington were here the first of the week from Ephraim on their way home.

Mrs. John Roberts of Vernal was a guest at the Mathis House the first of the week en ronto to Salt Lake City.

J hn Oliphant of Orangeville and C. Jensen of Ferron were among the Emery county delegation in Price during the week.

Judge Booth, Sam King, Monty Roberts and J. B Kellar of Provo were here the first of the week on their way to Emery county.

Ed F. Harmston of the Vernal country was in Price the first of the week and spread his autograph on the register at Hotel Clarke.

Mrs H. Hempstead of Little Rock, Ark , was a guest of the Hotel Clarke on Monday, coming in from the reservation en route to Salt Lake City.

Mrs N. C. Spalding of St Louis arrived here on Monday to visit a short time with her son, C. W. Spalding, and family of the Hotel Clarke.

Judge McConnell is expected to come in over the hot sands of the Uintah desert this week from the Vernal country and his mines in Indian Canyon.

Dr. Fields arrived from Ephraim Tuesday and is ready to enter upon his practice here He will have an office in the building west of Price Trading company.

Mrs. B R. McDonald has gone to Scofield, and with Mrs. H. A. Nelson of Castle Gate, will join a fishing party that will spend several weeks in the hills

W. W. Old, the life insurance song ster from Salt Lake City, came in Monday night from the West, registered at he Mathis House, and left in the morning for a pilgrimage into Emery county

Enos Bennion of Vernal was here during the last week looking after the sale of his wool, which he disposed of to Andrews & Co, of Manti. There was some 45,000 pounds of it, but the price paid was not made public.

Warren Foster was here the other day enroute to Salt Lake City, after a trip to Vernal, where he delivered a Fourth of July oration. He will give the Ashley Valley country a big writeup in Living Issues on his return home. The "great moral and religious" acknowledges an appreciated call.

Eastern Utah Advocate
July 20, 1899

Emery County.

The quarterly conference of the Emery Stake of Zion was held at Orangeville on Sunday and Monday, July 16th and 17th, 1899

There were present Of the Council of Apostles Elder John Henry Smith, Elder Jonathan G Kimball of the First Council of Seventies, the stake presidency, bishops of wards and a large attendance of officers and members from all parts of the stake

MORNING SESSION, JULY 16TH.

The conference was called to order by President Reuben G Miller. The choir sang hymn on page 260 Prayer was offered by Patriarch C G Larsen. Hymn by choir, 'How Firm the Foundation, Ye Saints of the Lord.'

President Miller made a few opening remarks in which he complimented the saints upon their attendance at the conference He stated that during the past three months he had visited all but one of the wards of the stake, and in closing expressed his hope that the spirit of the Lord would be with the people in the conference

Bishop Peter Johnson of Huntington, Bishop Hans P Rasmussen of Molen and Bishop Jasper Robertson of Orangeville gave good reports of their wards

The speakers were Elder Jonathan G Kimball of the First Council of Seventies and Elder John D Killpack, Jr The choir sang an anthem, which was followed by benediction by Orange Seely

Conference adjourned until 3 o'clock p m.

Hymn by choir, "Softly Beams the Sacred Dawning." Prayer by Patriarch Frederick Olsen. Hymn by choir, "A Holy Angel From On High." A ministering of Sacrament. Hymn by choir, "Prayer Is the Soul's Sincere Desire."

Bishop H. A. Nelson of Ferron and Bishop L. P. Overson of Cleveland reported their wards in good condition.

The speakers were Elders John H. Pace of the Stake Presidency, Apostle John Henry Smith and Elder Jonathan G. Kimball of the First Council of Seventies. The choir sang an anthem, "Come, Let Us Sing Unto the Lord." Benediction by Elder William Taylor.

Conference adjourned until 10 o'clock a. m., Monday, July 17th.

DURING INTERMISSION.

A priesthood meeting was held at 4 30. Good instructions were given to the brethren by Apostle John Henry Smith.

Ward meeting was held with the people of Orangeville at 4 00 p m. Apostle John Henry Smith and Elder Jonathan G. Kimball addressed the saints. Jasper Robertson wished to be released as bishop of the ward, but the people of Orangeville prevailed upon him to continue in the work. Mr. Robertson has been bishop of Orangeville for eighteen years.

MONDAY JULY 17TH—MORNING SESSION

Conference was called to order by President Miller. The choir sang hymn, "Praise Ye the Lord." Prayer by Elder N. L. Marsing. Hymn by choir, "Lord Thou Wilt Hear Me When I Pray."

The speakers were Henry G. Mathis of the Stake Presidency, Elders J. W. Nixon, A. E. Wall, Orange Seely and Jonathan G. Kimball and Apostle John Henry Smith. President Miller made a few closing remarks.

The general authorities were sustained as at the last general conference of the church, after which the stake authorities were presented and unanimously sustained as follows:

Stake Presidency—Reuben G. Miller president, John H. Pace and Henry G. Mathis, counselors.

Members of High Council—Elias Cox, John F. Wakefield, James Peterson, Sylvester H. Cox, Alma G. Jewkes, John Pearson, Christian G. Larsen, Jr., Frank M. Reynolds, Joseph H. Taylor, Oscar A. Wood, Niels P. Miller, Dios Crandall. Alternate—William Taylor.

Presidency of High Priests' Quorum—William Taylor, Niels P. Miller, Oscar A. Wood.

Patriarchs—Frederick Olsen, Alexander Jameson, Franklin W. Young, Christian G. Larsen, Charles Pulsipher.

Clerk of the Stake and High Council—Arthur W. Horsley.

Stake Board of Education—Reuben G. Miller, John H. Pace, Henry G. Mathis, James Peterson, Alma G. Jewkes, Peter R. Peterson, John D. Killpack, D. T. Thomander, secretary.

Relief Society—Anna U. Larsen, president Josie E. Childs and Ann Pulsipher, counselors, Amanda Ship secretary.

Sabbath School Board—Alexander Jameson, superintendent, Frank M. Reynolds and Jesse Washborn, counselors, Jesse D. Jewkes, secretary.

Y. M. M. I. A.—Joseph E. Johnson, superintendent, Alma G. Jewkes and Don C. Woodward, assistants, J. Fleming Wakefield, secretary.

Y. L. M. I. A.—Susannah Jukes, superintendent, Amelia Jewkes and May Miller, assistants, Amelia Larsen, secretary and treasurer.

Primary Association—Mary A. Sorensen, president, Levina VanBuren and Melvina Jack, counselors, Annetta Wakefield, secretary.

Religious Class Work—Alexander Jameson, superintendent, Uriah E. Curtis and Abanah Olsen, assistants.

SHORT STORIES.

The Advocate is getting out a new register for the Mathis Hotel. It will be a beauty

There is a scarcity of teams for work on the railroad grading up Whitmore Canyon

Arthur J Lee is he is about the only man in Price that did not go up to see the circus at Helper yesterday.

Sam Whitmore and Alf Ballinger went up to the head of Whitmore Canyon the other day on a prospecting trip

Fire Insurance written in the best companies doing business in Utah. See R W. Crockett at the Advocate office.

There is but little sickness in Price, according to the doctors This condition also holds good throughout the county.

The race track is in excellent condition and there will be lots of fun on the 24th for every admirer of good horse flesh.

There was a large crowd up to Helper from here yesterday to attend the circus Many went up by wagon and some on the train

About two miles of the iron for the railroad up Whitmore Canyon has been laid Some four miles of the grading has so far been done.

The Advocate office will be moved about the first of August to the Bryan building, which, in the meantime, will be fixed up to suit requirements.

Full line of legal blanks at the Advocate office at Provo and Salt Lake City prices Nearly two hundred different forms to select from Orders by mail promptly attended to

O C. Johnson was in from the Nine Mile country this week and filed his bond as a justice of the peace. W. H Don allson, who was appointed at Castle Gate, says he will not qualify.

Dun's Review of July 15th says of the Salt Lake business situation 'Bank statements show heavy increase in balances over last year, and collections are very good Trade is steady and improving"

There was a second fire at Fort Du chesne Saturday night that destroyed the quartermaster's stable, causing a loss to the government of several thousands of dollars. It is believed to have been of incendiary origin.

M P. Braffett received a telegram Sunday announcing the death of his father at Pawpaw, Ills, of old age Deceased was about 70 years old and was a prominent physician and respected citizen of his state for many years

Indian Agent Myton is giving sheepmen permission to graze their sheep on the reservation at the rate of $50 per thousand head for the season Sheepmen from Vernal paid him $1100 last week for the privilege of putting 22,000 head of sheep on the reservation

D R McDonald has for sale the wool clip of Charles Crouse of the Brown's Park country, and of which there is something like 60 000 pounds Louis Kabell of Uintah county is here and also has his clip up to the highest bidder There has been no sale as yet

News has been received here that ex Senator Cannon and others who lately took a bond on the Annie Lanrie mine will make their first payment of several thousand dollars when the same becomes due Carbon county citizens will get the largest part of the purchase price

For Pioneer Day, July 24th, a rate of one single fare for the round trip is authorized between any two stations on the lines of the Rio Grande Western Tickets will be sold July 23d and 24th, limited to July 4th on the going trip, with final limit July 25th. B. B McDonald, agent, Price, Utah.

The Rio Grande Western eating house is to have an addition of thirty feet built on the south end at Helper to be used for a lunch counter. Work has begun on the new chapel and the foundation is being laid A new building will be erected to the south of the depot to be used by Dr. Fisk and the assistant superintendent.

Tuesday was about the biggest day in the history of Helper. The Campbell Bros show exhibited there and there were big crowds from Price, Castle Gate and elsewhere In the evening there was a dance at Rooney's Hall, in the neighborhood of fifty to seventy five people being present from here The circus was about the ro tenest thing that has been along in many a day.

It is reported that the proprietor of the strip saloon has lately been hiring a woman to do the selling of the alcohol to the Indians. Agent Myton last week swore out complaints before United States Commissioner McConnell against all of the occupants of that resort, but when the officers went to serve the warrants the defendants had left the country. The officers are still looking for them

It will no longer be safe for Utah sports to attempt to fish or hunt on the reservation without a permit, as the agent keeps a party of white men and Indian police in the western part of the reservation continuously, looking after trespassers, with instructions to bring anyone to the agency they find on the reservation unlawfully If any are brought to the agency they will be prosecuted as trespassers

Parley P. Warren, who has been in Alaska, is expected to arrive home now at any time, his mother, Mrs S J. Warren, having received news that the vessel on which he sailed, the Servan, would arrive at some point on the Pacific coast the 11th of June His friends in Price will be glad to know that the young man prospered while in the frozen north, and returns with a goodly sum of money as pay for the many hardships and the exposure he has endured.

PERSONAL.

Mrs. William Potter has returned from Scofield.

Colonel Tadlock of Manti was here the latter part of the week on legal business

Tom Nichols went up to Salt Lake City yesterday morning on a short business trip.

Miss May Walker of American Fork was a guest at the Mathis House during the week.

Miss Louisa Westerberg of Salt Lake City arrived here last week to make her home in Price.

J. C. McNeill of Vernal was among the Ashley Valley people at the Mathis House this week.

Charles Andrews, the Manti wool buyer, was in town the latter part of the week, looking after business.

O. T. McCormick of the Salt Lake Business College was here this week in the interest of that institution.

Judge Rhodes of Moab was in town several days this week on legal business, having driven over from Vernal

Victor Rambaud came in Wednesday night from Colton where he has been for some time looking after his flocks

Robert Forrester was in from Sunnyside Monday and says things are moving along in good shape at the new coal camp.

Robert Craig, the Philadelphia wool buyer, was here this week and later left for the East. He was accompanied by Mrs. Craig

W. H. Donaldson has returned from a six weeks' visit to 'the old folks at home," back in the Shenandoah Valley of Pennsylvania.

Miss Linda Norrell of Salt Lake City, who has been visiting the family of F. E. Woods at Castle Dale, was here on Thursday last en route home.

Don C. Robbins was at the Hotel Clarke on Tuesday and left the next morning in the direction of Sunnyside, where he has some kind of a mining deal a working.

Dr A. J. Shores and wife of Salt Lake City and T. S. Wimmer and wife of Payson were here during the week, the guests of Mr. and Mrs. C. W. Spalding at the Hotel Clarke.

Harvey Douglas of Kansas City is at the Hotel Clarke. He represents a big cattle commission house at the city at the mouth of the Kaw, and is here looking up business for his firm.

Traveling Freight Agent Devereaux of the Santa Fe Route, and an old friend of the editor of 'the great moral and religious," was in town this week looking up business for his line.

District Attorney Woods of Castle Dale was here the other day on his way to Salt Lake City to have his face fixed, that is to get a new set of teeth Those that nature had given him were out. Having had them extracted, it made such a change in his facial expression that his most intimate friends here did not know him.

HOME MISSIONARIES.

Following is a list of the missionaries of Emery Stake of Zion, appointed to visit the wards of the stake on the dates named

Peter Christensen and Thomas A. Williams—Molen July 30, Ferron August 27, Orangeville September 24.

Samuel A. Williams jr and Nuel Beal—Ferron September 10, Molen September 24.

B. M. V. Goold and Andrew P. Nielson —Wellington July 30, Spring Glen August 13, Castle Gate August 27.

Lars P Larsen and John J. Thordareon—Castle Gate July 30, Spring Glen September 14 Wellington August 27.

J. W. Seely and Abanadi Olsen—Huntington August 27, Price September 10, Wellington September 24.

John Peterson and Jacob Sorensen—Cleveland August 13, Desert Lake September 10, Emery September 24

O. J. Anderson and Boye P. Peterson—Desert Lake August 13, Emery August 27, Ferron September 24

J. Fleming Wakefield and William Howard—Desert Lake July 30, Price August 13, Castle Gate September 10,

Joseph E Johnson and Peter Nielson—Orangeville July 30, Price August 27; Castle Dale September 10, Castle Gate September 24

John Oliphant and Allen Cox—Price July 30 Wellington August 13, Cleveland August 27, Spring Glen September 10.

L M Olsen and Chris Peterson—Spring Glen July 30 Castle Gate August 13, Desert Lake August 27, Wellington September 10.

George W. Stevens and Hans P. Rasmussen, Jr.—Emery July 30; Orangeville August 13, Castle Dale August 27; Lawrence September 24

M. A. Cox and J. D Killpack Sr—Huntington July 30, Emery August 13, Orangeville August 27, Castle Dale September 24

John Zwellen and John H Cook—Castle Dale July 30, Huntington August 13, Emery August 27, Orangeville September 10

Christian Peterson and John Pearson—Ferron July 30, Molen August 13 Lawrence August 27, Cleveland September 10.

Joseph H. Taylor and Christian G Larson, Jr —Lawrence July 30 Ferron August 13, Molen August 27, Huntington September 10.

SHORT STORIES.

William M. Roylance of Springville was at Hotel Clarke yesterday.

James Peterson, the photographer, is at Vernal, and is said to be doing a very nice business

The Hutchinson Bros are doing some painting at Castle Gate this week, and also have several jobs to do at Helper

The Advocate will be in its new home after this week in the Bryan building Our friends are invited to come in and see us there

Helper sent down a big crowd on the Twenty-fourth they were money spenders and backed the Glaser horse to a dark brown finish

J. F Rath is soon to move his short order restaurant to the old drug store building, next to Fitzgerald & Cos. Call and see him for a good steak

Victor Rambaud has a letter from the doctor who is waiting on Joseph Nougier at St Mark's hospital in which he says the injured man is getting along very nicely and will soon be out and able to return home. This will be good news to his many friends.

Charles S Maxwell, the Springville bank robber, now in the penitentiary, has filed in the state supreme court a notice of appeal of his case to the United States supreme court Maxwell, who is well known in Price was convicted of the robbery of the First National bank of Springville.

The Home Dramatic Company presented the comedy, "Confusion," at Town Hall, Friday evening there was a dance after the play that no doubt had the effect of making the crowd larger than it otherwise would have been Everybody thoroughly enjoyed both the play and the hop.

'The Battle of Santiago' was presented at Castle Gate Monday evening to a packed house by the Price Home Dramatic company. There was a dance after the show that was largely attended and most thoroughly enjoyed by those present Several couples were in attendance from Helper and Price

The Twenty fourth was the biggest crowd in Price for many a day. The program as announced in The Advocate last week was carried out with the exception of one or two numbers In the afternoon the greater part of the crowd found its way to the race course, where there was some fine sport.

George C. Whitmore is figuring on putting in a pipe line to carry the water from about a mile above the mines in Whitmore Canyon to his ranch below He estimates the cost at about ten thousand dollars per mile He and the new coal company operating in the canyon have not as yet come to an agreement on the water proposition

Special Indian Agent Harper came in Monday morning from Washington and left at once for White Rocks agency to have a conference with the leaders of the White River Utes The Indians have been wanting to return to their old reservation across the Colorado line, and it is to talk them out of it, as it were, that the special agent comes out at this time

Parley P Warren who has been in and around Dawson City, Alaska, the past eighteen months returned to Price last Friday, and says he has come back to stay. He prospered well while in that country but says people who are doing anything in Utah are foolish to leave here for the frozen north There are ten thousand miners and others there now out of work.

Judge McConnell was here the first of the week, driving in from the mines in Indian Canyon. He says his company has lately uncovered a new body of elaterite that is as good as any ever found in that section. The ore body is twenty-five feet wide and will be worked on an extensive scale. A new warehouse to hold twenty to thirty cars of ore at a time will be erected at the terminus of the Willow Creek branch, from which point shipments are now being made

Captain Guilfoyle, commander of the post out at Fort Duchesne, held a conference the other day with Old Sowowic, the chief of the White River Utes, in which the old murderer was told that if he and his people attempted to go back to Colorado, they would be followed by the cavalry and brought back. They persistently stated, however, that they were going, and it may be that there will yet be some dead Indians scattered along the Duchesne. This is the moon they have all along been waiting for in which to move. Sowowic's followers are said to be weakening under his leadership.

Salt Lake Herald Washington dispatch: "Although the Utah sheep raisers' delegation has won its request for temporary restitution of Uintah grazing privileges for this summer, it is not likely that it will be permitted in the future. The argument that seems to have prevailed with the land office was that the order was very unjust to the sheep owners for the present season. It is stated at the land office that the question is not permanently settled, but will be considered for her by the department this fall. There is no doubt that the recommendation of forest reserve agents will again be adverse to the practice, and that the report will be emphatic with arguments based on this summer's experience."

Price

PERSONAL.

Sam Whitmore returned to Salt Lake Tuesday evening

Miss Maggie McIntire spent the Twenty fourth at American Fork

Miss Nellie McMullin will not teach in the Price schools this year.

C. W. Spalding of Hotel Clarke made a short business trip into Emery county during the week

Misses Belle and Olive Boyd of the Nine Mile section visited friends here the first of the week

J. S. W. de Jong, a Chicago commercial man left his autograph on the register at Hotel Clarke Tuesday

Misses Annie Larsen and Isa McIntire went up to Salt Lake City Tuesday, attending the dance at Castle Gate enroute

Mrs A Ballinger, accompanied by Mrs Miller, visited friends at Salt Lake City the Twenty-fourth, returning Tuesday evening

Ernest Peyton left Cincinnati for Salt Lake City the first of the week. He will probably go to work for the Rio Grande Western again

Professor and Mrs J. W. Nixon were over from Huntington the first of the week and were guests of Mrs Bailie at the Mathis House.

Miss Mary Leonard, who has been in California attending the teachers' educational association, is expected to return to Price now at any time

Among the Eastern Utah arrivals at Hotel Clarke during the first of the week were W. C. Cassaday of Green River and James Sewall of Castle Dale

Mrs W. L. Warren of the Nine Mile section, who has been at Provo for a month under the care of Dr. Allen, returned on Monday and was met here by her husband

Mrs James Rooney of Helper was here Sunday visiting her mother, Mrs S J Warren, and also her brother, Parley P. Warren, the latter having just returned from the Klondike

Judge Van Natta was down from Helper to the races Monday. He made "the great moral and religious" an appreciated call while here. His fruit crop, he says, is about up to the average this year

SCARLET FEVER CASES.

Lena, the little girl of Mr. and Mrs D W Hollaway, was taken down with scarlet fever yesterday. Sheets have been put up on the door and openings between the postoffice and the living apartments, and every precaution taken to prevent the spread of the contagion. Great quantities of carbolic acid are being used and Dr. Pigd thinks there will be no spread of the fever so far as this case is concerned

A little child of A D Anderson, residing near the Hotel Clarke, also has a well developed case of fever.

LICENSE ORDINANCE.

An Ordinance regulating and licensing certain classes of business in Carbon county, Utah

The Board of County Commissioners of the county of Carbon ordains as follows

SECTION I

It shall be unlawful for any person to engage in any business hereinafter specified in Carbon county without first obtaining a license therefor as provided in this ordinance

SECTION II

Licenses shall be issued at the following rates

MERCHANTS

Any merchant carrying a stock of goods of fifteen hundred dollars or less shall pay a license of $2 50 per quarter year

Merchants carrying a stock of goods of more than fifteen hundred dollars and less than five thousand dollars shall pay a license of $5 00 per quarter year.

Any merchant carrying a stock of goods of more than five thousand dollars shall pay a license $7 50 per quarter year

HOTEL AND RESTAURANTS

Each hotel shall pay a license of $4 00 per quarter year.

Each restaurant shall pay a license of $3 00 per quarter year

PEDDLERS

Each peddler shall pay a license of $1 00 per quarter year.

BUTCHERS

Each butcher shall pay a license of $5 00 per quarter year for each market stall or stand

POOL TABLES

Each owner of a pool table shall pay a license of $3 00 per quarter year

TRAVELING SHOWS OR THEATER COMPANIES

Each traveling show or theater company shall pay a license of $3 00 for each performance

CIRCUSES

Each traveling circus shall pay a license of $5 00 for each exhibition or performance

SECTION III

No license named in this ordinance shall be issued for any time less than three months nor more than one year Provided that licenses for traveling theater companies shows or circuses may be issued for each exhibition or performance

SECTION IV.

It shall be the duty of the County Attorney to collect all licenses above named by a suit on the complaint of the County Clerk, County Sheriff or any Constable of the county where the party carrying on such business neglects or refuses to pay the license as required by this ordinance

SECTION V.

This ordinance shall take effect on September 1st, 1899 Provided, that all licenses now issued covering a period beyond September 1st, 1899, shall not be affected hereby.

H. A. NELSON,
Chairman of Board of Commissioners
Attest:
ROBERT HOWARD,
Clerk of Board of Commissioners.

Affirmative Vote { H A NELSON
GEORGE G FRANDSEN,
JOHN JAMES

I, Robert Howard, county clerk in and for the county of Carbon, state of Utah, do hereby certify that the above is a true and correct copy of an ordinance passed by the Board of County Commissioners at a meeting held July 11th, 1899 as appears of record in the Ordinance Book in my office

[SEAL]   ROBERT HOWARD,
County Clerk
First pub July 13, last pub Aug 8, 1899.

NOTICE

Notice is hereby given that there are now funds on hand to pay all warrants issued on the witness and juror fund at the last term of court.

ALBERT BRYNER,
Treasurer Carbon County.
Price, July 17, 1899

A Unique Ailment.

(Special Correspondence.)

Castlegate, July 26.—John Eddy, while up in the grove at the Pioneer celebration yesterday, felt a benumbed sensation in his right leg and foot, and on his arrival at home Dr. Asadoorian was called to examine the limb and found a curious ailment. The foot had swelled to an abnormal size and innumerable blisters had arisen on the leg between the ankle and calf. He treated it and when the blisters were punctured Mr. Eddy had a little ease. The medical books do not describe the ailment.

Castlegate Notes.

(Special Correspondence.)

Castlegate, July 26.—John H. McMillan took charge of the outside yard labor as foreman this morning. W. R. Ward having resigned.

Mrs. W. T. Lamph, Mrs. W. H. Lawley and part of their family are here from Castle valley to spend the holidays.

Miss Addie Cowley of Cleveland is staying with Miss Rhea Ricks.

Benjamin Williams of Cleveland is in town. He is in poor health and came up to see old friends and see if a change of climate would be of any benefit to him.

CASTLE GATE ITEMS

John Eldy, while up in the grove at the Pioneer celebration, felt a benumbed sensation in his right leg and foot, and on his arrival at home Dr. Asa Dorian was called to examine the limb and found a curious ailment. The foot had swelled to an abnormal size and innumerable blisters had arisen on the leg between the ankle and calf. He treated it and when the blisters were punctured Mr. Eldy had a little ease. The medical books do not describe the ailment

John H McMillan has taken charge of the outside yard labor as foreman, W R Ward having resigned

Mrs. W T Lamb, Mrs. W H Lawley and part of their families were here from Castle Valley to spend the holidays

Miss Addie Cowley of Cleveland is staying with Miss Rhea Ricks.

Benjamin Williams of Cleveland is in town. He is in poor health and came up to see old friends and see if a change of climate would be of any benefit to him

Price

SHORT STORIES.

George W Bodle has built a new stable and carriage shed at the Mathis House.

Pete Anderson is out again, after being under the weather for several days.

Miss Sarah Nielson has been appointed cook at White Rocks Indian agency at a salary of $500 per year.

The foundation for the Lowenstein store is well under way and the laying of brick will soon begin on the building proper.

The dance at Helper Monday night at Rooney's Hall was largely attended. Six or eight couples from Price were in attendance.

Noah Bartholomew will again take the Price and Vernal stage line and operate the same. Frank McCarthy has gone to Fort Duchesne.

J F Rath has rented the Hoffmann building next to The Advocate office and will hereafter conduct a short order restaurant there, moving from the McWilson property.

Chairman Nelson and County Attorney Hoffmann were in Salt Lake City this week negotiating the bond issue authorized by the board of county commissioners at its last meeting, and amounting to $1500.

Several couples went from Price up to Castle Gate to attend a wedding dance in the bowery there Sunday night, but when they arrived there was no dance and they were a very much disappointed crowd.

C. W. Spalding went over to Emery county the first of the week to see about a lot of sheep that he will ship to the Kansas City market about the 11th o' the month. There will be about fifteen cars in the lot

The 2 year old child of Section Foreman Atwood of Soldier Summit had its collar bone broken the other day by a box falling on it. Dr. Fisk of Helper dressed the fracture, and at last accounts the child was getting along nicely.

There are some forty five miners at work in the Sunnyside coal mines, but the force is not sufficient for the work in hand and Superintendent Forrester says he can put at least thirty five more men to work. He wants miners, however, and not laborers.

Robert McCune was down from Scofield the latter part of the week, where he has been taking orders for men's made-to-order clothing, and where business, he says, has been good with him for two or three weeks. He is representing a new house or two now, and has a fine line of samples to select from.

There are no new cases of scarlet fever in town, and the two reported last week are well under control of the physician in attendance, so that there is no danger of a spread of the disease.

"The Gilson Asphaltum company is shipping about a car load of its product a week," says Agent Arthur J Lee. "However, this output is likely to be increased at any time, as the demand for the material increases."

It is believed that this year will see the heaviest sheep shipment from the state of Idaho in its history. The Oregon Short Line has orders for over 800 double-deck stock cars for this traffic, nearly all being required for the Wood River branch, and the muttons being destined for Chicago.

It will be to the interest of anyone who desires good underclothing for grown people or children to come and examine our remnant outing flannels. We have just received a whole case. It costs nothing to examine, but you will surely buy. Emery County Mercantile company.

The Willow Creek branch of the Rio Grande Western is said to have been abandoned by the officers of the company, and if a line is built into the Vernal country, it will go in by way of Heber City. General Manager Dodge has lately been out over the Willow Creek branch and reported unfavorably on the proposition.

Tests of the coking coal discovered in the canyon to the east of Price by Robert Howard, Sheriff Allred, Tom Nichols, L. O Hoffmann and others have been made, and are most satisfactory. There are several veins of it, one of which is five feet in width. Some twenty five hundred acres have been located by the syndicate.

County Commissioner Dan Allen, who is also road commissioner to superintend the expenditure of Uintah's portion of the state appropriation for the repair of roads, has contracted for the delivery of the lumber and material for a new bridge across the Uintah at Fort Duchesne. Work upon the structure will commence in the near future.

The Advocate has received a letter from a gentleman at Ogden who is making inquiries as to the opening here for a photograph gallery. The field is a good one, and we have often wondered that it was not long since filled. If the gentleman comes he should bring along some double strength films, for there are faces here that would break down a six horse ore wagon in the middle of the street.

Joe Gavin, of the Colorado Midland freight department, was in Price for a couple of days last week loading the last of the wool for this year from this point. This consignment was captured by Paine & Lyne, of Salt Lake, and goes to Boston via the Rio Grande Western and Colorado Midland railroads. It was the clip of Louis Kabel of the Vernal country.

BIG FLOODS IN EMERY COUNTY.

Heavy Rains Prevail Throughout the Castle Valley Country,

STOPS RAILROAD TRAFFIC

Narrow Escape from Drowning of Milo Johnson of Price City.

WAS WASHED DOWN STREAM

With Horses and Wagon and Rescued with Difficulty—Was Dragged on the Bank by a Rope.

[SPECIAL TO THE "NEWS."]

Price, Utah, Aug. 4.—County Superintendent of Schools B. F. Luke of Emery county, and Milo E. Johnson, representing the Consolidated Wagon and Implement company of Price, had a very narrow escape from drowning on the road up from Emery county last night.

Heavy rains prevailed throughout Castle Valley all day yesterday. They were driving over from Orangeville and had reached Miller Creek, eight miles south of Price, which is a big dry wash, when a torrent of water came down upon them. The horses were completely inundated and were carried down the stream several hundred yards. The harness was cut loose and in trying to save the horses Mr. Johnson came near losing his life. He was thrown a rope by Mr. Luke and finally dragged out upon the bank.

STAGE AND TRAINS DELAYED.

The south stage with several passengers, due here at 8 o'clock last night, did not arrive until six o'clock this morning. A later rush of water than that detaining Luke and Johnson kept them out all night. There are a number of small washouts all along the line of the Rio Grande Western in the valley from Helper to Green River and beyond, and no trains ran through the night on the desert division.

The rain is falling heavy this morning and greater damage will no doubt result to railroad property, wagon roads and ditches.

PRICE.

Shipping Sheep—Asphaltum Shipments—Coal Miners Wanted—Scarlet Fever.

Special Correspondence.

Price, Carbon Co., Utah, Aug. 4.—C. W. Spaulding has gone to Emery county to drive into Price and other stations along the Rio Grande Western railroad fourteen car loads of sheep which he will market at Kansas City about the middle of the month. They were all raised in this part of Utah and brought in the neighborhood of $3.50 per head. Some will be loaded here about the 12th of the month.

ASPHALTUM SHIPMENTS.

President Baxter of the St. Louis Gilson Asphaltum company came in the other day from the East and left for the mines near Fort Duchesne, where he will look into the condition of the property generally. The company is at the present time shipping about five car loads of its product a month, but it is understood this will be increased in the near future to at least double this amount.

COAL MINERS WANTED.

Superintendent Robert Forrester of the Sunnyside coal mines is having considerable trouble in securing men to do the company's work in that camp. He now has some forty-five miners on the payroll, but could use as many more. He says, in explanation, however, that he wants coal miners and not laborers. The greater portion of the work is now done by contract and will continue to be until the railroad comes into the camp, which will be about the first of September.

H. G. Mathis, who was named by Governor Wells to superintend the expenditure of moneys on the Price and Vernal wagon road, has gone out with a force of men and will give the matter his entire attention now until the highways are put in first-class condition. His appointment is considered as good a one as the governor could have made. He is thoroughly honest and competent; there will not be a dollar thrown away out of the appropriation.

SCARLET FEVER UNDER CONTROL.

The epidemic of scarlet fever which threatened the city a short time ago is now considered a thing of the past. The case at the postoffice is well under quarantine, the premises having been most thoroughly disinfected, and there is no alarm to be considered from this source.

The 2-year-old child of Section Foreman Atwood of Soldier Summit had the left shoulder broken the other day by a box falling on it. Dr. Fisk of Helper dressed the fracture and the child is now getting along nicely.

Mr. Thomas Barton, a popular young business man of this city, where he has resided for several years, has gone to Mt. Pleasant, where he will make his home.

Several young people from this city attended the grand ball at Helper last Monday evening, the music coming from Leadville.

PRICE.

Vivid Description of Recent Terrific Rain and Hail Storm.

Special Correspondence:

Price, Utah, Aug. 7.—The oft repeated assertion that "hail fell as large as hens' eggs!" may be, and no doubt is in most cases a huge exaggeration. But after yesterday's terrible storm the citizens of this place are inclined to credit almost anything they hear of hailstorms. Some idea of the intensity of the downpour and the velocity of the wind can be conceived only when one views the destruction left in the trail of the storm. It was about 5½ miles in width and swept Carbon county from northwest to southeast. There is not a garden or in fact hardly any vegetation in Price that has not been totally destroyed. When the downpour started it came steadily for some time and then at intervals it seemed to come down in veritable bucketfulls. It didn't rain; it simply came down in unbroken streams! There seemed to be no prospects of intermission. It was interminable. About 4 o'clock yesterday afternoon one would have almost declared that all the aqua pura in the heavens was falling and that the foundation for a story calculated to completely eclipse the narrative of Noah and the ark was being laid.

"After rain comes sunshine" does not exactly fit the case here yesterday. After rain came hail which fell for more than half an hour. Whether or not it was an optical illusion is a matter for specialists to determine, but certain it is that the majority of the people here solemnly maintain that the hail was as large as hens' eggs.

In the track of the hailstorm oats have been greatly damaged. In some places the loss amounts to thousands of dollars.

Much damage was done in Emery county as the storm king raged fearfully there. From Vernal and Fort Duchesne come similar reports.

The alfalfa fields around Price are greatly damaged. Still other reports reach here that bridges are washed away and several people drowned. It is known that some bridges are missing, but little or no credence is placed in the death rumors.

Dr. W. P. Winters and Mr. Orange Seely did have a narrow escape from drowning, however, and this probably led to the starting of rumors.

These gentlemen made an attempt to drive over to Price from Castle Dale and when about two miles from here tried to drive over a deep washout that had been bridged. The bridge was not there. They were carried down the stream and finally lodged against a barbed wire fence. The buggy was lost likewise the horses and Dr. Winters lost a valuable set of surgical instruments.

The rains in the mountains have been exceedingly heavy and sheep owners have lost considerable. The Rio Grande Western trains are all late, a washing out of the grade in Whitmore canyon is reported. Word comes from Grand Junction that several engines are stopped there, that water tanks and pumping plants are washed away.

THE STORM'S RECORD.

The rain storms throughout Castle Valley for three or four days up to Monday last were the worst experienced for several years There was a very heavy downpour of rain at intervals of one to three hours during the day and night, accompanied by a terrific electrical display. Roads and bridges throughout this county, Emery and Uintah were in many instances washed out and there were several narrow escapes from drowning from swollen streams

Superintendent of Schools Luke and Milo Johnson were caught by the flood while trying to cross Miller Creek and came near losing their lives Their team and buggy was carried down stream a considerable distance, but they finally succeeded in reaching dry land in safety.

Orange Seeley and Dr Winters were coming in from Whitmore Canyon Sunday afternoon, and when try

Ben Stein is riding, or rather trying to ride, a new bike these days ing to cross a dry wash about two miles out were carried down stream, through or over a barbed wire fence and under a railroad culvert The doctor lost his case of surgical instruments, which he later recovered Mr. Seeley is short a pocketbook, containing valuable papers Both their horses were drowned and the buggy badly damaged

Freight train No 16, east bound, was ditched near Green River station Thursday night, and Engineer T. J McMahon and Fireman J. H. Whalen killed in the wreck There were no trains through here for two days or more, and many passengers were detained here in both directions

Considerable damage was done to growing crops of all kinds, and more especially by the hail storm of Sunday, which seemed to "have it in" for the gardens about town At Castle Gate and Helper there was some damage to the homes of those who live along the river banks

CASTLE GATE ITEMS.

Born, to the wife of John Hamel, a boy. Mother and child doing well

Last Thursday, while trying to jump over a steam heating pipe, Chas J. Carter slipped and fell on his left hand, fracturing the arm at the wrist.

E L. Carpenter, with a number of the Salt Lake educational board, was in town the other day, looking over the new stoker, with the object, if satisfactory, to put some in the schools of the city.

Extensive preparations are being made to welcome our four volunteers on their return They will be met at the depot by the entire population and escorted to the opera house, where they will be right royally entertained Castle Gate furnished five men for the Utah batteries, but one,

Corporal Chris Jensen, was killed near Manila.

Castle Gate citizens regret very much to hear of the accident to one of her soldier boys, Hans Sorensen, just when elaborate preparations are being made to give their townsmen a hearty reception on their return home

The committees are working in perfect harmony, and there is every reason to believe that Castle Gate will do herself proud in welcoming her volunteers It is to be hoped that Sorensen's injuries are not as serious as reported and that he will be here with the rest of the recruits

OLD FOLKS' REUNION.

The annual reunion of the old folks occurred at Cleveland on Wednesday evening of last week. The committee of arrangements appointed was composed of H H Oviatt, Jr, Lars P. Larsen, Sarah A. Cowley, Elroy Cowley, Chris Mortensen, Hy Bryson and Anton Crammer. This committee arranged a fine program and took great pains to see that every old person in town was provided with transportation to the hall. After a bounteous supper was served, the following program was rendered

Grand opening march	Led by the Old Folks
Opening remarks	Bishop L P Oveson
Song	H. E. Grenland
Stump speech	Hy Bryson
Song	Chris Mortensen
Remarks	Parian McFarlane
Song	Thomas N. Williams
Song	John W. Lewis and wife
Stump speech	A J Walton
Song	Thomas Richards and company
Stump speech	H H Oviatt, Jr
Step dancing	By all over 60 years
Recitation	Mrs Ollie Bryson
Song	Sarah Potter
Song	John P Davis
Song	Joseph Pringle

A very noticeable feature was the very few old people in the ward There was not a person over 75 years and only twenty-eight persons over 60 years of age

PERSONAL.

W C Brocker was down from Helper Monday evening

Mrs. Mary Shafer has gone to Ouray agency to remain some time

W E Taylor of Richfield was at the Hotel Clarke the first of the week

Mrs P Erickson of Murray was registered at the Hotel Clarke last Monday

W S Ashton of Vernal was in Price the other day going in to Salt Lake City

Orange Seeley and Dr Winters of Castle Dale were guests of the Hotel Clarke Sunday and Monday

Mrs E A Ireland of Salt Lake City was at the Mathis House during the fore part of the week

Mrs B R McBean and Master Holley have returned home from a protracted visit to Scofield

Bishop Hill of the Methodist church at Salt Lake City, was here yesterday en route home from Vernal.

J W Warf drove a party out to Vernal, leaving here this morning He will be absent about a week

Mrs H A Shaw and Mrs A Walker of Fort Duchesne were registered at the Mathis House during the week

Indian Agent Myton and Special Agent Harper were here Wednesday en route to the agency from Salt Lake City.

Tobe Whitmore has returned from a week's trip to Salt Lake City, accompanied by two of the junior Whitmores

Louis Smith has gone to Colorado, having become interested in a patent right for fixing bed springs He will work that territory.

Frank McCarthy came in from Fort Duchesne the first of the week and spread his John Hancock on the register at the Hotel Clarke

R J. Armstrong came in the other day from Bingham, nursing a sore hand, caused by a chunk of ore falling on him in a mine in which he was working

Charles O Walker, a surveyor from Colorado is here this week and thinks of locating in Price He is going into the hills for a while, but will return later

Joe Nougieur has returned from St. Mark's Hospital, and is at the home of Mrs Warren It will be some time, however, before he is able to look after his flocks

W. E. Banks, Sam Henry and B A Abel, who are selling buggies from an Iowa factory, are here this week and will try to dispose of several car loads of their goods

George W Feakins of the Great Rock Island Route was at the Clarke the fore part of the week, and returned to Salt Lake City Tuesday, after rounding up a number of shipments here.

SHORT STORIES.

Salt Lake s salt palace will be opened to the public on the 21st of the month.

The first watermelons of the season were received here yesterday by the Price Trading company.

C W. Spalding is still down in Emery county, getting his fourteen cars of sheep together for the Kansas City market.

Professor Hardy, the leader of the Emery Stake choir, has been engaged to give music lessons in the public schools of Emery county.

Billy Potter, Geo Callaway, Chub Millburn Jack Gentry and A. F. Redding made a short trip to Salt Lake City the first of the week.

The Carbon county teachers' institute will begin at Scofield the 28th of the month All teachers are required to attend, so announces County Superintendent Webb

Big crowds will go from Price, in fact all Eastern Utah, to Salt Lake City at the time the Utah volunteers come home The boys will arrive the 19th of the month

No civilians are allowed on the Fort Duchesne military reservation since the two incendiary fires there. The rule is very rigidly enforced by the commanding officer.

Messrs Ballinger and Whitmore have a deal on with Judge King for the sale of the Elgin group of claims in the Tintic mining district, and out of which they will get a considerable sum of money.

J. W. Burkhardt, a brakeman, had his leg broken at Farnham Monday evening while coupling Superintendent Welby's car on to a freight train He was taken to the hospital at Salt Lake City.

The Home Dramatic company has postpone the presentation of ' Joe, the Waif," until the evening of Tuesday, the 15th This is the last appearance of the Hutchinsons in Price, so they announce

The manure pile on the ground between town and the Mathis House is becoming very offensive and something should be done towards cleaning it up It is a disease breeder that should not long be permitted to exist.

The little child of Mr and Mrs Thomas Whalen fell down yesterday, cutting its tongue badly Dr Fred took several stitches in the injured member, putting the little one under the influence of ether, and at last accounts it was getting along nicely.

VOLUNTEERS' RECEPTION.

The good people up at Castle Gate are preparing to give the Carbon county volunteers such a reception as they have never had anywhere on their return home, the 20th of August, and every citizen of Price, in fact every precinct of the county, is invited to participate. There will be a grand parade of cavalry, floats, citizens on foot and the like, with the following program:

1—Address of Welcome,   W L Lamph
2—Inst. Music The Volunteers' Favorite,   Band
3—Song—The Old Brigade,.   W S Jones
4—Address—One Flag   Joel Ricks
5—Selection. ..   Prof Bartot's Orchestra
6—Song—The Vacant Chair,   Reese Quartette
7—Address—Our Dead Heroes.   David Crow
8—Duet—Violin and Flute,
    Prof Bartot and T G Reese
9—Song—Just As the Sun Went Down.
    ..   Ed Edwards
10—Address—The Army and Navy . ...
    H. A Nelson
11 Musical Selec.   Prof. Bartot's Orchestra
12 Song and Chorus—Star Spangled Banner,
    Reese Quartette
3—Address—The Volunteers,   H Y Caffey
14—Piano Solo   Prof Bartot
3—Closing Ode—"America".   All Present

After the exercises, which will be held at Knights of Pythias Hall, there will be a banquet spread for everybody in attendance. In the evening there will be a moonlight dance at the Bowery and a ball in the hall

The committee in charge of the affair and of which Billy Donaldson is chairman, is anxious that a cavalry company attend from Price. There will be no charge for feed for man or beast.

An attraction, and one that should draw a good crowd if nothing else will, is that beer will be five cents, all day and evening, and will be served both day and evening at Caffey's and at the Bowery.

Today's Salt Lake papers state that the Utah volunteers will arrive home on the morning of the 19th of August

Robert McKune is in Castle Gate, taking orders for clothing and will most likely remain until after the big reception to the returning soldier boys.

One of the little girls of Mr. and Mrs L M Olsen is sick of scarlet fever. This is the third case so far, but the other two are almost convalescent.

Dr Allen was down from Provo today, called here to see Mrs J M Whitmore, in consultation with Dr. Fisk of Helper. Mrs Whitmore is a very sick woman, so her friends believe

Trains are again running on time, with the exception of the noon passenger from the west which is more or less delayed by reason of the Southern Pacific not being on time at Ogden

Private William S Carter, who shot and killed Jack Thomas out on the Strip a few months ago, murdered Sergeant Jackson at Salt Lake City, Tuesday. Carter was pursued by almost the entire troop and shot down. The trouble grew out of an old grudge between the troopers of long standing

Salt Lake Herald
August 13, 1899

CASTLEGATE NEWS.

Several Accidents In This Live Coal Camp.

(Special Correspondence.)

Castlegate, Aug. 11.—This morning John ly bruised. Bartot is leading musician in ing coal, caught his right arm between two cars, the member being very serious. Bartot, while working at the Tipple dump, the coming reception to the volunteers.

George Cheshire, who is employed driving a team, came near getting his left leg broken this morning. As it is he will be laid up with a bruised ankle for several days.

Mrs. B. Marsing is slowly recovering, although she is not considered entirely out of danger.

Mrs. F. Latour is also very ill.

Dominic Preecco, an Italian miner, while at work this morning was badly hurt by a fall of coal, very severe injuries being sustained on the lower part of his body. Drs. Asadorian and Caffey waited on him and dressed his wounds. It appears that Preecco had tried to liberate the coal but failed, and when he got under it to mine it further, about a ton of it came down upon him. He is a married man but his family is in the old country.

The I. O. O. F. will organize a lodge here today. Some of the prominent men of the lodge are here to initiate about sixity aspirants into the secrets of the order. After the ceremonies a grand lunch will be served and the rest of the evening will be given over to fraternal greetings.

Deseret Evening News
August 14, 1899

PRICE.

Scarlet Fever Cases—Welcome to Volunteers—Burglary—Shipping Sheep.

Special Correspondence.

Price, Carbon County, Aug. 12.—Mrs. J. M. Whitmore, who has been at the point of death for several days with pneumonia and a complication of diseases, has rallied and there are now strong hopes by her family of her recovery.

SCARLET FEVER.

Price has now the third case of scarlet fever, but the disease is well quarantined by the city physician, Dr. C. H. Field, and there is thought to be no further danger of its spreading. Several citizens have sent their children out of town to avoid contagion.

Roy Gibson, for some time manager of the Western Union telegraph office in this city, has resigned his position to go with the Pleasant Valley Coal company at Sunnyside, the new camp in Whitmore canyon, as clerk to Superintendent Robert Forrester.

Mr. and Mrs. F. S. Leuthel, who have resided at Vernal for several years, where Mr. Leuthel has been county attorney for two terms, passed through here yesterday evening for Wichita, Kan., where they will reside in future.

WELCOME TO VOLUNTEERS.

Almost the entire town of Price will go up to Castle Gate next Monday where there is to be a grand reception to the returning Carbon county volunteers. There will be a literary and musical program, a big parade, and dancing in the bowery and in the Knights of Pythias hall in the evening.

PRINTING OFFICE BURGLARIZED.

The Advocate office was burglarized Saturday night by a tramp printer who had come along and worked for a few days. Entrance was effected through a rear door and the cash drawer broken open with a hatchet. A warrant was sworn out for the fellow, Guthrie by name, and Sheriff Allred is now out looking for the man. He was at Helper after the burglary, but escaped from Editor Crockett, who followed him and had him in charge, but there was no officer to be found, and he showed "the hot foot." Five shots were fired at him and one of the bullets from the editor's forty-five reduced the length of the fellow's coat tail about four inches. Guthrie also entered the office of Dr. Field, late of Ephraim, and stole a few dollars therefrom.

SHIPPING SHEEP.

The shipment of fourteen cars of sheep of C. W. Spalding, which were picked up in Emery and Carbon counties, were loaded on the cars at Mounds station and at Colton yesterday, and are now en route to the Kansas City market. Mr. Spaulding accompanied the shipment in person. There are a number of sheep buyers in this section, but the prices are ranging high and there are few changing hands to be put on the market. Some breeders are changing hands at a good figure.

The honey crop of Uintah and Emery counties has begun to move and one or two consignments for the East have already arrived here. William Roylance of Springville has an agent in both territories and will handle the biggest part of the two crops.

Salt Lake Herald
August 25, 1899

Castlegate's Volunteers.

(Special Correspondence.)

Castlegate, Aug. 23.—The reception held in honor of the four volunteers was in every respect a magnificent affair. The whole town turned out and about 200 visitors came in from the nearby settlements. The boys were met at the depot by the Uniform Rank, Knights of Pythias, Societi de Napoli, the I. O. O. F., school children and citizens. There was a great handshaking, and after that the parade was got into order by the marshal of the day, W. H. Donaldson, one of Captain Caine's troop. After parading the principal streets of the town, they stopped at the Knights of Pythias hall, where a programme was rendered, but owing to the immense crowd it was partly held on the outside. This detracted somewhat from the instrumental pieces on string instruments. After these exercises were over, a splendid banquet was served in the Latter-day Saints' church and in the district school house. In the evening there were dances held both in the bowery and in the hall.

Man Badly Hurt.

(Special Correspondence.)

Castlegate, Aug. 25.—This morning about 11:30, old man Reese, who is the supervisor of the sanitary department of this place, while going to the stables on his cart, met with a very severe and painful accident. The horse that was in the cart was a fractious one, and when going down the incline leading to the bridge crossing the river, it bolted. This un- balanced the driver and overturned the cart, pulling the old man about a hundred feet. When rescued it was found that he had several bad cuts on his head. One gash over his eye was a fearful one and required several stitches. Mr. Reese has been very unfortunate in being many times injured.

Many of the visitors who came to receive the volunteers are returning home.

Mrs. F. Latour was taken to the hospital in the city last evening.

Deseret Evening News
August 30, 1899

PRICE.

Grand Festival and Banquet in Honor of the Old Folks.

Special Correspondence.

Price Carbon Co., Aug. 30.—The old folks of Price and Carbon county are to have a day here next Friday, and nothing is to be spared by those having the affair in charge to make the day a pleasant one and one long to be remembered by those who attend the gathering. The work is in charge of various committees. Dinner will be served at 1 o'clock in the afternoon, to which all people over the age of 55 years will be seated. The old folks will be expected to assemble at the town hall at 10 o'clock in the morning and at which time the following program will be rendered.

Singing ....The Choir
Prayer ....Elder Heath
Singing ....The Choir
Address of Welcome, Bp. E. S. Horsley
Song...............................Geo. Downard
Speech ....Jens Peterson
Speech ....Monroe Allred
Song...............................Chas. W. Grames
Speech ....Ulrich Bryner
Speech ....N. L. Marsing
Speech ....Caleb Rhoads
Singing ....The Choir
Benediction ....E. W. McIntire

All persons over 14 years of age are invited to attend. There will be plenty to eat for all, and a general good time is promised all who may attend not only from this county but anywhere in the State, and Castle Valley in particular.

SHORT STORIES.

There has been an unusually large number of freighters in town this week.

Fresh fish and and oysters are b ing served to the patrons of the restaurants these days.

The new lunch room at Helper will be rea ly for occupancy the first of the week or thereabouts.

A. F. Redding, the butcher, has gone to Scofield, where he is working in the mines temporarily.

The Helper League Club is to give a big ball next Monday night at Rooney s Hall to which everybody is invited

M. E Johnson, the impliment man, is carrying around a bruised foot, the result of a horse having stepped on it.

There is talk among some of th y young people of the town of the organization of a social club to give two or three dances a month.

The foundation for the new chapel at Helper is about complete and work will begin on the building proper in a few days now

Doc Shores, of the Rio Grande Western special service, was sleuthing around town today. His business here he declined to divulge.

Dr. G. H. Keysor, the dentist from Salt Lake City, is at the Hotel Clarke and will remain until th 4th of Septem ber, so he advertises

Price public schools begin next Monday week.

The teachers in attendance upon the institute at Scofield will be given a banquet at the Union Pacific hotel there tonight.

State Land Commissioners McFarlane and Reese have gone out to Uintah county, passing through here the other day, to inspect state lands.

Charley Taylor has been busy the greater part of the week buying up cavalry horses to be shipped to California He has gotten hold of some good stock in Castle Valley.

J. H. Mease has sold his tradership business at White Rocks agency to A Q Bowen of Vernal. Mr. Mease contemplates giving most of his attention to the sheep business.

Lars Frandsen is stepping a little higher these days, the cause thereof being the arrival at his home the other day of a pretty girl baby. Mother and child are getting along nicely.

The Carbon County Teachers Institute convened at Scofield last Tuesday. The attendance is said to be most gratifying to Superintendent Webb and others directly interested.

Full line of legal blanks at the Advocate office at Provo and Salt Lake City prices Nearly two hundred different forms to select from. Orders by mail promptly attended to

There is a bran new baby boy at the home of Mr. and Mrs George G. Frandsen, of the regulation weight and a splendid pair of lungs. Georga isn't saying much, but nevertheless is stepping around with his head up and a smile as broad as the republican policy of expansion

The baby of Mr. and Mrs L M Olson which has been quite ill for several days, is now considered out of danger by the attending physician, Dr Field

The roof of the Lowenstein building is going on this week. As soon as enclosed work will begin on the interior, which will be finished up in elegant style

Arthur Hunter will go to work for Price Trading company in about two weeks, as soon as he has given the railroad company the requisite two weeks notice.

Attorney Braffett is considering the erection of a brick building which he will occupy as an office building. He has not yet decided on the ground, having several locations in view.

There will be a grand ball at Helper next Monday night, Labor Day, and to which Price people in general are invited. There will, no doubt, be a big crowd up from here.

Last week there was a general advance in the retail price of flour at Salt Lake City of from 10 to 15 cents the 100 pounds. When the mills begin to grind on new flour in a month or two prices are expected to come down

Heber Garff of Draper has been engaged as principal of the Vernal public schools. N. G Sewards, the former principal, will assume charge of the Merrill Ward schools as principal

Louis Kabell, the Vernal sheep and wool grower, has sold his herds to James Powers for twenty thousand dollars. Seven thousand head of sheep were transferred, the price being $2.75 per head. The delivery is to be made the 10th of September.

The grade of the branch road up Whitmore Canyon has almost reached Sunnyside camp and work is being rapidly pushed looking towards its early completion. The sooner the road is finished the quicker will substantial improvements begin in the camp

The Johnson family has been having a reunion at Huntington. The elder Johnson, father of M E Johnson, came to the country in 1857, but is now a resident of Grand county. Last Monday night there were 180 of his descendants at the home of M E Johnson, some being from as far as Oregon. The main gathering will be next Tuesday, however. Last Sunday night there was an informal meeting at the home of John Wakefield of Huntington and at which time there was a hundred, more or less, present.

PERSONAL.

Mrs. William Potter is in Salt Lake City.

Mrs. A. E. Gibson of Cleveland is visiting Mrs. Roy Gibson.

Judge Jacob Johnson was registered at the Hotel Clarke yesterday.

Miss Addie Cowley of Cleveland is visiting with relatives at Castle Gate.

Roy Gibson is expected in from Sunnyside for a few days about the 10th of the month.

Miss Mary Leonard is expected home tomorrow from the teacher's institute at Scofield.

R J Armstrong came in this morning from Denver, but will depart soon for Deadwood, S D

M M Riley of Moab came down from Salt Lake City last night and will be in town for a few days.

Mrs. Thomas Fitzgerald and babies are at home again from a visit of several weeks in Emery county.

William H. Price of Scofield was down during the week on business and registered at the Hotel Clarke.

Miss Emma Bodle of Salt Lake City is the guest of Mr. and Mrs. G. W. Bodle at the Mathis House.

N. Turner, one of the returning volunteers from Heber City, is in town visiting with friends and acquaintances.

Dr. Fell went up to Salt Lake the first of the week to meet his wife and will return home tomorrow evening.

G. T. Olson, the Emery merchant and stock grower, was in town today and will be here the balance of the week.

Colonel Casseday, the insurance man, was in town yesterday and will go down to Emery county before returning to Zion.

Miss Annie Larsen has returned from a ten days visit with friends and relatives at Ephraim, Cleveland and elsewhere.

J. W. Seely, Joseph F. Dorius J. W. Nelson and Ira R. Browning were among the Castle Dale people at the Clarke Hotel during the week.

Mrs E S Horsley is expected home this week from St. George, where she has been since may last at the bedside of her father, who has been at death's door He is sufficiently improved to permit of her returning home, which will be welcome news to the many friends of the family.

MRS. J. M. WHITMORE DEAD.

Wife of Prominent Price Merchant Passes Away—Almost a Tragedy.

(Special to The Herald.)

Price, Utah, Sept. 1.—Hannah Nixon Whitmore, wife of J. M. Whitmore, manager of the Price Trading company, passed away at 2 o'clock this morning. Deceased had been at the point of death for three weeks from pneumonia and a complication of diseases, two physicians, Dr. Allen of Provo and Dr. Fisk of Helper, being in almost constant attendance night and day. The funeral services will be held from the family residence tomorrow afternoon, and the remains are to be laid to rest in the private burying ground of the family at the home, which adjoins the city on the west. Bishop E. S. Horsley will conduct the funeral.

The deceased was born in Salt Lake City, Oct. 22, 1864, and was in her 35th year. She was the daughter of James Nixon, one of the old families of Utah, that first settled at St. George, in Washington county, and where most of her relatives, including her mother, now reside.

She was married to Mr. Whitmore about fourteen years ago, and they came to Castle valley and made a home. Of the union there have been seven children born, six of whom are living, the youngest being some 2 years of age. At her bedside when death came were her mother and children, husband and several near relatives.

Out of respect to the memory of Mrs. Whitmore the Old Folks' reunion and picnic, which was to have been held today, has been indefinitely postponed.

The late Mrs. Whitmore was a true Christian woman, and her death has filled many a household with sorrow.

After the death of Mrs. Whitmore and while friends were preparing the body an accident occurred that came near ending the life of Mrs. George W. Bodle, a sister of the deceased. Worn out with sitting up, the lady took from the dining room table a bottle that she supposed contained alcohol and swallowed a teaspoonful for a stimulant. It contained a deadly poison, and had been used as a lotion in the sick chamber. Dr. F. F. Fisk of Helper had remained during the night and had it not been for his presence Mrs. Bodle would have died before medical attention could have reached her.

The doctor gave it as his opinion that there was enough poison in the draught taken to have killed half a dozen people.

PRICE.

White Rock Agency Indian School—Interesting Carbon County News.

Special Correspondence.

Price, Carbon Co., Sept. 4.—The Uintah Indian boarding school at White Rocks agency opened today for the fall term. The attendance was as light as usual although the commissioner of Indian affairs had directed that a general round-up of the children on the reservation be made by the Indian police and school and Indian agent authorities. There are some 200 children on the reservation of school age, but heretofore not more than one-fourth of this number has attended the boarding school. The opposition among the Indian parents is due to the fact that in previous years a great number of children have died at the school, and the older ones of the tribe say the teachers and school authorities give the little ones "bad medicine," which takes them away. The school building has cost the government in the neighborhood of $40,000 and an appropriation of something like $15,000 a year is necessary to keep the school going for the school year.

Prof. J. W. Nixon, principal of the Huntington schools, left for home today, after attending the funeral of his sister, Mrs. J. W. Whitmore, which occurred here yesterday. He was accompanied home by his mother, Mrs. James Nixon of St. George, Washington county, who will remain there with her son and family for some time. Mrs. J. W. Foote, of Salt Lake City, a sister of the deceased, returned home this morning, accompanied by her husband who came in Saturday to be present at the funeral.

The Rio Grande Western railroad has made an exceptionally low rate from Carbon county points to Grand Junction, Fruit Day, and it is more than likely that there will be a big crowd on that occasion from along the line in eastern Utah. The round trip rate as announced is Price, $5; Helper, $5.50; Castle Gate, $7; and Scofield and Colton, $8.

FUNERAL OF HEBER THOMPSON.

The funeral services over the remains of Heber Thompson, who died at Spring

Eastern Utah Advocate
September 7, 1899

Members of the town board who prate about patronizing home industry give the contract for the town printing to an out of town concern, when it could have been done at home for less. A little criticism of some people has the effect of puncturing the cuticle

Daddy Jones and George Frandsen, it is said, came almost to personal blows at the meeting of the town board Tuesday night over the proposition of the town buying the scenery of the Sunday school now in the hall ' Fight dog, fight bear, nary a dog of ours there "

There is the best opening here in Price for a harnessmaker and a shoemaker of any small town in the West. Why one or both have not long since located here is a mystery that no one can explain.

With the new scenery that has lately been put in at Town Hall, Price should this winter be able to book some of the good traveling theatrical companies that play the other towns of the state.

As town clerk Hoffmann sends to Provo for blanks for the use of the town when he could obtain them at home for the same price, and save the express charges from Provo Mr. Hoffmann gets his living out of Price town and from Carbon county.

The Advocate bid $1 per page for the printing of the town ordinances in book form and agreed to duplicate the sample submitted. The Skelton company bid ninety-six cents per page and got the job. When the town pays the express on the work from Provo to Price, it will have cost more than if done at home. Town Clerk Hoffmann, who doesn't like

The Advocate, couldn't resist the temptation to throw a slur at "the great moral and religious" in the minutes of the record by saying something about the Provo firm being the "most responsible," or words to that effect. The Provo firm gets about two dollars less than The Advocate bid. Great saving, this.

HOME MISSIONARIES.

Following is a list of the missionaries of Emery Stake of Zion, appointed to visit the wards of the stake on the dates named

Peter Christensen and Thomas A. Williams—Molen July 30, Ferron August 27, Orangeville September 24

Samuel A. Williams jr and Nuel Beal-Ferron September 10, Molen September 24

B. M V. Goold and Andrew P. Nielson—Wellington July 30, Spring Glen August 13, Castle Gate August 27,

Lars P Larsen and John J. Thordarson—Castle Gate July 30, Spring Glen September 10, Wellington August 27,

J. W. Seely and Abanadi Olsen—Huntington August 27, Price September 10, Wellington September 24,

John Peterson and Jacob Sorensen—Cleveland August 13, Desert Lake September 10, Emery September 24

O. J Anderson and Boye P. Peterson—Desert Lake August 13, Emery August 27, Ferron September 24,

J. Fleming Wakefield and William Howard—Desert Lake July 30, Price August 13, Castle Gate September 10.

Joseph E Johnson and Peter Nielson—Orangeville July 30, Price August 27, Castle Dale September 10, Castle Gate September 24.

John Oliphant and Allen Cox—Price July 30, Wellington August 13, Cleveland August 27, Spring Glen September 10

L. M Olsen and Chris Peterson—Spring Glen July 30, Castle Gate August 13, Desert Lake August 27 Wellington September 10.

George W. Stevens and Hans P. Rasmussen, Jr—Emery July 30; Orangeville August 13 Castle Dale August 27, Lawrence September 24

M. A. Cox and J. D Killpack, Sr—Huntington July 30, Emery August 13, Orangeville August 27, Castle Dale September 24.

John Zwellen and John H. Cook—Castle Dale July 30, Huntington August 13, Emery August 27, Orangeville September 10.

Christian Peterson and John Pearson—Ferron July 30, Molen August 13, Lawrence August 27, Cleveland September 10.

Joseph H. Taylor and Christian G. Larson, Jr.—Lawrence July 30, Ferron August 13, Molen August 27, Huntington September 10

TRUSTEES' MEETING.

The town trustees met in regular session Tuesday evening, Monday being a legal holiday. All were present but Erastus Anderson.

The reports of Town Clerk Hoffmann and Judge Holdaway were read and approved, with the exception of 20 cents in the accounts of the latter, for taking bail in the case of John Doe, James Castle.

The report of City Marshal Anderson for the month of August showed receipts from sale of estrays of $3 50, which was approved.

Town Clerk Hoffmann reported that he had on the 5th day of August, 1899 posted the revised ordinances at three public places in Price town, to-wit, in front of the postoffice, in front of the town hall and in front of Price Trading company's store It was thereupon ordered by the president and the board of trustees of Price town that due and legal notice and publication of the revised ordinances of Price town had been given, said ordinances having been posted for a period of twenty days as required by law

Bids for printing the revised ordinances of Price town were received. The bid of R W Crockett at $1 per page and the bid of the Skelton company at 96 cents per page were opened. "The Skelton company being the lowest and most responsible bidder," it was ordered that they be awarded the contract.

The following accounts were presented and allowed by the board.

Joseph Jones, janitor and labor . .$14 00
J M Hutchinson, painting roof town hall
                                     $19.50
L O Hoffmann salary as town attorney.. 25 00
W M Allred, burning carcasses .   5 00
C W Allred feeding prisoners   ... 100
J C Berglund, work on city hall stage.. 8 00
Peter Anderson, salary etc   . 45.50
L O Hoffmann health books and blanks., 27 85
W A Thayn, surveying cemetery   14.50
Emery County Mer Co., supplies town hall 12.43

Albert Bryner was present with a proposition to sell the scenery in the town hall, belonging to the Sunday school, to the town for $100. The matter was laid over until the next regular meeting

Dr. C. H. Field, Seren Olson and Joseph Jones were appointed on the town health board. Dr. Field becomes city physician.

Price

PERSONAL.

F. F. Woods of Castle Dale was in town Monday.

Mr. and Mrs Sam Whitmore have returned to Salt Lake City.

Mr. and Mrs. George C. Whitmore have returned to Nephi.

Mr. and Mrs J W. Foote returned to Salt Lake City Sunday morning last.

Dr. C. H Field returned Friday morning from a short trip to Salt Lake City

Mrs C. W. Spalling visited with friends at Salt Lake City during the week.

The Misses Holdaway are at home from a few weeks' visit with friends and relatives at Springville.

Mr. and Mrs. B A. Van Duine of Vernal were guests of the Hotel Clark the first of the week.

Mrs. James Rooney has returned to her home at Helper after a short visit with her mother here.

Mrs Robert Howard left yesterday for a few weeks visit with friends and relatives in Salt Lake City.

R. A. Kirker came in the other day after several days absence and is quartered at the Mathis House.

Miss May Smith of Beaver was at the Mathis House the first of the week en route to the Vernal section.

Miss Dora Burton of Vernal was registered at the Mathis Hotel the other day en route to Salt Lake City.

Miss Lillie Kinder of Huntington was at the Mathis House the first of the week going to Salt Lake City.

Miss Mary Leonard has returned from her vacation in California, and says she never had a more delightful trip.

S. P. Snow of Orangeville was here the first of the week and spread his name across the register at the Hotel Clarke.

Miss Emma Bodle has returned to Salt Lake City after a pleasant visit of several days with relatives in this city.

Sergeant William Thornton came in from Fort Duchesne yesterday and was shaking hands with old friends here today.

Mr and Mrs George C. Whitmore come in Saturday from Nephi to attend the funeral of the late Mrs. J. M. Whitmore.

Miss T. M. Zielke, of Detroit, Mich, was here the first of the week, en route to Fort Duchesne where she goes to teach school.

H P Myton came in yesterday from White Rocks agency with his son, the latter being on his way to Denver to attend school.

Mrs Annie Kimber of Castle Gate, who has been the guest of Mrs Robert Howard for several days, returned home Monday evening.

J. P. Rudy, principal of the Vernal public schools, was here the first of the week, registered at the Hotel Clarke, having come in from the north

Mrs James Nixon departed Sunday for Huntington, where she will visit with her son, Prof. J. W. Nixon, for some time before returning to her home at St. George.

Miss Sadie Kimball, teacher in the public schools, is expected to arrive here from Scofield the latter part of the week. Miss Johnson will come in from Springville Saturday next.

Mr. and Mrs. George W. Bodle went over to Huntington yesterday to bring Mrs. James Nixon, Mrs. Bodle's mother, home from there, where she has been visiting for a few days.

Mr. and Mrs. Louis Lowenstein left Sunday evening for Salt Lake City, accompanied by Miss Ella and Master Sherman. Mr. Lowenstein will buy a big stock of new goods and the folks will visit with friends while absent.

William Ashton of Vernal was in the city the first of the week, accompanied by his daughters, Misses Ethel and Hazel, the former being en route to Salt Lake City, where she will attend St Mary's Academy. They registered at Hotel Clarke.

Deseret Evening News
September 7, 1899

PRICE.

Train Load of Fine Sheep Sent to Kansas City—Harness Maker Wanted.

Special Correspondence.

Price, Carbon County, Sept. 7.—Austin and Webb yesterday loaded at Colton sixteen car loads of sheep, making up an entire train of fine wethers, which were last night sent out to the Kansas City market. The mutton was picked up in Utah, Carbon and Emery counties and in Sanpete. It was a fine lot, and it is expected will bring the top of the market.

R. R. IMPROVEMENTS.

The Rio Grande Western railway is taking the split switches out of the yards here and replacing the same with more modern ones. There have been a number of accidents by reason of the split switches and it is to guard against these that the change is being made.

The Western is preparing to haul an unusually large amount of coal in the near future, and it is said the output from the Castle Gate and Scofield mines will amount to fully two hundred cars a day when a sufficient number of miners can be secured and for which the coal company is now advertising. There will be a big output from the Sunnyside mines as soon as the branch road is completed up there,

which will be in about two to three weeks hence.

John D. Boyd, for a long time resident of the Nine Mile section, has sent his family to Eureka, and he himself will go down to Arizona to work in the mines and prospect during the winter.

HARNESS MAKER WANTED.

Price offers a splendid opening for a harness maker and a shoe maker as well. Anyone who can combine the two is assured of a splendid business here. There is a great deal of harness repairing on account of the large number of freighters in and out of the town to Emery county and to the Ashley valley to the east.

President Reuben C. Miller has the poles all up for his eleven miles of private telephone line to his ranch, southwest of the city, and he will this week begin the stringing of the wires and put in the instruments.

Indian Agent Myton was here today with his son, en route to Salt Lake City, where Mr. Myton goes on business, and will send his son on to Denver to attend school.

Farmers throughout the Castle valley are busy now putting up their second crop of lucern and gathering in their wheat and oats, all of which are good crops.

PRICE.

Giant Powder Accident—Honey Shipments —Schools Opened—Coal Output.

Special Correspondence.

Price, Carbon Co., Sept. 11.—There came near being a frightful accident to record at [ ] per the other day. The parents of [ ] harley and Nella Johnson went away from home, leaving the boy, aged about 15 years, and the little girl, some two years younger, in charge of the house. They went to the cellar where there had been left a quantity of giant powder. They filled up an old iron pipe with the explosive, which, according to program, in such cases had to go off. Charley is short a big chunk of flesh from his left leg and foot, while the little girl was badly burned and bruised on the right side of her body and feet. When the quantity is taken into consideration, it looks as if only a kind Providence came to their rescue.

BIG SHIPMENTS OF HONEY.

The first car of strained honey from Ashley Valley was shipped out from here to the Chicago market yesterday by William M. Roylance of Springville. There are about nine more cars to be handled from that section, to say nothing about a large amount that will be shipped in the comb. The Emery county product has not as yet began to move, but some of it will be in during the coming two weeks. Mr. Roylance will get the most of this also.

The Price public schools opened for the fall and winter terms today, and the attendance will this year be the largest ever recorded in the history of the district.

COAL OUTPUT.

The Pleasant Valley Coal company is working all of its mines in Carbon county at full capacity, and the output the balance of the year will be the largest ever known. The company is having considerable trouble in getting a sufficient force of miners and at the present time want two hundred or more at Scofield, Castle Gate, Winter Quarters and Clear Creek.

The dipping pens at Colton have so far this fall put through the pens over 50,000 head of sheep and fully as many more are booked.

PRICE.

Medals for Volunteers — Indian School Children—Scofield Town Ordinances.

Price, Carbon County, Utah, Sept. 12. —Carbon county is to present her returning volunteers from the Philippines with medals, and the event is to occur at Castle Gate next Saturday evening if all goes well. There were seven of the boys from here, but one of them, Charles Jensen, never returned, having been killed in battle. His medal will be sent to his aged mother who lives in Denmark.

PUSHING R. R. WORK.

The graders who were lately taken off the Sunnyside branch of the Rio Grande Western to work on the Heber City line, will be returned in a few days and the road pushed to completion by the 16th of the present month.

INDIAN SCHOOL CHILDREN.

Reports from the Uintah and Uncompahgre reservations are to the effect that not much headway is being made in rounding up the Indian children and in getting them to the boarding schools at White Rocks and Ouray agencies, and it is thought Indian Agent Myton will yet find it necessary to cut off rations from the parents of children if he is to get them in. The Indian police are now scouring the country after the children under instructions from the Indian agent.

TOWN ORDINANCES OF SCOFIELD.

The town council of Scofield has adopted a new set of ordinances which will be printed in book form and will go into effect within the next thirty days. Titles to lots in the cemetery which have heretofore been clouded will be cleared up by one of the new ordinances which will prove a source of great satisfaction to many residents there.

CASTLE GATE.

Entertainment Given by Primary Association—Young Ladies Organize.

Special Correspondence.

Castle Gate, Carbon Co., Sept. 12.—A delightful entertainment was given last evening by the Primary association of this place, consisting of speeches, songs, duets, dialogues and recitations, all of which were creditably rendered. The song of Miss Vera Evans, only 10 years old, was a most meritorious effort, so also was the singing of Miss Mary Kimber. The people turned out in goodly numbers, and a dance finished up a well spent evening. The McDermaid-Harsel orchestra furnished music for the dance, this being their first venture in that respect, and they did well.

The young ladies of the ward meet tonight to organize themselves into an association.

The wife of Jas. Tedesco presented her husband with a baby boy. All doing well.

CASTLE DALE.

Serious Mishap — Freighter Thrown from Wagon and Severely Injured.

Castle Dale, Emery County, Sept. 12. —A very serious accident, which may prove fatal, took place here last night. A man by the name of Dalton, from Emery, just coming into town with a load of freight, was thrown from his wagon, the wheels passing over his thigh and hip, cutting a gash about six inches long on the inside of his thigh just below the joint, and it is feared he is also injured internally. His team left him and went to Orange Seely's stable, where it was found and cared for. Not knowing where the man was he was left in the street from nine o'clock in the evening until eight next morning perfectly helpless. He has a wife and three children at Emery.

Eastern Utah Advocate
September 14, 1899

Our county commissioners should make some change in the county road where the railroad runs through the cut in Spring Glen. It is the most dangerous crossing imaginable, no view being afforded to either trainmen or teamsters for a distance of over twenty five feet. Land is not so valuable in the vicinity of Spring Glen but that some change may be affected which will lessen the danger incident to the present crossing.

In The Advocate of the 24th of August this paragraph appeared. Last Thursday Mrs. Sarah Pratt and five children, who were driving from Price to Helper, were caught at the point indicated, by passenger train No. 3, which was running two hours late. Both horses were killed outright, and after the accident they were picked up by the train and taken to Helper. Neither the woman or any of the five small children were hurt which was most remarkable. The train did not whistle for the crossing. Ten dollars would change the road to run under the railroad track. This is only one of many accidents that have occurred at this point, to say nothing of many narrow escapes.

Price

SHORT STORIES.

County Treasurer Bryner is this week busy sending out tax notices. Taxes become delinquent on the 16th of November.

A. T. Ogren of Salt Lake City was here today, getting data together for the forthcoming edition of Polk's Utah Gazetteer.

Attorney Braffett has this week filed over fifty new suits in the the justices and district courts of Eastern Utah counties.

Price public schools opened Monday with about one hundred scholars in attendance, a very large enrollment for the first day.

Christensen's band from Castilla Springs was here today advertising that resort, and especially the attractions booked there for Saturday next.

About 50,000 head of sheep have so far been dipped at the pens of J. M. Miller at Colton and fully as many more are to go through.

The Advocate is getting out a handsome register for the Mathis Hotel Also one for the Rio Grande Western eating house at Helper.

The Advocate added several new names to its subscription list at Scofield last week. They can't do without "the great moral and religious in the great coal camp."

Price trading company will build a brick building on the ground to the west of their store, where the office of Dr. Field now stands, 20x24 feet, work upon which will begin in the near future.

The Carbon county volunteers will be given medals at Castle Gate Saturday evening next. There will be literary and musical exercises and dancing at the Knights of Pythias hall and at the Bowery.

Judge McConnell went through here Sunday for Meeker, Colo., to look up the titles to the asphaltum property for which he has a deal on with the Joe Leiter crowd, and which will go through for about $125,000 when the abstracts are satisfactory.

Charley Johnson, aged 15 years, and his little sister, Nelia, some two years younger, were left at home by their parents at Helper, last Thursday. They got into the cellar where there was a lot of giant powder. They filled up a piece of iron pipe with the explosive and began to have a real good time, as it were The powder went off so did a piece of the left leg of the boy and a portion of the right ankle of the little girl They were not seriously injured, however.

James H Heath this week found in the hills to the north of Price the greater portion of the tooth of some prehistoric monster, which he nor none of his friends can make out what it is or was He will likely send it to Salt Lake City. It is an inch or more in width and about three inches in length.

So successful has the Rio Grande Western dining car service been proved that the company has ordered another car. The Denver & Rio Grande has also ordered an additional diner, which will make eight in the service between Ogden and Denver. The Western had the biggest summer in its history for passenger travel and this helped the dining car service. The cars are being well conducted, however, which is the best drawing card of all and has made a reputation for the service.

Salt Lake City's Tribune of Sunday says "All the laborers and trackmen on the Rio Grande Western have been centered on the Heber line. Mile post 18 was passed Friday night, and the line it is now said, will be in operation not later than September 10. Tracklaying on the Sunnyside branch and other places has been temporarily suspended so all can work on the Heber line. Only two miles remain to be laid on the Sunnyside branch, and this will be finished as soon as the steel gang is released from Heber."

Miss Sadie Kimball left here Saturday last for Price, where she is to teach her second school term in the public schools there.

There is a new school teacher in town in the person of James W. Dilley, junior, who arrived last Thursday night. He has come to stay and is said to have as good a pair of lungs as any infant in this great coal camp.

H. H. Larll and some friends from Price are figuring on going out into the hills soon on a fishing and hunting trip, and will be absent several weeks

There is considerable activity in and around the Pleasant Valley coal mines here, at Winter Quarters and Clear Creek, the new property of the company.

The grading contract for the Winter Quarters No. 4 tramway is about finished. Jones & Jacobs of Salt Lake will look after the construction of the trestle work of the tramway. W. H. Jones of the firm, is on the ground now with a force of carpenters preparing the timbers.

Work on the grade for the Rio Grande Western branch from Scofield up to the Cleark Creek mines is being hurried forward. The railroad will very probably be at the mines by the 25th

Robert Forrester of the Sunnyside Coal company was in town on business the other day. He says the work at Sunnyside is going on nicely and the branch will likely be finished by the 16th

After spending vacation with their parents here, Miss May and Florence Kimball left the latter part of the week for Salt Lake, the former to resume her position as teacher in the city schools, the latter to attend Rowland Hall.

The Hutchinson Bros. of Price, have have been given the contract to paint $350 worth of scenery for the local dramatic company here, the latter to furnish the materials.

Scofield is the most prosperous now of any time in the history of the town. There is plenty of work for all, and the business men have no complaint to make

The Pleasant Valley Coal company wants coal miners for Sunnyside, Castle Gate, Scofield and the Clear Creek mines. Two hundred will be given employment.

The county teachers' institute which closed here a few days ago was the most instructive ever held in Carbon county. There were in attendance Professors Roylance and Marshal and Miss Bessie Kimball. The Carbon county teachers were Mrs Mary Crandall, Mrs H P. Lood, Misses Blanche Bent, Minnie Knight, Helen Bell, Sadie Kimball, Mary Leonard, Hannah Johnson, and Messrs J. W. Dilley, J. W. Bowman, William Terry. These represented the districts of Winter Quarters, Scofield, Castle Gate and Price only.

MISSIONARY REUNION

The elders of Emery Stake who have been on missions will hold a reunion at Huntington, September 28 and 29, when the following program will be rendered

Singing	The company.
Prayer	Chaplain J H Pace
Speech of welcome	D C Woodward
Response	President R G Miller.
Benefits of reunion	R. G Harmon
Song	Bishop Peter Oveson
Sketches from Missionary Journal	
	J D Killpack
Discussion on Spiritualizing the Scriptures	
	Elders A Brinkerhoff and N Curtis.

There will be a ball on the evening of Thursday, the 28th

THE SECOND DAY'S PROGRAM

Comparison of customs of Samoans and Americans	Abinadi Olson
Song	Henry Reid,
Attractions of Switzerland	Elder Schwallen
Missionary sketch	Alvin Thayn
Musical selection	J P. Wakefield Jr
Recitation	John Curtis

There will be a contest for the most amusing incident of missionary experience and for which a prize will be awarded.

THE PUBLIC SESSION.

Singing	Prof Hardy's choir
Speech	L. M Olson
Song	Villa Brinkerhoff
Missionary life of fifty years ago	
	John Duncan
Recitation	Mrs J D Killpack Jr
Bass solo	L. B Reynolds

Impromptu speeches, songs, and recitations are to follow

It is expected that all elders of Emery Stake who have ever been on a mission will feel interested to get together and renew the spirit of the work in which they were once actively engaged Their ladies are also invited.

CASTLE GATE ITEMS

Dominic Malano had his leg injuried Saturday morning by being stepped upon by a horse. The injury is painful though not dangerous.

H. A Nelson and B. F. Caffey were among the visitors from here to Salt Lake City the latter part of the week

J. M Madderly from Kyune was in town the latter part of the week, looking after business matters.

The district schools opened last Monday. The teachers this year are William Z Terry, principal, and Miss Helen M. Bell, and Miss Minnie A. Knight, assistants. It is expected that the school will be crowded to its utmost capacity. Night schools will also be held to benefit those who work in the mines.

Miss Annie Patterson and Thomas J. Hardee will be married at Scofield on the 16th inst.

A delightful entertainment was given Monday evening by the primary association, consisting of speeches, songs, duets, dialogues, and recitations, all of which were credibly rendered. The song of Miss Vera Evans, only ten years old, was a most meritorious effort, so also was the singing of Miss Mary Kimber. The people turned out in goodly numbers, and a dance finished up a well spent evening.

The young ladies of the ward met Friday night to organize themselves into an association

The wife of John Tedesco has presented her husband with a baby boy. All doing well.

Deseret Evening News
September 16, 1899

PRICE.

Large School Attendance — In Honor of Volunteers.

Special Correspondence.

Price, Carbon Co., Utah, Sept. 15.— There will be a big crowd from Carbon county towns at Castola Springs tomorrow to witness the match game of ball between Provo and Ephraim.

LARGE SCHOOL ATTENDANCE.

The registration of scholars at the commencement of the public schools this week is the largest in the history of the district, and the outlook is most flattering for a successful school year. Attendance will be made compulsory, and those scholars who have heretofore evaded going to school will be forced to come in.

IN HONOR OF VOLUNTEERS.

Many of the Price people will go up to Castle Gate tomorrow to be present at the presentation of the medals and to attend the concert in honor of the Carbon county volunteers there. There will be dancing at two places in the evening and a big spread for all.

CASTLE GATE ITEMS

The Ephraim band, under the leadership of Miss Christensen, paid this place a visit Thursday last, and gave a dance in the evening at Knights of Pythias hall

Mrs Eugene Santschi, accompanied by her son, left here Thursday last for Logan, where young Santschi, together with Joseph Halverson, are going to the agricultural college

Eugene Santschi, sr., has been sick with cholera morbus for several days, but is now able to be around

Superintendent W G Sharp paid us a short visit last week.

Assistant Superintendent H G Williams returned from Sunnyside Thursday.

Peter Delpeus, who has been suffering from dysentery, was on Sunday sent to a hospital at Salt Lake City.

Mrs Frank Latud, who has been in the hospital for several weeks died Sunday night. The remains were brought to Castle Gate for burial. Much sympathy is expressed for the bereaved husband. One little child is left with a sorrowing husband to mourn her loss.

Sunday morning the coal company made its first effort to run a man trip in the mines to convey the miners to their several entries. It is expected that the new method will be welcomed by all the colliers.

The presentation of the medals to the Carbon county volunteers which was to have occurred last Saturday evening at Castle Gate, has been postponed until next Saturday evening owing to an unlooked for delay in the arrival of the medals from Chicago

W H Donaldson spent the Sabbath at Price with his best girl.

Mrs Alice Markey and Frank Hallock were united in marriage last Friday, Judge Holdaway officiating They have moved out to the ranch belonging to Jack Egan, where they are to conduct the stage station

CLEVELAND NEWS

The anniversary of the young ladies Mutual Improvement association was celebrated with a very appropriate program and ball in the evening

The farmers are very busy these days cutting grain and threshing has commenced in earnest.

Drusilla, the little 4-year old daughter of Mr and Mrs Hyrum Oterstrom died on the 10th. The many friends extend their sympathy.

The Litesters family are on the improve, four of which have been very sick with typhoid fever.

Nelse Overson has gone to attend school at Ephraim Miss Nora and Jeneva, who were to accompany him, were detained on account of sickness

Mrs. Ollie Bryson departed for St. George on the 15th for her daughter, Mrs Flora McMullen and children, Mr. McMullen having died of the De Lamar poison It is hoped Mrs McMullen will like her new home.

Miss Annie May Larson, who has been making her home at Price for some time, is visiting her parents at Cleveland.

Little Jamie Alger, who had his leg broken a few weeks ago, is getting along nicely. The doctor thinks he will soon be able to get about on crutches

The temperature of the week ended September 18th was about normal the days being warm and nights cool Scattered showers fell in the eastern counties but the drouth still continues over other sections of the state Threshing is still quite general but is nearing completion Sugar beets are being dug and hauled to the factories as rapidly as possible Corn is being cut for fodder. The last crop of lucern is being secured The ground is too dry for fall plowing and seeding but some of this is being done Tomatoes are ripening very slowly The weather has been very fine for fruit.

SHORT STORIES.

Tobe Whitmore is out on the range this week, rounding up his horse crop.

There was a very poor house out Friday night to witness the play at Town Hall.

There are at the present time about eighty men at work at Sunnyside coal camp.

Work will begin in a few days on the new building of the George A Lowe Implement company.

L Wulfe of Salt Lake City has arrived here to run Callaway's barber shop while the latter is at Sunnyside.

Arthur J. Lee has been a sufferer from the quinzy for three weeks or more and seems to be unable to get relief.

L Lowenstein will get in his new brick building about the first of the month, if nothing unforseen happens.

Mrs Alta Howard, a midwife of Emery county, has located in Price and will practice her profession here

County Clerk Howard will this week draw the list of petit jurors for the October term of the district court.

The new bridge across the Uintah river at Fort Duchesne is under construction and will be completed before long.

Brick is being hauled onto the ground for the new building of the Price Trading company, which is to be put up at once.

Will Peyton, formerly night operator at Price, has enlisted in the signal corps and left for the Philippines last Saturday night.

The remains of Columbus Gentry, who suicided at Scofield last Sunday, were brought here last Tuesday and interred in the Price cemetery.

The thirteen year-old son of H. W. Curtis, of Ferron, who was stricken with paralysis on the first of September, died September 12th.

The children of Joseph Ande son have about recovered from the effects of the scarlet fever, and from which five or six were down at the same time.

Marriage license was issued this week to John C McKendrick and Betsie Honeck The former resides at Castle Gate and the latter is of Price

The infant child of J. M Whitmore, which has been suffering from a light attack of malarial fever, is some better and was out on the street Monday afternoon

There arrived at the home of Mr and Mrs H. W. Damon on Tuesday night a boy baby of the regulation weight. Mother and child are getting along nicely. Dr. Fisk of Helper was in attendance.

Gentry & Callaway have opened a saloon at Sunnyside on a homestead recently taken up by the former. It has been stated here that Superintendent Forrester has given it out that any one patronizing the place will be handed his time check.

There were twenty one people, big, little, old and young from Price to Castella Springs last Saturday. Everybody reports having had a good time Tom Baron was there from Mt. Pleasant and mingled with the feminine portion of the crowd.

There is but one criminal case so far filed to come up at the October term of the district court, that of the State vs John W. Lloyd, who recently shot and wounded a boy at Scofield when the latter was caught in the former's turnip patch.

Indian Agent Mynton says there are none of the Uintah, White River or Uncompahgre Utes off the reservation in Colorado, where the Indians are reported to be slaughtering game firing the woods and intimidating settlers The Indians are from the Navajo and Southern Ute tribes He has sent out policemen to drive them off and couriers to keep him posted as to the actual condition of affairs

Postmaster Holdaway says he is not running any bureau of information, though one might imagine that such is the case by the number of notices of various kinds posted up in front of the postoffice. The judge is a patron of and believes in encouraging newspapers, so that if the many notices which almost cover up the front of the building have disappeared some morning—well, don't blame it onto Judge Holdaway.

Attention is directed to the professional card of Dr P P Fisk of Helper, which appears elsewhere in this issue of The Advocate. Dr. Fisk will give a considerable portion of his time to his practice in Price. coming down each day on the afternoon passenger train In case he does not come on this train by reason of being called elsewhere, those who desire his services may reach him by wire by calling on B. H McDonald or the operator at the Rio Grande Western depot. There will be no charge for the telegraphic service.

SCOFIELD NEWS

There is more or less talk of the Union Pacific mines starting up again this winter

Professor Alexander has been lecturing here evenings on phrenology to big crowds

The Southern Pacific railroad is using about all the coal that comes from the mines here

A Madsen & Sons of Mt Pleasant have opened up a branch store here, carrying a big and complete line of goods

Contractor Sherrell has arrived from Salt Lake City with men to begin work on the new boarding house at Clear Creek.

The public schools under the principalship of Professor James W Dilley are doing well, and the attendance is the largest in the history of the district.

Preparations are being made to install the boilers in the new power house. The boilers will be of the Stoker pattern that have been successfully used at the Castle Gate mines.

Twenty five experienced miners are expected here from the East in a few days to work in the company's mines, and more are wanted here and at the other properties of the company

The vein now operated at No 4 mine is from seven to fourteen feet thick, but few accidents occur, and of them 75 per cent have been on account of men ruking too much, after being warned of danger.

War Conference was held here Sunday President David John of the presidency of Utah Stake, accompanied by Elders Albert Jones and Henry E Giles were in attendance from Utah county.

The new school house completed last season is found inadequate to hold the children of school age, and a room adjacent to the meeting house has been brought into use for the overflow from the district school house.

Deall Bros & Mendenhall have completed their contract for making the grade for the tramway at Winter Quarters, and tracklaying has now commenced It will be thirty days, it is thought, before No 4 will be ready to operate over the train.

A new shoot for No 1 mine is being built It will be completed in about two months—a gravity double track line will be run from the shoot at cut 1500 feet to the mouth of the mine. The coal at a distance of 1000 feet from the mouth of the mine will be brought out by electrical appliance.

There are now about 850 men and boys on the payroll of the Pleasant Valley Coal company, and about fifty horses are worked about the mines. The daily output of coal is 1,500 tons or sixty of the largest cars in use on the railroads. It is likely the output will be increased in the near future to 2000 tons a day.

The improvements to the Latter-day Saints' meeting house are a noticeable feature, and when the painter and glazier put on the finishing touches it will be an improvement that will add greatly to the appearance of the coal mining town. Bishop Thomas J. Parmley, in the dual capacity of bishop of the ward and assistant superintendent of the mine, by his courteous and fair treatment of all comers, holds the respect of the community.

Fortunately the fire at the Clear Creek mines last week, which was caused by the brattice cloth catching fire from a driver's lamp, did no great amount of damage, and the work in all parts of the mine is being rushed. W. H. Jones has moved his gang of carpenters up to the mine and they will prepare chutes, etc. As soon as the railroad reaches the mine shipments will be made. The coal from these mines is said to be of a very superior quality.

Columbus Gentry, an old resident of Carbon county, committed suicide Sunday last by hanging himself. He had been camping with his son, James, about a mile up Clear Creek canyon and was noticed to leave camp about 10 o'clock in the morning, with a piece of rope and some wire. Young Gentry was away at the time, but upon his return his wife, feeling uneasy, as Gentry had spoken at various times about doing away with himself, told him of the circumstances. He immediately began to search for his father and finally found him hanging from a stringer by a rope in a slaughtering pen about 100 yards from camp. The indications are that the old gentleman placed a ladder against the wall, climbed up, removed his hat and shoes, and binding his feet together with the bailing wire, secured the rope around the stringer and jumped off the ladder. A wire was found on the left wrist, as though he had thought to bind his hands but was unable to do so. He appears to have strangled to death. Gentry was 50 years of age. He had been married twice, his first wife being dead. His second wife left him about two months ago. He has been in poor health and unable to provide for her. This is given as the reason for his committing the act. An inquest held Sunday evening rendered a verdict in accordance with the above.

A case of heroic bravery has come to light in connection with the fire at the Clear Creek mines last week. When the fire was noticed the miners nearby endeavored to extinguish it, but finding their efforts were of no avail they ran out of the mine. By this time the brattice was burning fiercely. Upon investigation as to whether all the men were out so that the dip where the fire was could be closed up, it was found that one man was missing, and that he was working beyond where the fire had started. Foreman Thomas immediately called for volunteers to go with him in the mine to rescue the man. Several attempts were made by different ones but they were driven back by the flames, and the cry of "powder" caused a hasty retreat. Finally Heber Franklin, a young man whose work keeps him on the outside said "I will go." And accompanying Foreman Thomas they pressed on through the fire and found the man working away tamping a hole, entirely unconscious of the danger threatening him. They succeeded in getting out of the mine safely, when the fan was shut off and the dip closed up. The rescue was an act of great bravery on the part of Franklin, as his work keeping him on the outside, he was unacquainted with the exact lay of the land inside, and the danger of suffocation from black damp was great. He was the only man of the many standing by whose nerve did not desert him. It is stated upon good authority that ten minutes more of lost time would have resulted in the death of the miner who was at work and possibly a great loss to the company, as the supply of air could not be cut off while there was any hope of rescue, and that would have tended to feed the flames.

PERSONAL.

Tom Barton is expected in town Saturday from Mt Pleasant.

Miss Rose Bryner is visiting with friends at Manti this week.

Ernest Peyton went into Salt Lake City yesterday to have his eyes treated

L. M. Olsen was among the visitors from Price in Salt Lake City during the week.

Judge McConnell was down from Salt Lake City Monday and left in the evening for Colton.

Joseph J. Anderson of Emery and A. E Anderson of Fairview were at the Hotel Clarke during the week.

Mrs Sarah J. Warren returned Saturday from a short visit with her daughter, Mrs. James Rooney at Helper.

Mrs. Louis Lowenstein and Master Sherman returned Saturday from an absence of two weeks at Salt Lake City

Mrs Robert Howard returned last Saturday from Salt Lake City, where she visited friends and relatives for ten days.

Mr and Mrs C W Spalding and Mr. Spalding's mother were out on a fishing trip this week, taking their departure Monday.

W. H Kinnon of Denver and H. M Kahn and W. P Malsen of Salt Lake City were registered at Hotel Clarke Monday last.

Miss Ella Lowenstein will arrive from Salt Lake City Saturday, where she is attending school, to remain over Sunday with her parents.

City Marshal Anderson has gone to Gunnison to see his father who is in feeble health The elder Anderson is in his 99th year.

Mr and Mrs. A. Ballinger and a party of friends were up to the Price Trading company's coal mines last Sunday, where they spent the day.

Mrs George W. Balle and her mother, Mrs James Nixon departed last Saturday for Salt Lake City, where they will visit for some time

Hon. Orange Seeley of Castle Dale was here the other day en route home from Davis county, where he had been on a visit with relatives

M V Crockett, of Vinita, I. T., arrived in Price last Friday and will remain some time, having accepted a position with The Advocate.

Mr and Mrs A. Barnten, accompanied by Miss Groves, all of Salt Lake City, were registered at the Hotel Clarke during the forepart of the week.

William Potter and wife and H H Earll and wife of Scofield left here last Sunday for a hunting and fishing trip of several weeks in the mountains.

Professor I. W Nixon of Huntington was in town Tuesday on his way to Scofield, where he went in the interest of the Western Savings association of which he is the Eastern Utah agent.

Dr C H Field is packing up preparatory to leaving for Ham's Fork, Wyo, where he was located before coming to Price, and where his family are residing Mrs Field is not in good health, and she is anxious for her husband to return there and resume his practice During his short stay in this city Dr. Field has made many friends and built up a good practice The people here regret to see him leave.

Mr and Mrs. Irving F. Greene of Salt Lake City were at the Mathis Hotel last Saturday from Salt Lake City. Mr. Greene is credited with being the representative of Joe Leiter, and he was here trying to close up some deals for hydro carbon properties in this county. He is the stuff out of which good fellows are made and his many friends here are always glad to meet him.

Kay, the year-old son of Mr. and Mrs. Edward C. Lee, of Nine Mile, died Sunday morning of scarlet fever and the remains were brought here for interment. The many friends of the parents in this city, where they formerly resided, extend sympathies to the bereaved parents The child was remarkably bright for one of its age.

Salt Lake Herald
September 22, 1899

CASTLEGATE HAPPENINGS.

Sick Man Goes to the Hospital—Mrs. Latuda's Death.

(Special Correspondence.)

Castlegate, Sept. 18.—Peter Delpeas has been for the last few days a victim of dysentery, and he was last evening moved to the hospital.

Mrs. Frank Latuda, who has been in the hospital for several weeks, died last night, and will be brought to Castlegate for burial. Much sympathy is expressed for the bereaved husband. One little child is left with a sorrowing husband to mourn her loss.

This morning the coal company made its first effort to run a man trip in the mines to convey the miners to their several entries. It is expected that the new method will be welcomed by all the colliers.

Deseret Evening News
September 22, 1899

PRICE.

Gentry Interred at Price — Prospective Water Works—Politics.

Special Correspondence.

Price, Carbon Co., Utah, Sept. 19.—The remains of the late Columbus Gentry, who suicided at Scofield on Sunday last, were brought here this afternoon and the body interred in the Price cemetery.

Price is again without a butcher shop and if there is a good opening in the State for such a business, properly conducted, it exists here.

WATER WORKS.

Local capitalists are figuring on the building of a water works system and electric light plant, which is to be a private enterprise, selling water and light to the city and residents.

Local politics are demanding some attention in Price. There is a general sentiment of business men and taxpayers of the town that politics should be eliminated and men of business methods put in as trustees. Hon. Reuben G. Miller's friends are urging him to allow his name to be used on the citizen's ticket for president of the board of trustees of Price town.

Eastern Utah Advocate
September 28, 1899

CASTLE GATE ITEMS.

Saturday was payday at the mines.

Miss Annie Larsen is the guest of her sister and brother here this week.

Misses Ida McIntire and Jennie Branch visited with friends here Sunday evening.

Johnny Foote was here Saturday from Salt Lake City, mingling with old friends and acquaintances.

The Carbon county volunteers received their medals last Saturday night. There was a dance and literary exercises afterwards.

Bishop Scanlon of Salt Lake City held services here last Sunday for the Catholics. Large audiences were out to hear him.

John Potter and John Kay of Cleveland were here the latter part of the week, circulating among their many friends.

Frank Latuda, who lost his wife in the early part of last week is now called upon to part with his only remaining child. The little girl died Monday morning from cholera morbus.

Some eight or ten of Castle Gate's young men went down to Price Saturday evening to the Lowenstein ball and reception. They all say there was a fine crowd and a jolly good time.

Francisco Pasevento and wife left Saturday for Italy. For several days past Pasevento has been under the illusion that some one was trying to kill him and for several nights he has not dared to go to sleep, but has sat up with a loaded gun beside him.

SHORT STORIES.

Coun y warrants bought by R. W Crockett.

Marriage license was issued this week to Joseph Case and Margaret Wardell, both of Castle Gate.

President Miller and his counsellors were at Huntington last Sunday, where interesting services were held.

C. W. Spalding will make a shipment about the 5th of October of 2000 or 3000 head of sheep from Colton.

There is very little sickness in the county at the present time so far as The Advocate has been able to learn.

Steve Chipman has lately bought a band of about three thousand head of ewes which has about doubled his flocks.

J. N Whitmore will ship about 150 head of horses to the St. Louis market today, accompanying the stock in person.

Matt Thomas has lately bought up about forty calves in the Nine Mile neighborhood which he will feed this winter, and is after more.

The Emery County Teacher's association will meet on the 28th of October at Castle Dale and will take up the winter's work.

SHORT STORIES.

County warrants bought by R. W Crockett.

Arthur J. Lee is waiting on lumber to begin the erection of the building of George A. Lowe.

Thomas Murphy has been on the sick list for about a week, but is up again and around

Mr. and Mrs. J. L. Taylor have a bright baby girl which came to brighten their home the first of the week.

District court meets next Monday, the board of county commissioners the following Monday.

The town is almost depopulated this week, about everybody having gone into Salt Lake City.

Miss Mamie Robb has accepted a position with Louis Lowenstein as saleslady, and went to work the first of the week.

Tom Nichols cashed in his hog crop this week to C. H. Taylor, getting $12 50 out of a pig that he paid $1 50 for a few months ago.

There was a very nice dance given at the Mathis Hotel last Friday evening The crowd was small, but everybody present enjoyed themselves.

There was a big crowd from this part of Utah to Zion this week, attracted there by conference, the state fair, salt palace and other events. A great many will not return until about the 15th of the month.

The plate glass for Lowenstein's new brick was put in the first of the week and the firm will be ready for business in the new house in a few days at the farthest. An inventory is to be taken before the stock is finally removed.

Judge Holdaway is preparing to move the building until this week occupied by Louis Lowenstein to the ground west of the postoffice. The butcher shop building will be turned around to make room for it.

The city treasury was enriched to the extent of twenty-five dollars Wednesday morning by five gentlemen who were dallying with the pasteboards the night previous, and were called upon by City Marshal Anderson.

There is a new baby girl at the home of Mr. and Mrs. W. M. Allred The father is past 70 years of age and is stepping around this week as spry and chipper as many a man of half his years.

Dr. Fix was down today from Helper to see Riva, the little girl of Mr. and Mrs. D V. Holdaway, whom it was thought was threatened with pneumonia. He does not consider the case serious.

Salt Lake Herald
October 11, 1899

BOY SHOT DEAD.

Son of Thomas Arrowsmith Killed By Accident at Colton.

(Special to The Herald.)

Price, Utah, Oct. 10.—The 15-year-old son of Thomas Arrowsmith was accidentally shot and killed at Colton last night. The boy thought he discovered burglars in the store of his aunt, Mrs. J. V. Smith, and went to the saloon of his uncle, Hiram Smith, and notified the latter.

The two visited the store and found that they were mistaken. The boy then asked to look at the revolver which his uncle carried. The latter removed, as he thought, all the cartridges, but overlooked one. In passing the revolver to the boy it was discharged, the bullet piercing the heart. Death was instantaneous.

Eastern Utah Advocate
October 12, 1899
Price

SHORT STORIES.

County warrants bought by R W. Crockett.

A fine station building is to be built by the Rio Grande Western at Sunnyside.

Mr. Hepburn has ordered his drug stock and the same is expected to arrive here at any time now

Hy Herriman and family have moved to Eureka, where Mr. Herriman is at work in the mines.

The Colorado Midland and the Santa Fe had twenty seven car loads of sheep out of Colton the first of the week.

The regular term of district court will convene at Castle Dale next Monday. The calendar is a light one.

Tobe Whitmore will likely take another consignment of horses to the Eastern markets in the near future.

Quarterly conference of Emery stake will convene at Ferron next Sunday and will be in session Monday.

Notices have been posted for the election which is to be held next month for members of the town board.

Next Monday there will be an advance in freight rates from the east to Denver which will of course effect Utah merchants.

Typewriter paper in several grades and carbon papers for typewriter use carried in stock and for sale at The Advocate office.

R. J. Armstrong and family have lately moved into the Mc Wilson property from the building across the street from The Advocate office

Marriage license was issued last Saturday at Salt Lake City to John H. Eccles of Scofield and Hannah Davis of American Fork

Miss Gertrude Miller was operated upon last Sunday afternoon by Dr. Fisk of Helper, the physician removing her tonsils.

There is a brand new baby at the home of Mr. and Mrs. Hubbard Warren that arrived the first of the week. It is a girl. Dr. Fish of Helper is the attending physician

School district clerks' warrants in books of 100 and bound, can be used in any district in Utah, for sale at The Advocate office. Also blank contracts with trustees and teachers.

The Advocate takes orders for all kinds of printing. If it cannot be done at home we will send to Provo or Salt Lake City for it, and save you money at the same time making a small profit

Charley Taylor the other day shipped 425 head of cattle, 350 head of which were yearling heifers to the Kansas City market. They were unloaded at Denver en route.

Full line of legal blanks, location notices, blank deeds, contracts for school trustees, in fact, all blanks in use in Utah. Over 200 different forms. Prices the same as Provo and Salt Lake City. The Advocate, Price, Utah.

The Home Dramatic company presented "Oath Bound" and "Confusion" at Town Hall last Tuesday evening to a fairly good sized audience. The dance following the play was most thoroughly enjoyed.

J. U. Hutchinson went up to Salt Lake City the first of the week to engage his company for the winter season. The Imperial Dramatic company will open at Vernal on the 23rd of the month, where a week's engagement has been booked. Misses Maggie Jones and Sarah Larsen will be members of the company.

John H. Eccles of Scofield, who is a brother of David Eccles of Ogden, was in Salt Lake City the other day, says The Herald. With him was Peter Minnoch, who has for twenty two years been foreman of the Eccles Lumber company. Mr. Eccles recently opened the Scofield planing mill, and Minnoch will look after the plant until everything is in running order.

Iobe Whitmore came in Sunday from St. Louis, where he had been with four carloads of range horses which he put on the market there. Asked if the shipment was a profitable one, Mr. Whitmore replied 'Well, yes. I came back with money, and the fact is did better than I had anticipated. However, a man never does anything that he does not learn something and when I go back again I will get better prices than for this lot. I may ship out some more, but as to that I have not yet made up my mind."

Salt Lake Herald
October 16, 1899

CASTLEGATE NEWS.

Lively Incidents Occurring In Thriving Coal Town.

(Special Correspondence.)

Castlegate, Oct. 14.—Castlegate deer and bear hunters went out in a body this morning to hunt. Last Sunday a fine deer was brought into town by James Evans. While up one of the canyons he, with some more nimrods, say they saw a bear, so this morning they sallied forth to hunt bruin. Several crack shots are among them, and one or two experienced bear hunters, and it will not be surprising to see the party return with large game.

Born, to the wife of Alma Jones, last evening, a fine son.

There was a marriage in Italian town last evening, and the usual festivities were indulged in to an alarming extent. Some of these times there will be an inquest following.

Quite a number of brake-beam travelers were in town yesterday and this morning. One of them was minus a leg, but the way he tackled a freight train this morning was a surprise to the initiated; but they all got put off and as usual the coke ovens are their rendezvous.

A great deal of wanton destruction is going on among the young hoodlums of this town. Several windows have been broken of late belonging to the Mormon church. The authorities of the ward are determined to put a stop to it. A reward is being offered.

Salt Lake Herald
October 17, 1899

THE GROOM SHOT A WOMAN

TRAGEDY FOLLOWS WEDDING AT CASTLEGATE.

While Charivari Party Was Engaged In Efforts to Serenade Wedded Man Shot From Window.

(Special to The Herald.)

Castlegate, Utah, Oct. 16.—Pasquale Citerio, an Italian miner at Castlegate, was married in Price last Saturday and returned home in the evening. A charivari followed, the uproar outside continued until the patience of both were exhausted. So in a desire to scare off the disturbers of their peace, Citerio got up and reached for his gun and fired out of the window. The bullet struck Mrs. John Branco in the side. Mrs. Branco fell, but immediately jumped up and ran for home. Before reaching her house, however, which is but a short distance from Citerio's, she again fell and had to be carried home. Dr. Asadoorian was immediately summoned and made a careful examination of the wound and did all he could to ease the severe pain the woman was suffering. It was the doctor's opinion that the wound was dangerous if not a fatal one. This morning he says she cannot live. After learning the fearful consequences of his shot Pasquale got frightened and left town and made his way to Price and it is learned this morning that he has given himself up to the sheriff of this county.

Mrs. Branco is very much esteemed among her own people and is very prominent as a leader in their social gatherings. The young bride, Mrs. Citerio is being consoled with the thought that her husband fired the shot with the purpose to scare and not to hurt any one and hopes to see him home soon.

John Melloti and a few others having been notified of the action of Citerio, went down to Price this afternoon and an effort will be made to secure bail for him.

Salt Lake Herald
October 19, 1899

MRS. BRANCO DEAD.

Woman Shot During Charivari at Castlegate, Succumbs.

(Special Correspondence.)

Castlegate, Oct. 17.—Mrs. John Branco, who was shot on Sunday night, succumbed this morning. It is presumed that the deceased will be buried under the auspices of A. O. O. F., the bereaved husband being a member of that lodge.

Mrs. Branco was only 23 years old. She leaves a husband and a boy between 4 and 5 years old.

County Attorney Hoffmann is expected up today from Price, to see what can be done in the case of Pasquale Citerio, who fired the fatal shot. An inquest may be necessary to get at the facts in the case, for there are a good many rumors as to the killing, which can only be determined at an investigation.

Death Was Accidental.

(Special Correspondence.)

Castlegate, Oct. 18.—An inquest was held over the remains of Mrs. Genreffa Branco before Justice of the Peace J. Tom Fitch of Helper. A verdict of accidental death was rendered. The last sad rites of the awful tragedy ended this afternoon, when the remains of the dead woman were laid away. The ceremonies were conducted by the I. O. O. F. Consolatory remarks were made in the K. of P. hall by Bishop Lamph and Counselor Ricks. The band headed the procession. The ritual of the order was read at the grave.

PRIMARY STARY CONFERENCE

The quarterly conference of the Emery Stake of Zion was held at Ferron on Sunday and Monday, October 15th and 16th There were present of the First Council of Seventies, Seymour B Young and Joseph W McMurrin, Elder U G Miller of the Salt Lake stake, the Emery Stake presidency, bishops of wards and a good attendance of officers and members of the stake

The conference convened at 10 30 o'clock in the forenoon, Sunday, October 15th, President R. G. Miller presiding The choir sang hymn on page 362, " When Earth In Bondage Long Had Lain " Prayer by Oscar A Wood.

The choir sang hymn on page 88, ' Go Ye Messengers of Heaven "

President Reuben G. Miller arose and addressed the conference. He said " I trust the Lord will again favor us with His spirit during this conference as He has in the past " It reported the Emery stake as being in a good condition and said the people of Emery stake had cause to rejoice and thank the Lord for the blessings enjoyed by them

Elder Joseph W. McMurrin of the First Council of Seventies, addressed the Saints assembled He spoke on the law of tithing, stating that certain blessings followed the observance of that law He referred to the third chapter of Malachi, where the people had robbed the Lord in tithes and offerings, spoke of the mission of President Lorenzo Snow and the truthfulness of his word concerning the law of tithing The choir sang hymn on page 173, ' O, Awake my Slumbering Minstrel '

Benediction by Niels P Miller.

Conference adjourned until 2 p m.

The afternoon session was called to order by President Reuben G Miller The choir sang hymn on page 212, "Redeemer of Israel " Prayer by Patriarch Frederick Olsen.

The choir sang hymn on page 170, ' Hark Ten Thousand Thousand Voices "

Sacrament was administered. Bishop Alonzo Brinkerhoff reported the Emery Ward, said it was in a favorable condition.

Elder George Cluff, principal of the Emery Stake academy, addressed the conference upon the subject of church schools, and the education of the young men and women

Elder Seymour B. Young addressed the Saints assembled, spoke on the law of tithing, and President Lorenzo Snow s trip to St George. He then read from the doctrine to Covenants. Section 119 Gave figures showing the increase of tithing paid in corresponding months in different years Asked the blessings of the Lord upon the people, and a happy meeting of each other in the world to come

The choir sang an anthem, benediction by Bishop Calvin Moore.

Conference adjourned until Monday, October 16, 1899, at 10 30 o'clock a m.

At 7 30 Monday evening a meeting of the priesthood was held, showing a good attendance. The speakers were President Reuben G. Miller, President John H. Pace, Elder Joseph W. McMurrin and Elder Seymour B Young

Good instructions were given the brethren in regards to their duties in the church.

MORNING SESSION.

At 10 o'clock a. m. the conference was called to order.

The choir sang hymn on page 166, "We Thank Thee O, God, For a Prophet."

Prayer by Patriarch Franklin W. Young

The choir sang hymn on page 7, "Glorious Things of Thee Are Spoken."

The general authorities of the church were presented by President Reuben G. Miller and unanimously sustained, after which the stake authorities and officers were presented as sustained at the last quarterly conference and unanimously sustained

Bishop John Y. Jensen reported the Castle Dale Ward as being in good condition.

Elder U. G. Miller, of Salt Lake stake, addressed the conference, directing his remarks to the young people present.

Bishop Jasper Robertson reported the Orangeville Ward, said peace prevailed among the people and the tithing was increasing.

Elder Joseph W. McMurrin addressed the Saints upon the subject of prayer and exhorted the Saints to support the church schools of this stake.

The choir sang hymn on page 291, "Ye Wandering Nations Now Give Ear."

The benediction was pronounced and the conference adjourned until 2 o'clock p m.

AFTERNOON SESSION.

Conference called to order by President Henry G. Mathis, the choir sang hymn on page 66

Prayer by Elder John Zwallen, the choir sang hymn on page 61, "My God, the Spring of All My Joys."

President Henry G. Mathis addressed the Saints upon the necessity of being converted to the principles of the gospel, said we should seek to continually progress.

Elder Alexander Jameson spoke upon religion class work and the important branch of church education, gave notice of the Sunday school conference that will be held at Castle Dale on Saturday, October 21, 1899.

Elder Seymour B Young spoke upon the subject of true education or theology combined with book learning, spoke upon the subject of matrimony and our physical condition, read the revelation on the word of wisdom and explained the intent and meaning of that word.

President Miller made a few closing remarks, announced that the next quarterly conference would be held at Price, Carbon county, on Sunday and Monday, January 14 and 15, 1900, said it was desired that the stake board of education be present at the opening of the Emery Stake academy, which would take place on Monday, October 23, 1899, at Castle Dale.

The choir sang an anthem and the benediction was pronounced by President John H Pace. Conference adjourned for three months.

A citizen's non-partisan meeting was held at Huntington last Saturday evening at which the following were nominated for the town of Huntington A E Wall, president, D C Woodward, John W Lott, John L Brasher and Martin Jensen trustees There has been considerable discussion lately regarding disincorporation the citizens claiming that the benefits, if any, are not sufficient for the extra taxation, but at the meeting there was not decided opposition with the result of nominating a full board for the next two years The board is considered a good one, and the people expect to get the town out of debt

Dr James W Smith who lately resided at Scofield Utah died at Bel Air, on September 29th last, and was buried at Abingdon with Masonic honors He leaves no children, but his wife survives him At one time the deceased lived at Elko Nev, and it was there he married Miss Kate Darsey in the year 1881 Dr Smith was contemplating a year's study in the hospitals of New York, when he was taken with malignant tumor of the stomach, the cause of his death He was 47 years of age, and a member of Argenta Lodge No J of Salt Lake City.

SHORT STORIES.

Price

Jay L, the 3 year-old son of Mr and Mrs John L Willson, died last Saturday morning from membranous croup The funeral was held Sunday from the family residence The boy was a remarkably bright child and the parents have the sympathy of a large number of friends in their affliction.

The little girl of Mr and Mrs Bruce Wilson has been quite ill for several days with summer complaint.

Price Drug company is to have a big, nice, new stock of drugs in within the next few days.

John H. Holley of Salt Lake City will be the manager of the Pleasant Valley Coal company store at Sunnyside.

R R Lane, who has been night operator at the depot for several months, was called home to Galena, Kan, last Tuesday by the death of his brother, who was on the merchants' police force there. The telegram did not say anything more than that the brother was shot

Under an order from Judge Johnson, the estate of George Frandsen, deceased, is to be distributed by George G Frandsen, administrator to the heirs of which there are fourteen, Mrs George Frandsen, the widow, Lena Hanna, child of Joseph, (deceased), Annie, Lena George G, Ingobar, Maria, Lars, Hyrum, Erastus Peter, Heber, Orson and Christian The estate was appraised at $30 000, with a bond from the administrator of $50 000 and consists of real estate, personal property and cash The widow is given one third and the balance is divided up equally among the other thirteen To handle the estate properly has called for a great deal of good judgment and business sagacity on the part of the administrator, which has not been lacking, and when it came to a final settlement with the court there was not a cent out of the way in the accounts of George G Frandsen

CASTLE GATE ITEMS

Castle Gate deer and bear hunters went out in a body Saturday morning to hunt. Last Sunday a fine deer was brought into town by James Evans While up one of the canyons he, with some more nimrods, say they saw a bear. Saturday they sallied forth to hunt bruin Several crack shots are among them, and one or two experienced bear hunters, and it will not be surprising to see the party return with big game.

Born, to the wife of Alma Jones, Friday evening, a fine son

There was a marriage in Italian town Friday evening, and the usual festivities were indulged in to an alarming extent. Some of these times there will be an inquest following

A great deal of wanton destruction is going on among the young hoodlums of this town Several windows have been broken of late belonging to the Mormon church The authorities of the ward are determined to put a stop to it. A reward is being offered

Eastern Utah Advocate
October 26, 1899

Price

SHORT STORIES.

Next Tuesday is the last day of registration.

Tuesday, October 31st, is the last day of registration Have you registered?

C W, Spalding has his sheep running on private pasture near Scofield.

There will be a big crowd from Price to Helper tomorrow evening. Are you going? Salt Lake City music.

Miss Annie Lareen is sick at the Mathis Hotel. She returned from Salt Lake City about a week ago.

Flora, the bright little girl of Mr. and Mrs. Arthur J. Lee is sick with scarlet fever. Dr. Fisk is in attendance upon the case.

Brick work began on the new building of the Price Trading company last Monday morning and the walls will be up within a few days

George G. Frandsen went up to Salt Lake City Sunday evening to close up some matters in connection with the settlement of the Frandsen estate.

Truman A. Ketchum of Helper was ordered discharged from bankruptcy last week by Judge Marshall of the United States district court at Salt Lake City.

Arthur J Lee forwarded out to Fort Duchesne yesterday 150,000 feet of lumber to be used in the rebuilding of the stables, recently burned. The lumber came from Denver

Pete Anderson and a party of friends have been out in the hills for a week after deer. It is expected they will return with a number of carcasses, as Anderson never comes back empty handed

F. Crabtree formerly in the employ of the Rio Grande Western company at Ogden, arrived in Price the last of the week to relieve E. R. Lane, who was called to Galena, Kan, by the death of a brother.

Price D company's stock began to arrive yesterday and is being opened up and put on the shelves Mr. Hepburn will be ready for business the first of the week with the nicest line of goods ever brought into this part of Utah

Tickets for the grand ball and supper at the Rio Grande Western Hotel at Helper tomorrow night may be had of B R McDonald, at the depot There will be a free special train run for the accommodation of the crowd from here Tickets, including supper, $2 per couple

Robert Forrester says the railroad will be completed into Sunnyside this week, and that trains will be running into the new camp within a few days The town now has telegraphic connection with the outside world, the line having been completed some time ago

Poor Lo is here this week getting his freight out of the railroad warehouses There are some fifteen to twenty already in and more are to come Each Indian is trading ten dollars worth with the merchants here as authorized by Indian Agent Myton They will move with their stuff from now on until it is all gone.

Frandsen Bros are considering the matter, so George says, of building a hotel on the ground to the west of the home of Mrs. Frandsen, the mother. If they should conclude to build it will be a brick with all modern improvements and strictly up to date. The building would be on the corner of the lot and facing the main street from town to the court house

The preliminary examination of Pasquale Citerio for the killing of Mrs. Genof'a Branco was held before Justice of the Peace J. Tom Fitch at Helper last Thursday. The county attorney was there to conduct the prosecution There was only one witness examined, John Branco, the husband. The examination was waved in behalf of the defendant, and he was bound over in the sum of $500 to await the action of the district court.

The Imperial Dramatic company opened the season here Tuesday evening in "Comrades," and had a fairly good sized house to start out with They played Castle Gate last night, and the coming week are to be at Scofield and Winter Quarters, skipping tomorrow night on account of the dance and supper at Helper. The company returns here at 2 leave for Vernal, where a week's engagement will be played On the return the company will go through Emery county, and the Sanpete country.

H. W. Damon is building a neat four-room cottage north of the town hall about a block, which he and his family will move into as soon as completed and ready for occupancy.

Pasquale Citerio, who accidentally shot his sister in law at Castle Gate a few days ago, is in the county jail, to await trial at the next term of the district court in default of $500 bonds

There is a case of destitution in a tent above town at the brick yard that was reported yesterday and is now being looked after by Mrs. C. H. Empey and Mrs. John H. Pace and Bishop Horsley. The woman has been cooking for the men on the brick-yard and was taken ill a few days ago. Dr. Fisk was called to see her and thinks she should be a county charge. He offered to furnish medicines and give her his attention free of cost, while Mr. Dallinger was looking around to get her a house in which to live. The woman has four children, half breed Indians, and all of them are recent arrivals from the reservation.

The county commissioners meet again on the 29th of December.

The burned stables are soon to be rebuilt at Fort Duchesne, when another troop of cavalry is to be stationed there.

Judge Holdaway has been busy for a week moving the building formerly occupied by Lowenstein to the vacant lot near the postoffice.

Paul Hanten is at Castle Gate, where he is temporarily employed in the offices of the Pleasant Valley Coal company. He will later go to Sunnyside

A MODEL TOWN THIS

"The Pleasant Valley Coal company which operates the coal mines at Clear Creek, is going to make as pretty a little town as there is in Utah," said Charles Young of Scofield, who runs a boarding house for the miners at Winter Quarters, to a Salt Lake Herald reporter last Wednesday. "A contract had been let by the company for the construction of twenty frame cottages and forty or fifty more will be begun next spring

"These twenty will be finished within a few weeks," said he, "and they will be rented to miners with their families or without for that matter. Each house is to be as neat and convenient as can be made, with electric lights and water.

"The company has another method of building the town, too It will rent ground enough for a good sized yard on long time to miners who want to build their own houses. The rental has been placed at 50 cents per quarter, $2 per year. It is merely a nominal price, to get them to build.

"The company is endeavoring to build a town that will present a clean and creditable appearance. Scofield was built up by miners who constructed huts and shacks, and it presents a dilapidated appearance. When Clear Creek is finished it will be a model town."

PERSONAL.

James McCune of Helper has returned from California, much improved in health

Mrs A H Hilberts of Salt Lake wife of the cashier of the Rio Grande Western Eating House system, has arrived in Helper to remain permanently.

J. C. Wester of Park City came down Sunday evening to look after his interests at this end of the line.

Mrs Lewis C. Singleton has arrived from Cooley s Ranch, Ariz, to join her husband, Sergeant Singleton, here.

Mrs Anne A Frye of Salt Lake City is this week the guest of her daughter, Mrs Robert Howard.

Mrs H. A. Nelson is visiting with Mr and Mrs. D. R. McDonald this week.

Mrs James Rooney of Helper is in the city.

Robert Forrester came down Tuesday evening from Salt Lake City on his way to Sunnyside

Mrs O. G Russell of Helper has returned from Denver.

Roy Gibson was in yesterday from Sunnyside.

J. W. Warf is in Salt Lake City this week.

Miss Nellie Bowring arrived today from Salt Lake City to join the Imperial Dramatic company. Miss Chase and Will Hutchison will be here tonight.

THE CHAPEL DEDICATED.

The chapel at Helper was formally dedicated last Sunday evening. The cozy house was crowded to its utmost capacity and the services were most interesting Superintendent Welby and a party of friends came down from Salt Lake City in special cars Mr. Welby himself opened the exercises by a few well chosen words of welcome and congratulation Addresses were made by Major H. C. Hill, Dean Halsey of St. Mark's and Rev. W. M. Paden of the First Presbyterian church, all of Salt Lake City. The music by the choir brought from the capital was very fine and included solos by Mrs A. G. Andrews, Mrs. John Reed and Miss Miller. After the ceremony the visitors were shown the chapel, school and entertainment room, and other points of interest in the model railroad town.

Price

SHORT STORIES.

The town board meets in regular session next Monday evening

There will be a conjoint meeting at the town hall next Sunday evening.

Mr. and Mrs. Billy Potter are going to make their home at Scofield after this week.

The new bridge across the Uintah river near Fort Duchesne is now completed.

Professor Webb was here today en route to Wellington, where he will visit the schools.

Landlord Spalding has reduced the rates at the Hotel Clarke from two dollars per day to one-fifty.

The new home of Mr. and Mrs H W. Damon is nearing completion and will be ready to move into in about two weeks.

Do not miss trying the oysters and mountain trout at the lunch room. Fine steaks a specialty. J. F. Rath is the proper man to see.

Mrs Green, mother of Mrs. E R Hepburn, arrived in Price yesterday on a short visit to her daughter. She is en route to California

There are several bad cases of scarlet fever at Spring Glen and at Helper. Dr Iisk has been called to see a number of them and is enforcing strict quarantine regulations

The Rio Grande Western's steel gang on Monday resumed work on the Sunny side branch Only two miles remain to be laid with track, and this will be finished by the end of the week.

The two children of Mr. and Mrs Arthur J Lee, who have had the scarlet fever, are getting along as nicely as could be expected These are the only cases in town as far as known.

About one hundred of the White River Utes are off the reservation in Colorado hunting game, but Agent Myton will take no steps to return them until he is notified officially of the fact.

Pete Anderson came in last week from his deer hunt and while away bagged twenty seven fine bucks. The carcasses are coming in by wagon. M. P. Braffett and several others were out on a deer hunt this week.

The Imperial Dramatic company presented "Joe, the Waif" here Monday evening to a small audience. The play was given to a better house at Scofield last night. The company goes to Vernal and Fort Duchesne next week.

R. G. Miller is this week putting on the finishing touches to his private telephone line that is to connect his ranch and his residence in Price. It will be over nine miles in length when done and the best of material and instruments have been used.

Mr. and Mrs. Frank Houghton, of California, who have been visiting Matt Thomas and family for several weeks, departed yesterday for home. Mr. Houghton is an uncle of Mr Thomas and he is so well pleased with his stay in Utah he will return here next summer.

The editor of "the gr at moral and religious" is this week more or less knocked out by having been thrown from a buggy this side of Helper, Monday night. His injuries are not serious, but nevertheless are painful. Druggist Hepburn has sent in another order for court plaster and liniments of various brands.

Judge McConnell and associates are said to have another deal on for their gilsonite properties in Rio Blanco county Colo. Bert Seabolt will be in Utah from Boston soon to look out for the deal

Old Chief Chevanaux is soon to be sent to Salt Lake City to have an oculist operate on him in the hope of restoring his eyesight. There are three blind chiefs among the Utes around White Rocks agency. Old Sowowic, Chevaneaux and Tabby.

Tobe Whitmore says he will ship no more horses out this year.

Frank McCarthy will open his butcher shop as soon as the building is ready for occupancy.

Miss Jennie McMullin of Wellington has accepted a clerkship with Price Trading company.

Registration Agent Flack says there are more democrats on the registration lists than there are republicans.

Rath, the restaurant man, is figuring on occupying the new brick being put up by Price Trading company.

George Whitmore has a large force of men at work in Whitmore canyon, putting in the pipeline to his ranch.

Robert McKune came in yesterday from the west, where he has been selling gentlemen's made-to-order suits and the like. He will go out to Sunnyside in the near future,

Tom Fitzgerald was out on the streets today looking for election bets on almost any old proposition, but he could find no takers. The gang appears to be afraid of Fitz

Prudence Beardsley has been appointed administratrix of the estate of the late M. H. Beardsley of Helper. The estate consists chiefly of cash, real estate in Salt Lake City and personal property.

Indian Agent Myton was here yesterday on his way to Salt Lake City, where he goes with two inspectors who have been out on the reservations looking after things in general. Mr. Myton wants 200,000 pounds of oats for which he will pay $1.50 per hundred, delivered at the agency at White Rocks.

The cold and storm of a few days ago has given place to good weather, and the snow has disappeared except from the north hillside of the range, and owners of stock have been able to get their flocks and herds lower down with little loss from the storm, which caught many of them unprepared, and it was feared would be disastrous to stock that was well back in the hills.

Deseret Evening News
November 6, 1899

PRICE.

SCARLET FEVER EPIDEMIC

Threatens the Entire County of Carbon — Schools Closed in Price.

Special Correspondence.

Price, Carbon Co., Nov. 6.—The public schools here were closed this morning for two weeks or longer on account of the scarlet fever, of which there are several cases in the town.

A little child of Nathan Marsing, which has been in the schools, died last night, and there are several other cases that threaten to develop in the next few days.

At Spring Glen six miles west of here, there are some ten to fifteen cases that are being now looked after by the county board of health, but as these have been neglected, there is great probability of a widespread epidemic.

There are several cases at the town of Helper, Utah, also; Dr. Fisk, of Helper, has been notified by the board to look after and quarantine all cases at county expense.

CASTLE DALE.

Formal Opening of the Emery Stake Academy.

Castle Dale, Emery County, Oct. 25.—On Monday, October 23rd, was the day set for opening the first school semester in the new building, and although at one time it looked almost impossible to get it ready, it was gloriously accomplished, and at 12 a. m., the spacious hall was crowded, the students in the middle of the room and visitors around. Stake President Miller presided and called the meeting to order. The choir under the leadership of Elder Jameson and Andrew Mortensen from Cleveland at the organ rendered "Guide Us, O, Thou Great Jehovah," after which Apostle Lund opened with prayer wherein he invoked the blessing on the assembled people and dedicated that portion of the building which was finished, to the Lord, and sanctified it for the earnest labors of education.

There were short speeches delivered by the members of the old board as well as of the new, giving a review of the struggle in maintaining and building up the academy in Castle Dale, and

Brother James Peterson of this place was mentioned by several as a man worthy of praise and consideration from the whole Stake for his excellent work in pushing the building so far, and by having contributed of his own means until he now has about $700 coming to him besides liberal donations he had given.

Elder Nuttall and Apostle Lund also spoke and rejoiced in the hopeful and favorable beginning of the academy, and Brother Lund said: On behalf of the general Church Board of Education, I accept of this academy and pronounce it duly opened, and it shall be added to the Church schools in the land and may God grant that His choicest blessings rest over all its labors.

Elder George Cluff was then supported as principal of the academy, and deeply touched by the solemn occasion he accepted the position and promised to do his very best and satisfy all of his integrity and ability to carry on the work for which the people had shown him confidence and trust.

Eighty-five students are now enrolled and a number has applied for seats, as we expect more than 100 students this winter which is far more than the most sanguine would have dared to expect.—Emery County Record.

Eastern Utah Advocate
November 9, 1899
Price

DEATH OF MRS COWLEY

The many friends and relatives in Utah of W. Elroy Cowley will greatly sympathize with him in the death of his wife, Minnie, age 24 years, who died of typhoid fever Sunday, October 29th. It was a sudden and crushing blow to husband and relatives, who thought she had taken a turn for the better. She leaves two small children, Master Harry, old 3 years of age, and Lyons, 6 months old. She was a kind wife and loving mother. Funeral services were held in Town Hall, Cleveland, October 31st.

SHORT STORIES.

Mr. and Mrs. Doll Faucett have a case of scarlet fever, in mild form, at their home.

The children of Mr. and Mrs Arthur J. Lee are improving nicely, which is good news to their friends

There is a mill case of scarlet fever at the home of Mr. and Mrs. A. Ballinger, one of the little boys being sick

One of the children of N. L. Marsing died Sunday night of diphtheria and was buried the following day.

Dr. Fisk has been appointed on the health board of the town and will act in the capacity of health physician.

Mr McDonald's old dog, Rex, and a half dozen more canines, more or less, have been poisoned the past week.

There will be a chicken dinner Sunday from 1 o'clock in the afternoon to 8 in the evening at Rath's restaurant.

Do not miss trying the oysters and mountain trout at the lunch room Fine steaks a specialty. J. F. Rath is the proper man to see.

Mrs Stephens of Farnham and the mother of Mrs John Magann of Wellington, died last week at the age of 65 of quick consumption

Last Sunday was a field day with the sports in Price, the events being a wrestling match, a half dozen foot races and one or two jumping contests.

C. S. Hill, a Wellington boy who went to the war in the Philippines with the Utah batteries, is working here at the barber's trade, and writes his father that he is pulling down a hundred simoleans each and every month He will probably return home at no late day.

Tom Taylor and Ed Lee have been in for a week on matters business. Mr. Lee has rented a house in Springville and will soon send his family there for the benefit of the schools.

Wallace Liddell, the 14 year old son of Peter Liddell, died at Wellington last week and the remains were interred there. He had been a sufferer from a skin malady for several years.

The town board met in regular session Monday evening The only business out of the ordinary was the decision that the street committee expend about six hundred dollars draining the streets, two to the east of the town hall and the one to the west.

Price's public schools were last Monday dismissed on account of the scarlet fever. The town board on Monday evening passed a resolution forbidding the assemblage of persons at a public meeting of any kind. There will be no dances or theatres for at least two weeks

Charley Taylor is in today with about six hundred head of steers which he will ship out to the markets along the Missouri river. He will have sixteen or seventeen cars and they will most likely be divided up at Lincoln, Neb, and sent in smaller lots to Kansas City, Omaha and St. Joseph

Mrs Carrie Thomas has her new lodging house at Helper about ready for occupancy. There will be twelve to fifteen rooms Mrs. Thomas has lately bought there lots adjoining her property from the Price Trading company, situated on the lower end of the main street of the town, and for which she gave $100

W. J. Hill of the Wellington neighborhood, was in town Monday last and paid his respects in a substantial way to "the great moral and religious," which will go into his home for another year. Mr. Hill says there are a good many cases of typhoid fever in his section, but they are so far of mild form.

HOME MISSIONARIES

John F. Wakefield and Delos Crandall—Price, Nov. 12, Castle Gate, Nov. 26, Molen, Dec. 10.

James Petersen and Alma G. Jewkes—Cleveland, Nov. 12, Price, Nov. 26, Castle Gate, Dec. 10.

Christian G. Larson, jr., and Abiradi Olsen—Molen, Nov. 26, Huntington, Dec. 10.

John F. Pearson and William Howard—Ferron, Nov. 12, Wellington, Nov. 26.

Frank M Reynolds and J. W. Seely—Huntington, Nov. 12, Spring Glen, Nov. 26.

Joseph H. Taylor and John Oliphant—Cleveland, Nov. 26, Lawrance, Dec. 10.

Samuel A. Williams and Peter Christensen—Castle Dale, Nov. 12, Orangeville, Nov. 26.

Thomas A Williams and John Peterson—Molen, Nov. 12, Orangeville, Dec. 10.

B M V Goold and Lars P. Larsen—Wellington, Nov. 12, Price, Dec 10.

Andrew P. Nielson and John Thorderson—Desert Lake, Nov. 12, Spring Glen, Dec. 10.

Joseph E Johnson and L M Olson—Castle Gate, Nov. 12, Castle Dale, Dec. 10.

J. W. Nixon and A. E Wall—Orangeville, Nov. 12, Castle Dale, Nov. 26, Desert Lake, Dec. 10.

Orange Seely and O. J. Anderson—Lawrence, Nov. 12, Ferron, Nov. 26.

Jacob Sorensen and Boye P. Peterson—Emery, Nov. 12, Ferron, Dec. 10.

James H. Cook and Hans P. Rasmussen—Lawrence, Nov. 26, Emery, Dec. 10.

M. A Cox and Christian Peterson—Emery, Nov. 26, Wellington, Dec. 10.

John Zwallen and John D Killpick—Huntington, Nov. 26, Cleveland, Dec. 10.

Allen Cox and Christian Peterson—Desert Lake, Nov. 26.

Eastern Utah Advocate
November 16, 1899

SHORT STORIES.

There are several new cases of scarlet fever in town, but all are of mild form.

The Imperial Dramatic company has been playing to good houses at Vernal and Fort Duchesne.

Ed Lee will be in with his family this week from the Nine Mile section. They go to Springville for the winter.

The ladies of the Helper chapel will give a grand ball for the benefit of the chapel fund on Thanksgiving evening.

Matt Thomas is having the Mint Saloon repapered and otherwise fixed up this week. It is to be one of the neatest places in this part of the state.

Link Bros. of Helper, it is reported, will soon open a saloon in Salt Lake City. Lou Link has been up there several days looking out his location.

John Holley, a brother in law of B. R McDonald, is to be the manager of the Wasatch store at Sunnyside, which will be ready for business in about a week.

John B. Stidger, special agent of the United States land office at Salt Lake City, was here the first of the week on business in connection with some old timber cutting cases

There will be a grand ball at Sunnyside in the near future, that is as soon as the new boarding house there is completed Special trains will run from Scofield, Castle Gate, Price and intermediate points

Henry Mathis with a force of men went out Monday to finish up the work to be done on the Price and Vernal road under the state appropriation He will begin about four miles out from Price and work in places as far out as Soldier Canyon.

The stage from the south did not arrive last night until after 12 o'clock, being delayed by the rain and mud on the road. The driver walked his horses in from Castle Dale, a distance of thirty miles, and they were almost played out when they got here

Victor Rainband is back from Omaha, where he has been with two carloads of wethers and which he cashed in at $4 10 per hundred. He found the market better than he had anticipated and says there is a good demand for good fat stuff at Missouri river points.

Dr. C. E Pearson of Castle Dale, was married the other day at Salt Lake City and passed through here later for his home, accompanied by his bride, who came out to Utah to meet her former husband. The Advocate with other Price friends extends congratulations

C. E Tolhurst, a dentist, formerly of Salt Lake, and well known throughout Eastern Utah, who was arrested at Evanston some time since, charged with practicing without a diploma, has commenced suit in the district court at Evanston against Drs Cunningham and Keith Tolhurst alleges that they injured his name and business to the amount of $25 000

Newspaper stock and all printing papers have advanced under McKinley prosperity 40 per cent additional in the last thirty days and another raise is coming within the next thirty days, Don't kick, brother, if your printer charges a little more for your job work than he did thirty or sixty days ago, Republican prosperity comes high, but it seems we must have it.

Thomas Murphy has been confined to his bed for several days.

Miss Annie Frandsen is attending school at Provo this winter.

Nichols & Egan have lately added some elegant new glassware to their bar fixtures

B. R. McDonald has a fine St. Bernard pup that was sent him as a present from Denver friends.

John L. Willson is back again at the forge and bellows, ready for all work that comes his way.

Mark P. Braffett is home from Salt Lake City, where he has been for several days on legal business

Charley Taylor sold his six or seven hundred head of cattle he had in the yards here the latter part of the week to W. L. White of Salt Lake City, who shipped the most of them to the east in charge of Ben Heywood, who will look after their disposal at Missouri river points. Some two hundred of them were shipped to Lehi, where they will be fed at the sugar factory for the market.

H. A. Smith, E. A. Wilson, C D. Harding S H. Love, Alexander Camp bell, M. F. Eakle, D F. Collett, A. W. Gallacher, Thomas P. Page and others have organized a voluntary company, which they mean soon to incorporate under the name of the Eccles Canyon Coal company, says the Salt Lake Herald. They own 840 acres of coal land near Scofield, Utah, and 700 acres near Habs, a station on the Scofield branch of the Rio Grande Western railroad. The company has some very fine property The veins of coal run from five to thirteen feet thick. They have a number of men at work now and will put their first coal on the Salt Lake City market early next week.

The families of Hyrum and George G. Frandsen are visiting relatives in Sanpete county, and will be absent for some time.

Mrs. William Potter left yesterday for Scofield to join her husband, who was fortunate in securing a house there in which to move into.

General Fred Funston of Kansas will pass through Price Saturday on his way to the Philippines He will stop over in Salt Lake City a few days with friends.

The Advocate this week printed some elegant invitations for "a Chinese ball and supper," to be given under the auspices of Huntington Seminary tomorrow evening.

Mrs. Victor Rambaud has departed for France, and having sailed from New York last week, should have reached her home at Marseilles, by this time She will be absent for the winter.

Mrs. William Floyd and little daughter, Zella, arrived in Price from Huntington last Sunday and will reside here in future. Mr. and Mrs. Floyd will go to housekeeping in the Potter residence.

Ed Leo bought eight head of mules and several horses while in town this week and took them out to his ranch He was in the market for a bunch of cattle, but found nothing here that suited him.

There is to be another troop stationed at Fort Duchesne. It is troop K, of the Ninth Cavalry, and has been located for some time at Fort Baird, N. M. The troop is expected to arrive here this week on its way out

Arthur J. Lee has purchased the Noah Bartholomew property, and is now domiciled, as it were, under his own vine and fig tree. He will make his home in this section of the moral vineyard for some time to come

Sheriff Peter Jensen of Sanpete county was in town yesterday on official business as was also Sheriff Leamaster of Emery county. Mr. Jensen is an efficient officer and is a brother-in-law of our fellow townsman, Hyrum Frandsen,

County Clerk Howard made a short trip to Castle Gate today to look after a test as to the coking properties of some coal in which he and several other Price gentlemen are interested.

Colonel Dodge and a party of Western officials went through here this morning en route to Sunnyside for an inspection of the work now in progress there.

Peter Anderson and Miss Rosetta Bryner were married yesterday afternoon at the home of the bride's parents, Mr. and Mrs Ulrich Bryner, Bishop Horsley officiating There were a large number of friends of the contracting parties present.

The Deseret News of today says. ' In the case of the United States against the Price Trading company and A. Ballinger, the defendant today filed an answer to the complaint, in the federal court. The case is over some timber cut from the timber reserve and purchased by the defendant company. The complaint holds that the timber was cut in violation to the statute governing the timber reserve Of course the answer maintains that the transaction was legal, and that no law has been broken."

Hunting on correspondence of the Salt Lake Herald " ' The people here are now having the benefit of a republican administration in county affairs Our taxes are very much higher than before, and we are wondering if the tariff did it, or shall we lay it to the trust? Even the school land, the title to which still remains vested in the state, is taxed. Section 2,502 Chapter 1, Title 67, revised statutes of Utah, to the contrary notwithstanding The health of the people is very good, there being scarcely a case of sickness in town. The weather is fine and farmers are finishing their fall plowing."

Attorney Mark P. Braffett has a fine collection of Navajo blankets at his office which were sent him by a friend, a post trader on the reservation in Arizona,

E R Herburn and wife have moved into the house recently vacated by Mr. and Mrs. Victor Rambaud.

DIRECTORY.

EMERY STAKE OF ZION—PRESIDING
OFFICERS AND PRESIDENCY.

REUBEN C MILLER, President	Price
John H Pace First Counselor	Price
Henry G Mathis, Second Counselor	Price
Arthur W. Horsley Stake Clerk ..	Price

PRICE WARD

ERNEST S HORSLEY	Bishop
Albert Bryner	First Counselor
(Vacant)	Second Counselor

CASTLE DALE WARD.

JOHN Y JENSON	Bishop
Seth Allen	First Counselor
Peter Frandsen	Second Counselor

CASTLE GATE WARD.

E LAMPH	Bishop
Andrew Young	First Counselor
Joel Ricks	Second Counselor

EMERY WARD.

ALONZO BRINKERHOFF	Bishop
Peter Olsen	First Counselor
Peter H Gunderson	Second Counselor

CLEVELAND WARD

L P OVERMAN	Bishop
Erick Larsen ..	First Counselor
Thomas Parish	Second Counselor

FERRON WARD.

H A NELSON	Bishop
John L Allred	First Counselor
George Berry	Second Counselor

HUNTINGTON WARD

PETER JOHNSON	Bishop
Silas S Young	First Counselor
Don C Woodward	Second Counselor

LAWRENCE WARD.

CALVIN MOORE	Bishop
Ole Tutt	First Counselor
Bert Reynolds	Second Counselor

MOLEN WARD.

HANS HASMUSSEN..	Bishop
Hans C Hanson .	First Counselor
Daniel M Brach	Second Counselor

ORANGEVILLE WARD.

JAMES ROBERTSON	Bishop
Andrew Anderson	First Counselor
John Snow	Second Counselor

SPRING GLEN WARD.

EDWARD FULLMER.	Bishop
Tancum Pratt	First Counselor
Thomas Rhoades	Second Counselor

WELLINGTON WARD.

ALBERT E. McMULLIN	Bishop
Robert Snyler	First Counselor
Isaac Roberts	Second Counselor

Presidency of High Priests' Quorum.

WILLIAM TAYLOR	Ferron
NEILS P MILLER	Castle Dale.
OSCAR A WOOD .	.. Huntington

Stake Superintendents of Sunday Schools.

ALEXANDER JAMESON..	Castle Dale
F M REYNOLDS .	Castle Dale
JESSE D JEWKES (Sec and Treas) Orangeville

TOWN OF PRICE

Trustees	F S Horsley President
	G G Frandsen
	Joseph Jones
	Seren Olsen
	Erastus Anderson
Town Clerk and Attorney	L O Hoffmann
Marshal	Peter Anderson
Treasurer .	Albert Bryner
Street Supervisor	C F Bryner

SEVENTH DISTRICT COURT DATES

MAY TERM

May 8	Sanpete County	Manti
June 12 ...	Carbon "	Price
June 19	Emery "	Castle Dale
Aug 8 ..	Grand "	Moab
Aug 21 .	San Juan '	Monticello

SEPTEMBER TERM

Sept 11	Sanpete County	Manti
Oct 9	Carbon ' ..	Price
Oct 16	Emery ".	Castle Dale
Nov 11	Grand "	Moab
Nov 20 .	San Juan " ..	Monticello

CARBON COUNTY OFFICIALS

COMMISSIONERS.

H A Nelson..	Castle Gate
George G Frandsen	Price
John James..	Scofield

CLERK AND RECORDER.

Robert Howard	Price

TREASURER AND ASSESSOR

Albert Bryner .	Price

PROSECUTING ATTORNEY.

L O Hoffmann.	Price

SHERIFF.

C W Allred	Price

SUPERINTENDENT OF SCHOOLS.

H G Webb..	Castle Gate

SURVEYOR.

Alvin Thayn	Wellington

Salt Lake Herald
November 21, 1899

Castlegate Briefs.

(Special Correspondence.)

Castlegate, Nov. 20.—Last evening the wife of Christmas Davis died from inflammatory rheumatism. She had been a long sufferer from the ailment. She will be buried tomorrow. The ward authorities will have charge of the obsequies. The Knights of Pythias will also turn out, the husband being a member of that lodge.

L. M. Olsen and H. Fraick were Castlegate visitors yesterday.

The Young Men's and Young Ladies' associations of the L. D. S. are working up a concert, to come off on Thanksgiving night.

Eastern Utah Advocate
November 23, 1899
Price

SHORT STORIES.

S. N. Morris, proprietor of the Vernal stage line, was transacting business in Price this week.

The children of Mr. and Mrs. Doll Faucett have entirely recovered from the scarlet fever.

Emery County Mercantile company has already begun a display of its fine line of seasonable holiday goods.

R. G. Miller shipped a carload of fine wethers to O. G. Kimball at Scofield last Monday, which will be butchered there.

The public schools resumed Monday after a dismissal of two weeks on account of the scarlet fever.

Louis Lowenstein is getting in a fine line of holiday goods and he tells about them in this issue of The Advocate.

Thomas Murphy is out again after being confined to his home for several days with an attack of lung trouble.

Miss Annie Anderson, who has been employed at Hotel Clarke for some time past, departed Monday for her home at Emery

County Judge Nelson went out to Sunnyside Tuesday morning to look after the interests of the Wasatch Store company there.

The new town board at Scofield consists of Holly Earll, president, and J P. Curtin, William Forrester, A. Smith and Lars Jensen, trustees.

The buildings under course of repairing and belonging to Judge Hollaway will be ready for occupancy within the next week or ten days.

Steve Chipman was in town the latter part of the week and left Saturday for Nephi, where he will buy a large number of breeding ewes and put them on the range in the Nine Mile section

R G Miller has his telephone line completed and in working order between his ranch and home in this city. He says it is the most perfect of any line in the country.

Dell Van Wagoner, who has been ill with typhoid fever and also threatened with pneumonia, is no longer under the care of a physician, and will soon be able to get around.

Sheriff Jensen passed through here Monday on his way home to Sanpete county with a young man whom he picked out in the Ashley Valley and who is wanted across the range for seduction.

Price Trading company has bought heavily of holiday goods and say they will have the finest line ever shown in this part of Utah. The holiday display will be made in the new brick building now under course of construction.

J. T. Farrer, one of Green River's substantial citizens, came in today from Castle Dale, where he had been on business. Mr Farrer is one of the heaviest taxpayers in Emery county and had been there to look after his property interests

Dick Cotner came up from Sunnyside Wednesday and will remain several days. He says the dance to be given there the 25th of this month, has been postponed until the boarding house is finished, which will be a week or ten days yet

---

John James was down from Scofield the first of the week to attend the special meeting of the board of county commissioners. He says times are good in his end of the moral vineyard, everybody has plenty to do and there is not an idle man in the camps in that part of the county.

There has been a change in the character of the money order system which renders it more complete and efficient than ever. Instead of the money order with the ragged edges, torn to indicate the amount, the new money order is similar to a check and a receipt is given the sender for the amount.

A telegram from White Rocks to the Tribune says "The report that about 200 Indians from this reservation are over in Colorado hunting is without foundation. The Indian police returned from there a few days ago and say there are only six tepees over there—probably a dozen Indians—and they would have been back several days ago but one of their number is sick and they think he will die. Most of the Indians are here and expect to remain."

Judge D. W. Holdaway, our postmaster, while engaged last Monday in doing some repairing on one of his buildings, fell a distance of several feet to the floor from a scaffolding. He weighs over 200 pounds and in the fall his back struck a piece of scantling. He sustained severe bruises, but is at present resting easy.

"To discontinue an advertisement," says John Wanamaker, the largest advertiser in the world, "is like taking down your sign. If you want to do business you must let people know it. Standing advertisements when frequently changed, are better than reading notices. They look more substantial and business like, and inspire confidence. I would as soon think of doing business without clerks as without advertising."

The board of county commissioners met Monday evening in special session and ordered the creation of another county precinct at Sunnyside, which will most likely be known as No. 10. They also ordered the building of a bridge across the Price river at Castle Gate. James Harrison's bond as justice of the peace at Castle Gate was approved. He succeeds W. H. Donaldson, removed to Scofield.

CASTLE GATE BRIFFS.

Last evening the wife of Christmas Davis died from inflammatory rheumatism. She had been a long sufferer from the ailment. She will be buried tomorrow. The ward authorities will have charge of the obsequies. The Knights of Pythias will also turn out, the husband being a member of that lodge.

L M Olsen and H. Flack were Castle Gate visitors yesterday.

The Young Men's and Young Ladies' associations of the L. D S are working up a concert, to come off on Thanksgiving night.

SHE HAD NERVE.

A special to the Salt Lake Herald from Castle Gate says "Quite an exciting episode took place at Helper last Monday. Mrs. McCoombs was evicted from her home by Justice of the Peace J. Tom Fitch, who on some preteree or other put her household goods into the street. She got help and the goods were again put into the house. Fitch tried to stop them from being put back, but Mrs McCoombs got a gun and tried to perforate the hide of the justice

One shot was fired, then the justice concluded that discretion was the better part of valor, and made hasty tracks for the telegraph office and summoned up to his aid sheriff Allred of Price and County Attorney Hoffmann of the same place

"They came, but a compromise was effected and Mrs McCoombs at present still holds the fort."

Salt Lake Herald
November 24, 1899

CASTLEGATE NOTES.

Mrs. McCoombs Arrested For Assault and Battery—Big Funeral.

(Special Correspondence.)

Castlegate, Nov. 22.—The result of the eviction of Mrs. McCoombs of Helper and the firing of a gun is that Mrs. McCoombs has been served with a warrant of arrest for assault and battery with a deadly weapon, etc.

Special Officer Ketchum of the Rio Grande Western was in town today.

The funeral services over the remains of Mrs. M. A. Davis were held yesterday afternoon in the K. of P. hall. Remarks were made by Elders Young and W. Lawley. The town turned out to pay their last respects to the deceased, and quite a number followed the corpse to the cemetery, headed by the Castlegate brass band, the Uniform Rank of K. of P., the subordinate lodge of K. of P. and I. O. F.

Miss Addie Cowley left Castlegate this morning on a visit to her parents in Cleveland, Emery county.

A large number of Austrians who came here from Sunnyside as a result of the strike there, will leave tonight for Colorado and other points.

Salt Lake Herald
November 28, 1899

Castlegate Notes.

(Special Correspondence.)

Castlegate, Nov. 26.—Mrs. John Eddy sustained a severe fall last evening. She is nearly 70 years old. She fell upon her left shoulder and head, injuring herself severely.

J. F. Wakefield of Huntington was a Castlegate visitor today.

SHORT STORIES.

Arthur Honten is working for the coal company at Castle Gate.

Read what the Price Trading company have to say about holiday goods.

Proprietor Morris of the stage line has put on a new wagon with top cover that is a beauty.

Operator Worth has been sent to Castle Gate and E. M Peyton is again at the key in the office here.

Arthur J. Lee shipped out a carload of honey the first of the week to the east for William H Roylance.

Money to loan on farm and city property from six to ten per cent. Apply to J W. Warf, Price Utah.

Judge Holdaway is feeling much better, in fact was up on his feet yesterday and the day before for a while.

Frank Rath, the restaurant man, has put in a new range that is capable of baking anything from a spring chicken to a loin of beef.

Dr. Fisk has sent away for some vaccination virus and is prepared to take the start on smallpox should it break out in his territory

Lee, the 20 months old son of Mr. and Mrs. Al Baxter, died at Helper last Thursday of diphtheria. The remains were interred at Castle Gate.

Link Bros will close up their saloon at Helper as soon as their present license expires and will locate in business in Salt Lake City Lou Link is now there and will have the Salt Lake City place open and ready for business in a few days The Advocate regrets to see these men leave Carbon county. They are fair and honest in all their dealings and upright business men.

Chub Milburn celebrated his birthday last Tuesday. Several friends were invited in to help make way with a fine dinner cooked by his estimable wife.

There was a turkey shooting and several horse races out on the track last Sunday. Several parties will have cheap Thanksgiving turkey today.

Sheriff Preece went through here the other day with two prisoners for the penitentiary from Uintah county. One of them, Joe Nash, was lately convicted of incest.

Company K of the Ninth Cavalry came in Sunday from Baird, N. M , and started out on the march at once for Fort Duchesne. Captain Reid was in command.

There is a sweet baby girl at the home of County Clerk and Mrs. Robert Howard that came to gladden the household last Sunday afternoon. Mother and child are doing nicely.

E R Lane, who left here a few weeks ago for Galena, Kan , where his brother was killed, and who has been sick in Denver for several weeks, will return to Price to resume his position with the railroad company.

The Hutchisons presented "The Golden Giant Mine" at Town Hall last Friday night to a fairly good sized house, followed by a dance The company has been disbanded for a few weeks, but will return to Vernal and play through the holidays

Mrs. Ana A. Prye, mother of Mrs Robert Howard of this city, died at her home in Salt Lake City, October 30th, of pneumonia. Mrs Prye was in her seventy first year, and she had been enjoying the best of health up to within a few days before her demise for one of her advanced years Just a few days before her death she visited her daughter here, and in riding home on the train caught a slight cold which terminated in her death. She came to Utah from England thirty six years ago and has lived in Salt Lake City ever since. Several children survive her. She was an excellent Christian woman.

Rumors of smallpox at Ferron are unfounded.

Today is St. Andrews Day as well as Thanksgiving Day.

Two children of Mr. and Mrs. A. Ballinger have the scarlet fever in mild form

The Salt Lake Temple will close on Friday, December 23rd, and reopen on Friday, January 5th, 1900.

Attorney Mark P. Braffet is home from Salt Lake City, where he has been several days on legal business.

The county commissioners meet in regular session Friday, December 29th to wind up the business of the year.

Landlord Spalding of the Hotel Clarke invited in a number of friends today to eat turkey and celery and other good things.

James W. Burgess and Miss Lizzie Crow were married here Tuesday. Both are popular young people and have the best wishes of a host of friends.

All county warrants issued on the general fund for 1899 are now as good as the cash, according to a notice published in this issue by Treasurer Bryner.

Rumor has it that a popular young couple of Price will swear off living alone, and will unite their hearts and fortunes on New Year's day. A good resolution.

Andrews & Horsley have opened a butcher shop in one of the Holdaway buildings and start out with a nice line of meats of all kinds and a neatly arranged place.

S. N. Morris has bought the Hadlock property and is building a barn there for the accommodation of his stage stock. Mr. Hadlock will soon go to Moab to open a blacksmith shop.

Peter Anderson and James W. Burgess and their brides gave a wedding dance at Town Hall, Tuesday evening, that was largely attended by the friends of both couples and a jolly good time was had by all in attendance.

The Connecticut Insurance company of Hartford has cash assets of $3,720,000 00 with which to settle fire losses. R. W. Crockett is the agent for Eastern Utah. All policies written here in Price. No sending to Salt Lake City.

Price Lodge, Knights of Pythias, is considering the matter of selling the lot which the lodge owns next to The Advocate office on the west. There has been an advance in real estate and the lodge can make something by disposing of the property at this time.

The little 5 year-old son of Mr. and Mrs. Hy Frandsen was kicked in the mouth Tuesday evening by a horse. The boy was endeavoring to keep them from running out of the lot, when one of the animals whirled and struck the boy fairly in the mouth. Dr. Fisk was called and took a number of stitches and thinks the little fellow will have no permanent disfigurement.

CASTLE GATE NOTES.

The infant son of Mr. and Mrs. Alex Baxter of Helper, aged 18 months, was interred at Castle Gate cemetery Saturday afternoon. The child died Friday from diphtheria

The Knights of Pythias held their meeting Friday evening. The semi annual election of officers took place.

Pay day at the mines, though late, was none the less acceptable.

Mrs. Tholke and family left Saturday for Soldier Summit, where Mr. Tholke is now engaged as operator for the Rio Grande Western

About fifteen to twenty Italians have arrived in town, presumably to work in the mines here or at Sunnyside.

Mrs. John Eddy sustained a severe fall the first of the week. She is nearly 70 years old. She fell upon her left shoulder and head, injuring herself severely.

J. F. Wakefield of Huntington was a Castle Gate visitor Monday.

SHORT STORIES.

Tobe Whitmore is soon to sulp a fine bunch of cattle to the east.

Mathias Pattieson and Jessie Potter were married at Scofield last Thursday, Thanksgiving

Frank Horsley is in from the south, where he has been f r several days buying cattle for his butcher business.

Miss Nellie Holley left Tuesday evening for Castle Gate, where she has accepted a clerkship in the Wasatch Store.

Money to loan on farm and city property from six to ten per cent. Apply to J. W. Warf, Price, Utah

There was a pleasant dance at Town Hall Monday evening, attended by most of the young people of the town.

Billy Potter was down from Scofield yesterday packing up his household goods for shipment to the coal camp

There was a big dance at the meeting house at Welling on last Thursday evening, Thanksgiving, that brought out the biggest crowd for many months.

Spring Glen people danced in the meeting house Thursday evening. There were several in attendance from here, and all report having had a most pleasurable time.

There were heavy snows on the mountains to the west and north the first of the week and in consequence the sheepmen are wearing big, broad smiles

Parties in from Sunnyside say the operators there have again lost the coal vein, and that shipments have been temporarily stopped

Price merchants are all showing a splendid line of holiday goods. Judging from the displays there will be no occasion for anyone sending out of town for anything

Friends of Mrs B R McDonald will be glad to know that she is able to be up and around again. With her sister, Miss Holley, and the baby she visited Mrs H A Nelson at Castle Gate last Sunday.

Bartlett Borton, representing the New York Life, was here yesterday and the day before "taking the lives" of some of our citizens

Victor Rambaud has gone out on the desert and will give his herds his personal attention during the winter months

Jim Miller was down from Colton Tuesday. His business was the buying of a bunch of sheep, the deal for which was not finally consummated. He will be back again

Dell Van Wagoner and family have gone to Sunnyside, where they will reside in future. Mr Van Wagoner will be employed on outside work at the mines.

Beginning the first of next month, the subscription price of The Advocate will be one dollar and fifty cents a year. We are compelled to raise the price by reason of the fact that the paper upon which it is printed has advanced 40 per cent.

The sheriff and town marshal refused to allow a couple of nickle-in-the-slot machines to be operated here that were recently shipped in. Owners of machines in other towns of the county will be notified to take their machines out.

The postal service in Eastern Utah could be greatly improved upon. Not infrequently the mail for Price and surrounding territory is carried by here, much to the annoyance and inconvenience of the people who have important mail.

The cattlemen of this part of the state and others are protesting to the interior department against the granting of a lease of the Strawberry Valley grazing lands to any sheep outfit, but more especially the Swift syndicate.

Robert McKune is in town after an absence of a week or two in the towns to the west of here and a flying trip to Colorado. He is showing a fine line of samples of ladies and gentlemens goods to measure clothing and says that business has been good with him all along the line

Ed Lee brought in a car load of fine calves the first of the week which he accompanied east. He will unload at Denver and if the market there is not satisfactory he will go on to the river with them.

Hy Frandsen's little boy who was kicked in the mouth by a horse last week is getting along as well as could be expected and will be out in a few days.

Hy Frandsen came in the other day from a few days trip through the southern country, and reports that the ranges would be in splendid condition for sheep this winter with a good rain or two or snow within the next few days

Many herds of sheep are being driven in the direction of the San Rafael mountains by Carbon county and Eastern Utah owners. A rain or snow, according to reports, would put the feed in that section in excellent condition.

Judge Holliway is still confined to his room from the effects of the fall he had some days ago. He puts in the time sitting up in the old arm chair reading the life of Napoleon, the Bible, "the great moral and religious" and other high class literature.

Operator Worth and family have gone to Castle Gate. Mr Worth is holding down the day job there in the telegraph office, and will shave the average citizen after hours at twenty five cents per, devoting his spare time to studying medicine.

Salt Lake Tribune
December 14, 1899

Miss Frandsen's Funeral.
[TRIBUNE SPECIAL.]
Price, Dec. 11.—Miss Lena Frandsen, who died Sunday morning as a result of an accident by being knocked off the track by a Rio Grande passenger train, as reported in The Tribune of the 9th of December, was buried here in the Price cemetery.

Miss Frandsen was 22 years of age and was born in Mount Pleasant, Utah, coming to Price with her parents in 1885. Her father, who was bishop of Price ward for some years, died not long ago.

LIST OF JURYMEN

List of jurors selected by jury commissioners to serve as jurors in the district court of the Seventh Judicial district in and for the county of Carbon, State of Utah, for the calendar year A. D 1900

Winter Quarters—Thos Brown, W. L Jones, J. M. Leveridge, David T. Evans, Jas. Wallace, Sr , John Street, William Powell, Walter Clark. C N, Nublstein, Richard T. Evans Mathias Pattinson.

Scofield—David Burns, John D. Llewellyn, John P. Johnson, Robert Bishop, John Hunter, D. W. Nicholas, Andrew Gilbert, J. S. Robertson, Chas. Edwards, Adam Hunter, Wm. Murphy, J. E Ingles.

Castle Gate—B F. Caffy, Allen Cox, T. T. Lamph, Wm. Featherstone, Henry Wade, Michael Beveridge, D J.Thoma, E. Sintschi, T. L Reese, Reese Lewi, Grover Lewis, Robt Williams, Sr , Richard White, W. H Decker

Helper—P. A. Smith, Chas Iverson, L. M Link

Spring Glen—H. J. Stowell, J D Fullmer, Herbert Savage, Frank Wiseman, Robt W. Powell

Maude Maud—E. L Harmon, Ira D Lyman

Wellington—Thos Gale Thos Zandall, Geo. A. Willson, Abe Liddell, Laht Jeesen, J. S Birch, Jos. Roberts, B R. McMullin, A. W. Avery, John A. Powell.

Price—A. W. Horsley, Thos. Nichols, Frank Bryner, Lars Frandsen, C H. Empey, George Robb, R G. Miller, John L. Willson, H. D. Elliott, Lot Powell, A J. Lee, Thos. Fitzgerald, H. G. Mathis, Herman Bryner, J. M. Millard, Wilmer Burgess, Rasmus Frandsen, John S. Mathis, Seren Olsen

---

Several persons here have this week been vaccinated against smallpox by Dr. Fisk of Helper.

John L. Wilson and Nellie Pittman, both of Scofield, were this week granted license to wed by County Clerk Howard

Mr. and Mrs. Peter Anderson are keeping house in the residence until recently occupied by Hy Herriman and family.

Judge Holdaway has added considerably to the room at the post office by the removal of a partition, which at least gives him space enough in which to turn around.

Tole Whitmore got home Sunday from Denver, where he had been with two cars of good cattle, and which he sell there. He caught the market in fairly good shape.

Dr. C N. Ray, late of Ferron and who went to Salt Lake City to become physician at St. Mark's hospital, is voluntarily quarantined there. His face has broken out with pimples that may develop into a case of smallpox.

The Pleasant Valley Coal company is working its mines in this county at full capacity, and would put several hundred more men at work if they could be had. There is also a scarcity of coal miners in Colorado and Wyoming.

Mr. and Mrs. E. Santschi and family of Castle Gate will attend the great exposition in Paris next year Mr Santschi's home is in Switzerland. only a few hours ride from Paris, and he has not been back in something like twenty years.

THE COMMUNITY MOURNS

This community was horrified last Saturday evening and later went into mourning at a frightful accident which befell Miss Lena Frandsen, and a few hours later resulted in the death of the young woman.

Miss Frandsen had been to the store of the Emery County Mercantile company to make some purchases. Having finished she started from the store to her home.

Where the path crosses the railroad track she was struck by the engine of Passenger Train No. 3, which was about an hour late and was running at a high rate of speed.

Several persons who saw the accident rushed to the scene, the body being knocked or carried a distance of some thirty or forty feet to the west. Tender hands picked up the senseless and mangled form and bore it to the mother's home.

Dr. Fisk, who was at the depot waiting to take the train for Helper, was called, and later Dr. Allen, the old family physician from Provo, was summoned, arriving at 1 o'clock Sunday morning

An examination by the two physicians revealed that the right arm was crushed from the elbow to the shoulder, the shoulder broken and mashed, the ribs literally driven into the lungs, with several cuts and bruises about the body, and a wound on the head.

Pending the arrival of Dr. Allen, Dr. Fisk did all that could be done to relieve the intense suffering, but at 3 o'clock her spirit took its flight. She was conscious for a time, recognizing members of the family about her.

Miss Frandsen was about 31 years of age and because of her affliction, being a deaf mute, the favored child of the family—if there are such as favorite ones

Funeral services were held from the church yesterday. There was a large outpouring of friends of the family and citizens generally to pay the last earthly tribute to a good young woman

The funeral was under the direction of Bishop E. S. Horsley, and among the others participating were President R. G. Miller, L. M. Olson, Albert Bryner, John H Pace and E. W. McIntire

The widowed mother and sorrowing brothers and sisters have the heartfelt sympathy of everyone in the community in the untimely taking away of this loved one.

Eastern Utah Advocate
December 21, 1899

LIST OF JURYMEN.

List of jurors selected by jury commissioners to serve as jurors in the district court of the Seventh Judicial district in and for the county of Carbon, State of Utah, for the calendar year A. D. 1900.

Winter Quarters—Thos Brown, W. L Jones, J. M. Loveridge, David T. Evans, Jas. Wallace, Sr., John Street, William Powell, Walter Clark, C. N. Nubiateln, Richard T. Evans, Mathias Pattinson.

Scofield—David Burns, John D. Llewellyn, John P. Johnson, Robert Bishop, John Hunter, D. W. Nicholas, Andrew Gilbert, J. S. Robertson, Chas. Edwards, Adam Hunter, Wm. Murphy, J. E. Ingles.

Castle Gate—B. F. Caffey, Allen Cox, T. T. Lamph, Wm. Featherstone, Henry Wade, Michael Beveridge, D J. Thomas, E. Santschi, T. L Reese, Reese Lewis, Grover Lewis, Robt. Williams, Sr, Richard White, W. H. Decker.

Helper—P. A. Smith, Chas. Iverson, L. M. Link.

Spring Glen—H. J. Stowell, J. D. Fullmer, Herbert Savage, Frank Wiseman, Robt. W. Powell.

Minnie Maud—E. L. Harmon, Ira D. Lyman.

Wellington—Thos Gale, Thos. Zandall, Geo. A. Willson, Abe Liddell, Lehi Jessen, J. S. Birch, Jos. Roberts, B. R. McMullin, A. W. Avery, John A. Powell.

Price—A. W. Horsley, Thos Nichols, Frank Bryner, Lars Frandsen, C. H. Empey, George Robb, R. G. Miller, John L. Willson, H. D. Elliott, Lot Powell, A. J. Lee, Thos. Fitzgerald, H. G. Mathis, Herman Bryner, J. M. Millard, Wilmer Burgess, Rasmus Frandsen, John S. Mathis, Sören Olsen.

SHORT STORIES.

Tobe Whitmore has returned from Salt Lake City.

A. Ballinger was in Salt Lake City this week on business.

With smallpox all about us it would appear that vaccination is the proper thing.

Robert Forrester and W. J. Tidwell are down near Salina looking into some coking coal propositions.

Mrs. D. R. McDonald has gone to Castle Gate to be absent some time, visiting her sister, Mrs. H. A. Nelson.

There were several Indians in this week from the reservation after freight. Many new wagons were taken out.

Ed Lee will qualify and move the postoffice now at Brocks to his ranch, which will hereafter be known as Harper.

Salt Lake City owners have lately refused four dollars a head for sheep. Wool has been contracted for at twenty cents.

Dick Cotner has resigned his position as boarding boss at Sunnyside and will probably go to Clear Creek in the near future.

While in town this week Ed Lee had Dr. Fisk of Helper remove his tonsils, which have been bothering him for some time.

There will be a grand masquerade ball at Castle Gate Saturday evening which will be attended by a number of people from here.

The Pleasant Valley Coal company has contracted with the St. Louis Gilson Asphaltum company for a quantity of asphaltum to be used in making coke at Castle Gate.

County Clerk Howard and associates have had an analysis made of their coal, which shows it to be of very fine coking quality. The only question now seems to be as to quantity.

Mark P. Braffet closed out all of his supply of Navajo blankets this week, being besieged with calls for them by persons wanting to send them back East. He will get in a new supply of them in a few days.

Captain Guilfoyle and family and Lieutenant Walker and family went through here the other day en route to California, where they will spend a month or more, the officers being on leaves of absence.

Mrs. Hyrum Frandsen is suffering from nervous prostration, brought about through excitement incident to an accident to her little son a few weeks ago, when the lad was kicked by a horse. Mr. Frandsen who was on the San Rafael with his herds a few days ago has been sent for.

Parties in from Emery county say that Dr. Shepard, the occulist who was here a short time ago, has the smallpox and is quarantined at Castle Dale. G. T. Olson of Emery is down with the plague, having taken it since he went through here last Sunday. He had been east with a shipment of cattle. There are also several suspected cases at other towns in the county.

Salt Lake Herald
December 27, 1899

CASTLE GATE MINER DIES

WAS FATALLY INJURED IN AN ACCIDENT.

Skull Was Fractured and He Was Otherwise Hurt So That He Died After Reaching St. Mark's.

Peter Scalzo, a coke worker in the Castle Gate coal mines, was brought to St. Mark's hospital yesterday afternoon, suffering from injuries from which he died twenty minutes after reaching the institution. His skull was fractured at the base, and one of his arms was terribly crushed, the injuries being received in an accident at the mine.

Scalzo was 25 years old and a native of Italy. He has relatives at Castle Gate.

Eastern Utah Advocate
December 28, 1899
Price

SHORT STORIES.

Mrs. G. W. Bodle entertained a number of friends at cards one evening last week

Landlord Spalding served baked goose and other good things to his guests for Christmas dinner.

D R. McDonald spent Christmas day with his folks at Castle Gate, taking dinner with Mr. and Mrs. H. A. Nelson.

George W. Bodle has been installed as boarding boss at the Sunnyside mines, going through here for there a few days ago.

Tom Nichols entertained a number of friends at dinner Christmas day. His guests declare it to have been a spread fit for the gods.

Proprietor Norris of the Vernal stage line has gone to Idaho to bring back with him a car load of horses to be used on the road.

Miss Maggie McIntire returned from Thompsons last Saturday. She and her sister, Isabella, are going to attend the academy at Castle Dale.

The Imperial Dramatic company is playing to good houses at Vernal, where it opened for a ten nights engagement last Monday, Christmas

The mails from the east have been coming in very irregularly for the past ten days Delayed trains by reason of snow blockades is given as the cause

Several persons from here attended the grand masked ball at Castle Gate last Saturday evening A goodly sum was netted for the Knights of Pythias lodge, under the auspices of which it was given

There was a well attended dance at the Town Hall last Monday, Christmas night. Several persons from Helper, Castle Gate and surrounding towns were in attendance, and everybody had a thoroughly good time.

Mrs G. G. Russell made all the little kids of Helper happy Saturday night with a Christmas tree, and when this was over served them with refreshments, including all the delicacies dear to the stomachs of the little folks.

Mark P. Braffet has sent to Arizona for another installment of Navajo blankets which will be here in a short time. He could have sold a large number of them for Christmas presents, but his supply during the holidays was short.

Surveyors of the Rio Grande Western have been in this vicinity for some time running new lines from Helper to Grand Junction with the view of lightening up the grades and cutting out some of the sharp curves of the road. Work, it is said, will begin early in the spring.

The smallpox scare is not increasing in our county. Few new cases have developed in Emery, but are confined to a few families, and Dr. Pearson entertains now bright hopes for a successful arrest of the plague. No case is found in Ferron, none in Orangeville and only one case here in Castle Dale, which is the occulist, Dr. Shepard, who had been exposed to it in Emery. He is now in an isolated house outside of town and every precaution should be taken to hinder more cases Orange Seeley's house, where this patient stopped has been quarantined to be sure that nothing shall come from there and in order to ease the public mind.—Castle Dale Record.

Dr. Fisk is still doing a land office business in the matter of vaccination.

Genial Jimmie Loufbarrow is spending the holidays with his family in Salt Lake City.

Mrs A. Ballinger is under the care of Dr. Fisk of Helper. She has been indisposed for some time.

Sheep on the desert are reported to be doing well and in good condition. The late snows helped out the range wonderfully.

Matt Thomas & Co remembered many of their friends on Christmas day with a bottle of the stuff that cheers, and others with smokers.

Several persons about town are suffering from sore arms by reason of vaccination. In one or two instances persons have been obliged to take to their beds

The store and dwelling owned by Sid Southworth and occupied by Isaac Glaser, burned at Thistle Junction at 3 o'clock Saturday morning and was a total loss. Mr. Glazer had a stock of general merchandise valued at about $1200 and insurance for about half that amount. Mr. Southworth carried about $600 insurance on the buildings. Mr. Glazer says he lost over $100 in currency. Charles Glazer, who slept in the store. escaped by a window without saving his clothing or bedding The fire is said to have caught from the stove or flue.

W. C. Broeker, the Helper cigar dealer and barber, will soon move his stock and shop into a bigger building to the south of his present location. He has needed more room for some time.

Mrs. F. E. Woods and children came in yesterday from Castle Dale and left in the evening for Omaha, where they will visit with relatives for some time. Mr. Woods accompanied them a part of the way.

The brick for Emery County Mercantile company's store has been delivered on the ground, about one hundred and fifty thousand of them, and it is expected work will begin on the building early in the spring.

Reports from Colton are to the effect that the thermometer hovered around from 16 to 36 degrees below zero last week. The ice men are taking advantage of the conditions by harvesting thousands of tons of clear, thick ice.

DISSOLUTION OF PARTNERSHIP.
Notice is hereby given that the co-partnership heretofore existing between J. W. Gentry and J. G. Callaway, under the firm name of Gentry & Callaway, and doing business at Sunnyside, Utah, is this day dissolved by mutual consent, J. G. Callaway retiring and J. W. Gentry continuing the business of said firm, and assuming all bills and paying all debts of the said firm.
J W. GENTRY,
J. G. CALLAWAY.
Sunnyside, Utah, Dec 14, 1899

ROBBER'S ROOSTERS ARRESTED.

Officers Tuttle, Allred and Leamaster Succeed in Capturing Three of the Outlaws Who Were About to Ship Away Two Carloads of Horses.

[SPECIAL TO THE "NEWS."]

Price, Utah, Dec. 30.—Three bad men, horse thieves, cattle rustlers and sympathizers with members of the notorious Robber's Roost gang, were taken in at Ferron, Emery county, yesterday and are now in the county jail at Castle Gate. They are Joe Swasey, Lee McDonald and Peter Mickel, against whom the formal charge of stealing and driving off a band of horses will be made. Joe Swasey is a brother of the notorious Joe, for whom there is a warrant out and who is believed to be now in Canada and a son of the late Rodney Swasey of Provo, who was a banker of the Garden City.

McDonald comes from a respectable family at Molen, his father being a miner and known throughout Utah to all the old timers, while Mickel is a brother of Jim Mickel, who shot and killed Sheriff Burns of Sanpete county, about four years ago.

For some time now there has been considerable stock, both cattle and horses, missing from the ranges in the counties of eastern Utah. Suspicion pointed to these men; but there has been nothing to fasten their guilt until last Tuesday, when an Emery county merchant sent a check in here to have it cashed with the request that the party cashing it send the money by express to Mickel at Green River, where the money, some three hundred dollars, was wanted to pay the freight charges on two car loads of horses which were to be shipped east. Sheriff Allred in some manner got on to the money matter, and in the meantime he was in communication with Sheriff Leamaster, who was out looking for stolen horses.

Allred was joined here by Tobe Whitmore, who has lost heavily of stock in the past at the hands of thieves. They went to Green River in the hope that they might identify Whitmore's band, but none of his horses, it was subsequently proved, were in the bunch. Here they were met by Leamaster, and the two carloads of horses were located near the station, where they were being held until the money to pay the freight arrived. It was planned to ship last Thursday. The rustlers in some way got wind of the fact that the officers were after them as they deserted the stock and made for the San Rafael hills, in the southern part of Emery county. When it became known that the rustlers had fled, telegrams were sent out to Price and transmitted by telephone to Deputy Sheriff Tuttle at Castle Dale, who is also sergeant-at-arms of the lower Utah house and ex-sheriff of Emery county. He got track of the men and with assistance caught them at Ferron. Tuttle was wounded some time ago in a fight with the Robber's Roosters.

There were two carloads of the horses that they were going to ship, and among the lot was the only pair of work horses of a poor farmer at Castle Dale. The greatest part of the stolen stuff, however, was off the range. The officers have other members of the gang under surveillance and it is possible other arrests will follow soon.

TOWN HALL, PRICE.

Made in the USA
Columbia, SC
22 September 2018